Wonderful Counselor

The Story of Revelation,
Redemption
And the Return of Jesus Christ

Cynthia Sowa

TABLE OF CONTENTS

TABLE OF CONTENTS   **3**

PART ONE: CHRIST   **7**

   CHAPTER 1   **8**

      THE MESSAGE OF REDEMPTION OF EARTH AND MANKIND

      AN INTRODUCTION TO THE BOOK OF REVELATION

PART TWO: THE CHURCHES AND THE CHURCH AGE   **17**

   CHAPTER 2   **19**

      JOHN SEES THE DAY OF THE LORD

      Revelation 1

   CHAPTER 3   **36**

      THE CHURCHES OF EPHESUS AND SMYRNA

      Revelation 2:1-11

   CHAPTER 4   **55**

      THE CHURCHES OF PERGAMOS AND THYATIRA

      Revelation 2:12-29

   CHAPTER 5   **82**

      THE CHURCHES OF SARDIS, PHILADELPHIA, AND LAODICEA

      Revelation 3

PART THREE: TRIBULATION AS SEEN FROM HEAVEN'S VIEWPOINT   **103**

   CHAPTER 6   **105**

      THE CHURCH AGE ENDS

      Revelation 4

   CHAPTER 7   **124**

      EARTH'S TITLE DEED REDEEMED

      Revelation 5

CHAPTER 8   137

   SIX SEALS – TRIBULATION MIXED WITH GRACE

   Revelation 6

CHAPTER 9   157

   144,000 JEWS SEALED AND THE TRIBULATION
   SAINTS IN HEAVEN

   Revelation 7

CHAPTER 10   172

   GOD'S WRATH ON EARTH: THE FOUR TRUMPETS
   SOUND

   Revelation 8

CHAPTER 11   182

   THE LAST THREE TRUMPETS

   Revelation 9

CHAPTER 12   192

   THE MYSTERY OF GOD IS FINISHED

   Revelation 10

CHAPTER 13   201

   GOD'S TWO WITNESSES

   Revelation 11

**PART FOUR: TRIBULATION AS SEEN FROM EARTH'S
VIEWPOINT**   221

   CHAPTER 14   223

      THE RAPTURE OF THE CHURCH AND WAR IN
      HEAVEN

      Revelation 12

   CHAPTER 15   255

      THE RISE OF THE ANTICHRIST

      Background to Revelation 13

   CHAPTER 16   312

      THE BEASTS FROM THE SEA AND EARTH

Revelation 13

CHAPTER 17   **334**

THE FIRST 3 ½ YEARS OF TRIBULATION REVISITED

Revelation 14

CHAPTER 18   **355**

THE SAINTS VICTORIOUS OVER SATAN

Revelation 15

CHAPTER 19   **368**

SEVEN BOWLS OF WRATH

Revelation 16

**PART FIVE: TRIBULATION AS SEEN FROM SATAN'S
KINGDOM**   **397**

CHAPTER 20   **399**

BABYLON

Revelation 17

CHAPTER 21   **418**

BABYLON IS FALLEN

Revelation 18

CHAPTER 22   **431**

THE MARRIAGE OF THE LAMB AND THE BATTLE OF
ARMAGEDDON

Revelation 19

PART SIX: THE KINGDOM OF CHRIST   **451**

CHAPTER 23   **453**

THE THOUSAND-YEAR REIGN

Revelation 20

PART SEVEN: THE HOLY CITY AND ETERNITY   **490**

CHAPTER 24   **491**

A NEW HEAVEN AND EARTH AND THE NEW
JERUSALEM

Revelation 21

CHAPTER 25   **509**

JESUS' FINAL MESSAGE

Revelation 22

ACKNOWLEDGMENTS   **529**

SELECTED BIBLIOGRAPY   **530**

DETAILED TABLE OF CONTENTS   **533**

ENDNOTES   **554**

PART ONE: CHRIST

CHAPTER 1
THE MESSAGE OF REDEMPTION OF EARTH AND MANKIND
AN INTRODUCTION TO THE BOOK OF REVELATION

Amos 3:7: "Surely the Lord God will do nothing, but he revealeth his secret unto his servants the prophets."

Jeremiah 33:3: "Call unto me, and I will answer thee, and shew thee great and mighty things which thou knowest not."

Ephesians 1:17-19: "That the [G]od of our Lord Jesus Christ, the Father of glory, may give unto you the spirit of wisdom and revelation in the knowledge of him: The eyes of your understanding being enlightened; that you may know what is the hope of his calling, and what the riches of the glory of his inheritance in the saints, and what is the exceeding greatness of his power toward us who believe, according to the working of his mighty power."

Since the beginning of time, God has had a distinct plan for the creation that He placed on Planet Earth. Before He created man, He knew exactly how the entirety of human history would play out. He knew that Alexander the Great would both live, and conquer the known world. He knew that Isaac Newton would formulate a theory of gravity. He knew that Abraham Lincoln would be assassinated at Ford's Theater, and He knew that Johann Sebastian Bach would write brilliant music to His, God's, glory. He knew both the length of the Roman Empire and the winner of every Super Bowl that would ever be played.

More importantly, He knew the names of each human being who would ever be born and He knew which of those humans would accept His invitation to belong to Him. He knew exactly how He would bring salvation to a fallen world by sending His son, and He knew exactly when He would send His Son a second time in order to gather His people to Him. He knew what it would take to ultimately defeat mankind's greatest enemy, Satan, and He knew each step in the process of bringing about that defeat. The amazing thing is that He promised to share these plans with His people. That revelation of the mind of God is found in sixty-six books collectively called "The Bible." The book of Revelation is the last of those sixty-six books and it is the final installment given to us of God's secrets. It is the capstone of the plan of God.

REVELATION - THE UNVEILING

In Greek, the word for revelation is *apokalupsis*. It means the "unveiling," the "taking off of the cover." This book was written because God had every intention of keeping the promises He made in the three citations above. It was written for another purpose also, an even greater purpose. Although Revelation unveils the future, it unveils something much more important: Jesus. This book is, after all, called the "Revelation of Jesus Christ" and it unveils Jesus to us in a way that no other book in the Bible does, "for the testimony of Jesus **is** the spirit of prophecy" (Revelation 19:10, emphasis added). The New Testament begins with the Gospels. They are firsthand accounts of Jesus Christ as a man. Revelation is a firsthand account of Jesus as God. The Gospels present to us a picture of Jesus as the meek and lowly servant of man, the suffering savior who loved us enough to die for us. That picture is accurate. Revelation pictures Jesus as the Great King coming back to earth in power and glory. He will defeat every enemy, and at His feet every person who has ever lived will bow and confess His lordship. That picture, too, is accurate. One account is not complete without the other.

THE WRITER OF REVELATION

John the Apostle was one of those servants, spoken about in Amos, to whom God would reveal His secrets. He was referred to as the "disciple whom Jesus loved" (John 21:20), and he wrote the book of Revelation. John wrote Revelation sometime around A.D. 96 when he, himself, was in his nineties. He alone of the original thirteen apostles (including Mathias, Judas's replacement) had escaped the Imperial Persecutions with his life; instead the Emperor Domitian had exiled John to Patmos, an island off the western coast of Turkey. It was a barren, "god-forsaken," rocky island off the coast of Turkey in the open Aegean Sea; six miles wide and ten miles long, with no trees or rivers, the barest of vegetation, brutally cold in winter and certainly meant as a place of torment for the Beloved Apostle. In keeping with the nature of God, it was turned into the place where the glory of God was revealed to man in a way that it never has been, before or since. The place meant to torment John was changed into the place of unspeakable blessing for him. Such are the ways of God. As it was in the lowly manger, when Jesus first appeared on earth, so it was at this final unveiling. The mean and lowly became exalted and blessed, the crude and ugly became glorious beyond belief.

REDEMPTION PROMISED TO MAN AND TO THE EARTH

One of the critical messages of the book of Revelation is its promise of redemption (restoration) to the earth and to mankind (Revelation 21:5). "And when these things begin to come to pass, then look up, and lift up your heads; for your redemption draweth nigh" (Luke 21:28). God's plan of redemption involves the restoration of everything that has been lost because of sin: each of our souls, each of our bodies, the entire human race and Planet Earth.

The Bible begins in Genesis with the story of creation. We then see the fall of man as a consequence of Adam's choice to sin. At this point in time, mankind lost their existence in paradise and they lost their face-to-face relationship with God. They also gained some things: toil, disease, pain, and death. The history of man continued in this hopelessness until the New Testament announced the coming of God to earth in the person of Jesus. At the cross we did see the salvation of our souls, but we have yet to see God put an end to our existence of toil, disease, pain, and death. We hear the promise of such reclamation made in the Gospels, but exactly how it would happen was not made clear; that is until God sent one last message to earth through the final book in the Bible - Revelation. You see, Jesus had a message to send to His people after He had ascended into heaven. He would speak one more time. John was there when He spoke and John recorded the message for us. It is critical that we hear it.

Genesis, the first book of the Bible, chronicles the story of the *generation* (creation) of the earth and the *degeneration* of the earth (the Fall). Revelation, the final book of the Bible, tells the story of the *regeneration.* Titus 3:5 speaks of the regeneration of the soul, Matthew 19:28 speaks of the regeneration of the earth. Nowhere is it written that our bodies will be regenerated. They won't be. We will receive new bodies, not regenerated bodies. Our bodies now are not quite adequate for the ages. But everything else of God's creation is, and will be regenerated.

There is, however, another side to the story. That which cannot be redeemed will be destroyed by God's wrath, and Revelation records that fact also. The story is not complete without both sides of the story. It is interesting that Satan has attacked so strongly the two books of the Bible dealing with generation – Genesis - and regeneration - Revelation. The central story of Genesis, that God is Creator and that man is a fallen creature with a sinful nature, is roundly derided in this age. At least the story of Genesis is generally known. Satan's attack on Revelation has gone even further. It has been so successful that not only does the world not know of its existence, but even God-fearing, Bible-believing Christians don't understand it and refuse to even read it. How can God illumine that which we refuse even to examine?!

THE PURPOSE OF PROPHECY

God has prepared a mighty sign for the end of the age. It is the unmistakable, miraculous fulfillment of prophecy on a scale that the world has never before seen. In Matthew 24:34 and Luke 21:32, Jesus says that at the end of time much will happen in one generation. *Much* will happen in one generation. That is because prophecy is a catalyst. Catalysis is a chemical process that speeds up an action already in process. It does not *change* the process, it simply speeds it up. The fulfillment of prophecy will do this with the entire gospel process. There is no miracle like the miracle of prophecy being fulfilled. The world will be desperately searching for an answer to the confusion of the times; the Bible will have that answer. Christians had better be prepared with God's answer, or Satan will be right there to supply his fraudulent spin on what is happening. We have seen examples of this in recent church history. For instance, why didn't the Church speak out forcefully against the Jehovah's Witnesses' claim to be the 144,000 of Revelation? Because although they knew the

Jehovah's Witnesses were not, the Church had no idea who the 144,000 really were. So they kept silent, and a false religion ensnared millions. We cannot afford to do this in this most critical time that is approaching. We must be ready with an answer. Satan will certainly have his.

All biblical prophecy fits into one or more of three categories:

1. Prophecy concerning the nations.
2. Prophecy concerning the Jews.
3. Prophecy concerning the Church.

It is necessary to understand all three lines of prophecy in order to have an overview of end times. Different books in the Bible provide information on the different categories. As primary examples, Daniel concerns itself primarily with the nations, Ezekiel concerns itself primarily with the Jews, Revelation concerns itself primarily with the Church. The prophecy of what will happen to the heavens and the earth is woven into all three concerns: the nations, the Jews and the Church. Antichrist also connects with all three concerns.

DANIEL - THE NATIONS

The book of Daniel primarily concerns itself with the line of prophecy that records what will happen to the nations of the world. It is interesting to note that this vision concerning the nations was, in great part, given through a pagan king. This vision of the story of earth's nations culminates in Daniel 7:13-14: "I saw in the night visions, and, behold, one like the Son of man came with the clouds of heaven, and came to the Ancient of days, and they brought him near before him. And there was given him dominion, and glory, and a kingdom, that all people, nations, and languages, should serve him: his dominion is an everlasting dominion, which shall not pass away, and his kingdom...shall not be destroyed."

The culmination of the story of Planet Earth is that Jesus will come and establish His kingdom here and will reign in all glory and power. All the nations of the earth will then be subject to Christ and under His reign. Zechariah 14:9 bears this out: "And the Lord shall be king over all the earth: in that day shall there be one Lord, and his name one."

EZEKIEL - THE JEWS

The book of Ezekiel the Prophet primarily concerns itself with the line of prophecy that records what will happen to the Jews. This vision culminates in Ezekiel 36:25-28: "Then will I sprinkle clean water upon you, and ye shall be clean: from all your filthiness, and from all your idols, will I cleanse you. A new heart also will I give you, and a new spirit will I put within you: and I will take away the stony heart out of your flesh, and I will give you an heart of flesh. And I will put my spirit within you, and cause you to walk in my statutes, and ye shall keep my judgments, and do them. And ye shall dwell in the land that I gave to your fathers; and ye shall be my people, and I will be your God."

The culmination of the story of the Jewish nation is that they will return with their whole hearts not only to God the Father, but also to God the Son and will never be separated from Him again. Zechariah 12:10 again bears witness to this: "And I will pour upon the house of David, and upon the inhabitants of Jerusalem, the spirit of grace and of supplications: and they shall look upon me whom they have pierced, and they shall mourn for him, as one mourneth for his only son, and shall be in bitterness for him, as one that is in bitterness for his firstborn."

Furthermore, Israel's everlasting dwelling will be in the land that God has given to them.

REVELATION - THE CHURCH

And what about the Church? That story, as I already said, is primarily recorded in the book of Revelation. It is written to the Church and it concerns the Church. It takes up where the book of Acts leaves off (in a most abrupt manner - almost in mid-sentence) and tells the story of what will transpire from the time of John the Apostle, through the Church Age, through the Rapture, through the Tribulation, through the Judgments, through the Kingdom Age on earth and on into eternity. Why isn't this information common knowledge in the Church? If we deem necessary a study of Jesus' humble birth and the agony and humiliation of the cross, should we not also embrace the study of His triumph?

It is self-evident that the future can only play itself out in one way. Just because there are disparate views concerning how the future will happen does not imply that the future is not already decided and known by God. Not only does He know how the future will play itself out, He has recorded in the Bible exactly how it will occur. This foreknowledge of God's is the miracle of prophecy because it points to an omniscient (all knowing) and omnipotent (all powerful) Being. It is, then, incumbent upon us to understand the information that has been provided to us by God.

Generally speaking, there are three viewpoints of when Rapture (a term not used in the Bible, but that is understood to mean a catching up of the saints, both living and dead to heaven) will occur. The Pre-Tribulation view contends that it will happen prior to the beginning of the time of the Great Tribulation. The Mid-Tribulation view states that it will come in the middle of the Great Tribulation, and the Post-Tribulation view says that it will occur at the end of the Great Tribulation. But, there will not be both a pre-tribulation rapture and a mid-tribulation rapture, not to mention a post-tribulation rapture. There will be only one. And the way it will be is recorded in the Scriptures already. If we don't get it, it is not the fault of Scripture.

There are two ways of approaching a passage of Scripture. One way is to make it prove something that you have already decided, and if it doesn't quite fit, force it anyway, ignoring any inconsistencies. The other way is to find out exactly what the Scripture says *regardless* of your current belief. The first way forces the Scriptures to conform to your theology. The second method forces your theology to conform to the Scriptures. God blesses only one of these ways with wisdom and insight from Him. The other method is the sure road to confusion. Sadly, the road of confusion has been the road most frequently taken. To paraphrase Robert Frost, our desire with this book is to take the road less traveled, the road whereon the Scriptures are allowed to explain themselves. Then, the story, for the most part, will be clear.

A word of warning: There will be biblical Scriptures in this book that will disconcert you; possibly even annoy you. Hold on to those very Scriptures. If you honestly desire God's truth,

He will stretch you to accommodate them. He will *not* diminish them to accommodate you.

THE BLESSING OF REVELATION

Revelation is the only book in the Bible where we are specifically told that we are blessed if we read it (Revelation 1:3). No wonder there is blessing in this book; it unveils Jesus as God, Jesus as victor over Satan and the grave, Jesus as advocate, Jesus as ruler of the universe forever and ever. Given that, it also stands to reason why Satan has invested so much effort into keeping us away from this book: It heralds his doom. The Apostle Paul wrote in 2 Timothy 4:7 that he had a crown of righteousness waiting for him which the Lord, the Righteous Judge, would give him at the day of His appearing, and then he adds something very interesting to that statement: *"And not to me only, but unto all them also that love his appearing."* The crown for which Paul was waiting is also reserved for those who long for His appearing. But do most Christians long for His appearing? It seems to me that they fear it. Revelation, when it is understood, will completely remove that fear. You *will* long for His appearing. "If in this life only we have hope in Christ, we are of all men most miserable" (I Corinthians 15:19). This is an astonishing statement. I would not have the nerve to make a statement this strong, but Paul understood what the appearing of Jesus signified. I believe that at the end of the reading of this book we, too, will say the same thing, for Revelation will allow us to understand what compelled Paul to write this statement.

STRUCTURE OF THE BOOK

The structure of Revelation is as follows:

> Part 1. Christ (Revelation 1);
> Part 2. The Churches and The Church Age (Revelation 2-3);
> Part 3. Tribulation as seen from heaven's viewpoint (Revelation 4-11);
> Part 4. Tribulation as seen from the vantage point of earth (Revelation 12-16);
> Part 5. Tribulation as seen from the viewpoint of Satan's kingdom (Revelation 17-19);

Part 6. The Kingdom of Christ (Revelation 20);
Part 7. The Holy City and Eternity (Revelation 21-22).

Revelation is a unique book. It differs from other books of the Bible in that it was almost completely dictated by God. And what was not dictated was revealed by a supernatural vision. The book of Revelation is Jesus' last message to His people on earth. We are commanded to hear it. Let us be obedient.

PART TWO: THE CHURCHES AND THE CHURCH AGE

Figure 1   Part 2-3: Revelation 1 - 11

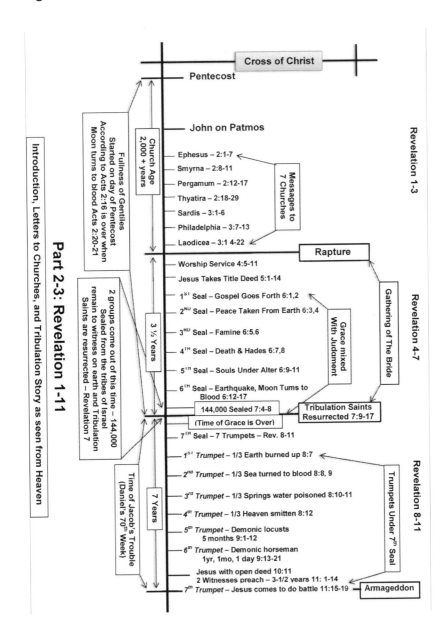

Cross of Christ

Pentecost

John on Patmos

Church Age
2,000 + years

Fullness of Gentiles
Started on day of Pentecost
According to Acts 2:16 is over when
Moon turns to blood Acts 2:20-21

Ephesus – 2:1-7
Smyrna – 2:8-11
Pergamum – 2:12-17
Thyatira – 2:18-29
Sardis – 3:1-6
Philadelphia – 3:7-13
Laodicea – 3:1 4-22

Messages to
7 Churches

Revelation 1-3

Rapture

Worship Service 4:5-11
Jesus Takes Title Deed 5:1-14
1ˢᵀ Seal – Gospel Goes Forth 6:1,2
2ᴺᴰ Seal – Peace Taken From Earth 6:3,4
3ᴿᴰ Seal – Famine 6:5.6
4ᵀᴴ Seal – Death & Hades 6:7,8
5ᵀᴴ Seal – Souls Under Alter 6:9-11
6ᵀᴴ Seal – Earthquake, Moon Turns to
        Blood 6:12-17
144,000 Sealed 7:4-8
(Time of Grace is Over)
7ᵀᴴ Seal – 7 Trumpets – Rev. 8-11

3 ½ Years

2 groups come out of this time – 144,000
Sealed from the tribes of Israel
remain to witness on earth and Tribulation
Saints are resurrected – Revelation 7

Grace mixed
With Judgment

Gathering of The Bride

Revelation 4-7

Tribulation Saints
Resurrected 7:9-17

7 Years

Time of Jacob's Trouble
(Daniel's 70ᵗʰ Week)

1ˢᵀ Trumpet – 1/3 Earth burned up 8:7
2ⁿᵈ Trumpet – 1/3 Sea turned to blood 8:8, 9
3ʳᵈ Trumpet – 1/3 Springs water poisoned 8:10-11
4ᵗʰ Trumpet – 1/3 Heaven smitten 8:12
5ᵗʰ Trumpet – Demonic locusts
        5 months 9:1-12
6ᵗʰ Trumpet – Demonic horseman
        1yr, 1mo, 1 day 9:13-21
Jesus with open deed 10:11
2 Witnesses preach – 3-1/2 years 11: 1-14
7ᵗʰ Trumpet – Jesus comes to do battle 11:15-19

Trumpets Under 7ᵗʰ Seal

Revelation 8-11

Armageddon

Part 2-3: Revelation 1-11

Introduction, Letters to Churches, and Tribulation Story as seen from Heaven

CHAPTER 2
JOHN SEES THE DAY OF THE LORD
Revelation 1

THE THEME

The first verse identifies the theme of this book: to reveal Jesus Christ. It is not primarily to reveal the future, although it does that. It is certainly not a coded message to the Church. Rather, it is written to reveal more of the mystery of Jesus to the world. The Bible is not complete without this book. One's understanding of Jesus is not complete without this book. What is even more missed by the Church is that this revelation is given *to* Jesus ("which God gave to him"). This is the crowning glory and reward for the completion of Jesus' work.

Wherefore God also hath highly exalted him, and given him a name which is above every name: That at the name of Jesus every knee should bow of things in heaven, and things in earth, and things under the earth; And that every tongue should confess that Jesus Christ is Lord, to the glory of God the Father (Philippians 2:9-10).

THE REVELATION OF JESUS CHRIST GIVEN BY GOD

It is clear in verse 1 that God sent and signified this last message *by His angel* unto John. John states emphatically that he was given this message by God. These are "fightin' words." This is God's message, not John's. Many students of Revelation have said that this book was not written by John the Apostle because the grammar and sentence structure are so very different from his other books. Apart from the fact that for the first two centuries the Church accepted that John was indeed the author, this verse explains any difference. These are *not* John's words, they are God's words. This is not John's work, it is God's work. Far from inducing doubt, the difference in construction between Revelation and the Gospel and Epistles of John lends credence to the divine construction of this book. John simply, as verse 2 states, bore record of the word and testimony of God and Jesus. This *is* consistent with John's other writings. The Gospel of John was written, according to the author, in order "that ye might believe that Jesus is the

Christ, the Son of God" (John 20:31). First and Second John were written to oppose false doctrine and evil spirits by asserting that Jesus is the Word of God, the only Christ, and that all who deny this are liars and antichrists.

It was not until the third century that authorship was attributed to anyone other than the Apostle. At that time, there were some who, out of a desire to escape Revelation's censure for certain doctrines, ascribed it to Cerinthus, a heretic of the first century. Even in the third century, however, most did not dispute the authorship of John. The Muratorian Canon, Clement of Alexandria, Tertullian, Origen, and Hippolytus were some of the most prominent voices that declared that John the Apostle was the writer of Revelation.

THE BLESSING
"Blessed is he that readeth, and they that hear the words of this prophecy, and keep those things which are written therein: for the time is at hand" (Revelation 1:3). When John wrote these words two thousand years ago he could not begin to know into whose hands they would reach, but he did know that whoever read his words would be very blessed by what they revealed. Again, this is the *only* book in the Bible that specifically promises a blessing to those who read it, and also to those who simply hear its words! Don't you know that Satan understands the power in these words?! I am sure that he does because he has worked hard for hundreds of years to convince Christian people and Christian leaders that they can safely ignore this book, indeed that it is safer to do so! We must decide to take this Scripture at face value and open this book and claim its blessing! If the Church does not understand and teach accurate prophecy, the false religions will teach false prophecy. Jesus warns of this same thing in Luke 21 when He says that the many false christs which appear in the end times will preach prophecy ("saying, the time draweth near" Luke 21:8).

When John records that "the time is at hand" he is not mistaken. Certainly, most of the book has not yet come to pass, however, the prophecies contained in Revelation 2 began to see their fulfillment in John's day. It is also necessary to understand that time is relative. A sense of expectancy is given to each hearer down through time, through each age. The words in this book have been applicable to every church era and time. The prophecies of Revelation will concern themselves not only with the Rapture and Tribulation, but also with the first-century Church and will continue with the Church through the ages. Therefore, the time is, indeed, at hand.

LETTERS TO THE SEVEN CHURCHES

In verse 4, John identifies to whom this letter is written: It is written to the Church. Although John is writing to seven specific churches in Asia (present day Turkey), his message is for an audience far broader than that. If there be any contention that this is not so, then logically, we cannot adopt any of the epistles' messages to any church except the church to whom it was written; i.e. Romans has a message *only* for the Church at Rome, Ephesians has a word *only* for the Church at Ephesus, and so forth. In other words, if one accepts that the Epistles have meaning for the entire Church throughout the ages, one must grant that same Canonical inspiration to Revelation also. The very number of churches addressed, seven, further emphasizes this. The number seven *always* signifies completion. It does not signify perfection in any way, as is many times erroneously taught, it simply means that the full picture of an issue is being presented. The full picture of the history and state of the Church is thus being addressed by Jesus.

Consider the local churches that are mentioned. They are all on the western coast of modern day Turkey. These churches were in a radius of eighty miles and the whole territory covered was no larger than the state of Pennsylvania. It seems almost impossible that churches so different could exist so closely together. As we will see, Smyrna is poverty-stricken and persecuted almost to death. She is one hundred miles from Laodicea, a church so wealthy it has need of nothing. The churches addressed are not the largest or the most important churches of that day, but they are representative of the Church in its fullness. The seven local churches are the complete picture of the Church and the Church Age. No new movement or new kind of church will arise outside of the picture of these seven. Any church outside of these seven types is a false church. This is important information to have when considering the validity of any deviant "Christian" movement, such as the Jehovah's Witnesses or the Latter Day Saints.

This is borne out by the earliest commentary that has been found addressing itself to this passage. It was written by the early Christian martyr Victorinus and makes clear how this passage was understood by the early Church. He wrote: "There are but seven churches in the whole world."

In an interesting aside, even though, in the first century, these seven Turkish churches perfectly represented the Church in her entirety, as reported by the Turkish government in the year 2010, Turkey is now considered to be 99.8% Muslim! And Christians alone do not even make up the remaining miniscule amount of .02%. In fact some missionary organizations put the number of Christians as low 3000. If that is true, that would means that Turkey is now the least Christian nation in the world.

GOD EXISTS OUTSIDE OF TIME

Grace and peace are given to the Church from "him which is, and which was, and which is to come." God had no beginning and He will have no end. He is eternal. That is very difficult for the linear-thinking human mind to grasp. But if man fails to grasp that point, he ignores entirely the fact that, although he does have a beginning, he, too, was created to become an eternal being with no end. Whether he will spend that eternity in joy or in despair, in heaven or in hell, is up to him. Although we have absolutely no say in the circumstances of our birth we have total control over where we will spend our next life. God is "not willing that any should perish," Peter tells us, so if a person faces an eternity of torment the fault lies with his choices.

THE SEVEN SPIRITS OF GOD

As has already been discussed, the number seven is symbolic of completeness. We have here the totality of God displayed, every facet of His unimaginable complexity represented, when we are shown the seven spirits that are before the throne. Six of those seven spirits are enumerated in

Isaiah 11:2, "And the spirit of the Lord shall rest upon him, the spirit of wisdom and understanding, the spirit of counsel and might, the spirit of knowledge and of the fear of the Lord." The question immediately arises as to why only six are named. I have come to believe that that is very deliberate on the part of God because He can never be completely defined by human terms. He is unknowable by the human mind and the unnamed seventh spirit symbolizes all of God that remains a mystery to the human race. But finally, here in Revelation, John is allowed to see, and apparently can comprehend the totality of God. It is the fulfillment of the promise given in 1 Corinthians 13:12 that we shall know as completely as we are known.

GOSPEL PROCLAIMED

Consider what John writes in verses five and six. He cannot get five verses into this book without presenting the gospel in its entirety. And how succinctly he does it! The fullness and desire of John's heart is so evident. And look at the promises given to the Christian! We are loved by Jesus, we are completely forgiven by Him, and then, unbelievably, we are ensconced as royalty in His kingdom forever and ever. This staggers the imagination. We share in the *rule* and *reign* of the King of kings, and through Him we wield a power over the kingdom of darkness and evil that hell cannot withstand! And this extraordinary promise is simply given by John in verses 5 and 6 as he goes on to even more glorious and sensational statements.

Notice that Jesus is called "God" in this passage. His equality with His Father is declared at the very beginning of this letter and if one dismisses that, one must argue with God Himself.

CHRIST COMES AGAIN

The matter of His second coming was very dear to the heart of Jesus. Almost every parable dealt with some phase of this event. Christ has not gone to heaven to stay there. He has gone, by His own admission, to prepare a place for those who will rule with Him. Consider this carefully; what other religion promises or even speaks of a return of their messiah? But to the Christian it is the integral promise. Jesus is coming back, we are not abandoned, and, further, the earth is not abandoned. All will be made right. Notice, in verse 7, John's response to this proclamation, "*Even so, amen.*" This is the first-century's version of "YES!!!"

Here, we are also given a great insight into the time of the return of Jesus. It is found in the response of earth to His coming. What is that response? "And all kindreds of the earth shall *wail* because of him." The earth does not rejoice to see Him, neither is the earth indifferent to Him; the earth despises His coming. How can that be if there are Christians on the earth when He comes? It is clear that the verse says *all* kindreds of the earth shall wail, and there is no mention of *any* rejoicing whatsoever. Thus, it is clear that the Christians have been raptured before this final return. (Rapture itself will be dealt with in great depth in a latter chapter.) Post-tribulationists are thus forced to re-examine their position only seven verses into chapter 1.

Notice also that this verse tells us how He comes: with the clouds. Hebrews 12:1 refers to the saints in this very way; as a collective cloud. It seems probable to me that Jesus is referring, not to the weather conditions when He returns, but rather to the fact that when He returns, He returns with the saints who, according to Revelation 19:14, accompany Him dressed in billowing robes of white linen that appear exactly like clouds when viewed from the earth. The point is Christ cannot return with the saints if they are not already with Him in heaven.

First Thessalonians 3:13 says "To the end he may [e]stablish your hearts unblamable in holiness before God, even our Father, at the coming of our Lord Jesus Christ *with all his saints*" (emphasis mine).

First Thessalonians 4:14 says "For if we believe that Jesus died and rose again, even so them also which sleep in Jesus will God *bring with him*" (emphasis mine).

Again, look at Jude 14 "Behold, the Lord cometh with ten thousands of his Saints."

Thus we see that Revelation 1:7 is a synopsis of the final coming of Jesus to the earth. He comes with His saints to a world that moans and wails and despairs when He descends to them.

"I am the Alpha and Omega, the beginning and the ending, saith the Lord, which is and which was, and which is to come, the Almighty" (Revelation 1:8). If you choose to argue with the words in His book, you are choosing to argue with the Almighty Everlasting God Himself.

JOHN'S VISION BEGINS

John has been exiled to Patmos by the Roman emperor Domition because of his Christianity. While suffering there he sees this most amazing vision of Jesus. Yet it was not really a vision, John was actually there with Jesus. At this time, Jesus tells John what he is to do; he is to write what he has seen, what is, and what is to be. Now John is the only one of the original twelve apostles still living. He is arguably the most exalted and interesting Christian on the face of the earth. But how does he identify himself? Simply, humbly, with no title, just "I John" not Bishop John, not Pope John, not even Pastor John. What a contrast with the spiritual leaders of today!

"I was in the Spirit on the Lord's day," he says. We twenty-first-century Christians with our twenty-first-century vernacular read this as "I was in the Spirit on Sunday." That is wrong. The Scriptures do not ever refer to Sunday in that way. (The oldest usage of that term for Sunday appears in a writing about A.D. 101, however, there is no evidence at all that the Church used the term "the Lord's Day" for Sunday until well into the second century.) But the scriptures *do* speak over and over again of a day of the Lord - the Lord's Day. That is: "a day when men hide in the rocks for fear, when the Lord shall roar out of Zion and the heavens and the earth shall shake, when Jesus comes with healing in his wings. That day that will burn as an oven, the day in which God will judge the world, the day for which all other days were made."[1]

The Jews were very familiar with *that* day spoken of throughout the Old Testament. The prophet Zephaniah describes it as follows, "The great day of the Lord is near, it is near, and hasteth greatly, even the voice of the day of the Lord: the mighty man shall cry there bitterly. That day is a day of wrath, a day of trouble and distress, a day of wasteness and

25

desolation, a day of darkness and gloominess, a day of clouds and thick darkness, A day of the trumpet and alarm against the fenced cities, and against the high towers. And I will bring distress upon men, that they shall walk like blind men, because they have sinned against the Lord: and their blood shall be poured out as dust, and their flesh as the dung. Neither their silver nor their gold shall be able to deliver them in the day of the Lord's wrath; but the whole land shall be devoured by the fire of his jealousy: for he shall make even a speedy riddance of all them that dwell in the land" (Zephaniah 1:14-18).

The New Testament adds Jesus Christ to the Old Testament's understanding of *that* day of the Lord. "Who shall also confirm you unto the end, that ye may be blameless in the day of our Lord Jesus Christ" (1 Corinthians 1:8). What John is saying here is truly remarkable. That Day had not occurred by the time Paul wrote his letter. That Day still hasn't come two thousand years later. But here John is saying "I was there, folks. I saw that day - The Lord's Day - and I'm going to tell you about it." Can you imagine the buzz that went up in the fellowships of believers when this letter was read out loud to them? Can you imagine the stir? What a claim! I doubt that any other living Christian would have been believed, but, "I, John" beloved Apostle, made it, so they listened.

As John finds himself present on that glorious Day of the Lord, he records that the first thing that catches his attention is a voice like that of a trumpet. When God was present on Mount Sinai giving the law, the Bible records that the same trumpet sound was the very sound of the voice of God. John immediately recognizes this voice of authority and begins to listen.

THE SEVEN CANDLESTICKS

John turns toward the voice and sees seven golden candlesticks. These are not dining table candlesticks, they are actually lampstands - tall, sturdy stands on which people would hang their lamps. The symbolism of the candlesticks is explained in verse 20. They are the seven churches that are about to be addressed. Further, because the candlesticks number seven - the number of completeness - the candlesticks represent the Church in its entirety and completeness. In other words, they symbolize the Church of Jesus Christ throughout her history on earth. In all cultures, truth and knowledge are likened to light. The Church then is the lampstand where the light resides and shines forth. The Church bears not her own light, but the light brought to the world by Jesus. And then John notices something incredible: Jesus Himself walking among the churches! "And lo, I am with you always, even unto the ends of the earth" (Matthew 28:20). Jesus is keeping His promise.

DESCRIPTION OF JESUS

This passage also gives us the only physical description we have of Jesus outside of Isaiah 53:2 and Daniel 10:5-6, and it is, in fact, identical to what Daniel recorded there, "Then I lifted up mine eyes, and looked, and behold a certain man clothed in linen, whose loins were girded with fine gold of Uphaz; His body also was like the beryl, and his face as the appearance of lightning, and his eyes as lamps of fire, and his arms and his feet like in colour to polished brass, and the voice of his words like the voice of a multitude."

John is seeing the resurrected person of Jesus and he is writing of how Jesus appears in heaven, of how He looks now and will continue to look through the ages. And he records a fascinating picture. Jesus is still in *human* form! Philippians 2:7 tells us that before Jesus came to earth as a tiny baby, He had the form of God, but He gave that up and assumed the inferior form of a human being with all the limitations which that meant. And He did it willingly. But once He did it, the change was permanent! Jesus would forever be found in the form of a man, never again to regain His former form. Only He can understand that sacrifice. We have only known the limitation of the human body, we have never been clothed in any form more glorious, so we don't even stop to think what a sacrifice that it was for Jesus to take "upon him the form of a servant, and [be] made in the likeness of men" (Philippians 2:7). It is somewhat like the story of the little mermaid, when, in order for her to be found in human form so as to be with her love, it was required of her that she surrender her form as a mermaid and also surrender and lose her most precious possession: her voice. Never again could she look back. Of course, that is a banal comparison, but it gives one the sense of the finality of the choice involved.

Consider, too, that no matter how adorable we might find a new little puppy, if someone were to suggest that we take on that form, we would resist. Why? Because as cute as that puppy is, it's much better to be a human. As nice as being a human is, it is much more exalted to be found in the form of God. But Jesus in effect said, "I love them... I love them so much that there is not one thing that it would cost me that I am not willing to give. And so I will leave my God form, I will not grasp it, I will not hold tightly to it. I will become human." And now John sees Jesus, still a man even in heaven, but what a glorious man!

His attire is both kingly (the sword) and priestly (the robe and girdle of Exodus 39). It is proper that it should be so because the priestly lineage of Levi and the kingly lineage of Judah have come together in Him.

His hair is white. Nothing in this picture of Jesus calls to mind old age or suggests that He is feeble or decrepit, therefore, I do not think the white hair is indicative of old age. Perhaps it is a reminder of His great suffering, perhaps it is symbolic of the wisdom of the ages that He possesses, perhaps it is indicative of His purity.

His eyes are "as a flame of fire." Eyes are symbolic of knowledge. The flame of fire speaks to purity because of the ability of fire to purge and make pure. Thus, He possesses perfect knowledge.

His feet are likened to brass. Whereas gold is the symbol of heavenly things, and silver is the symbol of redemption (it is no accident that Jesus was betrayed for thirty pieces of *silver*), brass is the symbolic metal of judgment. For instance, the altar in the temple on which was placed the sacrifice, was made of brass. His feet are brass because He has the power to execute judgment. All things are under his feet; feet speak of dominion.

"The Lord said unto my Lord, Sit thou at my right hand, until I make thine enemies thy *footstool*" (Psalms 110:1, emphasis mine).

"I have *trodden* the winepress alone: and of the people there was none with me: for I will *tread* them in mine anger, and *trample* them in my fury; and their blood shall be sprinkled upon my garments, and I will stain all my raiment" (Isaiah 63:3, emphasis mine).

Once, when David was conquering the land for Israel, he did not have time to go into Edom but he made clear his authority over it when he cast his shoe over into it (Psalms 60:8; 108:9). The book of Ruth makes it clear that the giving of one's shoe was the symbol of entering into contract with another. The foot and the shoe symbolize power and authority. That is why God commanded Moses to remove his shoes before approaching God's presence in the burning bush. The act of removing his shoes signified the humility of Moses and the suborning of his authority to God's authority. Now, John sees Jesus and sees that His feet are as burnished brass. Jesus is coming to execute judgment over the world. But He will execute that judgment with the eyes of perfect knowledge. It will be perfect judgment.

His voice is as the sound of many waters. Archibald Rutledge made a wonderful point when he wrote, "There are very few sounds in the natural world that are harsh. Even the massive rolling of thunder has about it something of solemn beauty. In anthems the sea rolls on the beach; and in the sunny shallows there are water-harps forever making melodies. The wind is a chorister. Many a wild bird can warble like an aerial rivulet. The world is really a melodious place, full of soft sounds and harmony. Man makes it riotous and blatant"[2] This is the Voice that orchestrated the sounds of Nature. The voice of God is the paragon of beauty and power. Psalm 29 describes that voice. It thunders. It is powerful and full of majesty, it breaks cedars, it divides flames of fire, it shakes the wilderness and forests, causing the cows to calve. Ezekiel says it sounds like the wings of the mighty cherubim. This is the voice that will call out our name from the heavens and bring us home!

SEVEN STARS

John records that He holds the seven stars in His right hand. The end of this chapter tells us who the seven stars are. They are the angels of the seven churches. The Greek word for angel simply means messenger. These angels might be spiritual beings or they might be the Christian leaders of the churches. The message to each of the churches is addressed to the angel of that church. That seems to signify a mortal, as a heavenly being would have no need of a message from John. Adding credence to that idea, we see that later on in Revelation, twice, an identified human being is called an angel by John. They appear angelic to John in their glorified states, however they are very clearly of the race of Adam.

However one chooses to interpret "angel," the more important point is that they are held in the right hand of Jesus. The right hand signifies authority. Jesus holds the authority over the Church, no one else: not any man, not any heavenly angel. It is His church. And from His mouth proceeds the sharp two-edged sword. Isaiah 55:11, Hebrews 4:12 and Ephesians 6:17 all tell us what this symbol represents. It is the Word of God. Remember that Paul tells us in 2 Timothy 3:16 that all Scripture is given by the inspiration of God, there is no private interpretation, one cannot pick and choose which Scriptures to believe. It flows from the very mouth of Jesus here. Jesus said when He was on earth that "the word that I have spoken, the same shall judge him in the last day" (John 12:48). This is about to happen.

THE COUNTENANCE OF CHRIST

John records that His countenance was as the sun. This is exactly how He looked on the Mount of Transfiguration, this is the complete glory of God upon Him. And, as with every other mortal who has beheld the glory of God, John could not abide it with his human body. He fell down as if dead. Now John was the closest friend that Jesus had when He was on the earth. John speaks of feeling free to rest with his head on Jesus' bosom at the Last Supper. There was intimacy between these two, but even John cannot stay conscious when he sees Jesus as God. How does Jesus respond? He ever so gently goes over to John, bends down and touches him with His right hand and says in effect, "John, don't be afraid, I am the one you knew. You are safe. I was dead and now I am alive and I will be alive for evermore." Then He says a most remarkable thing: "I have the keys of hell and of death."

THE KEYS TO DEATH AND HELL

When sin entered the world, death entered the world, and ever since death entered the world, it has been in the control of Satan. Hebrews 2:14 says "that through death he [Jesus] might destroy him that had the power of death, that is, the devil." The word used here for "hell" is the word for "the grave." Not only did Satan control death, he also had control of the bodies after they died. We see this in the Book of Jude when Satan is disputing with Michael, the archangel, over the body of Moses. When Moses died, Deuteronomy 34:6 says that God Himself buried his body and no man ever knew where. It is clear from Jude that God never gave that body over to Sheol (the grave), the domain of Satan, but kept it instead. Satan cried, "Unfair! You know that I have the legal right to all human bodies at death, now hand it over." Michael responded simply, "The Lord rebuke you." In other words, God always retains the ultimate authority in any situation, he always has the veto power. We will see later in this book the complete answer as to why God kept the body of Moses.

We see evidence of God's final authority over death in the ministry and teaching of Jesus. Matthew 16 tells us the story of when Jesus took his disciples to Caesarea Philippi. Caesarea Philippi had a widespread reputation for being a place of deep pagan worship and the disciples must have wondered why Jesus took them there. It is a beautiful place where an underground river bubbles forth from under the shadow of tall craggy cliffs. It is a place of many trees, much shade and the sound of water. But in the clefs of those crags can still be found statues of pagan gods. In fact, the Greeks believed that the mouth of this spring was an entrance to Hades. So when Jesus chose this very place to ask the disciples who men said he was and who they thought he was, and Peter replied, "Thou are the Christ, the Son of the living God," there was much meaning in Jesus' reply to that. I can see him looking around at the high rock face with all of the statues of demon gods perched upon it, and saying "upon THAT rock I will build my church and the gates of hell will not prevail against it." They were at the perceived gates of Hell! Jesus was telling them that Death and Hades themselves could not stand against the power of THAT rock! Death and Hades would fall to the power that Jesus wielded.

When Jesus first challenges Satan in regards to death, it is with Jairus's daughter. Jesus restores her to life almost immediately after she has died; in fact, her body is still warm. But hell knows what has happened, and its foundations begin to shake. Next, He raises the widow of Nain's son from the dead. The boy has been dead for a longer time when Jesus stops the funeral procession in order to raise him, but he has not yet been put in the grave. The foundations of hell crack farther. Finally we see the raising of Lazarus. When Jesus is called by Mary and Martha to come help their brother, He intentionally delays his coming until Lazarus has been dead for four days. When He comes to Bethany, He comes directly to the tomb. In a loud voice He demands that Lazarus come forth. He knows that Lazarus is not opposed to this command, but Satan is. Such is His authority, however, that the multitude sees Lazarus step out from his grave, still bound head to foot with the graveclothes. Imagine being able to witness that sight! Hell knew it must act. Immediately after this, the Bible says that "from that day forth they took counsel together for to put him to death" (John 11:53). John further recounts that they plotted to kill Lazarus also. Of course. Satan wanted that body back (four days in the grave indeed!), and he knew that he must stop Jesus. One week later, Jesus is dead. But that is not the end of the story. Jesus spent three days in the grave; they were three days of victorious battle. When Jesus defeated death, and rose from the grave, He rose with the keys to death and hell in *His* hands! Now He tells John that those keys are safely in His, Jesus', hands. As the old hymn stated so well, "He lives that death may die".

JESUS HOLDS THE KEYS

Due to the fact that we live on this side of the cross, we are sometimes blind in regards to understanding the absolute astonishment that the disciples experienced when they heard that Jesus had risen from the dead. I began to understand this on a very basic level one hot day in July in a town just north of El Paso, Texas. My husband and I had gone with our four daughters to an enormous water park to spend the day. While

I went with the two older ones to one part of the park, my husband stayed with the little ones, a two-and-a-half-year old and the baby, Bari, just eighteen months. Pete was the most protective of fathers, more protective even than I, but he took his eyes off of Bari for just a moment and she disappeared. When I returned with the two older girls about twenty minutes later, I found park employees who were busy trying to find my baby and a totally distraught husband. The water park had many, many water rides in addition to acres of grass and picnic tables and it was like looking for a needle in a haystack. My anguish was almost beyond bearing. Many kind people, including many young boys who were apparently gang members fanned out to help look. Three abreast, some began walking the "Lazy River" to see if her body might be found in the channel. I ran to the front entrance to see if someone was trying to sneak her out, but I could not bear the inactivity of simply waiting there, and so I ran back and forth like a crazed woman. An hour passed, the park was beginning to close. At this point, I was simply praying to find her body; the thought that she had been kidnapped was even more painful to consider. I imagined her disappearing over the United States border, twenty minutes away, never to be seen again. Finally, as the crowds all but disappeared at closing time we found her nonchalantly watching the ducks in a pond at the other side of the park. Although I clutched her to me all the ride home and all through the night, the terror of losing her did not leave me. All I could do was replay my constant thoughts of the long afternoon. I had begun then, in spite of myself, to plan her funeral, and the horror of losing her was still all too real. Now, in my mind, I walked through her funeral, pictured my mourning and inconsolable grieving in the days following her death, and then, incongruously, I pictured people running up to me saying, "Bari is not dead, she is alive and walking through town!" With every fiber of my being I felt what would be my confusion, my disbelief, my hope against hope that little Bari could somehow be alive. How I would run out that door to see for myself. How I would never be the same if somehow it could be true. And then suddenly I understood what it meant to the disciples when Jesus conquered death. All of those were their reactions: everything from despair to disbelief to astonishment and euphoria in the space of a few minutes. Jesus Christ conquered death, He was alive! And they were witnesses to it all. No wonder they turned the world upside down for Him in the years to come. He has risen, Alleluia! And now, after His ascension to heaven years before, He appears to John with the keys to death and hell in His hands.

Contemplate for a moment what a blessing it is to die on this side of the cross. When Jesus told His disciples that they would not see death, I think He was promising more even than eternal life. Jesus was telling them that He, Himself, would come for them; the Grim Reaper would not. Several years ago, the movie *Ghost* depicted the moments after death of some particularly evil characters. The depiction was quite graphic as horrid, demon-like creatures came to escort them out of this world and into the next one. The depiction is, if anything, tame compared to the reality of those who die outside of Jesus. No human will leave this life unescorted. And the reality is (sometimes without even realizing it), we each choose our escort.

THE BOOK'S MESSAGE OUTLINED BY JOHN

In verse 19, Jesus gives to John the outline of the book of Revelation. It will be composed of three parts: The things that he already seen (the vision of Jesus); the things that are (the letters to the churches in chapters 2 and 3); and the things that will happen in the future. Keep this in mind because many expositors of Revelation will interpret the scenes found in this book in light of past events. That is outside of the divine outline. Nothing that has occurred up to this point in human history has a place in this prophecy. This will be particularly important to remember when we deal with the woman and the child in chapter 12, and the war in heaven that is found in that chapter also. It is my contention that the Bible will always explain itself if we let it be true to itself instead of ignoring critical bits of information such as have just been given to us in verse 19. Revelation is a vision. It will not be simply told to John - he will actually see the Day of the Lord played out before his very eyes. At the same time, Revelation is not a "flash-back" either. According to Jesus, its purpose, besides the vision of Jesus, is to carry John into the future. The revelation will begin with the Church Age at the time of John, and will carry the saints through the entire Church Age until Jesus returns, on into the Great Tribulation and Armageddon, on through the thousand-year reign, and finally into eternity. The word "church" is not found after chapter 3 until the very last chapter of Revelation, when John uses it to identify who is the intended recipient of this letter. Why? The answer is telling. There will be no church found on the earth after the Rapture, only tribulation saints who will not be organized as a church because they will be fighting for their lives. Verse 19 also soundly contradicts a Preterist interpretation of Revelation that attempts to explain this book by suggesting that it is simply a coded book of first-century Christians speaking of their experience during the Imperial Persecution. It is, for the Preterists, simply a symbolic story. It was certainly not just that for John. It was a revelation.

As has already been mentioned, the final verse in this chapter explains the two symbols found in chapter 1. They are the seven stars and the seven golden candlesticks. Jesus says the seven stars are the angels of the seven churches and the lampstands are the seven churches themselves. Notice the word "mystery" used in connection with this explanation. It is clear that there is no mystery with the symbols themselves; they are interpreted. Instead, the word "mystery" intimates from the start that something more than just surface is intended with the churches. This mystery will be discussed in the next chapter.

CHAPTER 3
THE CHURCHES OF EPHESUS AND SMYRNA
Revelation 2:1-11

THE CHURCH AGE

Chapters 2 and 3 of Revelation concern themselves with the Church Age; that period of time between the beginning of the Church on the day of Pentecost and the return of Jesus for His Church. Seven churches are specifically addressed. We have already noted that they are representative of churches throughout time. As we will see, the letters to those churches are in a very interesting order. Indeed, two thousand years after John wrote this, it is clearly seen that the historical evolution of the Church has followed this identical pattern. Thus, although these are literal churches, and these letters were addressed to them, there is a prophetic miracle in play in chapters 2 and 3. In addition, each of these seven types of churches clearly is in evidence today. So the letters function in three ways: (1) to address a specific church in John's time, (2) to establish a type of church that would be representative of existing churches from then on,(3) to trace the history of the Church from the first century to the coming of Christ for His Church.

To each of the churches He will:

1. Identify Himself. Each identification will be different and personal, and will center on the aspect of Jesus which she most needs to heed. Each identification will be taken from the description already given of Christ in the first chapter.

2. Commend the church when and where applicable.

3. Reprove where applicable. "He who hath ears let him hear" is said to each church. He is pleading for them to heed Him and to reform. One of the great themes of Revelation is judgment, and, as the Scripture says, judgment must begin at the house of the Lord. So it is well and proper that before dealing with the world, Jesus firsts deals with the Church. Sadly, for the most part, the Church has ignored His warnings and pleadings for reform as steadfastly as will the world. The greatest weakness of the Church has been her insistence on

loyalty at the expense of self-cleansing. Submission is held in far higher esteem than purity and holiness. Voices from within who have cried out for cleansing and reform have been labeled disloyal, divisive, and heretical. For the most part, they have either been silenced or ignored. It is interesting to note that the Church of England has a cycle of required, structured Sunday Scripture readings that covers the entire New Testament *except* for chapters 2 and 3 in Revelation - the warnings to the churches. Wrote Richard Chenevix Trench, Archbishop of Dublin, Church of Ireland, "Under no circumstances whatsoever can the second and third chapters ever be heard in the congregation."[3] Contrast that with this quote from Martin Luther, one of the great reformers of the Church: "If I profess with the loudest voice and the clearest exposition every portion of the truth of God, except precisely that little point which the world and the devil are at that moment attacking, I am not confessing Christ, however boldly I may be professing Christ. Where the battle rages, there the loyalty of the soldier is proved, and to be steady on all the battlefield beside is mere flight and disgrace if he flinches at that point."

And speaking of Martin Luther, it is interesting to note that although the Catholic Church could tolerate all the corruption that Martin Luther was decrying, they could not tolerate Martin Luther. Until the hierarchy in each local church determines that the call to cleansing is critical, the church will remain polluted. But still the words of Jesus in chapters 2 and 3 echo down the ages.

4. Give a promise to the overcomers of each church. It will be different each time, and the promises will be cumulative until all that man has lost to sin is returned to the overcomers by the gracious hand of God. And who is an overcomer? The Bible answers this in 1 John 5:4-5, "For whatsoever is born of God overcometh the world: and this is the victory that overcometh the world, even our faith. Who is he that overcometh the world, but he that believeth that Jesus is the Son of God?"

Chapters 2 and 3 give assurance to the promise that Jesus gave to Peter in Matthew 16:18 that "upon this rock I will build my church; and the gates of hell shall not prevail against it." Although we will see that the onslaught of Satan against the

Church throughout history is powerful, unrelenting, and vicious beyond belief, when Jesus comes for her, she will be standing tall and waiting for Him. Hell will not win. Jesus said so. Revelation tells the story of the attack and it begins with the first-century church - Ephesus.

EPHESUS

Ephesus was both an important and magnificent city. The Romans called her "the crown jewel of Asia Minor." She was a seat of government and a center for trade, art, religion, learning, and wealth. The Temple of Diana, one of the Seven Wonders of the Ancient World, was located here as was a great temple dedicated to the emperor Domitian. The Temple of Domitian was modeled on the Temple of Zeus at Mt. Olympus and featured a statue of Domitian that was twenty-seven feet tall. Ephesus was a center of worship to Domitian who insisted that he was divine, not human, and required that the citizens there confess him as God. It may very well have been because of this fact that John, who had been living in Ephesus, was brought to the attention of the emperor and exiled to Patmos, because John, of course, would have refused to make such a confession. It was to Ephesus that John returned after he left Patmos, and it was here that Mary, the mother of Jesus, died. The name *Ephesus* means "relax" or "backslide" and, conversely, also means "desirable." This church was both - desirable and laudable in the eyes of the world, but found lacking (or backsliding) in the eyes of Jesus and in her relationship with Him. Ephesus is today a ruin.

HER CHARACTERISTICS, GOOD AND BAD

In the historical context of the Church, the church at Ephesus was a type of the church at the close of the Apostolic Age. Jesus is beginning the chronicle of the Church at exactly the place in time that the Book of Acts left off. Approximately forty years have passed since Paul founded this church, and at first blush she seems to be a model for churches everywhere. Jesus commends her liberally. It is clear from the letter that she is a working church full of good deeds. This does not escape Jesus' notice - it never does. She is true to the faith, doctrinally pure, with a steadfast opposition to evil. Evidently, the Elders of the church here have taken to heart the very last instructions and warning that were given to her by Paul in Acts 20:28-30. There, Paul warned them to faithfully watch over the flock, feed it, and keep it safe from men who would attempt to pervert the faith with false teaching, and thus draw away the sheep. Furthermore, according to 1 Timothy 1:3, Paul had left Timothy in charge of doctrinal matters at Ephesus, insuring a strong, solid foundation. Ephesus has also been faithful in enduring and bearing the burdens that accompany a walk with Christ.

But there is a deadly flaw in this church, so deadly that the removal of her candlestick is at stake. What is that flaw? She has left her first love. Where Christ was once her center, focus, and raison d'etre, He is being replaced. At first, Jesus was everything to them. After all, these were the people whose lives were so changed by Him that they set the world on fire. Then, gradually, the Church itself began to assume more importance than Jesus. We see this in many churches today. Church work as opposed to service to Jesus provides much of the motivation for good works. Money that was once spent on the spreading of the gospel is now spent on the church. Slowly, slowly the church becomes more important than Christ. The good and right things begin to take on a life of their own. Whereas before when a need was recognized and quickly met in the course of brotherly love, now perhaps a committee is formed to assess the need and the means for meeting the need. Meetings are held, a hierarchy is established, policy is formed, and finally help is given. Of course, after all that organization, the framework stays in place and the committee begins a life of its own. Lost, perhaps, is the urgent concern for people, replaced by bureaucracy; probably kindly bureaucracy, but bureaucracy nonetheless. Here we see that the Ephesians had lost the emotion; they were now just going through the motions.

THE FOCUS OF LOVE - THE CHURCH OR JESUS?

Love for *Jesus* is the root of all *true* Christianity, and while there is still health in her leaves and branches, this church has root rot. What is so interesting is that, because there is still so much health in this church at Ephesus - it is probably still experiencing great growth - this insidious disease is being missed by the Church. Only Jesus sees it. And he warns them. Notice how He identifies Himself to this church. "These things saith he that holdeth the seven stars in his right hand, who walketh in the midst of the seven golden candlesticks." He identifies Himself as having the power and preeminence over the Church. He holds the seven stars (angels to the churches) *in His hand,* and is found *in the midst* of the seven candlesticks (the churches). The church has been called into existence solely because of Jesus. But although they have a zeal for the truth and for the right, their love for Jesus is now secondary. Paul warned of this in 1 Corinthians 13 when he said that speaking with the tongues of angels, having the gift of prophecy, understanding all mysteries, having all knowledge and faith, doing all good works even to giving one's body to be burned, doesn't count for anything if the love is not there. Jesus says that this trend is so serious that He will remove their candlestick if they do not repent. "Repent and do the deeds as before or else I will remove your candlestick," He says. They are still doing the same things, only the motivation has changed, but that has changed everything in His eyes. In other words He says, "If you are doing these things for the wrong reasons, you might as well not do them." To place the love of the Church above one's love of Jesus is idolatry. However, when you love Jesus above all else, you will naturally love the Church. It will all be in balance. We see this balance of love for Jesus reflecting itself in love for the Church all through the book of Acts. Barnabas sold property to care for the needs of the saints. (The term "saint" will be used henceforth as it was originally used in the Bible, that is, as a term applicable to every believer. It will not be used to differentiate between different classes of believers - saints and then the rest of the Christians - as that distinction cannot be supported from a study of the Scriptures.) The office of deacon was initially established in order to meet the needs of Christian widows. Love of the brethren is a natural outgrowth of loving God.

Apparently, the Ephesians did not heed this rebuke for, indeed, her candlestick has been removed; there is no church in existence today at Ephesus. We, as individuals, must be heedful to mind this warning, also. If we fail to do so, if we put our ministries before our relationship with Jesus, we will also find that His light is gone from our lampstand. We might continue in our works, but the power, light, and holy anointing will be absent from them and from our lives. To abide in Him is more important than to do for Him.

THE NICOLAITANS - ECCLESIASTIC SEPARATION

In verse 6, the Ephesians are commended for hating the deeds of the Nicolaitans. There is no recorded movement or doctrine of Nicolaitans, so the word itself becomes very important to understanding what is being communicated here. The term *Nicolaitan* is a combination of two Greek words: *nico* and *laitanes*. *Nico* is the word for conqueror. *Laitanes* is the word for the laity, or common people. When combined we have a word that literally means "the conquerors of the laity." This is the beginning of the division of the priesthood and the laity. Jesus <u>died</u> to remove all barriers between God and us, but Satan is beginning to sneak them in within the doctrine of the Nicolaitans.

We are told in the Old Testament that there was an extremely heavy veil that hung in the Temple, separating the people from the presence of God that was contained in the Ark of the Covenant. When Jesus died, that veil was supernaturally torn from top to bottom signifying that there was now no separation between God and mankind. Furthermore, 1 Peter 2:9 is clear in stating that all believers are considered by God to be priests; there is no distinction or stratum with God. But the idea that there is a distinction among believers - a hierarchy within the Church - is being planted. We already see some people taking that veil and, in a manner of speaking, sewing it up and trying to tack it back into place, creating barriers between God and man. At this point, the Church is stringently resisting this movement and is commended by Jesus for doing so. Sadly, it will not always remain so.

Even in the most corrupt churches - of which Ephesus is not one - there will be overcomers and the first promise is now given to the overcomers. It is the restoration of access to the Tree of Life. This is significant. The first thing restored to man is the first thing that was taken from man: access to the Tree of

Life. When this access was lost, death began for all creation. Immunity from this curse must of necessity be the first restorative promise. Man was not created to die; man was created to commune eternally with God. But after sin entered the world, God, in mercy, had to allow death. Why?

Consider what Adam did when he brought sin upon himself. He brought curses upon himself. He brought pain, disease, torment, loneliness, and sadness. And he brought it not only upon himself, he brought it upon every human who would ever live. Knowing the evil, savagery, torment, disease, and pain that would be a consequence of sin, living forever in this climate would be unspeakable torture. Imagine a body wracked with disease and pain, from which it would never be released. Imagine the little children repeatedly abused and never having an end to the pain. Imagine the martyrs for the faith enduring unspeakable things that would have to stretch on forever. In fact, one of the most horrible aspects of the Tribulation that we will see will be a five-month period when, despite terrible torment, no one is allowed to die. No, God saw ahead and saw that death was a necessary mercy, but because death was a consequence of sin, death was not ever meant to be a permanent fixture for the people of God. When there is no more sin, death will no longer be needed.

The Tree of Life did not disappear when access to it was blocked. The Tree of Life was removed to heaven. Now, access to it will be restored to the overcomers. It is interesting to note that the leaves of this tree will be used for the healing of the nations on earth, but the fruit is reserved for the overcomers who dwell in the holy city that comes down from heaven (Revelation 22:2).

SMYRNA

Smyrna is known today as the city of Izmir, Turkey. She is situated at the head of a beautiful bay, much like San Francisco is, and she was considered the most beautiful city in Asia at this time. It was the birthplace of Homer. The root word of Smyrna means "bitterness" and this is indeed a bittersweet letter. There is not one word of reproach for this church from the mouth of Jesus. To the contrary, His tenderness and depth of feeling for the saints who live there are apparent. And yet the words are filled with foreboding. Smyrna was the site for much persecution during the Imperial Persecutions. Five hundred believers, and then later, eight hundred believers were martyred here at one time. The famous Christian, Polycarp, was Bishop of the church here, and was killed in a most gruesome way. Still, the church of Smyrna is a type of something much larger than just itself. History was swiftly propelling the first-century Church into two hundred years of intense persecution by Rome. This letter is a continuation of the story of the history of the Church down through the ages. Smyrna is also a type for every church that has known persecution, stretching all the way down to the churches facing persecution today.

UNDERGOING PERSECUTION

Jesus, knowing all that is about to happen - knowing that Satan is readying even now to open the floodgates of persecution against the Church - sends the Church at Smyrna and the Church, the Bride of Christ, a letter. Four points are clearly made. First, He, too, has suffered in the extreme. Ever so gently Jesus reminds them that He is not asking anything of them that He has not already gone through, and more importantly, has gone through with victory. There is nothing that will come against them that He has not conquered. Because He has conquered death, they can conquer death. Because He has conquered Satan, they can conquer Satan. Second, He knows what they are about to go through; nothing that Satan will do to the saints will catch Jesus by surprise. And because that is the case, He has already made provision in His Grace for everything that they are going to be called upon to go through. Third, He tells them not to fear. Fourth, He tells them that they will die but it will be all right. All of these words of Jesus apply to the saints down through history. There are things in each of our lives that are going to happen and they will be hard. They will catch us by surprise; they will not catch Him by surprise. He has already made provision for us out of His grace. It is enough to rest in that. And when we do, we will not fear because we know that it will be all right.

These assurances begin with Jesus' identification of Himself to this church: "These things saith the first and the last, which was dead, and is alive." He was the first to undergo suffering, and He has triumphed! So shall they because He will walk through this with them. He will truly be their light and their salvation. And, although they will die, they, too, will live forever.

POVERTY OR RICHES?

Jesus then commends them for their works, and gives assurance that He is aware of their tribulations and poverty. Jesus, however, holds a very different view than does the world concerning their poverty. He says that although by worldly standards they are indeed poor, He sees their condition and declares them rich. If ever a wealthy, prosperous, twenty-first-century Church needed to understand a spiritual principle it is this one. We do not understand rich. We are deceived and defrauded when it comes to perceiving what constitutes "rich." Now God understands rich. No one approaches His level of wealth. He alone has enough wealth to have perspective on what it means to be rich. And He shares that wealth and perspective with His children. He walks through His storehouse of unlimited treasures and He tenderly picks for each of us the exquisite gifts that He knows are most priceless. Sometimes they are treasures of health, or wisdom, or family, or friends, or wonderful talents, or a heart that truly knows Him. And, when He gifts us with these precious gems, we say "That's nice God, but give me the tinfoil. That's nice, but give me the paper. Give me the plastic. Give me the junk." We are like children choosing nickels over dimes because they appear larger.

How His heart must grieve over our foolishness and rebellion when we reject or demean His gifts. And indeed it is rebellion when we do this. We are in essence saying that what God has given to us is not adequate, it is not good enough and we deserve more, now give it to us! God knows our needs and He supplies them abundantly. We must absolutely come to rest in this truth if we are to go on in our walk of faith with Him. God is generosity personified. He delights to give to us the things that delight Him. We must learn to have His mind on this and not allow our fallen, inferior mind to deceive us as to what is of value. Paul understood this and wrote of it to the

Corinthians: "But in all things approving ourselves as the ministers of God ... as sorrowful, yet always rejoicing; as poor, yet making many rich; as having nothing, and yet possessing all things," (2 Corinthians 6:4,10). The Smyrnan Church had the light of Jesus; it was pure and undefiled. The Smyrnan Church was rich.

TARES IN THE CHURCH

In verse 9, Jesus refers to those who say they are Jews and are not, instead they are of the synagogue of Satan. This reference is also used in the letter to the Philadelphian Church, the only other church that was given no rebukes. It is a reference to those who claim to be God's chosen (the Jews were and are chosen of God, and so it is an understandable term to the first-century reader) and yet are not truly of the congregation of the righteous. Indeed, they are in the opposite camp, they are in the synagogue of Satan. They are the tares (weeds) that Satan has planted in the church. He only plants tares where there is wheat. Satan does not have need of tares in troubled churches - they are already out of balance and less than effective - but Satan always plants tares in the godly churches. Not all who are in the church are Christians and it is not the fault of the Church. "Don't worry", Jesus says. "I know who is who and also why they are there. Go on with your walk."

Nonetheless, Jesus warns them, these tares are part of their congregation even if disguised. In the very next verse Jesus tells the believers not to fear the things that they are about to suffer. It is very possible that these tares will speak words of discouragement, hopelessness, and unbelief to the Christians who are being persecuted in the days ahead. "I don't see how we're going to get through all this. All hope is lost, we might as well give up now. Woe is me. How could God allow this to happen?" etc., etc. Satan has planted these people in the Church. He knows what a well-placed word of fear or discouragement can do. The Christians are to counter these words with the words of Jesus that tell them to fear not. It is even possible that these tares will be traitors to the believers and will betray them to the authorities. It does not matter. God is in control.

FAITHFUL UNTIL DEATH

Although Jesus begins verse 10 with the comforting admonition to fear not, the rest of the sentence is bleak, indeed. He prophesies what awaits them - and it is suffering, imprisonment, tribulation, and death. This is the only church out of the seven that looks forward only to death, not to His return. In this way they are a type of the saints of the Tribulation period after the Rapture who, too, only have death as their way out. But this death will not defeat them; instead, they will overcome Satan. And further, Satan will be defeated on his own playing field with all <u>his</u> rules in force. How? Despite all of the torment that Satan will throw at them, nothing will crush them, nothing will defeat them, nothing will deter the force of God on the earth through His Church. The power of Grace will defeat the power of Satan. "But where sin abounded, grace did much more abound," (Romans 5:20). It does not matter who does the sinning; there will always be more grace in our lives if we will but accept it. So, there is grace for our own sins, but there is also grace in our lives when we suffer due to the sins of others. Consider the drunk driver who wipes out an entire family. That is not the sin of the family, but it is certainly sin on the part of the drunk driver. Many times the innocent bear the consequences of someone else's sin. It will be true for the Christians during this era. But the promise is that no matter how much sin is thrown into your life there is always more grace. Sin never has to win out. When you face trouble, you receive grace. When you face deep trouble you receive deep grace. There is never "not enough grace." This is the secret to living a victorious Christian life.

"And fear not them which kill the body, but are not able to kill the soul: but rather fear him which is able to destroy both soul and body in hell," (Matthew 10:28). Most of the time, we, when confronted with difficulty and tribulation, pray hard to be delivered from it. Many times God does deliver us, but many times the answer is not the promise of deliverance but the command to overcome. Deliverance makes it go away and leaves us relieved and thankful. But when, through the grace and power of God, we overcome, we are forever changed and find that our character is now more in the image of God's character. It is wonderful when He delivers us but it is glorious when we overcome. Do not despise the answer that says, "This time, you are to overcome" for what awaits is what awaited the Smyrnan Christians - the crown of life.

Fatima Al-Mutairi, a recent martyr for Christ in Saudi Arabia, well understood this. At the age of 26, she was murdered by her own brother – a member of the fanatical religious police in Riyadh – because she had shared her new-found faith with her Muslim family. She well understood the peril of doing so, but chose to publicly proclaim her faith in Jesus nonetheless. In a poem found after her death she wrote:

"Your swords do not concern me, not evil nor disgrace.

Your threats do not trouble me and we are not afraid.

And by God, I am unto death a Christian."[4]

"Blessed is the man that endureth temptation: for when he is tried, he shall receive the crown of life, which the Lord hath promised to them that love him" (James 1:12).

"Henceforth there is laid up for me a crown of righteousness, which the Lord, the righteous judge, shall give me at that day: and not to me only, but unto all them also that love his appearing" (2 Timothy 4:8)

THE DAYS OF PERSECUTION

The ten days in Revelation 2:10 are symbolic. Ten, in prophecy, is a small but indefinite number, or a number that is subject to change. An example of this is the ten virgins of Jesus' parable concerning His return. We see the same idea of a large but indefinite number when a large multiple of ten is used as with the ten thousand times ten thousand who stand before the judgment seat of God spoken of in Daniel 7:10. What Jesus is communicating by using the space of ten days is to say that they will not know beforehand how long the persecution will go on, but it does have an end; it will not last forever. There is much grace in not having a precise timetable. Imagine being only seventy-five years into the two hundred plus years of Imperial Persecution. It would be next to impossible not to give way to feelings of total despair. But with the future shrouded, each generation could hope that it would be the last generation to be so afflicted. And with each generation would also go the reassurance that Jesus would be with them to walk them through it and spread His wings of grace over them. They would not be delivered, but they would overcome!

OVERCOMERS DELIVERED FROM SECOND DEATH

The first thing that was restored to the overcomers was the Tree of Life. The second thing that is now restored is deliverance from the second death. Revelation 20:14 defines the second death as the lake of fire. After losing his access to the Tree of Life, man passed into judgment. The second promise saves us from judgment and punishment after we die. It is especially apropos that this promise concerning the second death should be given to those who are facing the specter of the first death. Again comes the word to "fear not them who can kill the body, but him who can destroy the soul" (Matthew 10:28). If you are delivered from the fear of judgment, you have nothing to fear!

By the very fact that the Smyrnan Church had to continually face the specter of death, she corrected what was so abhorrent to Jesus concerning the Ephesian Church. One cannot die in the ways they were forced to die without having Christ as one's central focus and love. Jesus was again the focal point of this church. He would not remain so in four of the next five churches.

ROMAN PERSECUTIONS

Between two and seven million Christians were killed during the Imperial Persecutions. As John was recording these words of Jesus, the Church had already been through the terror of the reign of Nero and now Domitian was emperor. After him would come Nerva for a short two years, and then Trajan would ascend to the throne in A.D. 98. Although Trajan did not actively seek out Christians, Pliny II wrote that thousands were put to death daily. Jesus' brother, Simeon, was killed during Trajan's reign, as was Ignatius, Bishop of Antioch. History records that Ignatius was killed by beasts in the Amphitheater.

POLYCARP

Hadrian became Emperor in A.D. 117 and he, too, persecuted Christians in moderation although it was he who first called the land of Israel by the name "Palestine", and he did so because he wanted to remove the God of Israel from remembrance. The next emperor, Antoninus Pius (A.D. 138-61) rather favored Christians but felt that he had to enforce the laws of the land. Polycarp, Bishop of Smyrna was killed at this time. Polycarp was a personal disciple of John the Apostle. He was an eighty-six-year-old man and was well respected by both the church and the community. Three days before he was arrested, he dreamed that his pillow became fire and consumed him. He awoke and prophesied that he would be burned alive. Persecution had broken out in Smyrna at that point, and believers were being thrown to the wild animals. On the day of his death, as Christians were being killed in the arena, the crowd began to call for the Christians' leader, Polycarp. The authorities sent out a search party to find him. After they had tortured two slave boys in order to find where he was hidden, they came to arrest him. It was a Friday afternoon and Polycarp was upstairs, resting. Instead of fleeing, Polycarp responded, "God's will be done."

Polycarp descended the stairs and welcomed the soldiers as friends, serving them food and drink. He then asked for an hour in which to pray. After being escorted to the Arena, the authorities began to reconsider. The Proconsul, especially, did not want to make this aged man a martyr and offered him his freedom if he would but curse Christ.

Polycarp replied: "Eighty and six years I have served Him. He has never done me wrong. How then can I blaspheme my king who has saved me?"

The proconsul then said: "Then do this, old man. Just swear by the genius [spirit] of the emperor and that will be sufficient."

Polycarp answered: "If you imagine for a moment that I would do that, then I think you pretend that you don't know who I am. Hear it plainly. I am a Christian." The proconsul threatened the wild beasts.

Polycarp replied: "Bring them forth. I would change my mind if it meant going from the worse to the better, but not to change from the right to the wrong." Polycarp was told he would be burned alive.

His reply was: "You threaten fire that burns for an hour and is over. But judgment on the ungodly is forever."

As the fire was being prepared, Polycarp prayed, "Father, I bless you that you have deemed me worthy of this day and hour, that I might take a portion of the martyrs in the cup of Christ... Among these may I today be welcome before thy face as a rich and acceptable sacrifice." His prayer was answered: the believers recorded that as his body was being burned, it smelled not like burning flesh, but like bread baking. He was finished off with a dagger. The Christians buried his remains on February 22 and set that day aside to be remembered as a day of triumph.

REIGN OF MARCUS AURELIUS

Marcus Aurelius assumed the throne in A.D. 161 and reigned for nineteen barbarous years. It was truly a reign of terror for the Christians. They suffered almost every conceivable torture under him. Many were thrown to the beasts in the Arena. Others were beheaded, whipped to death, or burned to death on a hot griddle. One martyr who was written about in these days was a woman named Blandina. She was apparently a very homely woman but full of faith. Contemporary accounts noted that never was it known for a woman to suffer so much for so long. When she was arrested, the torturers began to work on her. There was a succession of them from morning to evening. They reported that they were worn out, not she. She was whipped, roasted on a hot iron chair, enclosed in a net and thrown to a wild bull that tossed and gored her for some time. The torturers were amazed to see her breathing while her body was torn and laid open. Finally, she was sacrificed on an altar to a pagan god.

And what was the point to that? It was to glorify the name of Jesus. It is one thing for angels to give glory to God, they who live life under perfect conditions. It is quite another to have one little human being by the name of Blandina tossed and burned and gored and whipped and having her respond to this by simply praising the name of Jesus. That is glory to His name. Satan had thrown everything he could at her and she defeated him every time she opened her mouth. She completely understood what Paul meant as he wrote of his own life, "We are troubled on every side, yet not distressed; we are perplexed, but not in despair; persecuted, but not forsaken; cast down, but not destroyed; always bearing about in the body the dying of the Lord Jesus, that the life also of Jesus might be made manifest in our body. For we which live are always delivered unto death for Jesus' sake, that the life also of Jesus might be made manifest in our mortal flesh" (2 Corinthians 4:8-11).

Another martyr recorded at this time was a Christian named Lawrence. He kept the church's purse. It was rumored that the Church had much money and so Marcus Aurelius called for the arrest of Lawrence and then demanded to know where was the treasure of the church. Lawrence put his arms over the poor and answered, "These are the precious treasure of the church, these are the treasure, indeed, in whom the faith of Christ reigneth, in whom Jesus Christ hath His mansion place. What more precious jewels can Christ have, than those in whom He has promised to dwell?"

Aurelius replied; "Kindle the fire - of wood make no spare. Hath this villain deluded the Emperor? Away with Him, away with him: whip him with scourges, jerk him with rods, buffer him with fist, brain him with clubs. Jesteth the traitor with the Emperor? Pinch him with fiery tongs, gird him with burning plates, bring out the strongest chains and the fire forks and the grated bed of iron: on the fire with it; bind the rebel hand and foot and when the bed is fire-hot, on with him. Roast him, broil him, toss him, turn him. On pain of our high displeasure do every man his office, oh ye tormentors." All was done.

THE CHILDREN

Some of the most heart-wrenching tortures were the ones that pitted family loyalty against the loyalty to their most closely held Christian beliefs. One of these consisted of seizing the children of the believers and taking them down to the river and tying them to great dunking poles. As the parents watched, the children were lowered into the river and kept under the water until they almost lost consciousness. At the last minute, they were brought to the surface, coughing and sputtering. The parents were then told to deny Christ. They would not. The children were then lowered below the water and held while the parents were asked to reconsider their defiance. Over and over, the children were brought to the surface just in time, and over and over the parents had to make the decision to watch their children suffer and die rather than forsake the name of Jesus. Finally, of course the children were drowned, martyrs themselves to the cause of Christ. And still the Church grew.

REIGN OF SEPTIMIUS SEVERUS

Although the next emperor, Commodus, had co-ruled with Marcus Aurelius for the last three years of Aurelius's reign, he apparently did not inflict the same wrath on the Christians when he assumed solitary power. He was on the throne until A.D. 192. This easing seems to have lasted during the next year also when Pertinax and Didius Julianus reigned together. However, when Septimius Severus ascended the throne in A.D. 193, all changed.

Severus daily killed Christians by burning, crucifixion, and beheading. Saints were again thrown to the beasts in the Arena and boiling pitch was slowly poured over the bodies of others. The believers left no record of ever celebrating birthdays but they left many records of celebrating death days. They would meet on the anniversary of a believer's martyrdom and promise one another that they too, would hold fast to the faith when their time came.

Septimius Severus reigned until A.D. 211. Two others who ruled with him part of the time, continued in power. Caracalla reigned from A.D. 198 to 217, and Geta ruled from A.D. 209-12. The three emperors who followed these rather tolerated Christianity, and there was "peace" for the next eighteen years for the weary and sorely pressed believers. The three emperors who blessed the church in this way were Macrinus, Elagabalus, and Severus Alexander.

It is possible, as the believers saw almost two decades of peace descend on them, that maybe they dared to hope that the prophesied ten days of persecution were over and the world was safe once more? It was not to be, however, and persecution began again in A.D. 235 when Maximinus assumed the throne and changed tactics. Maximinus determined to go after the leaders of the Church, and did so fiercely, reasoning that without their leaders the remaining Christians would fall away. But as he killed the leaders, new leaders sprang up in their place. The Church continued to grow.

REIGN OF DECIUS

Not much is known about the following four emperors in regards to the believers. The rule of Gordian I, II, and III along with Philip, comprised the next eleven years. Much, however is known about the rule of Decius in relation to the Church. He became Emperor in A.D. 249 and ruled only for three years, but they were long, terrible years for the saints. Decius was determined to exterminate Christianity from the Roman Empire. One way that he ferreted out the believers was to require each person in the entire Roman Empire to have a certificate with oneself at all times that stated that one had sacrificed to the gods. Christians, of course, would not sacrifice to the gods, and thus had no certificate. Hence, they were easily recognizable. His violence towards those he apprehended was legendary, and because the persecution was not limited to certain areas, but was empire-wide, there was no hope of refuge for Christians. Origen, the most learned man of the ancient church was arrested and tortured at this time. Cyprian, Bishop of Carthage, remarked, "The whole world is devastated." It must surely have seemed so to the Church.

Trebonianus Gallus became Emperor in A.D. 251 and remained so until A.D. 253 when Valerian became Emperor. He was even more severe than Decius. Cyprian was himself martyred at this time. Valerian ruled for seven long years, and then, once more, Christians were able to catch their breath when an emperor who favored Christians, Gallienus, ruled for fifteen years. He was followed by Claudius II, about whom nothing in regards to the Christians is known, who ruled for two years. Aurelian assumed the throne in A.D. 270 and the persecutions began once again. They continued under him for five years. Probus (A.D. 276-82) and Carinus and Numerian (A.D. 283-84) followed Aurelian.

THE REIGN OF DIOCLETIAN

The last Imperial Persecution began right after this with Diocletian who reigned with the Tetrarchy from A.D. 284 until A.D. 305. It seems, in retrospect, that his reign was Satan's last attempt to destroy Christianity by persecution. It failed, but these final twenty-one years were, if possible, the worst of the years of the Imperial Persecution. It was Diocletian's stated aim that, under him, the name Christian would not only disappear from the face of the earth, it would disappear from history. The world would never again utter the name. He hunted down and put believers to death by every torture cruelty could devise. They were killed by beast, burning, stabbing, crucifixion and the rack. They were hunted down even to the caves in the forests. History records the severe whipping and beheading of a *seven* year old. But through all of this time the words of Jesus echoed that "upon this rock I will build my church and the gates of hell will not prevail against it" (Matthew 16:18). Rather than prevailing against the Church, the persecutions served only to strengthen and purify her. Diogenetus, an early church leader, wrote in description of the Christians, "They live in countries of their own, but simply as sojourners ... enduring the lot of foreigners ...They exist in the flesh, but they live not after the flesh. They spend their existence upon earth, but their citizenship is in heaven. They obey the established laws, and in their own lives they surpass the laws. They love all men, and are persecuted by all." And, incredibly, given the terrible persecution that they endured, their ranks swelled. Fully ten percent of the Roman Empire was accounted as Christian.

Eventually, Diocletian retired and a scramble for power ensued. The victor, Constantine, would usher in the next church age; the age of the Pergamos Church.

CHAPTER 4
THE CHURCHES OF PERGAMOS AND THYATIRA
Revelation 2:12-29

CONSTANTINE

It was October, A.D. 312. The fortunes of the Church were about to change. Constantine and his troops were marching toward Rome to battle against his adversary, the tyrannical Maxentius, for the position of emperor. The odds seemed to favor Maxentius as he had the greater army, but both men knew they needed supernatural help in order to prevail. Maxentius was relying on magical enchantments. Constantine was not sure on whom to rely. His mother, Helena, was a Christian. His father, Constantinius Chlorus, had abandoned her for political reasons and married the stepdaughter of the emperor Maximius. Constantinius Chlorus, although not a Christian, was a monotheist. Constantine decided to pray to his father's god. It was, apparently, his mother's God who answered. At a little after noon, Constantine saw the sign of the cross emblazoned across the sky and with it the words, *In hoc signo vinces* that translates, "in this sign you will win". Constantine and his entire army (who also saw the sign) were amazed. They accepted the vision and inscribed the sign of the cross on their armor. Although outnumbered, Constantine and his troops were victorious.

This account comes to us by way of the Christian Bishop of Caesarea, Eusebius, who was told it firsthand by Constantine, his friend. It was natural that Eusebius would become Constantine's friend because Constantine became the powerful patron of the Church. As Eusebius wrote in his Church History concerning the ascension to power of Constantine, "The whole human race was freed from the oppression of the tyrants. We especially, who had fixed our hopes upon the Christ of God, had gladness unspeakable." Along with his ally, Licinius, Constantine signed the Edict of Milan in A.D. 313, restoring to Christians full right as citizens. And he did not stop there. Constantine began to move toward making Christianity the state religion. It was actually the emperor

Theodosius who accomplished this, but Constantine saw to it that Christianity became the authorized faith of the Roman Empire by the end of the fourth century. The Imperial persecutions were forever over, the "ten days" of suffering were up. In fact, the Church was given a totally new temptation - the taste of secular power and favor. Let us now examine the words of Jesus given to this church.

THE CITY OF PERGAMOS

Pergamos was situated about sixty miles north of Smyrna. The city was built on a hill a thousand feet above the surrounding countryside, creating a natural fortress; the rest of Asia Minor was governed from there. Pergamos was the intellectual center of this area of the world. It boasted a 200,000-volume library. In fact, the word "parchment" is derived from its name. Pergamos' intellectual acclaim also came from the fact that it had a renowned teaching medical center there, a hospital dedicated to Aesculapius, god of medicine. The sign of the medical center was a coiled snake on a pole, the same sign as that of the American Medical Association today.

THE MIXTURE OF CHURCH AND STATE

The very name *Pergamos* means "mixture" or "marriage." The Church began to phase out of its status as a persecuted church into a church that now had the entire Roman government as her benefactor. The Church was beginning to be married to the State. Satan's tactics had changed. He saw that his relentless persecution was serving only to purify the Church and make her stronger. A new approach was needed - infiltration. Paganism began to enter the church at this time through pagan festivals and rituals. The Mass and the cult of the virgin and child was introduced. Remembrance of martyrs began to turn into idolatry of martyrs. Pictures, relics, and statues of "saints" (no longer considered to be a term referring to all believers) also made their way into their places of worship. In fact, even the places of worship had undergone a dramatic transformation. Up until now, the churches had never had permanent homes. In the beginning, Christians met in houses and in the synagogues, but the synagogues belonged to the Jews. Under Roman persecution, Christians had been forced to meet in the subterranean tunnels of Rome - the catacombs - and in other equally clandestine and base places. Now, Constantine was turning over the elaborate and richly decorated official Roman buildings, called basilicas, to the Church as places of worship. He gave them costly vestments and art works and the Church began to become wealthy. Sadly, the Church did not deal nearly as well with affluence and power as she had with want and persecution.

The Pergamos period of the Church was, in reality, simply a transitional period, because it would not be long before the next period, the Thyatiran Church was securely ensconced in power. The prophetic model of the Thyatiran Church is the archetypical Mediaeval Catholic Church.

Notice how Jesus identifies himself to this church as "he which hath the sharp sword with two edges." The two-edged sword has already been identified as the word of God. Jesus is stressing that He is the Imminent Word of God to the Church that was beginning to leave the word of God. He is also stressing that He is the authority on the word of God. Most in the world and even in the religious seminaries have fallen into a deception that they have the right to decide what, if any, of God's word they wish to believe and/or apply to their lives. This statement of Jesus comes against that thinking. The word of God stands in judgment of us, we do not stand in judgment of it.

We, too, in our personal lives can be susceptible to Satan's tactic of infiltration. Instead of obeying God's commandment to "come ye out from among them [the world]," many times we try instead to blend our social lives and viewpoints with our spiritual lives and viewpoints. Instead of being a light to our society, we tone down that light until it blends quite well with our surroundings. When we are so compromised, we open ourselves to the same rebuke from Jesus as did the Pergamum Church. We, as was the Pergamum Church, are called to change and challenge our society's mores, not accommodate ourselves to them.

There is another aspect to this identification of Jesus as the two-edged sword. The ruling powers at Pergamos had been given the "right of the sword," the power of life and death, by the emperor. In other words, they had no restraint upon what punishment they could inflict. The Church, too, was beginning to assume this power over the souls of its people, "sending" them to heaven or to hell. Jesus refutes this by saying that He alone wields the "right of the sword" and that He alone will determine the eternal fate of the people.

COMMENDATIONS BY JESUS

Pergamos is a working church and she is still holding fast to Jesus' name even in a place and time of great Satanic power. Although they are beginning to compromise the doctrine once and for all delivered unto the Church, they still hold great reverence for Jesus.

SATAN'S BASE OF EARTHLY POWER

Jesus makes an interesting statement in verse 13 when He identifies Pergamos as the place where Satan's seat is. The literal word used is "throne" and it denotes a capital, organization and hierarchy. This is the first reference in Revelation to Satan's organized system of power and adherents on the earth. It is not the last. Chapters 17-19 of Revelation deal with this concept in great detail. Suffice it to say at this point that the Bible is clear on the fact that Satan's organization of invisible principalities and powers is not found in hell, but rather here on earth. In fact, Satan will be at his most defeated state when he is finally consigned to hell. Hell was created by God as a place of punishment for Satan and his angels. The people who are also found there are there because they have chosen to align themselves with Satan and therefore share in his punishment. Be assured, Satan's domain is not hell, it is here on Planet Earth.

Three times in the Gospel of John, Jesus calls Satan the prince of this world (John 12:31; 14:30; 16:11). In Ephesians 2:2, the Apostle Paul calls Satan the prince of the power of the air, and in 2 Corinthians 4:4, he calls him the god of this world. Note that Paul calls Satan the god of this world *after* the death and resurrection of Jesus. Although Jesus' victory has removed Satan's legal right to the earth, it has not changed the fact that Satan is still recognized by heaven as the *de facto* ruler of this earth. The Apostle John tells us in 1 John 5:19

that the whole world lies in the evil one. This world, Planet Earth, is now the domain and territory of Satan although it will not always be so.

Apparently, there have been several locations on the earth where Satan has made his capital. The first of these was in Babylon and centered around the satanic Tower of Babel. The importance of this tower has been overlooked by most Christians. It was certainly not overlooked by God. He said He had to destroy it or else "nothing will be restrained from them [man], which they have imagined to do" (Genesis 11:6). God clearly saw that the need to destroy the Tower of Babel involved more than simply the need to deconstruct a multi-story building. The tower involved a high degree of satanic knowledge and information. The ziggurats that have been found throughout that area of the world are thought by most scholars to be attempts at reconstructing similar edifices as the Tower at Babel. Astrology began on the pinnacles of the ziggurats; indeed, they were occultic altars of every perversion. Occultic, mystery religions began here and spread throughout the world as the people were scattered. Nonetheless, Babylon remained the nerve center for the mystery religion cult until the days of Belshazzar when Babylon fell to the Medes and Persians. In his book, The Two Babylons, historian Alexander Hislop gives much documentation to show that Pergamos had inherited the religious mantle of Ancient Babylon. He writes that the mystery priests who had kept the secrets of their occultic religion since the days of Nimrod (again, the tower of Babel) were forced to migrate northwest to Pergamos where they established it as the greatest center of pagan religion of the time. Indeed, with one accord, historians note that Pergamos was a great religious center, headquartering both the cult of the emperor and the Greek pagan mystery religions. Mystery religions were occultic religions that appealed to people who wanted a deeper, more personal relationship with the pagan gods. This was "accomplished" through secret initiations, ceremonies, and rituals that led one by degrees deeper and deeper into the mysteries of Satan. The great altar of Zeus, one of the seven wonders of the ancient world, was found in Pergamos.

Apart from secular corroboration, Jesus here makes it clear that Satan has his throne in Pergamos. When Satan is next worshipped by the whole world, he will again sit on a throne. Satan's chief aspiration has been to be worshipped as god by the very beings that the real God created. All of the idolatrous systems in the world have come out of Satan's attempt to displace God as the ruler of the universe. He began in Babylon and, at the end of time, we will see that he will return there to rule the world. But at this point in time, we find him securely ensconced in Pergamos.

THE MARTYR ANTIPAS

Jesus makes mention of Antipas in verse 13 as the faithful martyr at Pergamos. There is no mention of Antipas in history. It is possible that he was a literal martyr who escaped the attention of historians; it is also possible that he is a type (or model) for all of the martyrs, none of whom have escaped the attention of God.

PERGAMOS'S FAULTS

Although Jesus commends this church for their works, their allegiance to His name, and their faith, He has "a few things against [them]." First He mentions that the doctrine of Balaam is creeping into the Church. The name "Balaam" literally means "destroyer of the people." Satan has changed tactics from outright persecution of the Church to infiltration of the Church. He does this by the two doctrines mentioned in the letter to Pergamos: the doctrine of Balaam and the doctrine of the Nicolaitans. We have already discussed the Nicolaitans but the doctrine of Balaam has not been mentioned before. This doctrine of Balaam will allow both fornication and idolatry to enter into the midst of the Church. Keep in mind that the first Council at Jerusalem had declared that nothing of the Jewish law would be bound upon the Gentile believers except "that they abstain from pollutions of idols, and from fornication, and from things strangled and from blood" (Acts 15:20). What a slap in the face of God it is for Satan to seduce the Pergamum Church to bring those very things into the church!

Idolatry is the act of worshiping someone or something other than God. At this point in the history of the Church, adulation of the "saints" and of Mary will turn into their outright worship by the leaders and people of the Church. The act of fornication or adultery is the act of joining oneself to someone to whom you do not belong. Adultery further means leaving the one to whom you belong in order to do so. Thus, fornication for the Church would be the act of joining with something or someone other than Christ. Here she is joining with the State. Daniel prophesied this very thing when he prophesied the rise and fall of Rome in Daniel 11:15-19. He also prophesied that as corrupting for the Church as that would be, she would not be defeated by it. Here we find that prophecy is coming true: the world system is beginning to infiltrate and contaminate the Church.

Historian Will Durant writes, "Paganism survived...in the form of ancient rites and customs condoned, or accepted and transformed, by an often indulgent Church. An intimate and trustful worship of saints replaced the cult of pagan gods...Statues of Isis and Horus were renamed Mary and Jesus; the Roman Lupercalia and the feast of purification of Isis became the Feast of the Nativity; the Saturnalia were replaced by Christmas celebration...an ancient festival of the dead [was replaced] by All Souls Day, rededicated to Christian heroes; incense, lights, flowers, processions, vestments, hymns that had pleased the people in older cults were domesticated and cleansed in the ritual of the Church...soon people and priests would use the sign of the cross as a magic incantation to expel or drive away demons... [Paganism] passed like maternal blood into the new religion, and captive Rome captured her conqueror...The world converted to Christianity."[5]

Still, the prophet writes, "But she shall not stand on his side, neither be for him" (Daniel 11:17). Although Rome corrupts the Church, she does not completely capitulate to Rome. Neither does Rome truly own her soul. Even in this soiled state she is still Christ's Bride.

BALAAM'S TEACHINGS

The doctrine of Balaam, also referred to as the error of Balaam in Jude 11, is the teaching and practice of mixing the things of God with the things of the world. It is the practice of the infiltration of error into a system by means of compromise. It will be what introduces fornication and idolatry into the Church.

The story of Balaam is found in the book of Numbers in the Old Testament. Balaam was a prophet. He was interesting in that he was a Gentile prophet, not a Jewish one. To him was given the prophecy that a star would lead seekers to the Christ child (Numbers 24:15), and he in turn prophesied that fact to a Gentile King - Balak. Balaam was the ONLY prophet to mention a star in connection with the coming of Christ. It was not a prophecy that was given to the Jews directly. Interestingly, only the Gentiles - the Wise Men of the East - knew to follow the star to Bethlehem, and the only Gentiles to see Jesus as a baby were those who followed the star.

So it is clear that Balaam was a voice for God, a genuine prophet, although not of the house of Israel. We are introduced to Balaam when Israel was still wandering in the desert for her forty years' penance. However, God remained with Israel and had just allowed her to destroy the Amorites and the people of Bashan. After these two decisive victories, the children of Israel pitched their camp in the plains of Moab. The Moabite king, Balak, was terrified. Not only had the Israelites been victorious against their previous enemies, they were enormous in their sheer numbers. Balaam's reputation as a prophet of God must have been widespread, because Balak sent emissaries with gifts of gold to Balaam, calling on him to help Moab saying, "Behold, a people came out of Egypt: behold, they cover the surface of the land, and they are living opposite me. Now, therefore, please come, curse this people for me since they are too mighty for me; perhaps I may be able to defeat them and drive them out of the land. For I know that he whom you bless is blessed, and he whom you curse is cursed" (Numbers 22:5-6, NASB).

Balaam had power, and he also had wisdom, because he responded to their offer to hire him to curse Israel by replying that he had to check with God first. Apparently, Balaam had not heard of Israel but it is clear that he knew their God. When he asked God what to do, God told him that under no circumstances was he to curse Israel, for God himself had blessed Israel. Thereupon, Balaam told the emissaries of Balak that he could not go with them to curse Israel. Balak did not give up; he sent even more distinguished emissaries (not to mention more gold) to Balaam with the promise to promote Balaam to very great honor if he would but come to Moab. Balaam held firm that he could not do other than that which God willed; however, he promised to ask God once more if he could go. Balaam was at this point in danger of compromise - he had a clear answer from God but he was not really happy with the answer. (Sounds like many of our prayers, doesn't it?) God told him that He would allow Balaam to go with the Moabites, but He absolutely forbade him to speak other than God's words concerning Israel. And, by the way, God was now angry with Balaam.

As Balaam traveled to Moab on his donkey with his two servants, God sent an angel to block the road, signaling His displeasure. This angel was very large and he had a drawn sword in his hand. Sadly, only the donkey could see the angel. Being a wise donkey, she turned aside into the field. Balaam was furious and hit the donkey, bringing her back onto the road. Soon the road took them through a vineyard that was walled on either side of the path. At this point, the angel reappeared. Once again, the donkey tried to bypass the angel, and this time Balaam's foot was crushed against the wall. The donkey was again hit. Finally, the road led to a very narrow place with no room either to the left or to the right of the path. When the angel reappeared, the donkey simply dropped in her tracks. This was not received at all well by Balaam who began to beat her severely with his staff. The donkey was then allowed by God to speak to Balaam, and she very understandably asked him why he kept beating her when she had done nothing wrong. Balaam, seemingly unfazed by his talking animal, replied that the donkey had made a fool of him, and furthermore if he had his sword with him, Balaam would have killed the donkey. The donkey asked if, in all the years that Balaam had ridden her, she had ever acted in that way before. Balaam had to admit that, no, the donkey had never acted up before. With that admission, God opened the eyes of Balaam and he, too, was able to see the mighty angel with the drawn sword. Balaam fell prostrate before the angel, face in the dirt, as the angel reproved him for his behavior towards his beast. The angel, who most probably was Christ, then told Balaam that, far from harming him, the donkey had saved his life because Balaam's way was perverse before him. Balaam was truly contrite and, admitting his sin, offered to return home. The angel of the Lord replied: "Go with the men: but only the word that I shall speak unto thee, that thou shalt speak" (Numbers 22:35).

When Balaam reached Moab, Balak took Balaam to a high place where Balaam could view the vast army of Israel. He called for seven altars to be built, and for animals to be sacrificed on them. It was an impressive moment. With all of Israel in view, Balaam opened his mouth and pronounced the blessing of God upon them. Balak was furious, but Balaam reminded him of their deal that he could only say what God gave him to say. Balak - desperate - suggested that they try again from a different place. (How typical - we assume that if we can only show God a different, more accurate, view of things that He will surely come around to our way of thinking!)   So they tried again, with the result of an even greater blessing on Israel coming from the mouth of Balaam. Finally, Balak commanded Balaam to shut up if all he could do was to bless Israel.

Balak's problem remained unsolved, however, and so the two of them agreed to try one more time. More altars were built, more animals were sacrificed, and the blessing that flowed from Balaam for Israel was truly awesome. In fact, it was at this point that he received the prophecy concerning Jesus arising out of Jacob and linking it with the star of Bethlehem. Balak was in a rage, and ordered Balaam to leave after reminding him that no pay or honors would be forthcoming.

Now about here things get interesting. In fact it seems almost impossible to understand what Balaam did next, after being so mightily used by God and so touched by his Spirit. According to Numbers 31:16, Balaam decided on his own to help Balak. What caused him to decide to do this is not recorded. Perhaps it was the lure of honor and riches, perhaps he felt sorry that he had let Balak down. Nevertheless Balaam went back to Balak and told him that although he, Balaam, could not curse Israel, he knew how to get God to do it. He advised Balak to tempt the men of Israel with the women of Moab. He advised Balak to introduce Moabite worship to the men of Israel. Now the way that the Moabites worshiped their gods was with gross sexual immorality. Balaam guessed, rightly, that the Israelite men might find this way of worship more appealing than the way they were being taught by Moses and Aaron to worship. Soon, Israel was deep into idolatry and sexual perversion, and God Himself cursed Israel with a great plague that caused the death of 24,000 Israelites. Balaam got to Israel through the back door by infiltration and compromise. Satan will do the same thing with this church.

Pointedly, the Pergamos church is warned by Jesus against this marriage of the things of God with the things of the world, the marriage of church with state. History bears witness to the fact that she did not heed the warning.

THE NICOLAITANS AGAIN

In addition to the doctrine of Balaam, Jesus rebukes the doctrine of the Nicolaitans, saying for a second time that He hates it. When Jesus *repeats* this statement, it is critical that we pay attention to Him on this issue. We saw this doctrine beginning to infiltrate the Church in the letter to the Ephesian church. It was the doctrine that taught that there were divisions between the saints within the church - a priesthood separate from the laity. Again, the word *nicolaitan* literally means "the conquering of the laity." Scripture teaches that all believers are part of the priesthood with Jesus as the High Priest. The doctrine of the Nicolaitans teaches that some Christians are priests and saints while others are not. Jesus has said twice now that this doctrine is repugnant to Him. Tragically, the *deeds* of the Nicolaitans in the Ephesian church have become the *doctrine* of the Nicolaitans in the Pergamos church. This teaching had now become institutionalized in the church, and by so doing, the false practices in the Ephesian church became the tenets of the Faith in the Pergamos church.

In verse 16, Jesus commands them to repent or else He will come and fight against them with "the sword of my mouth." The words of Christ, the Holy Scriptures, rebuked the teachings of the Pergamos church; there is no trace of her, physically, left today.

THE HIDDEN MANNA

The promises given to each overcomer in this church are twofold: hidden manna and a white stone. Furthermore, the white stone has a new name for each overcomer written upon it, the name being known only to the recipient. Let us first consider the promise of hidden manna.

Manna was the miraculous food that fell from heaven while Israel was wandering in the desert for forty years. It was a visible sign of God's provision for them. God had instructed them to place samples of the manna in the Ark of the Covenant as a reminder throughout the years of His protection and care for them. The hidden manna, then, was the manna that was hidden (or stored) in the Ark of the Covenant. The Ark of the Covenant was the most holy piece of furniture that Israel possessed. It was where the presence of the Living God manifested itself and was found in the Holy of Holies in the Tabernacle. The Tabernacle consisted of three different areas. The Outer Court, where the brazen alter for sacrifice was found, was open to all; the Holy Place was restricted to the priests; and the most sacred place, the Holy of Holies, was open only to the High Priest, and he could only enter it once a year. Thus, the hidden manna is in the most holy relic in the most holy place in all of Israel. No man was ever permitted to touch the Ark. In 1 Samuel 6:19 we read where *50,070* Bethshemites were slain because they simply looked into the Ark. Contrast that with this promise to the overcomers where they are being given the very contents of the Ark!! Nothing is withheld from the overcomers. The hidden manna thus speaks of the provision of God and of the special relationship of the believers to God.

When Adam sinned, he was forced to leave the garden and he lost the direct provision provided for him by God. Now, he would have to feed himself by the sweat of his brow. Except for that brief time in the wilderness wanderings, when God provided sustenance for His people in a miraculous way, that has been the rule of existence for man upon the earth. But now, once again, all that which was lost to sin is restored to the believer, and God will supply every need.

Keep in mind that this promise is being given to the overcomers in the church that has placed all sorts of barriers between the common Christian and Christ: Mary, "saints," popes, archbishops, bishops, priests, and even ritual. But the promise of Hidden Manna restores their standing as saints in and of themselves; they have their relationship with and standing before Jesus and His Father returned to them in full. And the promise is even greater when applied to the overcomers throughout the ages. We will once again have God walking in our midst, we will once again commune with Him face to face.

THE WHITE STONE

The white stone is reminiscent of one of the two stones that Israel used to divine the will of God for the nation of Israel, the Urim and Thummin. One stone was black; the other was white. We see the concept of white and black stones signifying votes of yes or no in many societies throughout history. White signified a "yes" vote, or acceptance, while a black stone represented a "no" vote. Our phrase "to blackball someone" has its roots in this custom. Man, through sin, has lost his association with God. It is up to God to accept man back into association with Him. The white stone given to the overcomer by Jesus Himself signifies acceptance by God and it also signifies the restoration of his relationship with God.

The new name written on the white stone and chosen by God, suggests that it is a new relationship. The Bible is clear that, in God's perspective, a name is indicative of one's meaning and value. Many are the examples where God either chose a person's name or changed a person's name. The reason was always because of the meaning of the new name. God Himself will rename each believer according to His full knowledge of us. This promise is also given in Isaiah 62:2 which reads, "...and thou shalt be called by a new name, which the mouth of the Lord shall name." We will join Abraham, Peter, Paul, etc., in having that incredibly personal gift from God. We will see ourselves from God's perspective, and our new name will be a constant reminder of our personal and individual relationship with God. It will also tell of our place and function in the New Jerusalem.

An interesting historical note concerns the aforementioned hospital at Pergamus. Although all who were dying were turned away for treatment there, if one was accepted and subsequently healed or improved, the custom was to place an inscription of thanks and praise to Aesculapius on white pillars of stone. Those pillars were placed on display at the entrance to the hospital. It is certain that those white stones must have readily come to mind as the saints at the church at Pergamos read this letter. The point could not have escaped them that Jesus was declaring that He alone was the ultimate healer of the rift between God and man, and that, far from turning away the dying, Jesus brought them the promise of both new life and new relationship with God.

THYATIRA

Thyatira was the home of Lydia, the affluent businesswoman converted by Paul and spoken of in Acts 16:12-15. She was, however, converted in the city of Philippi. Philippi was the major city in that part of Macedonia whereas Thyatira was a small, very obscure town of that region. The church there was also very small and many scholars have wondered at the fact that it was given the attention of this letter from Jesus. But its importance lay not as much in its existence as in the fact that it was a perfect example of the form that the Church as a whole would next assume.

WORSHIP JESUS

The Thyatiran Church is a type of the church in medieval history, covering approximately the years AD 500 to AD 1500. The Church was completely controlled by the Catholic papal system at this point and the viewpoint of God concerning her is very interesting. Note how He identifies Himself in verse 18, "These things sayeth the *Son of God.*" This is the only place in Revelation where He is so called. His most used name is Lamb, but to a church that is now worshiping mortals (Mary and various saints), He appears as the *only* Son of God. He *alone* is worthy of their praise and adulation. In fact, in Luke 11:27-28, when a woman began to praise His mother, Mary, calling her blessed, Jesus responded with correction saying, "... rather, blessed are they that hear the word of God, and keep it."

Again, you see that Jesus wants no distinction between believers in His church. Each one is a saint. Each one is a priest. And Jesus alone is to be worshiped.

The identification continues with the description of His eyes like a flame of fire and His feet like fine brass. As was noted in chapter 2, the eyes portray His perfect knowledge and His feet of brass signify His coming in judgment. Whenever judgment is in view, brass is the metal used. The serpent that was lifted up in the wilderness for Israel after they had sinned grossly with the Moabites was brass. The altar on which sacrifices were made for the sins of the people was brass. As has already been discussed, feet are a symbol of dominion and the *power* to execute judgment. The two symbols are now combined, feet of brass, which means that Jesus is coming to judge this church. Notice verses 22-23 and 26-27. He says that He will cast the wicked in her into great tribulation and death. Conversely, to the overcomers in this church He grants the power and authority to rule *sternly* (with a rod of iron) over the nations.

JEZEBEL - CHURCH APOSTACY

Jesus commends this church highly for her love (charity), service, faith, patience and works; all of which will increase over time. These please Him greatly but they, themselves, are not enough. "Notwithstanding" He says (in other words, "nevertheless..."), the same believers who are full of love, service, faith, etc. are in a church where immorality and idol worship are being taught, and regardless of the good works, sound doctrine is essential. The people truly love God but the Church does not have sound doctrine. There is a dichotomy in this church: the hierarchy and all the corruption that is entailed therein, and the laity who, for a thousand years, genuinely love and worship God.

Those who work apostasy in the Church are called Jezebel. Historically, Jezebel was a princess of Tyre, married to an Israelite king, Ahab. She was extraordinarily cruel and idolatrous. The mere fact that Jezebel was not Jewish should have prevented her from ever marrying any Jewish man, let alone the king. The fact that she did, gave her enormous power over the nation of Israel. The Bible says that Ahab was the worst of the worst of kings, and much of that was due to the influence of Jezebel. She used that influence to introduce the pagan god Baal into Israel. In Hebrew her name means "chaste, virtuous, without idolatry." Here Jesus makes her name synonymous with false doctrine; a doctrine that teaches something evil can be good, and the profane can be pure. It corrupts the church, all the while appearing to be chaste and holy. It is the profession of one ideal while being, in reality, the exact opposite.

Jezebel caused Israel to turn to witchcraft and whoredom (2 Kings 9:7) and to betray the God of their fathers. The people of Israel never completely rejected God outright, although some of their kings did, they just put Jehovah in the mix with the pagan gods Baal and Asherah, and that was enough to lead them totally astray. This is precisely what the leadership of the Church does during this period of history. As bad as was the fact that Pergamos tolerated false prophets, here they are the leadership! Jesus says this clearly in verse 20, Jezebel teaches and seduces the servants of God. She could not teach them if she were not in power to do so. The *deeds* of the Nicolaitans in the Ephesian Church became the *doctrine* of the Pergamons, but now it has become even worse. They have now become the *structure* of Thyatira. Jezebel was a heathen, impure, bloodthirsty woman who was exalted into queenly dominion over the people. This is exactly the case here concerning those in authority in the Thyatiran Church.

THE CHURCH CORRUPTED BY POWER

When Constantine moved his Imperial headquarters east to Constantinople, a power vacuum was created in the West. Because there was no civil authority to speak of in Rome, the Church took over much of the necessary oversight of the people. She handled the educational and welfare needs for the people and her influence was second to none. As the popes took over Roman civil government, so did ambition and greed overtake them. They acquired even more territory by coercion, fraud and war. Soon the popes were indistinguishable from the former emperors of Rome. They took the titles, function, pomp and riches that the emperors once had held. Along with the civil power that they inherited from the emperors, they added an enormously strong component - "the keys to heaven." Not only could they control a person's temporal life, they now taught that they could also control a person's eternal destiny. Although this teaching is contrary to all of the New Testament - God alone holds this power - it was, and is, accepted by most Catholics, then and now, that the Church has this power.

This combination of earthly and heavenly power proved too formidable for any other power to contest. Writing of the submission and humbling of Frederick I, Holy Roman Emperor and King of Germany and Italy, to Pope Alexander III, Catholic historian Fortunatus Ulmas records, "The next day Frederick Barbarossa ... kissed the feet of Alexander, and, on foot, led his horse by the bridle as he returned from solemn mass, to the pontifical palace... The papacy had now risen to a height of grandeur and power that it had never reached before. The sword of Peter had conquered the sword of Caesar!"[6] Indeed it had, except that it was not the sword of Peter, it was the sword of Constantine. Immortalized in painting is the scene of humbled Henry IV dressed in a hair shirt and barefoot in the snow waiting outside the closed door of Pope Gregory VII, begging forgiveness for his part in their quarrel in order that Gregory would allow him to enter heaven. What power on earth could fight against that perceived eternal power?

THE MEDIEVAL CHURCH

Much has been written about the Medieval Catholic Church. It is a dark picture of the church's leadership - concerning itself with power, rife with corruption, and lacking almost completely in any Christian virtue. Historian Carolly Erickson, in her book on Henry VIII Great Harry, writes, "The ways of the pope and the Roman Curia in the early sixteenth century were not those of sanctity and equity; corruption underlay every spiritual transaction, bribery every judgment of the papal posts as sinecures to be enjoyed in profitable splendor, neglecting all but their own aggrandizement. Vice and criminality of many kinds flourished in the papal city. It was widely believed that among the cardinals were some willing to use poison against one another and even against the pope. To the humanist Richard Pace the Eternal City appeared to be a perversion of everything holy, a monstrosity 'full of shame and scandal. There all faith, honesty and religion seem to have vanished from the earth" [7]

Cardinal Baronius in his <u>Ecclesiastical Annals,</u> wrote, "The Roman Church was...covered with silks and precious stones, which publicly prostituted itself for gold... Never did priests, and especially popes, commit so many adulteries, rapes, incests, robberies, and murders...[as in the Middle Ages]"[8]

Catholic historian R.W. Thompson writes, "It would be impossible to enumerate ... the outrages and enormities practiced in England during this gloomy period by kings and popes, who considered the assertion of any single popular right as a crime which God had appointed them to punish! More than a hundred murders were committed by ecclesiastics during the reign of Henry II, in which the parties were not even punished... The clergy had absolute power over their own body, and no appeal was allowed from their decisions. A layman forfeited his life by the crime of murder, but an ecclesiastic went unpunished. This was called one of the immunities of the clergy! [When the king tried to change this law] the pope refused his sanction and denounced it as 'prejudicial to the Church, and destructive of her privileges!'"[9]

CORRUPTION IN THE CHURCH

As always, with unlimited power came unlimited corruption. One pope, John XXIII (the first John XXIII, Baldassare Cossa, not the successor to Pope Pius XII) was a pirate before he was a pope. According to his secretary, he seduced two hundred virgins, matrons, widows and nuns. He was finally brought to trial after the Council of Constance removed him as pope. Writes Edward Gibbon in <u>The History of the Decline and Fall of the Roman Empire</u>, "The most scandalous charges [against him] were suppressed; the Vicar of Christ was only accused of piracy, murder, rape, sodomy and incest."[10] Lest this trial be seen as an attempt by the Church to try and deal with the corruption in its ranks as opposed to being a political move, it needs to be noted that upon Cossa's release from prison he was reinstated as the Bishop of Frascati and Cardinal of Tusculum. He was now qualified to cast votes on the selection of all future popes.

Along with sins of the flesh came the sins of avarice and greed. Brothels were not outlawed by the popes; they were taxed. Indulgences were sold, lands were confiscated. Anything the Church wanted, the Church took. The outrages that he observed while dealing with various popes caused Michelangelo to pen his scathing rebuke,

Of chalices they make helmet and sword

And sell by the bucket the blood of the Lord.

PURGATORY

The idea of purgatory was one of the most successful ideas in increasing both the spiritual power and the wealth of the Church. In theory, Purgatory is a state of being in which the deceased, although a Christian, must still expiate his or her sins. Because it is now impossible for the dead soul to do anything, the living must assume the responsibility. This was accomplished by paying the Church to say prayers for the deceased in order for the soul to be released from Purgatory. When Pope Gregory the Great introduced the idea in AD 593, there was much resistance to it. There was absolutely no scriptural basis for it and it took nearly 850 years for the Church to make it an official dogma. But once the idea took hold it was a veritable cash cow for the Church. Who could in good conscience take the risk that a family member was rotting away in purgatory when money could be paid to fix this? People would pay whatever it took to get out of purgatory and into heaven - never mind that Jesus had already paid the ultimate price for sin upon the cross.

Johannes Teazel coined a catchy phrase that stayed in the minds of the common people. It went, "Once the coin into the coffer clings, a soul from purgatory heavenward springs!" But just how many coins were needed was one issue that was never resolved by the Church. And so the people who "funded" their release from Purgatory before they died, leaving enormous bequests to the Church, could never really rest assured that they were safe. As the Council of Trent in 1545 made so clear, "If anyone says that after the reception of the grace of justification the guilt is so remitted and the debt of eternal punishment so blotted out to every repentant sinner, that no debt of temporal punishment remains to be discharged either in this world or in purgatory before the gates of heaven can be opened, let him be anathema."

In other words, "anyone who is fool enough to believe that the Cross alone can save you is, and should be, cursed." Speaking against this edict of the Council of Trent, of course, is the entire New Testament that teaches with one voice that the blood of Jesus is sufficient in and of itself to cleanse anyone of any sin. There is, however, no money in that good news; there is only salvation.

FALSE DOCTRINES AND PERSECUTIONS

Catholic historian and former Jesuit Peter de Rosa writes, "The cardinals had huge palaces with countless servants. One papal aide reported that he never went to see a cardinal without finding him counting his gold coins. The Curia was made up of men who had bought office and were desperate to recoup their enormous outlay. ...For every benefice of see, abbey and parish, for every indulgence there was a set fee. ...Dispensations were another source of papal revenue. Extremely severe, even impossible, laws were passed so that the Curia could grow rich by selling dispensations...[such as] from fasting during Lent. ... Marriage in particular was a rich source of income. Consanguinity was alleged to hold between couples who had never dreamed they were related. Dispensations from consanguinity in order to marry amounted to a million gold florins a year"[11]

NICOLAITANS IN POWER

The doctrine of the Nicolaitans was in full force. The division between the laity and the priesthood was complete and entire. Julian Hernandez was burned to the stake in Seville, Spain on December 22, 1560 because according to the charges brought against him he had, "Through his great efforts and incomprehensible stealth...introduced into Spain prohibited Books [Bibles and New Testaments] that he brought from far away places where they give protection to the ungodly [Protestants]...He firmly believes that God, by means of the Scriptures, communicates to the laity just the same as He communicates to the priest"[12]

THE INQUISITION

The darkest side of the Church in the Thyatiran Age was the renewed persecution against Christians. This time, almost unbelievably, it was done by the official church. It was called the Inquisition. It was the popes themselves who invented the Inquisition and made sure that it was both in force and enforced. Gregory IX, in 1233, handed the execution of the Inquisition over to the Dominicans with the understanding that all was to be done under his authority. The Grand Inquisitor of the Inquisition was always to be either an archbishop or bishop. They were no less cruel than the Imperial Emperors. To the contrary, to be able to impose the most extreme torture without a twinge of conscience became a mark of holiness and fidelity to the Church. Nor were their persecutions any more limited in scope. Eminent Historian Will Durant chronicles, "Compared with the persecution of heresy in Europe from 1227 to 1492, the persecution of Christians by Romans in the first three centuries after Christ was a mild and humane procedure. Making every allowance required by an historian and permitted to a Christian, we must rank the Inquisition, along with the wars and persecutions of our time, as among the darkest blots on the record of mankind, revealing a ferocity unknown in any beast."[13]

The sixteenth century did not see much improvement. On August 24, 1572, seventy thousand Huguenots were tortured and burned alive in a single day. This became known as St. Bartholomew's massacre. Considering only the years between 1540 and 1570, Europe saw at least 900,000 Protestants killed for their faith. In addition, the Spanish Inquisition had victims numbering in the millions. In matters of doctrine, no freedom of conscience was given at all. Writes church historian R. Tudor Jones, "The majority of the martyrs were ordinary people, including many women. ...The lengthy interrogations of scores of the people have survived and they concentrate on such topics as their beliefs about the Bible and its authority, transubstantiation, their attitude towards such Roman Catholic practices as the cult of saints, prayers for the dead and purgatory. One cannot but be impressed by the vigour and ability with which people...defended themselves, as well as by the immense courage of the sufferers in the face of unspeakable agony."[14]

`Jews and even Catholics who had no quarrel with the Church on doctrinal issues also became caught up in the machinery of the Inquisition. Whether because of a personal grudge, desire for revenge, or even envy on the part of an informer, no one was really safe.

Writes Dave Hunt, "When the inquisitors swept into a town an "Edict of Faith" was issued requiring everyone to reveal any heresy of which they had knowledge. Those who concealed a heretic came under the curse of the Church and the inquisitors' wrath. Informants would approach the inquisitors' lodgings under cover of night and were rewarded for information. No one arrested was ever acquitted. 'Heretics' were committed to the flames because the popes believed that the Bible forbade Christians to shed blood. The victims of the Inquisition exceeded by hundreds of thousands the number of Christians and Jews who had suffered under pagan Roman emperors. The Inquisition, established and repeatedly blessed by the popes, was an open assault upon truth and justice and basic human rights. It was the perfect setup for bigots, villains, enemies, and crazies with overworked imaginations to seek revenge, rid themselves of a rival, or gain personal satisfaction of having become important to the Church."[15]

INTERNAL REFORM

It is important to note that attempts to reform the Church came first from within. The name "protestant" comes from the word "protest". Protestants were first Catholics, and many Catholics were martyred who never considered themselves "Protestants" as we understand the term. Consider the story of Jan (John) Hus. Hus was a Catholic priest and preacher at the Bethlehem Chapel in Prague, Czechoslovakia. His teaching emphasized piety and purity in a believer's life. Heavily influenced by the writing of John Wycliffe, he taught that the Bible alone was the central authority in the Church, and that Christ - not the Pope - was the head of the Church. Although he defended the authority of the clergy, he preached that God alone could forgive sins. Further, he denounced the immoral and extravagant lifestyles of the clergy. With his emphasis on biblical preaching, he attracted a huge following; it was not uncommon for three thousand people to come to hear his sermons. Bethlehem Chapel itself was testament to Hus's teachings. On the walls were paintings contrasting the behaviors of Christ and the disciples with that of the popes and bishops such as a scene of Jesus walking barefooted along a road next to a scene of the panoply of the Pope on horseback in procession; or a painting of Jesus washing the disciples' feet side-by-side with a painting of people kissing the feet of the Pope. The point was not missed either by clergy or laymen.

As a consequence, the archbishop of Prague censored the writings of Hus and forbade his preaching. Hus only intensified his preaching, and began also to rail against the practice of indulgences. Hus was soon excommunicated and summoned to the Council of Constance to defend his teachings. Although promised protection by Emperor Sigismund, he was arrested upon his arrival and, soon afterwards, was condemned to be burned at the stake. His response? "I would not, for a chapel full of gold, recede from the truth." On July 6, 1415, he was led to his execution. His writings had already been declared heretical and great fires had been made of the manuscripts. It would have been understandable for Hus to feel that his life's work was destroyed and would never again influence the thinking of Christians. Rather than becoming despondent, Hus remained serene about his fate and about his ministry. He ended his life with an amazing word of prophecy. The literal meaning of the name Hus was "goose" and he may have been the inspiration behind the phrase "to cook one's goose" when he declared; "Today you will roast a lean goose, but a hundred years from now you will hear a swan sing, whom you will leave unroasted and no trap or net will catch him for you." One hundred two years later, Martin Luther, widely known as the Swan of Wittenburg, posted his famous ninety-five theses and the Reformation was launched in a way that would forever change history.

Hus's execution by fire only spread his ideas faster. We see the evidence of this in a letter from Pope Martin V to the King of Poland in 1429 when he writes: "Know that the interests of the Holy See, and those of your crown, make it a duty to terminate the Hussites. Remember that these impious persons dare proclaim principles of equality; they maintain that all Christians are brethren, and that God has not given to privileged men the right of ruling the nations; they hold that Christ came on earth to abolish slavery; they call the people to liberty, that is to the annihilation of kings and priests. While there is still time, then, turn your forces against Bohemia; burn, massacre, make deserts everywhere, for nothing could be more agreeable to God, or more useful to the cause of kings, than the extermination of the Hussites."

THE RESULTS OF PERSECUTION

The result of the Inquisition was the same as the result of the Imperial Persecutions. It only solidified and purified the Reformation. When Mary Stuart, daughter of Henry VIII, assumed the English throne, she determined to wipe out Protestantism in England. She soon became better known as Bloody Mary, and in the five short years that she reigned, she personally ordered three hundred Protestant Christians burned at the stake. Such was her cruelty that even the hearts of those who supported the execution of "heretics" were sickened. Historian Will Durant wrote, "As the holocaust advanced it became clear that it had been a mistake. Protestantism drew strength from its martyrs as early Christianity had done, and many Catholics were disturbed in their faith, and shamed in their Queen, by the sufferings and fortitude of the victims."[16]

As martyr Bishop Hugh Latimer was heard to call out as he was engulfed in flames with fellow martyr Bishop Nicholas Ridley: "Be of good courage, Master Ridley, and play the man. We shall this day, by God's grace, light such a candle in England as I trust will never be put out!"

So indeed it was to be. The times were swiftly advancing towards the age of the Sardis Church, the age of the Reformation, and, as Ulrich Zwingli would later state, "O, my beloved brethren, the Gospel derives from the blood of Christ this wondrous property, that the fiercest persecutions, far from arresting its progress, do but hasten its triumph!"

THYATIRA REFUSES TO REPENT

Verse 21 of Revelation 2 reads, "And I gave her space to repent of her fornication; and she repented not..." This church was not sincerely misguided. No, she had a knowledge of her wrongdoing and corruption and still refused to repent. Thus, divine punishment was prophesied to come upon her in the form of great tribulation and death according to verses 22 and 23. It is interesting to note that these times are considered the "Dark Ages" of history, complete with very short life spans for the people of this time, squalor, disease, and ignorance.

THE BLACK PLAGUE

In October 1347, a Genoese trading ship docked in Sicily with a crew of dead and nearly dead men. Black swellings the size of eggs in their armpits and groins oozed blood and pus, and boils covered the rest of their bodies. The Black Death had arrived in the world. It soon raged through Italy, North Africa, France, England, Switzerland, and Hungary. From there it spread to Scotland, Ireland, Norway, Sweden, Denmark, Prussia, and Iceland. From 1347 to 1350 - three short years - medieval Europe experienced perhaps the greatest calamity in human history. Incredibly, the world saw about twenty million deaths from the Plague. The estimate of one medieval chronicler is accepted as remarkably accurate by modern demographers when he wrote: "A third of the world died." Mankind has yet to come close to a scourge of that magnitude since. Indeed, it is possible that the world will only see this magnitude of death when the Seven Seals are opened after the Rapture.

Truly, death was visited on the children of Jezebel. It is interesting to note the response of the people at the time. To most people there could be only one explanation for the carnage: the wrath of God. His judgment of their sin seemed to be the clear reason for this punishment. One writer compared the plague to the Flood, an earlier indictment of the human condition from the divine hand of God.

TRUE BELIEVERS HOLD FAST TO THE TRUTH

A different message is given to "the rest in Thyatira, as many as have not this doctrine, and which have not known the depths of Satan." It is a message addressed to the true believers, not to the hierarchy, and it is a message of hope and encouragement. They are simply told to hold fast to what they have in Jesus. The evil is apparently so entrenched that they are expected to do no more than continue in the Faith and be true to Jesus even if it costs them their lives. God Himself will overthrow the system in His own grand time. There is no further burden given to them. And in God's time, not only was the system overthrown, the church at Thyatira itself can no longer be found in the physical realm.

Jesus speaks of the "deep things of Satan" that are known to the leaders of this church. This is an interesting concept. Paul in 1 Corinthians 2:10 speaks of the "deep things of God." It is clear that the human race has access to knowledge of both esoteric wisdom and esoteric evil.

DOMINION OF EARTH RETURNED TO SAINTS

To the overcomers in Thyatira, Jesus continues to restore all that has been lost by man to sin. "And he that overcometh, and keepeth my works unto the end, to him will I give power over the nations: And he shall rule them with a rod of iron; as the vessels of a potter shall they be broken to shivers: even as I received of my Father." Adam, and by extension mankind, was given dominion over the earth. That dominion has largely been lost through sin. Satan is now the prince of this world. This fourth promise restores the dominion lost by Adam's sin. The earth certainly is not in any way in our control. Pollution, weather, earthquakes are all beyond our ability to manage. In the world that God gave to Adam it was not to be so. That control will return to man. Be clear that WE do not regain that dominion, Jesus restores it to us by His grace. It cost Jesus His life to regain it from Satan, and His response is to simply return it to us. This is love.

This return of the dominion over the world to the overcomers is the fulfillment of the promise given by Paul in 1 Corinthians 6:2: "Do ye not know that the saints shall judge the world?" Yes, the saints will judge the world and will do so with a rod of iron. The word "rod" used here is the same as the word for "septre" used in Hebrews 1:8. It denotes power, authority and royalty. All will apply to the saints. "The heaven, even the heavens, are the Lord's: but the earth hath he given to the children of men" (Psalms 115:16).

Further, Jesus is promising that this will be righteous authority such as the authority that He Himself received from His father. This is very important because the Thyatiran Church has been overtaken by a fraudulent authority. The overcomers will rule justly and righteously, in a marked contrast to what they have seen demonstrated by their church.

"For the Lord taketh pleasure in his people: he will beautify the meek with salvation, Let the saints be joyful in glory: let them sing aloud upon their beds. Let the high praises of God be in their mouth, and a two-edged sword in their hand; To execute vengeance upon the heathen, and punishments upon the people; To bind their kings with chains, and their nobles with fetters of iron; To execute upon them the judgment written: this honour have all his saints. Praise ye the Lord" (Psalms 149:4-9).

THE MORNING STAR

A final promise is given to the overcomers: "And I will give him the morning star." This is a reference to Jesus as we see in 2 Peter 1:19, "And so we have the prophetic word made more sure, to which you do well to pay attention as to a lamp shining in a dark place, until the day dawns and *the morning star* arises in your hearts."

Here is a promise of a fuller understanding of Jesus Himself. Now we understand and know Him in a very incomplete way, but the promise is that we will know Him as we are known; as fully and as completely as He knows us. The believers are being given Jesus Himself in place of the idols that were so prevalent in the church of the Middle Ages. Jesus is indeed ours, we were created for Him and when we finally see Him face to face, we will wonder why we ever thought anything else was ever important.

CHAPTER 5
THE CHURCHES OF SARDIS, PHILADELPHIA, AND LAODICEA
Revelation 3

SARDIS

Sardis was the home of both King Croesus (of "rich as Croesus" fame) and Aesop. The word *Sardis* means "escaping few" or "remnant" which is apropos when considering that this is the church of the Reformation and of modern times. The predominant church today is a Sardian church. It thus behooves us to listen carefully to this letter.

To begin, Jesus identifies Himself to this church as the One who has the seven Spirits of God, and the seven stars (the angels of the churches). Jesus is stressing the fullness of God and the full work of His Spirit to Sardis. God wants His church to walk in the totality of His Spirit and thus reflect the completeness of His nature. This church does not; it is incomplete. This church has great need of the Holy Spirit because of its formality and its emphasis on right doctrine at the expense of relational commitment to Jesus. John 4:24 says, "God is a Spirit: and they that worship him must worship him in spirit and in truth." Sardis prides itself on its Truth and ignores the Spirit.

NO COMMENDATION FOR THIS CHURCH

Interestingly, there is no commendation given by Jesus for this church. Modern Protestants, on the other hand, revere this historical Church. This church to this day enjoys a reputation that it does not deserve. Jesus says she has a name that she is alive but that in reality she is not. That is because without the Holy Spirit, there is no hope of anything but death. "For the letter [of the law] killeth, but the Spirit giveth life" (2 Corinthians 3:6). The Sardian Protestant Church has passed out of the doctrine of a salvation by one's own works, but in doing so she has not come into the understanding of the Spirit-led life, much less the Spirit-led church. Her emphasis seems to be on a salvation based on correct doctrine. The substitution of a theology of salvation by understanding correct doctrine for the theology of salvation by works is no improvement. Nor is it any more balanced or powerful. Doctrine alone is no better than false doctrine. Both miss the point.

THE CHURCH- ORTHODOX BUT DEAD

In verse 2 Jesus tells them to strengthen the things that remain. In other words, the reform is not complete. The pride that has come to this church because of her doctrinal reformation has made her smug and self-satisfied. She is so full of self-commendation that Jesus has no desire to commend her Himself other than to obliquely refer to her reformation in the above-mentioned verse. Although this church is the most orthodox of the churches, she is also the most dead.

Writes Dr. Ernest Stoeffler, Professor Emeritus of Religion at Temple University, "During the seventeenth century the Reformed communion, like Lutheranism, found itself ever more tightly in the grip of a lifeless Orthodoxy. Reason was employed in the establishment of theological propositions, and hence exalted, while feeling was largely ignored. The major emphasis in the churches was on right belief as set forth by the theologians. Calvin's concern about the Christian life was paid only lip service."[17]

Again Dr. Stoeffler writes, "There was a widespread perception that the Reformation of the sixteenth century had indeed altered the theology and structures of western Christendom but had never succeeded in reforming the life of the church." He continues: "It is not surprising, therefore, that church life tended to be shallow, and that meaningful religious commitment on the part of church members was frequently lacking. Among both clergy and laity there was little awareness that in the biblical understanding of the Christian life, religious profession and an appropriate mode of daily living must go together"[18]

INFIGHTING

For the first time in history, the Church found herself gravely splintered. Then, as now, the different branches of the Reform movement fought one another almost as fiercely as they did Catholicism. Consider, for example, the matter of the

Communion. Reformers Huldrych Zwingli, Martin Luther, and Casper Schwenckfeld all held forth different interpretations concerning it, and all three groups celebrated this central rite of Christian faith and unity while in open warfare with other Christians.

Andreas Karlstadt, the professor at the University of Wittenberg who promoted Martin Luther to the doctorate in 1512, was an even more zealous reformer in many areas than Luther. He foreshadowed many positions that would be taken later by the Anabaptists and Baptists such as the idea of baptism for the believer as opposed to infant baptism. He and Martin Luther waged a war of words for years. Indeed, Luther called both Zwingli and Karlstadt "willful liars," "sect leaders," and "novices in the sacred Scriptures."

Many times what united different reform movements at all was simply their combined opposition to other reform movements, such as the despised Anabaptists (the precursors of the modern day Mennonites). Tolerance of other Christians was in as short supply then as it seems to be today. Freedom of religious expression was not any more present in Protestant countries than it was in Catholic countries.

Will Durant writes, "In order to permit peace among and within the states each prince was to choose between Roman Catholicism and Lutheranism; all his subjects were to accept 'his religion whose realm' it was; and those who did not like it were to emigrate. There was no pretense on either side to toleration; the principle that the Reformation had upheld in the youth of its rebellion - the right of private judgment - was as completely rejected by the Protestant leaders as by the Catholics."[19]

RESTORATION ONLY PARTIAL

This is not to say that the movement of the Reformation was not sorely needed. It was and there were many, many positive outcomes from it. They truly did save the things that were "ready to die." However, many Protestants tend to romanticize and idealize this church era without a clear picture of how much remained to be restored. Revelation 3:3 says as much when Jesus tells them to remember what they have learned - to keep it but to continue their repentance. Their concern with outward appearance over a life truly surrendered to Him threatens their relationship with Him. They rely on staid predictability and rational non-emotion and in so doing, grieve the Holy Spirit. He also warns them that they are in danger of having His coming surprise them as a thief in the night would. This is not a positive thing, and it is certainly not inevitable, else it would not be a chastisement to them. First Thessalonians 5:2 is often quoted from the pulpits, "For yourselves know perfectly that the day of the Lord so cometh as a thief in the night. For when they shall say, Peace and safety; then sudden destruction cometh upon them, as travail upon a woman with child; and they shall not escape." Rarely, however, is verse four, two verses down, read, *"But ye, brethren, are not in darkness, that that day should overtake you as a thief."*

Something is dreadfully wrong if the Church is caught off guard and surprised by the wonderful prophetic fulfillments that happen in the last days. The Sardis Church will be. Jesus' appearing will catch them off guard as much as it will the world. That is because this church does not know and does not teach prophecy. There were only two books in the Bible that Martin Luther felt did not belong there at all and thus were included in the Canon by mistake. One was James, the other was Revelation. Consider, too, how many Protestants know much of their Bible well, but yet have no concrete understanding of prophecy. Jesus is very stern here in His warning that this is unacceptable to Him. May His words fall on deaf ears no longer.

A SELF-RIGHTEOUS CHURCH

Verse 4 speaks of the overcomers who have not defiled their garment and who will walk with Jesus dressed in white. Sardis's main trade was in woolen garments. Several times the Bible speaks of garments in terms of righteousness - either the righteousness of God or their own "righteousness." Isaiah 64:6 reads, "But we are all as an unclean thing, and all our righteousnesses are as filthy rags." Most of the people in this church are content to be found in their own garments, that is, in their own righteousness. This is a self-righteous church; only the overcomers know that they have need of the righteousness of Christ. This church, while trumpeting salvation by faith, subtly whispers in self-congratulation, "and of course, salvation by knowledge of the truth." Jesus says to them, "you are wearing your own garments while pretending to be clothed in Mine."

We see this concept in the parable of the wedding feast in Matthew 22, "And when the king came in to see the guests, he saw there a man which had not on a wedding garment: And he saith unto him, Friend, how camest thou in hither not having a wedding garment? And he was speechless. Then said the king to the servants, Bind him hand and foot, and take him away, and cast him into outer darkness; there shall be weeping and gnashing of teeth" (Matthew 22:11-13).

Traditionally, wedding garments would be provided to all the guests by the father of the groom. The point that Jesus was making with this parable was that no one can go to heaven based on his own righteousness (garments). It takes the righteousness that is provided by the Father.

Consider Zephaniah 1:8, "And it shall come to pass in the day of the Lord's sacrifice, that I will punish the princes and the king's children, *and all such as are clothed with strange apparel.*"

When God is purifying Joshua the high priest as recorded in Zechariah 3, this is written: "Now Joshua was clothed with filthy garments, and stood before the angel. And he answered and spake unto those that stood before him saying, Take away the filthy garments from him. And unto him he said, Behold, I have caused thine iniquity to pass from thee, and I will clothe thee with change of raiment."

PROMISES TO THE OVERCOMER

Three promises are given to the overcomer and the first one - the promise of white raiment - is the fulfillment of God's promise given in the preceding verse. The Sardian overcomers will be found clothed in the righteousness of Jesus because they understand and claim for themselves Philippians 3:9-10 that reads, "And be found in him, not having mine own righteousness, which is of the law, but that which is through the faith of Christ, the righteousness which is of God by faith: That I may know him, and the power of his resurrection."

Genesis tells us that as a consequence of sin God had to clothe Adam. Now God will again clothe His people - this time in white garments of His righteousness.

The second promise given to the overcomer is that his name will not be blotted out of the Book of Life. If names are never blotted out of the Book of Life, as is many times taught, then this is a ridiculous promise. Jesus does not promise ridiculous things. Furthermore, both Exodus 32:32-33 and Psalms 69:28 make reference to the removal of names from the Book of Life. Psalms 69 speaks of both the blotting out of names from the Book of Life, and also of the absence of a name in the roll of the righteous. One of these actions is active (blotting out) and one is passive (*not* writing). Clearly two different things are in view here.

Heaven keeps many books. Ignorantly, the Church has taught of only one book kept in heaven, the Book of Life, but Scripture speaks clearly of other books. Revelation 20:12 speaks of the Book of Life, but speaks in the same sentence of other books, "And I saw the dead, small and great, stand before God; and the *books* were opened: and *another book* was opened which is the book of life: and the dead were judged out of those things which were written in the *books* according to their works."

Malachi 3:16 speaks of a book called the Book of Remembrance that is kept by heaven, but even so, Revelation 20:12's reference to "books" would require the existence of other heavenly records. Even in addition to the other books, two *different* books of life are mentioned in the scriptures: one is called the Lamb's Book of Life, the other simply the Book of Life. One records those that have found life through the sacrifice of Jesus the Lamb. The other simply records the names of all those who have ever lived upon the earth. The latter is the book spoken of here. Names are never said to be written in it, names are said only to be blotted out of it. It is apparent that physical life, not spiritual life, is what is being recorded. But for some, the judgment that is passed upon them is so severe that even the record of their names is purged out of existence. They are purged out of every written record kept throughout Eternity. This is not true of everyone who is not part of the Bride of Christ. Some names that are not in the

Lamb's Book of Life remain in the Book of Life. As will be discussed later, there are definitely degrees of God's punishment. This will be discussed in greater detail when John sees the Great White Throne Judgment in Revelation 20.

But glorious beyond the mere record of their names remaining in the records in heaven, the third promise given to the overcomers is that the names of the overcomers will be announced before God and His holy angels! And Jesus Himself will announce them! What a glorious, glorious promise. It will be the fulfillment of the words of Jesus recorded in Luke 12:8 when He said, "Also I say unto you, Whosoever shall confess me before men, him shall the Son of man also confess before the angels of God." He that hath an ear *let him hear*!

PHILADELPHIA

Philadelphia was a country town, not a sophisticated city at all. She was a wine market and the site of many earthquakes. The word *Philadelphia* means "brotherly love." Like Smyrna, the persecuted church, there is no reproof against this church. It is lovely in Jesus' eyes. Its trademark, its defining characteristic, is its love. When He walked upon the earth, Jesus told His disciples that the world would know that they belonged to Him by the evidence of their love. Not only is love *not* the first thing that comes to the mind of non-believers concerning the Church today, we barely tolerate one another! I find it amazing that Bible teachers assume the Church age that we are living in is the Philadelphian church age. We are not now the church of brotherly love by a long shot. There are few among us who would define our church experience as primarily being one of overwhelming love. The Church is still a divided, bickering church. This is not the Philadelphian church.

In that Church age, not only will there be overwhelming love for one another within the congregations, there will be overwhelming love among all the churches. The Philadelphian will be a powerful, doctrinally pure and united church. We will know that it is here when the world recognizes us as Jesus' disciples because of our love. When Jesus prayed that prayer, He spoke prophetically. The world *will* know it when the Philadelphian church is in full-flower. It will be the Church that Jesus comes for at Rapture. It will be the Church that the world and the false churches hate. The Philadelphian church age is not here yet (although some churches today are Philadelphian churches in spirit), and when it does come I believe it will be short-lived, as was the Smyrnan church. Just as the Imperial Persecutions produced the Smyrnan Church, something monumental will happen to produce the Philadelphian Church. I am sure it will be considered miserable by human standards but it will bring about something wonderful in the Church.

THE CHURCH UNITED

The Ephesian Church was very short lived - less than one hundred years. The Smyrnan Church lasted about two hundred years while the Pergamum Church lasted about three hundred years. The Thyatiran Church lasted for a very long time - about a thousand years. The Sardis Church has been the predominant church for only about six hundred years. Until the Sardis Church, the Church had always been a united church.

We are so used to being divided into different denominations that we rarely stop and think what an aberration this is in terms of overall church history. When the Philadelphian church arrives it will once again be a united church - believers of all different faiths will be supernaturally united, being truly the "Church of Brotherly Love." Something will bring them all together. It will most probably be some sort of persecution or intolerance on the part of the world that finally lets the Church understand that "who is not against Jesus is for Him." The Church, at the same time, will be Spirit-filled, functioning in truth and love; so the unity will not be because of compromise on the part of different denominations. No, the power of Truth will preclude that. It will truly be a Church united in heart and doctrine. The combination of the two variables - persecution by the world and the power of the Holy Spirit - could easily unite the Church in a way that has not been seen since the time of the Apostles.

The rest of organized religion, of those who call themselves Christians but are not, will at this point side with the world in opposing the Philadelphian Church. They will make up the Laodicean Church, the final church mentioned. The

Philadelphian Church and the Laodicean Church will exist side by side in the Last Days because the same events that conspire to form the Philadelphian Church will also form a backlash movement that, sadly, will also claim to be the Church of Christ. Two vastly different movements will both wear His name. The pretender, the Laodicean Church, will be the final church discussed.

KEY TO THE OPEN DOOR

Jesus identifies himself to the Church at Philadelphia as the One who holds the key of David. This key of David is spoken of in prophetic reference to the Messiah in Isaiah 22:22: "And the key of the house of David will I lay upon his shoulder; so he shall open, and none shall shut; and he shall shut and none shall open."

This identification of Jesus to a church is *very* interesting in that it is the only identification not found in John's description of Jesus in Revelation 1. Instead, it is found in Jesus' identification of Himself in verse 18 of that chapter, "...and I have the *keys* of hell and of death." The key of David is the power of resurrection over death. Only Jesus, the One who is Holy and True, holds it. In the very next verse, Jesus promises to use this key to set before them an open door. We see this open door in the first verse of the very next chapter. It is the open door to heaven; the saints' resurrection. The key is inextricably linked to the door. And that key will open the door of heaven for the Church that will experience the Rapture. I find it hard to understand why most Bible commentators explain this open door as an open door to evangelism. There is not one shred of supporting Scripture in this passage to augment that argument. The Bible always explains itself if given a chance. Every clue we need is in the first four chapters of the book. Furthermore, the task of evangelism is a task given to the Church; it would be a key she would hold, however, the key of David is held by Jesus alone. Evangelism is, indeed, a noble undertaking, but it is not what is in view here; the resurrection is.

If the reader is in need of more substantiation, let him consider Matthew 24:32-33. When speaking of the Rapture and the signs of the end Jesus says, "Now learn a parable of the fig tree; When his branch is yet tender, and putteth forth leaves, ye know that summer is nigh: So likewise ye, when ye shall see all these things, know that it is near, *even at the doors*" (emphasis mine).

When teaching of the Rapture in the parable of the ten virgins in Matthew 25, Jesus says in verse 10 concerning the virgins who missed the coming of the Bridegroom, "And while they went to buy, the bridegroom came; and they that were ready went in with him to the marriage: *and the door was shut*" (emphasis mine).

Speaking of those who will go to heaven, Jesus says in Luke 13:24-25, "Strive to enter in at the strait gate: for many, I say unto you, will seek to enter in, and shall not be able. When once the master of the house is risen up, and hath *shut the door*, and ye begin to stand without, and to knock *at the door*, saying, Lord, Lord, *open unto us*: and he shall answer and say unto you, I know you not whence ye are" (emphasis mine).

And, finally, consider the words of James 5: 9, "Grudge not one against another, brethren, lest ye be condemned: behold, the judge standeth **before the** *door*" (emphasis mine).

THE CHURCH WITH POWER

The Philadelphian Church will have miraculous power, as did the first-century Church. The literal meaning in Greek of the words "a little strength" is "miraculous power." This will be a Spirit-filled church. The first-century Church burst upon the world scene with boldness, faith, power and might. Jewish believers who had absolutely no cultural context for witnessing or evangelizing, went everywhere preaching the gospel. And wondrous signs followed the preaching. Just as with Jesus, the blind saw, the lame leapt, the dead were brought back to life, demons trembled. Will the Philadelphian Church possibly be able to compare to the Ephesian Church in this regard? Not only will she compare, she will surpass the Ephesian Church because, as Daniel 12:8-10 prophesied, in addition to the miraculous power given to her, prophetic knowledge will be opened up to the Philadelphian Church that heretofore has been kept from the Church. She will use that knowledge in power and boldness for Christ. The gospel will be preached in its fullness.

It seems that, since the completeness of the preaching of the Apostles, each particular Church age has stressed parts of Scripture while ignoring others. The Philadelphian Church will present both the spirit-filled gospel of power, and the inerrant gospel of truth. Once again we will see Acts 14:3 come to pass, "...therefore abode they speaking boldly in the Lord, which gave testimony unto the word of his grace, and granted signs and wonders to be done by their hands."

This is when we will see the fulfillment of Jesus' prophecy concerning the Church in John 14:12-14, "Verily, verily, I say unto you, He that believeth on me, the works that I do shall he do also; and greater works than these shall he do; because I go unto my Father. And whatsoever ye shall ask in my name, that will I do, that the Father may be glorified in the Son. If ye shall ask any thing in my name, I will do it."

Jesus says quite clearly here that the Church ("he that believeth on me", **not** just the Apostles) will do greater things than He did. We generally approach this passage with hearts of disbelief and try to explain it away by saying that in scope (or magnitude) the church will do greater things. Jesus simply says that the Church will do greater things. She will. She hasn't yet, but she will.

JESUS' NAME NOT DENIED

Two of the commendations given to this church are that they have kept His word (they are both scripturally pure and obedient to those Scriptures) and that they have not denied His name. From this we can see where two of the main spiritual battles in this age will be. One will be on holding fast to the belief of the inerrancy of the Bible, another will be in not denying the name of Jesus. This would seem odd to Christians of another era - of course Christians would cling both to their God and to their Scriptures! - but it becomes more understandable daily to present-time Christians because to take the Bible literally today is to invite scorn and ridicule. Furthermore, to insist that the way to the Father is by means of Jesus alone is seen as bigoted closed-mindedness.

This is not the first reference to the promise given to those who hold fast to the name of Jesus or the consequence to those who do not. Jesus Himself addresses this in Matthew 10:32-33 when He says, "Whosoever therefore shall confess me before men, him will I confess also before my Father which is in heaven. But whosoever shall deny me before men, him will I also deny before my Father which is in heaven."

Paul reiterates this in 2 Timothy 2:12, "If we suffer, we shall also reign with him: if we deny him, he also will deny us," while also stating in Romans 10:10 that "with the mouth confession is made unto salvation." Only the fool ignores these warnings and promises. The overcomer does not.

TARES IN THE CHURCH

We see in verse 9 the second mention of the tares that Satan sows in the churches that truly oppose him. In the Smyrnan Church the tares were linked with those who were possibly spies in their midst, reporting to the Emperor, but at the very least these tares were sowing seeds of fear and discouragement among the believers. At the time of the Philadelphian Church, the damage from the tares will again result in persecution, fear and discouragement. Keep in mind that the Laodicean Church will be in full-flower and will be opposing the Philadelphian Church to the greatest extent of her ability. But this time Jesus promises to punish publicly the tares. The promise is given that Jesus will make the tares come and worship at the feet of the true believers and to force this false group to acknowledge that the scorned believers, berated and persecuted by them is the true group of overcomers that are loved by Jesus.

This state of affairs is becoming more and more clear as one watches how true Christians are beginning to be treated in this nation. Scorn and ridicule are heaped upon them. They are called intolerant and unloving, and un-Christlike even by other churches because of their insistence on discerning between good and evil, right and wrong.

This criticism and scorn will abound both in the world and in the Church as time continues. It will not abate; it will increase. If a Christian is feeling timid now about disagreeing with the prevailing culture, I am truly afraid for him as the time for Jesus' return becomes shorter. The overcomer will stand on the Word, the pretender will not. And, says this blessed promise, the very people who said the believers were intolerant and un-Christlike will have to publicly acknowledge that they were wrong. When that will happen is not specified, but I strongly doubt it will be before Christ begins to judge the nations and to reign and rule on earth. Nevertheless, our vindication by Christ will come. Hang on to this promise, times are going to get very rough, criticism will get ugly. It does not matter. We are loved by the Son; we are overcomers because we have, as the next verse says, kept the word of His patience.

THIS CHURCH ESCAPES THE TRIBULATION
Another promise is given to those who keep His word at this time in history - they are promised that they will be kept from the hour of temptation that is going to come on the world during this time. In the Greek, "the" is a definite article. That means that this is a specific and definite time. It is not one hour of many, it is a unique and singular hour. This is the time of tribulation that has been prophesied throughout the Bible; it is "That Day" as the Bible so many times calls it. "And take heed to yourselves, lest at any time your hearts be overcharged with surfeiting, and drunkenness, and cares of this life, and so *that day* come upon you unawares. For as a snare shall it come on all them that dwell on the face of the whole earth" (Luke 21:34-35, emphasis mine).

The overcomers in the Philadelphian Church era will be kept from this time of tribulation. This is a clear promise. They are not promised to be kept from the worst of it, they are not promised strength to go through it, they are promised escape from it. This will be accomplished by the Rapture. Again, the time of the Rapture is pinpointed - it is before the hour of tribulation that will fall upon the earth. Consider Luke 21:34-36 once again. Verses 34 and 35 are quoted above, now add verse 36, "Watch ye therefore, and pray always, that ye may be accounted worthy *to escape all these things that shall come to pass*, and to stand before the Son of man" (emphasis mine). Again, Jesus does not tell us to pray for futile things, so if it were not possible to escape it, He would not command us to pray for that very thing.

The promise given by Jesus that they will escape THAT DAY is also proof of the prophetic mystery of the letters to the churches because this promise was not fulfilled in the first-century to the group of believers at Philadelphia who were the first recipients of this letter. No, it is a promise that is given by Jesus to the prophetic Church at Philadelphia that will exist at the time of His coming.

In verse 11, Jesus again refers to His coming for His church by informing them of how He will come. He says that He will come quickly. The Greek word used here for "quickly" implies "with speed or swiftness." It does *not* imply "soon." When Jesus says that He is coming quickly He is speaking of the manner of His coming, not its timeliness. After all, the Rapture is a rescue of the saints and it needs to happen very quickly. 1 Corinthians 15:52 says that it will happen in a "twinkling of an eye." More are the reasons to be ready.

THE OVERCOMERS' REWARD

The reward given here to the overcomers is that they will be made a pillar in the temple of His God, and that He will write upon them the name of His God, the name of the city of His God, and His –Jesus'- new name. Jesus' new name speaks of His new role. "In his days Judah shall be saved, and Israel shall dwell safely: and this is his name whereby he shall be called, *the Lord our Righteousness*" (Jeremiah 23:6). The writing of the name of God and Jesus upon our persons is a stupendous reward and I will write of it in depth when chapter 21 is under consideration. At this point, suffice it to say that Jesus is promising the saints that the fight is over, the victory is won, and it is a permanent victory.

In Genesis, God came down to man; now, with the giving of this reward, man will go up to God. Revelation 21:22 tells us that there will be no physical temple in heaven; the Lord God Almighty and Lamb are its temple. We are told here that we are the pillars in that temple. A pillar is not a decoration, it is a load-bearing device. As pillars are to an edifice, so are we an integral and indispensable part of the very dwelling of God. As George MacDonald once wrote, "[T]here is a place in God that only we belong in. Also as pillars, we have a job to do, even in Heaven." As the vision of Revelation continues to unfold, this will become more and more apparent. The saints have not finished their labors, they have just begun to work.

THE CHURCH'S FINAL FORM

Soren Kierkegaard once said, "Christendom has done away with Christianity without being quite aware of it." That statement defines the Laodicean Church perfectly and, sadly, that church will be the predominant church when Jesus comes. Do not confuse the Laodicean Church with the Philadelphian Church, which is the church for whom Jesus returns. The Laodicean Church and the Philadelphian Church will exist side by side. The two churches will play out the parable of the ten virgins; the Philadelphian Church will be taken, the Laodicean Church will be left. The Laodicean Church will be far larger, far stronger (in an earthly sense), and far more influential (again, in an earthly sense). This church exists today; all <u>seven</u> churches exist today. However, the Laodicean Church will be the final form that the Church will take.

Laodicea was a city in Phrygia, very near to Colosse; Laodicea had been the site of many battles. The last battle will be a spiritual one and it will pit the spirit of this world against the Holy Spirit. Laodicea literally means "rule of the people." It is the opposite of the Nicolaitan movement that sought to conquer the people. This time the people are totally in charge and the results are as disastrous as the opposite extreme. This is a man-centered, humanistic church. In fact in verse 20, we see Jesus standing outside this church knocking on the door. It is no longer His church.

THE TRUE WITNESS

Note how Jesus identifies Himself to this church: the Amen, the faithful and true witness, the beginning of the creation of God. To the church that is leaving the Word He identifies Himself as the Word - the true witness to the age of skepticism and unbelief. The role of the Church is to be a witness of the truth to the world. This church no longer holds the Bible to be the inspired word of God, and has ceased to be a witness to the truth. This is the final result of the man-centered seminaries that hold the Bible to be something other than the literal word of God. Thus, Jesus identifies their weakness by His role as the true witness.

Revelation 3:14 is the only place in the New Testament that "Amen" is used as a proper name. When said by God, "amen" means "it is and shall be so." It has the same meaning as "truly, truly" that was said by Jesus each time He imparted a new truth to the disciples. When said by men, "amen" means "so be it"; man accepting and obeying the revelation of God. Used here by Jesus as His proper name, He is establishing that He is the confirmation of God notwithstanding their unbelief.

The final identification - the beginning of the creation of God - is addressed to the church that embraces the theory of evolution and no longer believes in the Creation, Jesus identifies Himself as The Creator; the creation of God had its beginning with Him. Because Satan cannot create, he must challenge the truth that God can. This church believes the deception.

THE CHURCH DEPARTS FROM THE FAITH

This church is in rebellion to God. It will worship itself because it cannot hold to any authority other than itself. Departure from the faith on the part of the Church is a characteristic of the last days. Paul, writing to Timothy prophesies this when he says, "This know also, that in the last days perilous times shall come. For men shall be lovers of their own selves, covetous, boasters, proud, blasphemers, disobedient to parents, unthankful, unholy, without natural affection, trucebreakers, false accusers, incontinent, fierce, despisers of those that are good, traitors, heady, high-minded, lovers of pleasures more than lover of God; *having a form of godliness, but denying the power thereof,* from such turn away. For of this sort are they which creep into houses, and lead captive silly women laden with sins, led away with divers lusts, ever learning, and never able to come to the knowledge of the truth" (2 Timothy 3:1-7, emphasis mine).

In the next chapter he writes, "For the time will come when they will not endure sound doctrine; but after their own lusts shall they heap to themselves teachers, having itching ears; and they shall turn away their ears from the truth, and shall be turned unto fables," (2 Timothy 4:3-4).

These are not people who refuse to accept the gospel, these are people who, according to Paul, accept the gospel and then reject it; "Now the Spirit speaketh expressly, that in the latter times some shall depart from the faith, giving heed to seducing spirits, and doctrines of devils; speaking lies in hypocrisy; having their conscience seared with a hot iron; forbidding to marry, and commanding to abstain from meats, which God hath created to be received with thanksgiving of them which believe and know the truth" (1 Timothy 4:1-3).

Years before, when Paul wrote to the Colossian Church, he wrote words of warning about this situation to them in the first ten verses of chapter 2,

> For I would that ye knew what great conflict I have for you, and for them at Laodicea, and for as many as have not seen my face in the flesh; That their hearts might be comforted, being knit together in love and unto all riches of the full assurance of understanding, to the acknowledgment of the mystery of God, and of the Father, and of Christ; In whom are hid all the treasures of wisdom and knowledge. And this I say, lest any man should beguile you with enticing words. For though I be absent in the flesh, yet am I with you in the spirit, joying and beholding your order, and the steadfastness of your faith in Christ. As ye have therefore received Christ Jesus the Lord, so walk ye in him: rooted and built up in him, and stablished in the faith, as ye have been taught, abounding therein with thanksgiving. *Beware lest any man spoil you through philosophy and vain deceit, after the tradition of men, after the rudiments of the world, and not after Christ...* For in him dwelleth all the fulness of the Godhead bodily. And ye are complete in him, which is the head of all principality and power (emphasis mine).

THIS CHURCH NEITHER HOT NOR COLD

In verse 15, Jesus condemns the Laodiceans in part for their lukewarm nature. Historically, Laodicea had no water source of its own so it drew on two springs nearby. One was a hot spring in Hierapolis, the other was in Colosse and it was known for its cool, refreshing water. Laodicea built an aqueduct to pipe in water from both springs, but by the time both waters reached Laodicea and then joined together, they had become lukewarm with neither the healing benefit of the hot, nor the refreshing nature of the cool.

In the same way, the Laodicean church brings reproach upon the name of Jesus simply by claiming to wear it. Jesus says that because they are neither hot nor cold - because they stand for nothing, but still claim to be Christians - He cannot tolerate them and will vomit them out. It actually would be better if they did not wear His name at all. These are graphic and harsh words but they cannot be argued with. Jesus goes on to rebuke them further because of their worldly perspective that is completely lacking in spiritual insight. In this and in their earthly condition, they are the polar opposite of the Smyrnan Church. Laodicea is a rich church, apparently, maybe even extremely wealthy because they have stopped asking for donations. Laodicea states that she doesn't need them. Never, no matter how wealthy the church, have I heard this statement. It seems that in the end times, support of this religious system is so politically and/or socially expedient that need has nothing to do with donations; self-interest alone is enough to fuel contributions to it.

Apparently, this wealth and prideful attitude was symptomatic of the entire city of Laodicea. Earlier, an earthquake had destroyed the entire town and the emperor offered to rebuild it, but the city had turned down the offer, saying that they had need of nothing.

Spiritually, however, it is quite a different story. Jesus sees them as wretchedly poor and disabled. History tells us that once Thomas Aquinas came upon the Pope as he sat counting gold coins. The Pope reportedly remarked, "Thomas, the day is no more when the successor of St. Peter must say 'Silver and gold have I none." Thomas replied, "Neither can he say 'in the name of Jesus rise up and walk." The power of God is gone.

ALTHOUGH OUTWARDLY RICH, LAODICEA IS WRETCHEDLY POOR

Just as Jesus sees the poverty of Smyrna, but pronounces her rich, Jesus sees the wealth of Laodicea and pronounces her wretched, miserable, and poor. He warns them that they must find His gold, not theirs, if they are to be truly rich. And what is that gold? 1 Peter 1:6-8 tells us, "Wherein ye greatly rejoice

... that the trial of your faith, being much more precious than of gold that perisheth, though it be tried with fire, might be found unto praise and honour and glory at the appearing of Jesus Christ: whom having not seen, ye love; in whom, though now ye see him not, yet believing, ye rejoice with joy unspeakable and full of glory: receiving the end of your faith, even the salvation of your souls."

THIS CHURCH IS BLIND

In addition to telling them that they are poverty stricken, Jesus informs them that they are also blind. The city of Laodicea was famous throughout the world for its eye salve. People would travel from afar to purchase it. But Jesus counsels them to purchase from Him His eye-salve so that they will be able to have His insight and begin to see what is at stake here. Jesus is using this to point out that knowledge in the world's eyes translates to ignorance and blindness in His. As the old adage says, "none is so blind as he who will not see." Paul, in Ephesians 1:18, prays for "the eyes of your understanding being enlightened; that ye may know what is the hope of his calling, and what the riches of the glory of his inheritance in the saints, and what is the exceeding greatness of his power to us-ward who believe, according to the working of his mighty power." The Laodiceans are totally blind to this. They are only aware of their own "great" glory.

THIS CHURCH IS NAKED

Laodicea was also famous for its black wool. Beautiful garments were made from it and the clothing from there was a source of great pride. So the church there must be stunned to hear that in God's eyes they are naked. Although the trappings and vestments of this church will appear to be unequaled in splendor, Jesus tells them that it is as if they are wearing nothing. That is because they are dressed in their own righteousness, and, as we have discussed before, man's righteousness is as filthy rags to God. They need His righteousness in order to cover their nakedness.

GOD'S DISCIPLINE LEADS TO REPENTANCE

In verse 19 we are given great insight into the pattern that our own lives tend to follow. Jesus simply says that if He loves us He will chasten us. He does love us and thus we must expect the correction. Much, if not most of the trouble that we have in our lives is due to our own sin and rebellion. Jesus does not step in save us from ourselves. If we do not live in financial contentment with what He has given us, we will find ourselves mired in debt. If we live in the clutches of lust we must expect the consequences of shame and disease. Dishonesty in any respect will be revealed in the life of a Christian. Why? Because Jesus chastens whom He loves. If your sin hasn't been found out yet, don't worry, it will be. "For there is nothing covered, that shall not be revealed; and hid, that shall not be known" (Matthew 10:26). God is faithful to His promise. This is not to say that God does not give mercy, He does. However, He will not allow deep-seated sin to remain in the lives of believers without attempting to force us to repent. This, too, is mercy. Let us each, then, heed this verse and repent as He calls us to do.

JESUS CALLS US TO REPENTANCE

Of all the churches, this one is the most pathetic. Not one word of commendation is given to it by Jesus. And yet, although there is no hope for the church itself, Jesus calls out to individuals within the Church, pleading with them to repent. He loves them, He says, and in the oft-quoted verse 20, we see Him, outside of their church still knocking in the hope that *any man* might hear Him and open the door. If ever we see a picture of the importance of each individual person to God, this is it. What concern, love, and persistence are demonstrated here! Although He does not speak of His second coming to this church - they will completely miss it - He does offer this invitation to the wedding feast to anyone who would hear it, "If any man hear my voice and open the door, I will come in to him, and will sup with him, and he with me," (Revelation 3:20). And, some do respond, for, in the end, there are overcomers (true Christians) in this church. They have gotten past the Laodicean Church and, amazingly, heard and responded to the invitation of Jesus.

Concerning his offer to "sup" with Him, Jesus gave more information about that in Luke 12:36-37, "And ye yourselves like unto men that wait for their lord, when he will return from the wedding; that when he cometh and knocketh, they may open unto him immediately. Blessed are those servants, whom the lord when he cometh shall find watching: verily I say unto you, that he shall gird himself, and make them to sit down to meat and will come forth and serve them."

He does not just foot the bill, which He did with the sacrifice of his life, He does the serving! Love like this can hardly be comprehended by human minds.

FROM TRIALS TO TRIUMPH TO HIS THRONE

The final promise given to the overcomers is the ultimate promise beyond which it is impossible to go. Unbelievably, Jesus gives to the saints access to His very throne; to actually sit upon it with Him and then to rule and reign with Him over every dominion in His universe throughout the rest of eternity. He is giving to us what His Father gave to Him. What else could possibly be given to us?! There is nothing that He has that He withholds from us. Even if our lives here on earth were the most wretched ever known, it would be worth it all to be able to reign with Him throughout eternity. The pain in this life is nothing in comparison to the joy that awaits us.

With the final admonition for him who has an ear to hear what the Spirit is saying to the churches, there will be no more mention of the Church in the Book of Revelation, until the last chapter. The reason for this will become clear in the next chapter.

PART THREE: TRIBULATION AS SEEN FROM HEAVEN'S VIEWPOINT

Figure 2 Part 2-3: Revelation 1 - 11

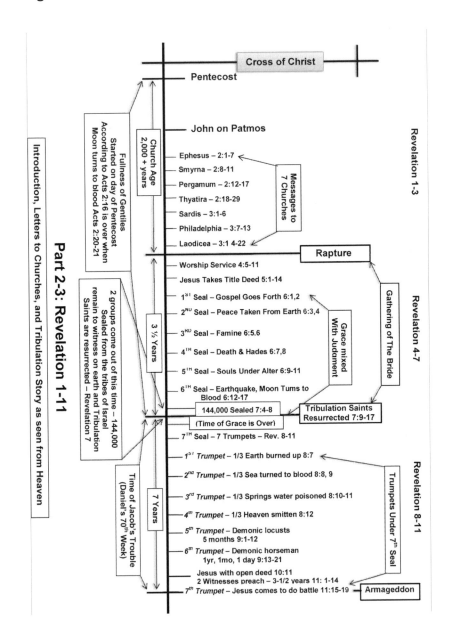

CHAPTER 6
THE CHURCH AGE ENDS
Revelation 4

END OF THE CHURCH AGE - THE RAPTURE

Up until this point, Jesus has been appearing to John on earth. Now, John is invited up into heaven. Prophets in the past have stood on earth and have seen things in heaven, but never before has a prophet gone into heaven and looked down on earth. (It is true that the Apostle Paul was caught up to the "third heaven," but it was not done so as a function of Paul as prophet. In fact, Paul was forbidden to speak or write of what he was shown there.) Chapter 4 also signals a time change. It opens with the phrase "after this." Remember that in chapter 1, John was supernaturally given the outline of Revelation. It consisted of: (1) the things that he has seen - the vision of Christ, (2) the things which are - the church age, and finally, (3) the things which shall be hereafter. Note the phrases "after this" and "I will shew thee things which must be hereafter" that appear in the passage above. With these phrases, we know exactly where we are in time. John has just finished telling the story of the Church age from the first-century until Jesus comes again. Then the voice from heaven tells John that he will now see what takes place after that. We know, then, that on a time line, we are right after the Church age: We are at the Rapture.

John himself is a type, or example, of the Rapture. He experiences the Rapture not as an individual but on behalf of the Church. Heaven's door opens and he hears a voice like the sound of a trumpet calling him up. This is consistent with what Paul says will happen to the believers at the Rapture, "Behold, I shew you a mystery; We shall not all sleep, but we shall all be changed; In a moment, in the twinkling of an eye, at the last trump: for the trumpet shall sound, and the dead shall be raised incorruptible, and we shall be changed" (1 Corinthians15:51-52).

Paul says again, "For the Lord himself shall descend from heaven with a shout, with the voice of the archangel, and with the trump of God and the dead in Christ shall rise first: Then we which are alive and remain shall be caught up together with them in the clouds, to meet the Lord in the air: and so shall we ever be with the Lord" (1 Thessalonians 4:16-17).

Although Paul does not name the archangel, Daniel does. It is Michael.

THE FUTURE TOLD FROM THREE DIFFERENT VANTAGE POINTS

The rest of the book except, of course, for the closing salutation, will deal *entirely* with future events. John is now going to tell the story of what happens between the Rapture and the final return of Jesus in three different ways and from three different vantage points. This is a common prophetic device. Daniel also gives his prophecy of the world governments to come three different times. Each time different details are given. Jesus does the same thing during His Olivet Discourse recorded in the Gospels. It only makes sense to approach a complicated subject in such a way. Imagine for a moment that you have been asked to outline a complete history of the world. It would be impossible to tell the story in a complete fashion without first breaking it up into sub-topics. You might first record the political history of the earth. Next you might discuss the art and literature. The history of medicine might come next, and so forth. John and the other prophets do exactly the same thing! To do it any other way would bog the prophecy down in details, so the prophet first gives an overview of the prophecy. With the next telling, more details are added now that the reader has a general idea of the prophecy. A third telling will render even more detail to the reader.

This is exactly what John is directed to do. First, he will tell the story of this time period from the viewpoint of heaven. That makes sense because everything begins first in heaven. Next, we will see the consequences of the heavenly action when he tells the same story from the viewpoint of the earth. Finally, he will add more detail when he addresses it from the viewpoint of Satan and his kingdom. Each view will be similar, but each view will offer different details. Revelation 4-11 will deal with the story of the earth from Rapture to the return of Jesus with His saints from the viewpoint of heaven. Revelation 12-16 will tell the same story from the viewpoint of earth. Revelation 17-19 will once again tell the same story, this time from the viewpoint of Satan's kingdom. To ignore this fact and to insist on a strict chronological reading of ancient prophetic material will predispose the modern reader to errors in interpretation.

THE ORGANIZED CHURCH DEPARTS

As the chapter opens, John sees an open door. Symbolically, a door means to come in while a window means to go out. This becomes apparent with an overview of prophetic understanding. When a door is used, people or creatures are always going in. When a window is in view, they are seen to be leaving. The raptured church, Philadelphia, was promised an open door. This is it. The true church is gone from the world and, as noted above, the word "church" is not mentioned again until the end of this book. There will be more who come to the Lord during the Tribulation, but the church as we know it, organized as it is now, will not be seen again on the earth. Thus, although the word "church" is not mentioned until the last chapter, the word "saint" appears in every chapter. Saints on the earth will be mentioned and saints in heaven will be mentioned. That is because all Christians are saints; some will have been raptured and are now in heaven, and some will have become Christians after the Rapture and will remain on the earth.

In Revelation 4 John does not record the details of *how* he gets to heaven. Possibly the details are not known to him yet; he simply finds himself caught up to heaven. But when John records this story again, from the earthly perspective, he will go into great detail. That story comprises chapter 12 of Revelation.

JOHN SEES THE THRONE OF GOD

We can safely assume that heaven is a completely new experience for John; he has not seen any aspect of it before. It is interesting, therefore, to note what part of it immediately catches John's attention and dwarfs every other feature by its glory. It is the Throne and He who sits upon it. It is an indescribable place of grandeur, greatness, majesty and dominion, and it is the throne that Jesus has promised that the overcomer will share with Him.

Daniel saw much the same scene in his vision of the Rapture that he records in Daniel 7:9-10: "I beheld till the thrones were cast down, and the Ancient of days did sit, whose garment was white as snow, and the hair of his head like the pure wool: his throne was like the fiery flame, and his wheels as burning fire. A fiery stream issued and came forth from before him: thousand thousands ministered unto him, and ten thousand times ten thousand stood before him: the judgment was set, and the books were opened."

THE RADIANT GLORY OF THE LORD

John is not speaking in symbols when He describes God, he is just describing heavenly things in earthly terms. The problem, of course, is that the beauty and brilliance that he sees cannot really be described in human terms. The Throne is the seat of the grandeur, greatness, majesty and dominion of the King of The Ages. It is indescribable in human terms. But John tries. He writes that the One on the Throne was to look at as a jasper and a sardine stone. Jasper is shimmering white with flashes of purple, while sardine is like a red/orange flame. Thus, John is met with a shimmering white brilliance with flames of red and orange. But all around these predominant colors are all the colors of the rainbow, emerald green apparently predominating. That is fitting in that green is the predominate color of the earth, just as blue is the predominate color of the sea. Even when man symbolizes the earth, green is the natural color that comes to mind. It is clear that God's original covenant with the earth - the rainbow- is in view here.

It is possible that something further is meant when John records that the One on the Throne resembles a sardine stone and a jasper stone. The breastplate of the High Priest has twelve stones set into it, each one representing one of the twelve tribes of Israel. The first stone listed in Exodus 28:17 is the sardius (or sardine) and the last one listed is the jasper stone. This might signify that the entire group of God's children is constantly upon His heart. Couple that idea with the rainbow around the throne and we understand clearly that we are the central focus of God's thoughts and plans.

THE RAINBOW

The rainbow found here is the original rainbow creation of God. The rainbow we see on earth is a copy of this one. Unlike the rainbows that we perceive to be semi-circular on the earth, this one completely encircles the Throne. The scene described here by John is amazingly similar to the one that Ezekiel describes in his first chapter, verses 26-28, "And above the firmament that was over their heads was the likeness of a throne, as the appearance of a sapphire stone: and upon the likeness of the throne was the likeness as the appearance of a man above upon it. And I saw as the colour of amber, as the appearance of fire round about within it, from the appearance of his loins even upward, and from the appearance of his loins even downward, I saw as it were the appearance of fire, and it had brightness round about. As the appearance of the bow that is in the cloud in the day of rain, so was the appearance of the brightness round about. This was the Appearance of the likeness of the glory of the Lord. And when I saw it, I fell upon my face, and I heard a voice of one that spake."

THE COVENANT OF GOD WITH THE EARTH

The rainbow is the sign of the covenant between God and earth; between God and all flesh, not just human flesh (Genesis 9:13-14). It was given to Noah and his family as a sign that God would never again destroy the earth with a flood. The covenant remains in effect; we can personally testify to that each time it rains and we see a rainbow. God considers that covenant so sacred that His very throne is set in the middle of it. It is constantly before Him. The world that we see today is not the same world that God created and set Man in its midst. This is a fallen world, full of weeds, pollution and toxins. Nonetheless, God will not destroy the world; He will purify and cleanse it.

Interestingly, the Bible tells us that the physical world itself has knowledge of God and memory of its pristine state. That seems like a most unbelievable statement, but consider Romans 8:19-22, "For the anxious longing of the creation waits eagerly for the revealing of the sons of God. For the creation was subjected to futility, not of its own will, but because of Him who subjected it, in hope that the creation itself also will be set free from its slavery to corruption into the freedom of the glory of the children of God. For we know that the whole creation groans and suffers the pains of childbirth together until now" (NASB).

The earth anxiously awaits the time that Jesus will redeem it and restore it to its former beauty and freedom. The curse of sin will be lifted even from the earth. Another Scripture that speaks of cognizant ability on the part of the earth is found in Luke 19 when Jesus entered Jerusalem and was met by the multitudes singing "Hosanna" and waving palm branches. The Pharisees rebuked Jesus and told Him to still His disciples. Jesus replied in verse 40, "I tell you that, if these should hold their peace, *the stones* would immediately cry out" (emphasis mine).

1 Chronicles 16:31-33 speaks of the rejoicing and praise given to God by the physical world, "Let the heavens be glad, and let the earth rejoice: and let men say among the nations, The Lord reigneth. Let the sea roar, and the fulness thereof: let the fields rejoice, and all that is therein. Then shall the trees of the wood sing out at the presence of the Lord, because he cometh to judge the earth."

This exhortation is repeated in Psalm 96:12, and in Psalm 98:7. Isaiah 44:23 commands,

"Sing, O ye heavens; for the Lord hath done it: shout, ye lower parts of the earth: break forth into singing, ye mountains, O forest, and every tree therein: for the Lord hath redeemed Jacob, and glorified himself in Israel." In an interesting side note, astronomers have now discovered that stars "sing" and have even recorded the songs which are played in some observatories. Until now, no human had ever heard the voices of the stars, but since they were created, they have been singing for their creator.

THE EARTH TO BE REDEEMED NOT DESTROYED
Thus, it is prophesied over and over that, at the coming of the Lord in judgment, the earth will rejoice. It will rejoice because the coming of Jesus will herald the fact that the earth will be purified, cleansed, and set aright. Creation longs for that day. *But...* that day will come with the rainbow set firmly

around the throne; with the covenant securely in force. God will not destroy the earth. God will purify the earth. The primary Scripture that speaks of how this will happen is in 2 Peter 3. This passage is so important that we must consider almost all of the chapter:

> This second epistle, beloved, I now write unto you; in both which I stir up your pure minds by way of remembrance: That ye may be mindful of the word which were spoken before by the holy prophets, and of the commandment of us the apostles of the Lord and Saviour: Knowing this first, that there shall come in the last days scoffers, walking after their own lusts, and saying, Where is the promise of his coming? For since the fathers fell asleep, all things continue as they were from the beginning of the creation. For this they willingly are ignorant of, that by the word of God the heavens were of old, and the earth standing out of the water and in the water: Whereby the world that then was, being overflowed with water, perished: But the heavens and the earth, which are now, by the same word are kept in store, reserved unto fire against the day of judgment and perdition of ungodly men. But, beloved, be not ignorant of this one thing, that one day is with the Lord as a thousand years, and a thousand years as one day. The Lord is not slack concerning his promise, as some men count slackness; but is longsuffering to us-ward, not willing that any should perish, but that all should come to repentance. But the day of the Lord will come as a thief in the night; in which the heavens shall pass away with a great noise, and the elements shall melt with fervent heat, the earth also and the works that are therein shall be burned up. Seeing then that all these things shall be dissolved, what manner of persons ought ye to be in all holy conversation and godliness, Looking for and hastening unto the coming of the day of God, wherein the heavens being on fire shall be dissolved, and the elements shall melt with fervent heat? Nevertheless we, according to his promise, look for new heavens and a new earth, wherein dwelleth righteousness.

EARTH PURIFIED BY FIRE

What Peter is saying here is clear: I, Peter, am not telling you anything new. This teaching is all through the Scriptures. The prophets have laid it all out for you. But, at the end times people will begin to scoff at the notion that there will be a Second Coming. It will be an idea that will give great amusement to the world. Christians who actually believe that Jesus will return for them as He has promised, will be seen as unsophisticated, ignorant idiots. One of the arguments the world will make is that the world is exactly as it has always been. Not so! They forget the state of the world before Creation and they also forget that the world had once been destroyed by a worldwide flood.

Peter goes on to say that the world will change once again, and this time it will be destroyed by fire. The question arises, then, as to what is meant by "destroyed"? Peter makes that clear, also. He certainly does *not* teach that nothing will be left of the world, that it will be totally annihilated by fire. Although this is what is most commonly taught today, it is not what Peter taught at all.

To begin with, in verse 6 Peter says that the world, "being overflowed with water, perished," or was destroyed. It certainly was; however Planet Earth still remained after the Flood. It was decidedly different, but it was still Planet Earth. We understand that concept so clearly that we have terms for it: antediluvian (before the flood) and postdiluvian (after the flood). So shall it be when God destroys it by fire. It will be completely different, but it will still be Planet Earth. In fact, God Himself limits His destruction the second time more than the first time. Genesis 8:21 records God's promise to the earth, "...neither will I again smite any more every thing living, as I have done."

THE EARTH NOT ANNIHILATED

There are forty-nine different Hebrew words for the English word "destroy." We must be diligent to understand what meaning is in view. Verse 10 says that "the heavens shall pass away with a great noise and the elements shall melt with fervent heat and all the works that are therein shall be burned up." The Greek word used here for "pass away" is *parerchomai*. It does not mean annihilation or termination. It means to pass from "one condition of existence to another." We use the term "pass away" to speak of death in exactly that way. When a person dies, he is not annihilated nor does he cease to exist. He exists in a different form, but he exists. What Peter is saying is that the earth will pass from one form to another, exactly as it did before as a result of the Flood. Isaiah 34:4 has this exact time in view, "And all the host of heaven shall be dissolved, and the heavens shall be rolled together as a scroll: and all their host shall fall down, as the leaf falleth off from the vine, and as a falling fig from the fig tree."

The very next chapter of Isaiah records the new condition of earth, "The wilderness and the solitary place shall be glad for them; and the desert shall rejoice, and blossom as the rose. It shall blossom abundantly, and rejoice even with joy and singing: the glory of Lebanon shall be given unto it, the excellency of Carmel and Sharon, they shall see the glory of the Lord, and the excellency of our God."

Verse 11 of this passage in 2 Peter says that all things on earth will be dissolved. When we speak of something dissolving, it, too, implies a changed state of being. Ice dissolved remains water, it is simply water in a changed state. Ice destroyed is altogether different. Sugar dissolved in coffee remains in the coffee, its form is just different. The word translated "dissolved" in this passage in Peter, literally means "to loose." It is translated that way in Matthew 21:2, "You will find a colt, *loose* her." The translators could have as easily rendered that, "You will find a colt, dissolve her," except that the meaning would not have been clear. Again, the same word is used in John 11:44 when Jesus, referring to Lazarus who has risen from the grave, tells the people to "unbind" him. "Unbind" is the same word as "dissolve." It is also the same word that John the Baptist used, when, speaking of Jesus, he said "I am not worthy to loose his shoes."

This unbinding of all things on earth will allow for a changed earth. In the same way that the rope bound the colt and the graveclothes bound Lazarus, something has the world bound up against its will. That something is sin. The bonds of sin must be loosed from the earth and it, too, must be set free from the curse.

This time spoken of in Peter is the time that Hebrews 12:26-27,29 is speaking of when it says, "Whose voice then shook the earth: but now he hath promised, saying, Yet once more I shake not the earth only, but also heaven. And this word, Yet once more, signifieth the removing of those things that are shaken, as of things that are made, that those things which cannot be shaken may remain... For our God is a consuming fire."

God is going to put the earth aright, He is not going to destroy it.

The Psalmist, in Psalm 102:25-26, speaks of this change of the earth in terms of the earth changing as one changes clothes: "Of old hast thou laid the foundations of the earth: and the heavens are the work of thy hands. They shall perish, but thou shalt endure: yea, all of them shall wax old like a garment; as a vesture shalt thou change them, and they shall be changed."

THE EARTH WILL REMAIN FOREVER

According to Scripture, the earth cannot be annihilated because God has made it clear that He has created it to abide forever.

"They that trust in the Lord shall be as mount Zion, which cannot be removed, but abideth for ever" (Psalms 125:1).

"One generation passeth away, and another generation cometh: but the earth abideth for ever" (Ecclesiastes 1:4).

"I know that, whatsoever God doeth, it shall be for ever: nothing can be put to it, nor any thing taken from it: and God doeth it, that men should fear before him" (Ecclesiastes 3:14).

"For thus says the Lord, The whole land shall be a desolation, Yet I will not execute a complete destruction" (Jeremiah 4:27, NASB).

No, the earth will not be destroyed, it will be redeemed and put aright. It will end up as it was when Adam And Eve were in the Garden of Eden, a perfect work. "And he shall send Jesus Christ, which before was preached unto you: Whom the heaven must receive *until the times of restitution of all things*, which God hath spoken by the mouth of all his holy prophets since the world began" (Acts 3:20-21, emphasis mine). When John sees the finished work - earth in its purified state – he says, in

Revelation 21 that he saw a new heaven and a new earth. It certainly looks brand new to him. But contrast John's perspective with that of God's perspective found in verse 5 of that same chapter. God recounts what He has done and He says, "Behold, I make all things new." NOT "all new things" but "all things new." He has made the world new, He has not made a new world.

The cleansing of earth will be a perfect work, and as such, will come from the hand of God, not man. *Man* clean up the earth?! What a ridiculous thought! Man has polluted and destroyed the earth. It will take God to clean it up. The plagues that we will see later on are *not* random nuclear missiles shot off by human governments. The plagues are the means of God's cleansing of the earth. With them, He will eradicate every trace of sin that has etched itself onto the earth. The Bible says that that was also the reason for the flood, "And God looked upon the earth, and, behold, it was corrupt; for all flesh had corrupted his way upon the earth. And God said ... behold, I will destroy them with the earth" (Genesis 6:12-13).

THE TIME OF THE EARTH'S CLEANSING

Some have erroneously taught that this passage in 2 Peter refers to the time after the thousand-year reign of Jesus upon the earth. But verse 10 clearly places this at the Day of the Lord, *not* a thousand years later. Isaiah 66: 15-16 also links the Day of the Lord with fire when it says, "For, behold, the Lord will come with fire, and with his chariots like a whirlwind, to render his anger with fury, and his rebuke with flames of fire. For by fire and by his sword will the Lord plead with all flesh: and the slain of the Lord shall be many."

When we look closely at the Day of the Lord, which we will in later chapters, we find that the last seven plagues each carry fire. The Bible teaches that both blood and fire cleanse. The Day of the Lord will cleanse with fire that which has refused cleansing by the Blood of the Lamb, but it will do so with the Rainbow securely fixed around the Throne, and with the promise of the Rainbow firmly in the mind of God Almighty.

THE TWENTY-FOUR THRONES AND THE TWENTY-FOUR ELDERS

As noted before, the first thing that captures John's attention in heaven is the Throne and the One who sits upon it. The next thing he notices is the twenty-four thrones that are placed around the Throne. He sees twenty-four men with great authority - elders - sitting upon these thrones. These are saints. They wear the clothing of the saints, and they wear crowns and sit upon thrones. Only the saints have the promise of any of these. In the Old Testament, each city had elders that judged the people of that city. The saints have now come into the work of judgment.

- "To execute upon them the judgment written: this honour have all his saints" (Psalms 149:9).
- "The Ancient of days came, and judgment was given to the saints of the most High; and the time came that the saints possessed the kingdom," (Daniel 7:22).
- "Do ye not know that the saints shall judge the world?" (I Corinthians 6:2).

Twenty-four is a significant number. First Chronicles 25 tells us that there were exactly twenty-four Israelites who were chosen to be prophets before the Lord at any given time. The chapter before, 1 Chronicles 24, records that there were exactly twenty-four orders of priests. There were exactly twenty-four Patriarchs recorded in the Old Testament. Twenty-four seems to be the number that God chose both to minister to Him and to administer for Him.

Twelve is the symbolic number of the redeemed. This was represented in the Old Testament by the twelve tribes, and in the New Testament by the twelve apostles. In the holy city, the city of the redeemed, there are twelve gates and twelve foundation stones. It is possible, then, that the twenty-four saints in view here are representative of Old Testament saints as well as the New Testament saints in light of the fact that the twelve tribes of Israel and twelve apostles add up to the number twenty-four.

It has been theorized that these twenty-four elders might be the twenty-four patriarchs recorded in the Old Testament because of their stature and antiquity. While I doubt that only the Old Testament saints are represented here, whether they are simply New Testament saints, simply Old Testament saints, or a combination of both, the fact remains that the twenty-four elders are functioning in their ruling and judging capacity.

LIGHTNINGS, THUNDERINGS, AND VOICES FROM THE THRONE

In God's dealings with man, mercy always comes before judgment. Noah preached for 120 years before God sent the Flood. The Nation of Israel was warned time and again about her abominations before being taken into captivity by the surrounding nations. And the smallest amount of repentance on her part was enough to stay God's hand from punishing them for decades. Each of us has a lifetime on earth to respond to His love before facing His Throne of Judgment. We see the same principle in play here. First, John saw the rainbow - mercy indeed - but now he sees the lightnings and thunderings and voices proceeding from the throne. They warn of the judgment and wrath that is about to come upon the world. The seven lamps of fire are identified as the seven-fold Spirit of God, the Holy Spirit. The Holy Spirit, too, has ceased to take the form of a dove, symbolizing peace and mercy, and has now taken the form of flaming torches prepared for battle as in the days of Gideon. The Age of Grace is coming to a close, the age of judgment is beginning to dawn. It is important to note that the flaming torches are not a symbol of the Holy Spirit, they are the manifestation of Him as were the tongues of fire at Pentecost. Here is the *power* of the Holy Spirit.

Psalm 97 speaks of the throne of God in a similar vein to these verses in Revelation: "The Lord reigneth; let the earth rejoice; let the multitude of isles be glad thereof. Clouds and darkness are round about him: righteousness and judgment are the habitation of his throne. A fire goeth before him, and burneth up his enemies round about. His lightnings enlightened the world: the earth saw, and trembled. The hills melted like wax at the presence of the Lord, at the presence of the Lord of the whole earth."

A SEA OF GLASS

John's eye now moves outward from the Throne and he sees a sea of glass like crystal encircling the Throne and also in its midst. When humans have been allowed a glimpse into heaven, they have consistently seen this sea. Ezekiel saw this heavenly scene and recorded it in Ezekiel 1:22: "And the likeness of the firmament upon the heads of the living creature was as the colour of the terrible crystal, stretched forth over their heads above." Ezekiel viewed this sea from his perspective on earth and so it appeared as a crystal ceiling to him because he viewed it from below. John sees the sea in its proper perspective, and thus, not as a ceiling.

When Moses, Aaron, Nadab, Abihu and the seventy elders went up on the mountain to meet with the Lord as written in Exodus 24, they, too, saw this view of heaven. Verse 10 records, "And they saw the God of Israel: and there was under his feet as it were a paved work of a sapphire stone, and as it were the body of heaven in his clearness."

THE CRYSTAL SEA REPRESENTED IN THE TEMPLE

God revealed to Moses how he wanted the Tabernacle designed. Hebrews 8:5 tells us that the Tabernacle and the furnishings therein were patterned on the actual items that are in heaven. The pattern of the Temple was also supernaturally given to a man -David. "All this, said David, the Lord made me understand in writing by his hand upon me, even all the works of this pattern" (1 Chronicles 28:19). The Temple featured this sea but it was fashioned of brass. It was situated in front of the altar. Brass is the metal of judgment, and when the nation of Israel approached the altar of God they were facing the judgment of God. Later, Ahaz, one of the wicked kings of Israel, dismantled it and chopped up the sea and the Chaldeans carried it into Babylon. This so displeased God that it was one of the reasons that He sent Israel into captivity.

Now John is seeing the original sea in heaven itself and this time the sea is crystal, not brass. The symbolic meaning of the sea is given later in Revelation 17:15. There it is interpreted as being "peoples, multitudes, and nations, and tongues." There are countless masses of people before the Throne of God. They are the saved of the race of Adam, the saints are not facing judgment for they are clothed in the righteousness of Jesus. The sea is crystal; the people are pure.

THE FOUR LIVING CREATURES

In the midst of the sea and around the Throne of God are four spiritual "beasts" that John calls, in Greek, "the four living creatures." The Living Creatures that surround the throne are full of eyes and are described as resembling a lion, a calf, a man, and an eagle in flight. We are given insight into the Living Creatures by their features. The lion suggests kingly characteristics, the calf those of a servant. Man is representative of rulership of the earth, which was bestowed on him by God, and the soaring eagle suggests to us access to heaven. All of these are reminders of different aspects of Jesus as He interacts with the world. They will also be characteristics of the Overcomers when Jesus comes for them.

The very number used here (four) is the symbolic number of the earth. There are four seasons, four points on the compass, four winds, etc. When God interacts with earth, He consistently chooses the pattern of four. Thus these creatures have interaction with earth.

Other prophets had seen these creatures and called them by different names; cherubim (Ezekiel), seraphim (Isaiah), morning stars (Job), living creatures (Ezekiel and John). Isaiah 6:1-3 reads, "In the year of King Uzziah's death, I saw the Lord sitting on a throne, lofty and exalted, with the train of His robe filling the temple. Seraphim stood above Him, each having six wings; with two he covered his face, and with two he covered his feet, and with two he flew. And one called out to another and said, Holy, Holy, Holy, is the Lord of hosts, The whole earth is full of His glory" (NASB).

Notice verses 6 and 7 of this same chapter in Isaiah, "Then flew one of the seraphims unto me, having a live coal in his hand, which he had taken with the tongs from off the altar: and he laid it upon my mouth, and said, Lo this hath touched thy lips; and thine iniquity is taken away, and thy sin purged."

Ezekiel records these same coals of fire as being administered by creatures he calls cherubim.

And he spake unto the man clothed with linen, and said, Go in between the wheels, even under the cherub, and fill thine hand with coals of fire from between the cherubims, and scatter them over the city. And he went in in my sight....and one cherub stretched forth his hand from between the cherubims unto the fire that was between the cherubims, and took thereof, and put it into the hands of him that was clothed with linen: who took it, and went out....And as for their appearances, they four had one likeness, as if a wheel had been in the midst of a wheel. When they went, they went upon their four sides; they turned not as they went, but to the place whither the head looked they followed it; they turned not as they went. And their whole body, and their backs, and their hands, and their wings, and the wheels, were full of eyes round about, even the wheels that they four had....and every one had four faces: the first face was the face of a cherub, and the second face was the face of a man, and the third the face of a lion, and the fourth the face of an eagle. And the cherubims were lifted up....This is the living creature that I saw under the God of Israel by the river of Chebar; and I knew that they were the cherubims. Every one had four faces apiece, and every one four wings; and the likeness of the hands of a man was under their wings. And the likeness of their faces was the same faces which I saw by the river of Chebar, their appearances and themselves: they went every one straight forward (Ezekiel 10:2,7,10,14,20-22).

Although Ezekiel here records that one of the faces resembled a cherub, in other accounts he renders it as the face of an ox. Isaiah records that the creatures had six wings, Ezekiel sees four. On this basis, most expositors have decided that the two creatures are entirely different creatures. But that seems nonsensical to me. It is entirely possible that Ezekiel saw only four of the six wings. The roles of the cherubim and seraphim are identical, and the descriptions of the two are too similar to be entirely different classes of creature. Ezekiel's description of the creatures (to whom he gives the same name as did John) had all four creatures with all four animal characteristics (lion, calf, man, eagle), whereas John saw each creature with a separate face. Again, it is entirely possible that John saw only the face that each creature was presenting forward and did not notice faces to the sides and back. This is even more understandable when one considers that the cherubim in Ezekiel were in motion whereas the living ones in Revelation were stationary.

Lucifer (Satan) was created as the chief of these creatures. He is called the "covering cherub" in Isaiah. The "covering cherub" was apparently the chief, or most important, cherub. It was closest to the Throne and to the glory of God and thus "covered" the glory of God. In fact, the name Lucifer means "the bearer of light." He caught and transmitted the very glory of God. When Satan appeared in Eden, the form he took in the Garden was the form that the Hebrews called a *seraph*. We translate it as serpent. Seraph is a Hebrew word that literally means "burning, poisonous serpent; venomous snake, fiery winged dragon." Satan took the form closest to the form in which he was created. (It must be remembered here that the serpent was not a snake as we recognize snakes until God cursed it. It was more like the fiery winged dragon of myth. It was only after God cursed it that the serpent was forced to crawl upon its belly.) Again, the terms seem to be interchangeable - Satan was a cherub (plural: cherubim) who took the form of a seraph (plural: seraphim.)

Here in Revelation, John sees what he terms Living Creatures around the Throne. The Temple depicted four cherubim overshadowing the Mercy Seat (the place of the presence of God) in the Tabernacle. Thus Living Creatures are synonymous with cherubim. Interestingly, it was these creatures that were sent to guard the Garden of Eden when Adam and Eve were expelled from there. "Therefore the Lord God sent him forth from the garden of Eden, to till the ground from whence he was taken. So he drove out the man; and he placed at the east of the Garden of Eden Cherubims, and a flaming sword which turned every way, to keep the way of the tree of life" (Genesis 3:23-24). Every time judgment falls upon the earth the four Living Ones call the signal. They are about to do so now.

WORSHIP BEFORE THE THRONE

Before every great event in heaven that is recorded in Revelation we will see that first there is worship. That is because praise precedes power. Always. Here and in our lives also. A most wonderful event is about to happen in chapter 5, and so we see worship in chapter 4. To begin with, the Living Creatures give glory and honor and thanks to God, surrounding the Throne with cries of "Holy, holy, holy" that never cease. Isaiah 6:4 tells us that when they praise God, it is with such ardor that the doorposts of His temple shake and His temple is filled with smoke. "Holy, holy, holy" is their response to God and to everything God does and has ever done. They have been witnesses to the actions of God throughout all time, and there is nothing God has done that has not been holy. This is not simply repetitive praise. As they view the actions of God, "Holy" is the response they give. "Look what He has done. Holy." "Oh see what He has created. Holy." "See, He has redeemed mankind. Holy." "Look how He loves them. Holy." As they meditate upon Him, their only possible response is "Holy," and they say it continually.

Next we see the twenty-four elders, who are representative of all of the saints, entering into the worship service after already passing through the Bema Seat Judgment of Jesus, and as they do so, the realization of who Jesus is and what He has done has so overcome them that they remove their own crowns and place them where they belong; at the feet of the only One among them worthy of praise and glory - Jesus.

Many have taught on the subject of the crowns that await the Christian, stressing that they are the result of lives lived in holiness here on earth, and that some Christians will have large crowns while others possess smaller ones. If, in fact, that is so, we see here what happens to those crowns. They end up at the feet of Jesus, for no glory can remain with us when we are in the presence of God. Once again, the saints are equal one to the other as they fall down and worship Jesus. They are, as the Scriptures teach, joint-heirs; that is, heirs holding all things in common together. There is no strata here, no hierarchy, no differing class of saint, only all of the saints in one accord worshiping their Savior. All present realize that even one's righteousness is a result of the righteousness of Christ. No personal claim can be held and no personal claim is held.

Once again, the great praise that is given is given to the Lord as Creator. Recognizing that the Godhead is the Creator of the Universe is central to Christian doctrine. It is also most threatening to Satan who cannot create, and thus is the author of the theory of evolution. One sees no Darwinians assembled here in heaven; only those who know fully from whence all blessings flow.

CHAPTER 7
EARTH'S TITLE DEED REDEEMED
Revelation 5

EARTH IS YET TO BE REDEEMED

Chapter 5 of Revelation is a pivotal chapter. It centers around a book in the hand of God. It is a critically important book that must be opened. Like removing the sword Excalibur from the stone in the Legend of King Arthur, only one who meets very specific requirements may open it. Initially, no one in the entire universe is found who can meet those requirements. This is beyond tragic, this is catastrophic, as witnessed by John who weeps *greatly* when no one can be found. What does this all mean? As puzzling as this chapter might be to the Twenty-First Century reader, it was not to John. He recognized the significance of the scene immediately. Nor was it puzzling to the readers of John's age. This was familiar stuff. This was right out of the Old Testament. This was their custom of Redemption. The theme of chapter 5 is the redemption of the earth.

EARTH STILL IN THE HAND OF SATAN

When man sinned, he lost his soul, his body, and the earth. Jesus redeemed man's soul at Calvary, the saints have received their new bodies at Rapture, but the earth is still in the hands of Satan. The earth has been Satan's since Adam lost dominion of it when he sinned in the Garden of Eden. Jesus made that clear in John 12:31 when he called Satan "the prince of this world." He makes the same statement in John 14:30 and John 16:11. Satan himself declared this ownership to Jesus *who did not dispute it* when he tempted Jesus during the forty days in the wilderness. Luke 4:5-6 records: "And the devil, taking him up into an high mountain, shewed unto him all the kingdoms of the world in a moment of time. And the devil said unto him, All this power will I give thee, and the glory of them: for that is delivered unto me; and to whomsoever I will I give it."

Although Calvary canceled Satan's legal claim to the earth, it did not remove him from its rulership. Thus, even after

Calvary, Paul in 2 Corinthians 4:4, calls Satan the "god of this world", and in Ephesians 2:2 he calls him "the prince of the power of the air." Furthermore, in 1 John 5:19, the same John who is writing this book of Revelation says (in the literal Greek) that "the whole world lieth in the evil one."

Redemption is not complete until all that has been lost by sin is restored. In fact, Acts 3:21 *promises* the "restitution of all things." Before Rapture occurs, men's souls have seen redemption. After Rapture, our bodies will be perfect once again. But, at that point, as it has since Eden, the earth will still lie in the power of the evil one. It, too, must be reclaimed and Satan will oppose every step.

GOD HAS OWNERSHIP OF EARTH

The earth belongs to God by virtue of His having created it. "The earth is the lord's, and the fulness thereof; the world, and they that dwell therein. For he hath founded it upon the seas, and established it upon the floods" (Psalms 24: 1-2). Paul quotes this verse in 1 Corinthians 10:26; it is a critical verse. God is now going to take earth back, based on the ages-old principle of His, called "redemption."

When God led the people of Israel into the Promised Land, He allocated the land first to each tribe and then to each family within the tribe. The source of wealth was found completely within land ownership. How else could one grow crops? How else could one support livestock? Without land, one was doomed to be a servant of someone who did own land. It was important to God that the playing field be equal for all of His people; thus He divided up the land. He also knew, because He knew human nature, that the playing field would not remain equal. Some people would lose their land, some people would buy up the land of others. As concerns those who lost their land, their families would effectively be cut off from the hope of prosperity forever. Whether a man lost his land because of sloth, drink, gambling, poor judgment, whatever, that man had lost the hope of his family until the year of Jubilee. The year of Jubilee happened every fifty years. In that year, all land reverted back to the original owners, all debts were considered paid, all indentured servitude forgiven. The playing field would once again be level.

GOD'S LAW OF REDEMPTION OF THE LAND

Like most of God's great ideas, after a while this one, Jubilee, did not continue to be observed. Knowing this would happen, and also knowing that fifty years would be most of a whole generation's life span, God instituted another law. He established the "Law of Redemption." This law stated that the land could be reclaimed. It could be bought back for the disinherited offspring by someone who met three criteria: he had to have the original purchase price of the land, he had to be a kinsman, and he had to want to do it. In other words, he had to want to, he had to be able to, and he had to be in a related family to do so. Thus, elaborate means were taken to insure the possibility of redemption whenever land changed hands. A deed was drawn up that listed exactly the boundaries of the land, the purchase price of the land, the original owner of the land, the purchaser of the land, and the date of the transaction. The deed would be signed by both parties, rolled up (at this time in history it was, of course, a scroll), sealed, and given to the heir, so that, if anytime he was able to, he could redeem his inherited possession. The kinsman who chose to reclaim the land for his family member was called "the redeemer."

It is important to note that land was the "inherited" possession of the heir, but it was simply the "purchased" possession of the buyer. The rights of the one who had it as an inherited possession always superseded the rights of the one who had only a purchased possession. A purchased possession was, by definition, temporary. At *any* time, a kinsman could demand the return of the property if the conditions of the sale could be met. What if the buyer had just erected buildings on the land? What if crops had been planted and were ready to harvest? Too bad, because the rights of inheritance always superseded the rights of purchase.

We see an example of this with the story of Ruth and Boaz in the book of Ruth. Ruth is the widowed daughter-in-law of Naomi. Naomi, also a widow, must sell the land of her sons. Boaz, who is a kinsman, agrees to buy it because he wants to marry Ruth. He tells Naomi that he will redeem her land and will marry Ruth and will have heirs with Ruth and thus her children can have back their inheritance. But there is a kinsman closer than Boaz who has first right of refusal. Boaz goes to the city gates before the elders of Israel(whom we have just discussed in conjunction with the twenty-four elders seen in heaven) and asks that kinsman if he wishes to redeem Naomi's land. The kinsman replies that yes, he absolutely does. No problem, says Boaz, but you must know that Ruth goes with the deal. The kinsman immediately loses interest and Boaz is free to redeem Ruth's inheritance. They, by the way, become the great-grandparents of King David.

We also see an example of redemption in the life of Jeremiah the prophet. Jeremiah had been told by God that Israel was destined for captivity. After proclaiming this to the people of Israel for quite some time, Jeremiah received a vision from God in which he was told that if a kinsman came up to him and offered to sell Jeremiah land that was his by the right of inheritance, Jeremiah was to do so. This puzzled and upset Jeremiah greatly because it would make no sense to buy land if he believed that Israel was destined for captivity. But God showed him that by redeeming the land it was a testament to the fact that there was hope that Israel would one day be released from bondage and would return to her land. Thus the act of redemption was a concrete act of hope on the part of Jeremiah. And so Jeremiah obeyed God.

THE TITLE DEED TO THE EARTH

In light of this, consider chapter 5 of Revelation. The sealed book in the hands of God in verse 1 is the actual title deed to Planet Earth. Although no explanation of it is given, it is obvious to the Jewish reader. The book is never said to be read; what is in it is apparently known. The fact that it is sealed means that it is subject to redemption.

God has the rights to earth, but God gave the earth in its fullness to man. "The heaven, even the heavens, are the Lord's: but the earth hath he given to the children of men" (Psalms 115:16). God created the earth for man and He gave it to Adam as an inheritance for him and Eve but also for all the people that would come after them. Adam, in his innocence, probably did not know what he had. But Satan knew what Adam had. And Satan knew that there are laws that God has set up and by

which He lives.   Satan, knowing that there are immutable
eternal laws of God, knew that if he could get Adam to forfeit
his inherited possession - the earth - by sinning, it would then
become Satan's.

THE TRICKERY OF SATAN

Now Satan lusted after the earth.   It was truly a glorious
creation.   Not only that, Satan hates mankind and seeks to
harm him because God created all of this earth for him.
Furthermore, God has called man to be in relationship with
Him.   This enrages Satan.   He is the fiercest, most intense
enemy that the human race has.   So Satan went to Eve (the
more vulnerable of the two), with a proposition: disobey God by
eating the forbidden fruit, and become like God yourselves.
When Adam and Eve agreed, they lost everything, for
themselves, and for us as their heirs.   And worse, Adam,
through sin, lost it all to Satan.

But the earth is man's *inherited* possession; it is but
Satan's *purchased* possession, liable to redemption at any time
if a redeemer could be found.   Not one of Adam's race was able
to qualify; their very souls were part of the lost possession (as
were their bodies).   But according to the immutable laws of
God, the redeemer had to be a kinsman - the redeemer had to
be human! What a quandary! Not only that, this kinsman
redeemer had to be able to pay the price.   What was the price?
Sin lost the possession; a completely sinless life was necessary
to buy it back.   Thirdly, this sinless, kinsman redeemer had to
be willing to do it.   As the words to the old carol said, "Long lay
the world in sin and error pining." It seemed hopeless for earth
and her people.

We see this hopelessness in the first few verses of this
chapter.   The sealed book, the title deed to the earth, is in the
hand of the One on the Throne, and, when the angel asks who
is able to take and open the seals, thus putting in motion the
reclamation of earth, *no one* in heaven, on earth, or under the
earth is found who is worthy.   No wonder John weeps
uncontrollably! It seems that the situation is doomed.   When all
seems lost, one of the elders says to John, "Weep not: behold,
the Lion of the tribe of Judah, the Root of David, hath prevailed
to open the book, and to loose the seven seals thereof"

(Revelation 5:5). Jesus is our Redeemer! As 1 Corinthians 15:45-47 says, Jesus became the second man, the last Adam. Jesus as God was not our kinsman, Jesus as man was. Further, Jesus was the only one able to pay the price and defeat sin. Finally and most critically, Jesus was willing to pay the price.

JESUS - OUR KINSMAN REDEEMER

The redemption price was paid and our debt was canceled at the Cross. Jesus is our sacrifice. We will never understand, while on earth, what it cost Jesus to redeem us. All of the forces of heaven and all of the forces of hell did battle in that body for three hours. The prophets foretold that He would be lifted off the earth and the Cross accomplished exactly that. He was lifted off the very ground of the earth because He took on Himself every sin, every disease, every curse that had ever and would ever inflict itself upon man, and that cosmic battle between good and evil needed to be fought suspended between heaven and earth. It was. It was centered in the body of one human being, Jesus. That battle is inconceivable for the human mind to comprehend. Jesus bore the weight of all that sin, disease, and curse and that was far worse than simply the punishment of the cross upon one human body. It also explains why Jesus died in three hours. Most who died by crucifixion lingered for days, and the people were amazed that Jesus was dead in such a short time.

But far more than simple crucifixion was at play here. God was forced to turn His face from His son. Even God could not look upon so much concentrated evil. But Jesus bore it, and more importantly, Jesus defeated it. And our souls, bodies, and the earth were redeemed. The reclamation of those things redeemed, however, is not a simple task. When Jesus went to Hades and left with the keys to death and hell, all the souls that were His were recovered. Each soul that will come to Him has been with Him ever since. The bodies are not recovered until the Rapture. This will entail an enormous fight between the angels of God and the angels of Satan. (We will discuss this in chapter 14) When John sees this remarkable throne room scene in chapter 4, Rapture has happened although John has not written about it yet, and the souls and the bodies of the saints have arrived safely in heaven. But Satan is still in possession of the earth.

This struggle for rulership of the earth is the point of the parable of the absentee landlord recorded in three of the Gospels. A man planted a vineyard, hired laborers, and left for a far-away country. After a season, he sent his servant to gather the fruit from the husbandmen. The husbandmen beat the servant and sent him packing. So the landlord sent another servant who was treated even worse. After sending a third servant with the same result, the landlord reasoned that it was necessary to send his beloved son. Surely, he thought, they will respect him. But when the husbandmen saw the son they reasoned that if there were no son then there would be no heir. So they killed the son in order to have the vineyard to themselves. What, Jesus asks, will the landlord do? He will surely come and destroy the husbandmen. God, of course, is the landlord; and the world, under the prodding of Satan, killed His only Son, after killing the prophets - the servants whom God had sent. But the inheritance of the vineyard will not go to Satan and his cohorts. No, God will avenge all evil.

THE LAMB

Now, in chapter 5, with the saints gone to heaven, it is especially true that Satan is in control on earth. The saints are no longer there to oppose him in any way. Granted, this possession of the earth is illegal; Satan is a squatter. But it is going to take enormous power and authority to remove him. John is looking for a power that can match that of Satan's as the voice of the Elder announces the coming of the Lion of Judah. Turning, expecting to see a lion, he sees instead a lamb. And he sees not simply a lamb but a butchered, slaughtered lamb! "Lamb" is Jesus' redemptive name. As the Lamb of God, Jesus paid the price; as the Lion of Judah, He will now take possession. The Greek word used here for lamb is the word that means a very gentle, domesticated lamb, a pet lamb, as it were, not just a barnyard animal. But this gentle lamb has seven horns and seven eyes. Horns are symbolic of power or strength. The biblical examples of this are numerous. Psalm 18:1-2 reads, "I will love thee, O Lord, my strength. The Lord is my rock, and my fortress, and my deliverer; my God, my strength, in whom I will trust; my buckler, and the *horn of my salvation,* and my high tower." "For thou art the glory of their strength: and in thy favour our horn shall be exalted. For the Lord is our defense; and the Holy One of Israel is our king" (Psalm 89:17-18). "He hath dispersed, he hath given to the poor; his righteousness endureth for ever; his horn shall be exalted with honour" (Psalm 112:9).

Eyes, as we have already discussed, are symbolic of knowledge. Seven is the number of completion. The Lamb of God has complete knowledge and power. The picture is of a gentle lamb but a lamb with total power and total knowledge. It will take both to oust Satan from the place above all places in the universe that he claims as his own - the earth. This power and knowledge are the seven Spirits of God that are sent forth into the earth. Here we see the Father on the Throne, Jesus the Lamb of God, and the Holy Spirit sent forth into battle upon the earth. We have here the Trinity in action.

THE TITLE DEED TO EARTH IS RECLAIMED
"And he came and took the book out of the right hand of him that sat upon the throne" (Revelation 5:7). This action will go unnoticed upon the earth but the consequences will soon be felt. When Antichrist is firmly ensconced in power and Satan seems for the first time to be in complete control and possession of the earth, the sealed book, the title deed to earth, is in heaven in the hands of Jesus! Satan is about to be evicted. Nothing since Calvary will have the effect on the earth that this simple action of Jesus taking the scroll will have. It signals the end of the millennia of horrors that the world has seen under the dominion of Satan and his cohorts. The black clouds that have kept this world in darkness are about to be broken up. And only Jesus can do this. Only Jesus dares to evict Satan.

Heaven never underestimates the power of Satan, only the uninformed on earth do that. I am convinced that when Job speaks of Leviathan in Job 41, he is describing Satan. No animal truly fits the description of Leviathan, Satan does. No man ever tried to make a covenant with an animal, but Job 41:4 says they do with Leviathan, and many a man has made a pact with the Devil. Consider how God describes Leviathan (Satan) to Job,

Lay thine hand upon him, remember the battle, do no more. Behold, the hope of him is in vain: shall not one be cast down even at the sight of him? None is so fierce that dare stir him up... Who can open the doors of his face? His teeth are terrible round about. His scales are his pride, shut up together as with a close seal. One is so near to another, that no air can come between them. They are joined one to another, they stick together, that they cannot be sundered... his eyes are like the eyelids of the morning. Out of his mouth go burning lamps, and sparks of fire leap out. Out of his nostrils goeth smoke, as out of a seething pot or caldron. His breath kindleth coals, and a flame goeth out of his mouth...His heart is as firm as a stone; yea, as hard as a piece of the nether millstone. When he raiseth up himself, the mighty are afraid... The sword of him that layeth at him cannot hold: the spear, the dart, nor the habergeon. He esteemeth iron as straw, and brass as rotten wood. The arrow cannot make him flee: slingstones are turned with him into stubble. Darts are counted as stubble: he laugheth at the shaking of a spear. Sharp stones are under him: he spreadeth sharp pointed things upon the mire. He maketh the deep to boil like a pot: he maketh the sea like a pot of ointment. He maketh a path to shine after him; one would think the deep to be hoary. Upon earth there is not his like, who is made without fear. He beholdeth all high things: he is a king over all the children of pride (Job 41: 8-10, 14-21, 24-34).

But *God* can fight against Satan. God says, "Who then is able to stand before me? Who hath prevented me, that I should repay him? Whatsoever is under the whole heaven is mine" (Job 41:10-11). And now is the time that God is going to reclaim what is His. Jesus is about to open the book, the title deed of the earth. He will do so by opening its seven seals one by one.

THE CLEANSING OF CREATION

All of the action in Revelation will come from the opening of the seven seals of the book. The breaking of the seals will set in motion the most violence the world has ever known. The action will come from three directions: heaven, earth, and the unseen world of Satan. Evil spirits taking terrifying forms will be turned loose on the world by the millions. The world that has scorned the mercy of God will experience the wrath of God. These judgments will not be the work of a callous or capricious god. Each will have a purpose; each will be necessary. Each will purge some vestige of sin. Every one will be a part of the tremendous task of the regeneration of the earth. Sin has had countless years to work its destruction upon the face of the earth. Sin has left its mark. We live with it daily and accept it as normal, but it is not. Polluted air is not from God. Rancid toxins have seeped into our soil. Our seas and rivers are spoiled beyond belief. All of the results of sin must be erased. God intends to have a world like the world that He created and pronounced good. He will have a world with not the faintest mark of sin upon it. Only God knows the depths to which sin has penetrated the original perfect creation. If He were to leave out one of the plagues, one of the purifications, then some portion of the world would be left uncleansed.

This world is part of the inheritance of the saints of God. "...Ye were sealed with that holy Spirit of promise, which is the earnest of our inheritance until the redemption of the *purchased possession,* unto the praise of his glory" (Ephesians 1:13-14). As heirs, we will be present when the seals are opened. We will be in heaven. The Rapture will have happened.

THE BEGINNING OF THE END

When Jesus comes and takes the book out of the hand of God, all of heaven resounds with praise. This is truly the most momentous event to have happened since the Cross. Heaven and creation have been waiting for this moment since the Fall of Man. There is a great outburst of joy at the realization that the reign of Satan is about to be over. Good and evil have been fighting over Planet Earth since the Garden of Eden. Now God the Son is about to go forth and destroy evil. Nothing that has been stolen from God will remain stolen. Truly, the meek will inherit the earth. To be meek in the Biblical sense is to cease to look out for one's own interests, to cease fighting one's own battle, knowing that it is enough to realize that God is ultimately in charge and He will prevail. Meekness has the connotation of great confidence and security, *not* weakness. The milquetoasts will not inherit the earth, the meek will.

The four beasts and the twenty-four elders fall down before the Lamb with harps and golden vials of incense. In the Old Testament harps were used to accompany prophecy. The prophesies of thousands of generations are about to be realized. So are the prayers of thousands of years. The golden vials are said, in verse 8 to contain the prayers of the righteous. Every time someone recited the Lord's Prayer and said, "Thy kingdom come, thy will be done on earth as it is in heaven," that prayer was heard and saved. Now that prayer is about to be answered. Every time a Christian prayed, "Maranatha; Lord come quickly," that prayer was heard and saved. Every time we have asked, "Jesus come and let your glory shine," He has, in effect, said, "I will begin to do it now through you if you but let me, but I will do it completely in the coming days." We have been living on a planet ruled by the most vicious and evil being that the universe has ever seen. Only the grace of God has ameliorated the effect of his power and rule. Now the prayers throughout the ages that pled for the end to violence and to evil, the prayers that pled for truth and goodness to rule upon the earth are presented to Jesus. The power to go forth and reclaim earth is His and He now will respond to the prayers of the ages.

THE SONG OF REDEMPTION

"And they sang a new song" (Revelation 5:9). A new song is now heard in heaven. It is interesting to examine that song. Nothing in it, except for opening of the seals, is new at all to us! We have sung it or ones like it thousands of times. It is a song of praise to Jesus who alone is worthy; who alone can meet the qualifications of Redeemer. It praises Him for dying for our sins and for redeeming us to God on that basis. It praises Him for allowing us to rule and reign with Him (the Greek is clear when it reads in verse 10: "And hast made *us* unto our God kings and priests: and *we* shall reign *on the earth*"). How can that song be a new song? Because it is the first time that a song of redemption has been sung **in heaven**!

Angels and the other denizens of heaven have never had to be redeemed, thus they have never been able to present this praise to Jesus. But the saints know this song! They, alone, know it and they sing it in glory to Jesus. The word "redeemed" that is used in verse 9 is the Greek word for purchasing a slave out of the slave market. We who "once were lost but now am found, was blind but now see" understand the magnitude of the sacrifice of Jesus. We who once were wretched, dumb, and blind praise Jesus for being our Redeemer. And heaven echoes the praise for the very first time. What an incredible moment! What a wonderful song! Catherine Hankey, the writer of the hymn "I Love to Tell the Story" understood this and penned it when she wrote:

And when, in scenes of glory
I sing the new, new song,
'Twill be the old, old story
That I have loved so long.

Of the saints who are singing this song, there is not a people nor a nation, nor a tongue, nor a tribe not represented. The grace of God is full and complete. It has reached everywhere.

ANGELS AND THE CREATION JOIN IN THE PRAISE

The angels now join in the praise. They *say* with a loud voice the praises of God, they do not sing. "Hark the Herald Angels Sing" to the contrary, angels are never said to sing. There is not one verse in the Bible that records that the angels ever sang or are even able to. In Job 38:7, another praise service in heaven is recorded. It seems to have happened much earlier in earth's history. The morning stars (the living ones) sang and the angels did not; they shouted! Singing praise is apparently reserved for the four living ones (the cherubim, including Lucifer before he fell) and mankind. I believe that this is why God loves our praise so much. We are able to praise Him uniquely. And when we do not, heaven cannot duplicate it.

The angels praise the Lamb for being worthy to receive all that belongs to Him - power, riches, wisdom, strength, honor, glory and blessing. Then creation itself begins to join in. (Does earth hear this?) All of the creatures (creatures, not people) in heaven and on earth and under the earth [who are they?] and in the sea begin to praise Jesus. Why? Because, they too, are about to be set free from the effects of a sin-scarred world.

And this cacophonous celebration continues. What an incredible scene! Finally one of the four beasts says "Amen" and the elders fall down before the Lamb once again in silence. There has never been a praise service like this one in the history of the universe! And *we* will be there, we will be a part of it all.

CHAPTER 8
SIX SEALS – TRIBULATION MIXED WITH GRACE
Revelation 6

THE SEALED BOOK - AN OVERVIEW OF THE TRIBULATION PERIOD

The book sealed with seven seals, the title deed to the earth, is now in the hand of the Lamb and the time has come to break the seals. This will begin the period of time commonly referred to as the Great Tribulation. Our word "tribulation" is taken from the Latin word, *tribulum*. A tribulum was actually a threshing sledge, a tool used to separate the wheat from the chaff. That is exactly what the Great Tribulation will accomplish. The first six seals, terrible as they will be, will be mixed with grace because the primary purpose of these first judgments is to eternally save any on the earth who might yet come to Jesus. God does not leave any stone unturned, He does not stop trying to save those whose hearts will turn to Him, if not before, then through these judgments. His mercy endures forever. The prophet Isaiah spoke of these times and the reasons for these times when he wrote, "With my soul have I desired thee in the night; yea, with my spirit within me will I seek thee early: for when thy judgments are in the earth, the inhabitants of the world will learn righteousness. Let favour be shewed to the wicked, yet will he not learn righteousness: in the land of uprightness will he deal unjustly, and will not behold the majesty of the Lord" (Isaiah 26:9-10).

As a consequence of the opening of these six seals, some will come to righteousness but some will be hardened. The events under the seals will be a catalyst for both reactions. The final seal, the seventh, will not be merciful. It will bring forth pure judgment upon the earth. When the seventh seal is opened it is a time of terror for the world.

The opening of the seals will accomplish two other things. They will begin the purging of the scars that sin has etched upon the physical world and they will bring mercy to the persecuted tribulation saints by forcing Antichrist to deal with the consequences of the seals. This will deflect him from his single-minded persecution of the tribulation saints. It will not stop him, it will simply buy the saints some time.

THE FIRST SEAL OPENED

As Jesus opens the first seal, the time of the Great Tribulation begins for the world. John hears a thunderous voice. He identifies it as coming from one of the four beasts or living ones. As has already been discussed, four is the symbolic number of the earth. The earth is certainly in view here. It occupies all of the thoughts of heaven. The King James Version of the Bible records the living one as saying "come and see." The Greek word here translated "come" can be translated either "come" or "go!" The phrase "and see" is not found in the Greek text. Given that the translation of the word used by John can be rendered either "come" or "go" in English, in this instance, the more accurate translation would be "Go!" The living one is not talking to John, he is giving an order to someone else that is overheard by John. We see who that someone is in verse 2. It is a rider upon a white horse. The living one is sending him forth from heaven to the earth. In verses 3-8 of chapter 6, John sees three more riders upon three different colored horses: red, black, and pale. They will be ordered to go forth by the remaining three living ones. Each living one will oversee one of these four riders of the Apocalypse.

The prophet Zechariah recorded seeing horsemen in heaven in Zechariah 1:7-10: "Upon the four and twentieth day of the eleventh month, which is the month Sebat, in the second year of Darius, came the word of the Lord unto Zechariah, the son of Berechiah, the son of Iddo the prophet, saying, I saw by night, and behold a man riding upon a red horse, and he stood among the myrtle trees that were in the bottom; and behind him were there red horses, speckled, and white. Then said I, O my lord, what are these? And the angel that talked with me said unto me, I will shew thee what these be. And the man that stood among the myrtle trees answered and said, These are they whom the Lord hath sent to walk to and fro through the earth."

In the beginning of chapter 6, Zechariah again speaks of these horses: "And I turned, and lifted up mine eyes, and looked, and, behold, there came four chariots out from between two mountains; and the mountains were mountains of brass. In the first chariot were red horses; and in the second chariot black horses; And in the third chariot white horses; and in the fourth chariot grisled and bay horses. Then I answered and said unto the angel that talked with me, What are these, my lord? And the angel answered and said unto me, These are the four spirits of the heavens, which go forth from standing before the Lord of all the earth. The black horses which are therein go forth into the north country; and the white go forth after them; and the grisled go forth toward the south country. And the bay went forth, and sought to go that they might walk to and fro through the earth: and he said, Get you hence, walk to and from through the earth. So they walked to and fro through the earth."

Are the patrollers of the earth seen by Zechariah the same riders that John views? Clearly, one of them is different. The speckled (or dappled) horse in Zechariah is replaced by the pale green horse in Revelation. That horse is ridden by Death and Hades. Death and Hades have a specific function at this time that will be unique to this time. That is why Zechariah does not see the pale green horse. However, the number of the patrolling horses is always four, the number of the earth. God apparently has different horses for different purposes, of which four are always in use at any given time. Truly, we are being given a fascinating glimpse into the spiritual world as we behold these riders.

THE WHITE HORSE AND RIDER - THE FIRST HORSEMAN OF THE APOCALYPSE

It is commonly taught that the rider on the white horse is Antichrist and he will now go forth. I believe that the Bible contradicts that view. Let us look first at the symbolism; white. The saints are dressed in white. Jesus Himself will come out of heaven riding a white horse. Nowhere is white used symbolically any differently from this. Adherents of the antichrist view will argue that Antichrist is the false christ and thus is disguised in righteousness. Symbols are never used this way. Symbols symbolize what they mean. One does not read them backwards or in reverse fashion. Prophecy would be meaningless if that were so. This is not symbolic "back-masking"; to render it such is to invite confusion to the highest degree. White means white, white does not mean "pretend white." This rider is righteous. This rider is holy. The mission of the rider is righteousness. The mission of the rider is holiness. Furthermore, the rider rides out of heaven. Antichrist is *not* in heaven, nor is he sent forth by heaven. He is the work of Satan, not God. To suggest otherwise is reprehensible. Paul states this in 2 Thessalonians 2:7 when he says that the spirit of Antichrist which is the spirit of lawlessness, is already at work in the world. But the Holy Spirit constrains it - it can only go so far. At the time of the coming of Antichrist to power, the Holy Spirit will step out of the way (not, however, out of the world) and allow Antichrist his time of power. Allowing this situation is a completely different thing than causing it. God will allow it but Satan will empower and cause it to happen.

THE FIRST HORSEMAN IS RIGHTEOUS, NOT EVIL

There are other symbols in play here. The rider holds a bow. A bow is the symbol for the proclamation of God's word, that is, for preaching. In Habakkuk 3, Habakkuk prophesies when he asks and answers four questions. He states that the Lord Himself rides upon horses of salvation with the bow that Habakkuk says is the proclamation of His word. (The "word" itself is symbolized by a sharp sword.) This is not unusual symbolism; it is found even in paganism. Consider Cupid with his bow as he shoots his victim with the arrow of love. The bow is very symbolic of the act of sending forth or proclaiming. Thus, the rider under the first seal is dressed in righteousness and armed with the proclamation of God's word.

A crown is given to the rider. The Greek word used here for that crown is *stephanos*. The *stephanos* crown is the crown that will be worn by Christ and His saints. It is a crown of victory or triumph. Always. Satan and Antichrist wear a different kind of crown: a *diadema*. Thus far, then, we have the rider leaving heaven, clothed in righteousness proclaiming the word of God, and wearing the crown of victory.

John records next that this rider goes forth conquering and to conquer. The Greek word used here for conquering is *nikao.*

It is translated "conquering" only one other place in the entire New Testament. That is in Romans 8:37: "Nay, in all these things we are more than conquerors through him that loved us. For I am persuaded, that neither death, nor life, nor angels, nor principalities, nor powers nor things present, nor things to come, nor height, nor depth, nor any other creature, shall be able to separate us from the love of God, which is in Christ Jesus our Lord."

Nikao is usually translated as "to overcome." It is the word that is used seven times chapters 2 and 3 of Revelation when speaking of the saints. "To him that overcometh I will give..." Jesus says there. God uses it in Revelation 21:7 when He says, "He that overcometh shall inherit all things: and I will be his God, and he shall be my son." John uses *nikao* when he writes in 1 John 5:4-5, "For whatsoever is born of God overcometh the world: and this is the victory that overcometh the world, even our faith. Who is he that overcometh the world, but he that believeth that Jesus is the Son of God?" It is blasphemous to assume that Satan overcomes in this way.

So, this rider, dressed in righteousness, preaching the word of God, wearing the crown of the Lord and His saints and going forth to conquer as only we who belong to the Lamb can conquer, is the Antichrist?!!! No, this holy rider is riding out of heaven having the everlasting gospel and its proclamation upon his lips. He is going forth to conquer with the Word of Christ. He will conquer the hearts of the people which will conquer Satan. That is the conquering in view here, not the world dominion by Antichrist. We must take the Bible at face value. To twist the Scripture in order to place the Antichrist in heaven at this point is more than disingenuous, it is dangerous to the accurate understanding of all that happens after this point in time. Some argue that because Antichrist is the "false christ" one must take what the Bible says and reverse it. Thus we are told to read some Scripture straight, and some Scripture backwards. Again, this is not unmasking the Word, this is "backmasking" the Word. And if we begin to "backmask" the Scriptures like this, we will be led only into confusion and darkness. The Bible is true to itself, its symbolism is true to itself. It requires no machination on our part.

THE PREACHING OF THE GOSPEL FROM HEAVEN

The concept of the preaching of the saving message being the first seal opened makes sense when you consider the character of God. Mercy is always the first thing offered to man by God. If, however, the mercy is rejected, judgment will surely follow. This is the consistent teaching of the whole Bible. It remains consistent in the book of Revelation.

Keep in mind that this vision is from the viewpoint of heaven. When John records this vision from the viewpoint of earth, this is what he writes, "And I saw another angel fly in the midst of heaven, having the everlasting gospel to preach unto them that dwell on the earth, and to every nation, and kindred, and tongue and people, Saying with a loud voice, Fear God, and give glory to him; for the hour of his judgment is come: and worship him that made heaven, and earth, and the sea, and the fountains of waters" (Revelation 14:6-7).

The Bible could not be more clear: the gospel will be preached from heaven. Thus the vision from the viewpoint of heaven and the vision from the viewpoint of the earth are entirely consistent. What does John mean when he writes that the everlasting gospel is preached? The word "gospel" simply means "good news." Good news has been preached from heaven before, so the idea is not a new one. The angels announced *from heaven* that Jesus had been born on the earth. That time, the news that Messiah had come was given to a select few. At this time, the news that Messiah is coming again, this time in judgment, will be given to all. God is nothing if not fair.

But why is the gospel being preached from the skies? Because it has been extinguished from the face of the earth. Although we have not seen this view yet, Satan, through Antichrist, is in total control of the world. All communication avenues are completely under his authority: every newspaper, every TV and radio station, even every publishing house. Consider also that at the beginning of this tribulation time, every saint has been caught up to heaven. There is no one left on the earth who can witness to the glory of God. But God is not dependent on newspapers, radios, televisions, or satellites to get His word out. He will use the saints from heaven! For indeed, these angels (or messengers) are the saints. They are wearing the clothing of saints, the crown of saints, and are conquering as only the saints are said to conquer. The Bible is well able to explain itself! The gospel cannot be preached on earth so the gospel will be preached from heaven and it will be preached by those to whom it was given to preach it - the saints.

THE ENTIRE WORLD HEARS THE GOSPEL

When Jesus spoke of the times of the end He prophesied this. Matthew 24:14 says, "And this gospel of the kingdom shall be preached in all the world for a witness unto all nations; and then shall the end come." Many have been taught that the Rapture cannot happen until the entire earth is evangelized. The Bible does not mention Rapture, the Bible mentions the end of the world. That is not Rapture. But the end of the world will not come until the entire world has heard the saving message of the Good News of Christ. God will keep His word. Evangelical organizations report that as the population of the world increases, we are falling farther and farther behind in evangelizing the world. We are not gaining on the world, the world is gaining on us. That will not defeat God. God has mighty plans. And God has "amazing grace" for His world. There has never been a time on the earth when God could not look down and find a righteous remnant, even if that remnant consisted of only a few souls. Now that the Christians have been raptured, God must have a new remnant of righteous people. He will accomplish this for the earth; its people will never belong entirely to Satan.

THE SECOND SEAL OPENED - THE SECOND HORSEMAN OF THE APOCALYPSE

We now see the second rider of the Apocalypse and he is sent from heaven to remove the false peace that has deceived so many which Antichrist has brought to the earth. This will be more completely addressed when the earthly viewpoint is under consideration, but for now, consider what the Apostle Paul prophesied in 1 Thessalonians 5:1-3, "But of the times and the seasons, brethren, ye have no need that I write unto you. For yourselves know perfectly that the day of the Lord so cometh as a thief in the night. *For when they shall say, Peace and safety; then sudden destruction cometh upon them, as travail upon a woman with child; and they shall not escape"* (emphasis mine).

Daniel prophesies in Daniel 8:25 that the Antichrist will destroy many by peace. In other words, by means of peace it will be possible for Antichrist to come to power and thus to destroy many. Luke 17:26-30 tells us the conditions that will be prevalent when Jesus returns for His people (the Rapture), "And as it was in the days of Noah so shall it be also in the days of the Son of man. They did eat, they drank, they married wives, they were given in marriage, until the day that Noah entered into the ark, and the flood came, and destroyed them all. Likewise also as it was in the days of Lot; they did eat, they drank, they bought, they sold, they planted, they builded; But the same day that Lot went out of Sodom it rained fire and brimstone from heaven, and destroyed them all. Even thus shall it be in the day when the Son of man is revealed."

Life is good, people are prosperous, all is well. And then as suddenly as the Flood came upon them, as suddenly as Sodom was destroyed by fire, peace will again be taken from the earth. This happens under the second seal when the horseman upon the red horse rides forth from heaven.

Red is the color of blood, it is a symbol of war and the shedding of blood. Satan's false "millennium" will be over. Mankind has been deceived, lulled into believing there was peace when really there was no peace. The show is now over. Violence and war will become the state of the world. So pervasive will be the lack of peace that even the animal kingdom will begin to prey upon the human population.

The first mission of the seals is to bring people to repentance. The gospel has been preached under the administration of the first seal. The remaining seals (excepting the fifth) will add fuel to the fire of godly conviction. The administration of the seals will also serve to purify and cleanse a sin-scarred planet. Finally, the opening of the seals will harass Antichrist with the very bedlam they are creating in his world. He will be kept busy "putting out fires" all over his domain.

This is again the hand of a merciful God because, although we have not seen it yet, Antichrist has begun the persecution of those who have come to Jesus through the work of the first horseman - the preacher of the gospel from heaven. Now part of Antichrist's attention will of necessity be turned away from their persecution and onto restoring order in his kingdom. There will literally be no peace on Earth. Besides the wars, there will be terror in the streets. Violence will be the rule of the day. Just as Adolph Hitler's full attention was taken away from the extermination of the Jewish race by the war he had to win in order to accomplish his goals, so will Antichrist's attention be diverted from the total extermination of Christians.

A great sword is given to the second horseman. This is not the Greek word for an ordinary sword. Its meaning is "having the very power of life or death." The Second Horseman has this power given to him and death prevails. Jesus predicts this time of tribulation in Luke 23:28-31 when He says, "Daughters of Jerusalem, weep not for me, but weep for yourselves, and for your children. For, behold the days are coming, in the which they shall say, Blessed are the barren, and the wombs that never bare, and the paps which never gave suck. Then shall they begin to say to the mountains, Fall on us; and to the hills, Cover us. For if they do these things in a green tree, what shall be done in the dry?"

His last sentence is truly chilling. When said, Israel was about to kill the Son of God. As horrible as that was, Jesus says that the era (the tree) in which He was living and speaking was one of life and health in comparison to the days of The End at which time the "tree" will be dead. It is unfathomable how bad times will get when the truly depraved are in power! These horsemen signal but the *beginning* of the time of the dry tree.

THIRD SEAL OPENED - THIRD RIDER OF THE APOCALYPSE

God is the God of the harvest. He is the author of all good gifts. The very world in which we find ourselves is a gift from His hand. He will now, as He has many times in His dealings with mankind, use His authority over the elements in order to demand the attention of earth. Man has ignored His word, man cannot ignore His power over their environment. The third seal will strike there.

The third horseman rides with a pair of balances in his hand. This is the horseman of famine. When wheat is abundant, it is sold by gross measure and no attention is paid to a few hundred grains either way. Not so when wheat is scarce. Every grain will be measured and weighed. Famine follows war as surely as night follows day. A worldwide famine will now exist. Cities have storehouses of food for only a few weeks. Trucks and trains are constantly running to bring new stores of food to the cities. When transportation breaks down so will the food supply and shelves will very quickly be barren. Not only that, war brings destruction to the crops themselves, so soon there will be no food to bring even if the trucks could run! Add to the mix adverse weather conditions (completely under the control of God), and the earth has a famine of epic proportions!

But again we see mercy in the mission of the horseman. Verse 6 tells us that he has sound words of advice for the earth if they will but listen. The horseman is the famine administrator much as Joseph was for Egypt in the time of the great famine during the reign of Pharaoh. "For these two years hath the famine been in the land: and yet there are five years, in the which there shall neither be earing nor harvest. And God sent me before you to preserve you a posterity in the earth, and to save your lives by a great deliverance" (Genesis 45:6-7).

The work of this horseman is to prevent famine from wiping out mankind. The "measure" spoken of in the words of warning is equivalent to the amount of food it would take to meagerly feed one person for one day. The penny mentioned was the equivalent of the average wage for one day. It will take a day's wages to buy enough food for one person. What about the food for the rest of the family? What about money for housing, gas, electricity, etc? These will be hard times indeed. Even if one has money, one must deal with the scarcity of available food. Barley is mentioned along with wheat. Barley is animal feed. Humans will be reduced to eating animal feed in order to survive.

The horseman sounds a warning to protect the oil (the source of which was olives) and the grapes. Olives and grapes grow wild. Thus, with all able-bodied men fighting, a stern warning will be given to the people not to harm the things that need no cultivation and will grow on their own.

FOURTH SEAL OPENED - THE FOURTH HORSEMAN OF THE APOCALYPSE

The fourth horseman comes to reap what the three before him have sown. He is said to ride upon a pale horse. The Greek word used here for pale is *chloros*. This is the root word of our word "chlorophyll." Chloros indicates life. (A brown, withered plant lacks the life producing chlorophyll.) But with this horse and its rider we have a strange dichotomy. The horse is a pale green (chloros) indicating life, but its rider is Death. At this point in time, death will predominate over life in the overall effect on earth. The pale green horse, then, becomes almost a caricature of life; its pale green color the loathsome color of a corpse or of decaying flesh. As we see here with the fourth horseman, Death will now ride Life.

Death will now claim one fourth of the earth's population. That is an enormous percentage of those living. They have died from the wars, the famine and from wild beasts. As mentioned above, when the horseman takes peace from the world, it is taken even from the natural kingdom. After the Flood, God gave to Noah a protection that is recorded in Genesis 9:2, "And the fear of you and the dread of you shall be upon every beast of the earth, and upon every fowl of the air, upon all that moveth upon the earth and upon all the fishes of the sea; into your hand are they delivered."

The natural fear that keeps predatory animals away from the habitations of man has apparently ceased. Not only do men worry about dying from other men, they must now fight off the wild animals! Possibly even the tame animals are affected and domesticated pets rise up against their owners. This fierceness will certainly be exacerbated by the privation caused by the worldwide famine that has surely impacted the animal kingdom also.

Interestingly, the word used here for "beast" is the same word that is used for the poisonous snake mentioned in Acts 28:5. Apparently snakes and other reptiles (and most probably even creatures in the sea) also turn malevolent. Animal attacks are apparently commonplace at this time, because it is one of the primary reasons given for the enormous number of deaths. Can one even imagine times like these? There is no food, there is war, civil unrest, riots, and only God knows what else, and now, when one leaves one's front door, even the tree squirrels are a mortal threat. Terror must surely reign upon the earth!

DEATH AS A PERSONA

Hell follows death. Hell as used here is the same word in the Greek as "grave". Here in chapter 6 and also in chapter 20, death is seen as a persona - a specter, a presence; not just an experience. We are told that death will be thrown in the Lake of Fire. One cannot throw an experience into the Lake of Fire. The commonly portrayed specter of death as a tall, shadowy, hooded creature may not be that far off. Since Jesus conquered death, death has no power over believers. In fact, Christians are promised by Jesus that they "will not see death." Although Jesus was speaking primarily of Christians having eternal life when He promised them that they would not see death, there may be more to that promise than is generally supposed. Death, He says, will not come for you; I will. You will never have to encounter Death. Thus, it is clear that this Rider of the Apocalypse does not come after the Christians who are now on earth. But the unrepentant and ungodly *will* see Death and he will be terrifying.

DEATHS ARE FROM HAND OF GOD AND HINDER THE ANTICHRIST

The deaths that result from the fourth horseman are not from the hand of Antichrist; they are straight from the hand of God, and are completely controlled by Him. "For thus saith the Lord God; How much more when I send my four sore judgments upon Jerusalem, the sword, and the famine, and the noisome beast, and the pestilence, to cut off from it man and beast?" (Ezekiel 14:21).

Death rides out of heaven, sent by the heavenly command to "GO." Again, the purpose of this is, in part, to hinder Antichrist and to deflect him from tormenting the new believers.

What are Death and The Grave doing coming out of heaven? "I am he that liveth, and was dead; and, behold, I am alive for evermore, Amen; and I have the keys of hell and of death" (Revelation 1:18). Jesus completely controls death and it is used by Him both as a blessing and a curse. Here, it is a blessing for the believers and a curse for the wicked.

The word translated "hell" here is actually "hades." Hades is a place of waiting after one has died. It was established by God and it, too, is controlled by Him. Hades will now accept the souls of those who die under this plague. It will not accept the souls of those killed because of their commitment to Christ. They wait at an entirely different place. We see that place as the next seal, the fifth, is opened.

FIFTH SEAL OPENED

Here is evidence that the preaching of the gospel from heaven has had effect upon the earth, for we see *saved* souls now. Because this is the heavenly view we have not seen what has been happening on the earth. We have only seen the heavenly origin of the plagues. Now the tribulation Christians are in view only because they are dead and we see their souls under the altar. We are seeing, for the first time, the evidence of Antichrist's onslaught against the Christians on the earth. Some mid- and post-tribulationists have argued that these souls are the souls of all the Christians who have ever lived and they are all awaiting the Rapture. The Scripture contradicts this because it specifically states that all who are dead have been martyred. They have *all* been slain for the word of God. That is, thankfully, not true of all Christians who have died. The vast majority have died deaths other than as martyrs. But to be a Christian during the reign of Antichrist is to sign one's own death warrant, and here we see the evidence of that.

The souls under the Altar are also evidence that Revelation cannot be read strictly chronologically as some insist because, although the evidence of Antichrist's actions are apparent in Revelation 6, he, himself, does not appear until Revelation 13.

THE MARTYRS' BLOOD AVENGED

There is one question on the mind of every tribulation Martyr: How long will God refrain from avenging their blood on those who dwell on the earth? God is a righteous judge and He will administer the justice that the world does not and cannot give. The last verse of the song of Moses reads, "Rejoice oh ye nations with his people: for he will avenge the blood of his servants and will render vengeance to his adversaries, and will be merciful for his land and his people" (Deuteronomy 32:43).

Jesus also said in Luke 18:7; "Now shall not God bring about justice for his elect, who cry to him day and night and will he delay long over them? I tell you that he will bring about justice for them speedily." Christians must give their personal ideas of vengeance up to the only One who has the right to vengeance. After all, it is His law that has been violated, it is His standard that has been breached. Ultimately it is not we who are violated, it is God, and God alone has the wisdom to address the violation.

THE CHRISTIAN EXPERIENCE OF THE GRAVE

Man is a tripartite being consisting of body, soul, and spirit. (His maker, God, is a triune being consisting of Father, Son, Spirit.) Each of these different parts (body, soul, and spirit) passes through the death experience. We have in this passage an insight into life after death - one of the few in the Bible. Here is clear evidence of soul awareness in the person while the body waits in the grave and the spirit awaits heaven. It seems to indicate that heaven is not the immediate abode of the soul or body after death. Heaven, given other Scriptures, may be the abode of the spirit of a person. We know that when Jesus died His spirit went immediately to the Father, His soul went into Hades, and His body went into the ground. We know our bodies go into the ground. I have come to believe that the spirits of the believers also go to be with the Father and that their souls await the glorious resurrection in a place like Paradise.

THE MARTYRS WEAR THE CLOTHING OF THE BRIDE

White robes are given to the tribulation saints in anticipation of their union with Jesus. These garments were promised to all of the overcomers in Revelation 3:5. They are the clothing of the Bride. By giving them to these souls under the altar, Jesus makes it clear that He considers them to be part of the Bride and they will need the necessary clothing to attend the wedding feast (Matthew 22:1-14) that is still in the future. In Revelation 7 we are told that they will be fed by Jesus, led by Jesus and comforted by Jesus, just as He has ministered to the rest of His body. Revelation 20:4 tells us that these tribulation saints will sit upon thrones with Jesus, judging and reigning with Him. This honor is reserved for the Bride *only*.

RESURRECTION OF THE TRIBULATION SAINTS

As with the first part of the resurrection, the resurrection of the souls under the alter will happen en masse. Souls and bodies do not trickle up to heaven. There has been one great resurrection, the Rapture, and there will be a second phase to it. That will be the resurrection of all of the tribulation saints *at one time.* They are told here that they must wait until all who will be killed by Antichrist have been killed by him. When we see this scene from the earthly perspective in Revelation 13, they are given a more specific answer: three-and-a-half years. Time is an earthly concept, not a heavenly one, and so the answer is not given in years in chapter 6. If you will notice, not one period of time has been given during all of chapter 6. This is not to say that heaven is not aware of time, it is simply to say that times will be more freely given when the story is told from the earthly perspective. At that time we will be told that three-and-a-half years is the amount of time that Christians will be persecuted by Antichrist. It will only take him that long to hunt them all down and exterminate them.

THE SIXTH SEAL OPENED

As if life has not been terrifying enough on Earth, the manifestations under the sixth seal become the deafening final call for the repentance of those still living. Like the darkness and great earthquake at the crucifixion, this sign from God cannot be ignored. First, there is a great earthquake, but to call it simply a great earthquake is an understatement. At its conclusion, not a mountain nor an island is in its former place. As one who lived through the 1994 Northridge earthquake in California, I find that I simply cannot comprehend the terror and destruction that would cause this. The 6.8 magnitude of the Northridge quake destroyed buildings, caused freeways to topple, began fires from broken gas lines, took some lives and shattered others. An earthquake that would not leave one single mountain in its original place staggers the imagination.

Further, it will appear that the sky is falling in upon earth, because, besides the earthquake, meteors will rain upon earth. The horror is inconceivable. The Bible compares it to a fig tree regaled by such a wind that its *green* fruit, not its ripe is thrown to the ground. Jesus says in Luke 21:25 when speaking of these times of signs in the sun, moon, and stars that there will be distress with "perplexity." The Greek word used here for "perplexity" is the word with a closer modern meaning of "no way out." The terror cannot be overstated.

The sun will turn black as a sackcloth made of hair and the moon will turn red as blood. Both sackcloths and hair shirts are apparel of penitence and mourning. The primary lights of earth now don this symbol. These signs are very significant for another reason. They are prophesied elsewhere, both in Joel 2 and in Acts 2 (quoting Joel). The context is the Day of Pentecost when the Holy Spirit comes upon the 120 in the upper room. They began to speak in languages other than their own and the people from the diverse nations who had gathered for the feast were amazed that they were hearing their native tongue. Others accused them of being drunk, and at that point Peter stood up and explained what was happening. He assured them that the disciples were not drunk, but that what the people were witnessing was what Joel had prophesied would happen hundreds of years before.

> And it shall come to pass in the last days, saith God, I will pour out of my Spirit upon all flesh: and your sons and your daughters shall prophesy, and your young men shall see visions, and your old men shall dream dreams: And on my servants, and on my handmaidens I will pour out in those days of my Spirit; and they shall prophesy: And I will shew wonders in heaven above, and signs in the earth beneath; blood, and fire, and vapour of smoke: The sun shall be turned into darkness, and the moon into blood, before that great and notable day of the Lord come: And it shall come to pass, that whosoever shall call on the name of the Lord shall be saved (Acts 2:17-21).

THE AGE OF GRACE IS OVER

What Joel was prophesying was the Age of Grace. Peter was saying It has come today, on Pentecost. Now the Church pays great attention to the beginning of the Age of Grace. It was announced by the outpouring of the Spirit upon the disciples, as witnessed by the diverse tongues they spoke. It is universally agreed that the Day of Pentecost began the Age of Grace. What is largely ignored is that Joel and Peter both announce the signs of what will *end* the Age of Grace. It will begin with the outpouring of the Spirit. It will end with notable signs in heaven and on the earth. Two of these signs are the darkening of the sun and the blood-likeness of the moon. When these signs happen, the Age of Grace is over. These signs did not happen at the time of Pentecost, so the only reason to quote them was to bracket the end of the age as clearly as the first signs bracketed the beginning of the age. Here we see the fulfillment of these signs under the sixth seal. The Age of Grace does not end with the rapture, for it includes the souls under the fifth seal, the tribulation saints. It ends three and a half years later, under the sixth seal.

After the Age of Grace is over, not a single Gentile will enter into the Kingdom of Heaven. God will then turn His attention to the Jews as Paul prophesies in Romans 11:25-26, "...blindness in part is happened to Israel, until the fulness of the Gentiles be come in. And [then] all Israel shall be saved." As we will see, this is completely consistent with the view of things given by John in Revelation. Except for the conversion of the Nation of Israel, not a single other convert is recorded after the sixth seal.

From this point until Christ comes with the saints at Armageddon will be a period of seven years. *Now* begins the Seventieth Week of Daniel, the Rapture does not begin the countdown. What is meant by the Seventieth Week is the reference in Daniel 9:24-26 that reads as follows, "Seventy weeks are determined upon thy people and upon thy holy city, to finish the transgression, and to make an end of sins, and to make reconciliation for iniquity, and to bring in everlasting righteousness, and to seal up the vision and prophecy, and to anoint The Most Holy. Know therefore and understand, that from the going forth of the commandment to restore and to build Jerusalem unto the Messiah the Prince shall be seven weeks, and threescore and two weeks: the street shall be built again, and the wall, even in troublous times. And after threescore and two weeks shall Messiah be cut off, but not for himself: and the people of the prince that shall come shall destroy the city and the sanctuary: and the end thereof shall be with a flood, and unto the end of the war desolations are determined."

What Daniel is saying is this: God is going to continue to plead with you Israelites for a space of seventy more "weeks." A "week" was a Jewish term that meant seven years, it was as common an expression to the Jews as the expression "decade" is to us. Thus seventy weeks would be seventy times seven years (490 years). Daniel further divides the 490 years into two segments; the first 483 years (69 weeks) and the last seven years (one week). He says that at the end of 483 years, Messiah will come and he will be killed ("cut off"), *but not for himself!* In other words He will be killed not because of Himself, but for the benefit of others. This prophecy was fulfilled perfectly and in its entirety. Exactly 483 years after Daniel wrote this, Jesus came as Messiah and was killed for our sins. One week - seven years - remains of the prophecy. With one accord, the prophecy teachers teach that this last week begins at the Rapture. But why on earth would it?! The seventy weeks of Daniel have nothing at all to do with the Gentiles! And the fulness of the Gentiles is not up until the moon turns to blood as it does here, under the sixth seal. After that God will turn His attention to the Jews and not before, for all of the Gentiles who will come to Him have come to Him at this point in time. Their number is now complete. That is exactly when Paul, quoted above in Romans, says that God will deal with the Jews.

So, although the prophecy teachers put the Seventieth Week at the Rapture, Revelation, Joel, Acts and Romans all put it in a different place altogether - after the Age of Grace. I am going to side with John, Joel, Peter, and Paul on this one. This means, then, that the time between Rapture and Return of Jesus is ten-and-a-half years, not seven. We are given the time that elapses from the first to the sixth seal; it is three-and-a-half years. Add to it the Seventieth Week - seven years- and the sum total is ten and a half years. This will be covered in more detail later on, and we will see why the times given in Revelation make a seven-year time span between the Rapture and the Second Coming of Jesus an impossibility.

When the stars fall from heaven and the mighty earthquake hits the entire earth, all of humanity is affected from the mighty to the slaves. Although slavery as a recognized part of any civilization is now almost unheard of, slavery will once again be instituted into the political order under Antichrist. In fact, slavery will be spoken of several times in Revelation. Human misery will fuel the great prosperity of Antichrist. His great cities will be built upon the back of human suffering. Life will not be held sacred, if indeed it ever really has been (witness the abortion and euthanasia laws of today).

TOTAL REJECTION OF GOD BY THE WICKED

The afflicted on earth do not cry out to God for mercy. Instead, the kings and the slaves of the earth will together lift their prayers to Nature (the mountains) to fall on them. Jesus prophesied exactly this in Luke 23:30-31, "Then shall they begin to say to the mountains, Fall on us; and to the hills, Cover us. For if they do these things in a green tree, what shall be done in the dry?" This was also prophesied in Hosea 10:8; in addition, the reason for the destruction of the earth was given there. It was because of the high places of Aven, which means "idolatry". The passage is as follows: "The high places also of Aven, the sin of Israel, shall be destroyed: the thorn and the thistle shall come up on their altars; and they shall say to the mountains, Cover us; and to the hills, Fall on us."

They beg the hills to cover them from God and from the Lamb. *And from the Lamb!!* The unrepentant know from whence come these disasters, the preaching from heaven has been heard! Furthermore, the *unsaved* understand the concept of Jesus as the Lamb, as the atoning sacrifice made for the world. There is more understanding of this concept in three-and-a-half years of preaching than there has been in two millennia of earthly preaching! The word of God has gone forth so completely and so perfectly during this time that every human being on earth understands the concept of Jesus as Lamb. Today, many who even consider themselves Christian do not truly understand this concept. This is weighty proof of the preaching from heaven. Why else would the world, in three and a half years, understand so well what most have never understood before? Tragically, although by the time of the sixth seal everyone on earth understands, they would still rather be dead than be God's.

"For the wrath of God is revealed from heaven against all ungodliness and unrighteousness of men, who [suppress the truth]" (Romans 1:18).

"For the Lord of Hosts will have a day of reckoning against everyone who is proud and lofty, and against everyone who is lifted up, that he may be abased" (Isaiah 2:12).

"For the great day of his wrath is come; and who shall be able to stand?" (Revelation 6:17).

Chapter 7 of Revelation answers that question.

CHAPTER 9
144,000 JEWS SEALED AND THE
TRIBULATION SAINTS IN HEAVEN
Revelation 7

TWO GROUPS SAVED OUT OF THE TRIBULATION

Chapter 7 presents to us the two saved groups that come out of the first three-and-a-half years of the Tribulation. The first group (verses 1-8) is on earth, the second group (verses 9-17) is in heaven. The members of the first group are still alive, those in the second group have all been killed. The first group is relatively small (144,000 souls), the second group is countless. The first group is comprised entirely of Jewish men. The second group is comprised of every nation, tongue and tribe found on earth. The two groups seemingly could not be more different, but they have one great factor in common. Each group has come about because the people in them have repented and accepted the Lord. They have done this because of the work of the six seals in chapter 6 of Revelation.

The first group, the 144,000 Jewish men who are found on earth, are the first of the nation of Israel to be converted to Jesus at this time. They are the firstfruits of the nation of Israel that will come in its entirety to the Lord.

The second group, in heaven, is comprised of those who have been martyred by Antichrist. He has hunted them down and murdered them in every place on earth that his influence can reach. The word of God has been preached from heaven, has been heard worldwide, and the response of this uncountable group gives testimony to its efficacy. This would not make sense if it is assumed that the tribulation saints themselves are responsible for converting the world. How could they? They are running for their own lives. They cannot buy a bottle of water, they cannot pawn a wedding ring. They cannot rent a motel room to escape the cold for even a single night. How is it that they are erecting satellite stations to proclaim the gospel? How are they financing the overseas missions? No, the preaching has been in the hands of the Raptured saints and it has been heard by every nation, kindred, people and tongue on the earth. This second saved group is comprised of the souls that we saw under the fifth seal, only now their number is complete and they have been resurrected. They are the tribulation saints who have been killed by Antichrist.

MAJOR CHANGES IN EARTH'S ENVIRONMENT

After the great earthquake an eerie stillness comes upon the world. The winds completely cease to blow, there is not even a breeze. Air quickly stagnates without any wind currents so pollution will hang over the cities as a toxic cloud. The smoke from refineries will go up and will stay up. Exhaust fumes will go up and will stay up. The atmosphere will soon become unbelievably foul. People will scan the sky for clouds, hoping for a cleansing rain but there will be no rain. There will be no clouds because there will be no wind to bring those rain clouds inland. In addition to all of this, the coastal cities will notice something very strange; the absence of waves. The oceans will be as still as the air because without wind to move the water, the waves will cease also. The strangeness of it all will be overwhelming and, in it, the people will see the portent of more horror to come. They will be right. Something of immense importance is about to come from the hand of heaven. Six of the seals that bind the book in the hand of the Lamb have been broken and opened. This has taken three and a half years (the time is given when the story is told from the earthly perspective). One seal remains, and it will take another seven years to complete the opening of the final seal.

THE RIGHTEOUS PROTECTED FROM GOD'S WRATH

The seventh seal will be different from the first six. It will consist of pure wrath. All who would accept the saving grace of the Lamb have come to Him. Only the evil and defiant remain upon the earth (excepting Israel). So horrible will be what is about to come forth from heaven that it is necessary to divinely protect those who belong to God. So before the four angels are allowed to hurt the earth and the sea, the angel bearing the seal of the living God appears. He says to the four angels who hold the four winds that they must wait until the righteous have been protected by the seal of God upon their foreheads. Although we have not seen this, Antichrist has required that his seal be placed upon the foreheads or hands of all under his control. God will now place His seal upon the foreheads of those who belong to Him.

The judgments of God that are about to come upon the world differ from natural disasters. God does not promise believers divine protection from accidents and floods and earthquakes, but He always promises us special protection from His wrath. Consider the Flood. Consider the plagues of Egypt. Consider even Sodom and Gomorrah when the righteousness of Abraham saved the less than righteous of his family. In concert with this principle of God, the Rapture must occur before the Tribulation. There is about to be a time of pure unmitigated wrath but it will not touch God's people. Thus, the 144,000 are sealed against that day.

GOD RENEWS HIS RELATIONSHIP WITH THE JEWS

As was said previously, God will never look down upon the earth and see it bereft of any righteous. Now that Antichrist has been successful in hunting down every Christian, God will turn His attention to Israel, and the Jews will come back into their former place as the chosen people. This is the fulfillment of what was spoken about by Paul in Romans 11:25-27, "Blindness in part is happened to Israel, until the fulness of the Gentiles be come in. And so all Israel shall be saved: as it is written, There shall come out of Sion the Deliverer, and shall turn away ungodliness from Jacob: For this is my covenant unto them, when I shall take away their sins."

Chapter 7 finds the first mention of the Jews in Revelation. Twelve thousand souls from twelve tribes of Israel have accepted Jesus in a mighty fervor and are declaring Him as Messiah to the rest of Israel. This has occurred after the Rapture. They are exempt from the persecution of Antichrist because they are on Mount Zion, and Mount Zion is the one place on the face of the earth that Antichrist never reaches. It is God's holy mountain. Later, it will be seen that the Ensign of God spoken of by the prophet Isaiah has come to rest upon Mount Zion and the presence of God now dwells there. What is the Ensign of God? I believe that it is the long-missing Ark of the Covenant.

Although Israel as a country will be affected by the plagues of God, these 144,000 will be completely under the protection of God. Ezekiel 9:3-4 prophesied this long ago, "And the glory of the God of Israel was gone up from the cherub, whereupon he was, to the threshold of the house. And he called to the man clothed with linen, which had the writer's inkhorn by his side; And the Lord said unto him, Go through the midst of the city, through the midst of Jerusalem, and set a mark upon the foreheads of the men that sigh and that cry for all the abominations that be done In the midst thereof."

This protection of God's will extend not only to them concerning the wrath of God upon the earth, God will also supernaturally protect them from the hand of Antichrist when he comes against Israel in three-and-one-half years. It will be a continual thorn in the flesh to Antichrist that he cannot come against the 144,000 in any way, and it will be a testimony to both Antichrist and to the world of who, ultimately, is in charge.

JEWS TO SUFFER TRIBULATIONS BUT FIND JESUS

The opening of the seventh seal begins the time of Jacob's Trouble that is spoken of in Jeremiah 30:7-9, "Alas! For that day is great, so that none is like it: it is even the time of Jacob's trouble; but he shall be saved out of it. For it shall come to pass in that day, saith the Lord of hosts, that I will break his yoke from off thy neck, and will burst thy bonds, and strangers shall no more serve themselves of him: But they shall serve the Lord their God, and David their king, whom I will raise up unto them."

This seven years, the seventieth week of Daniel, is the time that God will sift them and, through calamity, draw them unto Him, "For, lo, I will command, and I will sift the house of Israel among all nations, like as corn is sifted in a sieve, yet shall not the least grain fall upon the earth... And I will plant them upon their land, and they shall no more be pulled up out of their land which I have given them, saith the Lord thy God" (Amos 9:9,15).

Up until now, the attention of the Antichrist has not been on Israel. It has been on exterminating the Christians and on dealing with the consequences of the first six seals. And now he will sign a peace treaty with Israel that will assuage any fears that she may have of his intentions. But in three and a half years he will break that treaty and will focus on annihilating Israel as he has annihilated the Christians. Antichrist knows that if he can defeat prophecy he can defeat God. Indeed, Psalm 138:2 tells us that God magnifies His word above even His name. This tells us how solemn and true is every pronouncement that comes from the mouth of God. If Satan can nullify God's eternal covenant with the Jews, Satan will have won.

But God intends to use the persecutions from the Antichrist for His own purposes. Just as it took Adolph Hitler to bring the Jews to their land, so it will take the horrors of Antichrist to bring the Jews to Jesus. God has destined these 144,000 Jewish souls to begin the reclamation of His people. They may not even be aware themselves that they represent an equal grouping of the twelve tribes, it may just seem very random to them. But God will know.

The 144,000 are the first of the house of Israel to understand that Jesus is Messiah and they have begun to preach this to the rest of Israel. *Christians* are awaiting the *second* return of their savior. *Religious Jews* have continued to await the *first* coming of their messiah, but when Christ returns as The Lamb, He will also come as the King of the Jews, and both the Jewish and Christian dispensations will come to an end at the same time. Both are looking for the coming of Christ. This does not negate the fact that this is His second coming. Nor does it negate the fact that before this time, the Christians have risen to meet Him at the Rapture and will return with Him at the Battle of Armageddon. It simply means that this is the time that the prophecy of Zechariah 12:10 is fulfilled, "And I will pour upon the house of David, and upon the inhabitants of Jerusalem, the spirit of grace and of supplications: and they shall look upon Me whom they have pierced, and they shall mourn for him, as one mourneth for his only son, and shall be in bitterness for him, as one that is in bitterness for his firstborn."

"Thus saith the Lord God; Behold, I will take the children of Israel from among the heathen, whither they be gone, and will gather them on every side, and bring them into their own land: And I will make them one nation in the land upon the mountains of Israel; and one king shall be king to them all: and they shall be no more two nations, neither shall they be divided into two kingdoms any more at all: Neither shall they defile themselves any more with their idols, nor with their detestable things, nor with any of their transgressions: but I will save them out of all their dwelling-places, wherein they have sinned, and will cleanse them: so shall they be my people, and I will be their god. And David my servant shall be king over them; and they all shall have one shepherd: they shall also walk in my judgments, and observe my statutes, and do them. And they shall dwell in the land that I have given unto Jacob my servant, wherein your fathers have dwelt; and they shall dwell therein, even they, and their children, and their children's children for ever: and my servant David shall be their prince for ever" (Ezekiel 37: 21-25).

"And they shall be mine, saith the Lord of hosts, in that day when I make up my jewels, and I will spare them, as a man spareth his own son that serveth him" (Malachi 3:17).

"And to this agree the words of the prophets; as it is written, After this I will return, and will build again the tabernacle of David, which is fallen down; and I will build again the ruins thereof, and I will set it up: That the residue of men might seek after the Lord, and all the Gentiles, upon whom my name is called, saith the Lord, who doeth all these things. Known unto god are all his works from the beginning of the world" (Acts 15:15-18).

THE FIRST SAVED GROUP IN CHAPTER 7 - JEWS FROM THE TWELVE TRIBES

All of the twelve original tribes of Israel are mentioned in chapter 7 except for Dan and Ephriam. Ephriam was the son of Joseph; Joseph was not originally named as a tribe by God, but he is mentioned here. Ephriam, then, is covered under Joseph. Dan is left out completely. Dan was situated the farthest north of any of the tribes and was the first tribe to go into idolatry. In fact, the tribe of Dan was always associated with idolatry in the latter times of the Old Testament. Dan had become so corrupted by idols that the entire tribe is missing from Israel by the time 1 Chronicles 1-8 records the genealogies of all of Israel. Dan became "The Lost Tribe of Israel" and he has never been found to this day.

One receives great insight into the mercy of God when it is realized that when, in Ezekiel 48, the location of each tribe is given in the Millennium (the thousand-year reign of Christ after He comes back to the earth with the saints), the location of Dan is the first location given. It will lie north of Damascus, far into Syria. God will restore Dan to the kingdom of Israel after it has been the "lost tribe" for centuries, and He will do this before he parcels out the land to any other tribe. Restoration is always foremost in the heart of God.

The order and the meaning of the names of the tribes are very important. Genesis 49:1 tells us that the prophecy associated with the names of the tribes concerns the last days. The order listed here is not the usual order in which the tribes are listed. There is a reason for this. Dr. Joseph Seiss writes: "All Jewish names are significant, and the meaning of those which here are given is not hard to trace. Judah means 'confession' or 'praise' of God; Reuben, 'viewing the Son'; Gad, 'a company'; Asher, 'blessed'; Nepthalim, 'a wrestler' or 'striving with'; Manasses, 'forgetfulness'; Simeon, 'hearing and obeying'; Levi, 'joining' or 'cleaving to'; Issachar, 'reward' or 'what is given by way of reward'; Zebulun, 'a home ' or 'dwelling-place'; Joseph, 'added' or 'an addition'; Benjamin, 'a son of the right hand, a son of old age'. Now put these several things together in their order, and we have described to us: Confessors or praisers of God, looking upon the Son, a band of blessed ones, wrestling with forgetfulness, hearing and obeying the word, cleaving unto the reward of a shelter and home, an addition, sons of the day of God's right hand, begotten in the extremity of the age" [20]

Clearly that describes these of Israel. They are praisers of God who, as a nation, have always forgotten the ways and the goodness of God, but now they will hear and obey the word and will receive their reward. They are an addition to the family of God; sons who have come at the very end of the age. When one sees the purpose and the prophecy in these names it is immediately apparent that neither Dan nor Ephraim fit. Dan means "judged" or "judging." This group is neither. Ephraim means "increase." There is no increase to the numbers here. It is fixed and predestined at 144,000. We will be given more information about these 144,000 when the story is told from the viewpoint of earth.

THE SECOND SAVED GROUP IN CHAPTER 7 - THE TRIBULATION SAINTS

The second group in Revelation 7 is that which is comprised of the tribulation saints, last seen under the fifth seal. Now they have been resurrected. They knew that it would cost them their lives when they responded to the heavenly preaching, but they came joyfully anyway. They understood completely what Jesus meant when he said in Matthew 10:34-39: "Think not that I am come to send peace on earth: I came not to send peace, but a sword. For I am come to set a man at variance against his father, and the daughter against her mother, and the daughter in law against her mother in law. And a man's foes shall be they of his own household. He that loveth father or mother more than me is not worthy of me: and he that loveth son or daughter more than me is not worthy of me. And he that taketh not his cross, and followeth after me, is not worthy of me. He that findeth his life shall lose it: and he that loseth his life for my sake shall find it."

They have been betrayed by friends and family; they have been hunted down throughout the kingdom of the Antichrist and have met death by execution, starvation, dehydration, and exposure. Truly, to accept Jesus in that day will be a death sentence. Knowing that, they have chosen Him anyway and have suffered horribly. What is their response to their fate? "Salvation to our God which sitteth upon the throne, and unto the Lamb." Nothing else is important now.

THE SECOND PART OF THE FIRST RESURRECTION

We see the saints with their resurrected bodies clothed in white robes. This is the second phase of the *first* resurrection. The first resurrection brings to heaven those who will rule and reign with Jesus throughout eternity. The first *phase* of the resurrection was the Rapture that brought forth the righteous in Christ from their graves, and lifted the living saints to heaven. The resurrection of all of those who have been martyred by Antichrist for their faith - the tribulation saints - will be the second and final phase of the resurrection of the righteous. It will occur at the end of the sixth seal, three-and-a-half years after the Rapture takes place. The Church is now complete.

There will be yet another resurrection at the end of Revelation. It will be comprised of those who do not know Jesus and of the wicked dead. That is the *second* resurrection.

Jesus spoke of these two resurrections in John 5:25-29. Most readers miss the fact that two resurrections are indicated here. The first of those is when those who hear the voice of the Son of God, whether living or in the grave, shall live. Who can hear the voice of Jesus? "My sheep hear my voice" (John 10:27). Jesus states that those who hear shall live. This apparently stuns and amazes the listeners, for Jesus goes on to say, "Marvel not at this: for the hour is coming, in the which *all* that are in the graves shall hear his voice and shall come forth; they that have done good, unto the resurrection of life; and they that have done evil, unto the resurrection of damnation."

Those in the first resurrection will be judged on the basis of their standing in Jesus and upon His righteousness. Those in the second resurrection will be judged by their own works. This is exactly what Revelation 20:12 states when it tells of the second resurrection, "And I saw the dead, small and great, stand before God; and the books were opened: and another book was opened, which is the book of life: and the dead were judged out of those things which were written in the books, *according to their works*," (emphasis mine).

In 1 Corinthians 15, the Apostle Paul speaks, in detail, of resurrection. He, too, teaches that there is a definite order to the Resurrection; as he puts it, "every man in his own order." Christ, Paul writes, was the first to be raised, second will be those that belong to Christ. It is not until the end of the thousand-year reign that Christ will deal with His enemies. Although Paul does not mention the thousand-year reign by name, he tells us that Christ will deal with His enemies when he destroys death; Revelation 20:14 tells us exactly when that happens. It happens at the end of the thousand-year reign.

TRIBULATION SAINTS HERALD JESUS' RETURN TO EARTH

As John sees the resurrected tribulation saints, he notes that they hold palm branches in their hands. Thousands of years before, mankind responded to the hope that Jesus was coming in triumph, to rule and to reign, in just the same fashion. The people shouted hosannas and waved palm branches as Jesus entered Jerusalem in the last week of His earthly life. And although it seemed to them that He met with total defeat just a few days later, in reality, it was a triumph over sin and the grave. In a few years, after the opening of the seventh seal is completed, Jesus will return to earth in complete triumph over Satan and his forces. He will, at that time, reign as the conquering king that the Jews expected thousands of years before. And when He does, these blessed tribulation saints who have given up everything for Jesus, are given the privilege of waving the palm branches and singing hosannas to Jesus before His second triumphal entry into Jerusalem. Again, just as before, His holiness and authority demand it. Jesus said of his first entry into Jerusalem that if the people had been silent, the very rocks would have cried out. The same is true now. The first time Jesus entered Jerusalem, he entered it as Redeemer. Now these saints prepare his way into Jerusalem as he comes a second time as King of Kings and Lord of Lords. There is amazing symmetry in the Scriptures!

The tribulation saints are now wearing the robes that were given to them while they were under the fifth seal. At that time they could not wear them as they had not yet been resurrected. This is the clothing of the righteous when they receive their new bodies. The robes have been washed in the blood of the Lamb and been made white. Even the martyrdom of these saints is not enough to allow them to be clothed in their own righteousness. Heaven understands that even a great degree of human righteousness still falls far short of the standards of God. *Only* the righteousness of the Lamb will suffice. Jeremiah 2:22 graphically points this out: "Although you wash yourself with lye and use much soap, the stain of your iniquity is before Me, declares the Lord God," (NASB). The tribulation saints now join the rest of the raptured and resurrected believers and together they make up the Bride of Christ.

When last we saw these saints, they were concerned with the judgment of their persecutors. Now that they are with the Lamb, He and He alone fills their thoughts and tongues. They give Him praise for their resurrection. The angels, the elders, and the Living Ones join in the praise and worship. Heaven seems to be unable to refrain from worship and praise! It is a joyous throng indeed that is found around the throne!

One of the elders approaches John and asks him about this second group - the great multitude clothed in white with palms in their hands. Who are they? he asks John. John implies that he does not know, but that he would like to know, and he is sure that the elder does know. John knows the saints, angels, etc., but he does not know this group. That is because he has only seen things from the perspective of heaven; he has not seen the persecution taking place on earth. So the elder tells him that these are they who have come out of the Great Tribulation, and have given their lives for the Lamb who has given His life for them.

THE TIME OF THE "GREAT TRIBULATION"

The elder refers to this time as the "great" tribulation. Heaven has seen many tribulations, persecutions and martyrdoms happen on the earth, but heaven has never seen the likes of this one. That is a truly remarkable statement given the horrors that have come upon the godly over all the years of human existence. It is almost inconceivable to think that the persecutions that the Smyrnan Church era faced will pale in comparison to this time. In and of itself, it is a statement that summarizes how truly horrific the conditions have been for the tribulation saints for the past three-and-a-half years. Jesus prophesied this time and the coming seven years of terror in Matthew 24:21-22: "For then shall be great tribulation, such as was not since the beginning of the world to this time, no, nor ever shall be. And except those days should be shortened, there should no flesh be saved: but for the elect's sake those days shall be shortened."

We get a glimmer of what they have endured when we are told what they will never again have to experience: hunger, thirst, exposure. The reason for this will become clear when this story is told from the viewpoint of the earth. Antichrist will institute an economic system whereby one must take his mark, a 666, upon one's body in order to buy or sell anything. Christians, of course, cannot accept this mark, and so the ability to buy any food, drink or housing (even the ability to purchase a tent) will be impossible for them. So, while they are on the run from Antichrist for their very lives, every possibility for survival will be denied them. They, who have literally died from starvation, will hunger no more. They, who have felt their tongues swell up and had their bodies wracked with thirst, will thirst no more. They, who have had the sun beat down upon them mercilessly, and they, who have frozen in the snow banks will now be sheltered by the very wings of God.

THE LAMB AND THE SHEPHERD

"For the Lamb which is in the midst of the throne shall feed them, and shall lead them" (Revelation 7:17). The *New American Standard Bible* translates this as follows, "For the Lamb shall be their shepherd." That is one of the most beautiful paradoxes in the Bible. Only Jesus could be both Lamb and Shepherd, and be both simultaneously. Isaiah 53:6 expresses the same paradox, "All we like sheep have gone astray; we have turned every one to his own way; and the Lord hath laid on him the iniquity of us all."

Jesus is both the sacrificial lamb and the shepherd for all the wayward lambs under his mighty care. Because He is our Lamb, he is our Shepherd.

We, in this day and age, do not shepherd flocks as the shepherds of biblical times did. A shepherd literally lived with his flock. He walked with them as they grazed all day, keeping an eye out for their natural predators. He led them to food and to water. At evening, he led them home where, after checking them thoroughly for disease and wounds, he laid himself down at the door of the sheep enclosure and slept with them all through the night. The shepherd's body was constantly between the flock and the perils outside the pen. The shepherd never took a vacation - the sheep would perish without him - and he was with them through every stage of their lives. No wonder the sheep knew the voice of their shepherd!

Once in a while, a little lamb would be born to the flock that had a mind of his own and refused to come under the direction of the shepherd. This imperiled the life of the little lamb, and so the shepherd would set out to change the behavior of the lamb. He would use his staff to pull the lamb back in away from danger, and he would use his rod to discipline it. This would usually suffice, but if it did not, the shepherd had two choices. He could give up on correcting the behavior and let the lamb take his chances in the cruel world of nature, or he could take a rather drastic step of discipline that might cause the lamb pain, but that would surely save his life. Because of the love that the shepherd felt for his flock, it was the second choice that was most often taken. The shepherd would take the lamb and break each one of his little legs, setting the bones so that healing would soon be possible. This rendered the lamb entirely helpless. The shepherd was then responsible for every facet of its survival. He would place the helpless lamb around his neck and proceed to carry the little lamb everywhere that he, himself, went. (We have seen these pictures of Jesus with the little lamb around his shoulders, and most probably did not think to question why.) He would hand feed the lamb, and scoop water with his hands for the lamb to drink. The little lame lamb would sleep closest to the shepherd at night and would never leave his presence during the day. Eventually the legs would heal and the lamb would be set free. But the lamb seemed never to choose freedom again. In fact, when one saw the flock, one could immediately tell which of the lambs had its legs broken for it would be the one who never left the side of the shepherd for the rest of its life. There was a bond that formed between the shepherd and the lambs that were completely dependent upon him that the other lambs did not share.

These tribulation saints are like those little lambs. Of a surety, these were wayward lambs because, for whatever reason, they did not belong to Jesus at the time of the Rapture and they were left behind. But the horrors of tribulation have caused them unspeakable pain and they have come to be totally reliant on their shepherd, Jesus. It is He who has allowed them to live through this time, and even though they have been martyred by Antichrist, they have never left Him. Now we see them in Heaven, never leaving the side of the Shepherd again, "and [he] shall lead them unto living fountains of waters: and God shall wipe away all tears from their eyes" (Revelation 7:17).

NO TEARS IN HEAVEN

There will be neither tears nor sorrow in heaven. Sorrow is part of the earthly experience, not the one in heaven. In meditating on this verse, it has given me insight into our experiences on earth, as Solomon probably also had when he wrote, "For what hath man of all his labour, and of the vexation of his heart, wherein he hath laboured under the sun? For all his days are sorrows, and his travail grief; yea, his heart taketh not rest in the night" (Ecclesiastes 2:22-23). Life here can be brutish and short. Why must we weep here and know such sorrow? Putting aside that this is a fallen planet whose ruler is Satan, I think that there is a deeper answer. First Corinthians 13:12 promises that we shall know God as He knows us. That is truly remarkable. Those who belong to Him will be able to plumb the depths of His being and understand Him as we are now understood by Him. There will be no tears in heaven. At that time, it will be impossible for us on earth to come to understand him as "Comforter" as "Rock of our Salvation" as our "mighty fortress" as "our very present help in times of trouble" for when we get to Heaven there will be no troubles there. No, man is learning that part of His nature now, while on the earth. We will know him as king of Kings and lord of Lords much more clearly then; we learn to know Him as our "balm of Gilead" now. I truly believe that He allows us to know sorrow in our lives in order to allow us to know Him completely and entirely. He wants us to learn to rely on Him to soothe our hearts when nothing else can.

Prisoners of War have spoken often of how, when the torture was too much to bear, the only things that could keep them sane were God and the God-given love for their families. The more that was taken from them, the more they realized what they still had. It is rare that people get to this dramatic point of despair, but when they do, their only hope is God. There are times when only God can sustain you, nothing else is able to. You will never know that Jesus is all you need until Jesus is all you have. The sweetness that exudes from lives that have suffered in the Lord is very apparent to other people. All other distractions have been lost and there is a trust, a selflessness, and an understanding of God that common lives do not share. If God has made your cup sweet, drink it in thanksgiving. But if God has made your cup bitter, then drink it in communion with Him. He will come to you, and He will reveal himself to you. It is a high privilege and honor indeed.

CHAPTER 10
GOD'S WRATH ON EARTH: THE FOUR
TRUMPETS SOUND
Revelation 8

GOD'S WRATH IS USHERED IN BY THE BREAKING OF THE
SEVENTH SEAL

The seventh seal will loosen the wrath of God upon the world in a way that the world has never seen. It will be wrath without the mixture of mercy. The plagues under the seventh seal have a two-fold purpose: First, to strike hard at Satan and his kingdom, and second, to purge the earth of the consequences of man's sin. The former judgments had as their primary purpose the saving of souls. That is now complete. All who remain upon the earth, excepting the 144,000 Jews who have been sealed, are here by choice; they are here because they have rejected God. Now God will judge them, and only the nation of Israel will repent and turn back to Him.

THE SEVEN TRUMPETS

With the breaking of the seventh seal, every seal that sealed the title deed to the earth has been broken. Now, under the seventh seal, comes another series of seven; the seven trumpets that sound under the seventh seal. The number seven signifies completion. This will complete the mighty redemption work of Jesus. Each trumpet will signal action from the throne of God toward the earth. When the final trumpet has sounded, the title deed will lie open and the legal demands of eternal justice will have been met. At that point in time, the time for taking back Planet Earth from Satan, the time of the redemption of the inherited possession, will have arrived.

After the seventh seal there is silence in Heaven for about half an hour. This is the first time that a time frame has been given. It is given by John who is estimating it. After the tumultuous rejoicing we saw in chapter 7, the silence now is deafening. Thirty minutes of silence after all of the unbridled joy, praise, and worship must indeed be somewhat chilling. Heaven recognizes the importance of the seventh seal and responds with gravity and solemnity. The climax of the ages has arrived and it is terrible.

In the Old Testament, trumpets were sounded for seven different reasons:

1. They were connected first with war. Numbers 10:9 commands that before the Israelites ever went into war they had to sound the trumpet. We are walking into war now, in fact it will be the crucial battle in the cosmic war between good and evil that has waged for eons.

2. Trumpets were also connected with the voice, majesty, and power of God. This has been the prevailing theme of Revelation and it is certainly displayed here.

3. Third, trumpets were connected with the convocation of the people and the moving of the camp in the wilderness. Trumpets were to sound before any move. Now, Jesus and the saints and all the forces of Heaven are preparing to move out and take back earth.

4. Trumpets were used to proclaim the great festivals. The wedding feast of Jesus and His Bride is soon to be and it will be magnificent.

5. Trumpets were blown at the announcement of royalty. Jesus will soon take His rightful place as King over all the earth.

6. Trumpets were used to indicate that the wicked were about to be overthrown. Satan's doom is now announced from the heavens.

7. Trumpets were commanded to be sounded when the foundation of God's Temple was about to be laid. Now is the time for the culmination of prophecy that will establish God's temple and throne and dwelling place for ever and ever, amen.

And the seven angels who stand before God are given their trumpets...

The seven trumpets that shall soon sound forth in spiritual battle are reminiscent of another battle, the Battle of Jericho. That battle was the first battle fought in the taking of the Promised Land. Seven trumpets were in view there also, given to seven priests. God had promised Israel the land and He further promised them that He would give it to them by His power, not theirs. For six days they came to the city that was walled and thus impregnable.   For six days the people assembled, marched once around the city in total silence with only their trumpets sounding, and then left. On the seventh day they appeared as usual, marched around the city seven times instead of once, blew the seven trumpets, and lifted their voices in a great shout of triumph. The walls crumbled, and Israel rushed upon the city with complete and total victory. The city was taken by shouts and trumpets God will now take back the entire earth with these seven trumpets and the great shout of triumph from Jesus. Earthly trumpets and shouts sufficed when the foe was earthly, this time it will take spiritual warfare. This time, because the battle is with Satan, it will be fought in the supernatural realm with heavenly trumpets and the authority of the very voice of God.

PRAYERS GO UP TO GOD - JUDGMENT COMES DOWN

Another angel offers the prayers of the saints mixed with much incense as an offering to God upon His golden altar, the copy of which, when found on earth, was also set before the presence of God (Exodus 30:6). The act of the angel in offering the incense was given on earth as a priestly function and, since we are priests before God with Jesus our high priest, this angel is most probably a saint. When this story is told in Revelation 15 all of these angels wear the clothing of saints. Again, the word for "angel" simply means messenger from God, and saints certainly qualify. The idea of incense and prayers being linked is found several times in the Bible. For instance, Psalm 141 reads, "Let my prayer be set forth before thee as incense". These prayers before the altar are very specific prayers. They are the prayers that are about to be answered, including prayers for the judgment of God's enemies. Jesus is going forth to take back the inherited possession, the earth, for the people of God, and He is going to defeat evil at its source. Probably millions of prayers have been prayed for exactly these things - that the forces of darkness be utterly defeated and that God's will is finally done on earth as it is in heaven. And they have been noted and saved for thousands of years. Now they will be answered. As the smoke rises from the altar, it alone brings the prayers before God. No one else dares to speak. The gravity of the situation demands nothing less than awestruck silence as God goes forth to conquer Satan.

The angel now steps forward to the altar, fills his censor with fire from the altar, righteous judgment, mingled with the incense of the prayers and throws it to the earth. Power and prayer join together and, as a result, the world will forever be changed. Voices and thunder fill the silence. The judgment of God, that has been ignored and dismissed by the earth, now makes itself felt. "Woe to the inhabitants of the earth." Lightning, but no rain, and an earthquake grip the world. It is but the beginning as the trumpets prepare to sound. The King is coming!

THE FIRST TRUMPET - JUDGMENT OF FIRE, HAIL AND BLOOD

The first angel sounds the first trumpet, and the world catches fire. God has used this same plague on His enemies before; the sixth plague visited upon Pharaoh in the times of Moses was hail stones and fire that ran along the ground. This time the hail and fire are mingled with blood, making the plague even more revolting. "And I will shew wonders in the heavens and in the earth, blood, and fire, and pillars of smoke" (Joel 2:30).

This is the time that the prophecy of 2 Peter 3 will be fulfilled, the time when the earth will be destroyed by fire. Indeed, it will seem that the whole world is on fire. One third of the forests on earth are consumed (one third of the fruit trees included) and there is not a patch of grass left anywhere. Even the green grass is gone, and it takes a considerably hot fire to burn green grass! The famine will of course worsen with this firestorm. The food supply has taken another hit that it could ill bear. Fodder for animals will now be almost non-existent. In fact, the Greek word used here for "grass" is *chloros*. It is, in particular, grass that is used for feeding cattle. Not only will the famine worsen, the destruction from the far-ranging fire will also make the land more vulnerable to floods and mud slides.

Note that one-third of the trees are destroyed. We will see that one-third of the sea will become blood, one-third of the sea creatures will be destroyed, one-third of the fresh water sources will become poisoned, and finally, one-third of the heavenly lights will be darkened. One-third is a fraction that, when seen in Scripture, is many times linked with evil or impurity. One-third is the inverse of the Trinity that is mathematically represented as 3/1. It is also the number of the evil angels who joined Satan's revolt eons ago. Now, when the purging of sin from the earth is in view, one-third is the fraction used when describing the cleansing action taken.

In 1 Chronicles 16:31-33, David prophesies about the time on earth when Jesus returns and reigns. Not only man rejoices, so does the physical planet. "Let the heavens be glad, and let the earth rejoice: and let men say among the nations, The Lord reigneth. Let the sea roar, and the fulness thereof: let the fields rejoice, and all that is therein. Then shall the trees of the wood sing out at the presence of the Lord, because he cometh to judge the earth."

What is left of the trees, fields and sea after the first trumpet has finished its purging will ultimately rejoice and resound with praise to the Lord. But the trees that God does not want are gone, as are the animals that God does not want. Many end-times teachers teach that what we see under the first four trumpets are the results of war and nuclear destruction. NO!! Every bit of this is from the hand of God. The action begins in heaven and is experienced on earth. God is cleansing, mankind is not destroying! How would we know which third of the trees to burn up? How would we know where to cleanse the ocean? The Bible never says that a contiguous third of the sea turns to blood, it simply reports the fraction of the ocean that is affected. God, and God alone knows where to point His "holy laser" to eradicate the contamination of thousands of years. We see perfect symmetry when destruction is controlled by God whereas there has always been anarchy when destruction is under the control of man. By the end of the sounding of the trumpet, the earth will have thrown off the bondage of sin and will rejoice in its pristine condition. It will, finally, have been set aright, and now will the desert be able to bloom as the rose.

THE SECOND TRUMPET – ONE-THIRD OF THE SEA TURNS TO BLOOD

As the second angel sounds, fire again hits the earth. This time it is in the form of a mountainous object that is on fire and lands in the ocean, rendering it polluted with blood. God did this before, again with the plagues against Pharaoh. Note that the object that is said to fall from heaven is not a literal mountain. When people argue that one cannot know what is symbolic and what is literal when studying Revelation, that is nonsense. This is the steadfast rule: If something is not to be taken literally, one is always given the indication that it is not. Here is a perfect example; John writes "*as it were* a great mountain." It is not a mountain, it is something that is reminiscent of a great mountain. If it were a literal mountain, John would say so.

ONE-THIRD OF SEA CREATURES DIE, ONE THIRD OF SHIPS DESTROYED

Again, as during the time of Moses, the waters become blood; this time it affects one-third of the oceans. One-third of the sea creatures are destroyed along with one-third of the ships. The food supply was hit under the first trumpet, the food and water supplies in the oceans are hit under the second. When Antichrist first began to reign, he brought the greatest prosperity the world had ever seen. Some of that wealth is still left. Granted, there are very few necessities like food, but there are luxuries like yachts still in evidence. After the fire hits earth under the first trumpet, some people will say, "No problem. I've got a yacht. I'll sail out to sea. I'll escape all of this. God can do what He will, but I will not have to suffer, I am on the sea. He cannot hurt me on the ocean. The sea can't burn." Now, they, too, will be hit. Does it begin to dawn on them that there is no escaping God? Probably not. Even the pollution of the water leaves them arrogant. "Maybe," they reason, "we don't have to worry. After all, we still have the rivers, the streams, and the lakes. There is still potable water." They have reckoned without the third angel.

THE THIRD TRUMPET - FRESH WATERS POISONED

When the third angel sounds his trumpet, a flaming star from heaven falls upon a third of the fresh water sources, poisoning them at their sources. Water has now become more precious than gold. The name that God gives to the flaming star (meteorite?) is Wormwood. The meaning of wormwood is "bitter." Prophetically, it is a punishment for idolatry. Consider Jeremiah 9:13-15, "And the Lord saith, Because they have forsaken my law which I set before them, and have not obeyed my voice, neither walked therein; But have walked after the imagination of their own heart, and after Baalim, which their fathers taught them: Therefore thus saith the Lord of hosts, the God of Israel; Behold, I will feed them, even this people, with wormwood, and give them water of gall [poisoned water] to drink."

Consider also Deuteronomy 29:17-18: "And ye have seen their abominations, and their idols, wood and stone, silver and gold, which were among them: Lest there should be among you man, or woman, or family, or tribe, whose heart turneth away this day from the Lord our God, to go and serve the gods of these nations; lest there should be among you a root that beareth gall and wormwood."

In a coincidence that is truly chilling, the Ukrainian word for "wormwood" is the word "Chernobyl." And indeed, the meltdown at Chernobyl on April 28, 1986, released lethal particles equal to ten Hiroshimas, poisoning both water and air. Even considering that, the punishment is just. Their hearts are poisoned against God, their bodies will be also. And the fourth angel lifts his trumpet to his mouth.

THE FOURTH TRUMPET - CELESTIAL LIGHTS DARKENED

"And the fourth angel sounded, and the third part of the sun was smitten, and the third part of the moon, and the third part of the stars; so as the third part of them was darkened, and the day shone not for a third part of it, and the night likewise" (Revelation 8:12).

When the fourth trumpet is blown, an eerie darkness comes upon the earth. All of the celestial lights seen from the earth - the sun, moon and stars - are darkened by one-third. A third of the daylight is removed and the nighttime is likewise affected. The world will now be without natural illumination for a third of the day and a third of the night. The fact that God, Himself, will disturb all of His creation, the heavens included, is prophesied in Haggai 2:6 and quoted in Hebrews 12:26, "For thus saith the Lord of hosts; Yet once, it is a little while, and I will shake the heavens, and the earth, and the sea, and the dry land."

Even the heavens are polluted. When I say heavens, I do not mean God's dwelling place, His throne room. That is holy. No, I mean what we would commonly refer to as "outer space." After all, man has been to space and left his litter there. Satan, too, has had free reign in space, "For we wrestle not against flesh and blood, but against principalities, against powers, against the rulers of the darkness of this world, against spiritual wickedness *in the heavenly places*" (Ephesians 6:12). God will have to clean up the heavens also.

When this part of the story is told from the perspective of the earth in Revelation 16, more details are given. During the night, the people experience darkness and extreme cold, then they experience a sun that shines with a heat so intense that it actually scorches them. When in the cold, the people long for the heat, but when in the heat they beg for the darkness and the arctic cold to return. Christian martyrs who suffered under the Communist regime told of similar torture. They would be stripped and chained in cells that were heated to an extreme degree. After passing out, they would be thrown into freezing cold rooms. Their bodily reactions were studied and monitored as they struggled to survive. Most did not. This will probably prove to be true under the fourth trumpet also. But, unlike the Christian saints in the USSR, the people on earth at this time have chosen the wrath of God over His mercy. As the angel says later in Revelation, "They deserve it."

JUDGMENT COMBINED WITH CLEANSING

It must always be kept in mind that judgment is not the only thing going on here. The earth is being cleansed. Before God can put the earth aright, he must rip out and destroy what is polluted. It would be easier if God were simply dealing with a clean slate as He did when He first created the world. It is much harder now because He has to purge what doesn't belong before He can begin to make it right. This is what God is doing now. As 2 Peter 3 said would happen, the earth is being purged with fire, but, praise God! the rainbow is still around the throne. The earth will not be annihilated, it will be cleansed. Because of Adam's sin, the very ground has been cursed. It cannot remain so for the King is coming to rule and to reign! Every trace of sin will be eradicated, every unnecessary pest will be tracked down and killed. Every weed will die. Every pollutant in air, ground, or water will be destroyed. What science has spent the last half of the twentieth century trying to accomplish will be accomplished by the agents of God in seven years! Every destructive thing that Satan and mankind and sin have done to the earth will be hunted down and healed. The meek will inherit the earth, but it will be a cleansed and purified earth. And the Lord Jesus Christ shall rule over His creation.

AN EAGLE APPEARS IN HEAVEN WITH AN OMINOUS WARNING

At this time, before the fifth angel sounds his trumpet, an ominous sign appears. The King James Version reads that an angel different from those we have seen flies throughout heaven at this point. In actuality, according to the Greek, it is an eagle not an angel that flies through heaven. This eagle most definitely is a saint. Scripture compares the children of God to eagles in Isaiah 40:31 when Isaiah says, "But they that wait upon the Lord shall renew their strength; they shall mount up with wings as *eagles;* they shall run, and not be weary; and they shall walk, and not faint".

The comparison is made again in Matthew 24:27-28 speaking of the return of Jesus for the saints, "For as the lightning cometh out of the east, and shineth even unto the west; so shall also the coming of the Son of man be. For wheresoever the carcase [body] is, there will the *eagles* be gathered together."

The eagle proclaims with a loud voice "Woe, woe, woe, to the inhabiters of the earth..." As if things have not been bad enough, the eagle announces that far more and far worse is about to come upon the world. So far, just physical plagues have tormented the earth. A whole new realm of torment is about to be opened up under the remaining three trumpets: the supernatural. Woe to the earth indeed, for hell itself is about to be loosed on the earth.

CHAPTER 11
THE LAST THREE TRUMPETS
Revelation 9

As bad as things have been up to now, its about to get worse. Why? Because the supernatural evil powers that are bound deep in the Underworld are about to be loosened. The abyss that has contained them is about to be opened and they will ascend upon mankind.

THE FIFTH TRUMPET -THE KEY TO THE REALM OF DARKNESS

The fifth trumpet is blown, and after it has sounded John sees a star that, according to the Greek, had been in heaven but had since fallen to the earth. (The word used for "fall" in the Greek is in the perfect tense that means that it is already past.) John records that the star is given the key to the Abyss - the bottomless pit. How can a key be given to a star? The answer lies in Revelation 1:20 that has already explained the meaning of this symbol: a star is an angel. This, then, is a fallen angel and he will now be allowed to open the Abyss and let loose the profane and unholy forces of evil. Based on Isaiah 14:12, I believe that this angel is Satan, "How art thou fallen from heaven, O Lucifer, son of the morning! How art thou cut down to the ground which didst weaken the nations!"

Although the forces of the Underworld are Satan's, he does not have total control of them for God always retains the veto power over everything. But now the world has rejected God, sided with and worshipped Satan, asking for him and his administrations. God will now grant their request and they will experience fully what it is to live under the government of Satan.

The first four trumpets brought forth wrath from the Throne and it was directed toward the earth itself. Now that God has given the key to the abyss to the fallen angel, Satan, Satan will afflict the people on the earth. Woe, indeed to the inhabitants of earth! Chapter 9 is the record of the culmination of Satan's hatred toward the race of Adam; toward, unbelievably, even those who follow and worship him! Satan hates the entire race of mankind. Aligning oneself to him does not in one whit ameliorate his violence toward one. The world has asked for Satan and will now get him!

We have seen the keys to hell and death mentioned in chapter 1. Here is another key, the key to the unseen realm of demons and evil spirits of every kind. These spirits have, to a great degree, been locked up for the protection of man. They will now be loosened. It is interesting to note that there is an occult teaching of long standing concerning a place that they call "Hidden Earth." Hidden Earth is the residence of unseen spiritual forces that the occultists endeavor to tap. Revelation 9:1 may give credence to the idea that that place does exist.

DEMONIC LOCUSTS

A great swarm of locusts are released as the bottomless pit is opened. It is such a great number that the air is darkened as they are let loose. These are not ordinary locusts, their description makes that clear. They resemble centaurs, a horse/man amalgam, with the faces of men and the bodies of horses. Their hair is long and they wear a crown. Their teeth are ferocious, like the teeth of lions, and they wear armored breastplates. They have wings and poisonous stingers in their tails. Some have theorized that they are helicopters being described by a first-century man. I, personally, have never seen a helicopter with the face of a man and the torso of a horse. I have also somehow missed the ones with long hair and stingers. That is because helicopters do not look like the above description of John's. These are not helicopters. What they are, are legions of demonic beings who have been imprisoned in the Abyss for centuries. This abyss has been alluded to before in the Scriptures as being a holding place for malevolent beings. When, in Luke 8:31, Jesus delivered the Gadarene demoniac from his legion of demons they pleaded with Jesus not to send them to the "deep," their term for the Abyss. Their argument was that it was not yet their time for imprisonment, and Jesus apparently agreed as He sent them into a herd of swine. The swine then ran over the cliff and drowned. After that we are not told the journey of those evil spirits. We don't know what happened to them, but we do know that they didn't go to the Abyss. But some demons are there and have been there for thousands and thousands of years. We have witnessed the impact of evil spirits upon men, but these captive spirits are far worse; so bad, in fact, that they have been kept off the earth until now.

When Jesus sent out the Seventy as recorded in Luke 10:17-18, they returned with joy saying "Lord, even the devils are subject unto us through thy name." Jesus responds to them by telling them that He was aware of this because He saw Satan losing power in the spiritual realm; "falling from heaven" is the exact phrase used. Then, still in relation to the spiritual realm that they are discussing and the spiritual war they are fighting against Satan and his forces, Jesus makes them a promise, "Behold, I give unto you power to tread on serpents and scorpions, and over all the power of the enemy: and nothing shall by any means hurt you." Jesus is not promising them protection against physical agents - against scorpions, snakes, mosquitoes, tarantulas, milk allergies, and the like. No, Jesus is calling these demonic beings scorpions and serpents. This has biblical precedent as Satan himself took on the form of a serpent when he first chose a physical form. The locusts mentioned here in Revelation 9 are twice linked with scorpions, each time concerning their ability to harm men. Furthermore, these infernal locusts are the satanic opposite of the Living Ones. As the Living Ones had the characteristics of an eagle, a man, a calf and a lion, so these locusts have the characteristics of a man, a lion, a flying creature (the wings) and a horse. Up until now, they have been bound in order to protect mankind. Now they are set free.

THE LOCUSTS HAVE BOUNDARIES

Although God has allowed them to be freed, He is still setting their boundaries, and they are ultimately serving His purpose. "The Lord hath made all things for himself: yea, even the wicked for the day of evil" (Proverbs 16:4). They are forbidden to touch the grass, the trees, indeed, any growing thing. This is another indication that they are not actual locusts. Normal locusts would devour crops, grass, etc., however, these locusts must scrupulously avoid what ordinary locusts would consume. God has already destroyed the trees and grass that He wants destroyed, the remaining trees and the grass that have now sprung up are not allowed to be harmed.

The remaining people, except for those who are sealed with God's seal, are an altogether different story. They are, without exception, evil, and thus the locusts can indiscriminately attack them. Thus, it is clear that these infernal beings have intelligence in that they are able to discriminate between those who have God's protection about them, such as God's hedge around Job, and those who do not. They are well able to follow orders. They are not allowed to kill the people. That the locusts have it in their power to do so is understood by the command that they must not. They are only allowed to torment. The time that they are allowed to torment men is five months. It is possible that some men have escaped the effects of the first four trumpets, but no one living except for those sealed with the seal of God's protection will escape the torment of the demonic locusts. Closed doors, caulked windows, bricked chimneys, etc. will not prevent the hoards of locusts from entering every dwelling and from tormenting all who are found there.

NO DEATH PERMITTED FOR FIVE MONTHS

There is found under the fifth trumpet an occurrence that the world has never experienced in all its millennia of existence: the cessation of death. This pause in the natural cycle of things lasts during the entire span of the locusts' torment, five months. This is the exact length of time of the duration of The Flood (Genesis 7:24), another great time of God's cleansing, purging, and mighty judgment. It has been stated that time is not a heavenly concept. So it seems odd to find a time given here until one considers that John is overhearing the divine limitation that the angel places upon the infernal locusts. They do deal in time, so here a time limit is set.

At first blush, this removal of death from the human experience might be taken as a wonderful gift, but verse 6 tells us that the opposite is true. Men long for death and actively seek it but it is denied to them. What this verse tells us is truly astonishing. Men will attempt to die and they will not be able to - their spirit will not leave them. This in no way stops the body from accepting the consequences of the suicide try, thus the man who puts a gun to his head and pulls the trigger will not die but his head will be open and bleeding and in enormous pain. The woman who jumps off the high building will be left with a shattered body, but she will live. Trains will run over those who position themselves on the tracks, but the mangled bodies will continue to writhe in torment. Imagine, too, the sight of these suicide attempts as they continue to present themselves to the living! Even horror writer Stephen King has not imagined something so macabre and horrific. And when the time is up (it is never indicated that the evil people know how long the time will last) and the first person dies, the entire world must breathe a collective sign of relief. Of all of the woes, it is conceivable that this is the worst, for, again, death is a grace note from God, an escape from a sinful and fallen world. When He removes this grace, even for a short time, the consequences of this removal are unimaginable to the sane person.

KING OF THE LOCUSTS

Verse 11 tells us that there is a king over these fiendish creatures. This king is *not* Satan, but one of his princes. There is an evil hierarchy just as there is a heavenly one. Ephesians 6:12 sheds some light on this concept as it lists some of the offices in the satanic kingdom: principalities, powers, and rulers of the darkness. Jeremiah 10:11 calls them gods (lower case g), but prophesies that they shall perish from the earth and from under the heavens at the coming of the wrath of God (upper case g).

This satanic hierarchy (or should I say lowerarchy?) Is another indication that we are not dealing with earthly locusts for Proverbs 30:27 records, "The locusts have no king, yet go they forth all of them by bands." It is clear from the context of this verse in Proverbs that the writer is speaking of earthly locusts as he groups them with ants, badgers, and lizards, all common creatures to us. These locusts in Revelation 9 are an altogether different class of creature. The name of their prince in Hebrew is *Abaddon*, and in Greek it is called *Apollyon*. This is an indication that the locusts will affect both Jews (except for the 144,000 who have been sealed by God) and Gentiles. In both languages the name means the same: destroyer. This, of course, is the satanic opposite of the name of Jesus that in the Hebrew means "savior." The people on earth have rejected and cursed the Savior and have embraced the Destroyer. This is the consequence. And still, two more woes await...

SIXTH TRUMPET - FOUR SATANIC ANGELS RELEASED

When the sixth angel sounds, a voice is heard from the four horns of the golden altar. Leviticus 4:34 tells us that the blood of the sacrifice for the sins of the people was to be placed on the horns of the altar. The blood on the horns in heaven belongs to Jesus; His voice compels the release of the four evil angels. No other authority could release them. Possibly, the blood of the martyrs cries out for justice in much the same way that we are told the blood of Abel cried out to God from the ground for justice in his murder by his brother Cain. The blood of the wicked people on earth will now be required as a recompense for their sin.

"GENERALS" OF AN EVIL FORCE

The sixth angel is told to loose the four angels that have been bound and have been destined for exactly this time to bring vengeance upon the wicked. These are evil, not good angels. That is clear from the fact that they are bound; good angels would never have to be restrained in any way. In fact, the fact that they are bound indicates that they are particularly dangerous. Any angel is powerful beyond our comprehension (one righteous angel destroyed 185,000 enemies of Israel in only one night), so the malevolence and violence of these four must be awesome indeed. They, like Abaddon, are high up in the hierarchy of Satan. They have under their command two hundred million evil creatures. It is possible that they are the evil archetypes of the Four Riders of the Apocalypse, as they ride their satanic horses through the earth, killing a third of mankind. Nonetheless, these loathsome spirits are under the authority of God Almighty and they will be used of Him for His purpose. When Philippians 2:10 speaks of all creation bowing their heads and bending their knees to Jesus Christ and recognizing Him as Lord, it says that even the "things under the earth" shall do so. Even the evil spirits must recognize His authority, do His bidding, and laud him as Lord of the Universe.

John says that these four dangerous angels are bound at the river Euphrates. This was a river in the Garden of Eden, where the race of Adam began. It is in the land of Shinar where ancient Babylon was sited. This is the place where every evil and heathen religion had its beginning. It was here that the powers of evil first made an attempt against the human race. It was here that the first murder was committed. And it was here that the satanic government and system of Babylon first supplanted the godly government and system of Eden. Thousands of years hence we find evil waiting just under the surface in order to seize the opportunity to break forth once again. There is an occultic teaching that there are places on the earth that are conducive to the entry of unseen powers and forces. If that is true, then surely this is the primary place of Satan's entry to the earth.

The number of these angels is four. As has been stated before, four is the symbolic number of man and of the earth. There are four points on the compass, we speak of the four corners of the earth, there are four seasons and four winds. These angels have been reserved for this period of time during which they shall come against mankind. The Greek says that they are prepared for *the* hour, day and month and year, not *an* hour, day, month and year. They are prepared for this specific time. The time given also indicates how long they will be loose upon the earth. They are the generals of an evil force that will now seek out and kill men.

Notice again that John freely gives times after the Rapture. It is Rapture that is the secret and that must be kept from Satan. Notice also that the very fact that times are so freely given is a nail in the coffin of Post-Tribulation Rapture theology. If, as everyone agrees, the time of the Rapture is a secret, how could Rapture be missed if it is the final event to happen? All it would take is to note the different events under the seals, calculate the times given, and one could precisely pinpoint the day of the Rapture.

THE EVIL FORCE AND THEIR ACTIONS DESCRIBED

As John describes these angels, they are dangerous and loathsome in the extreme. They inspire terror. (In contrast, heavenly angels always inspire worship.) John sees two hundred million horses but they are not horses as we know horses. These are satanic horses. They are more reminiscent of dragons, having the heads of lions and breathing out fire and smoke and sulfur (brimstone). Their tails are like snakes with poisonous fangs. The creatures that sit upon the horses seem to come from the pit of hell itself. Their breastplates match the eruptions out of the horses' mouths being of fire and brimstone and jacinth (orange).

As the horses ride freely over all of the earth, they decimate the entire human population by a third. Under the five months of the locusts, men sought to die; now they can hardly escape death. One in three is dead within the space of little over a year. As the horses approach them, the people are killed by being burned up, suffocated by smoke, or poisoned by gasses. If they somehow escape all of that, they must withstand the horses' departure as their deadly, whipping, lashing tails strike out, biting like serpents. Imagine the terror induced as the horsemen are sighted on the horizon!

JOEL'S VISION OF THIS SAME SATANIC ARMY

Joel saw a vision of these creatures and recorded it in the second chapter of his book. Reading from Joel 2:1-10: "Blow ye the trumpet in Zion, and sound an alarm in my holy mountain: let all the inhabitants of the land tremble: for the day of the Lord cometh, for it is nigh at hand; A day of darkness and of gloominess, a day of clouds and of thick darkness, as the morning spread upon the mountains: a great people and a strong; there hath not been ever the like, neither shall be any more after it, even to the years of many generations. A fire devoureth before them; and behind them a flame burneth: the land is as the garden of Eden before them, and behind them a desolate wilderness; yea, and nothing shall escape them. *The appearance of them is as the appearance of horses; and as horsemen, so shall they run.* Like the noise of chariots on the tops of mountains shall they leap, like the noise of a flame of fire that devoureth the stubble, as a strong people set in battle array. Before their face the people shall be much pained: all faces shall gather blackness. They shall run like mighty men; they shall climb the wall like men of war; and they shall march every one on his ways, and they shall not break their ranks: Neither shall one thrust another; they shall walk every one in his path: *and when they fall upon the sword, they shall not be wounded.* They shall run to and fro in the city; they shall run upon the wall, they shall climb up upon the houses; they shall enter in at the windows like a thief. The earth shall quake before them; the heavens shall tremble: the sun and the moon shall be dark, and the stars shall withdraw their shining."

A SATANIC ARMY - NOT THE CHINESE ARMY

In light of these verses in Revelation and in Joel, it is inconceivable to me that it is generally taught that this horrific and evil visitation upon man is no more than the Chinese Army. The "logic" of that teaching stems from the number of the horsemen which is two hundred million. It is then deduced that the only army that could field a force of that size would be the Chinese. Overlooked completely is the fact that this is not a human army, besides which, the Chinese people along with every other race of people have been greatly decimated by this time because of the preceding plagues. Furthermore, why would God exempt the Chinese from His wrath at this time given that they are no less wicked and rebellious than all the others who remain upon the earth? Finally, it is a rather anemic thought that with all that has happened to the earth previous to this, God saves his "woe, woe, woe to the earth" for the idea that the Chinese Army is coming! No, that explanation is patently absurd: This is not a scene out of a Tom Clancy thriller, this is a scene out of J.R.R. Tolkien's book, The Lord of the Rings! What is in view here is the supernatural world of evil, just as were the locusts under the fifth trumpet. Another consequence of this unleashing of Satan's forces is that when Jesus does finally defeat Satan utterly, Satan can never claim that God withheld his (Satan's) forces from him. The problem for Satan is that he is driven to use all in his power against mankind and thus, unwittingly, furthers the will of God in this day.

NO REPENTANCE - SIN FLOURISHES

One would think that living through this time of the horsemen would be enough to cause anyone to repent and turn to God, but verse 20 tells us that *not one soul* repents, and even more unbelievingly, not one soul turns from worshiping Satan! Even after all that his government and administration has meant to the earth, not one person changes his or her mind. Man has become like his god. Mankind understands the cosmic battle between good and evil and mankind chooses evil. "For every one that doeth evil hateth the light, neither cometh to the light, lest his deeds should be reproved" (John 3:20).

It is important to note the sins that are listed at the close of this chapter. They are murder, drugs (the literal meaning of the word *pharmekia* in the Greek, which is here translated "sorceries"), sexual sin and thefts. These are the same sins that brought on the Flood. This generation is as reprobate as the generation of Noah. That generation was utterly destroyed; this one shall be also.

CHAPTER 12
THE MYSTERY OF GOD IS FINISHED
Revelation 10

JESUS DISPLAYED IN HIS GLORY

The scene in chapter 10 of Revelation presents a marked contrast to chapter 9. Chapter 9 records unspeakable havoc and destruction as the Underworld is opened in order to torment the earth. Chapter 10 records the most glorious scene since we saw God upon His throne in chapter 4. Again, as in chapter 4, we glimpse the rainbow and the little book...and Jesus, but with a difference now. This time, the rainbow is not around the Throne of God; it is around the head of the mighty angel. This time, the book is not rolled up and sealed with seven seals; the seals have been broken and the book lies open. This time, Jesus does not appear as a slaughtered Lamb, He appears in His complete glory. His face is as the sun in its radiance, and His feet are as pillars of fire. Jesus is coming in the clouds with the rainbow around His head, keeping God's covenant with the earth even in this terror. Despite the opening of the seven seals and the loosening of the purging that it contained, the earth is still here, the race of Adam lives. The Rainbow Covenant is sacred and intact.

THE MIGHTY ANGEL IS JESUS

How is it that we know that the mighty angel is, indeed, Jesus and not simply another angel? There are seven reasons why the identity of the mighty angel is undeniable. First, the description given could only be given about Divinity. He is clothed with a cloud as Jesus, in several Scriptures, is said to be clothed. Second, who else could possibly have the rainbow around his head? Only the one who made the Rainbow Covenant. Third, John has already described in chapter 1 the face of Jesus as if it were indeed the sun, and His feet as pillars of fire. We see that exact description here. Fourth, who has had the little book as a possession since it was taken out of the hand of the One on the Throne? Jesus, and it has not left His possession. He has, one by one, broken the seven seals that held it closed in chapter 5. (Although some have attempted to obfuscate the understanding of this passage by insisting that this little book is not the same as the "small book" of chapter 5, that idea is not substantiated in any particular Scripture. No other scroll has been or will be mentioned in Revelation except for that scroll that is the title deed to the earth. After all, Revelation is dealing with the redemption of the earth. It is the only document that is relevant.)

Fifth, who else but Jesus could claim victory over the previous ruler of the earth (Satan) by placing mighty feet upon the territory in dispute? Sixth, as this mighty angel continues to speak to John in the next chapter, chapter 11, He says He will give power to HIS two witnesses. And finally who else could possibly declare that the Eternal Time had come to file legal claim in the Celestial Courthouse of Total Justice, declaring intent of the Right to Possession? ONLY THE REDEEMER! Now, according to the custom of Redemption, with the title deed present and opened, Jesus takes formal and legal possession of Planet Earth by placing His right foot upon the sea and His left foot upon the earth for both are His. God told Israel that Canaan was legally her possession wherever the Israelites' feet trod. The feet of Jesus are as pillars of fire as he treads His rightful possession. The redemption of the earth cost Jesus His life. He now makes claim upon it.

There is some understandable confusion as to the identity of the angel because most translations read, "And I saw another mighty angel..." In the Greek, it reads, instead, "And I saw another angel, mighty." There has been no other mighty angel spoken of. No, John sees another angel, but with a difference, this one has far more power than the others; he is mighty. But why did John refer to Jesus as an angel in the first place? I cannot presume to know, but I do have some ideas. John is writing as things unfold before him. He sees another celestial being and possibly he calls each of them an angel for want of a more precise understanding of heavenly things. We know for a fact that later on in Revelation he labels as an angel another believer whom he does not recognize as being human because he is seeing that believer in his, the believer's, resurrected body. John lets this identification stand because it is clear to him, as He continues to see more detail concerning the celestial being, that those details further identify the mighty angel.   John, for all the reasons given above, is confident that the reader will understand that this angel could be no one other than the Son of Man.

This identification of Jesus as an angel has biblical precedence. When the Angel of the Lord appears to Balaam in Numbers 22, He tells Balaam that he, Balaam, is to speak only the words that He, the Angel of the Lord, gives him to speak. Balaam then identifies that angel as God Himself when referring to who will give him the words to speak.   Clearly, Jesus here appears to a human in an angelic form, much as He does to John in Revelation 10. It appears that we humans miss the nuances of heaven on a regular basis.

JESUS TAKES FINAL AND LEGAL POSSESSION OF EARTH

As Jesus places His right foot upon the sea and His left food upon the earth, He cries aloud with a triumphant voice, much as the lion roars after conquering his prey.   This too, was prophesied long ago in Isaiah 42:13-16: "The Lord shall go forth as a mighty man, he shall stir up jealousy like a man of war: he shall cry, yea, roar; he shall prevail against his enemies. I have long time holden my peace; I have been still, and refrained myself: now will I cry like a travailing woman; I will destroy and devour at once. I will make waste mountains and hills, and dry up all their herbs; and I will make the rivers islands, and I will dry up the pools. And I will bring the blind by a way that they knew not; I will lead them in paths that they have not know: I will make darkness light before them, and crooked things straight. These things will I do unto them, and not forsake them."

Since the Redemption price was fully paid at Calvary, Satan's dominion over man, the earth, and the grave has been breaking down.   Each time a human soul accepted the redeeming blood of Jesus and renounced Satan's claim to his soul, another thread of the power of Satan has snapped. Now the Redemptive Work will be finished entirely. Jesus is now coming to kick Satan off of Planet Earth entirely and bind him in chains.

This scene is too glorious to comprehend. But if we are His, we will see it. We will be there, just as was John. Our Lord and Savior will prevail, and the shout that comes from that mouth will stir our hearts and thrill us as no other sound has ever done before.

THUNDERS OF JUDGMENT

After the shout has stopped ringing through the universe, seven thunders will utter their voices. They are called *the* seven thunders. They are distinct and unique and we have seen them before in chapters 4 and 8. They are the Judgment Thunders. They come from the Throne of God. At this point, they say something incredibly important and profound. John begins to record what he has heard the thunders say when he is stopped. This is the very first time that John is kept from recording information, but the information that John overheard is so important that it must be kept secret until that day. Mind you, it is not being kept secret from us, the saints; it is being kept secret from Satan. A mighty battle still awaits, and the knowledge and strategy in the announcement of the seven thunders is apparently critical to the culmination of the Universal War between Good and Evil. So, we do not know what it is that the seven thunders say, but when this day comes, we, too, shall be in heaven and we will hear for ourselves the words of the seven thunders. Until then, we shall wait, knowing only that Jesus Christ, our Lord and Master, shall prevail against and conquer all of His enemies --- the malevolent forces of Darkness and Evil.

DELAY NO LONGER IN FINISHING THE MYSTERY OF GOD

As the thunders fade away, Jesus, with His feet firmly planted on both earth and sea, lifts His hand up to heaven and swears by the Creator of the Universe, His father, that there will be no more delay, but that in the days when the voice of the seventh angel shall begin to sound, the mystery of God shall be finished. This, too, was prophesied by Daniel long, long ago. Daniel records it in the last chapter of his book: "And I heard the man clothed in linen, which was upon the waters of the river, when he held up his right hand and his left hand unto heaven, and sware by him that liveth for ever that it shall be for a time, times, and an half; and when he shall have accomplished to scatter the power of the holy people, all these things shall be finished" (Daniel 12:7).

LENGTH OF TIME TO FINISH GOD'S WORK

John records that it will take some days for the sounding of the seventh angel to be completed. Daniel tell us how long that will be --- a time, times, and a half. That is the Jewish reckoning for three-and-a-half years. The time given in the very next chapter, chapter 11, until the seventh trumpet is sounded is also exactly three-and-a-half years. We are right on track as concerns the days of the sounding of the seventh angel.

Earlier, reference was made to the fact that the time span between Rapture and the Return is a total of ten-and-a-half years, not seven years as is commonly taught. The seven-year time span refers only to the Jews because it is the time of Jacob's Trouble. It begins three-and-a-half years after the Rapture. The time span just given by Daniel and John is another reason why seven years is not adequate. We know that the opening of the first six seals takes three-and-a-half years. We have just been told that the days of the seventh angel (the sounding of the seventh trumpet under the seventh seal) will take another three-and-a-half years. Those two time spans together already total seven years. But we must also factor in the times of the first six trumpets (or angels) that have been recorded in Revelation 8-9. We have been told the time frames of two of those trumpets: trumpet number five lasts at least five months, trumpet number six lasts one year, one month and one day. Those two trumpets alone last a bit over a year-and-a-half. So the times given so far since Rapture already add up to eight-and-a-half years without factoring in the times of trumpets numbered one through four. The seven-year time span so frequently referred to is simply inadequate.

UNDERSTANDING THE MYSTERY

Verse 7 of chapter 10 speaks of the mystery of God that has been revealed to his servants the prophets. The beginning sentence of Wonderful Counselor quoted Amos 3:7, "Surely the Lord [G]od will do nothing, but he revealeth his secret unto his servants the prophets." Daniel 12:10 further enlightens the revelation process when it says "...None of the wicked shall understand; but the wise shall understand."

It takes the gift of the Holy Spirit to understand the things of God. The natural mind cannot understand those things. Just because a secret is revealed does not mean that it is understood. The mystery of the first coming of Jesus was revealed in the prophets but it was not understood until after the Resurrection. It takes the understanding that only God can shine on a revelation in order to comprehend the revelation. Colossians says this same thing when Paul speaks of the mystery of the coming of Christ to the earth, "Even the mystery which hath been hid from ages and from generations, but now is made manifest to his saints" (Colossians 1:26).

Daniel prophesied that his words would remain a mystery until the time of the end, but that at that time of the end, knowledge would increase. Habakkuk said the same thing about his vision of the End Time. The grace of God is such that we live in a time in which the Spirit of God is quickening revelation knowledge to all who would seek it. If we, like the Sardian and Laodicean Church, close our eyes and hearts to this knowledge we will answer for our rebellion.

DOMINION OF EARTH RETURNS TO MAN

The voice from heaven commands John to take the little book, the title deed to the earth, out of the hand of Jesus. In this action, John is a type of the saints. Jesus has redeemed earth for mankind and will give the dominion over it back to the Race of Adam. This is precisely what His intention was from the beginning of time. Psalms 8:3-8 declares this when the psalmist writes: "When I consider thy heavens, the work of thy fingers, the moon and the stars, which thou hast ordained; What is man, that thou art mindful of him? And the son of man, that thou visitest him? For thou hast made him a little lower than the angels, and hast crowned him with glory and honour. *Thou madest him to have dominion over the works of thy hands; thou hast put all things under his feet*: All sheep and oxen, yea, and the beasts of the field; The fowl of the air, and the fish of the sea, and whatsoever passeth through the paths of the seas."

The first chapter of Ephesians deals at length with this concept. Paul explains that all things in heaven and in earth will come together in Jesus when the time is right in the sight of God. Not only we but also the earth (here Paul calls it "the purchased possession") will be redeemed, and this redemption of the earth is our inheritance in Christ. In fact, the gift of the indwelling of God in the form of the Holy Spirit is God's down payment, His "earnest money" to us as regards our inheritance. In verse 18, Paul prays an interesting prayer for the saints that God would allow them to understand what riches and glory are involved with this inheritance. Most of our eyes have been sealed shut when it comes to the hope and promise of our inheritance of the "purchased possession," earth. Like Esau who sold his birthright for a mess of porridge, we have dismissed and ignored the "riches of the glory of His inheritance in the saints" (Ephesians 1:18).

The title deed to earth is now back in the hands of man, as typified by John the Apostle.

Because of His birth at Bethlehem, God in the form of Jesus is now a member of the Race of Adam. He, of course, will assume the preeminent reign over earth, but we, as His Bride, will ascend to His throne with Him and will also rule over earth. This scene in Revelation 10 is very telling in regards to the character of Jesus and to His love for us. The battle against sin and Satan has been borne entirely by Him; He and He alone has defeated Satan. It has cost Him enormous suffering, and yet, when He holds aloft the open title deed to earth, when He stands with one foot on the earth and one foot on the sea, when he lifts His hand to heaven and swears that there shall be time no longer, that the mystery is almost finished, notice what He does with the fruit of the victory. He gives it to John on behalf of all of the saints!! They are foremost in His mind, and all that He has done, He has done out of love for them. Now, there is an inheritance!

OBTAINING THE PROMISED INHERITANCE IS BOTH SWEET AND BITTER

Acting in obedience, John takes the little book out of the hand of Jesus, and Jesus commands of him a peculiar thing. John is told to eat it. He is further told that the taste of it is sweet, but the absorption of it will be bitter. How like many of the promises and commands of God this is. The promise itself is sweet, but the working out of the promise can be bitter indeed. Consider the promise that we will be changed into the likeness of Jesus. A more sublime promise cannot be found in the entire Bible. But when we begin the change in our lives, we soon find that it comes at the cost of dying to our self, to our wants, desires, and plans for our lives. It comes at the cost of learning to turn the other cheek, to bless those that curse you and pray for those that despitefully use you. Is it worth it? Yes. Is it easy? Never. It will cost much for the saints to regain dominion over earth, but the promise is sublime. No wonder Paul wants us to appreciate this, our inheritance. All the best stories in the world are bittersweet. This is the very best story and it is bittersweet indeed.

It is interesting to note that the eating of this scroll was foreshadowed in Ezekiel 3. Ezekiel was given a book of lamentations, mourning, and woe for the house of Israel. Although it was bitter news indeed, Ezekiel, too, was told to eat it and as he did he remarked that the taste was as honey in his mouth. I believe there is enormous symbolism here, I have only scratched the surface of it. Let me only add that by eating the book, John has taken complete possession of it. It is his, and the saints, forever. As Jesus promised on the Mount of Olives, the meek *will* inherit the earth! It will be then also, when we receive our inheritance, that we will finally understand the cost of that inheritance. We will finally appreciate what price Jesus paid. As for the little book, it is never mentioned or seen again in Revelation.

WE WILL BE ETERNAL WITNESSES

Jesus says one more thing to John. He tells him that he will prophesy again before many people, nations, tongues, and kings. Remember that John is an old, old man now and in exile on the Island of Patmos. There was no speaking tour for him after he was released off of Patmos. He did not prophesy worldwide after this. After being released from exile he returned to Ephesus and there he died. This cannot refer to a mission of John's while he lived on earth. This is future. This may refer to the part that John will play in the preaching of the eternal gospel from heaven. However, John was given this prophecy *after* he receives back dominion over the earth. John, as a type of all the saints, is being told that there is apparently *eternal* witnessing to do. After all, Isaiah says of Jesus, "Of the *increase* of his government and peace there shall be no end" (Isaiah 9:7).

The saints will continue in heaven what was given them to do on earth - proclaim the Holy name of Jesus.

CHAPTER 13
GOD'S TWO WITNESSES
Revelation 11

THE JEWS WILL COME TO JESUS

The story of Revelation 11 is the story of the fulfillment of Romans 11. In verses 25-26 of Romans 11, Paul states that a spiritual blindness has come over Israel, their hearts have been hardened and they will not recognize Jesus as Messiah because of it. The hardening of Israel is not complete and total, of course; Jews have continued to come, one by one, to Jesus throughout the centuries, but for the most part Jews have been the most intractable opponents of Christianity. But in verse 26, Paul makes a staggering prophecy. He says that when all of the Gentiles who are going to come to Jesus have come to Jesus, *all* of Israel will be saved. No word is ever given of how this will happen throughout the rest of the New Testament until we get to Revelation 11. There, the entire story is given in amazing detail.

It took Adolph Hitler to bring the Jews back to their land. It will take an even greater catastrophe --- Antichrist --- to bring them to Jesus as Savior. That they will come is without doubt. Not only Paul, but Moses, Isaiah, Micah, and Zechariah have prophesied the same. Just before Israel was to cross over the Jordan River into Canaan, Moses said to them in Deuteronomy 4:20, 30-31: "But the Lord hath taken you, and brought you forth out of the iron furnace, even out of Egypt, to be unto him a people of inheritance, as ye are this day... When thou art in tribulation, and all these things are come upon thee, *even in the latter days,* if thou turn to the Lord thy God, and shalt be obedient unto his voice; (For the Lord thy God is a merciful God;) he will not forsake thee, neither destroy thee, nor forget the covenant of thy fathers which he sware unto them."

"But Israel shall be saved in the Lord with an everlasting salvation: ye shall not be ashamed nor confounded world without end" (Isaiah 45:17).

"But thou, Bethlehem Ephratah, though thou be little among the thousands of Judah, yet out of thee shall he come forth unto me that is to be ruler in Israel: whose goings forth have been from of old, from everlasting. *Therefore will he give them up, until the time that she which travaileth hath brought forth: then the remnant of his brethren shall return unto the children of Israel"* (Micah 5:2-3).

"And I will strengthen the house of Judah, and I will save the house of Joseph, and I will bring them again to place them: and they shall be as though I had not cast them off: for I am the Lord their God, and will hear them" (Zechariah 10:6).

I am sure that the reason why Satan conspired to have Hitler attempt to annihilate the entire Jewish race was in order to defeat these prophesies. And if the word of God was defeated, then God Himself is defeated. Hitler proved no match for God and neither will Antichrist. Indeed, God will use both for His purposes for His children Israel.

ISRAEL'S SPIRITUAL CONDITION ASSESSED

A measuring rod in the form of a reed is given to John and he is told to measure the temple of God and those that worship therein. It is therefore immediately clear that the Jews are in view here for they are the ones who worship God in His temple. When John is told to measure them, what is implied by that measurement is spiritual measurement. Historically, the standard of measurement of a cubit was predicated on the length of the right arm of the king. Now, this measurement and evaluation is based on the strong right arm of the King of Kings. John is evaluating and judging them in accordance with the standard of God. Ezekiel had this same exact vision where Jesus appears to him and measures the Temple. Ezekiel 40-42 tells of the vision in great detail, and Ezekiel 43 gives the culmination of the measurement. Israel is found greatly wanting, indeed, the measuring rod was found in the form of a reed as it is in Revelation, and the reed was an instrument of chastisement. This chastisement of the Lord's will lead them to repentance and renewal. As Ezekiel 43:7-9 states: "Son of man, the place of my throne, and the place of the soles of my feet, where I will dwell in the midst of the children of Israel for ever, and my holy name, shall the house of Israel no more defile, neither they, nor their kings, by their whoredom, nor by the carcases of their kings in their high places... Now let them put away their whoredom, and the carcases of their kings, far from me, and I will dwell in the midst of them for ever."

JUDGMENT UPON ISRAEL

This chastisement comes upon Israel now as the city of Jerusalem is about to be overrun by the Gentiles because, at this time, Antichrist will break the covenant of protection he signed with Israel three-and-a-half years earlier and will invade Israel with his forces. But all is not lost because, as we see in this chapter, Antichrist must contend with the Two Witnesses and with their preaching, which Antichrist is powerless to stop.

Although John writes of measuring the temple, when he wrote this, there was no Temple. It had been destroyed in A.D. 70, and John was writing this some twenty-five years later. At the end of Revelation is a stern injunction to the Church not to edit John's letter. In fact, curses will be placed on anyone who does. Had it not been for that injunction, the Church most likely would have assumed at this point that John was becoming feebleminded and would have excised this passage. But John knew exactly what Jesus had told him. He was as confident of the future as he was of the past, and he knew that the temple would have to be rebuilt. I write this on the eve of the year 2011, and as of yet there is no temple. For almost two thousand years, this prophecy of John's has stood unfulfilled, but it is sure. The first temple, Solomon's Temple, was one of the wonders of the ancient world. It was the most costly and resplendent building on earth at its time. In fact, the Queen of Sheba fainted when she first saw it. It was built by David's son, Solomon, at a pinnacle of Jewish history. It was built in gratitude to God Almighty for sustaining blessings upon Israel. When next the temple is rebuilt by the Jews, it will be built not in gratitude, but in unbelief. It will be a monument to Israel herself, not to God. For this, Israel will be judged and found wanting.

John is told not to measure the outer court of the temple. This was the only area of the Temple to which the Gentiles were allowed to come, thus it was called the Court of the Gentiles. The meaning of this instruction to John is thus: There is no point in evaluating the rest of the world, it is not God's. The only spiritual work that God will do will be with the nation of

Israel. The rest of the world is hopeless. As was mentioned above, John is now told that the Gentiles will occupy Jerusalem for forty-two months. That is exactly three-and-a-half years, exactly the time that Daniel has said is remaining before Jesus comes with His saints. Jesus discusses this occupation in the Olivet Discourse: "For these be the days of vengeance, that all things which are written may be fulfilled. But woe unto them that are with child, and to them that give suck, in those days! For there shall be great distress in the land, and wrath upon this people. And they shall fall by the edge of the sword, and shall be led away captive into all nations: and Jerusalem shall be trodden down of the Gentiles, until the times of the Gentiles be fulfilled" (Luke 21:22-24).

For these last three-and-a-half years, Antichrist will overrun Palestine, attempting to force the Jews to worship him. The only place in Israel that Antichrist never reaches is Mount Zion. All of the rest of the Jewish territory is his. But, even in this bleakest of times, God's mercy is manifest toward the Jews. This time His mercy takes the form of two Jewish men, God's two witnesses. These two men will do two things: (1) they will stand up and war against Antichrist, (2) they will lead Israel to Jesus.

THE TWO WITNESSES

Jesus now tells John the story of these two witnesses. John does *not* see this in a vision, he is told this by Jesus and John records what he is told. He is told that the two witnesses of Jesus will be empowered of God to go from their abode in heaven to Israel and prophesy to her for three-and-a-half years. It is significant that there are two of them because, according to Judaic law, a fact is established by the mouths of two witnesses. The witnesses wear sackcloth that is what the Old Testament prophets wore when mourning over the condition of the people of Israel. Jesus calls them the two olive trees and the two candlesticks standing before the God of the earth. The significance of this is that although they are men, they come out of heaven. It is clear then that they are not men who are currently living on the earth, they are men who have lived on the earth in previous times. When Jesus calls them the two olive trees, He is giving us significant insight. The reference is to Zechariah 4. Zechariah there records a vision that he has had that concerns two olive trees that stand by a golden candlestick in heaven. An angel appears to explain the vision to him and starting in verse 11 Zechariah asks about the olive trees: "Then answered I, and said unto him, What are these two olive trees upon the right side of the candlestick and upon the left side thereof? And I answered again, and said unto him, What be these two olive branches which through the two golden pipes empty the golden oil out of themselves? And he answered me and said, Knowest thou not what these be? And I said, No, my lord. Then said he, These are the two anointed ones, that stand by the Lord of the whole earth"

As the two olive trees, the witnesses will bring the olive oil (symbolic for the Holy Spirit) to Israel. As the two candlesticks, the witnesses will bring the light to Israel. Remember that in Revelation 1, the churches were identified as the golden candlesticks because they brought the light of God to the world. The churches are gone and have been gone from earth for several years so the appointed candlesticks to the Jews now show up.

WHO ARE THE TWO WITNESSES?

As part of their ministry, and to establish their God-given authority, the Two Witnesses perform miraculous signs. They are the only two men on the face of the earth that frighten Antichrist. They are the only two enemies that he is unable to control, and, further, they are the only two that are able to torment him. They will wander freely throughout Palestine preaching Jesus to the Jews and Antichrist will be powerless to stop them. Scripture tells us why. Fire proceeds out of their mouths to devour their enemies thus making them impervious to attack. This passage does not mean that they are fire-breathers, it means that they have the ability by their words to call down fire from heaven. Furthermore, they shut up heaven so that it does not rain for the entire three-and-a-half years of their prophecy and in so doing they worsen the famine and consequently the food supply. In addition, they have the power to turn the waters to blood and to smite the earth with plagues at their whim. These were the exact works of two other prophets in the Old Testament: Moses and Elijah.

Moses smote Egypt with bloody waters and diverse plagues when contending with Pharaoh over freedom for Israel. He also called forth fire upon the earth (Exodus 9:23-24). Elijah, too, called forth fire from heaven upon his enemies at least two times. One was when he confronted the 450 prophets of Baal in 1 Kings 18:17-40, the other time that is recorded in the Bible is when he confronted two of King Ahaziah's captains and their companies of fifty soldiers in 2 Kings 1:10-12. "And Elijah answered and said to the captain of fifty, If I be a man of God, then let fire come down from heaven, and consume thee and thy fifty. And there came down fire from heaven, and consumed him and his fifty. Again also he sent unto him another captain of fifty with his fifty. And he answered and said unto him, O man of God, thus hath the king said, Come down quickly. And Elijah answered and said unto them, If I be a man of God, let fire come down from heaven, and consume thee and thy fifty. And the fire of God came down from heaven, and consumed him and his fifty"

The apostles James and John made reference to this when they asked Jesus if they should do the same to His enemies, "And when his disciples James and John saw this, they said, Lord, wilt thou that we command fire to come down from heaven, and consume them, even as Elias [Elijah] did?" (Luke 9:54).

In addition, Elijah stopped the rain from falling on earth during his time of ministry. "And Elijah the Tishbite, who was of the inhabitants of Gilead, said unto Ahab, As the Lord God of Israel liveth, before whom I stand, there shall not be dew nor rain these years, but according to my word" (I Kings 17:1). The Old Testament does not record how long the drought lasted, but twice the New Testament does. Consider James 5:17: "Elias [Elijah] was a man subject to like passions as we are, and he prayed earnestly that it might not rain: and it rained not on the earth *by the space of three years and six months*" (emphasis mine). Luke 4:25 gives the same information. That is the exact period of time for which the Two Witnesses will seal up the heavens!

God Himself said that He waged war against all the *gods* of Egypt when He smote Egypt with plagues, and now, as before, a supernatural battle will wage on both sides --- good and evil.

So far, then, we have established that the witnesses come down from heaven to earth, and that they perform the exact wonders that Moses and Elijah performed when they lived on earth. But there is more. Luke 24:2 tells us that two *men* appearing in likeness to angels, dressed in dazzling apparel, witnessed the resurrection. Two men in white clothing also witnessed the Ascension and affirmed the Second Coming of Jesus in Acts 1:10. Two men in a glorified state also appeared with Jesus on the Mount of Transfiguration, and, according to Luke, what was discussed then was the departure (exodus) of Jesus from the earth. That would have included His death, burial, resurrection, and ascension. That time, however, the two men are identified; they were Moses and Elijah. Why would Jesus be discussing the particulars of His upcoming death with Moses and Elijah? It is perfectly logical if, indeed, all three of them knew that Moses and Elijah would bear witness to the death, resurrection, and ascension of Jesus by reenacting them in the last days.

Both Moses' and Elijah's bodies were kept from Satan after their departures from this earth at a time when Satan controlled both death and the grave. Elijah never died and was translated (raptured) to heaven. Moses died, but God himself came for the body and buried it in a place that no man ever found. The Scripture does not say if that place was actually on the earth. The fact that Moses' body had been kept from Satan was the cause of a great dispute between God and Satan. Jude 9 gives us a titillating look into the spiritual realm when he writes, "Yet Michael the archangel, when contending with the devil he disputed about the body of Moses, durst not bring against him a railing accusation, but said, The Lord rebuke thee."

It is readily apparent that Elijah is a type of the Christians who will not see death, but will be raptured while they remain living. Moses, on the other hand, is a type of those who die in the Lord and of the hope they have of resurrection from the grave.

Moses and Elijah each represent two other great concepts. Moses is the archetype of the Law, Elijah is the archetype of the Prophets. Over and over, the Bible speaks of the two things that will most convict and convince the Jews: the Law and the

Prophets. The Synagogue service of Jesus' day consisted of two readings: one from the Torah and one from the Haphtorah, the Prophets. When Jesus was revealing himself to the two men on the road to Emmaus the Scripture says, "And beginning at *Moses and all the prophets*, he expounded unto them in all the scriptures the things concerning himself" (Luke 24:27). Paul writes in Romans 3:21, "But now the righteousness of God without the law is manifested, being witnessed by the law and the prophets."

Paul repeated this to the Roman governor Felix in Acts 24:14, "But this I confess unto thee, that after the way which they call heresy, so worship I the God of my fathers, believing all things which are written in *the law and in the prophets*" (emphasis mine). Again, Paul writes a few chapters later in 26:22: "Having therefore obtained help of God, I continue unto this day, witnessing both to small and great, saying no other things than those which *the prophets and Moses* did say should come."

Paul, in chains in Rome, spoke often of this as recorded in Acts 28:23: "And when they had appointed him a day, there came many to him into his lodging; to whom he expounded and testified the kingdom of God, persuading them concerning Jesus, *both out of the law of Moses, and out of the prophets*, from morning till evening" (emphasis mine). Finally, Philip, speaking of Jesus to Nathanael, said, "We have found him, of whom Moses in the law, and the prophets, did write, Jesus of Nazareth, the son of Joseph" (John 1:45).

The very last words of the Old Testament before four hundred years of silence were concerning Moses and Elijah: "Remember ye the law of Moses my servant, which I commanded unto him in Horeb for all Israel, with the statutes and judgments. Behold, I will send you Elijah the prophet before the coming of the great and dreadful day of the Lord: And he shall turn the heart of the fathers to the children, and the heart of the children to their fathers, lest I come and smite the earth with a curse" (Malachi 4:4-6).

Incidentally, the Hebrew word for "curse" used here is the word for "utter destruction". God was speaking of nothing less than pure and undefiled wrath upon a sinful world.

DOES THE RETURN OF ELIJAH AND MOSES FIT JEWISH TRADITION?

That Elijah would come again was completely accepted and anticipated by the Jews. It still is, in fact they set a place for Elijah at each Passover celebration. John the Baptist came in the spirit and power of Elijah and could have been their Elijah had they but repented and accepted Jesus as Messiah. Jesus makes this exact statement in Matthew 11:14, Matthew 17:11-13, and Luke 1:17. But because the Jews rejected Jesus as Messiah, the original prophecy stands and will be fulfilled.

But what of Moses? John 1:21 makes clear the Jewish tradition regarding the second prophet who would appear with Elijah. They ask two distinct questions: "Are you Elijah?" and "Are you the Prophet?" The Jews were expecting two men, only one of whom had been named (Elijah), who would appear before the Day of the Lord. Given that it is the Law and the Prophets that have been chosen by God to reveal Jesus to Israel; given that the miracles performed are the miracles of Moses and Elijah; given that Elijah never died; given that the body of Moses was guarded and kept by God since his death, never falling into the hands of Satan; given that it was with Moses and Elijah that Jesus discussed His death; given that a type of both the dead and the living speak to the promise of Resurrection; how can we conclude otherwise to the identity of these *His* two witnesses --- two men in dazzling white who were witnesses to His resurrection at the tomb, His ascension, and His coming again?! The two witnesses must be Moses and Elijah.

IS ENOCH ONE OF THE TWO WITNESSES?

I know that some insist that the second witness must be Enoch who, like Elijah, was also translated by God. There is not one thing that points to Enoch as being one of the Two Witnesses in the Scriptures. Enoch, unlike Elijah, is not even Jewish, predating, as he does, Abraham. Historically, Jews have been open to instruction only by other Jews, Gentiles, for the most part, need not apply. So why would God send one Jew and one non-Jew to the Nation of Israel? Adherents of this idea point to Hebrews 9:27 which states that it is appointed unto man once to die and after this comes the judgment. In a narrow and legalistic interpretation of this passage, they insist that God cannot use as one of the witnesses a man who has died because he cannot be made to die again. First of all, God can do anything and use anyone He wants, He is "Lord of the Sabbath, the Sabbath is not lord of Him." Secondly, they conveniently choose not to consider all of the other exceptions to this principle found in the Scriptures. What about the widow of Zarephath whose son Elijah raised from the dead, and the Shunammite woman's son who was raised from the dead by Elisha? What about the man who, when dead and buried in the sepulcher of Elisha, simply touched the bones of Elisha and lived again? What about Jairus's daughter, the widow of Nain's son, and Lazarus, all of whom were raised from the dead by Jesus? And finally, what about the many bodies that came to life and walked around Jerusalem after Jesus' resurrection? Do the legalists who view Hebrews 9 as an iron-clad rule mean to suggest that those people are still living? The idea is preposterous.

And what of Enoch himself? He also breaks this principle because he never died. If it is appointed unto man once to die, how did Enoch get by without dying? Enoch himself shows that Hebrews 9 is a principle, not an unbreakable rule that God *must* observe. Ah, but Enoch *must* die, they say. That is why Enoch must come back as one of the Two Witnesses, in order that he does die because every man must die. Oh? Paul vehemently refuted this theory in 1 Corinthians 15:51 when he wrote; "Behold, I shew you a mystery; We shall not all sleep [die], but we shall all be changed." He wrote again concerning this in I Thessalonians 4:17; "Then we which are alive and remain shall be caught up together with them in the clouds, to meet the Lord in the air: and so shall we ever be with the Lord." Hebrews 9 is an extremely valuable verse because it decries the idea of reincarnation as opposed to resurrection. It, however, does not bind the hand of God in any way.

MOSES AND ELIJAH CONTRASTED

The lives and personalities of Moses and Elijah could not be more diverse. Moses was brought up in extreme luxury in the palace of Pharaoh. He was educated there, and that would have meant the finest education which that time could give.

Elijah, on the other hand, was a rough and solitary man; dwelling in hills, caves, and desolate ravines all throughout Palestine. Very akin to John the Baptist, he wore a loincloth of skin and wrapped himself in a hairy cloak. Contrasted to the educated and urbane Moses, Elijah was a wild and ascetic man. According to the Bible, Moses was the meekest man who ever lived. Elijah was a very confrontational, almost anti-social man. When not confronting and accusing kings, or hewing false prophets to pieces, he could be found in melancholy isolation. What a pair they must make when they show up again in Israel! What a stir there must be as their identities become known!

And so the two men most revered in Judaism will roam Jerusalem preaching the astounding news (to Jews!) that Jesus is indeed Messiah. Incredibly, the Jews will have Moses to explain to them the symbolism of Christ in the Law and they will have Elijah to explain the words and meanings of the prophets. And both the Law and the Prophets have as their ultimate message the person of Jesus. Moses will reveal to them the significance of the Passover lamb and its blood upon the doorposts as realized in the death of Jesus upon the cross. He will explain to them their own temple furniture and how it symbolizes Jesus. The Law was given by God in the first place in order to prepare Jewish hearts to receive Jesus. Now it will be explained to the Jews by the very person who first brought it to their nation. Elijah will open to the Jews the ways in which the coming of Jesus fulfilled all of the prophecies concerning the coming of the Messiah. He will also explain to them the prophecies that deal with His imminent second coming. The effect upon the Jews will be electric. What happens next will only bring home more clearly the point that Jesus is Messiah.

TWO WITNESSES KILLED ON GOD'S TIMETABLE

For three-and-a-half years, these two witnesses have tormented Antichrist and he has been powerless before them. He has sought to kill them to no avail, but, then, suddenly he succeeds! Antichrist, at this point must take this as a sign of his superior strength against Jehovah God and, as Satan did upon killing the Son of God, must assume that he will soon be victor of the universe. But Revelation tells us that they are killed only when their testimony is completed. All is according to the timetable of God.

And speaking of the timetable of God, this verse is in a very unfortunate place for those who insist that Revelation's timetable begins in chapter 1 and goes straight through to chapter 22. If that is the case, how is it possible that the Beast (Antichrist) is killing the witnesses when he does not even appear on the earth for two more chapters? It does not make any sense if one interprets Revelation in that manner. It makes perfect sense, however, if one begins the story anew in chapter 12, understanding that this is the second time the story is being told. John will then tell it from the viewpoint of earth and new details will then be revealed. This is exactly how most prophecy is written. And this is how Revelation is written. If only we will be true to the details given, we can have understanding of the Scriptures.

Antichrist kills the Two Witnesses, and he kills them by crucifixion. (This must be Satan's favorite death.) We know this because verse 8 tells us that they are killed in Jerusalem where *also* our Lord was crucified. (Although some English versions of the Bible leave the world "also" out of the passage, this is not true to the Greek which includes the word *kai* which means "for also" in this context.)

Death by crucifixion of the Two Witnesses makes perfect sense. They will re-enact the death, resurrection, and ascension of Jesus. That is why they were discussing it all on the Mount of Transfiguration, and were, most probably, the two men in dazzling white both in the tomb and at the ascension of Jesus!

It is clear that the place where the two witnesses are killed is Jerusalem because that is where Jesus was crucified. Here it is spiritually called Sodom and Egypt. Sodom was an immoral place under judgment. So, now, is Jerusalem. Egypt signifies bondage and slavery. That, too, is the case here.

I have noted that Moses and Elijah re-enact the death, resurrection, and ascension of Jesus. That is true. What is left out is the burial of Jesus. The two witnesses are not buried. Possibly, Satan has fought so long and so hard against God to kill these men that he needs to continually view his victory over them. Possibly he is attempting to prevent the resurrection of these two bodies as happened to Jesus. Or maybe Antichrist is acting in the tradition of brutal tribal warfare that displays the bodies of conquered enemies as trophies. For whatever reason, he leaves their bodies in the street for all to view. And all do view them. John writes, "And they of the people and kindreds and tongues and nations shall see their dead bodies three days and an half, and shall not suffer their dead bodies to be put in graves. And they that dwell upon the earth shall rejoice over them, and make merry."

As reasonable as that sounds to us as twenty-first-century Christians, think a moment how the first-century Christian must have received this. The whole world able to view two bodies in a street in Jerusalem?! The idea was preposterous! Maybe, if one climbed up on a rooftop, one could see the bodies a couple of blocks away, but all of Jerusalem see them? All of Israel see them? All of the world see them? Truly, John was mad. But the injunction at the end of Revelation remained, and so these verses were not tampered with. Indeed, until the advent of satellite TV, this verse was impossible to understand. And yet John saw it and recorded it and the verse now stands the test of time. We are the uninformed and ignorant ones, not the words of prophecy.

WITNESSES' DEATH BRINGS SATANIC CELEBRATION

With the death of these two witnesses, the concept of a Christmas-type celebration breaks out all over again. It must have been a long and dreary ten-and-a-half years since peace was taken off the face of the earth and customs such as Christmas would have long disappeared. But here, with these two "enemies" defeated, the customs of Christmas (sans Christ, of course) come surging back. In the space of three days, the time Jesus was in the grave, presents are bought, sent and received!

Every eye is now glued to the televised picture of these two bodies in the street. That scene has usurped all other TV programming. When I first taught Revelation in 1982 and reached this verse, the people in the class found this very hard to swallow. What of the sitcoms? What of the game shows and soap operas? What of the other world news they asked? Who in the world could just watch two dead bodies for days?! And then came the infamous O.J. Simpson white Bronco chase where we watched one car drive the 405 Freeway for hours. At that point I felt totally vindicated. Indeed, news stations were that banal. Since that incident a few years ago, I have, from my living room in Southern California watched many a car chase lasting for hours, watched many a hostage stand-off situation, watched many a fire burning for hours. And when the tragedy of September 11, 2001, occurred, the coverage went from hours to days. This TV coverage of the dead bodies of the witnesses is not so far-fetched after all! Couple that with the fact that these two witnesses are truly hated by the world and to them are ascribed every plague, evil, wrong, and scourge happening on earth. The interest in their death cannot be overrated; if one doubts that the bad times are over, one has only to go to one's TV set to see their lifeless bodies and so be convinced and consoled.

TWO DEAD WITNESSES RESURRECTED

The two bodies, dead for three-and-a-half days, now have a most gruesome appearance. They have been lying on the street exposed to the elements. The bodies, mouths and tongues would be extremely bloated and swollen. Assuming that the witnesses have been taken down from the cross and laid on their backs, the blood in the bodies would have begun to settle in the backs and faces making them a deep purplish red. The hands and feet would now be black and the legs, arms and torsos would be bright pink and bright green (from gangrene). If the heat happens to be high, the effects would be intensified and maggots could easily have invaded the bodies. The odor from the bodies would be the foulest odor imaginable because of the decomposition. Now, suddenly these two foul bodies are changed in an instant as they rise to their feet! In view of all watching their TV screens or their computer monitors! No one can claim that the bodies are stolen this time as they did at the resurrection of Jesus. This happens in full view of the entire world and great fear falls upon mankind. As if that were not enough, a great voice is heard from heaven saying, "COME UP HITHER." With their enemies watching, Moses and Elijah ascend to heaven in a cloud - just as did Jesus.

JEWS' RECOGNITION OF JESUS AS MESSIAH IS PRECURSOR TO ARMAGEDDON

Again, just as happened after the death of Jesus, a great earthquake rocks the land. It is such an enormous earthquake that one-tenth of the city is destroyed and seven thousand men are killed in it. But, all of the Jews who are left finally see the light, see the connection to Jesus, and give glory to God. "For the children of Israel shall abide many days without a king, and without a prince, and without a sacrifice, and without an image, and without an ephod, and without teraphim: Afterward shall the children of Israel return, and seek the Lord their God, and David their king; and shall fear the Lord and his goodness in the latter days" (Hosea 3:4-5). "And I will pour upon the house of David, and upon the inhabitants of Jerusalem [exactly where this story takes place], the spirit of grace and of supplications: and they shall look upon me *whom they have pierced* [past tense], and they shall mourn for him, as one mourneth for his only son, and shall be in bitterness for him, as one that is in bitterness for his firstborn"(Zechariah 12:10, emphasis mine).

"They shall look upon me" the Scripture says. They *are* able to look upon Him because at this point He is coming back with all His saints. This is the time of Armageddon.

The Law and the Prophets as personified by Moses and Elijah have shown the Israelites the identity of Messiah. By recreating the ministry, death, resurrection and ascension of Jesus, the Jews accept what they once completely rejected. When Jesus came as a babe in the manger, the Jews were looking for a conquering King and they rejected a suffering Savior. Jesus said as much in Luke 19:44 when he told the Jews that they "knewest not the time of thy visitation." They missed it because they were predisposed to what role they thought the Messiah should take. In the last public sermon of his ministry, Jesus, the week before His death, went a final time to the Temple. He went in sorrow and in frustration at the rejection of Him as Messiah by His people, by the hardness of their hearts and by their unbelief. It is then that He gave voice to His lament that He would have gathered them together as a hen gathers her chickens but they would not. Speaking prophetically, He left the Temple saying, "Behold, your house is left unto you desolate. For I say unto you, Ye shall not see me henceforth, till ye shall say, Blessed is he that cometh in the name of the Lord" (Matthew 23:38-39). And so it has remained with the house of Israel. In contrast, the Gentile believers, used to only the "crumbs off the Jews' table" when it came to a relationship with God, immediately and joyfully accepted Jesus as Savior. Now, they, along with any Jews who, before now, have accepted Jesus as Savior, are coming back with Jesus as He comes. He is coming as that conquering King to the Jews; the conquering King the Jews always looked for and expected. It will end up just as they thought. But what a price will be paid by them. Jesus will come back with His Bride, the Church. Because the Jews rejected the first coming of Jesus as Suffering Savior, they will now settle for the far less exalted position of "friend of the Bridegroom"; a biblical phrase with somewhat the connotation of a best man at a wedding. Nonetheless, by Jesus' coming and by their acceptance of Him as Messiah, Israel will be saved from certain destruction at the hands of Antichrist. They will also finally have their king, their Jewish king, Jesus, and He will rule in His holy capital, Jerusalem, over the entire world for the next thousand years.

THE SEVENTH ANGEL BLOWS HIS TRUMPET/ THE KINGDOM OF DARKNESS BECOMES THE KINGDOM OF LIGHT

John informs us that with the ascent of the Two Witnesses and the great earthquake that kills seven thousand, the sixth trumpet (the second woe) is over. The next verse records that, indeed, the seventh angel now sounds his trumpet. Jesus, Himself, told John in Revelation 10 that "in the days of the voice of the seventh angel, when he shall begin to sound, the mystery of God should be finished, as he hath declared to his servants the prophets." The same account is given when John tells the story from the viewpoint of the earth. Revelation 16:17 records, "And the seventh angel poured out his vial into the air; and there came a great voice out of the temple of heaven, from the throne, saying, It is done." It is done. "And he shall reign forever and ever." The prayers of the saints who said, "Thy kingdom come, thy will be done" will now be answered. Christ will now take possession of the earth. Jesus has come and begun to reign. What can be left of the story? Again we have a clear signpost that the story is at an end and will be told again starting in the next chapter. When we ignore God's signposts, we open ourselves up to total confusion. That is why many have such a hard time with Revelation. It need not be so.

The great manuscripts record that instead of saying "the kingdoms [plural] of this world are become the kingdoms [plural] of our Lord, and of his Christ", the actual phrasing is "the kingdom [singular] of this world is become the kingdom [singular] of our Lord and of his Christ." This makes far more sense. There are only two kingdoms: the light and the darkness; the good and the evil. Now we are told that the kingdom of darkness (the kingdom of this world) has become the kingdom of light (the kingdom of our Lord and of his Christ). What a joy it is for us to have this recorded! Evil is defeated, it does not win! Remember this as you toil in this world and it seems that justice and goodness are rare commodities indeed. That is true now while this world is ruled by the Ruler of Darkness, but that is only a temporary truth. God will prevail, Satan will falter and fail. Evil will be defeated. The gates of hell will not prevail.

WORSHIP IN HEAVEN

Before Jesus comes to begin to reign, there is, as there always is, a worship service in heaven. The twenty-four elders, saints every one, fall upon their faces and worship God. If only we would learn the principle of prayer and worship before action! *Everything* that happens on earth is a result of something that has already happened in heaven.

ARMAGEDDON ARRIVES

"And the nations were angry." This is a bit of an understatement. This is a reference to Armageddon when Antichrist assembles all of the earth together to destroy every vestige of anything Jewish. Only God stands between the Jews and total annihilation. God is enough.

"Behold, the day of the Lord cometh, and thy spoil shall be divided in the midst of thee. For I will gather all nations against Jerusalem to battle; and the city shall be taken, and the houses rifled, and the women ravished; and half of the city shall go forth into captivity, and the residue of the people shall not be cut off from the city. *Then shall the Lord go forth, and fight against those nations, as when he fought in the day of battle.* And his feet shall stand in that day upon the mount of Olives, which is before Jerusalem on the east, and the mount of Olives shall cleave in the midst thereof toward the east and toward the west, and there shall be a very great valley: and half of the mountain shall remove toward the north, and half of it toward the south" (Zechariah 14: 1-4, emphasis mine).

Although Armageddon is dealt with very briefly at this point in Revelation, John will be shown the battle later in much more detail. Suffice it to say now that this is a time of judgment and reward. Jesus will judge the nations and reward the saints with authority over the remaining people of the earth.

AWARENESS OF SIGNS THAT COME BEFORE RAPTURE

At the end of verse 18, John makes another statement that must have seemed enigmatic to the first-century reader. He writes that the Lord will destroy them that destroy the earth. Until the explosion in 1945 at Trinity Site in Southern New Mexico, which was the culmination of years of secret work on the creation of an atomic bomb, to even *threaten* the whole world had been beyond man's capability. People have argued that what John meant was the "whole known world at that time." But John is not making the statement; the twenty-four elders who are in heaven are making the statement in praise to Jesus and from the vantage point of heaven, the entire world is known to the elders! They know that at the point in time when this will occur, the capability will exist to destroy the whole world. This puts a nail in the coffin of the idea of an imminent rapture - a rapture that could have happened at any point since Pentecost until now. According to the Scriptures, it could not. Certain things had to be fulfilled. So far we have seen that the Jews had to be back in Israel (and the Scriptures make it clear that every Jew will be there, not just some), the temple had to be rebuilt, and the capability of total world destruction had to exist.

But, some say, that could all happen after the Rapture takes place. WHAT??? We have seen what happens since the rapture. Peace is taken from the earth, every plague imaginable has been loosed upon the earth, fire has raged, waters are turned to blood, supernatural torment abounds. Who in the world is going to have the resources, the time or even the desire to build incredible temples and cities? Antichrist will not; he will be busy fighting against God and trying to keep his empire from destructing. No, if it cannot happen after the Rapture, then it must happen before the Rapture. Jesus said there would be unmistakable signs before His coming. "And when these thing begin to come to pass, then look up, and lift up your heads; for your redemption draweth nigh. And he spake to them a parable; Behold the fig tree, and all the trees; When they now shoot forth, ye see and know of your own selves that summer is now nigh at hand. So likewise ye, when ye see these things come to pass, know ye that the kingdom of God is nigh at hand" (Luke 21: 28-31).

There are more signs that must be fulfilled before Rapture. We do not know exactly when Rapture will take place, but we can be sure that the time is coming when the signs are fulfilled. God never intended us to be totally unaware, He intended us to be on the watch and ready. More will be said about this when Revelation 13 is discussed.

THE HEAVENLY ARK IN HEAVEN

The final word that John gives concerning the heavenly view of the times between Rapture and Armageddon is this: "And the temple of God was opened in heaven, and there was seen in his temple the ark of his testament: and there were lightnings, and voices, and thunderings, and an earthquake, and great hail." The temple is opened and the Ark is revealed. The Ark was the sign of God's protection and presence. So full of the presence of God was it that the Jews were forbidden to touch it on pain of death. It will continue to be so until the time that Jesus himself, God in person, reigns over Israel (Jeremiah 3:16). Both the earthly Ark of the Covenant and the earthly Temple are copies of the heavenly ones. The Ark was the only furniture in the Tabernacle that specifically looked forward to the coming of Jesus. The Ark was covered by the Mercy Seat that stood for atonement for the sins of the people. The Ark also symbolized the possession of the land. It was carried before Israel when they went into battle. It disappeared during the days of Josiah and it has not been seen since. Isaiah 11:11-12 speaks of the "ensign" which shall appear in the latter days that will lead the people of Israel out of captivity once again. I believe that this is the original Ark of the Covenant and that it has been kept safe and will reappear at the appointed time according to the timetable of God.

Here, with John, we see the heavenly ark. It appears just before the Second Coming and the restoration of all things to the Jewish nation. It is accompanied by lightning, voices and thundering because judgment to the world will accompany the promise.

THE GREAT EARTHQUAKE

John records "an earthquake." Here again is another incredible understatement. This one is such an understatement that it reminds me of Genesis 1:16, when Moses declares that, "God made two great lights; the greater light to rule the day and the lesser light to rule the night: *he made the stars also*" (emphasis mine). The creation of the incredible system of stars, planets, comets, and so forth, is included almost as a footnote! The Bible is never hyperbolic, to the contrary, it is minimalist in the extreme, even when recording mind-shattering events. This earthquake is an example. It is the greatest earthquake that ever hit the world. It is the earthquake that changes the degree of the polar axes and forever changes the topography and climate of Planet Earth. More will be said about this at a later time.

The record of the heavenly view of the ten-and-one-half years between Rapture and the Battle of Armageddon is now complete. Revelation 12 will begin to tell the story anew, beginning again at the Rapture; but this time John will see it from the vantage point of the earth. It will be as spellbinding as the first story has been.

PART FOUR: TRIBULATION AS SEEN FROM EARTH'S VIEWPOINT

Figure 3 Part 4: Revelation 12 - 16

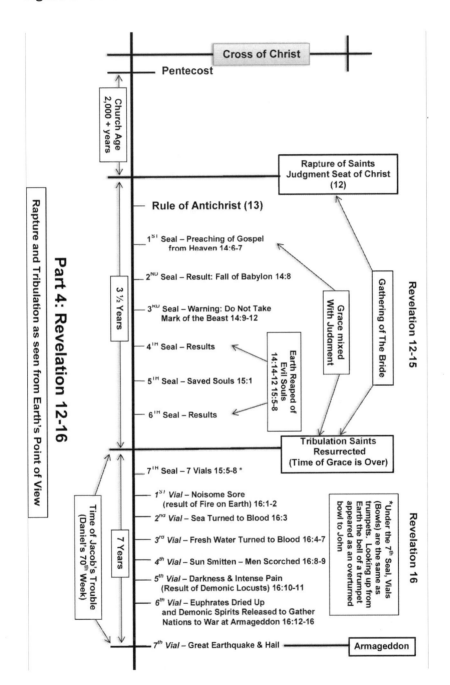

CHAPTER 14
THE RAPTURE OF THE CHURCH AND WAR IN HEAVEN
Revelation 12

JOHN'S VISION CONTINUES - THE FUTURE DISCLOSED, NOT THE PAST

As we begin Revelation 12, it is necessary to remember the divine structure of this book. It is clear that it is divine because it was given by Jesus Himself at the end of Revelation 1 when he told John, "Write the things which thou hast seen, and the things which are, and the things which shall be hereafter (after these things)." We see, then, that the divisions are: (1) the things seen (things past); (2) the things which are (things present); (3) the things which shall be (things future). Only one thing in Revelation was history when Jesus gave this direction, and it was the vision of Jesus that John saw in Revelation 1. The present would be the Church Age that was outlined in Revelation 2 and 3.

Note that Revelation 4 begins with this phrase "after this." Beginning with Revelation 4, everything that John sees would be in the future. Thus, from Revelation 4 on, everything John saw was prophetic, and prophecy does not concern itself with things past. Obviously. A prophecy that deals with past events would be oxymoronic. Revelation 12 is, like the rest of the book, prophetic. Therefore, it does not describe a past event. To further corroborate this, the Greek word translated "wonder" in verse 1 ("And there appeared a great wonder") is *semeion*. W. E. Vine, noted Greek scholar, says that its literal meaning is "tokens pertaining to *future* events" (emphasis mine). Joseph H. Thayer, another greatly respected Greek authority defines its meaning as being "of signs portending remarkable events soon to happen." This is the word used by Jesus in Luke 21:11, "And great earthquakes shall be in divers places, and famines, and pestilences; and fearful sights and great signs shall there be from heaven." So, too, does Acts 2:19, "And I will shew wonders in heaven above and signs in the earth beneath; blood, and fire, and vapour of smoke." The obvious context is that these things will happen in the future. Revelation 12:1 is no different. Revelation does not deal with past events. The word "revelation" means "unveiling." One does not unveil past events, they are already unveiled by the mere fact of their having been.

EVENTS OF REVELATION 4-11 NOW SEEN FROM EARTH'S VIEW

Revelation 12 begins again the story of exactly what has transpired in heaven during the course of Revelation 4-11. This time the story is told from the perspective of earth. The perspective of heaven was given first because everything that happens on earth begins in heaven. We will now see the time from Rapture to Armageddon as the earth will experience it. Up until now, we have seen the time frame from Rapture to the return of Jesus at Armageddon from the heavenly perspective. And so, we have seen the tribulation saints (the souls under the altar under the fifth seal, and, later, those same souls praising Jesus in heaven), but we have not seen any details at all as to how they came to be martyred. We have not seen the rise of Antichrist, nor have we seen his world system. All of this will now be revealed with the earthly view of the same events.

As said earlier, this method of telling a story, with or without symbols, and then retelling it with different emphasis, is a common prophetic device. This is the device used in Daniel when he has four different visions concerning the same topic: the world empires present at Daniel's time, and the world empires to come. Although the visions concern themselves with the empires, each vision is different and each one gives us different details. Jesus employs this same prophetic device during His Olivet Discourse in the Gospels, where He recounts what will be the signs of His coming back. He tells the story, then He goes back to the beginning and fills in details.

Revelation 4 (the beginning of the heavenly view) began by the trumpet call to John to come up to heaven. A door in heaven is opened up to him and he is caught up to heaven. Revelation 12 (the beginning of the earthly view) opens with the vision of the woman, the child and the dragon. Both chapters begin with the same occurrence: Rapture.

A WOMAN - THE VISIBLE CHURCH

There appears in heaven a great wonder: A woman clothed with the sun, the moon under her feet, and a crown of twelve stars upon her head. A woman, symbolically, represents a religious system. The woman pictured here is the symbol of the visible Christian Church. Later on in Revelation we will see another woman who will symbolize a different religious system. That will be the Great Harlot that represents the religious system of Satan. What is meant by the "visible" church? It is the church that is apparent to the world; the people who attend services on Sunday and/or who say that they are Christian. But Jesus Himself said that not all who called him "Lord, Lord" were His. Remember that the church type that is strongest and most visible to the world at the Rapture is the Laodicean church. That is the church where Jesus is on the outside, knocking at their door to come in. This is the church that Jesus says He will vomit up. But, at the time of the Rapture, along side the Laodicean church will exist the loving, powerful, and doctrinally pure, church of Philadelphia. To understand fully the symbol of the pregnant woman of Revelation 12, one must integrate the prophetic words of Revelation 3. Jesus, Himself, identified them both as churches, but only one of them would be taken at the Rapture. Here, again, we see the same prophecy played out. Only the child is taken; the woman is left.

Even now, not all the people in the church are really Christians. And only God knows who, indeed, belongs to Him. Those people, those who truly belong to Jesus, make up the "invisible" church within the "visible" church. The woman is the visible church, made up of both believers and un-believers. The invisible church, the "true believers," is symbolized by the child that the woman carries. The child is found in the body of the woman and is part of her, but at the same time he is a separate entity. So it is with the true believers. They are found within the Church, but yet they comprise a group entirely their own.

The woman is clothed with the sun. The sun is the symbol of light. Likewise the Church is the custodian of the light, the Truth of God. Jesus said to her, "Ye are the light of the world." Not only that, but, I believe that the true Church will be in its purest earthly form at the time when Jesus comes for her. After all, He is coming for His beloved Philadelphian Church, His Bride without spot or blemish. The trials that will happen at the end of the church age will create two opposite churches. Not only will the Philadelphian Church, the church of brotherly love, result from them, so also will the Laodicean Church. That church will be comprised of Christians who have become apostate, and also those who were false believers from the beginning. Although both churches are found in the woman, the heavenly light around the woman is a consequence only of the true church, the child that she carries.

The moon is under the feet of the woman. Feet are the symbol for dominion. The moon, as the antithesis of the sun, is symbolic of the darkness; thus, the Church is victorious over evil and darkness. She wears a crown - she is royalty before the birth of the child. Indeed she is, for part of her is the Bride of the very Son of God, a bride without spot or blemish. But notice also, the condition of the woman after the birth. She is a fugitive, not one trace of her exalted position remains. That is because all the glory rested in the child. When she is without the child, she is without any glory. The Church only had this standing before God because of the true saints - the overcomers. Without them, she is only the Laodicean Church, naked and poor and blind.

The number of stars in her crown is twelve (Revelation 1:12). Twelve is symbolic for the actions of God upon the world. The number representing God is three; the number of the world is four; three times four equals twelve. At the present time, God acts upon the world primarily through the Church, so it is fitting that she is crowned with twelve stars. Remember also that there were also twelve tribes of Israel, there were twelve original apostles.

This woman is about to deliver a baby. This delivery will be the Rapture. The baby is the symbol for the overcomers, the true believers, the "invisible church." Their birth will be the Rapture itself. Isaiah, Micah, and Paul all use this exact symbolism.

"*Like as a woman with child, that draweth near the time of her delivery, is in pain, and crieth out in her pangs;* so have we been in thy sight, O Lord. We have been with child, we have been in pain, we have as it were brought forth wind; we have not wrought any deliverance in the earth; neither have the inhabitants of the world fallen. *Thy dead men shall live, together with my dead body shall they arise.* Awake and sing, ye that dwell in dust: for thy dew is as the dew of herbs, and the earth shall cast out the dead" (Isaiah 26: 17-19, emphasis mine).

"Before she travailed, she brought forth; before her pain came, she was delivered of a manchild. Who hath heard such a thing? Who hath seen such things? Shall the earth be made to bring forth in one day? Or shall a nation be born at once? For as soon as Zion travailed, she brought forth her children" (Isaiah 66:7-8).

"Therefore will he give them up [the nation of Israel], until the time that she which travaileth [is in labor] hath brought forth [has given birth]: then the remnant of his brethren shall return unto the children of Israel" (Micah 5:3). (This prophecy says that the rest of the Jews will come in after the Rapture, which indeed, they do.)

"But of the times and the seasons, brethren, ye have no need that I write unto you. For yourselves know perfectly that the day of the Lord so cometh as a thief in the night. For when they shall say, Peace and safety; then sudden destruction cometh upon them, *as travail upon a woman with child*; and they shall not escape. But ye, brethren, are not in darkness, that that day should overtake you as a thief. Ye are all the children of light, and the children of the Day: we are not of the night, nor of darkness" (I Thessalonians 5:1-5).

The symbol of a woman in labor always indicates a resurrection or a deliverance. This is a constant throughout the Scriptures. Jesus, himself, tied this symbolism into His own death and resurrection in John 16:16-22 when He spoke of the disciples' sorrow over His death. "A little while, and ye shall not see me: and again, a little while, and ye shall see me, because I go to the Father...*a woman when she is in travail hath sorrow, because her hour is come: but as soon as she is delivered of the child, she remembereth no more the anguish,* for joy that a man is born into the world. And ye now therefore have sorrow: but I will see you again, and your heart shall rejoice, and your joy no man taketh from you" (emphasis mine).

Jesus clearly links the analogy of the birth of the woman with His own resurrection.

Just as labor pains increase in frequency and intensity as a woman progresses through labor, so, too, will the signs which indicate the coming of Rapture increase in frequency and in intensity as Rapture draws nigh. These signs will be dealt with at great length in chapter 15.

The woman, too, in Revelation 12 longs for the delivery; she is in pain. This is spiritually accurate if she is the Church. Not only do the saints await their release from earth, the Laodicean Church wants them gone as fervently as they wish to be gone. After all, True Believers are always an insult and an embarrassment to Enlightened Free-Thinkers. But someone else is also obsessed by this birth. The dragon stands before the woman in order that he might kill and consume her baby as soon as it is born.

POWERFUL SATANIC CONFEDERATION OPPOSES GOD'S PLAN

There can be no dispute over the symbolism of the dragon for verse 9 identifies him as Satan. John describes him as a great, red dragon with seven heads and ten horns and seven crowns upon his heads. One cannot have a complete view of either the spiritual or physical world without the story of the parallel force. One must contend with this truth. Out of the vastness of the universe we find only two confederations - one evil and one good. The dragon symbolized the one that is evil. As stated before, seven signifies completion, therefore with the seven heads on the dragon, we have the picture of Satan in all his power throughout the ages.

Satan has a mighty confederation of evil, both demonic and human, numbering millions upon millions. There is vast power behind him, for principality after principality have fallen in line behind him. Because of his dominant state over humans and their planet, the very humans born here were made his slaves and servants. It was against this entrenched, overwhelming evil that Christ Jesus rose up to battle. It was a battle so horrible that it wrung even His mighty soul with unspeakable anguish, both as He sweat great drops of blood in the Garden of Gethsemane, and upon the cross itself. Because of that battle, every captive who so wished could exit slavery for liberty in Christ. Notwithstanding that, many have not, and so here is Satan, at the end of the age, in command on earth with his terrible power.

The seven heads of Satan signify the six major empires that have been in place on earth throughout the history of man: Egypt, Assyria, Babylon, Medea-Persia, Greece, and Rome, and the worldwide empire that is now in place as John sees this scene, the empire of Antichrist. That is because the world empires (not necessarily individual nations), have always been controlled by Satan. He is the power behind the kingdoms of this earth; he is the ruler of this world.

Consider the temptation of Christ in the wilderness. Satan came to Jesus with the three most potent temptations he had in his power. One temptation appealed to Jesus' flesh (His hunger). One appealed to His pride (letting the angels catch Him as He threw Himself off the mountain). But the most powerful one was the one that Satan saved to the last. That one appealed to Jesus' mission. Jesus had come, in part, to wrest control of the earth away from Satan. God had mandated that the redemption of the earth, along with the redemption of human bodies and souls, be accomplished by the Cross. But Satan came to Jesus and offered Him a shortcut. "You can have the governments of the world," said Satan, "just worship me." The temptation to Jesus was to fulfill His mission by bypassing the Cross. After all, it would result in almost the same end, just by different means; easier means, and not God's means. This would not have been a temptation had not the world governments been Satan's to give. But Jesus looked His greatest temptation in the eye and defeated it by His obedience to the will of God, submission to the Cross. Daniel had prophesied long ago that all the territory that had been usurped by Satan would be redeemed by God, but it had to be done on God's terms. It was.

Knowing that Satan would be the force behind every world government might have been the reason why God so clearly favored small and independent settlements of people. Genesis 1:28 records that God wanted mankind to spread out all over the earth. He gave the same commandment to Noah after the flood in Genesis 9:1. The tower of Babel was, in part, rebellion against this commandment as the people of the earth said, "Go to, let us build us a city and a tower, whose top may reach unto heaven; and let us make us a name, *lest we be scattered abroad upon the face of the whole earth*" (Genesis 11:4, emphasis mine).

SEVEN HEADS - TEN HORNS - SATAN'S HISTORIC POWER OVER KINGDOMS OF WORLD

If the seven heads represent the complete picture of the power of Satan in human government throughout history, the ten horns signify the nations that came out of the Roman Empire after her fall. They correspond to the ten toes of Daniel's vision. They are in view here because prophecy mandated that they would remain until the coming of Antichrist. He has now come and the ten nations will be the nucleus of the seventh world empire; the empire controlled by Antichrist.

Daniel saw these ten horns in his vision of the four beasts, recorded in Daniel 7. Because it was prophetic and because prophecy does not concern itself with past events, Daniel did not speak of the first two world empires. He only told of the empire that was currently in place - Babylon - and the four that would come after it. He prophesied that the eagle (Babylon) would be followed by the bear (Medea-Persia), that would conquer Babylon and who would also add new territory to its empire. This was symbolized by the bear having three ribs in its mouth, and, true to Scripture, the Medea-Persian empire conquered three empires: Babylon, Lydia, and Egypt.

The leopard followed next in Daniel's vision. It symbolized Greece. This leopard was unique in that it had both four wings and four heads. Alexander the Great was the mighty Greek warrior who conquered the Medea-Persian Empire, and when he died, it was divided up among his four generals. Prophecy is amazing in its detail!

The final beast (Rome) was not identified as a recognizable animal, it was only said to be completely different from the other beasts. It was said to be both dreadful and terrible and exceedingly strong. This was where Daniel saw the ten horns; they were upon the head of the fourth beast. No other beast (empire) was prophesied to control the world after this until the very end of time that would see the reign of Antichrist. Instead, the Roman Empire would remain broken up into a small number of countries that would remain independent until the coming of Antichrist. In prophecy, ten symbolizes a small but indeterminate number. It does not have to indicate exactly ten countries any more than the Imperial Persecutions of the Smyrnan Church had to last exactly ten days. There may very well be exactly ten countries in the last days scenario, but it is not mandated by Scripture that it be so.

SATAN TAKES WORLD CONTROL

Since the collapse of the Roman Empire, there has not been a one-world government. There have been world powers and there have been attempts at world control, but none have succeeded. None will succeed until Antichrist comes upon the world scene. Daniel sees exactly that when he records that a very odd thing happens among the ten horns - a little horn (Antichrist) comes up among them and takes control. The dragon (Satan) now controls the ten horns completely.

Revelation 12:4 records that Satan drew the third part of the stars of heaven and cast them to the earth in order to help him kill the child. Most expositors explain this as the initial rebellion in heaven when Satan and his angels were thrown out of heaven. True, they were forced to leave the presence of God, but they certainly were not confined strictly to Planet Earth. If that were true, Paul would not have called Satan the "prince of the power of *the air*" nor would he have said in Ephesians that we wrestle with these satanic powers and principalities *in the heavenly places*! Furthermore, that particular rebellion of Satan and his angels is past, and *prophecy does not concern itself with past events*! Finally, it was not Satan who cast the third part of the stars of heaven to the earth, it was God who did so as a consequence of their rebellion.

Therefore, what this Scripture is saying is that at this time, in preparation for the birth of the child, Satan will marshal all his forces, which number one-third of all of the angels, and he will cast them to earth. This will mean increased Satanic activity upon earth. We know conclusively, because of Scripture, that Antichrist will appear on earth before the Rapture. When he does, he will come with amazing signs and wonders that will deceive many. He may also prepare the human population for this with a greater frequency of "alien" encounters (demonic encounters). It may mean increased psychic powers being manifested in people on earth. By whatever means, Satan will prepare the earth as best as he can for this fight, and then he will gather his forces together to himself on the earth to prevent the new-born baby from living. He will use every force at his command to attempt to kill the child. What does that mean? It is made clear when we see what happens to the child when he is born. Verse 5 tells us that he is caught up to God and to His throne. That is exactly what Satan is attempting to defeat by bringing to bear all his force in the killing of the child. Satan is going to war to prevent the Rapture!

It is impossible to estimate what would comprise a third part of the angels of heaven. Would it be millions? Would it be billions? We do not know. But we do know that Satan was the most beautiful and powerful creation that God ever made. And when he left, he left with a third of the force of heaven. The two sides, Good and Evil, have fought ever since. But they have not fought a battle like this since the initial rebellion of Satan. That is because both sides know what this war is going to mean. One side will lose and, for that side, too much would be lost. In a less serious way it would be like Kennedy and Khrushchev with their hands on the atomic button during the Cold War. To push that button would have to be an act of final desperation for the weaker side. It becomes such a situation for Satan at the Rapture and he goes to war.

It has been about two thousand years since Calvary, and yet the bodies of the believers still remain in their graves. Satan fought mightily over the resurrection of one single human, Moses. Imagine how he will fight over the resurrection of millions of bodies! It now becomes very clear why the timing of Rapture must be such a secret. Jesus said that only the Father knew the exact time, even He [Jesus] did not. Why? Because as a man, Jesus might have allowed Satan access to that fact and the element of surprise would have been forever lost. You see, Satan is a formidable foe and heaven never underestimates him. Only the foolish on earth do that. The safe arrival of all of the souls that belong to Jesus, whether dead or alive, will bring about a war in the heavens the likes of which the Universe has not seen since the first rebellion in heaven! This is a war of universal proportion, of unparalleled magnitude. When the Church goes to Jesus, it signals Satan's doom. He must stop it at any price. That is why Paul prayed: "I pray God your whole spirit and soul and body be preserved blameless unto the coming of our Lord Jesus Christ. Faithful is he that calleth you, who also will do it" (I Thessalonians 5:23-24). Notice that Paul prays specifically for the spirit and soul and body of each Christian. The spirit, soul, and body of Jesus each went a different place after his death and it seems probable to me that ours will too. It is at Rapture that those triune parts will be reunited, so Paul prays that they each be preserved. If Satan allows that reunification of the Bride of Christ, he has lost everything.

Because of its extreme importance and because of the fierce opposition of Satan to it, all of the forces of heaven will be needed to accomplish the Rapture of the saints. Michael is the commander of the heavenly army of God. Not only is he is the only archangel ever named, he is mentioned by name whenever force is required in order to see that God's will is done. First Thessalonians 4:16 tells us that the raptured saints will hear three sounds: the shout of the Lord, the voice of the archangel, and the trumpet of God. The fact that Revelation 12 mentions the involvement of Michael dovetails perfectly with the account in Thessalonians and lets us know, once again, that the story of Revelation 12 is the story of the Rapture. Now, Michael and his angels will war against the dragon and his angels. Michael and his angels will prevail.

THE CHILD - WHO IS HE?

The child is said to be a "man child." The literal Greek rendering is "a son, a male." The Greek word used here for son is *huios*. According to W.E. Vine, the word primarily signifies the relationship of offspring to parent. Indeed, in Scripture, the word "son or sons of God" is used exclusively for directly created beings of God. Adam was called a son of God, as were angels. We are allowed to be called sons of God, directly created by Him, when we are spiritually born again. Furthermore, to use the word "son" as opposed to "child" has an additional import. According to Jewish law, it was the <u>son</u> who received the inheritance of the father. Hence, the word "son" denotes a promise that the word "child" does not.

However, the use of the word "son" does not exclude female believers. Jesus uses *huios* in a very significant way in Matthew 5:9 when He says, "Blessed are the peacemakers, for they shall be called the sons of God," and also in verses 44-45 when He says, "Love your enemies, and pray for them that persecute you; that ye may be sons of your Father which is in heaven." Clearly, no one would dispute the fact that women are included in this instruction and reward. Galatians 3:26-28 makes this fact clear when Paul writes: "For ye are all the children of God by faith in Christ Jesus. For as many of you as have been baptized into Christ have put on Christ. There is neither Jew nor Greek, there is neither bond nor free, there is neither male nor female: for ye are all one in Christ Jesus."

We will all, male and female, receive the inheritance as "sons of God", because we all, male and female, are part of the Bride (*another* gender specific term but feminine this time).

Why, then, emphasize the maleness of the child? It must be understood that the Greek word, *arsen* used for "male" in the text, is neutral in gender. The meaning, then, is like the meaning of the word "mankind." We easily understand that to encompass the human race - both male and female - even though the word used is "man". The child, then, is not limited to men only or even to just one man. Just as the Woman, denoting the visible Church, is understood to encompass both male and female believers, so, too, does her child, denoting the overcoming church, encompass both male and female believers.

But special emphasis is placed upon the masculine qualities of this church by the use of the term "manchild." We would all agree that traits may be considered masculine or feminine while being possessed by either sex. For example, nurturing and tender care are considered to be feminine traits but are quite admirable when possessed by men. Here, then is a child possessing traits that seem to be markedly masculine. This makes perfect sense. As Joseph Seiss writes: "Here are men and women, in multitudes upon multitudes, of whom the world was not worthy, alike pervaded with the highest qualities of virtue, courage, self-denial and strength. They are all conquerors. They all have overcome the world, triumphed over the powers of darkness, won the race of faith, and through the grace of God possessed themselves of titles to everlasting crowns and honours. Their masculinity in these respects is unquestionable and most intense, whether they be men or women as to sex. Nor is this so true and characteristic of any people that have lived, or that shall live, as it is of the true children of God of all time. Here we find all the noblest and best of the race, and the embodiment of the highest virtue and wisdom that ever pulsated in the arteries of humanity. Here is the proper 'man child' if ever there was or will be one upon earth"[21]

Many have said that the man child must be Jesus because it is He alone who will rule the nations with a rod of iron. This is incorrect. Again let me quote Revelation 2: 26-27, which is His promise to those who overcome in the Thyatiran church, "And he that overcometh, and keepeth my works unto the end, to him will I give power over the nations: *And he shall rule them with a rod of iron*; as the vessels of a potter shall they be broken to shivers: even as I received of my Father." We have already seen that each of the promises to the overcomers of each church are for every overcomer in every age. Thus, the overcomers - those who will be raptured whether living or dead - are told that they will rule the nations with a rod of iron! Psalm 149:5-9 promises the saints that exact promise: "Let the saints be joyful in glory: let them sing aloud upon their beds. Let the high praises of God be in their mouth, and a two-edged sword be in their hand; To execute vengeance upon the heathen, and punishments upon the people; To bind their kings with chains, and their nobles with fetters of iron; To execute upon them the judgment written: this honour have all his saints. Praise ye the Lord."

Although the occurrence of Rapture fits the symbolism of the birth of the child perfectly, it is missed by most commentators. The most common explanation of these symbols is that the woman pictured in Revelation 12 is Israel and Jesus is the child. Does the story fit? No. First, the woman here is in an exalted position *in heaven*. Israel was not in this glorious position, Israel is never said to be involved in spiritual warfare. If she had the light of God's wisdom, how did she miss Jesus' coming? She had already killed the prophets who had come her way, and then she rejected and killed Jesus. This is not light, this is darkness. The Church, on the other hand, *is* greatly involved in heavenly matters: Ephesians 2:6 tells us that Christians are even now *seated in the heavenly places* in Christ Jesus.

A second problem with the idea of the Woman as Israel is that the woman here does not kill her baby. The baby is never in any danger from her. For the analogy of Jesus and Israel to fit, the child here would have to be killed by the woman. The child is not, in fact, he is *never* killed. Thirdly, the woman in Revelation flees to the wilderness for three-and-a-half years after the birth of the baby. This is mentioned twice! Satan did not chase Israel around the wilderness for that time but Satan will do exactly that to the Church after the Rapture, *and* he will do it for exactly three-and-a-half years!

The earth did not help Israel for three-and-a-half years after the birth of Jesus, and, further, verse 17 speaks of the "other offspring" of the Woman. The Church will have the tribulation saints as other offspring but the nation of Israel did not ever produce any other offspring. Some say that the Church is Israel's offspring, but the Church is never spoken of as being born of Israel, the Church is born of God. Although Israelites were called the natural branches and the Gentiles were called the grafted-on branches, the tree was Jesus! Israel did not birth the Church, Jesus did. If the Woman is Israel, then, who are her other biological offspring?

Another very important part of the story in Revelation 12 is the catching up of the child immediately after the birth. Jesus was not caught up to God immediately after his birth. To the contrary, he ascended to God *under his own power* thirty-three years later. And finally, there was no war in heaven over the ascension of Jesus. The war for our souls was over at that point, having been fought and won at the Cross. There will be, as has been mentioned, a future war between Michael and Satan. It will be over the resurrection of the bodies of the saints and it will take place at the Rapture. Revelation 12 tells us that at that time the great accuser of the brethren will be thrown down. Although that fits the time line of the Rapture perfectly, it does not fit at all the time of the birth of Jesus, for

Satan has continued to accuse the Brethren two thousand years and counting!

THE TRUE/VISIBLE CHURCH IS CAUGHT UP BY THE RAPTURE

The phrase "caught up" used here in conjunction with the child, implies a rescue out of great danger. The record of this in Daniel 12:1-2 describes the same thing when he uses the phrase "shall be delivered": "And at that time shall Michael stand up, the great prince which standeth for the children of thy people: and there shall be a time of trouble such as never was since there was a nation even to that same time: and at that time thy people shall be delivered, every one that shall be found written in the book. And many of them that sleep in the dust of the earth shall awake, some to everlasting life, and some to shame and everlasting contempt."

The word that Daniel uses for "delivered" is the Hebrew word *malat*. It means "to rescue, specifically to bring forth" with the implication that the action is necessary because the situation is a gravely dangerous one. Paul uses a Greek word with similar meaning *harpazo* in 1 Thessalonians 4:17 when he teaches about Rapture: "Then we which are alive and remain shall be *caught up* together with them in the clouds, to meet the Lord in the air: and so shall we ever be with the Lord." *Harpazo* means "to be snatched up quickly, to take by force." It was the word used in Acts when Philip was caught up and carried away when he was with the Ethiopian eunuch. It was the word used when Paul said he was caught up to the Third Heaven. It is the word Jude uses when he tells us to rescue believers who are entangled in deadly sin, "pulling them out of the fire." Perhaps the most vivid picture of intended force is in John 6:15, "Jesus, therefore, perceiving that they were intending to take Him by force (*harpazo*) to make Him King, withdrew again to the mountain by Himself alone."

Harpazo is *not* a word that is ever used of the Ascension of Jesus. Two words are used in Scripture for that event. The word used for the ascension in Luke is *anaphero*. It means to "carry up." The word *analambano* is used in Mark and Acts. The meaning is "to take to oneself." This is exactly what God did to Jesus, He received him as a father receives a son. No force of any sort is implied in the usage of either of these words. That stands in marked contrast to the word used for Rapture. The two events, Rapture and the Ascension of Jesus, are completely different events. It is we who will be caught up, Jesus ascended! Jesus' ascension was a visible statement of victory, not rescue! War did not break out in the heavens when Jesus ascended, an unbelievable war will break out over Rapture. Further, Michael had nothing to do with the ascension of Jesus. He has much to do with the rapture. Paul tells us that the voice of the archangel will be present at Rapture, Daniel tells us that Michael goes to battle ("stands up") in order to facilitate resurrection. John, too, tells us that Michael is involved. Michael is the one who wars with Satan and his angels in order to facilitate our safe arrival to heaven. At Rapture, we will hear the voice of Jesus as He calls us to Himself, but Michael's voice is also heard as he calls forth his forces; the trumpet sounds, and the battle over us begins.

If symbolism is used as a prophetic device, it is consistent within the example. Thus, a symbolic woman would give birth to a symbolic child. You would never have a symbolic woman giving birth to a literal child nor a literal woman giving birth to a symbolic child. It is much like the grammatical rule against mixing singular nouns with plural verbs. A case in point is given in this very vision. Satan is, by necessity, symbolized. The symbol is explained as being Satan, but it is the Great Red Dragon, a symbol and not the literal Satan, who interacts with both the symbolic woman and the symbolic child.

THE WOMAN IS NOT MARY - THE CHILD IS NOT JESUS
Given the truth of this, many then reply that the woman is Mary and the child is still Jesus. Ignoring the fact the dragon remains symbolic and so must the woman also, the story does not fit the birth of Jesus. There is simply no getting around that fact. We see in the symbolic picture that the child is caught up to heaven immediately after his birth. In order for this to be a picture of Jesus and Mary, Jesus would have had to have been caught up from the manger.

Consider also, the symbolism of the woman escaping to the wilderness. Although Joseph and Mary were warned in a dream to leave Bethlehem and flee into Egypt, the timing is not right for it to fit Revelation 12; it did not happen immediately after Jesus' birth. In fact, Jesus was probably around two years old when Joseph received his warning from God to flee with Jesus to Egypt. And although the woman is alone in her flight in the story, Mary was not; Mary was accompanied by her husband. Some have stated that the three-and-one-half years spoken of here is meant to indicate the time of Jesus' ministry on earth. But the three-and-one-half years spoken of here has nothing to do with the child and everything to do with the persecution of the woman's other children. And, Satan did not come after the other children of Mary! However, the Great Red Dragon does come after the tribulation saints, and he does it for exactly three-and-a-half years.

THE WOMAN AND CHILD ARE FUTURE EVENTS, NOT PAST

The supposition that the woman is Israel or that the woman is Mary does not fit the God-inspired outline that was given to John at the beginning of Revelation. He was told, in reverse order, to write the things that were future (the birth of Jesus was past); the things which are present (the birth of Jesus was not); and the things which he, John, had seen. John had not been present at the birth of Jesus! He had certainly not seen it, he had only been told of it. Not one of the criteria in Revelation 1 is met if one considers the woman and child as being the story of the birth of Jesus. The Bible is never less intelligent than we are. The best we can hope for from prophecy is not a close approximation. We are never forced to say, "Ah, well, this is the best God could come up with, this is the closest He could get, and we'll just have to make do." To the contrary, prophecy is perfect in every detail. It is one of the greatest proofs of the power and omnipotence of God, and also, one of His greatest miracles. If we find ourselves slamming square pegs into round holes, we know we are off in our interpretations of prophecy.

One of the obvious facts about a study of Revelation is that it is either new information as concerns facts or new information as concerns the fitting of facts given elsewhere in the Bible. In other words, Revelation strings and fits all of the facts given elsewhere in prophecy together while presenting much new information. No one reads Revelation and says

"Yeah, yeah, I knew that already." And Revelation 12 is a long chapter. Why would it take up much space reviewing something extremely familiar to any reader of the Bible such as the birth of Christ? It makes no sense at all.

So the story does not fit the birth of Jesus in any way. The Greek words in which it was originally written do not fit, the divine outline given to John does not fit, and the symbolism is not constant and thus does not fit. The symbolism, however, fits the story of the Rapture perfectly. The miracle of prophecy is that it is exact and perfect in every detail. To turn this prophecy of the woman into the birth of Jesus is to make a sham of the exactness of prophecy. Further, the birth of Jesus is past, not future. Prophecy and history are oxymoronic - they are opposites. How is it possible to prophesy the past? And what would be the point? The Old Testament prophesied many particulars of the birth of Jesus in order that the people might recognize the birth of the Son of God when it occurred. Matthew and Luke then recorded the occurrence of that birth. The Book of Revelation has no need to revisit it for any reason. Especially when one notes that not one new detail is given! Ah, but if the story of the woman and her child is the story of Rapture then many, many insights into the experience are revealed here. That is the point of the book and of the prophecy.

JOHN'S VISION IS A TRUE PICTURE OF THE RAPTURE

The visible church (the woman) consists of both true and false Christians. The true Christians, the overcomers, are symbolized by the man child. In him is found all the glory of the woman for she is wretched and pathetic after the birth. In him is also the promise of power and authority, for the saints will rule the world with a rod of iron. The Rapture's exact timing, although expected to occur by both the Saints and Satan (the dragon), is kept secret. When it does happen, a great war breaks out in heaven; Michael and his angels battle Satan and his angels. As a consequence, two things will happen: the saints will arrive safely to heaven and Satan will be kicked out of heaven. To have the saints take over his vantage point will mean his doom, and, furthermore, Satan will have to give up the one thing that he *to this day* still holds: the bodies of the saints. Here, Satan loses even that very last stranglehold on the saints. The bodies of the saints are as free as their souls and spirits. Satan has fought against the resurrection of every single person throughout history; the Rapture will enrage him. The rage of Satan over his loss is terrifying. Imagine all of the power of all of the hate, anger, and evil of Satan harnessed and arrayed against one event. That is a war! Dependent simply upon human strength, we would be helpless before Satan. So, Michael goes to war. On our behalf. And we arrive safely in heaven, there to be forever with our God.

After the catching up of the child, there is a wilderness (persecution) time of exactly three-and-a-half years where the woman (what remains of the Church on the earth) and her subsequent offspring (the tribulation saints) are hunted down by Satan. This corresponds exactly to the time frame of the Great Persecution of the tribulation saints by Satan that occurs after the Rapture. It is, in fact, the first three-and- a-half years of the Great Tribulation; the time of grace mixed with judgment.

SCRIPTURE CONSISTENT IN IDENTIFYING THE TIME OF RAPTURE

The timing of Rapture is consistent throughout prophecy. It is before the Great Tribulation and it also precedes the Second Coming of Jesus to earth. Chapters 4-11 of Revelation have shown us the condition of the earth since the opening of the first seal. It has been war, famine, pestilence and plague for the last ten-and-a-half years. No time on earth has ever been so dissolute and so desolate. But that is not the picture of conditions right before the Rapture as given by Jesus in Luke 17:26-28. He describes the conditions then as calm and prosperous: "And as it was in the days of Noah, so shall it be also in the days of the Son of man. They did eat, they drank, they married wives, they were given in marriage, until the day that Noah entered into the ark, and the flood came, and destroyed them all. Likewise also as it was in the days of Lot; they did eat, they drank, they bought, they sold, they planted, they builded."

Matthew 24:29-31 discusses the timing of the Second Coming and it is clear that Rapture has already occurred:

"Immediately after the tribulation of those days shall the sun be darkened, and the moon shall not give her light, and the stars shall fall from heaven, and the powers of the heavens shall be shaken: And then shall appear the sign of the Son of man in heaven: and then shall all the tribes of the earth mourn, and they shall see the Son of man coming in the clouds of heaven with power and great glory. And he shall send his angels with a great sound of a trumpet, and they shall gather together his elect from the four winds, *from one end of heaven to the other.*"

When Jesus returns, this passage says that He returns with His elect. And He gathers them together before He comes. Where does he find them? From one end of *heaven* to the other. Not from one end of the *earth* to the other! Why not? Because they can no longer be found on earth. They have been raptured earlier to heaven!

Paul, in Colossians 3:4 also tells us that when Jesus appears at the Second Coming, we will appear with Him. That necessitates that we have first gone to Him, which we have, at the Rapture. He repeats this in 1 Thessalonians 3:13 when he says: "To the end he may [e]stablish your hearts unblamable in holiness before God, even our Father, *at the coming of our Lord Jesus Christ with all his saints.*"

This prophecy is not original with Paul. According to the Bible, one of the very first men who ever lived, Enoch, prophesied the very same thing. This is the same Enoch who never died, but was translated to heaven. Jude quotes him in Jude 14, "And Enoch also, the seventh from Adam, prophesied of these, saying, Behold, the Lord cometh with ten thousands of his saints."

Jesus describes what will come upon the earth during the time of Tribulation and He commands the disciples to "watch ye therefore, and pray always, that ye may be accounted worthy to escape all these things that shall come to pass, and to stand before the son of man" (Luke 21:36). Why would Jesus tell them to pray to escape all of these things if, in fact, it were impossible to do so? If all are resigned to going through the Tribulation, then it seems a cruel joke for Jesus here to hold out hope of escaping it. But, of course, it is not a cruel joke on the part of Jesus. He is saying that the righteous will escape

Tribulation and those who walk in righteousness need not worry.

Remember, too, the promise given to the Philadelphian Church in Revelation 3:10: "Because thou hast kept the word of my patience, I also will keep thee from *the* hour of temptation, which shall come upon all the world, to try them that dwell upon the earth."

Paul adds more detail about the Rapture in I Thessalonians 4:13-18: "But I would not have you to be ignorant, brethren, concerning them which are asleep, that ye sorrow not, even as others which have no hope. *For if we believe that Jesus died and rose again, even so them also which sleep in Jesus will God bring with him.* For this we say unto you by the word of the Lord, that we which are alive and remain unto the coming of the Lord shall not prevent them which are asleep. For the Lord himself shall descend from heaven with a shout, with the voice of the archangel, and with the trump of God: and the dead in Christ shall rise first: Then we which are alive and remain shall be caught up together with them in the clouds, to meet the Lord in the air: and so shall we ever be with the Lord. Wherefore comfort one another with these words" (emphasis mine).

We are told exactly what to expect at the Rapture. We will hear the shout of Jesus, the voice of the archangel calling forth his angel warriors, and the trump of God. When we do, the graves of the saints will open and they will be caught up to the Lord. Immediately after that, the living saints will be caught up also and we will meet Jesus in the air, where He has descended from heaven. Jesus will not return to the earth itself until he comes at Armageddon and places His foot on the Mount of Olives.

Who exactly will be raptured? The Gospel of John records Jesus' answer to this question when Jesus said, "Verily, verily, I say unto you, The hour is coming, and now is, when the dead shall hear the voice of the Son of God: and they that hear shall live." And they that hear shall live. It is that simple. But won't everyone on earth and in the grave hear the shout of Jesus, the voice of Michael, and the trump of God? Apparently not. When God spoke from heaven the third and final time while Jesus was on earth, some heard it and some simply heard thunder.

"My sheep hear my voice," Jesus said. Those who do not have Jesus as their shepherd do not hear His voice today. And so it will be at the Rapture. If one's heart is tuned to Jesus, the shout will be deafening in that day. For the others, the moment of Rapture may pass completely unnoticed. On that great day, everything will be riding on the condition of one's relationship with Jesus.

TIMES SECRET BEFORE RAPTURE - SPECIFIED AFTER RAPTURE

A careful study of prophecy shows that only times before the Rapture are kept secret. Times after the Rapture are freely given. After the Rapture, the timetable could not be more specific; it is given in years, weeks and days so that there can be no doubt as to when the prophesied events will occur. From the span of time that the tribulation saints will be persecuted by the Beast to the span of the Two Witnesses' ministry, events are laid out in detail. Now, if there is either a mid-tribulation rapture, or a post-tribulation rapture, how could it possibly come upon the world like a thief in the night? It is impossible! Anyone could read Revelation and know exactly how close the world was to the coming of Jesus. Only with a pre-tribulation rapture can the timing remain secret.

Consider, also, that the Rapture is planned by God to be a great sign to unbelievers. During the Great Tribulation, plagues, war, and famine are the orders for the day. In the midst of such calamity, Rapture would be lost in the noise. But, Rapture in the midst of peace (of which there is none after the Rapture) would be an enormous sign. Imagine the stir on that day, if just the graves at Arlington National Cemetery were to be involved. At Arlington are found acres upon acres, row upon row of graves. At Rapture, thousands of these graves would be found open and empty, while thousands of others would remain completely undisturbed. In a time of tranquility, that scene of "randomly" opened and disturbed graves side by side with undisturbed graves repeated on a global scale, would have to qualify as one of the most frightening experiences in human history. In marked contrast, with the panic, death, and supernatural terror which is omnipresent during Tribulation, empty graves at that time would be seen as just another horror, barely worth mentioning. The same applies for the missing living. In a time of prosperity, each person would be noted and missed. In a time of war, earthquake, famine, plague, who would question a person's disappearance? There would be too many explanations for it. The Rapture, in part, is meant to bring unbelievers to Christ. For that reason, it is written, "For when they shall say, Peace and safety; then sudden destruction cometh upon them, as travail upon a woman with child, and they shall not escape" (I Thessalonians 5:3).

HOW THE RAPTURE WILL IMPACT THE WORLD

A pre-tribulation rapture would also explain the absence of the United States in prophecy. Although America is the most dominant world power today, she is not mentioned, except maybe very peripherally, in Scripture. Israel, Iraq, the European nations, Egypt, even little Lebanon, play the major roles at the end. Now, consider for a moment, the current distribution of Christians throughout the world. And consider what would happen to the governments of the world at the coming of Rapture. Speaking in generalities, Africa would not be much affected except, perhaps, nations like Kenya and Ethiopia. The Jewish, Moslem, Hindu, and Buddhist countries would barely see a ripple in their everyday life. China, percentage wise, would not be very impacted, either. Indeed, the enormous population found there might experience relief that many were missing. Europe, although Christian in name, is cold to the things of God. At least at this point in time, there is not much revival or interest in things spiritual in Europe. Yes, there would be some consternation and upset in those countries, but nothing on a grand scale. Now imagine how the Rapture would impact America. Much of the population would be gone. Not only that, nowhere in the world are Christians as evenly disbursed in every strata of society as in the U.S. From the Supreme Court Justices to the homeless, Christians can be found at every level of government, academia, society, and business. Thus, every facet of life would be thrown into a panic. Senators, FBI agents, firemen, insurance appraisers, professors, newscasters, CEOs, and salespeople at the local Wal-Mart, would be gone. Houses would be vacant, businesses would be empty. The stock market could not function, at least for a period of time, for many players would be gone. It is impossible to imagine any phase of American business, political, or personal life that would remain unaffected.

Imagine, too, the potential for fraud and criminal activity. Bank accounts would sit idle, property would sit unclaimed. False assumption of identity in order to access these assets would be the order of the day. It would be necessary to implement an entirely new identification system. This will surely present the opportunity for the mark of the Beast to be implemented. America, more than any other country would be decimated by Rapture, and it is doubtful, given the horror that breaks forth on the earth right after Rapture from the seven seals of God, that she would be able to recover. She would be a broken nation, watching as other powers came to prominence on the world stage. Clearly, those are the halcyon days for the empire of Antichrist, not for America. It all fits prophecy perfectly.

SATAN LOSES HIS PLACE IN THE HEAVENS

"And there was war in heaven." We have already touched upon the fact that, according to Jesus and to Paul, Satan's abode is still the heavenly places. Jesus apparently kept watch on Satan there in the heavenly places even while He, Jesus, was on the earth. Upon the return of the seventy disciples whom He had sent out, they announced with joy that even the demons were subject to them. Jesus already knew this. He had seen into the spiritual realm and consequently remarked that, "I beheld Satan as lightning fall from heaven," (Luke 10:18). What Jesus was telling the seventy was that He saw Satan's power diminishing as they went forth in the name of Jesus, and as Satan's power diminished, the security of his dwelling place in the heavens became more and more threatened. Here, in Revelation 12, we see that Satan will lose entirely that place.

Jeremiah 10:11 also placed the abode of Satan in the heavens even as he prophesied Satan's removal from there. Jeremiah places the pre-Rapture abode of Satan very specifically: not on earth and not in the highest of heavenly places (that is the abode of God), but rather in the under-heavens. Although this may, at first, seem a novel thought, other places in the Bible refer to the strata of heaven. For instance, the gospel will be preached in mid-heaven according to Revelation 14.

Many, many times in the Bible, Satan and his forces are called the host of heaven. Consider Acts 7:42, 2 Kings 17:16, 21:3,5, 23:4-5, and Isaiah 24:21 as but a few examples. And to further remove any doubt on the subject of where evil now has its abode, consider Ephesians 6:12, "For our struggle is not against flesh and blood, but against the rulers, against the powers, against the world forces of this darkness, against the spiritual forces of wickedness *in the heavenly places*" (NASB).

SATAN RULER OF THIS WORLD - NOT RULER OF HELL

"Isn't Satan the ruler of hell," one may ask. No, absolutely not. Satan is the foremost victim of hell. Hell was created by God in order to punish Satan and his angels according to Matthew 25:41. Those mortals who align themselves with Satan will likewise find that it is their destination, but they are secondary inhabitants. Satan is as anxious to remain as far away from hell as is anyone else. Do not confuse hell with the grave, which, for a time Satan did control. However, although Satan was master of the Grave and the unseen world of death before the time of the crucifixion, now those keys are also in the hands of Jesus . There are evil, malevolent spirits which are kept in chains by God and which are loosed during the great time of the Wrath of God, but for the most part, Satan and his forces are free to come and go upon this earth and in the atmosphere above. This war between Michael and Satan in Revelation 12 will end all of that.

SATAN CAST TO EARTH - HIS DOOM IS SEALED

All of the forces of heaven, both good and evil; the forces of both Michael and Satan will war in the most stupendous battle which has ever been seen since the beginning of time. Only one other battle comes close and that was the battle that saw the removal of Satan and his angels from the uppermost levels of heaven, the dwelling place of the Lord Most High. The outcome of this next battle will see as its results two things: Satan and his forces will be completely purged from heaven and will be cast down to earth as their only dwelling place, and the raptured saints will arrive safely to heaven.

(For those who interpret this battle as the Great Rebellion in heaven when Lucifer and his angels were expelled from heaven, have they ever questioned why the telling of this story comes here, after the birth of the child? Even for those who hold that the woman is Israel and the child is Jesus, it seems a strange place to tell the story of the initial rebellion of Satan.)

Again, one sees why the Rapture is such a secret. When Satan loses his vantage point in the heavenly places to the saints, it will seal his doom. He must keep the Bride of Christ from her extraordinary destiny. The Rapture, the mass resurrection of all of God's people throughout the ages, will then present to him his greatest peril. Not only will they arrive in untold masses, these people are the very heirs of God, the very Bride of God's son!

SATAN IS STILL POWERFUL

Satan, today, is much more powerful than we like to suppose. The Bible calls him the *great* red dragon. Yes, he was dealt his death knell at the Cross but he is not yet dead. The mortal wound has been inflicted upon him by Jesus, but Satan wields great power even in his death throes. I once heard the story of an official in India whose job necessitated travel to rather far-flung outposts. The outposts were rarely visited, but small houses had been built there for the convenience of the official when he did arrive. Once, coming upon one of the houses with his aide, they saw through the window that it was inhabited by an enormous python. The python had curled himself around much of the furniture and was at rest. The official knew that he had but one chance to kill the serpent, for if his shot missed, it would alert and enrage the snake and they would be in grave danger. His aide took careful aim and shot the snake square in the head. It was a mortal wound, but it did not immediately kill the beast, for the beast was large and powerful. The man reported that it took well over an hour for the serpent to die and in that hour, it thrashed and writhed in such a way that by the time it was dead, it had completely destroyed everything in the house.

This is exactly how we must view Satan. The fatal shot was delivered to him at Calvary. But he is powerful even in his death throes and that is why he is still able to inflict such carnage upon Planet Earth. Satan is a formidable opponent. Heaven never underestimates him, only the uninformed on earth do so. Although his doom is certain and his defeat was ordained at the Cross, he still commands enormous power and cunning. Never think for one minute that this world is not his to influence, it is. He rules here, not *de jure* (by law), but certainly *de facto* (in fact). However, with the removal of his heavenly vantage point at Rapture, Satan loses an enormous advantage. Not only do the saints now occupy that vantage point, but Satan himself is confined to earth. This is a great limitation to his power, however, as regards his presence on earth, he will now be at the height of his influence. All of his force, all of his demons, all of his dominion, powers and principalities, and he, himself, will now be concentrated on Planet Earth. Woe, indeed, to the inhabitants of earth!

ASCENT OF SAINTS - DESCENT OF SATAN

When Daniel sees his vision in Daniel 7, he records a courtroom-like scene at this point. Verses 9-10 read thusly: "I beheld till the thrones were cast down, and the Ancient of days did sit, whose garment was white as snow, and the hair of his head like the pure wool: his throne was like the fiery flame, and his wheels as burning fire. A fiery stream issued and came forth form before him: thousand thousands ministered unto him, and ten thousand times ten thousand stood before him: *the judgment was set, and the books were opened*" (emphasis mine).

With this in mind, it is interesting to consider the information given in Revelation 12:10-11: "And I heard a loud voice saying in heaven, Now is come salvation, and strength, and the kingdom of our God, and the power of his Christ: for the accuser of our brethren is cast down, which accused them before our God day and night. And they overcame him by the blood of the Lamb, and by the word of their testimony; and they loved not their lives unto the death."

This is recorded immediately after Satan's fall from heaven is announced and the voice begins by saying "Now." This indicates that the two events are linked. It is clear that the ascent of the saints must be accompanied by the descent of Satan. But Satan does not "go gently into that good night." After his failure to prevent the Rapture, Satan changes tactics. Force has not prevailed, now he can only resort to God's justice. Satan will appeal on legal grounds: He will argue before God, the legality of the Rapture. Satan will challenge the right of the saints to occupy heaven. This is not unknown in the spiritual realm. We see an example of opposing sides arguing their case, with God as the ultimate judge, in Zechariah 3. There, Joshua, the priest who came out of Babylonian captivity with Zerubbabel to rebuild the Temple is seen presenting his case to God. "And he shewed me Joshua the high priest standing before the angel of the Lord, and Satan standing at his right hand to resist him."

LEGALITY OF RAPTURE - SATAN ARGUES BEFORE GOD

Because God is the personification of justice, God gives Satan the opportunity to argue his case. Satan's challenge is heard in the highest court in the universe, the Judgment Seat of Christ. Both Daniel and Revelation allude to a judgment of the saints. This is not the Great White Throne Judgment at the end of time, nor is it the Judgment of the Nations when Jesus divides the sheep from the goats after Armageddon. This is the Bema Seat Judgment of Christ. Paul talks about this in II Corinthians 5:10 when he says: "For we must all appear before the judgment seat of Christ; that every one may receive the things done in his body, according to that he hath done, whether it be good or bad."

According to this verse, we who are Christians will be held accountable for all of our actions upon the earth. How can this be possible if God has truly forgiven all of our sins and not only has remembered them no more, but has removed them as far from us as the East is from the West? The answer to this is that God has forgiven and forgotten our sins. He is not the one who accuses us. But there is someone who remembers and who will accuse us. Satan is "The Accuser of the Brethren," not God! In fact, we get our word "devil" from the Greek word *diablos* which literally means "slanderer." Notice that he is called the accuser of the <u>brethren</u>. There is no need for him to accuse the unsaved, they are his already. But the arrival of the brethren to heaven will bring our slanderer to his feet. He will spring into action in order to convince the Judge of the Universe that a mistake has been made concerning the salvation of each and every saint. It is the Devil himself who has noted our sins and who has never forgotten even one of our failings. He and his minions have monitored our lives almost as closely as Jesus has. And he has his notes in order. All the ammunition that he has gathered against us, will be used against us on that day.

This is a trial scene, and a very sobering one. One by one, he will challenge our right to remain in heaven. Now, the human condition is a condition of both sin and the denial of that sin. Even after living a lifetime with ourselves, most of us consider that, overall, we are quite lovely human beings. I fear that Satan will not present our case in quite that light. There are things that each of us has done hoping that nobody else would ever know. There are other things that we have done and completely forgotten about. There are attitudes that we have displayed and acts that we have committed that we have effectively blocked out of our consciousness. But Satan will uncover even the *hidden* evil in our lives and bring it to light.

Now, if at this moment, we muster our own defense, we are lost. As Job, himself a very righteous man, said, "If I justify myself, mine own mouth shall condemn me: if I say, I am perfect, it shall also prove me perverse" (Job 9:20). If, in the solemnity of that Court, with the gravity of the charges brought against us, we attempt to defend ourselves with a recounting of the good moments in our life, our defense will be pitiful and useless. That is because no one who has ever committed even one sin is worthy to remain in heaven. Heaven is for God and the god-like; the sinless creatures who have never had one rebellious thought, much less action. Our anemic defense of personal righteousness will crumble like a house of cards. It is probable, too, that in the very recounting by Satan of the cruelty which abounded in our life, and the weakness and selfishness of it will, in its entirety, overwhelm us to the point where we cannot even begin to muster a plausible reason for God to spare us. For the first time in our lives we will fully understand the consequences of each of our sins, small and great, as the Accuser paints in great detail the effects that they had on ourselves and on others. We will understand how even a sharp or careless word wounded and crushed the spirit of our little children, how our smug attitudes caused so much pain to souls who were searching for truth. But all this is necessary even if it is Satan who brings it about because finally we will begin to hate sin as God hates sin.

It is no wonder, then, that Satan has spent centuries convincing people that their own good lives will earn them heaven. He knows that argument is completely without merit in the Court of God, and by convincing them to use it, he, Satan, will secure their souls for eternity.

SAINTS' DEFENSE AGAINST SATAN'S ACCUSATIONS

In light of that, whatever will we do?! We will do as these saints do. We will answer truthfully that every charge against us is completely true and accurate. BUT we will testify to more. The word "testimony" is a legal term. It concerns evidence given under oath. And, here, we are in a trial which involves our eternal souls. At this critical time, the word of our testimony will be the same as is given by each saint here, "I am covered by the blood of the Lamb and it matters no longer what I have done. Praise God, I am covered by the blood of the Lamb! It is on the basis of His righteousness that I am worthy of heaven, not on the basis of my righteousness. And no fault whatsoever can be found in the Lamb. He, and only He, is sinless."

"And when you were dead in your transgressions and the uncircumcision of your flesh, He made you alive together with Him, having forgiven us all our transgressions, having canceled out the certificate of debt consisting of decrees against us and which was hostile to us: and He has taken it out of the way, having nailed it to the cross" (Colossians 2:13-14, NASB).

On the basis of this testimony, Satan will be rendered powerless against us.

According to Scripture, a fact is established by the mouth of *two* witnesses. John said earlier in 1 John 2:1 that when we sin we have an advocate with the Father who is Jesus Christ the righteous. An advocate is the same as a lawyer, one who pleads our case for us. And now, in this most serious of all court cases, our lawyer, Jesus, approaches the bench. He will confess our name before the Father, He will claim us as His own, and with that admonition we are safe for all eternity! Our remorse will turn to a joy that is impossible to overstate.

SAINTS ARE OVERCOMERS EVEN OF SATAN

"And they [the saints] overcame him [Satan]." As Arthur Bloomfield wrote: "The saints are overcomers of Satan. They have met him on his own ground, Planet Earth, and they have come off victoriously. By the opposition of Satan, God has developed a people with a strength of character and a nobleness of soul that would have been impossible to create directly. This character is found only in the race of man. Angels have lived lives under perfect conditions. How could it ever be said of them that they "love[d] not their lives unto death"?" That is why the angels are sent to minister to us. Although now our estate is one that is lower than theirs, that will change. We are told that, at that time, we will even judge the angels. Each time Satan hands a believer a hardship or even a tragedy and he responds, not with rancor and bitterness, but with faithful thanksgiving to his God, praise to God abounds throughout the universe. The natural man would not react so. Only those whose character has been changed into the likeness of Jesus would be able to respond thusly.

SATAN'S RAGE DIRECTED AT THOSE LEFT BEHIND AND THE TRIBULATION SAINTS

The heavens are told by the heavenly voice to rejoice because all things satanic and evil have been removed from there. Likewise, the earth and sea are told that woeful times are upon them because Satan will now take up residence in them. And, as evil and cruel and bloodthirsty as Satan has always been, now he is worse because he is filled with a rage that even he has not known before.

"And the serpent cast out of his mouth water as a flood after the woman, that he might cause her to be carried away of the flood. And the earth helped the woman, and the earth opened her mouth, and swallowed up the flood which the dragon cast out of his mouth." Just as the dragon is symbolic, so too is the flood that proceeds out of its mouth. Satan is the dragon. A flood is an intuitively understood symbol of an overwhelming, inescapable situation. Here, it is persecution from the hand of Satan that now comes upon the woman (what remains of the church) and her offspring (the tribulation saints). But supernatural help is afforded her during her time of tribulation that will last for three-and-a-half more years. Just as a flood of persecution will flow from the mouth of the serpent (Satan), so will the earth help the woman. The earth will help the woman by means of the plagues that God will send upon the earth during the first six seals. This is because the plagues will distract and torment the Kingdom of Antichrist so that his full attention cannot be given to the persecution of the woman and to her subsequent offspring (the tribulation saints). The plagues are designed in part to help the woman and hinder the dragon. Although Satan will send forth a flood of overwhelming persecution, other events will keep commanding his attention. Verse 14 says that the woman is given two wings of a great eagle. That was exactly God's promise to Israel when he brought plagues against their tormentor, Egypt. "Ye have seen what I did unto the Egyptians, and how I bare you on eagles' wings, and brought you unto myself," (Exodus 19:4). Those plagues, which were, in fact, miracles of God, helped Israel. They will now help the Christians, and will slow Satan's hand, allowing three-and-a-half years more for people to respond to the gospel of Christ. Even now, even in her weakened condition, Satan does not and cannot prevail against the Church. The promise of Matthew 16:18 is still standing firm, "Upon this rock I will build my church; and the gates of hell shall not prevail against it." The promises of God are forever true.

CHAPTER 15
THE RISE OF THE ANTICHRIST
Background to Revelation 13

Revelation 13 chronicles the rule of Antichrist after the Rapture and his interaction with the saints. It does not give us the particulars of his rise or his effect upon the rest of the world. We must go to other biblical prophesies and other prophets for this information.

Antichrist is called by many names in prophecy. Daniel calls him the "little horn," the "vile person," and the "raiser of taxes." Isaiah calls him "the Assyrian," Habakkuk calls him "the Chaldean." Ezekiel calls him "Gog" and the "Prince of Tyrus." Paul calls him the "man of sin." John simply calls him the "beast."

DANIEL'S FIRST VISION

The book of Daniel chronicles the rise of Antichrist in great detail. He does it in conjunction with an overall prophetic outline of human history from his, Daniel's, time until the coming of Jesus at Armageddon. The first of these prophesies is found in Daniel 2:31-45 and it came as a dream to King Nebuchadnezzar, the Babylonian king who ruled in the times of Daniel. The dream of the king was extremely disturbing and Nebuchadnezzar sought out his sorcerers, astrologers, and magicians to tell him its meaning. But Nebuchadnezzar was nobody's fool; he refused to tell them the dream itself, rightly supposing that if they could supernaturally interpret the dream then they could supernaturally divine it. The seers, all too ready with an interpretation, could not manufacture the dream. Daniel, a Jewish prophet who was a captive in Babylon along with the rest of the Jewish nation, requested an audience with Nebuchadnezzar and described to him both his dream and its interpretation. It was as follows: "Thou, O king, sawest and beheld a great image. This great image, whose brightness was excellent, stood before thee; and the form thereof was terrible. This image's head was of fine gold, his breast and his arms of silver, his belly and his thighs of brass, His legs of iron, his feet part of iron and part of clay. Thou sawest till that a stone was cut out without hands, which smote the image upon his feet that were of iron and clay, and brake them to pieces. Then was the iron, the clay, the brass, the silver, and the gold, broken to pieces together, and became like the chaff of the summer threshing floors; and the wind carried them away, that no place was found for them: and the stone that smote the image became a great mountain, and filled the whole earth.

"This is the dream; and we will tell the interpretation thereof before the king. Thou, O king, art a king of kings: for the God of heaven hath given thee a kingdom, power, and strength, and glory. And wheresoever the children of men dwell, the beasts of the field and the fowls of the heaven hath he given into thine hand, and hath made thee ruler over them all. Thou art this head of gold. And after thee shall arise another kingdom inferior to thee, and another third kingdom of brass, which shall bear rule over all the earth. And the fourth kingdom shall be strong as iron: forasmuch as iron breaketh in pieces and subdueth all things: and as iron that breaketh all these, shall it break in pieces and bruise. And whereas thou sawest the feet and toes, part of potters' clay, and part of iron, the kingdom shall be divided; but there shall be in it of the strength of the iron, forasmuch as thou sawest the iron mixed with miry clay. And as the toes of the feet were part of iron, and part of clay, so the kingdom shall be partly strong, and partly broken. And whereas thou sawest iron mixed with miry clay, they shall mingle themselves with the seed of men: but they shall not cleave one to another, even as iron is not mixed with clay. And in the days of these kings shall the God of heaven set up a kingdom, which shall never be destroyed: and the kingdom shall not be left to other people, but it shall break in pieces and consume all these kingdoms, and it shall stand for ever. Forasmuch as thou sawest that the stone was cut out of the mountain without hands, and that it brake in pieces the iron, the brass, the clay, the silver, and the gold; the great God hath made known to the king what shall come to pass hereafter: and the dream is certain, and the interpretation thereof sure."

Daniel begins his interpretation of future world dominions with Babylon, the empire that was in place at the time he was writing. That was the head of gold. At that time Babylon was considered impregnable, so it is easy to imagine the astonishment that met Daniel's next pronouncement - that another, *inferior,* kingdom would conquer her. But, this, indeed happened, and the story is chronicled in Daniel 5:27 and Isaiah 44-45, even naming Cyrus, the Persian king who would conquer Babylon. The Medes and the Persians (notice that the arms and breast of silver in the vision correctly noted the two-part characteristic of this kingdom) over-ran Babylon and subdued her.

The history of the fulfillment of that prophecy is an interesting one. Babylon was a magnificent city. The Hanging Gardens of Babylon were one of the wonders of the ancient world. The city was completely surrounded by an impregnable wall, eighty feet thick, three hundred feet high, and also set thirty-five feet below the ground in order to thwart attempts to dig under the city. A full four-horse chariot could easily be turned around on the top of this wall. Within the city walls were fifty streets; twenty-five running north/south, twenty-five running east/west. Down the middle of the city ran the Euphrates River that divided the city into two halves. At each place where a street intersected the river there were iron gates and sentries manning the gates, thus there were fifty gates. Between those gates and the city was dug a moat, causing anyone entering the city to first disembark and then be ferried to the city. Babylon was impregnable. Over-arching the river, the ruins of at least one drawbridge have been discovered which allowed the two sides of the city to be traversed by foot traffic.

Babylon was an esthetic and engineering marvel. And Cyrus coveted her. Thus he laid siege to Babylon but without effect for Babylon was totally self-sufficient. As his only hope, Cyrus dug a lake bed which would serve to divert the river in case a night would ever come when the gates along the river would not be shut. Years passed; Nebuchadnezzar, the king who reigned over Babylon when Daniel received this vision had died and Belshazzar his grandson now reigned in his place. Although Nebuchadnezzar had learned under Danicl's tutelage to revere Jehovah, Belshazzar did not. Upon his ascension to the throne, Belshazzar decided to hold a huge and lavish feast to exalt himself. He called for the sacred Jewish temple vessels and profaned them by drinking from them. This caused great delight for the guests who were present. Egged on by their delight, he then passed them around for all present to use all the while praising the pagan gods.

The atmosphere was uproarious and drunken, but solemnity was immediately established when suddenly, and from out of nowhere the finger of a hand appeared to all present at the feast and began to write upon a wall. Written were the words *mene, mene, tekel, upharsin.* The Babylonians, although not understanding the foreign words, were terrified of the finger and the writing. It is recorded that Belshazzar turned white and lost control of his bowels because of his terror. He cried for an interpreter of the words and Daniel was once again remembered. Daniel was found and, although at this time almost ninety years old, he was brought into the great banquet hall. He translated the words for Belshazzar, bringing more terror into his heart. The meaning was as follows, "God hath numbered thy kingdom and finished it [this was written twice]. Thou art weighed in the balances, and art found wanting. Thy kingdom is divided, and given to the Medes and Persians." At that exact moment, Cyrus was engaged in turning the course of the Euphrates into his manmade lake and the army was standing ready to march into the city, for in the midst of the drunken celebration, the Babylonians had forgotten to close the gates! Sure enough, the kingdom of silver - the kingdom of the Medes and Persians - was established.

Daniel then prophesied the rise of a third kingdom, a kingdom of brass, which would conquer the Medes and the Persians. Greece, under Alexander the Great, did exactly that. The prophesied fourth kingdom, the kingdom that would follow Greece, would be a harsh and strong kingdom, a kingdom of iron. It would not fall before another power and would not have a successor, it would simply break into pieces. This was the exact fate of the kingdom that conquered Greece, Rome.

After the empire of Rome, Daniel said that there would be no real world empire, there would simply be remains of the Roman Empire. That fact is symbolized by the statue's feet. They are the successor to the Roman legs of iron - the ten toes would neither be able to unite and control the world, nor would they disappear from the world scene. This, too, has come to pass; its history was the history from the Middle Ages to the present time. Although the independent countries that now occupy the territory of the Roman Empire tried to form alliances by every means from marriage to decree and from treaty to war, they never united. The grand schemes of emperors from Otto I to Napoleon have always come to naught. Further proof of the truth of this prophecy was the failure of Communism to overrun the world, although it looked at times in the Twentieth Century as if it would. Biblically, It was impossible for Communism to triumph. Had it happened, prophecy would have been defeated, for prophecy has decreed that the nations of Europe will remain independent of one another until the coming of Antichrist.

This is an important point. Many current eschatologists teach that the countries will come together into a federation that will produce the Antichrist. Daniel says the opposite. He says the countries will stay divided until the coming of the man, antichrist, who will, for his own purposes, unite them.

Daniel described a stone from the hand of God shattering the statue. This stone is Jesus and His kingdom that will be established upon the earth at the Second Coming of Jesus Christ. But notice that when this stone, Jesus, strikes and demolishes the statue, the statue is completely in place and standing. The stone hits the statue upon its feet - the remains of the Roman Empire - but Daniel clearly states that *all* of the statue is destroyed - the feet, the iron (legs), the brass (torso), the silver (arms and breast) and the gold (the head). In fact, Daniel stresses this point by mentioning it twice. The statue *in its entirety* will constitute a final empire; the empire of Antichrist. It will be the prophetic and historical era symbolized only by the toes, but the territory involved will be that of the entire statue *because the entire statue is shattered by the stone.* This will be the territory of Antichrist. Antichrist will begin with control over the territory of the Roman Empire, but his empire will eventually include all of the four world empires of Nebuchadnezzar's vision. Today, the gold, silver, brass, and iron have all disappeared as being recognizable kingdoms. Only the iron and clay of the feet are left. Thus, something extraordinary is on the horizon: Someone will appear and reclaim the territory symbolized by the entire statue. Ezekiel 38 outlines the same general area, but adds in verse 9, "and many people with thee." So the empire is probably even larger than depicted in Figure 4.

Figure 4 Antichrist's Empire

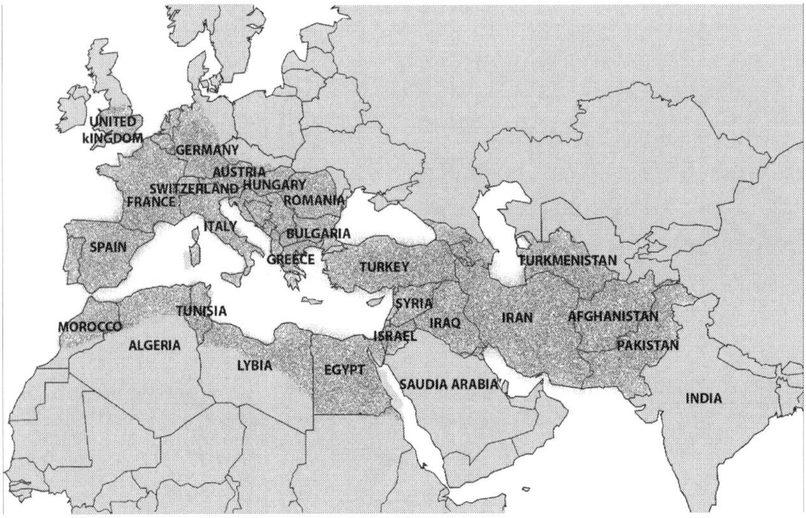

Notice that China and Russia are absent from this territory. Contrary to the teaching of many prophetic teachers, China and Russia are not central to Antichrist's plan.

DANIEL'S SECOND VISION

Daniel has a second vision of the coming world empires that is recorded in chapter 7. That he has a second vision concerning the same events is significant. When Joseph interpreted the two dreams of Pharaoh concerning the famine that would afflict Egypt, he said, "And for that the dream was doubled unto Pharaoh twice; it is because the thing is established by God, and God will shortly bring it to pass," (Genesis 41:32.)

This second vision of Daniel's builds on the information already given in the first vision. This time, many more details are given concerning the kingdom of Antichrist. The second vision uses different symbols - animals instead of parts of the statue - possibly because animals can show action whereas the statue cannot. The symbols are changed from the first vision, but the interpretation of future events remains constant. In the second vision, Daniel sees four great beasts arise from out of a very tumultuous sea. The first beast is like a lion with eagle's wings. Again, this is Babylon. The wings of the lion are plucked, and a man's heart is given to it. The man is Nebuchadnezzar and Daniel records in chapter 4 exactly how this came to pass. One year after the prophecy was given to Daniel, Nebuchadnezzar was walking in his palace when he remarked, "Is not this great Babylon, that I have built for the house of the kingdom by the might of my power, and for the honour of my majesty?" The words were still in his mouth when a voice spoke from heaven saying, "O king Nebuchadnezzar, to thee it is spoken; The kingdom is departed from thee. And they shall drive thee from men, and thy dwelling shall be with the beasts of the field: they shall make thee to eat grass as oxen, and seven times [seven years] shall pass over thee, until thou know that the most High ruleth in the kingdom of men, and giveth it to whomsoever he will." That very same hour, Nebuchadnezzar went mad; eating grass and living outdoors, his hair growing like eagles' feathers and his nail like birds' claws. At the end of seven years, Nebuchadnezzar lifted his eyes to heaven and his faculties were restored to him. In his own words, he "blessed the most High, and I praised and honoured him that liveth for ever, whose dominion is an everlasting dominion, and his kingdom is from generation to generation."

The second beast in Daniel's vision is likened by him to a bear which rises first on one of its sides and then the other. Again, this is the two-sided empire of the Medes, an ancient kingdom, and the Persians, a recent kingdom. The bear has in its mouth three ribs, and the commandment is given it to devour much flesh. Historically, this is accurate. The Medo-Persian Empire conquered three nations; Babylon, Lydia, and Egypt (the three ribs) and therefore the bear did devour more than did the lion (Babylon). The third beast to arise was similar to a leopard with four heads and four wings upon its back. This was the kingdom of Greece, and very interestingly, Alexander who died before he turned thirty-three, chose to divide his empire between his four generals. Hence, we have the four heads and wings as the symbol of Greece.

Daniel then sees an unfamiliar beast - he describes it as frightening and terrible, and exceedingly strong. It devours everything. This is the Roman Empire. And, again, coming out of the symbol for the Roman Empire, Daniel sees ten horns, just as before he had seen ten toes. Now, the Jews did not crown their kings, they anointed them with oil which was carried in a horn. Therefore, the Jewish symbol of a kingdom was a horn. We see then, that ten kingdoms will arise out of the Roman Empire. Again, no separate animal arises after Rome. In Daniel's vision, Rome is not conquered, Rome simply ceases to be except for the individual nations which come out of her.

Daniel's vision continues. He sees, from among the ten horns, a little horn appear. The little horn quickly and violently subdues three of the ten horns. When Daniel examines this little horn he sees that in it are eyes like the eyes of a man and a mouth speaking great things. Daniel is seeing the Antichrist: "Then I would know the truth of the fourth beast, which was diverse from all the others, exceeding dreadful, whose teeth were of iron, and his nails of brass; which devoured, brake in pieces, and stamped the residue with his feet; And of the ten horns that were in his head, and of the other which came up, and before whom three fell; even of that horn that had eyes, and a mouth, that spake very great things, whose look was more stout than his fellows. I beheld, and the same horn made war with the saints, and prevailed against them; Until the Ancient of days came, and judgment was given to the saints of the most High; and the time came that the saints possessed the kingdom. Thus he said, The fourth beast shall be the fourth kingdom upon the earth, which shall be diverse from all the kingdoms, and shall devour the whole earth, and shall tread it down, and break it in pieces. And the ten horns out of this kingdom are ten kings that shall arise: and another shall rise after them; and he shall be diverse from the first, and he shall subdue three kings. And he shall speak great words against the most High, and shall wear out the saints of the most High, and think to change times and laws: and they shall be given into his hand until a time and times and the dividing of time.

But the judgment shall sit, and they shall take away his dominion, to consume and to destroy it unto the end. And the kingdom and dominion, and the greatness of the kingdom under the whole heaven, shall be given to the people of the saints of the most High, whose kingdom is an everlasting kingdom, and all dominions shall serve and obey him. Hitherto is the end of the matter. As for me Daniel, my cogitations much troubled me, and my countenance changed in me: but I kept the matter in my heart," (Daniel 7:19-28).

There is much information in this second vision. To begin with, the little horn is *not* one of the original ten; it comes up from among them. Secondly, the little horn has human characteristics, unlike the other ten. It is clear, then, that we see a man arise out of the territory of the ten horns. The man appears first and then creates the nation. Although the commentaries teach that the nations come together and then the man comes to the fore, Daniel says that the toes will *never* come together until Antichrist has taken back all the territory implied in the symbol of the statue. The nation that produces Antichrist will be a nation of no great significance at first. The man at the head of this nation will grow in importance until he becomes greater than the nation. From that point on, the nation is more or less forgotten but the man becomes the dominating world figure. He will conquer three nations that stand up against him and he will do so ruthlessly. With his superior military might and the economic prosperity that he will bring, there will be no need for Antichrist to conquer any more nations. And after this, no nation will come up against him, they will willingly come under his control. After Antichrist's initial show of force, we are told in Daniel 11 that he acquires the rest of his kingdom by flattery and treachery. No more force is needed, his territory is willingly given to him.

Truly, Antichrist will captivate the world. Verse 25 says that he will think to change times and laws. Laws are understandable. There are many just laws that would stand in the way of a tyrant such as he. The accepted standards of justice, fairness, goodness, rightness, and morality will have to give way in order for him to hold sway. But what about the times? Why would he choose to change times? On this side of the prophecy, no one can answer with certainty, however, at least one thought does spring to mind: The common practice of historical dating. Although most historians now use CE (common era) BCE (before the common era), in the more laic common usage, years are now referred to as being either B.C. or A.D., both of which date from the birth of Jesus. Even atheists and pagans, by and large, adapt to that accepted practice. However, one can readily see how that particular dating system would stick in the craw of the man who has put himself directly in opposition to Jesus Christ in every way possible. Indeed, how could he tolerate the dividing of all human time according to the birth of his mortal enemy, Jesus? When he has total power, it might be one of the very first things that he outlaws. Furthermore, Daniel 2:20-21 tells us that the setting of times and the seasons is God's perquisite. This, then, is further proof of the extent of the rebellion of Antichrist and is simply another encroachment of his on the authority of God. In any case, it is telling that Antichrist is able to change any facet of human life that he chooses to and no one is able to stand against him.

The eyes of the little horn are specifically mentioned by Daniel. It has often been said that the eyes are the window to the soul. Adolph Hitler, possibly a crude proto-type of Antichrist, had mesmerizing eyes. Gustl Kubizek, Hitler's almost constant companion as a youth, in his book, The Young Hitler I Knew: "Never in my life have I seen any other person whose appearance was so completely dominated by the eyes"[22] Eyes are symbolic of intelligence. According to Scripture, Antichrist's will reflect diabolical and amazing intelligence that will both awe and deceive the world.

Daniel also mentions the mouth of the Little Horn that, he says, speaks great things. Revelation 13:5-6 reads as follows: "And there was given unto him [Antichrist] a mouth speaking great things and blasphemies; and power was given unto him to continue forty and two months. And he opened his mouth in blasphemy against God, to blaspheme his name, and his tabernacle, and them that dwell in heaven."

Antichrist will talk his way into power by flatteries and promises of peace and prosperity. He will be a spell-binding public speaker. His charisma will mark him as a "natural" for the times and people will rejoice that he has finally been "discovered" by the world. All (except those who know what to expect prophetically) will fall under his spell and by means of his words be deceived. Again, using Hitler as an example, it is enlightening to read what Ulrich de Maiziere, a member of Hitler's General Staff, had to say about Hitler: This man emanated an almost indescribable demonic effect on individuals which only a few were able to escape and which one can't really understand if one hasn't experienced it oneself."[23]

So upset by this vision is Daniel that, at its conclusion, he feels that he cannot tell the vision to anyone. If Daniel is upset by the vision, imagine the condition of the state of the people who will live through the rise of the Antichrist to power! And remember, this is before the Rapture. Armed with the true word of God, Christians will be able to minister to thousands of searching unbelievers in those days.

DANIEL'S THIRD VISION

The giving of a third vision by God on this same subject of the history of the coming world empires lets us know the significance of this topic in the mind of God. The primary theme of Daniel's third vision is the particular empire of Antichrist. In fact, he gives very little attention to the other empires. Because it is nearing the end of the Babylonian Empire and because prophecy is concerned with future, not past events, Daniel does not even mention that kingdom. He begins his vision with the symbol of the Medo-Persian Empire; a ram with two horns, the last one to appear being the taller horn. Again, the latter horn (or kingdom), Persia, was indeed the stronger kingdom of the two. He sees the ram pushing westward, northward, and southward while no beast is able to withstand him. That is the case until a male goat with one horn "ran unto him in the fury of his power," (Daniel 8:6). The goat breaks the horns of the ram and then tramples the ram into the dust. The goat is Greece, the horn is Alexander the Great. The great horn, Alexander, is broken, and in his place four notable horns appear. These, again, are Alexander's four generals who assumed leadership of the Grecian Empire after the death of Alexander. This interpretation is clearly stated by the heavenly man who appears before Daniel in chapter 8.

The third vision then takes up with the "little horn," not concerning itself with the Roman Empire at all. As Daniel 8:9-17 says: "And out of one of them [the four horns of the goat] came forth a little horn, which waxed exceeding great, toward the south, and toward the east, and toward the pleasant land. And it waxed great, even to the host of heaven; and it cast down some of the host and of the stars to the ground, and stamped upon them. Yea, he magnified himself even to the prince of the host, and by him the daily sacrifice was taken away, and the place of his sanctuary was cast down. And an host was given him against the daily sacrifice by reason of transgression, and it cast down the truth to the ground; and it practised, and prospered. Then I heard one saint speaking, and another saint said unto that certain saint which spake, How long shall be the vision concerning the daily sacrifice, and the transgression of desolation, to give both the sanctuary and the host to be trodden under foot? And he said unto me, Unto two thousand and three hundred days; then shall the sanctuary be cleansed. And it came to pass, when I, even I Daniel, had seen the vision, and sought for the meaning, then, behold, there stood before me as the appearance of a man. And I heard a man's voice between the banks of Ulai, which called, and said, Gabriel, make this man to understand the vision. So he came near where I stood: and when he came, I was afraid, and fell upon my face: but he said unto me, Understand, O son of man: for at the time of the end shall be the vision."

With almost one accord the commentators say that the little horn - the transgressor of desolation - is Antiochus Epiphanes. Antiochus Epiphanes was the Syrian ruler who inspired the Maccabean Revolt by setting up a statue of Jupiter in the Holy of Holies, forbidding circumcision, commanding the sacrifice of swine, and destroying the Jewish sacred books. Granted, Antiochus Epiphanes was evil, but as far as persecution of the Jews is concerned, Antiochus doesn't begin to approach Adolph Hitler, and even Hitler is not mentioned in prophecy. To interpret Antiochus as the Little Horn, the commentators must ignore history, for the facts of the time of Antiochus as he interfaced with Israel do not fit the details of this prophecy. For one instance, Antiochus was Syrian and Syria is not a part of any of Daniel's visions. Furthermore, the angel Gabriel says quite plainly in verse 17 that Daniel must, "Understand, O son of man: for *at the time of the end* shall be the vision" (emphasis mine). The time of Antiochus was not "at the time of the end," it was 170 years before the birth of Christ. Who then is the Little Horn? Daniel, in his second vision, has already identified the Little Horn as the last world ruler. The last world ruler will be Antichrist. The times of Antiochus are long gone at the time of the end, but the times of Antichrist are not. That *is* his appointed time!

In addition to the stated times being consistent with the rule of Antichrist, the Little Horn has already been identified as being the symbol of Antichrist. The symbols of Daniel are and must be constant. One can't have the head of gold symbolizing Babylon at one point in time, and at another point in time have it symbolizing Rome. The same is true of the symbol of the Little Horn. If it symbolizes the last world ruler who is specifically said to war against the saints until the coming of the Ancient of Days in his second vision, then the little horn will remain constant in ensuing visions. Consider, too, that Daniel mentions this "transgression of desolation" three other times, in Daniel 9:27, Daniel 11:31, and Daniel 12:11, and every time it is always in reference to the Antichrist. This is exactly as Jesus Himself understood this vision for he connected the "transgression of desolation" with the persecution of the Jews by Antichrist, not Antiochus. He also referred to it as being in the future, not the past! This is recorded in Matthew 24:15-21: "When ye therefore shall see the abomination of desolation, spoken of by Daniel the prophet, stand in the holy place, (whoso readeth, let him understand:) Then let them which be in Judaea flee into the mountains: Let him which is on the housetop not come down to take any thing out of his house: Neither let him which is in the field return back to take his clothes. And woe unto them that are with child, and to them that give suck in those days! But pray ye that your flight be not in the winter, neither on the sabbath day: For then shall be great tribulation, such as was not since the beginning of the world to this time, no, nor ever shall be."

It goes without saying that Antiochus's time was long past by the time Jesus was born. It also goes without saying that Antiochus will have nothing to do with the time of the Great

Tribulation. But, according to both Daniel and Jesus, the Little Horn will. The Little Horn can be no one other than Antichrist.

Arthur Bloomfield clearly points out what Daniel has managed to do: "He began with his own time when the Babylonian Empire was at its height. He predicted the fall of Babylon and the rise of the Medes and the Persians, usually known as the Persian Empire. He foresaw the dramatic fall of the Persian Empire and the rise of the Empire of Greece under the leadership of Alexander the Great. He saw the breaking up of Alexander's Empire into four parts. He called all three of those empires by name. The only one he did not name was the last one, the Roman Empire. He told Nebuchadnezzar about the rise of the fourth world empire and how it would break up into many nations, and that these nations would exist until the coming of Christ to set up His Kingdom, which would be an everlasting kingdom. Daniel predicted the dramatic rise of a man who will hold sway over a large part of the earth until he is defeated by the coming of Christ."[24] It behooves us to pay attention to what Daniel has to say about the little horn, because when the little horn stands up, everything on Planet Earth will change forever.

Verse 9 tells us that Antichrist will move southeast and toward the pleasant land. The pleasant land is Palestine (Psalm 106:24). In order to move southeast, then, he must begin in a place northwest of Palestine. Of all the places on the map that are northwest of Palestine, one is of great interest: Germany. The country of Germany, as its borders are now defined, is half in and half out of the historical area of the Roman Empire. Thus, it qualifies as both being one of the ten horns, and yet separate from them. The little horn could arise in a part of Germany that would qualify as another distinct horn as the little horn is said to be in Daniel's second vision. I find it interesting, too, that Hitler came out of Germany. If Hitler was an attempt on the part of Satan to produce the Antichrist, Satan certainly got the area right! The prince of the host of haven referred to in verse 11 is Satan himself. Satan will completely control the little horn.

Habakkuk, too, speaks of the eastward movement of "the Chaldean," or Antichrist. And Habakkuk adds an interesting detail: "He will heap up dust and take it." Dust is Antichrist's weapon of conquest! This made no sense in times past; it makes terrifying sense in today's age of nuclear weapons and biological warfare. Antichrist will first conquer three nations in the old Roman Empire, but from the very beginning he will aim towards Palestine.

"And in the latter time of their kingdom, when the transgressors are come to the full, a king of fierce countenance, and understanding dark sentences, shall stand up. And his power shall be mighty, but not by his own power: and he shall destroy wonderfully, and shall prosper, and practice, and shall destroy the mighty and the holy people. And through his policy also he shall cause craft to prosper in his hand; and he shall magnify himself in his heart, and by peace shall destroy many: he shall also stand up against the Prince of princes; but he shall be broken without hand. And the vision of the evening and the morning which was told is true: wherefore shut thou up the vision; for it shall be for many days. And I Daniel fainted, and was sick certain days; afterward I rose up, and did the king's business; and I was astonished at the vision, but none understood it" (Daniel 8: 23-27).

"A king of fierce countenance and understanding dark sentences..."The phrase "dark sentences" means diabolical knowledge that is usually not understood by men. The power and the understanding of the king are satanic. Further, 2 Thessalonians 2:9 says that he is coming with *all* power. All of the world will wonder at him whose coming is after the working of Satan.

"He shall destroy wonderfully..." The New American Standard Bible translates this as follows, "He will destroy to an extraordinary degree and prosper and perform his will; He will destroy mighty men and the holy people." Revelation 13:4 asks, "Who is like unto the beast? Who is able to make war with him?"

It is a rhetorical question for, indeed, no one can. In fact, his power will be due to his superior knowledge. He will be in the same position as was the United States when she, and only she, had the knowledge of the atomic bomb. The United States was able to bring World War II to a close because no one could war against her. So, too, will it be with Antichrist in his day. He will have access to knowledge that is unknown even to the great scientists of his day. Prophecy is never an exaggeration; if anything, it understates future events. Prophecy has outlined an horrific scenario which will facilitate the rise of Antichrist. It cannot be downplayed. The world will come right up to the brink of disaster. Satan will be there, waiting to propel Antichrist onto the world scene, as he watches it happen. Satan is all too ready to see the world destroyed if he cannot rule it through his puppet, Antichrist. God will put aside His restraining power and allow Antichrist access to the world stage. Antichrist will "save" the world. He will have scientific knowledge that no other man alive on earth has comprehended. He will understand the "dark sentences," and he will be able to make war against all who will stand in his way in a way that renders their defenses obsolete and their offenses tame and ineffective.

"By peace [he] shall destroy many." Although in possession of the ultimate in warfare technology, and although he has already used that technology to subdue three countries, for the most part Antichrist will use peace as a weapon of deception that will lead to the people's destruction. Remember 1 Thessalonians 5:3 which states, "For when they shall say, Peace and safety; then sudden destruction cometh upon them, as travail upon a woman with child; and they shall not escape." As a man, Antichrist will never conquer the whole world, but as Satan, his influence will be universal. He will rid the world of fear and restore to them hope, peace, and prosperity.

"And I Daniel fainted, and was sick certain days." Although his previous vision was so disturbing that Daniel could not bring himself to share it even with his closest companions, this vision was so disturbing and distressing that Daniel actually lost consciousness. After coming to his senses, the memory of it made him physically sick for days. The very frightening thing to keep in mind is that Daniel simply saw what was destined to happen to produce the Antichrist; the Christian Church of that day will live it.

DANIEL'S FOURTH VISION
The world-wide famine in the times of Pharaoh would change the course of history. It's importance cannot be underestimated. Thus God gave two dreams to Pharaoh

concerning it. God has now doubled that number of visions for the subject of the coming world empires. We are dealing with a very weighty spiritual matter here.

The fourth vision of Daniel's was very straightforward; he saw a man clothed in linen with a girdle of fine gold. The body of this man resembled a beryl stone. This was a precious stone to the Jew and was one of the stones found upon the breastplate of the high priest. The color meant is uncertain as beryl stones can range from being colorless to blues and violets, and also to yellows and browns. His face had the appearance of lightning, while his eyes appeared to be lamps of fire. His arms and his feet were as brass, and his voice was the voice of a multitude. This is remarkably similar to the vision that John had of Jesus in Revelation 1. In fact, Daniel was seeing Christ and Christ had a final message for him concerning the last days. Before giving the message to Daniel, though, Christ tells him something very interesting. He tells Daniel that He had intended to come to him right away, but that the prince of Persia (modern day Iran) had come against him and had waged battle with Christ for twenty-one days until finally He and Michael the archangel were able to prevail. How very interesting that the prince of Persia, a demonic entity, sought so hard to keep this final message out of the hands of Daniel, and thus out of the hands of all who would later read Daniel's book. What was this message? "Now I (Christ) am come to make thee understand what shall befall thy people in the latter days: for yet the vision is for many days" (Daniel 10:14). Satan did not want this outline of the final days to be given to or understood by men. Christ now commences to tell Daniel that there would be three more kings who would arise in Persia and that the fourth and final king would be richer than all who had gone before. This king, through his strength, would stir up the realm of Greece. History records that all this happened exactly as prophesied. The fourth king of Persia was Xerxes, and his invasion of Greece raised up Alexander the Great.

Christ went on to say that the mighty king of Greece would rule with great dominion and would do exactly as he wished. After this king, Alexander, the kingdom would be broken up and would be divided into four parts. He then prophesied of

Rome in verses 5-19 of chapter 11 of Daniel; chronicling both her rise and fall.

Verses 20-45 go into great detail about Antichrist. Some very interesting details are given. Beginning in verse 20, Daniel records, "Then shall stand up in his estate [as a successor to Rome] a raiser of taxes in the glory of the kingdom: but within few days he shall be destroyed, neither in anger, nor in battle. And in his estate shall stand up a vile person, to whom they shall not give the honour of the kingdom: but he shall come in peaceably, and obtain the kingdom by flatteries." The mystery of this two-part manifestation of Antichrist -the raiser of taxes who is soon killed, and the vile person who supplants him - will be dealt with in great detail in the next chapter. It is important to remember one more detail in conjunction with it; verse 38 says that Antichrist will worship Satan whom Daniel calls "the god of forces: a god whom his fathers knew not." This is an interesting point. One of the main premises of New Age thought is to let go of one's rational thought processes and listen to your "inner voice." The next step is to allow oneself to be a channel for higher intelligence. Become a "channeler." An example of this was in the movie "Star Wars". Luke Skywalker prevailed at the end because he let "The Force" direct him. Antichrist will also be led by "The Force," or as Daniel calls him, "the god of forces." The force, under either name, comes in and takes over one's mind if invited to. It can come in by visualization, occult meditation, drug use, etc. But it is an evil, unholy force; it is the force that will be worshipped by Antichrist.

Daniel calls Antichrist "a raiser of taxes to the restoration of the kingdom." At the time of the birth of Christ, a decree went out from Caesar Augustus that all the world should be taxed. When a decree goes forth like that again, Antichrist will have come.

ANTICHRIST WILL APPEAR BEFORE THE RAPTURE OCCURS

The rise of Antichrist will happen before the Rapture. He will be firmly in place as the predominant world ruler while Christians still remain on the earth. Today, the most common position taken as to the timing of his rise is that it happens after Rapture. This is erroneous, but this error is not a new one. Paul dealt with it even in his day and age with the Thessalonian Church. The Thessalonian Church of the first century was undergoing so much persecution that she began to surmise, and then teach, that the Rapture had already occurred and that somehow the Christians there had missed it. They were afraid that they had been left behind, and were now experiencing the reign of the Antichrist. Paul wrote the entire letter of 2 Thessalonians in order to put their minds at ease by explaining once again the timing of the Rapture. And in chapter 2 of that letter, he places the Rapture squarely *after* the rise of the antichrist. "Now we request you, brethren, with regard to the coming of our Lord Jesus Christ, and our gathering together to Him, that you may not be quickly shaken from your composure or be disturbed either by a spirit or a message or a letter as if from us, to the effect that the day of the Lord has come. Let no one in any way deceive you, for it will not come unless the apostasy comes first, and the man of lawlessness is revealed, the son of destruction, who opposes and exalts himself above every so-called god or object of worship, so that he takes his seat in the temple of God, displaying himself as being God. Do you not remember that while I was still with you, I was telling you these things? And you know what restrains him now, so that in his time he may be revealed. For the mystery of lawlessness is already at work; only he who now restrains will do so until he is taken out of the way. And then that lawless one will be revealed whom the Lord will slay with the breath of His mouth and bring to an end by the appearance of His coming; that is, the one whose coming is in accord with the activity of Satan, with all power and signs and false wonders, and with all the deception of wickedness for those who perish, because they did not receive the love of the truth so as to be saved. And for this reason God will send upon them a deluding influence so that they might believe what is false, in order that they all may be judged who did not believe the truth, but took pleasure in wickedness" (II Thessalonians 2:1-12, NASB).

"With regard to the coming of our Lord Jesus Christ, *and our gathering together to Him.*" This can only refer to Rapture since we are not gathered to Him at the Second Coming, we come back with Him at that time. Paul clearly states in verse 3 that that day, the Rapture, will not come until the apostasy comes, and the man of lawlessness - Antichrist - is revealed. Again, Rapture will not come until the man of lawlessness is revealed. What restrains him now, the Holy Spirit, will continue to do so until He is taken out of the way. Some misread this passage by saying that the restraint will continue until the Church is taken out of the world. First, it takes God, Himself, to restrain Satan. If the Church could do it, why haven't we done it?!! Second, the Bible does not say "taken out of the world," the Bible says "taken out of the way." The point, here, is that the Antichrist cannot pick and choose his own time. The timing will be entirely up to God, not up to the Church, and when God decides that the time is right, He will step out of the way and allow Antichrist to exert his influence. The Holy Spirit will *never* be taken out of the world. If the position is taken that He will, who will indwell the new believers, the tribulation saints? Are they not Christians, have they not accepted Jesus, do they now not receive the promised gift of the Holy Spirit. Let me repeat, the Holy Spirit will *never* be taken out of the world. He will, however, stop restraining evil for a time and allow Antichrist his designated time on earth. Granted, Antichrist is different after the Rapture than he is before, both in power and manifested malevolence towards Christians in particular, but his initial ascent to power comes before the Rapture. Another fact to be considered is that Antichrist's rise to power is predicated on the spirit of deception that is over the face of the earth. After the breaking in heaven of the first seal, Satan's satanic spirit of deception is greatly weakened on the earth. And the breaking of the first seal is the *first* action that Jesus takes toward the world. Thus Antichrist must rise before the Rapture.

Why, then, do you suppose that so many Christians believe that the rise of the Antichrist occurs after the Rapture? I believe that this is a deliberate deception fostered by Satan. Consider for a moment that you are Satan and you are planning to send your man, Antichrist, and that, after all, you are the god of deceit and deception and lies. And your mortal enemy is the Church and the understanding of end time events is given to that Church by God. Would you encourage an understanding and belief in those people that they need to be on the lookout for this man? Would you teach them to recognize him or would you encourage them to not worry about him? Would not your teaching stress that they need not worry about him because they would be long gone in the Rapture before the world would ever see him? I believe that Satan is doing his spade-work in the Church, teaching believers to not worry about the one thing that they most need to be on guard about if they are to affect the non-believers around them and save them from deception. It all depends on if the Christians know their Bible as to whether he succeeds.

THREE PROPHETIC TIME ZONES BEFORE THE RAPTURE

If, then, the rise of the Antichrist comes before the Rapture, it behooves the Church to recognize the prophetic signs that are given concerning the time of his rise. There are three distinct time zones during the build-up to Rapture. However, they will all happen in their entirety in just one generation. Once the clock starts ticking, it will take very little time. The three time zones are:

1. The buildup to a world crisis, at the apex of which Antichrist will come to prominence.

2. The working of satanic signs and wonders by Antichrist that will convince the world that he is the new Christ. As the world comes to believe this, Antichrist will effect major changes in the economic, political, religious, and geographic spheres of the world.

3. "As in the days of Noah" is how Jesus described this time. The meaning is that these days will be like the condition of the world prior to The Flood when Noah was both preaching and building the ark. They were days of extraordinary peace, prosperity, and skepticism concerning the coming wrath of God. When the world is securely in those days of Noah, look for the imminent coming of Jesus.

All the great men of history are products of their times. So, too, will be Antichrist. The times will produce him and propel him to prominence. What if George Washington or Abraham Lincoln had been born either a hundred years earlier or later than they were? Our nation's history would most likely have been remarkably different. In an historically critical time, two things are factors: the unique person or persons, and the unique times which forge the circumstances that allow the man to come forward. The antichrist will be pivotal to world history. So, too, will be the times that produce him. Therefore, it stands to reason that we cannot look first for the person, we must look for the times. That is exactly what biblical prophecies instruct us to do, however, it seems that is not what most Christians are doing. They are intent on identifying the man although they are ignorant about the times that will produce him. They then erroneously identify men such as Kissinger, Gorbachev, King Juan Carlos of Spain, etc. as being the antichrist.

Antichrist will appear on the world scene just when it looks as if the earth and all who dwell in her are rushing headlong into annihilation. He will appear and he will save the day. In turn, he will be revered by an unknowing and deceived humanity. Much information is given about Antichrist in scripture and he will fulfill every detail.

TIME ZONE ONE

#1. *Worldwide Deception.* The first sign of the build-up to the world crisis that will produce Antichrist will be a worldwide deception of all the peoples of the earth. We just read in II Thessalonians 2:1-12 where the coming of Antichrist is linked with a great deception that will permeate the thought processes of mankind. "And for this reason God will send upon them a deluding influence so that they might believe what is false, in order that they all may be judged who did not believe the truth, but took pleasure in wickedness." When the disciples asked Jesus what would be the signs of His coming and of the end of the world (the very things we are asking two thousand years later), the very first thing Jesus said was, "Take heed that no man deceive you," (Matthew 24:4). (An interesting side note is that as Jesus answers their questions, he is sitting on the Mount of Olives. That means He is sitting on the exact spot where He will return to earth at the Battle of Armageddon, but He mentions none of this to His disciples.)

Revelation 12:9 reiterates the deceptive abilities of Satan. This deceptive spirit will be potent, causing even Christians to leave the truth. Paul prophesies this in I Timothy 4:1 when he writes, "Now the Spirit speaketh expressly, that in the latter times some shall depart from the faith, giving heed to seducing spirits, and doctrines of devils." Those who would argue the possibility of this must argue with the words of Paul, not with me.

The time is coming when world events will divide the Church between those who will follow the greatest deceiver who will ever live and those who will hold fast to the gospel delivered once and for all. The scriptures are very clear about the Great Apostasy which will occur before the Rapture. Apostasy is not a term used of non-believers. Apostasy is a term that describes one who has once embraced Christianity but then has rejected it. Apostasy means "to fall away." Peter is clear that the greater judgment rests upon apostates, far more than simple non-believers. "For if after they have escaped the pollutions of the world through the knowledge of the Lord and Saviour Jesus Christ, they are again entangled therein, and overcome, the latter end is worse with them than the beginning. For it had been better for them not to have known the way of righteousness, than, after they have known it, to turn from the holy commandment delivered unto them. But it is happened unto them according to the true proverb, The dog is turned to his own vomit again; and the sow that was washed to her wallowing in the mire" (2 Peter 2:20-22).

"Now the spirit speaketh expressly..." The Spirit is forced to speak expressly because this fact will be so contested by many within the Church! Deception will be the prevailing state of these times. The most complete and universal program of deceit ever known will be foisted upon the world. Satan is called "the father of lies" by the scriptures; this era will be his masterpiece. The conditions at the end will bring forth such a climate of deceit that only those believers who are fully Spirit-filled, i.e. who have enough oil for their lamps, will stay awake. Jesus sounds this warning in Matthew 24:24 when He says, "For there shall arise false Christs, and false prophets, and shall shew great signs and wonders; insomuch that, if it were possible, they shall deceive the very elect." In order to understand this verse we must understand that the word "if" in the phrase "if it were possible," is a first-class conditional clause meaning "if, and it certainly is, possible." With this understanding the verse now reads, "For there shall arise false Christs, and false prophets, and shall shew great signs and wonders; insomuch that, if, and it certainly is, possible, they shall deceive the very elect." This is strong stuff, so strong that I stand amazed at the church teachers who tell people not to worry about being on their guard, it will all take care of itself. This is the antithesis of what Jesus and the Gospel writers warned the Church to do. And, as always, the truth is on the side of Jesus, therefore, the Church needs desperately to be told to be alert, to be aware, to be on guard against the coming deception of Antichrist. The Church will be here at the rise of Antichrist, the Church will be present when the winds of deception blow strongly upon the world. The Church must raise her voice against the deception with the truth of Jesus.

One of the central biblical truths that will be most scorned at this point will be the doctrine of the return of Christ. Even with the apostasy prevalent today in the very liberal seminaries within the Church, the doctrine of the Second Coming has not been met with undue derision and scorn. It may be questioned, it may even be dismissed, but it is not now met with extreme hostility and even hilarity. It will be. Satan will soon turn his attention to the doctrine of the Second Coming, central to the Christian faith and ever her hope, and will attack it as systematically and effectively as he has attacked the doctrine of Creation. Mark that development, it is prophetic. "Now learn the parable from the fig tree: when its branch has already become tender, and puts forth its leaves, you know that summer is near: even so you too, when you see all these things, recognize that He is near, right at the door" (Matthew 24:32-33). Deception will be the hallmark of these times. To some degree, being human has meant being vulnerable to deception and error, but this will be deception on a heretofore unimaginable scale. Some of the seemingly most spiritual people will be completely taken in by Satan's program. The deception will be worldwide and complete; it will be Satan's masterpiece. It will prepare the way for the next sign ... the rise of false christs.

#2. *The Rise of False Christs.* After warning the disciples not to be deceived, the next thing Jesus mentioned was the rise of many false christs who would deceive many people. Starting almost immediately after the ascension of Jesus, false christs have begun to appear. At the time of the end, however, we will see a special situation. These false christs will not simply be false teachers and cult figures; they will say "I am Christ." They will claim to be God. In years past, I found this hard to imagine, for I felt that they would simply be laughed off of the world religious scene. I no longer find myself incredulous. The entire New Age, eastern philosophy so in vogue at present has completely changed popular thought. Now, to say that we are all one with God, and, in fact, each hold god-consciousness, makes this claim to be Christ almost respectable. What will make it completely respectable, is the New Age teaching that Christ was simply one of a long line of avatars; messengers sent to the earth at appropriate times in order to enlighten mankind. Christ was one, Mohammed was one, Buddha was one, and soon another (or many others) will come to earth. The new avatars will be "way-showers" as were all who came before them. This will also explain the apparent conflict between claims; in other words, how can one be Christ if another one is claiming to be him at the same time? Simple, many can be christs. Even Christ was simply a "christ"!

So instead of competing claims, we have claims reinforcing one another. In the Greek, Mark and Luke leave out "Christ" completely when they record the claims of this time. Instead they say that the false christ will simply claim to be "I Am." This claim is, if possible, even more blasphemous than the claim to be Christ. "I AM" is what Jehovah God called Himself. The fact that there will be many of these false christs, and that they will be so readily received, shows that this time will be one of great religious fervor. There are few cults in times of apathy but there are many in times of revival. Although there *will* be great, godly revival at this time, do not mistake the fervor of the false christ for holy or godly fervor. It will simply be religious fervor, as were many eras of paganism.

There is one more amazing aspect to these false christs: they will preach prophecy! Luke tells us that they will preach that "the time is at hand," that is "the end is near." This preaching will be Satan's attempt to counteract the great spiritual power that will be evident at this time in the Philadelphian Church. The various messages which have been brought by the myriad of false christs throughout the ages have always been specifically geared to the times and they have twisted the true message of God given for that time. Consider the rise in popularity of occultism in the nineteenth century which was designed to blunt and prevent the results that the so-termed "Great Awakening" outpouring of God's Holy Spirit was having on the entire United States at that time. Consider the New Age Movement that appeared at just about the same time as the Jesus Movement did. It was, and is, a war for the minds and souls of the people. Today in contrast to the "Truth of God" we have "true enlightenment." The times that will produce Antichrist will also be times of great prophetic fulfillment. And, if God's people are not there for the world with prophetic knowledge, Satan's people will be. They will tailor their message so that the interpretation of the signs point, not to God, but to Antichrist. There is a very strong admonition given by Peter to believers to be ready with an answer of why Christians have hope when times seem hopeless to the World: "Be ready always to give an answer to every man that maketh you a reason of the hope that is in you with meekness and fear" (I Peter 3:15).

It is imperative, then, that Christians learn their Bible, their entire Bible. Possibly one-fourth of scripture is prophetic; that leaves an enormous window of vulnerability for the average Christian. "My people are destroyed for lack of knowledge" (Hosea 4:6).

Because conditions on earth will be changing so quickly, it will not escape anyone's notice that things prophesied long ago are coming to pass. Fulfilled prophecy is one of the most amazing miracles of the Bible. Last-days prophecy fulfillment has been ordained by God to bring in countless souls before the return of Jesus. Woe to the church if she fails in this task! The void will be filled by the false christs.

#3. *Wars and Rumors of Wars.* Along with a great spirit of deception and the coming of false christs will come the next signpost that Jesus gave to the disciples: Wars and rumors of wars. Jesus was not talking about the conditions of war that have been prevalent for the centuries that man has been upon the earth. So familiar are we with wars and rumors of wars, that many eschatologists discount this sign entirely. They do this to their great peril. Surely Jesus was aware of the history of mankind, therefore He had to have something very different in mind when this warning was given by Him. He is fully aware that there have been few years, if any, where there has been widespread peace upon the earth. Therefore, the scale and intensity of the wars and the rumors have got to be greatly magnified from the usual "same ol', same ol'" in order for this to be a sign. This intensity is a twentieth-and-twenty-first century phenomenon in several ways.

First, global knowledge of war is recent. In years past, a war involving the Incas would have passed unnoticed in China. Now, news reporting is truly on a global scale. It is understood that no local war can be written off as isolated from a world context because, at any moment, events can escalate it from the local sphere into the global sphere. Second, up until the development of nuclear weapons, man's ability to destroy the world was also localized. Now, we know all too well that it is not.

For wars and rumors of wars to be a sign of the last days, we have to be talking about the terror and uncertainty present during war and during the talk of war to be a universal terror. The whole world will seem to be exploding with conflict everywhere and all at once. The rush to annihilation by mankind will be the talk on everyone's tongue. Civility and control will seem a thing of the past as terrifying rumors and destruction unfold daily. Any one of a number of unstable leaders could destroy all traces of human life, and it appears that the threat of that is constant. The anxiety and uncertainty experienced by human kind will be unprecedented in the annals of history. This *will* be a sign of unmistakable import. It will be such a troubling and fear- provoking sign that Jesus felt compelled to tell his brethren to "*be not terrified.*" Even Christians at this point will need supernatural reassurance that mankind will not destroy the world because every sign will point in that direction.

At this point in human history, the conflicts and tension will be so universally high that there will be only two choices available to the world: either man will destroy it (and himself) or prophecy will be fulfilled. Keep in mind, however, that Jesus states that these are but the "birth pangs" that come before the birth [i.e. Rapture]. "The end is not yet." Many will mistake all of this for the time of Tribulation and will wonder, "Where is the coming of Jesus?" It is very possible that the mid-trib viewpoint will be much in vogue because it will seem that the Rapture failed to happen on a pre-trib timetable. This is, of course, not true. Everything is on schedule, a pre-trib schedule, Christians have just not been taught the prophetic signs that will accompany the Rapture.

The Gospel of Luke sheds even more light upon this time because, along with listing wars and rumors of wars, Luke adds that there will be "commotions." We must understand the Greek import of this word, because, to our ears, it sounds more like an overturned table at a backyard barbeque than anything that would be truly terrifying. The word "commotions" in Greek might best be described as "internal strife and unrest." "Instability" describes the situation in twenty-first century verbiage. Picture the Watts Riots in the 1960s. Picture Los Angeles after the Rodney King verdict. Picture unrestrained rioting and looting. Picture the gang scenes from "A Clockwork Orange." That is the picture in view here. The unrest will be everywhere on the national scene, but the violence will also reach into almost every neighborhood, even staid neighborhoods which have never seen anything approaching this. Terror will truly abound. But, "be not terrified."

A very clear picture of these times is given by the prophet Habakkuk. Habakkuk was somewhat of a mystery man; very little is known about him. He was from Judah but it is not known in what part of Judah he resided. He appeared out of nowhere, gave an extraordinary prophecy to the world, and then seemed to disappear back into oblivion. But God knew the importance of this message, and saw fit to save his prophecy, giving him a book in the Bible. Habakkuk begins his prophecy with these words; "The burden which Habakkuk the prophet did see." And what a burden it was! The book of Habakkuk chronicles the rise of the Chaldean (the name by which he calls the Antichrist) and the times surrounding that rise. He uses the following words to describe it: Violence, iniquity, grievance, spoiling, strife, contention, and wrong judgment. A reading of the corresponding time in Daniel paints the picture even more bleakly. Add to the wars, the rumors of wars, and the internal unrest a picture of total government corruption. During these times of injustice and personal grievance, no justice will be available to the aggrieved. As Habakkuk wrote in chapter one, verse three: "Therefore the law is paralyzed, and justice never prevails. The wicked hem in the righteous, so that justice is perverted." (NIV) The spoilers of property, the illegal confiscators of property will find no threat to their tactics of violence and falsehoods in the judicial courts of that day. The corruption will allow all spoils to the highest bidder, or the bidder with the greatest political influence. Daniel 8:23 prophesies, "And in the latter time of their kingdom, when the transgressors are come to the full, a king of fierce countenance, and understanding dark sentences, shall stand up." The king of fierce countenance is Antichrist. What is meant by "when the transgressors are come to the full" is that corruption is so extensive that it presents a threat to the entire fabric of government and civil justice. The systems of government under which citizens will live will be completely evil. It is almost impossible for modern day Americans to understand a system that is so completely rigged and corrupt. But, that will be the state of all governments of this time, even in America. Perhaps, for us, that is the most chilling prophecy of all. When Habakkuk was given his vision, he was so shaken and dismayed by it that he refused to record it. It seemed to him that God had lost and that the Chaldean would take over the world. The horror of that was so complete that he could not record it. He told God that he would simply wait for a different vision! God answered him thus, "Write the vision, and make it plain upon tables, that he may run that readeth it. For the vision is yet for an appointed time, but at the end it shall speak, and not lie: though it tarry, wait for it; because it will surely come, it will not tarry." In other words, "Habakkuk, the vision that you saw is inescapable. It will come, it will happen. *At the end* it will become plain and the people will need to have your knowledge. You must write what you have seen, no matter how distressing it may be." Few prophecies in the Bible are so strongly emphasized.

The first two chapters of Habakkuk have only one subject, Antichrist, although he is not initially identified. Instead, the conditions surrounding his ascent to power are described in detail. Habakkuk writes of widespread misery; of confiscation of private property, of roving bands of thugs (the "commotions" of Luke), of terror and tyranny reaching into every neighborhood, and, again, of the widespread corruption in society. And when this happens there is no justice, no recourse in the courts. This will distress even the Christians but it shouldn't. Jesus specifically told us to "lay not up for yourselves treasures upon earth, where moth and rust doth corrupt, and where thieves break through and steal" (Matthew 6:19). I don't think we will realize how much of our security truly rests in our possessions and in our government until that security crumbles. Once again, our security will have to be placed totally in Jesus.

The vision of this situation was so grim that Habakkuk despaired for humanity. He saw the world becoming totally dark with no apparent hope of deliverance. It seemed to him that the entire world would be lost and God's program of redemption would be brought to an abrupt end. The people who live through this time will feel exactly the same way. The church *must* have the light and knowledge of what is going on and they must share it with the world.

Chapter 1 of Habakkuk deals with the coming and destruction of the Chaldeans, but in verse 7 the subject changes from the plural to the singular as translated in the Septuagint Version of the Old Testament. Most probably what is meant by the term "Chaldeans" (plural form) is the system of government that will be found at the end of the times before Rapture. But at verse 7, we see the appearance of Antichrist (singular form) chronicled. From then on, he is *the* Chaldean. It is no longer the system that is in view, Antichrist completely eclipses the system. As Habakkuk describes him, he is terrible and dreadful, he shall come to work violence and he shall deride every weapon that is fashioned against him. Most ominous is the verse that says that he will impute his power unto his god. His god is Satan. The power behind him is Satan's. The plan and genius behind him is Satan's. His knowledge and power are given to him by Satan. No nation will be able to withstand him. As hopeless as this may seem, it is not. Keep in mind that this short time of total domination is given to him by God, and he cannot come into his time until

God allows it. Even when the world is completely under his sway, God holds the veto power and God decrees the duration of his rule.

Why does God allow Antichrist this power? Habakkuk answers this in 1:12, "Art thou not from everlasting, O Lord my God, mine Holy One? we shall not die. O Lord, *thou hast ordained them [him] for judgment*; and, O mighty God, *thou hast established them [him] for correction*" (emphasis mine). In other words, through Antichrist there will come to the earth both judgment and correction. The evil will rise to the top in order for God to chasten and judge it. There is another, even more critical, result that is recorded in 2:14, "For the earth shall be filled with the knowledge of the glory of the Lord, as the waters cover the sea." As unlikely as it might seem, these times will point many people to Jesus because of their great despair and hopelessness, and if Christians are as disheartened as are unbelievers, then a great opportunity will be missed. I am reminded of the words of J.R.R. Tolkien in his book The Fellowship of the Ring where he writes of the perilous times facing that fictional world:

"I wish the ring had never come to me, I wish none of this had happened," said Frodo.

"So do all who live to see such times," replied Gandalf, "but that's not for them to decide. All we have to do is decide what to do with the time given us. There are other forces in this world besides the will of evil."

And so it will be now. The Church must take hold of this courage.

#4. *Natural Disasters.* Coupled with the wars, rumors of wars, internal strife and lawlessness, and the breakdown of the justice system will be an increase of purely natural disasters. In times past, when the people ignored God's word to them whether spoken or written, He responded to their apathy with natural disasters. True to form, earthquakes, famines, pestilence, fearful sights, and great signs from heaven are all mentioned by Jesus as occurring at this time. These, of course, will be from the hand of God and will serve to further destabilize the social systems. The pitch of pure fear and terror at all of this instability is hard to imagine on this side of the events. Security, peace, and hope, will all be in extremely short supply. The whole world will be staggering under the weight of seemingly impossible problems. This is all in the plan of God, and under His control. But only a few will recognize and understand that fact. The only people who will be able to witness in times like these are the people who know what God intends to do.

#5. *The Appearance of Antichrist.* As Habakkuk recorded, extraordinary times will produce an extraordinary man, Antichrist. In order to prepare the way, the world will walk into an experience that has never been faced before by the world or by the church. This will be a time of total terror, men's hearts will fail them, they will die from fear. The world will seem to be rushing toward destruction; violence will be the rule of the day. Famines, pestilence and earthquakes will be all too commonplace. All hope of survival will be gone. Everyone will be looking for Jesus to come *at that time* to rescue them. But He will not come. Someone else will appear on the world scene. At the last minute a man will rise up with a singular power to prevent the destruction of the world, bring the world back to its senses and bring about world stability. The terror will come to an abrupt end by the appearance of Antichrist. He will, without doubt, be the most sensational man besides Christ who will ever appear on the face of the earth. He will produce an hypnotic effect on the world. When the world is in a state of hopelessness and fear with no way out, here will be a man who seems to know exactly what to do and how to do it. Jesus, Himself, said that Antichrist would be equipped with "all power." Never mind that the knowledge to do so is satanic, it will only seem to be supernatural, not evil. At this point, and to its utter ruin, the world will pin its hopes on Satan's man.

TIME ZONE TWO

#6. *Satanic Signs and Lying Wonders.* Paul tells us in 2 Thessalonians 2:9 that the coming of Antichrist will be accompanied with all of the power of Satan and will manifest itself with signs and wonders that will support his lies. If anything further were needed to convince the world that their hope lay in the direction of this man, the lying wonders will do it. His demonstration of power will be so spectacular, so sensational, so amazing, that the world will fall at his feet. In fact, Satan's demonstrations of power are described in the same manner as is the witness of God Himself to the message of the Gospel. Both are accompanied with signs, wonders and miracles, but the Gospel is also accompanied with the gifts of the Holy Spirit. Antichrist's demonstrations of power will not be accompanied by the Spirit of Truth, no, the counter-spirit to the Spirit of Truth will be released: the Spirit of Deception. No wonder the world will be deceived! The mid-trib position taken by some Christians during the buildup to world crisis (what Jesus called "the birth pangs"), mistaken by them as the first part of the Great Tribulation, will very possibly now pass into a period of predominant post-trib thought. The rationale will be thus, "Hmm, we have passed through Tribulation and now an amazing man has appeared doing all manner of great signs and wonders. This has to be Christ. This is his post-trib appearance." Both positions will be born out of an ignorance of what the Bible says about the times of the end.

Conversely, if Christians know their prophecy, it will be impossible to miss the fact that this man is Antichrist precisely because of the miracles that he will perform. Do not think for one minute that Satan cannot perform miracles, his power allows much latitude in the spiritual realm. Consider the miracles that Pharaoh's magicians were able to do. That will be child's play in comparison to the wonders of Antichrist, and just as Jesus' miracles drew the people to Him, so, too, will the wonders of Antichrist draw the world to Satan's man. His demonstration of power is going to be so spectacular, so amazing, so sensational that no one who is looking for him can miss him.

The decision to look for him will be the rub. Part of the plan of deception being prepared even now by Satan is the idea that Christians will not be here at the rise of Antichrist. And, of course, if they won't be here, why bother to learn the signs of his coming? When Christians fall into this deceptive plan, and many teach that Antichrist's rise comes after the Rapture, it throws those who listen to those teachers off their guard, making them very vulnerable to this spirit of deception. It is dangerous to teach that none of these things can happen before the Rapture; Christians must be prepared. This was the precise point of Jesus when He told the parable of the Ten

Virgins. What was the danger to them? Sleepiness, inattention, ennui, complacency. Jesus understood well what would be the tenor of that time, and He explicitly warned Christians to be on guard, to watch, to not fall asleep. Their voice will be the only voice raised against Antichrist. If they are silent, all mankind will be deceived. The world will love this man and those who speak against him will be ridiculed and soon hated. If you recognize him and speak out, trust me, you will not be the toast of too many cocktail parties. "True," they will say, "he did wipe out three nations, but look what he's done for the economy!" But when these things begin to come to pass, rejoice!, for it will be in that same generation that Jesus will return.

#7 . *A New Church Era.* The Age of the Philadelphian Church will now give way to the Age of the Laodicean Church. The Philadelphian Church will continue to exist and exist with power (it is she for whom Christ shall return), however, the Laodicean Church will now be far larger, far more prominent, and far more influential of the two churches as concerns the world arena. Because the Laodicean Church will be the predominant church, it is a given that this church will embrace Antichrist as readily as will the world. They are blind, Jesus said, and they will miss the spiritual battle that will rage. This will not be the first time that the Church has been deceived. During the rise of Adolph Hitler, many Christians in Germany embraced Hitler as the gift of God to Germany. Known as "German Christians," they were entrenched in the church leadership positions. Their spokesman, Hermann Gruner, made it clear for what they stood: "The time is fulfilled for the German people in Hitler. It is because of Hitler that Christ, God the helper and redeemer, has become effective among us. Therefore National Socialism is positive Christianity in action.... Hitler is the way of the Spirit and the will of God for the German people to enter the Church of Christ."

It was against this prevailing attitude on the part of the German Church that men like Dietrich Bonhoeffer and Martin Niemoller strove. They were not successful. Neither will be those who seek to warn the Laodicean Church. Blind she is and blind she will remain. She will be totally taken in by Antichrist. Preachers will extol the virtues of Antichrist, he will be praised from pulpits over all the world. To speak against him, will invite scorn and outrage. It will take great courage on the part of Christians to proclaim that this adored man is the son of Satan. Nonetheless, it will be demanded of them by God.

#8. *Great World Prosperity.* It is quite possible that a worldwide economic crisis will accompany the world instability that will produce Antichrist. If so, it will not remain after his coming. In fact, Antichrist will bring about the greatest prosperity and the greatest tranquility that has ever been experienced on earth. "For when they shall say, Peace and safety; then sudden destruction cometh upon them" (1 Thessalonians 5:3). As Ezekiel 28:4-5 prophesied about Antichrist, "With thy wisdom and with thine understanding thou hast gotten thee riches, and hast gotten gold and silver into thy treasures. By thy great wisdom and by thy traffic hast thou increased thy riches, and thine heart is lifted up because of thy riches."

What will result will be world prosperity to a degree that has never been experienced before. It is wealth - across the board wealth - that is almost beyond comprehension. Everyone will be happy. Remember, the Church at this time is the church that says, "I am rich, and increased with goods, and have need of nothing." I have never heard a church say, "Don't give, I don't need anymore." This church will. And it is not simply America that will be the Land of Plenty. It will be a worldwide phenomenon. Zechariah 9:13 talks about the city of Tyre, located in Lebanon, where silver and gold will be as dust in the streets. It is not too difficult to understand this prosperity given world peace and a united world government. A truly free, worldwide market would certainly bring about world prosperity. Without trade restrictions of any sort and with global cooperation and the full employment that would follow, the line between the haves and the have-nots would soon disappear.

A case in point is the United States, herself. Because there is free trade, common language, common law, and common currency between the states, all of them prosper. Imagine for a moment if crossing from North Carolina into South Carolina was the same as crossing from America into Mexico. Imagine having to be subject to tariffs, passport restrictions, immigration restrictions, long lines, etc. at each state's border. But because that same political situation does not apply to the US and Mexico, it is easy to contrast the difference between the two countries which are, after all, as contiguous as are North and South Carolina. The world is rich enough in global resources; it is the politics and economic restrictions of the nations of the world that keep those nations in poverty. And not only would the underdeveloped countries prosper, there would also be full employment and increased prosperity in the developed countries as they produced the goods necessary to the well-being of the third world countries.

Why does Antichrist bring this prosperity to the world? Out of concern for man's well being? NO, he knows that the way to men's hearts is through their pocketbooks. Their increased wealth will make them adoring, lethargic, and accepting. Because of Antichrist's economic genius, because of the prosperity he brings to the world, he will be greatly revered. As we have seen in the late twentieth century, much can be forgiven a world leader if the economy is good. Imagine, then, a charismatic leader, working miracles, who also is able to bring peace out of tumult, and prosperity - incredible prosperity - out of depression. No one will consider him evil, no one will link him with the prophesies of Antichrist! No one, that is, except for those who know the signs.

#9. *The Building of Great Cities.* Another sign of the times immediately preceding Rapture will be the building of great cities. At least two ancient cities will be rebuilt. One will be in Lebanon and one will be in Iraq. Their splendor and opulence will be staggering. Lebanon's city, Tyre, will be the political capital of Antichrist, and Babylon, located in Iraq, will be the religious and commercial capital of the world. At first blush, this sounds ludicrous. It seems as likely as saying that Yuma, Arizona, will overtake Washington, DC, as the center of political power, and South Bend, Indiana, will become the financial center of world trade. Nonetheless, the Bible is specific. Tyre and Babylon will be the two major cities of the world at this point in time. They will both be monuments to the greatness of Antichrist. Babylon will once again be one of the wonders of the world as she was in the ancient world. She will be the greatest and costliest city ever built. Furthermore, only one other city, Tyre, will come close.

We are given insight into the grandeur of Tyre in Zechariah 9:3 which says, "And Tyrus [Tyre] did build herself a strong hold, and heaped up silver as the dust, and fine gold as the mire of the streets." The rebuilding of Tyre is assured because Ezekiel takes three chapters to describe the destruction of Tyre and he describes her destruction in a way by which Tyre has never been destroyed. She will have to be rebuilt in order to be destroyed that way. Ezekiel 28 describes the king of Tyre; he is Satan. The power of this prophetic sign is that when Tyre and Babylon, two inconsequential places today, assume their strategic importance on the world scene, there will be no denying the miracle of biblical prophecy.

Some will argue that, even though it is clear in prophecy that there will be grand cities during the reign of Antichrist, they could be built after the Rapture. The Bible is clear that they could not. We have seen the times after the Rapture; they are times of chaos and terror. Who is going to be able to build grand cities? Remember that the people of the world will be looking for animal feed to eat because the famine will be so extreme after the Rapture, and while not foraging for anything edible, they will be looking to find some water somewhere that has not been poisoned, or else they will be seeking some refuge from the infernal demon locusts in addition to trying to cope with numerous other horrors. No one will be designing and building metropolises.

#10. *Expansion of Egypt Across Africa.* When Egypt expands across Africa, gobbling up country after country, look for the Rapture, it is near. She will come up out of nowhere and will become a major world power. Although poor now, this will change dramatically. The Bible says that in the future there will be a huge lake formed south of Aswan. It is now there, Nassar Lake, created by the construction of the Aswan Dam. Isaiah suggests that there will be canals and ponds that are offshoots of the lake, full of fish, supporting the population. Egypt will, in fact, become so powerful that she will have visions of conquering the world for herself. Although a part of Antichrist's kingdom, this power of hers will foster some degree of independent action, and she will be a troublesome satellite in

Antichrist's orbit. Although there will be an uneasy coalition between Antichrist and Egypt because of their common enemy, Israel, at times there will even be warfare between the two. Jeremiah discusses Egypt in Jeremiah 46:7-10. "Who is this that cometh up like a flood, whose waters are moved as the rivers?" he asks. When Jeremiah wrote this the days when Egypt was a major world power were already gone. And never since that time has she reappeared again as a world power. But Jeremiah saw Egypt rising up once again to that status and he recorded it. He prophesied that Egypt will eat up lands as far as Lebanon, the border of Antichrist's kingdom, before she is stopped. At the point at which she is stopped, Egypt will head a confederation of nations that, according to Jeremiah and Ezekiel, will include Morocco, the Sahara, Sudan, Ethiopia, Libya (Put), and Algeria (Lud). Daniel also prophesied the rise of Egypt. She is the "King of the South" mentioned in Daniel 11. There will be Egyptian principalities and governors over all of the lands of the confederation. This is astonishing prophecy when one considers the poverty of Egypt today.

Since the time of Joseph, the story of Egypt has been intertwined with the story of Israel. It will continue to be so until the last days of her history. She will play a major role in the coming crisis in Israel, which will also be a sign of these end times.

#11. *Antichrist Attempts to Annihilate Every Living Jew.* Israel is not an accident. She is a planned nation in a planned location and God is not done dealing with Israel, nor will He ever repent of His everlasting covenant with her. He will not rest until there is a complete restoration of Israel to Himself. This restoration will consist of three steps (1) the return of the Jews to the land of Israel, (2]) the return of the Jews to God, (3) the coming of the Jews to Jesus as their Messiah. World War I freed the land of Palestine from the Turks, but there was no mass exodus by Jews to Palestine. It took Hitler to convince the Jews of the necessity of a homeland. Even so, although the land has been returned to the Jews, the Jews have not completely returned to the land, and many who have returned, have returned in unbelief. But the Bible states that every Jew will at some point be back in Israel, and furthermore, will come to believe fully in Him and in His Son. This has not happened but it will. The following is the story of how it will happen.

Consider that although the ancient land of Israel is now occupied by its rightful heirs, although there is now a national homeland for any Jew who wishes to claim it, the Jews, as a nation, have only returned to their land, language, and culture, they have not returned to God. Furthermore, the credit for their return to Israel is reserved for themselves, no glory is given to God. Israel, today, is, for the most part, a secular nation. Although there is an orthodox movement present there, it is highly controversial even in Israel. It took Hitler to return the Jews to the land. It will take even more to turn them to God; it will take Antichrist.

"And you, son of man, prophesy to the mountains of Israel and say, 'O mountains of Israel, hear the word of the Lord. Thus says the Lord God, "Because the enemy has spoken against you, 'Aha!' and 'The everlasting heights have become our possession,' therefore, prophesy and say, 'Thus says the Lord God, "For good cause they have made you desolate and crushed you from every side, that you should become a possession of the rest of the nations, and you have been taken up in the talk and the whispering of the people."'" 'Therefore, O mountains of Israel, hear the word of the Lord God. Thus says the Lord God to the mountains and to the hills, to the ravines and to the valleys, to the desolate wastes and to the forsaken cities, which have become a prey and a derision to the rest of the nations which are round about, therefore, thus says the Lord God, "Surely in the fire of My jealousy I have spoken against the rest of the nations, and against all Edom, who appropriated My land for themselves as a possession with wholehearted joy and with scorn of soul, to drive it out for a prey"'" (Ezekiel 36:1-5, NASB).

This prophecy concerns the land. It is even addressed to the land, "Prophesy to the mountains..." The prophecy is given to the hills, mountains, trees and streams because God is saying to the land, "Land you belong to me and I am going to restore you to the people that should be in you and then, as a consequence, you will bloom." We see this beginning to happen now in Israel simply because some of the Jews have returned.

At the time of the fulfillment of this prophecy, the land will once again be occupied by the enemies of Israel, nonetheless Israel has to be occupying some portion of it because the last verse says that the Arabs (Edom) are planning to cast them out. The time, therefore, is after the return of the land to the Jews but before the return of all of the Jews to the land. And every Jew will at some point return to Israel. God made a promise to Israel in Ezekiel 34:11-16 to search out and find every sheep that is His and to return it to the mountains of Israel. Verses 12-13 read as follows: "As a shepherd seeketh out his flock in the day that he is among his sheep that are scattered; so will I seek out my sheep, and will deliver them out of all places where they have been scattered in the cloudy and dark day. And I will bring them out from the people, and gather them from the countries, and will bring them to their own land, and feed them upon the mountains of Israel by the rivers, and in all the inhabited places of the country."

God promised the same thing to Moses stressing that His intention to recover every single Jew extended even to outer space! Nehemiah 1:8-9 reads, "Remember, I beseech thee, the word that thou commandedst thy servant Moses, saying, If ye transgress, I will scatter you abroad among the nations: But if ye turn unto me, and keep my commandments, and do them; though there were of you cast out *unto the uttermost part of the heaven,* yet will I gather them from thence, and will bring them unto the place that I have chosen to set my name there" (emphasis mine).

When, in Ezekiel 36:10, God talks about the promise of restoring the land to Israel He says it is for "all the house of Israel, even all of it." "All of Israel" is emphasized twice. When God emphasizes something in this way He is saying, "Get this, this is important." And here He is saying that this prophecy involves every single Israelite alive. Israel, each part of her, is going to come back to the land. Furthermore, when Moses is prophesying about this time in his last address to the Israelites in Deuteronomy chapters 28-30, he says in Deuteronomy 30:4-5 that, "If *any* of thine be driven out unto the outmost parts of heaven, from thence will the Lord thy God gather thee, and from thence will he fetch thee: And the Lord thy God will bring thee into the land which thy fathers possessed, and thou shalt possess it; and multiply thee above thy fathers" (emphasis mine).

That every Jew has returned to Israel is certainly not the case now, nor will it be the case when the Arab nations plot to cast them out of the land that is occupied. And it is while this remains the situation in Israel, before all the Jews in the world return within her borders, that the Arabs will rise up to reclaim the land that Israel now occupies.

The prophet Obadiah speaks of this confederation of Arab states that will align with Egypt to destroy the Jews. The desire on the part of the Arabs to drive out the Jews and take their land will be what brings about the second crisis in Israel, the crisis that will return them to God. Antichrist will already be on the world scene and will be revered by the world. He will set about to create a momentum of hatred against the Jews, much as did Hitler after ascending to power. There will, however, be a crucial difference. Hitler's sphere of influence was confined to the nation of Germany; Antichrist's sphere of influence will be the entire world. Once again, the Jews will be blamed for every evil found in society, and a hatred for them will be systematically engendered. Antichrist will then propose a "solution." He will propose, as Hitler did before him, that the world rid itself of every Jew found upon its face. There is diabolical intelligence behind this "final solution." If there are no Jews to be found on earth, prophecy concerning Israel in the end times cannot come to pass, and God's word (and thus, ultimately, God) will be defeated. Why? Psalm 138:2 tells us that God holds His word even above His name. Therefore, if prophecy fails, Satan wins it all.

When one understands that it was Satan, ultimately, who was behind Hitler and his plans for world domination, one begins to understand why Hitler, in the last days of the war, acted as he did. Although Nazi troops desperately needed supplies and ammunition, Hitler used almost every available train to transport, not food and guns to the troops, but Jews to the death camps. His generals were in equal parts dismayed and livid, but no one could go up against Hitler's decision. They failed in their attempts to reason with him because they were, in actuality, fighting different wars. The Nazi hierarchy was fighting the Allied Forces, while Hitler was fighting God.

Satan understood, and so directed Hitler, that it was not enough to defeat the Allies; their only hope lay in defeating God and to do so meant the total extermination of every Jew on the face of the earth. Adolph Hitler failed in that attempt but Satan will commandeer the rise of another who will propose the same "final solution" yet again.

Apparently Hitler had some inkling of this because, in a 1982 PBS interview with his personal aide, the aide described the last day of Hitler's life before he committed suicide. Hitler told his aide that he had decided to end his life and the aide declared that he would also, pledging his ultimate loyalty to Hitler even in defeat. The aide was upbraided by Hitler and told that he could not do so. When the aide, despairing, replied that he would not know what to do without his Fuhrer, Hitler commanded him to "serve the man who is coming after me." It is a chilling but entirely accurate prophecy.

And so, the nation of Israel will be sent into Egypt to die. But how do the Jews end up in Egypt in the first place? Deuteronomy 28:64-68 reveals that to us. It is the final solution of Antichrist. "And the Lord shall scatter thee among all people, from the one end of the earth even unto the other; and there thou shalt serve other gods, which neither thou nor thy fathers have known, even wood and stone. And among these nations shalt thou find no ease, neither shall the sole of thy foot have rest: but the Lord shall give thee there a trembling heart, and failing of eyes, and sorrow of mind: And thy life shall hang in doubt before thee; and thou shall fear day and night, and shalt have none assurance of thy life: In the morning thou shalt say, Would God it were even! and at even thou shalt say, Would God it were morning! For the fear of thine heart wherewith thou shalt fear, and for the sight of thine eyes which thou shalt see. *And the Lord shall bring thee into Egypt again with ships,* by the way whereof I spake unto thee. Thou shalt see it no more again: and there ye shall be sold unto your enemies for bondmen and bond women, and no man shall buy you" (Deuteronomy 28:64-68, emphasis mine).

First, God will scatter Israel throughout the nations of the world and then when they are scattered, the Lord will bring the Jews back into Egypt once again. But at this time they will come in ships. This cannot be explained by arguing that Moses is threatening them with a return to Egypt at the time that he spoke, for then they could have marched right back into Egypt. There would have been no need for ships. No, Moses is looking forward to a time when the Israelites will once again return as slaves to Egypt, but this time, instead of being indigenous people, they will be transported there from all over the world.

When will that be? When a man arises who has control over the nations of the world and who also has a pathological hatred for the Jews. Hitler had the hatred, but although he came close, he did not have the worldwide power. Antichrist will fulfill both criteria. He will engender a universal hatred for the Jews. And due to the spirit of deception that will be on the world he will be believed. Using his enormous power and influence over the nations of the world, Antichrist will offer those nations an option. "You are welcome to remain in my sphere of peace and affluence. There is but one criterion: Get rid of your Jews, every Jew found within your borders. Send them to Egypt where I have a settlement waiting for them. If you refuse, not only will you not share in my bounty, you will come under my wrath."

Keep in mind that his wrath has already been observed by the world because Antichrist has destroyed three nations who rose up against him when he came to power. So, although some nations may balk, most will not. In fact most of the people in the world apparently will embrace the plan. They may do so hesitantly at first because, after all, the world will remember World War II. They will remember how good people in Germany inexplicably did horrible things to the Jews. But that remembrance will be counterbalanced by other thoughts: "I do have a family to feed. I've got to think of my own safety. And Antichrist is so wise! He is so extraordinary! Maybe he knows something we don't know. Maybe the Jews are the problem. Who are we to say that they are not? Clearly, Antichrist has established his credibility. We need to listen to this man. I know it sounds insane, but has he been wrong yet? Well, maybe he is right about the Jews also." And so the program of Antichrist's will begin.

In the end, very few will speak out against the deportation except for the same little "odd ball group" that doesn't trust this man in the first place: The Christians. Hopefully, they will rise up in protest, but if the Christians do protest the action it will only serve to make them even more despised and reviled by the general population than they were before. The conscience of the world will be uneasy about this anyway; they will not want to be reminded of their cowardice.

But the Christians will have to have the courage to stand for the right against the prevailing winds of public opinion. Even today, when there are no legal or financial sanctions levied against Christian expression, many, many Christians are effectively silenced simply by not wanting to appear to be out of the mainstream of prevailing public thought. The sad but unmistakable fact is that Christian beliefs and mores will only be considered more extreme, not less, as the last days approach. That does not make their beliefs invalid, it only makes them unpopular. Revelation 21:8 speaks of those who will have a part in the lake of fire, the second death. Along with the unbelieving, the abominable, the murderers, etc. are listed the fearful. I am convinced that the fearful are listed because they did as much damage to people by refusing to stand for the convictions of God as did the abominable. Theirs might be sins of omission rather than sins of commission, but they are every bit as harmful to the work of the kingdom. C.S. Lewis made this point wonderfully well in The Screwtape Letters when he wrote: "...courage is not simply one of the virtues, but the form of every virtue at the testing point, which means, at the point of highest reality. A chastity or honesty or mercy which yields to danger will be chaste or honest or merciful only on conditions. Pilate was merciful till it became risky."[25]

Apparently "the carrot and the stick" of Antichrist's program for the Jews will be too powerful for any nation to refuse, for every Jew in every part of the world will find himself sent into Egypt to die as Ezekiel says, "with fury poured out." If one knows prophecy one absolutely cannot miss that the architect of this program is the man whom the Bible calls the Antichrist. The intensity and cruelty of this program is hard to conceive until one remembers the Holocaust. And this will be far worse. It will take some time for this planned annihilation to take place and it will not be a complete success. Some Jews apparently escape the desert for more populace parts of Egypt because Isaiah 19:18 says that five cities of Egypt will speak Hebrew.

And what of the Jews who are in Israel at that time? Antichrist will attack Israel and, with the help of the Arab nations, he will scatter the Jews in all directions, north, south, east and west, out of Palestine. They will be scattered as far as Ethiopia and Iraq. Keep in mind that Antichrist is so intent upon this because he knows that Christ is coming as King of the Jews and if Satan can annihilate the Jews, he can prevent the Second Coming. That is Antichrist's plan; God has another.

Both Ezekiel 20:33-38 and Deuteronomy 28:63-68 record the future of Israel when the "final solution" seems destined to succeed at last. Ezekiel writes: "As I live, saith the Lord God, surely with a mighty hand, and with a stretched out arm, and with fury poured out, will I rule over you: And I will bring you out from the people, and will gather you out of the countries wherein ye are scattered, with a mighty hand, and with a stretched out arm, and with fury poured out. And I will bring you into the wilderness of the people, and there will I plead with you face to face. Like as I pleaded with your fathers in the wilderness of the land of Egypt, so will I plead with you, saith the Lord God. And I will cause you to pass under the rod, and I will bring you into the bond of the covenant: And I will purge out from among you the rebels, and them that transgress against me: I will bring them fourth out of the country where they sojourn, and they shall not enter into the land of Israel: and ye shall know that I am the Lord."

"And I will cause you to pass under the rod." Passing under the rod denotes an extremely close inspection and a judgment. It is a shepherd's term. When the sheep that had been grazing all day would be gathered into the fold for the night, the shepherd would stand at the doorway and extend his rod, forcing each individual sheep to pass under it. As it did, the shepherd would check to see if anything were wrong with the sheep. It might be a bald spot, a sore, or a festering scratch underneath the wool that needed attention. Likewise, Israel will pass under the rod. God will minutely examine her, passing judgment on her miserable spiritual condition. But there in the deserts of Egypt, He will reconcile Israel to Himself and He will deliver her from her bondage. And in the same way that the good shepherd accounts for every single sheep under his care, so, too, will God account for every single Jew alive in the world. As was just quoted in Ezekiel, God will meet them there in the desert and plead with them face to face. Deuteronomy 30:1 speaks of the hand of God gathering the Jews from all the nations of the world in order to cause them to repent and turn to Him. He will chasten them (cause them to "pass under the rod"), and will purge the rebellious Jews entirely, but the remaining Jews will repent and turn back, realizing that if they do, God will, as always, keep His end of the covenant. He will recover by His strong hand the scattered Jews and the captive Jews. He will then deliver them, miraculously leading them out of Egypt and back into their own land as Isaiah 11 records. Verses 11 and 12 are particularly noteworthy: "And it shall come to pass in that day, that the Lord shall set his hand *again the second time* to recover the remnant of people, which shall be left, from Assyria [probably the empire of Antichrist, because he is called the Assyrian in prophecy], and from Egypt, and from Pathros [area north of Ethiopia], and from Cush [Ethiopia], and from Elam [area east of Babylon], and from Shinar [Babylon], and from Hamath [area north of Palestine], and from the islands of the sea [far distant lands]. And he shall set up an ensign [symbol] for the nations, and shall assemble the outcasts of Israel, and gather together the dispersed of Judah from the four corners of the earth."

According to Isaiah 18, the ensign of God will reappear in Ethiopia. And as it moves it causes the destruction of Israel's enemies. When it reaches Egypt, one by one the Jews will begin falling into place behind it. Israel, all of Israel, will walk out of Egypt where, up to now, they have been imprisoned in the bowels of one of the strongest nations on the earth in that day; sent there to die by the order of the strongest dictator who has ever lived. And no one will stop them! Why? There will be no army, there will be no weapons. There will be no human power behind them at all. The only power will be the supernatural protection of God as exemplified by the ensign.

I believe that the ensign will be the long lost, but always protected, Ark of the Covenant, the most holy relic of all Israel. It will show up when it is most needed, and as it afforded the

Israelites protection and victory in battles long ago, so shall it do so once again. The Jews will walk out of Egypt as the Ark goes before them with not a stick, with not a club, with not a gun, with not a bow, with not an arrow. They will march naked or at best dressed in rags, their skeletal frames displaying the marks of malnutrition and torture. The Ark and the Israelites will march through Egypt until they reach the Red Sea. When they get to the Red Sea it will once again part for them as it did with Moses. "And the Lord shall utterly destroy the tongue of the Egyptian sea; and with his mighty wind shall he shake his hand over the river, and shall smite it in the seven streams, and make men go over dryshod. And there shall be an highway for the remnant of his people, which shall be left, from Assyria; like as it was to Israel in the day that he came up out of the land of Egypt" (Isaiah 11:15).

"I will bring them back from the land of Egypt, And gather them from Assyria; And I will bring them into the land of Gilead and Lebanon, Until no room can be found for them. And He will pass through the sea of distress, And strike the waves in the sea, So that all the depths [of the river (KJV)] will dry up; And the pride of Assyria will be brought down, And the scepter of Egypt will depart. And I shall strengthen them in the Lord, And in His name they will walk, declares the Lord" (Zechariah 10:10-12, NASB).

"And it shall come to pass, when all these things are come upon thee, the blessing and the curse, which I have set before thee, and thou shalt call them to mind among all the nations, whither the Lord thy God hath driven thee, And shalt return unto the Lord thy God, and shalt obey his voice according to all that I command thee this day, thou and thy children, with all thine heart, and with all thy soul; That then the Lord thy God will turn thy captivity, and have compassion upon thee, and will return and gather thee from all the nations, whither the Lord thy God hath scattered thee" (Deuteronomy 30:1-3).

Once again they will cross over the Red Sea on dry ground. The whole thing will be miraculous from beginning to end! As the nation of Israel was born in Egypt in the days of Joseph for the first time, so shall a new, spiritually enlightened Israel begin in Egypt.

The scenario is incredible. In order to begin to get a handle on the significance of this scene, one must realize that these Jews are at least as hopeless as were the Jewish concentration camp victims. Imagine every Jew walking out of every Nazi death camp unaided by any weapon; a rag-tag army of concentration camp victims simply picking up and walking out with every German soldier helpless before them! What an incredible testimony to the miraculous, sovereign power of Jehovah God! He alone will return them to their promised land, and the Ark will come to rest on the top of Mount Zion. And when it is all said and done, every Jew will now be in Israel; not because they moved there of their own accord, but because every Jew in the world had been sent into Egypt to die, and those who survived and who repented have, en masse, been led into their Promised Land by Jehovah's mighty hand alone. Mount Zion is also the place where the 144,000 will stay after the rapture. They will be safe there because the Ark of God will be there. It is the one place that neither Satan nor the Antichrist ever reach or control. It is God's holy mountain. As Obadiah 17 records, "But upon mount Zion shall be deliverance, and there shall be holiness; and the house of Jacob shall possess their possessions."

This deliverance of the Jews will signify the nation "born in a day" as Ezekiel 37 describes. Egypt will be severely punished for her inhumanity toward the Jews; she will be utterly destroyed by God. So toxic will that destruction be that neither man nor animal will be found within her borders for forty years (see Ezekiel 29:12).

There is a third and final step in God's dealing with Israel, and that step will result in Israel's acceptance of Jesus as Messiah. The story of that was the story of Revelation 11. We read that the Two Witnesses will appear in Jerusalem preaching that Jesus is the Messiah. This will enrage Antichrist and he will also bring the wrath of the whole world down upon Israel. Fifty percent of the city of Jerusalem will go into captivity as Antichrist's forces storm and overcome the city, but with the appearing of Jesus and the saints at the end of the ten-and-one-half years of Tribulation, Jerusalem, along with the rest of the Jewish nation will be rescued and will be forever reconciled to God and to His Son. As is said seventy-plus times in Ezekiel alone, "And they shall know that I am God." This is the reason for fulfilled prophecy.

#12. *Rebuilding of the Temple.* After the Jews' return, they will recapture all of the land that, historically, was promised to them by God.   This is because the Ark will be in their possession and will go before them. They will then set about to rebuild The Temple. When they begin this rebuilding, the land will be theirs and the Moslem Dome of The Rock will no longer be an impediment. One of the reasons that Bible students can know that the previous events will happen before the Rapture is because the prophets put the rebuilding of the Temple after the return of the Jews to their land and to God. There is no prophecy that speaks of rebuilding the Temple in unbelief. From the rebuilding of the Temple after the Babylonian Captivity to the rebuilding at the end of the days, the scriptures speak of the rebuilding of God's house by a believing and penitent people. So the rebuilding must come after the spiritual restoration of the nation of Israel and that happens, according to the Bible after He pleads with them in the desert. That is one side of the time frame.

The other side is established by the fact that the Temple *cannot* be built after the Rapture. The circumstances that will face the world at that time will not allow it. Solomon's Temple was a spectacular site in the ancient world.   Some archaeologists speculate that there was more gold in Solomon's Temple than is known to exist in the world today. Hence, the new Temple must be built in times of *great* prosperity. The Temple will have to be built before the Rapture; it cannot be built afterwards. The times will be too catastrophic for such an enormous and expensive undertaking after the Rapture. Although Israel will be in a covenant of peace with Antichrist for part of the Tribulation, she will still be experiencing the famine, pestilence, and plague that have come upon the world. It took forty-six years to build Herod's Temple which was not even as grand as Solomon's Temple. The building of the Temple is not a simple undertaking.

Once again, the signs before the Rapture are unmistakable. The only way to miss them is to not know them.

We have considered many signs in the second time zone before Rapture: the building of great cities, the expansion of

Egypt across Africa, the crisis in Israel, and the rebuilding of the temple; it goes almost without saying that the arena of world importance will concern the Middle East. It will not concern the US, China, or Russia, but will instead center on Jordan, Syria, Iran, Egypt, Lebanon, Ethiopia, Iraq, and Israel. One has to wonder at the eschatology that preaches otherwise.

TIME ZONE THREE

Before considering the final time zone before the return of Christ, let us review what already has taken place. Time zone one: the buildup to a world crisis propels the man, Antichrist, to world attention. After he gains power, the stage is set for the implementation of his political and economic program for the world that will comprise the second stage. The culmination of this political and economic program will bring the world to the third and final stage before the Rapture. This time was referred to by Jesus as days like "the days of Noah." Its hallmark will be an extraordinary and worldwide time of peace, safety and prosperity. All of the preceding occurrences will solidify Antichrist's stranglehold upon the empire of the world. The stage will have been set for the final act before the Rapture: A repeat of the "Days of Noah."

#13. *The Earth at Rest – Peace and Prosperity.* "But of that day and hour knoweth no man, no, not the angels of heaven, but my Father only. But as the days of Noah were, so shall also the coming of the Son of man be. For as in the days that were before the flood they were eating and drinking, marrying, and giving in marriage, until the day that Noah entered into the ark, And knew not until the flood came, and took them all away; so shall also the coming of the Son of man be. Then shall two be in the field; the one shall be taken, and the other left. Two women shall be grinding at the mill; the one shall be taken, and the other left. Watch therefore: for ye know not what hour your Lord doth come. But know this, that if the goodman of the house had known in what watch the thief would come, he would have watched, and would not have suffered his house to be broken up. Therefore be ye also ready: for in such an hour as ye think not the Son of man cometh" (Matthew 24:36-44).

The prophecies concerning the "days of Noah," that incredible time of peace, prosperity and tranquility, have confused many. After all, Jesus himself prophesied times of war, rumors of war, internal strife, and calamities in connection with His coming. What is not remembered is that when Jesus spoke of these times he added, "All these are the *beginning* of sorrows." Times do not remain in turmoil. No, the antichrist appears on the world scene and transforms it to an unbelievable degree. War is replaced by peace, instability is replaced by stability, economic crisis is replaced by extraordinary prosperity. All that he requires in return is complete control. That will quickly be accorded him by a panicked world. Only spiritually aware Christians will know that all is not right. Even the demand to turn over the world's Jews will be accepted by the nations in order that they might continue to share in the boom times controlled by Antichrist. Peter prophesies in 2 Peter 3: 3-4 that the world will scoff at the idea of Jesus' return. This is not the case when the world is in dire straits before the appearance of Antichrist. At that point, believers and non-believers alike will be praying for Jesus' return. But remember what Jesus said, "Therefore be ye also ready: *for in such an hour as ye think not* the Son of man cometh" (Matthew 24:44, emphasis mine).

Peter writes that the scoffers will say, "Where is the promise of his coming? For since the fathers fell asleep, all things continue as they were from the beginning of the creation" (2 Peter 3:4). The normalcy of the world situation is surely not in view in the turmoil that will proceed the rise of Antichrist. No, Peter is speaking of the "days of Noah."

Paul, too, places the Rapture in times of tranquility, not panic. "For yourselves know perfectly that the day of the Lord so cometh as a thief in the night. For when they shall say, Peace and safety; then sudden destruction cometh upon them as travail upon a woman with child; and they shall not escape" (1 Thessalonians 5:2-3).

In the Matthew passage, Jesus describes the time at which He is coming. Notice how He refers to the Rapture immediately after describing the "days of Noah." He did not refer to it earlier in Matthew 24 when he was listing the signs of wars, rumors of wars, etc. No, Jesus pinpoints His return for us exactly.

This is the time right before the return of Jesus for the saints (Rapture), and things are exactly as Paul describes them. The world will say it has both peace and safety. The two do not necessarily go together. Now, in the US, we have peace but we do not really live in safety. Other times have seen safety but not peace. An example of this has been wartime in earlier generations. Granted, there was no peace, but the then predominately rural and small town landscape of the nation predisposed people to safety, at least on the home front. During the time of Antichrist but before the Rapture, peace and safety will go hand in hand. This prosperity and peace will bring about both enormous personal wealth and enormous personal indifference to the things of God. Jesus himself wondered, in Luke 18:8 "Nevertheless when the Son of man cometh, shall he find faith on the earth?". That lack of faith in the Son will produce a vacuum in the spiritual lives of man that will then be filled with a counterfeit faith. The end times will see a return to idolatry and, eventually, the worship of man himself.

#14. *Wealth and Indifference.* Incredible wealth, both national and personal, will bring about the greatest test that the Church has ever known. The Smyrnan Church was tested with persecution; the Philadelphian Church will be tested with prosperity. Of the two, prosperity is a far more deadly test. It will be at this time that the Laodicean Church will be in full-flower although it will exist side by side with the Church of Brotherly Love - the Philadelphian Church. The Laodicean Church, as a whole, will abysmally fail the test. The Philadelphian Church, as a whole, will overcome it. The story of this dichotomy is found in the parable of the Ten Virgins. "Then shall the kingdom of heaven be likened unto ten virgins, which took their lamps, and went forth to meet the bridegroom. And five of them were wise, and five were foolish. They that were foolish took their lamps, and took no oil with them: But the wise took oil in their vessels with their lamps. While the bridegroom tarried, they all slumbered and slept. And at midnight there was a cry made, Behold, the bridegroom cometh; go ye out to meet him. Then all those virgins arose, and trimmed their lamps. And the foolish said unto the wise, Give us of your oil; for our lamps are gone out. But the wise answered, saying, Not so; lest there be not enough for us and you: but go ye rather to them that sell, and buy for yourselves. And while they went to buy, the bridegroom came; and they that were ready went in with him to the marriage: and the door was shut. Afterward came also the other virgins, saying, Lord, Lord, open to us. But he answered and said, Verily I say unto you, I know you not. Watch therefore, for ye know neither the day nor the hour wherein the Son of man cometh" (Matthew 25:1-13).

Jesus is the Bridegroom. He is coming back for his Bride, the Church, here signified by the virgins, but He is coming back at a time that is unspecified. The Church is simply told to watch and wait. There is a test involved here for her. It is a very unusual test. It does not require suffering, it requires the need to remain constant in her anticipation of His coming. The passage very clearly states that the Bridegroom will tarry, He will not come when He is expected to. Is there pain, is there tribulation for His Bride when he delays His coming? No, to the contrary, things are so easy, so normal, that the temptation is to lose her fervor, to lose her ardor.

Hebrews 10:25 gives a warning to the Church to not forsake the fellowship of other believers but to encourage one another. And then is added a very interesting exhortation, the exhortation to be even more diligent about this "as ye see the day approaching." The day spoken of here is the Day of the Lord. For the Christians, that day will dawn at the Rapture. Hebrews is saying that as the times build up to the time of Rapture it will become critical for the Church to support one another. Otherwise the lethargy that will be so prevalent in the world will put them to sleep also. The very same people who were on the edge of their seats praying fervently, promising God anything if He would but save them just a short time ago will be some of the people who are now saying, "Church? We'll get to Church soon, but this Sunday I'm going shopping for a new boat."

By the percentage given in the parable, fully half of the Church will succumb to the prevailing spirit of complacency and will sleep on until it is too late, and the Bridegroom is at the door. Remember, the Laodicean Church was categorized by her lukewarm attitude. She wasn't in, she wasn't out; she was simply there. This perfectly describes the world situation right before the Rapture; peace, safety, complacency, and a self-congratulatory attitude. After all, where are the signs of His coming? We've made it thus far, we can afford to take it easy. This lulling, deceptive spirit is so pervasive that even the overcomers nod off. The test, the trial, is to stay awake! But, somehow at that point, a warning is sounded! Somehow the virgins know that Jesus' coming is near, He is nigh unto the very door! But alas, the oil (symbolically, *always* the Holy Spirit) is in short supply. Indeed, fifty percent of the virgins have run dry. They turn to the remaining Spirit-filled believers for a quick fix, but that does not help. One must have one's own relationship with the Bridegroom, one cannot depend on another's. The Holy Spirit's indwelling in one life is not transferable to another. The relationship is far too personal for that.

And so, the foolish virgins scurry off for answers. While they are seeking, the Bridegroom comes. And the wise virgins, who are tuned to His voice, will hear it and will meet Him. Then the door is shut. Remember the symbolism of the door discussed when the letter to the Philadelphian Church was in view: it is the entrance to heaven. The foolish virgins are left to go through the Tribulation. It is important to note that they still have a chance at Redemption. This experience is bound to awaken some of them and they convert whole-heartedly to Christ. If Christians have done their job and have continued to preach the news of Jesus returning for them (the Rapture), then when Rapture does occur it will be a tremendous sign to the world that those crazy Christians were right, and thus, maybe they were right about all the other things they said about God. Many many conversions will come about because of the sign of the Rapture. The cost to those who would not believe before the Rapture is that they will have to live through the Tribulation. But their souls can be saved. Why do I say that so emphatically? Because the writer of Hebrews did. "And as it is appointed unto man once to die, but after this [cometh] the judgment" (Hebrews 9:27). Judgment comes after a person's death, not before. Each man has his entire life to decide for or against God before his decision is judged. These foolish virgins are not dead, they have missed the Rapture but they are still alive. Therefore they still have the opportunity to repent. Many of the earliest tribulation saints that were under the Fifth Seal may very well have first been "foolish virgins."

#15. *The Return of Idolatry and the Exaltation of Man.* Along with the signs of peace, prosperity, wealth and indifference will come another great sign: The return of idolatry and the exultation of man himself. This is evident in the prophecies of Isaiah when he speaks of what God will rectify when He comes. In order to undo these things, they must be present. Isaiah 2:10-21 speaks of the Day of the Lord and what He will find when he comes, "Enter into the rock, and hide thee in the dust, for fear of the Lord, and for the glory of his majesty. The lofty looks of man shall be humbled, and the haughtiness of men shall be bowed down, and the Lord alone shall be exalted in that day. For the day of the Lord of hosts shall be upon every one that is proud and lofty, and upon every one that is lifted up; and he shall be brought low: And upon all the cedars of Lebanon, that are high and lifted up, and upon all the oaks of Bashan, And upon all the high mountains, and upon all the hills that are lifted up, And upon every high tower, and upon every fenced wall, And upon all the ships of Tarshish, and upon all pleasant pictures. And the loftiness of man shall be bowed down, and the haughtiness of men shall be made low: and the Lord alone shall be exalted in that day. And the idols he shall utterly abolish. And they shall go into the holes of the rocks, and into the caves of the earth, for fear of the Lord, and for the glory of his majesty, when he ariseth to shake terribly the earth. In that day a man shall cast his idols of silver, and his idols of gold, which they made each one for himself to worship, to the moles and to the bats; To go into the clefts of the rocks, and into the tops of the ragged rocks, for fear of the Lord, and for the glory of his majesty, when he ariseth to shake terribly the earth."

It is not hard to see the beginnings of the worship of man even today. The Self-Esteem Movement has long argued that each person needs to feel good, nay, needs to feel almost ecstatic about himself. At the same time, this feeling of self-esteem is said to be totally independent of any character or actions of the person. One needs to feel good about oneself period. It does not matter that one does things that are wrong, hurtful, or selfish. Thus, self-worth is totally divorced from one's conscience. It is then but a small step to the Me Decade; "I am the only one who matters." Outdated concepts such as loyalty, charity, honesty, patriotism and a basic concern for the needs of others fall quickly by the way. Couple that with the fact that Satan is now sowing the seeds of idolatry and the exultation of man today with the New Age Movement, and this prophecy no longer seems so far fetched. Of course, man as a god himself (or woman as goddess herself) is the core of the New Age doctrine, but, beyond that, it is preparing man for the leap to idolatry. Back in the early 1990s, I read a newspaper account of a towering statue of a man 300 feet tall made entirely of bread being towed out to sea as an offering to the sea from a contrite and humbled humanity. The idea behind the offering was that man had only taken from the sea, and thus had abused her abundance, without even the proper thanks or recompense. The statue of bread was man's gift back to the sea. This symbolic gesture was afforded quite a bit of newsprint. Although paganism such as this may seem quaint and silly now, it is but a harbinger of things to come. In the midst of our scientific, empirical mode of thinking, the idea of a return to idolatry by most of mankind is almost beyond belief, yet it is mentioned in many, many prophecies dealing with the latter times. Again, as was evident in the days of Noah, the world will be immersed in idolatry and the unspeakable sins that accompany it. Amazingly, even the Jews will succumb to idolatry.

In many ways, this is the hardest prophecy to understand. Although the Jews had centuries of idol worship behind her, indeed it was her besetting sin, after her return from captivity, she never went into idolatry again. In fact, all of her rebellions as a conquered nation against her political rulers from Antiochus Epiphanes to the caesars of Rome, were over resisting state-mandated idol worship. Nonetheless, the Bible is clear that Israel will join in the world-wide deception of idolatry even after her wilderness experience in Egypt. Satan understands, even if Israel does not, that while Israel is in covenant relationship with God, he, Satan, is helpless to come against her. Thus he must lead her into idolatry in order for Israel herself to step out of God's protection. The missing piece in her lasting fidelity to God will be the final step in God's plan for her: Her acceptance of Jesus as God and as her Messiah which will be accomplished through the ministry of the Two Witnesses.

THE RETURN OF JESUS FOR HIS PEOPLE

Prophecy has a special place in the program of God. It is God's weapon prepared against Satan at the time when Satan's power is greatest upon the earth. There is no miracle more sensational than prophecy when it is being fulfilled. All of Satan's power, signs, and lying wonders will only serve to prove the accuracy of the Word of the Lord God Almighty as they are being played out. Those with the Spirit of God will discern the truth and the signs of the day. Those without the Spirit of God will enter into the grandest deception that the world has ever seen. There will be so many miraculous fulfillments of prophecy that people generally will be looking for the coming of Christ. They will also be looking for Him to come and rescue them from the coming world crisis, a crisis so serious that the future of mankind will hang in the balance. Christ will not come when he is looked for, longed for and expected. Instead, the Antichrist will come and "save the world." Things will quiet down, the Antichrist will bring about the greatest time of peace and prosperity ever known in history. No longer will Jesus' coming be looked for, indeed, it will be scoffed at. Jesus has not come, the miracles and signs will cease and a great feeling of security will spread over the world. The parabolic ten virgins will begin to nod off. Many within the church will say, "Well, the preachers were wrong. The Lord did not come after all." It is when they think not that the Son of Man will indeed come.

CHAPTER 16
THE BEASTS FROM THE SEA AND EARTH
Revelation 13

THE BEAST FROM THE SEA

Revelation 13 is a picture of the Antichrist solely as he interacts with the saints. Remember that Revelation is the book of prophecy that concerns itself with the Church. Because the rise of the Antichrist is an area of prophecy that primarily concerns the nations, we do not read of the rise of the Antichrist in Revelation. The information given to us in Revelation will concern itself with the treatment of the Church by Antichrist and he will have no control over her until he is established in power. Thus when we see the Antichrist pictured here, he has already risen to power. This picture is a continuation of the picture we saw in Revelation 12. Remember that in John's letter (the Book of Revelation) there were no artificial chapter headings. So there is no break between Revelation 12 and 13. The dragon (Satan) was in view there as he set about to make war with the people who become Christians after the Rapture. They have become Christians as a result of being left behind at the Rapture or because of the preaching of the saints from heaven which will be discussed later.

The Beast Rises Up. The first thing that John sees in Revelation 13 is a seven-headed beast with ten crowned horns, rising up out of the sea. The seven heads of the beast are the seven world empires that have existed throughout history. They have always been under the control of Satan. Notice that the crowns are not on the heads, they are on the ten horns. That is because at this point in time six of these seven world empires, Assyria, Egypt, Babylon, Medeo-Persia, Greece, and Rome, are already history. All of the power that formed and sustained these world dictatorships now rests in the ten horns of the seventh and final world government of Satan's. Power like that is unimaginable to us; it will take the power of God to defeat it.

When Daniel saw the vision of this final beast who would appear on the world scene, he, too, saw the ten horns upon the head of the beast. The ten horns are interchangeable with the ten toes of Daniel's vision spoken of in the last chapter. This is the kingdom of Antichrist. By using the symbolism of a horn, Daniel is stressing the power and authority of Antichrist over these ten nations. When Daniel prophesied about Antichrist at this point in time after the Rapture, he chronicled the fact that by this time, Antichrist has already subdued and conquered three nations. Clearly Antichrist is the dominant world figure in the times immediately preceding the Rapture.

The beast wears the name of blasphemy. It is anti-God and anti-Christ in every aspect of its being. Blasphemy is nothing new to earth, but John calls this "the name" of blasphemy. He is not speaking of normal, everyday blasphemy, he is speaking of the source, the wellspring, behind every blasphemy which has ever been uttered under heaven. It is possible that the "name of blasphemy" spoken of here is the name of the evil spirit which is behind every word of blasphemy. That blasphemous spirit will be powerful indeed, empowered by the great authority that Satan now has over the earth, and it will also be the primary influence upon the culture at that time. We now have a culture that is becoming more and more blasphemous, especially in the realm of television, motion pictures and art (witness the Maplethorpe exhibit, and the dung-smeared Madonna), but it pales in comparison to what will come. No one will be able to fight against that blasphemous spirit; it will control the minds of the whole world except for the committed Christians. It will be the lodestone of the times and the pivotal characteristic of the rule of Antichrist.

At the end of Revelation 12 we saw the Dragon (Satan). When John's view shifts in chapter 13 he sees the emergence of a second evil, the Beast. It rises up out of the sea, whereas the Dragon has fallen from heaven onto the earth. Scripture tells us that the Beast's coming is after the working of Satan so we know that the Dragon and this Beast are inextricably linked. The sea is a symbol for masses of people; thus, the Antichrist will rise up from humanity and will be human. But I believe that something else is implied by his rising out of the sea; that implication being Antichrist's dual nature, both human and satanic, just as Jesus' dual nature was both human and divine. Both Isaiah and Job call Satan by the name "Leviathan" and both place him in "the sea." Job's description of Leviathan in Job 41 could only apply to Satan, especially the last verse when Job says of him, "He beholdeth all high things: he is a king over all the children of pride." Isaiah, prophesying of the great and terrible Day of the Lord, also calls Satan Leviathan. He says in Isaiah 27:1, "In that day the Lord with his sore and great and strong sword shall punish leviathan the piercing serpent, even leviathan that crooked serpent; and he shall slay the dragon *that is in the sea,*" (emphasis mine). The sea, therefore, seems to have a dual meaning here, indicating both the human and satanic origins of Antichrist. His satanic origins will become clearer when we discuss his fatal wound.

The Beast's Kingdom as Seen by John and Daniel. John does not describe the beast in either human or satanic terms, because John has different information even than that to impart. John says that he is like a leopard, although his feet are like the feet of a bear, and he has a lion's mouth. These are the same beasts that appeared in Daniel's second vision but now we see them in reverse order. That is because Daniel was looking forward in time and John is looking backward through time. Daniel was prophesying, John is simply recounting history. Daniel used the symbol of a lion for Babylon, the bear for the kingdom of the Medes and Persians, the leopard for Greece, and Rome he simply called the beast. But because all four symbols are named, the leopard, the bear, the lion, and the beast, we know that all four kingdoms and their territories will be under the control of the Antichrist. The great image of Daniel's first vision is up and standing. And the power and authority over all of that territory belongs to Satan. Verse 2 says that the dragon, Satan, then gives Antichrist "his power, and his seat and great authority." Satan is going to invest into this man everything that is at his disposal to give him.

The Beast's Fatal Wound and Recovery Provide Satan with a Body. One of the Beast's heads receives a fatal wound. That head can only be Antichrist because the other six heads of the beast belong to history. This fatal wound of Antichrist and his apparent recovery are two of the most fascinating prophesies in the Bible. They are spoken of here by the Apostle John and are also spoken of by Daniel. This is the point: Antichrist will be killed and yet he will live. It will be the greatest deception of

Satan's career, for make no mistake, this is completely the work of Satan. Satan will have two reasons for killing Antichrist.

First, the reappearance of Antichrist after his death will be Satan's answer to those nagging questions that the population is having about the Great Resurrection of God's at Rapture. "See," Satan will say, "I, too, have resurrection power. I too am God." And Satan's claim to be God is really at the crux of the great spiritual battle between good and evil which has raged throughout time.

The second reason to kill Antichrist is to furnish a body for Satan, for no matter what Satan claims, he does not have the power of the resurrection. That belongs exclusively to Jesus. Neither can Satan create for himself a body. Satan has appeared in the form of a serpent and also as an angel of light, but he has *never* appeared as a man. He has not been able to. Holy angels, interestingly enough, can, because the power to do so comes from God. Hebrews 13:2 tells us that some have even entertained angels never knowing that they were doing so because they were clothed in human form, but God has never and will never give a body to Satan. The closest that Satan has ever gotten to that was through demonic possession, but even so, the body used by him belonged to another soul. It was never Satan's body. Thus he is forced to use the bodies of humans to satisfy his cruelties and his lusts. For instance, he uses humans to sexually abuse little children in order to satisfy his own lust. Oh, he passes on that lust to the human, but it never ceases to be the lust of Satan. He uses humans to torture, to murder, to steal and to destroy because he has no body to do it himself and his sadism must be satisfied. He also uses human mouths to defame, to curse and to lie. No wonder Jesus tells Christians to stop letting Satan use their bodies and instead to present their bodies as a living sacrifice to God.

Satan demands to be Worshipped "in Person". Satan has another reason for wanting a body because his desire has always been to be worshipped in person, not just in spirit, by God's creation, man. It is not enough for Satan to be worshipped vicariously through idols of gold, silver, brass, iron, wood, or stone, or even through a human being, even if that human is as close a copy to him as Antichrist will be. No, his ambition and pride compel him to have God's creation, man, fall down at his, Satan's, feet and be worshipped by him.

Now, as was stated above, Satan has never had a body. That is why the fact that Jesus came *in the flesh* is so galling to him. One of the praises that Jesus had for God was that God had prepared for him a body. It was a truly miraculous thing and a thing that Satan has never been able to duplicate. Hence we have insight into why John wrote in John 4:2-3, "Hereby know ye the Spirit of God: Every spirit that confesseth that Jesus Christ is come in the flesh is of God: And every spirit that confesseth not that Jesus Christ is come in the flesh is not of God: and this is that spirit of antichrist, whereof ye have heard that it should come; and even now already is it in the world."

The spirit of Antichrist cannot confess that Jesus came in the flesh because to do so would give Jesus a power that Satan does not have. And so the evil spirits must remain silent. But all of that will seem to change when Antichrist lives after his fatal wound. This death and reappearance of Antichrist will be the means whereby Satan will acquire a body. But what kind of body will it be in reality? To understand that, we must look at this murder of Antichrist closely.

The Predicted Murder of Antichrist. Details of this murder are given in Revelation 13, in Revelation 17:8-11, and also in Daniel 11:20. Daniel tells us that a man will rise to the forefront of the world scene who will restore the glory of the kingdom (Satan's kingdom). This is Antichrist, but Daniel tells us that he will not last very long. "Within a few days", according to Daniel "he shall be destroyed, neither in anger, nor in battle. And in his estate shall stand up a vile person, to whom they shall not give the honour of the kingdom [Antichrist will not be given the title of King]; but he shall come in peaceably, and obtain the kingdom by flatteries."

"Within a few days" means "in a very short time.. After Antichrist comes to the forefront, he will last but a short time before the "vile person" takes over. The vile person is Satan and he will reign in the place of Antichrist because Antichrist will be murdered. Isaiah 14 also bears this out. It is a prophecy of the end both of Satan and Antichrist, and they are inextricably linked. Antichrist is the ruler of the earth initially, empowered by Satan. Then Satan goes one step further and rules in person. How?

Antichrist's Death Analyzed. First, let us look at Antichrist's fatal wound and his apparent recovery. According to John in Revelation 13:3, Antichrist is definitely killed, his death is not a fraud. "And I saw one of his heads as it were wounded to death." "As it were" is a strong expression in the Greek. It is almost an overstatement as would be, "He was killed dead" in English. The expression is so strong, definite and intensified that nothing less can be grammatically understood here except that real death is meant. Furthermore, John calls the wound both fatal and deadly. The argument cannot be scripturally made that his death is faked. And yet he continues to live!

The method of death is intriguing. According to Revelation 13:14 the weapon used is a sword, which is a rather archaic weapon. Daniel 11:20 tells us that this wound is received neither in anger nor in battle. This, then, is not a typical murder in the sense that we generally assume that some level of anger is needed in order to take a life, for those who kill Antichrist, strange as it may seem, are not the least bit annoyed with him. No, in fact Antichrist has done everything according to plan, but Satan simply needs his body. It is also not an assassination; to assassinate the world leader would require anger at something at least on the part of somebody. And, as if this isn't riddle enough, Antichrist apparently recovers. Is this an actual resurrection? No, Satan does not have the power to resurrect, but I think it is as close as Satan can come to a resurrection. So we must deal with two seemingly mutually exclusive facts: First, the wound of Antichrist is fatal, he dies and it is not a faked death, but second, he lives! Satan cannot restore life and God will not restore this particular life so how then do we reconcile this information?

A Cloned Body? It is possible that the answer will be found in the sciences. I think that the "resurrected" body of Antichrist will be a brand new body but it will exactly resemble the first one. I think that it will be something akin to a cloned body of Antichrist's but with a totally missing soul, for, after all, each soul comes from God. It will be a body that Satan can then completely possess. At long last Satan will acquire a body.

About seventy-five years ago, the possibility of cloning - the breeding of genetically identical copies of an individual organism - was recognized by John Burdon Sanderson Haldane, an English biologist. He chose the new word "cloning" because it comes from a Greek word meaning "a cutting" as from a plant. And, interestingly, Dr. Joseph Mengele, "The Butcher of Auschwitz," was fascinated by the idea. He was intently researching cloning at Auschwitz in the 1940s. Given the parallels between Adolph Hitler and the coming antichrist, I don't think the interest was coincidental.

I first surmised the idea of this satanic resurrection coming to be through the machination of a cloned body in 1979. As I would share this theory in my classes I was met with disbelief and shock. Who could possibly clone a human body? The idea seemed ridiculous. Now, twenty-some-odd years later, it does not seem far-fetched at all. One of my own highly reputable medical sources has told me that it has, in fact, already occurred although information about it has been effectively suppressed. I have even been told in what country it has happened. Regardless of the truth of that information, does the cloning theory fit the facts of scripture? In Revelation 17:8, John describes the "vile person," the resurrected Antichrist. Notice how he does so, "The beast that thou sawest *was, and is not...* and they that dwell on the earth shall wonder...when they behold *the beast that was, and is not, and yet is."* John is trying his hardest to explain an unexplainable thing, at least unexplainable to his first-century audience. "The beast existed and now he doesn't exist but yet he still does." See, John knew that he was looking at the exact same creature and yet it was fundamentally different in a way that he couldn't really pinpoint. Actually, John's description is an amazingly perfect description of cloning by a first century writer. He reiterates this conundrum in verses 10-11 of the same chapter when he writes, "And there are seven kings: five are fallen, and one is, and the other is not yet come; and when he cometh, he must continue a short space, And *the beast that was, and is not, even he is the eighth, and is of the seven,* and goeth into perdition" (emphasis mine).

The seven kings spoken of in Revelation 17:10 are the kings of the seven world empires: Egypt, Assyria, Babylon, Medea-Persia, Greece, Rome, and the coming empire of Antichrist. At the time John is writing this five are history, one, Rome, is in force as he writes and one is not yet come, Antichrist. But when he comes he will last for a very short time and then there will be an eighth although the eighth is not really a real eighth, it is really one of the seven previously described kings, but, still, somehow it is an eighth. So, actually, the last king is the seventh and also the eighth king, in some unexplainable way he is both! John sees both the seventh head, Antichrist, and the eight head (Satan in a replica of Antichrist's body) and he is struggling to get the concept across that although they are different creatures they are the same. After all, the concept of cloning would be an unimaginable thought to a first-century church. (I can sympathize, I had the hardest time, myself, in the twentieth-century church!)

The Fatal Wound. Does this theory of cloning stand up against the description given of the wound - a sword wound, given neither in anger nor in battle? Yes. Picture not a battlefield but instead, a hospital. Picture not a warrior's sword but a surgeon's sword, a surgical knife, killing the unknowing, unwilling donor, Antichrist, on an operating table, not in anger but with cold-blooded calculation as detached as a researcher dissecting a laboratory rat. A second body, an exact replica of the first, is there waiting to be inhabited. Satan himself provides the soul for this soulless body, completely possessing it, and although not of the Adamic race, it is as close as Satan could possibly come to reproducing the miracle of Christ the Divine becoming Christ the Man. Then it would be possible for the body of Antichrist and the cloned body of Antichrist possessed by Satan to be the same and yet fundamentally different. And Antichrist, the man who had completely given himself up to the service of Satan, would, in the end, be betrayed by Satan his master. As always, given Satan's hatred for each one of God's creations, even those who give themselves up to Satan's service, are ultimately destroyed by him.

I must also state that when Antichrist appears, science could easily be far advanced genetically from cloning and that it might be an altogether different procedure that produces the eighth beast. Nonetheless, I find it plausible that the answer of the false resurrection of the beast lies somewhere in the genetic sciences.

SATAN'S FALSE SIGN OF "RESURRECTION"

In order for the world to appreciate this resurrection, the death of Antichrist will have to be heralded long and loud, far and wide. His body probably will lie in state as the entire world comes to pay homage and to mourn for the man who "saved the world". If ever it was unpopular to oppose Antichrist it will be doubly so at this point in time and the "rebellion" of the Christians will seem to the world to be even more egregious and infuriating. Then after the world has wailed and sobbed at his death, wondering what will become of Planet Earth without him, the Beast will miraculously re-appear, the new body of Antichrist will of necessity have to be the exact age that Antichrist was when he was murdered. Although this is not scientifically possible now, who can state with certainty that Satan's "understanding of the dark sentences" cannot engineer it then?   Adam and Eve certainly sprang forth as full-grown creatures, it is not an impossible concept, and Satan will attempt to counterfeit God in every detail.

Satan fully understands the power of the sign of resurrection. Witness the power that Jesus' resurrection had two thousand years ago. Because, under His own power he came out of the grave to be seen by men again on earth the world still knows His name, and many still follow Him. The "resurrection" of Antichrist will have much the same impact initially. They will say, "We've only heard of Jesus' resurrection, but we've seen this resurrection! There can be no doubt that it happened." And so the deception will grow.

Signs of the Times. Another clue to these times is given to us by Jesus when he said, "But as the days of No[ah] were, so shall also the coming of the Son of man be" (Matthew 24:37). In the days of Noah there was also an attempt by Satan to genetically alter the human race. Genesis 6:1-8 gives us the story of why God decided to destroy mankind. The "sons of God" mated with the "daughters of men" producing a race of giants. When chronicling this, Enoch called the sons of God angels. He was, of course, referring to fallen angels. Ancient Hebrew scholars understood this passage to be referring to angels also. There are many biblical arguments that can be made which support this idea, but suffice it to say that if that were indeed the case, as I firmly believe it was, then the genetic tampering with God's creation of humanity has been strongly on the mind of Satan since antediluvian times. How apropos that it be used by him as his final great deception!

ALL NATIONS WORSHIP THE POWERFUL BEAST

As a consequence of this "resurrection," the people of the earth will worship Satan whom they fully understand is the one behind the miracle. They do not confuse him with God; they worship him for whom he is. And they worship the beast. Apparently, Antichrist will be equal to or surpass any other man who has ever lived, at least in surface attributes. "Who is like unto the beast?" they ask. According to Daniel, he is handsome, politically astute, a spellbinding orator, a genius and a spiritual leader with supernatural knowledge, understanding even "the dark sentences." He is certainly the most powerful man alive, for "who is able to make war with him?"

And how does Antichrist respond to this giftedness? He blasphemes God, God's dwelling place, and the raptured saints that are now in heaven. All of Satan's pride, hatred, arrogance, and violence will feed this blasphemous spirit. Although Antichrist is completely empowered by Satan, ultimately it is God who has given him everything that is his because everything that can be given is under the control of God. Revelation 13:5-7 says he was given his oratorical ability, his power, his authority. If God did not step out of the way and let Antichrist ascend to power, Antichrist never would have gained power. Everything that is happening now is according to God's timetable and God's plan, not Antichrist's! But Antichrist will not acknowledge that this opportune time and his attributes of intelligence, oration, etc. have been given to him by God; he will take them as being of his own manufacture. Thus, his arrogant, posturing, hateful, and violent words will be aimed against God Almighty and against all of heaven.

As he assumes total control of the government of Planet Earth he will cry with a voice that fills all the airwaves that he, Antichrist, cannot be stopped even by God, that his power is absolute, that he will be worshipped by every living creature of God or else they will cease to live, that every mind will be controlled by his dark thoughts; that, ultimately, he has defeated God and has won the final cosmic battle of the Universe! And it will seem, for a time, that Antichrist is right.

SATAN RAGES AGAINST SAINTS BOTH IN HEAVEN AND ON EARTH

Satan will rage against the saints in heaven because he bears towards them unfathomable anger. It was their resurrection, Rapture, that caused his downfall from heaven. This, incidentally, is another instance in which the Scriptures support a pre-tribulation view. Satan would not be raging against the saints in heaven if Tribulation came later, say mid-trib or post-trib, because that event would still be future. But because Rapture has occurred, because the raptured saints have defeated Satan, and because those saints are safely out of his reach and even more insulting, are occupying his former territory, Antichrist can only spew venom against them and continually blaspheme their memory to those left on earth. This is an important point because he must convince the people left on the earth that those who were taken in the Rapture were not taken because they were good and holy people; no, they disappeared because they were evil, sub-human people. If you find it hard to believe that the people left on earth can be convinced of that, think of how many people already call the holy, profane and the profane, holy in our society today. Antichrist will be the ultimate spin doctor. It won't even take him long to rewrite history as concerns Rapture, given the spirit of deception that pervades the world.

As malevolent as he will be towards the raptured Christians, he will be far more malevolent to the Christians he *can* reach, those still alive on earth. He begins to kill each and every one of them, hunting them down and ferreting them out with a ferocity and determination not seen on earth since the days of the Imperial persecutions. That was during the time of the Roman Empire, and it is no coincidence that persecution against Christians begins the minute the next, and final, world empire is established. The extreme cruelty and thoroughness of the persecution at this time is understood when one realizes that in three-and-one-half years Antichrist is able to do what two hundred years of persecution under the emperors of the Roman Persecution never succeeded in doing. Unlike the Roman Emperors, Antichrist will find and decimate the entire Christian population. Although some scriptures imply that possibly a very few escape death, to state that with certainty is not possible. Suffice it to say that Antichrist succeeds in locating the believers with a thoroughness that is beyond our wildest imagination. Daniel 7:21 prophesied this exact persecution and its consequences: "I beheld, and the same horn made war with the saints, and prevailed against them". We were also told that this would happen in Revelation 12:17 where we read, "And the dragon was wroth with the woman, and went to make war with the remnant of her seed, which keep the commandments of God, and have the testimony of Jesus Christ." We see now just how fierce the war against them will be.

The length of this persecution of the tribulation saints is told to us in verse 5; it is exactly forty-two months, three-and-a-half years. It will be worldwide, involving every kindred, tongue, and nation. There will be only one spot on the entire face of the earth that Antichrist will not be able to control. That place will be Mount Zion where the Ark of God will rest at this time and where the 144,000 will abide. Scripture tells us over and over again that Mt. Zion will never be moved, it will abide forever.

NOT EVERYONE WORSHIPS ANTICHRIST

Such will be the power and fury of Antichrist's persecution that every single person who is not a believer will choose to worship him. Indeed, without the power of Christ it will be impossible to resist him. Verse 8 states this in a very revealing way. It says that only those whose names are written in the Lamb's Book of Life will defy Antichrist. Remember that the Lamb's Book of Life is different from the Book of Life. The Lamb's Book of Life records the names of all who belong to the Lamb while the Book of Life records the names of the living.

Thus, the Lamb's Book of Life is a subset of the records in the Book of Life for not all who have ever lived belong to the Lamb; only the Christians do. Verse 8 also tells us that the Lamb, Christ, was slain before earth was even created by God. How can this be? We have a definite date in time when the Crucifixion occurred and it was certainly after earth was created and peopled. Yes, but remember that time is a human concept. God does not deal in time and the essential fact of the Crucifixion was such a certainty that God reckoned it as completed even before the fall of the human race in the Garden of Eden. This means that when Adam chose to rebel against God it did not come as a surprise to God and, further, that God had already made provision for that fall.

Both Psalm 139:16 and 2 Timothy 1:9 tell us that each believer was known to God and belonged to him before the world even began. The Psalm states, "Thine eyes did see my substance, yet being unperfect; and in thy book all my members were written, which in continuance were fashioned, when as yet there was none of them." Timothy states, "[God] hath saved us, and called us with an holy calling, not according to our works, but according to his own purpose and grace, which was given us in Christ Jesus before the world began." This verse says something very deep. It says that when God contemplated creating the Universe, the first thing He did was to write down each of our names. We were thought of first, before God created a blade of grass, before God created the Pacific Ocean, before there were clouds in the sky, before there were mountains, before the first sunrise or sunset was envisioned by the Creator. Before any of this, we were thought of and known personally to God. Understanding that, how can we ever think that God has forgotten us or our needs? It is impossible!

(Having said that, it is important to clarify that I am not presupposing that there is no free will on our part in accepting the gospel. To the contrary, God, knowing everything, always knew who would respond to His call throughout human history. In fact, 1 Peter 1:2 says that God predestined us *according to His foreknowledge.* It was not a capricious decision on His part, it was based on His knowledge of who would respond.)

FOR THE TRIBULATION SAINTS JUSTICE WILL SURELY PREVAIL

Revelation 13:9-10 seems at first blush to be juxtaposed upon the text: "If any man have an ear, let him hear. He that leadeth into captivity shall go into captivity: he that killeth with the sword must be killed with the sword. Here is the patience and the faith of the saints." But it is not a juxtaposition. These verses are, in my opinion, inserted here for a particular audience: Those tribulation saints who will read them when all hope seems to be lost. Jesus began His message to each of the seven church eras with the words, "If any man have an ear, let him hear." It is no accident that Jesus, here, is repeating those words. He is alerting us to the fact that an eighth and final group of Christians need a message specifically tailored for them just as much as any other era of the church age did. In fact, these same words will have the exact effect upon the tribulation saints when they read them as did the letter to the Smyrnan Church have upon the martyrs during the Imperial Persecutions. The end-time saints will also know that their faith must be in Jesus; that Jesus knows what will happen to them and that not one of the plans of Satan will catch their Savior unawares. Don't fear, Jesus says to them as He once said to the martyrs at Smyrna; you will die but it is meant to be. And finally, and maybe most importantly to the tribulation saints, justice will surely prevail. Those that send you into captivity will themselves be captives of the Lord Most High, those who kill you will themselves be killed. We see the tribulation saints claiming this very promise when we see them again when the fifth seal is opened.

Revelation 13:10 is written for the tribulation saints. It is going to sustain them, it is going to uphold them. It is going to encourage them and it is going to guide them because it tells them that the sufferings of His saints will not go unnoticed by God. He will both acknowledge the sacrifices of the saints at this time and he will avenge them when He comes in power and glory. This, then, will be their perseverance and faith: Jesus will win out and He will repay.

It will also settle for the tribulation saints the question of whether or not they should expend any energy fighting against the beast or his system. No, will be the answer given to them from God. Antichrist is far too strong for them, this is his appointed time and, seemingly, he will be allowed to overcome them. But in reality he will only be able to kill them and then they will be with God forever and will witness His great victory and retribution over Antichrist and his minions. Fear not who is able to kill the body, fear him who is able to destroy both the body and the soul. Mankind is not capable of defeating this man (so much for Kingdom Theology!); God and God alone can and will defeat him. Do not be dismayed, saints, yours is the winning side regardless of how distressing and hopeless things appear to be.

This same encouragement to simply persevere and have faith has been given to the saints three other times before in the Book of Revelation. We first saw it given in the letter to the Smyrnan Church as they were walking into two hundred years of intense persecution. "Fear not what you are about to suffer," Jesus tells them. He will bring them through, they are not to fight. The second time was seen in the letter to the Thyatiran Church that was so corrupted. No other burden was placed on them except to repudiate for themselves the deep things of Satan and to hold fast to the things that they had been given by Jesus. In His own time, God would reform the Church. The third time that this admonition was given was when the souls under the altar were seen asking God how much longer this horror of Antichrist would go on. They, too, were told to rest until the plans of God were played out upon the earth. With this verse, those same tribulation saints are being told while they are still on earth that this is not their fight to wage. It is God's, and He will win it.

THE BEAST FROM THE EARTH: THE FALSE PROPHET

"And I beheld another beast coming up out of the earth; and he had two horns like a lamb, and he spake as a dragon" (Revelation 13:11). We see here the appearance of a third beast, the first being the dragon, the second being the beast who rises out of the seas. The Antichrist is not alone upon the earth, and, in fact, he has a companion who is hardly less remarkable than he is himself. This companion will be the one who will lead the world into the religion of Babylon; the satanic, one-world religion of the Dragon. So it is extremely fitting that this third beast is identified in Revelation 19:20 as being the False Prophet. He will perform all manner of miracles and so will weave a web of deception around all who do not have the discernment of the Holy Spirit. This third person will round out the full complement of the Satanic Trinity. It will consist of Satan, Antichrist, and the False Prophet. The False Prophet performs the antithetical role of the third person of the Holy Trinity, the Holy Spirit. Interestingly, 2 Thessalonians 2:9 uses the Greek word *dunamis* when describing the power of Antichrist. It means miraculous power, a miracle in itself. Hebrews 1:3 uses the same Greek word when describing how God upholds all things. Just as the Holy Spirit empowers the miracles from God so will the False Prophet empower the miracles from Satan. Just as the Holy Spirit brings truth and enlightenment from God to humans so will the False Prophet bring lies and deception from Satan to humans. Just as Satan is the Anti-God and the Beast is the Anti-Christ so will the False Prophet be the Anti-Spirit. And just as the Holy Spirit never exalts Himself but turns all praise to the Father and the Son so, too, will the False Prophet encourage and direct all worship and praise toward Satan and Antichrist. After all, Satan must plan for the religious instinct that resides in man. The religious instinct is one of the most powerful elements in the human experience. Whether for good or evil, man is inspired, dictated to, and drawn by religion. The purpose of this religion will be to deify and to worship Satan.

This beast, the False Prophet, comes up out of the bowels of the earth, unlike Antichrist who came up out of the sea (the masses of humanity), and the dragon who fell from the heavens. The coming and oppression of this man had been prophesied in Psalms 10:17-18 where we read this prayer, "Lord, thou hast heard the desire of the humble: thou wilt prepare their heart, thou wilt cause thine ear to hear: To judge the fatherless and the oppressed, *that the man of the earth* may no more oppress" (emphasis mine). The bowels of the earth from whence he comes house the spirit world according to scriptures such as I Samuel 28:13 and Ezekiel 32:24, among others.

Coincidentally, it has been a long-held occultic belief that the spirits of the "other world" are in a place called "middle earth," a place located under the surface of earth. This is more confirmation that the Second Beast is the Anti-Spirit. Exactly what type of being he will be, human or otherwise, is not clearly spelled out and different theories abound. It is possible that the exact nature of this beast will not become apparent until his coming, but suffice it to say that he is a potent and malevolent being indeed. His appearance is as a lamb but his words are dangerous in the extreme, being the words of the dragon itself. Whereas Jesus is portrayed as both Lion and Lamb, the False Prophet is portrayed as both Lamb and Dragon. Jesus warned of this very thing in Matthew 7:15 when He said, "Beware of false prophets, which come to you in sheep's clothing, but inwardly they are ravening wolves."

Notice that the False Prophet appears as a sheep with two horns. Horns are symbols of power. He has two distinct areas of power and they are the same two areas of power that all of the false religions, which have ever existed, have carved out for themselves. The focus of worship of every false religion has never been directed at God but has, instead, been directed to one of two places: The natural world (tree worship, water worship, worship of Mother Earth, etc.) or the supernatural world of demons and evil spirits. The False Prophet will combine both arenas, hence his two horns. Noted eschatologist Joseph Seiss foresaw this and over one hundred years ago wrote the following description of the False Prophet: "Therefore he is at once a naturalist and a supernaturalist, - a scientist and a spiritualist, - a Rationalist, yet asserting power above ordinary nature and in command of nature. In other words, he claims to be the bearer of the sum total of the Universal Wisdom, in which all reason and all revelation are fused into one great system, claimed to be the ultimatum of all truth, the sublime and absolute *Universeology*. And professing to have everything natural and supernatural thus solved and crystallized as the one eternal and perfect Wisdom, he must necessarily present himself as the one absolute apostle and teacher of all that ought to command the thought, faith, and obedience of man. The possession and exercise of the two horns of religious power certainly can mean nothing less than this."[26]

SATANIC "PROOFS OF DIVINITY"

"And he causes..." is said of the False Prophet eight times in these few verses. He is the administrator of Satan's program over all of the earth. He forces the world to worship Antichrist but his is not simply a brute show of force over the peoples of the earth. He uses both Old Testament and New Testament signs of divinity to deceive the masses. The New Testament sign of the Living God is the sign of the Resurrection. The False Prophet points to the "resurrection" of Antichrist as sufficient proof of his godhood. One of the Old Testament signs of the authority of God was the ability to call down fire from heaven. Moses did this, Elijah did this, and now the False Prophet does this as continuing proof of the divinity of Satan/Antichrist. Further this fire from heaven counterfeits the power of the Holy Spirit as it was the Holy Spirit who baptized the one hundred and twenty people in the Upper Room on the Day of Pentecost with cloven tongues of fire. As has been mentioned, 2 Thessalonians 2:9 tells us that the coming of Antichrist will be after the working of Satan and will be accompanied with all power, signs, and wonders that will support the lies (lying wonders).

A SATANIC IDOL AND DEMONSTRATIONS OF POWER

The False Prophet is ever in the presence of Satan/Antichrist, and he demands that an image of Antichrist be built by the humans. He then is able to make the image "come to life," causing it to speak. Furthermore, verse 13 says that he makes fire come down from heaven in the sight of men. It does not say it comes down in the sight of blithering idiots. The signs and wonders of the False Prophet are not parlor tricks perpetrated upon a backward, naive people. The speaking image, the fire from heaven, and the other wonders and miracles will be played out in front of probably the most sophisticated audience that could possibly be found in the history of mankind. This will be an audience of people used to the technical wonders of the twenty-first century if not an even later century, an audience raised on the incredible special effects industry of Hollywood; all in all, a very savvy group of consumers. And yet the miracles convince. Of course they do! They are empowered with *all* the power that Satan has at his disposal. And believe me, that is an enormous amount of power.

Another power is at his disposal, the power of life and death: For whoever chooses not to worship the Beast is summarily killed. This means that Christians face certain martyrdom, it will simply be a matter of time. Whereas before when Satan attempted to wipe Christians off of the face of the earth he found himself thwarted, this time he will succeed. It is Satan's time of total domination over earth. The majority of humans have asked for this, whether it was done ignorantly or not does not matter, and this is what they have received. Long ago, another king made a statue of himself and passed a law decreeing that every person in the kingdom had to bow down and worship the image. That king was Nebuchadnezzar; that kingdom was Babylon. Three men refused - Shadrach, Meshach, and Abednego. They were threatened with being burned alive. To that threat they replied: "Our God can save us. Whether or not he will is up to Him, but he can save us. Either way, we will not bow down before the idolatrous statue." For that rebellion, they were thrown alive into a furnace so hot that the men who threw them in were immediately killed by the heat of the furnace. But their God spared Shadrach, Meschach and Abedmego, and when they were released not even the smell of smoke remained on their bodies. The God of Shadrach, Meschach, and Abednego is the God of the tribulation saints who, too, will have to defy the king and refuse to worship his image. But this time, God will not intervene. The cost of being a disciple of Jesus at this time is at the cost of one's life.

THE MARK OF THE BEAST AND ITS CONSEQUENCES

The method by which the worship of the Beast will be assured and the rebellion of the Believers discovered will be the forced branding of each human body with the mark of the Beast. It will be administered in one of two places on their bodies, the forehead or the right hand. Because the right hand is much less conspicuous, it can be surmised that it will be the most prevalent place for people to receive the mark. Perhaps the forehead will be reserved for those who are hyper-loyal to the Beast and to his government. I can see now that the choice of a forehead marking could be made into a badge of honor at that time, immediately indicating those who are the hard-core adherents of Antichrist.

There is another more practical reason for the choice of two places; not everyone has a right hand but I have yet to meet a human without a forehead. Thus, there will be no excuse for anyone to refuse the mark, the choice whether or not to do so will have to be made by every person alive at this point in time. One can either choose Jesus or one can choose Satan. There is no other option available and there is no avoiding the choosing.

To further complicate the lives of non-adherents to the Beast's system, there will be another turn of the screw. Because it may take some time to hunt down and eradicate everyone without the mark of the Beast (there will be a huge number of non-compliers), a method will be needed to expedite the process. Therefore, a law will be instated that demands the existence of the mark in order to complete any financial transaction whatsoever. Groceries cannot be bought; one will not be able to buy even a stick of gum without the mark, and even the purchase of a cup of coffee will simply be a pipe dream without it. Rent or mortgage payments cannot be made without the mark, and even if the mortgage is paid in full, the taxes cannot be paid without the mark, so those without the mark will lose the ability to own or rent a home. Likewise, even a motel room cannot be rented for the night, a campground site cannot be had. The number of deaths from starvation, dehydration, and exposure will become enormous. And so every day the choice will have to be made again; will I live or will I remain faithful to God?

At this time we see an interesting upheaval of the world's social structure. Apparently the great, egalitarian society that Antichrist promised to the world at the beginning of his rise has not remained in place. Verse 16 clearly states that there are now rich and poor and small and great. But the world has gone even further into degradation than they were prior to Antichrist, for now slavery is a large part of the world's society. There will now be a free class of people and a bond (or slave) class of people. As in George Orwell's classic parable, <u>Animal</u>

Farm, I wonder if anyone will even take note of the incremental steps that Antichrist will take as he convinces people of slavery's need in society, all the while continuing to convince those people of the equality of his system?

The word that John uses for the "mark" of the Beast is made up of two Greek characters that stand for the name of Christ, but with a chilling addition in the middle of the two; a figure of a crooked serpent. That particular mark can be chosen, so too can the name of Antichrist (whatever that turns out to be), or his number. The number that is associated with Antichrist is the number 666. The number six has evil implications in Scripture, in fact, "six" in Greek is the word "hex." (As a side note, during Hitler's reign of terror, although there were many concentration camps scattered throughout Germany and Poland, only a few of those camps were set up primarily to exterminate the Jews. Those few were known as the "death camps" and they numbered exactly six.) Here, again, Satan takes to himself the number six, but this time it is given to him in triplicate. Why? In the number 666 we are given evidence of the Satanic trinity, three sixes, one each for Satan, Antichrist, and the False Prophet.

THE BEAST: NOT A COMPUTER NOR A SYSTEM BUT A MAN

Over the years, many books have been written speculating on the identity of the Beast. Those that named a particular person have---and this really goes without saying---been found to be false. Others have put forth the idea that Antichrist is not a man at all; he is a system. This particular theory found many adherents during times of crises such as World War II or the Cold War. The systems that were indicted were different, identified perhaps as Fascism or Communism, but the idea that the Beast represented a system remained. In the last few decades a new idea has gained supporters, and that is the idea that the Beast is the Computer, usually some behemoth computer in another country that has the capability to track the movements of every human on earth. That doesn't take a computer anymore, only a Global Positioning System which is available now in everything from cars to cell phones. The sad truth is that all of this brainpower could have been applied elsewhere if heed had but been given to Revelation 13:18, "Here is wisdom. Let him that hath understanding count the number of the beast: *for it is the number of a man;* and his number is Six hundred threescore and six." Antichrist, for all of his otherworldly ability and cunning, will be human and, as a human, will be found to be the greatest traitor to that race of all who have ever lived.

CHAPTER 17
THE FIRST 3 ½ YEARS OF TRIBULATION REVISITED
Revelation 14

MOUNT ZION - SAFE REFUGE FOR THE 144,000 JEWS

John now turns his attention from Antichrist and the False Prophet and their totalitarianism over all of the earth to Mount Zion. What a relief it must have been for him to do so! A greater contrast between two scenes can hardly be imagined. Whereas earlier in Revelation 13, the scene before John's eyes was one of complete evil and blasphemy, and one in which the righteous were suffering mightily at the hands of Antichrist, the scene now before John is one of holiness, purity and righteousness. It is the one bright spot on the face of the earth. But God has always had at least one. Never has He been forced to look down upon the world and give it up as being totally corrupted and in the control of the Evil One. Even now, at the zenith of Satan's power, that power of evil is not total. There are still overcomers, there are still those who belong to God. And those overcomers are found in every tongue, tribe, and nation - a billion points of light, if you will. There is one spot upon the earth that is totally undefiled by Antichrist. That place is Mount Zion.

Over and over in the Bible Mount Zion is spoken of as being the City of God and as abiding forever. Mount Zion is also the only place on earth that will be kept from the reach of Antichrist. We see the truth of those prophecies in Revelation 14. The very first thing that catches John's eye as he looks from the kingdom of Antichrist to Mount Zion is that The Lamb is present there. Jesus Himself is present on Mount Zion. This may be because the Ark of the Covenant is now lodged there, and the Ark has always been, for the Jews, the dwelling place of God upon the earth. With Jesus are the 144,000 Jewish Christians that we first saw in Revelation 7. Ten of the original Twelve Tribes of Israel are represented with 12,000 men each. The tribes of Ephraim and Dan are missing, but Ephraim is represented by his father, Joseph, who was not included in the names of the original twelve tribes. The tribe of Levi was considered to be "God's portion" and thus was not generally listed among the twelve tribes. It is listed here, however, but Dan, who is usually included, is here omitted, keeping the number of the tribes at twelve, the historic number. We come, then, to a full complement of 144,000 men: 12 tribes times 12,000 men each.

144,000 SEALED WITH THE NAME OF GOD AND JESUS

This company of Christian Jewish men is mentioned thirty-three times in the Psalms. They are protected by the presence of the Lamb and of the Ark. If they were to step but one foot off of Mount Zion they would surely be killed by Antichrist. In the same way that Antichrist is identifying his adherents by sealing their foreheads with his diabolical mark, so, too, are these 144,000 sealed in their foreheads with the name of both Jesus and God. The *King James Version* of Revelation 14:1 quoted above mentions only the name of God, however the Greek reads, "having the name of him and the name of the Father of him having been written on the foreheads of them." It is very curious to note that the Jehovah's Witnesses have claimed that they are the 144,000. It is a major tenet in their belief. My question is, what in the world are Jehovah's Witnesses doing with the name of Jesus on their forehead? They clearly deny the deity of Jesus and His equality with God! They would be the last to be sealed with the name of Jesus, but once again, because the Church has remained silent on Revelation for so many thousands of years, the cults have appropriated prophecy unto themselves and have distorted its meaning.

THE TASKS OF THE 144,000

The existence of these 144,000 sealed Jewish men was prophesied by Ezekiel when he wrote of them in Ezekiel 9:4, "And the Lord said unto him, Go through the midst of the city, through the midst of Jerusalem and set a mark upon the foreheads of the men that sigh and that cry for all the abominations that be done in the midst thereof". They have come to Jesus during the first three-and-one-half years of the Tribulation. Remember that the story of the Tribulation has begun again in Revelation 12, but this time it is from the standpoint of those on the earth.

We see the 144,000 once again because their story is being told once again. They are not in heaven as are the tribulation saints because they haven't been killed; they are being protected on Mount Zion. The reason that God has not allowed them to be killed is that they have not completed the tasks assigned to Israel, prophesied in Daniel 9:24, which must be completed prior to Israel's anointing of the Most Holy, Jesus. Those tasks are to finish the transgression and to make an end of sins, to make reconciliation for iniquity, to bring in everlasting righteousness, and to seal up the vision and prophecy. Earlier in verse 11, Daniel wrote, "All Israel have transgressed ...therefore the curse is poured upon us, and the oath that is written in the law of Moses the servant of God, because we have sinned against him." Thus, the first task is to repent as a nation and turn back to God. The 144,000 are the voices crying out in the wilderness to do this.

The second task, to make reconciliation for iniquity, has already been done because it could only be done by Christ himself. This He has done by His atoning death upon the cross. The message that this has been completed will be given by the 144,000 to the rest of the Jewish nation. The third task, to seal up the vision and prophecy, refers, I believe, to either the roles of the Two Witnesses or to some event which is still in the future and which will prove the prophecy that God gave to Daniel. The Jews will have an active role in this. When this is done, then Israel will receive Jesus when He comes again as their Messiah and long-awaited King and will complete the tasks given to them by anointing the most Holy, Jesus Christ, King of the Jews.

HEAVENLY VOICE AND EARTHLY VOICES JOIN IN A NEW SONG

After seeing the Lamb and the 144,000 thousand standing on Mount Zion, John then hears a voice from heaven. It is the incredible sound of the mightiest of mighty waterfalls, something akin to Niagara Falls perhaps, with that deep, resonant sound filling every airwave. But it is not the sound simply of the rush of majestic waters, it is also the sound of a mighty thunderstorm with peals of thunder overlaying the sounds of the falling, rushing waters. It is the voice of God, described many times before in exactly this way. That, by the way, is the same voice that will announce each believer's name at the Throne of God in heaven. Surely to have that experience alone would be fully worth any trial that might be visited upon one on earth!

And then, just as the sounds seems so majestic and powerful that one feels one cannot live before its presence, the sweet strains of music played by ethereal harps are heard all throughout the air. This is the sound of the 144,000 joining with the voice from heaven in a new song of praise. That it is the sound of harpers is quite apropos. The commandment to praise God with the sound of harps is given numerous times to the children of God from Genesis to Isaiah. We have already seen in Revelation 5 that the saints round the Throne praise Him with harps. Now the saints who are still on the earth join their voices to the praise of the Lord God Almighty. The song they sing is a song that has never before been heard in the universe. It is their particular song to God, born of their particular experience of overcoming in His power.

Just as the saints in Revelation 5 sang a new song to the Lamb, so these saints sing of their special relationship with Jesus. In a very real way, this is true of every single human being who has turned his life over to Jesus. This is true for you, too, if you wear His name. No one else has lived your life. No one else has been through exactly what you've been through. In fact, there is not another single person who has ever lived who has had the touch of Jesus in exactly the same way that you have. You have a praise to give Him, and if you don't sing that praise, it won't ever be sung. But imagine that praise service in heaven when each mortal there sings out his particular praise to God! The diversity of song within the unity of spirit will be the most harmonious and glorious sound ever to have filled space in the Universe. Point and counterpoint, melody and harmony will reach their zenith as each believer looks into the face of The Lamb and pours out his heart in thankful praise for what God has done in each life.

144,000 VIRGINS

Revelation 14:4 tells us that these 144,000 are virgins, never defiled by women. There are two views regarding the meaning of that. One is that they are actual virgins; 144,000 men who have never been with a woman. The second view focuses on the phrase "defiled by women" because the Bible is very clear on the point that the marriage relationship does not sexually defile a believer in any way. Reference Hebrews 13:4 which says, "Marriage is honourable in all, and the bed undefiled: but whoremongers and adulterers God will judge." Therefore, marriage would not have defiled these men. In addition to this point, the Bible sometimes refers to chastity and purity in the lives of believers in a strictly spiritual fashion. Second Corinthians 11:2 says, "For I am jealous over you with godly jealousy: for I have espoused you to one husband, that I may present you as a chaste virgin to Christ." So it is possible that the purity and chastity of these men are a reflection of their single-mindedness to Christ and speaks to the fact that there is no adulterating influence of the world on their lives. This will be especially noteworthy in these times because the Bible says that the last days will be like the days of Noah where immorality was rampant and "every imagination of the thoughts of [man's] heart was only evil continually" (Genesis 6:5). At any rate, these 144,000 men are certainly chaste in every way now, for no women are said to be abiding on Mount Zion at this time!

144,000 FIRSTFRUITS

This company is called the "firstfruits" to God and to Jesus. They are the firstfruits of the nation of Israel, firstfruits in the context that even though all of the Nation of Israel will finally accept Jesus as Messiah at the end of the time of Tribulation when He comes in victory, these 144,000 are the first to do so during Tribulation. The very term "firstfruit" is indicative of more fruit to come. Romans 9:25-28 quotes both Hosea and Isaiah concerning the prophecy given to them that Israel will be totally restored to God. The promise that He will finish the work in that race of people is confirmed. Later in Romans 11:25-26, Paul states emphatically that all Israel shall be saved, adding in 2 Corinthians 3:15-17 that the veil that now hides their hearts from Jesus will be taken away.

They Preach to Israel, Not to the World. It is taught many times that the 144,000 will witness of Jesus to the world. This is absolutely not true. The fullness of the Gentiles spoken of by Paul is now completed and was so at the end of the sixth seal. That means that God's work among the Gentiles is finished and complete. Only Israel remains to be dealt with by God's grace, and the 144,000 are God's instruments to do exactly that. They do not preach to the world, they preach to Israel. Historically, Jews have always ministered to their own people, they do not proselytize Gentiles. When this is reflected upon, it shows us that the Apostle Paul and his companions were even greater agents of God's grace than we understand at first because of their willingness to share God's good news with the Gentiles. Considering the existence of evangelical groups such as "Jews for Jesus", the desire of most Jewish converts still seems to be to minister to their own.

They Always Follow the Lamb. "These are they which follow the Lamb whithersoever he goeth." This again speaks to their purity, and single-minded devotion to the Lamb, Jesus. They do not stray from Him; wherever He leads them, they follow. If He leads them to still waters, they go. If He leads them into battle, they go. If He leads them into persecution, they willingly go; they are the sheep, He is the shepherd. That is exactly the position and commandment given to every believer who has ever belonged to Jesus. The commandment to follow Him, however, has been a bit of a hit-or-miss proposition in most every Christian life. It is not the case with these 144,000; they follow the Lamb wherever He goes. And when Jesus returns triumphant, they will join the rest of the saints in no longer following the Lamb, but rather in having an even more blessed position and station: that of having the Lamb be in their very midst.

Their Tongues Are Pure. Another fact that speaks of their holiness is the fact that in their mouth no guile can be found. If one wants to evaluate the life of any Christian, it can best be done by evaluating how controlled his tongue is. Our spiritual maturity can pretty well be determined by how disciplined our tongue is. The Bible itself states this in James 3:2-8, "For in many things we offend all. If any man offend not in word, the same is a perfect man, and able also to bridle the whole body. Behold, we put bits in the horses' mouths, that they may obey us; and we turn about their whole body. Behold also the ships, which though they be so great, and are driven of fierce winds, yet are they turned about with a very small helm, whithersoever the governor listeth. Even so the tongue is a little member, and boasteth great things. Behold, how great a matter a little fire kindleth! And the tongue is a fire, a world of iniquity: so is the tongue among our members, that it defileth the whole body, and setteth on fire the course of nature; and it is set on fire of hell. For every kind of beasts, and of birds, and of serpents, and of things in the sea, is tamed, and hath been tamed of mankind: But the tongue can no man tame; it is an unruly evil, full of deadly poison."

Apparently, these 144,000 have tamed their tongues, and by reporting that fact, John gives us almost full understanding of the condition of their lives, because the tongue seems to be "the last frontier" when it comes to holiness. When we get our tongues under control, we are controlled people. We may not drink ourselves into a stupor, we may not steal nor murder, we may not even gamble away our children's milk money, but we still say ugly things. The entire lives of these men are described by describing the state of their tongues. They are godly.

JOHN AGAIN SEES THE SIX SEALS OPENED - THIS TIME FROM THE EARTH

The scene now changes. Something compels John to look away from Mount Zion and upward into the skies. There he will see from the vantage point of earth what he has already seen from the vantage point of heaven: The opening of the first Six Seals. From heaven, he saw the Four Horsemen of the Apocalypse ride forth under the command of God. He will also see them now but they will appear to him to be angels as he stands upon the earth and looks up. Verses 6-20 of this chapter will tell the same story as did Revelation 6, but different details will be given. Why, when there is so much information to relay to John (and, hence the rest of the Church) would the same information already relayed simply be repeated? It is not. It is the same principle that attorneys use when they call several witnesses to relate each of their account of the same incident. It is both to corroborate the truth of the situation and to bring forth differing details. The whole Bible is written in this manner.

The story of Melchizedek, King of Salem, is an example of this. Genesis tells us the basic story of the meeting between Abram and him. It tells us that Melchizedek was a priest before God, that he brought bread and wine to Abram who then gave to him a tithe, after which Melchizedek blessed Abram. But one has to continue to read almost through the entire Bible in order to get to Hebrews where we learn that Melchizedek had no father, no mother, no beginning of days and no end of days. Psalm 110:4 tells us that Jesus Himself is a priest after the order of Melchizedek. Genesis mentions none of that.

Moses is another example of this. Deuteronomy records his death and burial and even tells us that God himself buried Moses (a first!), but it does not tell us anything else. Jude, the penultimate book of the Bible and a one-chapter book, gives us an amazing fact: Satan was furious that God kept the body of Moses and demanded that God return it. We might never have been able to understand why unless we had also been given the Gospels that recorded the story of the Transfiguration where Moses and Elijah appeared to Jesus in glorified bodies to discuss Jesus' upcoming death. Elijah never died, so that body was with God and thus could appear on the Mount of Transfiguration, but what if Satan had held Moses' body?! He would have been absent. God, knowing that Moses' body would be needed, kept it, enraging Satan. Finally, Revelation 11 gives us the final installation of the story when it tells us how Moses comes as one of the two witnesses to Israel at the time of the end. Once again, the story is not neatly given, with every "i" dotted and every "t" crossed. The Bible demands more attention and study out of us than that.

Not even leaving the Pentateuch, a third example springs to mind - that of the Wilderness Wanderings of the Israelites. Again, many details are found in Deuteronomy: The number of years spent wandering, the cloud that followed them by day and the pillar of fire that followed them by night, the feeding of the multitude first with manna and then with quail, etc. However it takes looking at Psalms 78 to realize that manna is the food of the angels and it takes reading Nehemiah to discover another amazing detail of the wanderings. After spending forty years in the heat and dust of the wilderness, constantly journeying, dealing with a water shortage most of the time, Nehemiah tells us that none of their clothes wore out and neither did their shoes! This is after wearing their clothes for forty years in an hostile climate and wearing clothes that were not even made of polyester! This was miraculous. Imagine, also, wearing shoes that had to march through a desert for forty years and did not wear out. My high heels need new heel taps after two weeks of use on the streets. This detail, the very preservation of their clothes, speaks to the mercy of God. The Israelites are wandering in the first place because they sinned but God says, "I know you're here because of unbelief and disobedience, but I love you and I will take care of every little detail even in your punishment".

The Bible is replete with example after example of the need to tie all sixty-six of its books together, to approach studying it as a systematic endeavor, but let me quickly mention an example as concerns prophecy: The four visions of Daniel concerning the future of the nations of the earth. When we looked at these visions in detail in chapter 15, we saw that each one concerned itself with the same prophecy, but that different details were given each time. Because of that we have a more accurate and complete picture. That is exactly the purpose of the retelling of the opening of the six seals from heaven's viewpoint in Revelation 6, and from earth's viewpoint here in Revelation 14. We should welcome the greater detail, not stress over the fact that we are given a re-visitation of an earlier enlightenment.

What this chapter in Revelation will do for the reader is to enlighten him as to the pronouncement of the Horseman/Angel as each seal on the Little Book - The title deed to the earth - is opened in heaven. We saw that as the First Horseman rode out of heaven in Revelation 6 he did so on a white horse with a bow and a *stephanos* crown signifying victory and that he went forth to conquer for heaven. Here we see what he says and we find that it is the Everlasting Gospel of Christ that is preached to every person who dwells on the face of the earth. Isn't this just like the God that we know, love and worship! First comes mercy, then comes punishment only if the mercy is rejected. Before war, famine, before pestilence and curses, the First

Horseman preaches the Good News of Jesus' saving grace to every human being who finds himself in the empire of the Antichrist.

GOSPEL PREACHED FROM HEAVEN: EXPECTED AND EXPERIENCED

But isn't preaching from heaven just too weird a thought to be contemplated? Apparently It wasn't to Paul who knew it would occur and even warned in Galatians 1:8 that, "But though we, *or an angel from heaven*, preach any other gospel unto you than that ye have received, let him be accursed" (emphasis mine). Blessedly, the gospel that is proclaimed in Revelation 14 is not a false gospel but the gospel once and for all delivered. The writer of Hebrews (probably Paul himself) quoted an Old Testament prophecy that one day God's word would be preached from heaven. Consider the warning in Hebrews12:25-27: "See that ye refuse not him that speaketh. For if they escaped not who refused him that spake on earth, much more shall not we escape, if we turn away from him that *speaketh from heaven:* Whose voice then shook the earth: but now he hath promised, saying, Yet once more I shake not the earth only, but also heaven. And this word, Yet once more signifieth the removing of those things that are shaken, as of things that are made, that those things which cannot be shaken may remain" (emphasis mine).

The quote here is from Haggai 2:6-7 and it is concerning end times. That is made clear in the context that includes the warning about the impending shaking of the world, which happens at the time of the end.

Not only is heavenly preaching expected, it was experienced. Consider the birth of Jesus. "And there were in the same country shepherds abiding in the field, keeping watch over their flock by night. And, lo, the angel of the Lord came upon them, and the glory of the Lord shone round about them: and they were sore afraid. And the angel said unto them, Fear not: for, behold, I bring you good tidings of great joy, which shall be to all people. For unto you is born this day in the city of David a Saviour, which is Christ the Lord. And this shall be a sign unto you; Ye shall find the babe wrapped in swaddling clothes, lying in a manger. *And suddenly there was with the angel a multitude of the heavenly host praising God, and saying,* Glory to God in the highest, and on earth peace, good will toward men" (Luke 2:8-14, emphasis mine).

Granted, the angels only appeared to the shepherds on earth that time but it does not change the fact that the preaching was other-worldly. Consider, too, the fact that it has been prophesied by Jesus Himself that the end of the world will not occur until every human ear has heard the gospel of Christ. Lest we think that we are moving closer to that goal, missionary societies say otherwise. We are falling behind, not gaining ground, in our quest to evangelize the world. As concerns world population percentage-wise, we are not even holding our own. And yet, the prophecy will come to pass. Before the end of the world, every human on the face of the earth will have heard the gospel. In fact here it says, "every nation, and kindred, and tongue, and people" will have the everlasting gospel preached to them. Consider, too, that the Church has been laboring for two thousand years to reach the entire world with the gospel and has not finished the task. Now, the entire world, with all the Christians gone who could proclaim the message of the Cross, must hear in the space of three-and-one-half years! It will take the miraculous intervention of God to get it done and it will be done from heaven.

It is very possible that it will be the saints themselves who do the preaching. I say that for two reasons: first, the commandment to preach the Gospel has been delivered to the Church and it is her responsibility. Second, the saints in their post-raptured bodies could very well resemble angels when viewed from earth's perspective. After all, the word "angel" in Greek simply means "messenger," and we have already seen that the letters to the churches were written to the "angels" of the churches. Because heavenly angels would have no need of written instruction from John, the possibility is great that humans are the angels to whom John refers. Certainly in this passage, the saints, who now occupy heaven, could be the messengers that God continues to appoint as the proclaimers of His gospel.

The Angel Who Preaches Is Not a Broadcasting Satellite. Some end-times preachers teach that when verse 6 talks about the angel preaching from heaven it is talking about a giant

Christian radio station with a giant satellite that finally gets the job done. If that is so, why hasn't it happened by now? The technology is certainly in place. Yes but, the argument goes, the cost is too prohibitive now. And that will change?! All that will change in the three-and-one-half years that follow the Rapture will be an incomprehensible outbreak of war, famine, wild animal attacks, pestilence, plague, and earthquakes. It is highly unlikely that the cost will go down. And what group of Christians will have the ability to organize or fund the giant satellite? The Bible clearly says that they won't even be able to buy a carton of milk or rent a campsite. How will they finance this? And that hardly matters anyway, given that they wouldn't have the time to organize it because they are being hunted down and killed as fast as Antichrist can identify them.

It is also posited by these preachers that the satellite is not yet in place because there are too many governmental regulations at this time. Does anyone seriously think that if the United States government is putting up obstacles now that Antichrist himself will be more lenient when he is in power? The idea is patently absurd. It is not within the realm of possibility that Antichrist, who has worldwide dictatorial powers will sit idly by while the largest Christian broadcasting satellite ever conceived is launched, even if we suspend belief about the possibility of its financing and organization ever happening.

No, the preaching will be under God's direction and control. He knows that with no Christians left on the face of the earth to share about the atonement of His son, Jesus. that He will either have to leave the world in ignorance or He will have to have the saints share from heaven. Before God destroyed the earth with the Flood, He had Noah preach for one-hundred-twenty years to warn the people of impending doom. This time the world only has three-and-a-half years to hear and to heed. Again, given God's mercy, the warning to repent comes before the judgment. Verse 6 is clear, the gospel is preached from heaven. Only those who feel they must limit God and His grace and mercy can argue.

No Partial Rapture. The fact that the gospel is preached from heaven also attacks the mistaken belief that God will be forced to leave some Christians on the earth in order to preach during the time of the Tribulation. Proponents of this viewpoint argue that some Christians who deserve to be raptured based on their relationship with Jesus will, nonetheless, be denied the Rapture because somehow the Gospel must be given to the Post-Rapture world. It will be, but, unlike their argument that lacks any scriptural basis on which to base a partial Rapture, the passage here describes how the Gospel will be given to a world bereft of Christians.

Revelation 14:6 is clear on what exactly is preached. It mentions the "everlasting gospel," but it also mentions the commandment to fear God and give Him glory. This will be a warning that will counteract what the False Prophet is commanding the people on earth to do, which is to fear the Beast and worship him. A line is drawn, each person must decide whom to believe and whom to obey - the preaching from heaven or the despot on earth.

Further, the angel warns that they are living in a world that God Himself created and that there is a heaven above them where He resides. The angel specifically mentions the creation by God of heaven, earth, the seas and the fountains of water. These are the first four areas that will be affected by the coming plagues. God has made the heavens, the earth, the seas, and the fountains of waters and God retains control over them even now. This proof of His authority is like the plagues that God sent on Egypt in the days of Moses and Pharaoh in that those plagues were directed at gods whom the Egyptians worshipped. As an example, the Egyptians worshipped the Nile River. The first plague saw the entire Nile turned to blood. The message to Egypt was unmistakable: The God of the Israelites was far more powerful than their god.

The same message concerning the authority of God, Creator of heaven and earth, is being delivered to the earth now. At this point in time Antichrist is claiming that he is the controller of earth and heaven, that he is God. The voice from heaven says "NO!" Did Antichrist make heaven, earth, seas, and fountains of water? If not, you had better consider Who did, and that is to Whom you direct your worship. The theory of evolution that has prepared the world to disbelieve and discount The Creator has also prepared the world for the deception of these times. After all, if man has evolved from protozoa status, who can deny that he can evolve into godhood like Antichrist?

The lie that denies the fact of God's direct hand in the creation process of earth is not benign. Satan well understands that fact; sadly, many Christians do not. They are quite sanguine in their acceptance of this great lie of evolution. God as Creator was always the message that the early Christians preached to the pagan. Note Paul's response to the people of Lystra in the following passage when he and Barnabas were misidentified as being gods after Paul healed a cripple there: "And when the people saw what Paul had done, they lifted up their voices, saying in the speech of Lycaonia, The gods are come down to us in the likeness of men. And they called Barnabas, Jupiter; and Paul, Mercurius, because he was the chief speaker. Then the priest of Jupiter, which was before their city, brought oxen and garlands unto the gates, and would have done sacrifice with the people. Which when the apostles, Barnabas and Paul, heard of, they rent their clothes, and ran in among the people, crying out, And saying, Sirs, why do ye these things? We also are men of like passions with you, and preach unto you that *ye should turn from these vanities unto the living God, which made heaven, and earth, and the sea, and all things that are therein*" (Acts 14:11-15, emphasis mine).

Paul preached the same message to the populace of Athens when he arrived there, saying, "Ye men of Athens, I perceive that in all things ye are too superstitious. For as I passed by, and beheld your devotion, I found an altar with this inscription, TO THE UNKNOWN GOD. Whom therefore ye ignorantly worship, him declare I unto you. *God that made the world and all things therein, seeing that he is Lord of heaven and earth, dwelleth not in temples made with hands;* neither is worshipped with men's hands, as though he needed any thing, seeing he giveth to all life, and breath, and all things; And hath made of one blood all nations of men for to dwell on all the face of the earth, and hath determined the times before appointed, and the bounds of their habitation; That they should seek the Lord, if haply they might feel after him, and find him, though he be not far from every one of us" (Acts 17:22-27, emphasis mine).

GOD AS CREATOR IS FOUNDATIONAL TO SALVATION

But what does Creationism have to do with salvation? Why, with all of the doctrinal points that might be addressed, is it the one emphasized *from the heavens*? One must understand that Satan is thoroughly threatened by the concept of God as creator. When God is revealed as being preeminent in power and authority in the universe, He is then revealed as being more powerful than Satan. The theory of evolution is no accidental happening in the scientific world. Since its wholesale acceptance, Creation no longer points to God. It is clear that one could not convince Paul that Darwinism or the Blind Watchmaker Theory was compatible with Christianity's view of God's role in creation.

THE SECOND ANGEL FORETELLS THE FALL OF BABYLON - ANTICHRIST'S CAPITAL

On the heels of the first angel's announcement comes the announcement by a second angel. At first blush, the two seem to have no relation but they are inextricably linked and they both hit hard at the authority of Antichrist and at the power of his kingdom. The second angel announces that Antichrist's great capital, the greatest city in the world at this point in time, Babylon, is fallen. If one will remember, the second horseman was the horseman from heaven who removed peace from the earth. The second horseman initiated the action; the second angel sounds the warning to the world's people. War and strife begin to break out all over the planet, and peace is even being taken from the animal kingdom. This removal of peace by God will resonate all throughout Antichrist's kingdom and impact even its crown jewel, Babylon. She will be no more. Although when this announcement is made by the angel, Babylon is still glorious and prosperous, the angel announces that Babylon is a wasteland already.

The initial response of people may be to call this announcement ridiculous given that their eyes clearly tell them that Babylon is not fallen, but the authority and solemnity of the angel must give them pause. What they don't understand, but somehow sense, is that God is not bound by time as mere mortals are. Many have been the times when future events were announced in the present tense under God's direction. A case in point was the taking of the city of Jericho by the Israelites under the leadership of Joshua. "Now Jericho was straitly shut up because of the children of Israel: none went out, and none came in. And the Lord said unto Joshua, See, I *have given* into thy hand Jericho, and the king thereof, and the mighty men of valour" (Joshua 6:1-2, emphasis mine). The battle was not even begun and yet God says that it is already done. And it was; all that needed to happen in order for the humans to understand what God understood was the passage of time. As Romans 4:17 declares, "God...quickeneth the dead, and calleth those things which be not as though they were." We are limited by time and experiences; God is not. It is a done deal when God first speaks it into existence. The same holds true for the fall of Babylon. It is a fait accompli even though it hasn't happened yet.

Isaiah was given the same message about the fall of Babylon in Isaiah 21: 6-9: "For thus hath the Lord said unto me, Go, set a watchman, let him declare what he seeth. And he saw a chariot with a couple of horsemen, a chariot of asses, and a chariot of camels; and he hearkened diligently with much heed: And he cried, A lion: My lord, I stand continually upon the watchtower in the daytime, and I am set in my ward whole nights: And, behold, here cometh a chariot of men, with a couple of horsemen. And he answered and said, *Babylon is fallen, is fallen;* and all the graven images of her gods he hath broken unto the ground" (emphasis mine).

Another aspect of the heavenly view besides the removal of peace from the world which will ultimately lead to the destruction even of Babylon, is the attack again upon the power and authority of the Beast. Even while the first angel is proclaiming God as creator of heaven and earth, many people might respond by thinking, "Well, so Antichrist didn't create them, but look at what he did create; that marvelous wonder Babylon." And Babylon will indeed be an unbelievable city when Antichrist is finished with it. Babylon will be rebuilt before the Rapture takes place. The time spoken of here is after the Rapture and it is a time of total war and strife. No one is building now, the world is in chaos! The rule is this: If something cannot happen after the Rapture then it must happen before the Rapture. Babylon cannot be built after the

Rapture in times of war, plague, famine, etc. Therefore, it must be completed before the Rapture. The world has never seen the likes of a city which the Bible tells us Babylon will be. The very streets will be paved with gold. Man will pride himself on this great work. And then the angel appears proclaiming God's dominance over even Babylon, the very center of Antichrist's control.

Why Babylon Will Be Destroyed. The angel goes on to explain why the city will be destroyed. It is not a capricious destruction; because of Babylon every single nation on the face of the earth has been forced or has chosen to drink of the wine of her incredibly debauched and profane actions. I am sure that the debauchery that will be part and parcel of everyday life in those times will be staggering and sickening. The angel speaks of the wrath of Babylon's fornication; the wrath of her unspeakable evil. Whose wrath is it? It is not speaking here of God's wrath. It is speaking of Satan's wrath against the human race that causes him to lead them into degradation. You see, every sin that we commit, even the "pleasurable" ones, are conceived in Satan's hate and anger, which is ultimately aimed against God but also against God's special creation, man. And those sins, even the most self-pleasuring and self-serving ones, are intended to destroy the very one who chooses them.

If only we as humans could ever see sin through Satan's eyes, I feel its power would forever be lost on us. And when we begin to see sin through God's eyes, we will begin to understand why God hates it so, in part because it is anathema to His very nature, and in part because of its total destructive ability on man and even the earth itself.

THIRD ANGEL GIVES WARNING CONCERNING THE BEAST

The third angel now follows with his pronouncement as the preaching continues. His grave warning is aimed against worshiping the Beast or even his image and also against receiving his mark, 666, in one's forehead or on one's hand. The angel also reveals the consequences of disobedience on this point. The consequences described comprise one of the strongest preachings on hell found in the Bible. One ignores this pronouncement at one's everlasting peril. Martin Luther hated this book, Revelation, because he saw a God that he didn't want to see, a God of wrath and punishment. Too bad, says John, this too, is God. One cannot argue that God is unaware of hell or that it exists without His permission. That point is strongly made in the assertion that all hell exists "in the presence of the holy angels, and in the presence of the Lamb." You can take your scissors to this verse, I won't. The angel also states that hell lasts for ever and ever. There will be no rest for those who receive this mark.

Taking the Beast's mark is a guarantee of eternity in hell. The question arises as to why the third angel is sent with this warning at this time. The answer is because the corresponding horseman in Revelation 6 is the horseman who brings the worldwide famine to earth, and thus the temptation to take the mark of the Beast will now increase substantially.

Although the system of the Beast, which has required the Mark in order to buy or sell anything in the marketplace, has been in effect for a while, one must consider that whenever a new project or system is put into place it is a bit loose in the beginning stages before the screws really begin to tighten. It will be the same with the system of the Mark of the Beast. When the system is first instigated, no doubt one will see the Beast's government employees and the hyper-patriotic immediately show up and take the mark. Societal pressure will be intense. But a lot of people will drag their feet; they will take a wait-and-see attitude. "My friend works at Albertson's. She can get me groceries," will be a commonplace refrain. The produce stands and farmers' markets will be slower to require the mark and many without the mark will depend on access to them. This may, indeed, work for a while but the screw will be inexorably tightening. And then the God-induced famine will hit. Things will change. The friend at Albertson's can no longer even guarantee that there will be food for herself on the shelves, much less for a friend. And furthermore, no one will get one bit without that cursed mark. Immediately, the need for the mark will be paramount to survival. Under this famine, food will be so scarce that a day's wages will buy starvation level substance for the worker only, none for the spouse and none for the children. Further, one will work all day for food only, not for housing, clothing, electricity, etc.

But it is at this precise point in time that the third angel will appear and will sound the warning that if one succumbs to the pressure to take the mark, one will be tormented in hell forever. After all, even death by starvation has an end point; Hell does not. Choose wisely, the angel warns, for no choice will have an excuse; the warning has been sounded from heaven and all have heard. Each person on earth will have to decide whether to choose short-term survival or long-term salvation. We today make the same exact choice but somehow our choice is more masked from us, more removed from consequence. It will not be so at this point: You take the mark, you go to hell. Decide. The clear drawing of this line is divine grace. No one will be able to say, "if only I'd known," because all will know. And because all will know the consequence of the mark, many will refuse it and many will be saved. It will be clearly spelled out by the angel that it will be far easier to face any death meted out by Antichrist than it will be to face God's judgment.

TO LIVE IS HELL - TO DIE IS CHRIST

Verse 13 assures the tribulation saints that God has ordained and allowed this time. They will have to go through it, they will have to die, but it will be okay, Jesus will walk with them as they face death, and their reward will be worth *anything* required of them. However, there will be no escaping the fact that it will be much better to be dead than to be alive if one is a Christian. Without the mark, one will watch oneself and one's family slowly starves to death. Stomachs will gradually distend from hunger and tongues will turn black from lack of water. People's resolve against taking the mark will falter, but then they will remember the voice from heaven. It will be their preservation and their inspiration. The end facing each Christian at this point will be inescapable martyrdom; therefore death is not something to be avoided and fought against, but rather something to be embraced. All the trials of earth will finally be over and there will be rest on the other side. And as each Christian is killed, each death will be met by the heavenly pronouncement that yet another soul has come off victorious from the beast.

"And their works do follow them" says the Spirit. What are their works? Have they orchestrated great missions, have they built great churches, have they preached great sermons? No, they have simply stood their ground and not compromised with evil. They have remained faithful and true at a time when every societal pressure is against them. They have made the statement with their lives and finally with their deaths that Jesus was more important to them than anything found on earth. And that fact is so glorifying to God that He insures that their obedience will never be forgotten but will be remarked upon throughout the rest of eternity. As Francis of Assissi said, "Preach the gospel at all times; if necessary use words." It will be our deeds, not our words, that follow us to heaven.

THE REAPING OF SOULS - SAVED AND UNSAVED

The fourth, fifth, and sixth seals in Revelation 6 all concern themselves with death and judgment and we see the same thing in Revelation 14. There, as here, there are only two categories: the saved and the unsaved. In chapter 6, the saved were found under the fifth seal and the unsaved were found under the fourth and sixth seals. Here, the souls are reaped by the angelic messengers into the same two groups; saved and unsaved. The Son of man, Jesus, directs the reaping of both groups.

The Saved. The first group reaped is the saved; "the harvest of the earth is ripe", the angel says. These are the same words used by Jesus in John 4:35 when He said to His disciples, "Behold, I say unto you, Lift up your eyes, and look on the fields; for they are white already to harvest." This harvest is a harvest of eternally saved souls. Jesus will now reap what He has planted. This announcement by the angel as to the reaping that Jesus is about to do, is the corollary to the scene of the souls under the altar that was seen under the fifth seal in Revelation 6, for it is the souls of the tribulation saints which are about to be reaped. It is important to note that Jesus Himself does the reaping of these souls. He comes for them because they belong to Him. In contrast with that, the angel who is the Angel of Fire executes the second reaping, the reaping of the unsaved souls.

The Unsaved. The Angel over Fire announces the second reaping, a reaping symbolized by overripe grapes. Just as the white field of harvest is a symbol of the righteous, a harvest of grapes is symbolic of a harvest of wickedness. Isaiah 63 asks the question: "Who is this that cometh from Edom, with dyed garments from Bozrah this that is glorious in his apparel, travelling in the greatness of his strength? I that speak in righteousness, mighty to save. Wherefore art thou red in thine apparel, and thy garments like him *that treadeth the winefat?* I have trodden the winepress alone; and of the people there was none with me: for I will tread them in mine anger, and trample them in my fury; and their blood shall be sprinkled upon my garments, and I will stain all my raiment. For the day of vengeance is in my heart, and the year of my redeemed is come" (verses 1-4, emphasis mine).

The prophet Joel explains: "Let the heathen be wakened, and come up to the valley of Jehoshaphat: for there will I sit to judge all the heathen round about. Put ye in the sickle, for the harvest is ripe: come, get you down: *for the press is full, the vats overflow;* for their wickedness is great" (Joel 3:12-13, emphasis mine).

Those in this harvest are the people who are killed by the rider of the Pale Horse, the fourth horseman of the Apocalypse, Death, and those who are killed under the sixth seal when the mighty earthquake occurs. The slaughter of the wicked is so great that John records that their blood comprised a river that was high enough to reach to the bridle of a horse. Even more ominous than that is the fact that the Age of Grace is now over. Not one Gentile is ever recorded as being saved after this. Only more horror awaits the earth as the time comes for the opening of the final and most horrific seal, the Seventh Seal of the title deed to the earth.

CHAPTER 18
THE SAINTS VICTORIOUS OVER SATAN
Revelation 15

THE TRIBULATION SAINTS REAPPEAR - SAME STORY, DIFFERENT VIEWPOINT

The angel's warning in Revelation 14 not to take the mark of the Beast, nor the mark of his name, nor to worship him or his image has borne fruit and we see the results of that fruit in Revelation 15. Countless numbers of people, out of the even larger group symbolized by the sea of glass, have heeded that warning and, as a consequence, have been martyred. This is the same group of people that we saw in Revelation 7:9-17. It is another indication that we are in the second telling of the same story given in Revelation 4-11. The appearance of the tribulation saints follows the sixth seal in both accounts.

This is the second sea of glass talked about in Revelation. The first sea of glass was seen by John in Revelation 4 and was comprised of the raptured saints. The sea of glass in view here is comprised of the tribulation saints. This time the sea of glass is mingled with fire. Fire is symbolic of the power and presence of the Holy Spirit, and the point that is being made here is that not one single person could have withstood the persecution and the temptation of that tribulation time unless the Holy Spirit was in complete control of that person's life. The very symbolism of the sea of saints is marked by the undeniable authority of the Holy Spirit over their lives.

THE TRIBULATION SAINTS VICTORIOUS OVER SATAN

Just as when Satan killed Jesus and thought, very prematurely as it turned out, that hc had defeated God Himself, Satan in the form of Antichrist will now rejoice that he has wiped out every last vestige of Christianity upon the face of the earth except those on Mount Zion who will command Satan's attention next. He will once again exult in the fact that to all appearances he has defeated God. But heaven does not record it that way. Heaven records it thusly: "And I saw as it were a sea of glass mingled with fire: *and them that had gotten the victory over the beast, and over his image, and over his mark, and over the number of his name*, stand on the sea of glass, having the harps of God" (emphasis mine). Heaven sees things from quite a different perspective than does earth. Granted, these souls were not delivered from Satan's persecution, but a much more spiritually powerful experience occurred here. They overcame Satan by the power of the Holy Spirit within their lives.

When Roman soldiers went into battle, they were not to worry about the outcome of the battle, the outcome of the campaign, nor the outcome of the war. They were to worry about one thing and one thing only. Each soldier was given one square meter to defend, about three feet each way. He was to fight and die for that one square meter. That was his sole responsibility. No enemy was to take it from him. And you see, if each soldier were steadfast in his job, the battle would be won. We, too, have been given one square meter to defend by his power in this overarching battle between good and evil. That one square meter is our life; our tiny time on earth; our tiny sphere of influence; our one square meter. It is a small fight, but it is a vicious fight. Satan is absolutely determined to win each and every square meter.

Robert Louis Stevenson wrote: "The world has no room for cowards. We must all be ready somehow to toil, to suffer, to die. And yours is not the less noble because no drum beats before you when you go out into your daily battlefields, and no crowds shout about your coming when you return from your daily victory or defeat."[27]

For the most part, ours will be obscure battles, not fought out before the cameras, but do not ever believe the lie that they are unimportant. They are critical. Without you, your one square meter will go undefended. What would that mean? We don't need Frank Capra's *It's A Wonderful Life* to spell it out for you. It means that the primary protection for your children will not be there. They will have to depend on the other lives that peripherally intersect theirs. It means the good, and the peace, and the strength, and the comfort that you bring to your spouse will be absent. It means that the cleansing and patching up of the wounds of your friends who are also engaged in their battle might go unattended. It means that the courageous stand for morality and right that your voice is ordained to utter in the workplace, in the neighborhood, in the PTA meeting, at the soccer game, and in the classroom will be silenced and more darkness will hover over an already dying world. And it means another thing.

Besides the many victories that God will affect through you if you stand your ground and love Him with all your strength, a most amazing thing will happen. You will cease to pick apart the lives of the others who are fighting alongside you. You will not have the time nor the inclination. You will simply want to encourage them to stand their own ground in the fight. No more will we draw our sword and fight and wound one another - we will stand shoulder to shoulder and fight our one common enemy - the Prince of Darkness.

There is an important lesson for each one of us here. Almost without fail, when we are faced with trial and difficulties, we pray for deliverance from them. Sometimes God grants that prayer, but many times he says to us instead, "It is not in My plan to deliver you this time. Instead, it is My will that you live through this and overcome this trial by the strength and power of My Name, and when you do, you will be forever changed." One way is easy and gratifying to our flesh, the other way is difficult and strengthening to our souls. One way speaks to the power of God to defeat any obstacle faced by humanity, the other way speaks to the power of God to transform weak and sinful creatures into His very likeness. When, by His mighty power, He delivers us, He gets the praise; He gets the glory. And when, by His power, we overcome, He gets the praise; He gets the glory. "In all these things we are more than conquerors through him that loved us" as Romans 8:37 tells us.

GOD'S GRACE HAS TWO MANIFESTATIONS

There are only two possibilities for us when we put our troubles in the hand of God: He's either going to take them away or He's going to give us the strength to come through them victoriously. If God has made your cup sweet, drink it in thanksgiving. If God has made your cup bitter, drink it in communion with Him. We're thankful when we drink the sweet, but we learn of Him and become more like Him in the bitter. Without exception, each one of this countless number comprising the sea of glass has tasted victory in the second way. They have overcome every conceivable trial and temptation thrown at them by Satan, and in so doing have come off victorious over him.

It is beyond our comprehension to understand what these tribulation saints have been through, but through it all the Love of Christ has sustained and kept them and now they are in the presence of the Lord God Almighty. At this point in time all their suffering is behind them, but for many days they had to live in the reality of Christ's presence and victory because their own reality seemed too hard to bear. Their ability to do so has been in the understanding and acceptance of this truth: "Who shall separate us from the love of Christ? Shall tribulation, or distress, or persecution, famine, or nakedness, or peril, or sword? As it is written, For thy sake we are killed all the day long; we are accounted as sheep for the slaughter. Nay, in all these things we are more than conquerors through him that loved us. For I am persuaded, that neither death, nor life, nor angels, nor principalities, nor powers, nor things present, nor things to come, Nor height, nor depth, nor any other creature, shall be able to separate us from the love of God, which is in Christ Jesus our Lord" (Romans 8:35-39).

I tell you when these saints get to heaven they will be able to teach year-long seminars on that verse; they have had to live it every day.

THE SONGS OF MOSES AND THE LAMB ARE SUNG

And now these overcomers hold harps of God and sing the Song of Moses and the Song of the Lamb in total understanding of what spiritual victory costs and what it means. Long ago Isaiah prophesied in Isaiah 30:30-33 that the power that would bring down Antichrist (called by him "The Assyrian") would be accompanied by the music of the tambourine and the harp (or lyre). Here we see that prophecy fulfilled.

It is significant that one of the two songs lifted in praise to God by these Tribulation saints is the Song of Moses. The Song of Moses was first sung at the Red Sea crossing when Moses led the children of Israel out of Egypt. It is recorded in Exodus 15. The nation of Israel sang this song one more time when Moses was preparing for his death and thus giving his final instructions to the nation. [See Deuteronomy 32.] The song rejoices over the defeat of Israel's enemies, and of her deliverance. It speaks of the justice of God, of the care of His children, and, interestingly, of His anger against devil worshipers who are ultimately destroyed by God. Each one of these praises is integral to the situation that the tribulation saints have lived through under the reign of Antichrist. Note the following verses in light of the experience of the tribulation saints: "Thy right hand, O Lord, is become glorious in power: thy right hand, O Lord hath dashed in pieces the enemy. And in the greatness of thine excellency thou hast overthrown them that rose up against thee: thou sentest forth thy wrath, which consumed them as stubble... The enemy said, I will pursue, I will overtake, I will divide the spoil; my lust shall be satisfied upon them; I will draw my sword, my hand shall destroy them. Thou didst blow with thy wind, the sea covered them: they sank as lead in the mighty waters. Who is like unto thee, O Lord, among the gods? Who is like thee, glorious in holiness, fearful in praises, doing wonders? ... Thou in thy mercy hast led forth the people which thou hast redeemed: thou hast guided them in thy strength unto thy holy habitation. The people shall hear, and be afraid: ... Fear and dread shall fall upon them; by the greatness of thine arm they shall be as still as a stone; till thy people pass over, O Lord, till the people pass over, which thou hast purchased. Thou shalt bring them in, and plant them in the mountain of thine inheritance, in the place, O Lord, which thou hast made for thee to dwell in, in the Sanctuary, O Lord, which thy hands have established. The Lord shall reign for ever and ever" (Exodus 15:6-7, 9-11, 13-14, 16-18).

There is also prophecy in the Song of Moses concerning the rule and reign of Jesus from Jerusalem at His second coming. "Thou wilt bring them and plant them in the mountain of Thine inheritance, The place, O Lord, which Thou hast made for Thy dwelling, The sanctuary, O Lord, which Thy hands have established. The Lord shall reign forever and ever" (Exodus 15:17-18, NASB). With what joy will that be sung by the saints, in anticipation of His near return and reign on the earth!

THE SONG OF MOSES PROCLAIMS VICTORY BOTH PAST AND FUTURE

When this song was first sung, it was sung in victory: The Israelites had just witnessed their great deliverance from Pharaoh. When it is sung by the tribulation saints it will be sung in faith because their vindication has not yet happened; it is still future. But so great is their confidence in their Lord God that they sing of this victory, as did the Israelites in the past tense. God calls each of us to live in that same confidence. Begin to thank Him, praise Him, and trust Him even before we see His answers come. Learn to walk by faith and not by sight, trusting completely in Him. Sing, as do these saints, the song of praise ahead of time.

The other song that is sung is the Song of the Lamb. It is a glorious song. "Great and marvelous are thy works, Lord God Almighty; just and true are thy ways, thou King of saints. Who shall not fear thee, O Lord, and glorify thy name? For thou only are holy: for all nations shall come and worship before thee; for thy judgments are made manifest" (Revelation 15:3-4).

The title "Lord God Almighty" as used here, appears five times in the Psalms, and nowhere else in the Bible. What an awesome title it is, and it is understandably the one that springs to the collective mind as the tribulation saints stand before the Throne of God. "Thou King of the Saints," they add and, in a praise incomprehensible to the unsaved, they sing "Just and true are thy ways." There is not a trace of bitterness in them for giving up their lives under Antichrist's reign of terror. They have been able to comprehend that which few are able to grasp while yet living on earth: That God's ways, even when they demand sacrifice and pain, are perfect, good, holy, and righteous. Not one of them asks, "Why in the world did you make me go through what I did?" Instead, they come into the presence of God with praises on their lips for being counted as worthy to suffer for His name. This is a company of people who have been through an almost unimaginable nightmare for the sake of the name of Jesus, and yet what do they say to Him when they first see Him? "Just and true are thy ways."

GOD'S PERSPECTIVE

Sometimes in our lives when we are confronted with our trials and worries, it is easy to get a little frustrated with God. That is because, after all, He is God and He could fix the things that are driving us crazy if He just would. Many times, it is at this point that Satan takes this thought and begins to go to work on it, telling us, "You know, if God really were a good god he would fix it. He would end all suffering, he would make things perfect." We forget that God *did* make things perfect; it was Satan and it was man's free will in choosing sin that brought to an end the perfect world. But instead of remembering that, we reason that things are not going well for us for either one of two reasons: 1) God is not able to fix it, or, 2) God is not willing to fix it. Now, at some point we will be able to break free of those lies of God's inability and His unconcern and be able to see our lives from the perspective of God. The hope is that we will accept it now, while we are still on earth, but even if we never see it here, there will be a time coming in heaven when we, with all our hearts, will say, "Just and true are thy ways, O Lord. There is not one thing that happened to me that was not just and true by Your standards." We will understand and rejoice in the fact that God was more interested in our holiness than in our happiness, because our holiness is eternal, our earthly happiness is not. C. S. Lewis once wrote: "If you think of this world as a place intended simply for our happiness, you find it quite intolerable; think of it as a place of training and correction and it's not so bad."[28] God is using this small amount of time that we have on this earth to prepare us to reign in His kingdom. Most of us do not naturally learn those lessons, nor do we alter our character without the impetus of adversity. We have one window of time - our life - to learn His lessons and to be molded into His likeness, and so He brings things into our lives that allow us to grow up. And the people we are after we've been through our lessons with Him ought not to faintly resemble the people we were before.

HOW DO WE RESPOND TO TRIALS?

Nonetheless, we retain our choice to rebel against those trials. We can respond with bitterness or we can respond with trust in His just and true ways. After all, the same sun that melts butter also bakes clay. Either we become softened or we become hardened. These saints in Revelation 15 have been tortured and slaughtered by Antichrist. But they have also come off victorious from the beast. They lost their lives, but they won their battle.

I have a friend who had spent a long time building up a printing shop when he decided that he wanted to get out of the printing business and do something else. He sold his business to another Christian man in his congregation. The money from the sale of his business represented the fruits of years of labor and it was all he had financially. The problem came about when the man who bought it never paid my friend a red cent. Oh, the buyer took over the business, he took over all of the equipment, took over the customers, he just never paid his bill. Many people counseled my friend to sue the man. After all, he had stolen years of my friend's life and all of his money. But my friend responded, "No, he's my brother. God clearly tells us not to take our brother to court. I am not going to sue him and this man can keep my business. God will have to work on him, but I am going to do what God is calling me to do." My friend never got his money. He and his family went through terrible financial times for many years. Now Satan says, "We sure got ol' Max. We took his job, we took his money, we took years out of his life. We put gray hairs on his head, we beat that man up. Boy, we got him!" But heaven says "Max came off victorious from the beast. He came off victorious from the enemy. He did the righteous thing, and glory was given to God because that human, through the power of Jesus Christ, did, indeed, do the holy thing. The power of God is mighty." Just and true are thy ways, O Lord.

Also found in the song of the Lamb is the certainty that the unbelievers will be gone when God prevails, for "all nations shall come and worship before thee". This is a fulfillment of Zechariah's prophecy when he wrote in Zechariah 14:16-17: "And it shall come to pass, that every one that is left of all the nations which came against Jerusalem shall even go up from year to year to worship the King, the Lord of hosts, and to keep the feast of tabernacles. And it shall be, that whoso will not come up of all the families of the earth unto Jerusalem to worship the King, the Lord of hosts, even upon them shall be no rain."

JOHN'S VISION OF THE HEAVENLY TEMPLE

As the song ends, the Holy of Holies, the Temple of the Tabernacle of the Testimony as it is called here, is opened in heaven. This is the original Holy of Holies, a pattern of which was given to the Israelites to incorporate in the earthly Tabernacle. "And let them make me a sanctuary; that I may dwell among them. According to all that I shew thee, after the pattern of the tabernacle, and the pattern of all the instruments thereof, even so shall ye make it" (Exodus 25:8-9). The writer of Hebrews said the same thing when he said in 8:5 that the Tabernacle was a shadow of heavenly things, made according to the pattern to Moses on the Mount of Sinai.

The Holy of Holies was the dwelling place of God on earth. It was separated from the rest of the Tabernacle by an enormously heavy full-length curtain. The High Priest, and only the High Priest, was allowed to enter it once a year in order to make supplication for the forgiveness of the nation's sins. In other words, God was removed from the people, and could only be approached through the mediation of the High Priest, and even that access was extremely limited. When Jesus was crucified, the Temple Veil that separated the Holy of Holies from the rest of the Temple was torn in two, without human hand, *from top to bottom* signifying that the barrier between God and man had been destroyed by Jesus' death. Soon after this happened, the Temple was destroyed by Roman forces.

Now, we see through John's eyes, the original Holy of Holies which is in heaven. The Temple is open; God is again dealing with Israel.

GOD DEALS WITH ISRAEL'S REBELLION WITH JUDGMENT FROM HIS TEMPLE

Historically, judgment against the sins of the people came out of the Temple. Because that was where the judgment originated, it was also where the atonement was made for the sins of the people. The Temple was also where the people were called to come to worship because it was the dwelling place of

God. The Mercy Seat, the covering of the Ark, was representational of Jesus. When Israel rejected the Messiah, she rejected the Mercy Seat and, in reality, everything else symbolized by the Temple, and in that state of rebellion she has since existed.

But now we are entering Daniel's seventieth week, the final period of time in which God will deal with Israel and the Temple and all that it signifies is again in play. Now, with the Mercy scorned, Judgment must come forth out of the Temple onto Israel. "Thus saith the Lord God; Behold, I will take the children of Israel from among the heathen, whither they be gone, and will gather them on every side, and bring them into their own land: And I will make them one nation in the land upon the mountains of Israel; and one king shall be king to them all: and they shall be no more two nations, neither shall they be divided into two kingdoms any more at all: Neither shall they defile themselves any more with their idols, nor with their detestable things, nor with any of their transgressions: but I will save them out of all their dwelling places, wherein they have sinned, and will cleanse them: so shall they be my people, and I will be their God. And David my servant, shall be king over them; and they all shall have one shepherd: they shall also walk in my judgments, and observe my statutes, and do them. And they shall dwell in the land that I have given unto Jacob my servant, wherein your fathers have dwelt; and they shall dwell therein, even they, and their children, and their children's children for ever: and my servant David shall be their prince for ever. Moreover I will make a covenant of peace with them; it shall be an everlasting covenant with them: and I will place them, and multiply them, and will set my sanctuary in the midst of them for evermore. My tabernacle also shall be with them: yea, I will be their God, and they shall be my people. And the heathen shall know that I the Lord do sanctify Israel, when my sanctuary shall be in the midst of them forevermore" (Ezekiel 37:21-28).

SEVEN ANGELS WITH SEVEN VIALS DISTRIBUTE GOD'S WRATH ON EARTH

Seven angels come out of the Temple, each wearing the clothing of saints and thus indicating the possibility that they are, indeed, saints who have, to John, the appearance of angels. It is certainly possible that the saints have been handed the golden vials of judgment over the earth, given the fact that judgment of the world has already been given into the hands of the saints (1Corinthians 6:2-3). Regardless of who the seven are, they are given the authority to distribute the wrath of God over the face of the earth by virtue of the fact that they have been handed the seven golden vials, or as we would refer to them today, bowls.

These seven vials or bowls are the same repositories of God's wrath as are the seven golden trumpets that John saw under the seventh seal in Revelation 8 and 9. When John recorded those earlier chapters, he was in heaven and he saw things at their point of origin. Now he is upon the earth, looking up into heaven, and is seeing things from the perspective of a recipient, not the originator. Thus, what he saw as a golden trumpet when he was in heaven now appears to be an overturned golden bowl from earth's perspective. (The bowls are all seen as overturned in chapter 16.) They are overturned because out of them the last seven plagues will rain down upon the earth. The point is this: The bowls and the trumpets are one and the same. The overturned bowl is simply the bottom of the trumpet that is all that could be seen of the trumpet from the perspective of earth. If you doubt this, lift a trumpet over your head and stare into its bell, ignoring everything else above that bell. It appears to be, especially at a distance, an overturned bowl. Thus, John's description of the golden bowls found in Revelation 15 and 16 is an accurate description of what he was able to see from the standpoint of earth, and is in no way in opposition to his description of the trumpets described in Revelation 8 and 9.

GOD'S WRATH IS FOR CLEANSING THE EARTH AND FOR JUDGMENT UPON THE BEAST

It is important to remember that the wrath which will be seen upon the earth as a consequence of these golden vials/trumpets comes directly from the hand of God and is completely under His control. Many commentators have ignored this crucial fact and have written and taught that the wrath under the seventh seal is a consequence of nuclear wars waged by warring men. They fail to understand the reason for the wrath of God at this point. It is not simply retribution against the Beast and his followers; no. Jesus is going forth to take back the inherited possession, the earth, for the people of God. And when He takes it back, it is going to be a cleansed earth; cleansed of every trace of sin, of every pollutant, of every impurity; cleansed of even the scars of the sin and pollution which have etched themselves upon the earth. And just as He cleansed the world with water at the Flood, this time He will cleanse the world with fire. How in the world could He trust this amazingly accurate cleansing to man?! Man was the source of all of the pollution and impurity in the first place, and never in the history of the world has he been able to eradicate it. And now, the willy-nilly launch of nuclear weapons will somehow do the job? No, they would only add more pollution to the world; they would only intensify the curse already upon the earth. It will take God, and God alone, to oversee the first total cleansing of the earth since The Flood. The vials are under the control of God, to Planet Earth's everlasting protection.

GOD'S WRATH IS HOLY, BLAMELESS AND PURE

With the understanding of the intent and purpose of the coming wrath of God upon the earth, we see that the holiness and goodness of God is in no way compromised by dispensing this wrath. The final verse of Revelation 15 bears this out as the entire Temple is filled with the overwhelming glory of God as He issues the bowls of wrath to the seven angels. This is the Shekinah Glory of God: the visible manifestation of the divine presence. The smoke that now fills the temple is the same manifestation of God's presence as was the Pillar of Cloud by day and the Pillar of Fire by night which led and sustained the Israelites during the Wilderness wanderings. So intense and extreme is the presence of God in the Temple that no man is able to enter the Temple for any reason until the cessation of the coming seven plagues that will be poured out of the seven bowls of wrath. The overwhelming glory of the Lord that resides in the Temple while the Wrath is being played out on earth, allows no thought of injustice to be attached to that wrath. Not only is the wrath necessary to cleanse and repay evil, the wrath is, as is its Originator, holy, blameless, and pure.

CHAPTER 19
SEVEN BOWLS OF WRATH
Revelation 16

Revelation 16 begins the chronicle of the Wrath period of the Tribulation. It is comprised of the time that begins at the opening of the seventh and final seal on the scroll of the title deed to the earth (the book found in the hand of God in Revelation 5), and lasts until the Battle of Armageddon is fought. No mercy toward the inhabitants of earth (except for those Jews who belong to the Lamb) will be manifested during this time. Mercy has already been offered by God to earth, but it has been scorned and spurned by those who will now feel His wrath. Because no mercy will be found, this time of Wrath will not commence until the tribulation saints are safely in heaven and the 144,000 Jews are sealed with the seal of God. When the seventh seal is opened, seven bowls (or vials, as the *King James Version* calls bowls) of wrath will be found waiting under it. They correspond exactly to the seven trumpets that were seen in Revelation 8 and 9.

FIRST VIAL: GOD'S WRATH BEGINS

The first trumpet affected the earth; so does the first bowl. When John was experiencing this period of time from heaven's perspective, he recorded that the sounding of the first trumpet sent hail and fire mingled with blood down upon the earth. Now, from earth's perspective - the pouring out of the first bowl - he records what results from that fiery, bloody hail: Grievous and horrible sores appear on the bodies of the worshipers of the Beast. A "noisome" sore is a weeping, draining, pus-filled sore. It is very possible that these are similar to the radiation sores that inflicted the bodies of the victims of the bombs that fell on Hiroshima and Nagasaki. It is possible that they are even worse than that.

SECOND VIAL: ADDITIONAL INFORMATION OF THE SEA OF BLOOD

Again, we see exactly the same scenario as happened under the second trumpet. The second vial affects the sea; so does the second bowl. Under the second trumpet we were told that one-third of the seas were turned to blood, one-third of the sea creatures died, and one-third of the ships were destroyed. John here reports that every living creature found in the affected seas will die. In other words, the description of the wrath under the second trumpet had the entire body of sea creatures and ships on the earth in view when it states that one-third die. Here, under the second bowl, John sees only the affected seas when he tells us that all in them perish. We have two bits of information: one-third of the seas are affected and, within them, all die.

It is easy to understand how the creatures in the sea would die in oceans turned to blood, but what about those on ships and boats perched on top of the "water"? Apparently, the properties of water that allow ships to float will be missing from the blood that now fills the seas, and all of the ships will sink. Those on the ships who have sought refuge in the sea from the fiery hail thinking that they have outsmarted God, will find that there is no hiding from His justice.

The resulting death will be even worse than from the hail. Generally when one drowns, one swallows water and, as a consequence, the lungs fill with water and cannot take in air. Here the people will be forced to swallow not water but blood that will fill their lungs and drown them. Worse than simply drinking in and drowning in blood, will be the fact that it will not even be living, oxygenated blood. No, it will be like the blood found in a decaying corpse. My sister is a mortician, and she has told me that many times she can actually identify the disease that afflicted a person by the smell of his blood as she embalms him. Sometimes the stench of the blood is too much for her to take. This will be the type of blood by which these people will drown. The terror and disgust that these worshipers of the Beast will feel as they die is hard to imagine.

THIRD VIAL: FRESH WATER ALSO TURNED TO BLOOD

The third trumpet affected rivers; so, too, does the third bowl. We have already seen the earth pummeled with bloody, fiery hail under the first bowl. The seas are turned to blood under the second bowl, and now, under the third bowl, the very sources of fresh water on the earth are contaminated with the same curse of blood; this is just as happened under the third trumpet. This is not capricious judgment on the part of God. A point is being made by these plagues of blood, and that point is recognized and praised by the angel in charge of the waters. This is fitting judgment for those who have shed the blood of the saints. Now, as a consequence of their bloody deeds, these evil people will find themselves literally drowning in blood. This pronouncement by the angel also seems to suggest that judgment will fall most heavily on those who are guilty of hunting down and putting to death the saints of God. However, all on earth (except for the Jewish believers) have rejected the Living Water that Jesus offers and now they will be forced to drink from the well of their own actions; a filthy, putrid, cursed, and bloody well. Although drinking blood is an abomination to God, these people are so defiled that He, Himself, gives the blood to them to drink. A greater indictment from God is hard to imagine; it speaks to their complete depravity and cruelty.

HEAVEN'S HOSTS CONCUR WITH GOD'S JUDGMENTS UPON THE EARTH

Within this passage is a small glimpse into the heavenly hierarchy. We are told that there is an angel specifically in charge of earth's waters. This fact lends itself to the speculation that there might be angels in charge of each facet of man's existence. We know from Daniel that there are holy and demonic angels who have been assigned to nations and who come into conflict with one another. It will be interesting to find to what extent we, while on earth, had our senses dulled to the mighty spiritual forces that were surrounding us in every avenue of our lives.

It is also interesting to note that within these territorial assignments as exemplified by the angel over the waters, there is not a trace of indignation over what God chose to do over his, the angel's, domain of the waters. Heaven understands that all of creation, including each life and each soul, is God's to do with as He wills. The angel realizes full well that the waters of earth have been polluted by man's sin just as has everything else on the face of the earth and, because of that spoiling and sin, they, too, must pass under the judgment and purification of God. Oh, that man would ever grasp that fact and submit to that sovereignty! The Angel of the Waters has spent millennia watching man spoil and ruin his beautiful waters. He has watched while his rivers actually caught fire because of the pollution within them. Now, God turns them to blood. Does the angel say, "I thought they were bad before, but now look at them"? No, he rejoices and gives praise to God because he understands what is necessary to clean up the waters. Sometimes things have to get worse before they can get better.

There is a correlation to this in our lives. If we have an area that we keep from God, a "besetting sin" so to speak, the fact is that, if you are God's child, He will not let it remain. He will begin to work on you to give it up to Him. The hope in the situation is that one can begin to give it up immediately and let God free him. But if one doesn't, just like the rivers we see here, things are going to get worse in order to allow them to get better. God usually provides some grace by cushioning us from the results of our sins, but if we do not repent and turn from them, that cushion will be removed and the full force of our sins will hit our lives. Whatever the sin --- anger, lying, pornography, drunkenness, drug use, gambling, overspending, etc. --- we can either get free or we can see our personal water "turned to blood" as God strives to cleanse and purify our lives.

FOURTH VIAL: PURIFICATION OF THE EARTH BY FIRE

The fourth trumpet affected the sun; so, too, does the fourth bowl. It is under this vial that the earth is literally purified with fire. This is the time of which Peter prophesied when he wrote in 2 Peter 3:10, "But the day of the Lord will come as a thief in the night; in the which the heavens shall pass away with a great noise, and the elements shall melt with fervent heat, the earth also and the works that are therein shall be burned up."

Although many of the plagues contain the element of fire, this one is the most intense and extreme. The resulting heat will make it seem as if the sun has exploded. But just as the earth was still standing after the flood, so will it be after this plague. The rainbow is still around the Throne. Isaiah 24:5-6 bears this out when, speaking of this time, it records, "The earth also is defiled under the inhabitants thereof, because they have transgressed the laws, changed the ordinance, broken the everlasting covenant. Therefore hath the curse devoured the earth, and they that dwell therein are desolate: therefore the inhabitants of the earth *are burned, and few men left*" (emphasis mine). Granted, not many men are left, but some are! The earth is not annihilated.

In Revelation 15 we saw the worship service of the tribulation saints and we were told that in it they sang the Song of Moses. The Song of Moses prophesied the very event now happening. "For a fire is kindled in mine anger, and shall burn unto the lowest hell, and shall consume the earth with her increase, and set on fire the foundations of the mountains. I will heap mischiefs upon them; I will spend mine arrows upon them. They shall be burnt with hunger, and devoured with burning heat, and with bitter destruction: I will also send the teeth of beasts upon them, with the poison of serpents of the dust. The sword without, and terror within, shall destroy both the young man and the virgin, the suckling also with the man of gray hairs" (Deuteronomy 32:22-25).

Malachi 4:1 also prophesies of this day: "For, behold, the day cometh, that shall burn as an oven; and all the proud, yea, and all that do wickedly, shall be stubble: and the day that cometh shall burn them up, saith the Lord of hosts, that it shall leave them neither root nor branch."

REPROBATE HEARTS DO NOT REPENT EVEN THOUGH IN FIERY TORMENT

When Revelation speaks of this time under the fourth trumpet we are told that it is dark one-third of the day. The information now given under the fourth bowl/vial seems to suggest that there is intense heat for two-thirds of the day and then the sun completely disappears, plunging the world into a eight-hour period of intense cold. So, for sixteen hours the people must cope with a world on fire as they long for the darkness, and then as soon as it comes, they are enveloped in frigid cold and they long again for the merciless heat. It is possible that the alternate cycles of extreme heat and then extreme cold are part of the purifying and cleansing process for the earth. Some have theorized that it may be at this time that the ozone layer is removed; that layer being a primary shield for the earth against the strength of sun upon the earth. Whatever the reason, the torment is unspeakable.

This very torture was used in some Communist concentration camps, and the survivors spoke of the complete breakdown of the human body when forced to endure such extremes over and over. But Antichrist's people now go through this torment without one thought of repentance. They have experienced famine, thirst, fires, sores, heat, cold, lawlessness, wild beasts and they will soon encounter the demonic world in all its rage; all without once considering submitting to the Lord of the Universe who is controlling this. Some have taught that the purpose of hell is to reform people and that when they spend time there, they will repent and thus there will be no need for an everlasting hell. This passage teaches us the exact opposite lesson. It teaches us that some hearts are totally reprobate. The hearts found here certainly are, because we see them respond, not in repentance and reform, but in blasphemy and the cursing of God repeatedly. It can be safely assumed that all people who find themselves in the Lowest Hell (as Deuteronomy 32:22 divides hell), find themselves there because of the same rebellious, blasphemous spirit that controls these people. This is one reason why I believe that the Bible teaches that there are different degrees of punishment. Jesus himself taught this in Luke 12:47-48, Matthew 5:22, 16:27, 23:14, and Paul refers to this fact in Romans 2:6. The fact is inescapable that those merely ignorant of God's will would not respond as these do. When we see these people who have the very heart of Satan, we are given to clearly understand that as long as sin lasts, hell must last, for sin shows no sign of abating in these hearts even during the severe punishment of the vials. It must be assumed that these hearts would remain eternally evil no matter how many chances to reform and repent they are given.

FIFTH VIAL: DARKNESS, TERRIBLE PAIN, BUT NO DEATH

Simple darkness does not cause pain, but these people gnaw at their tongues because of the pain. This does not make sense unless one couples the fifth trumpet with the fifth vial. Under the fifth trumpet, the sun is completely darkened because the bottomless pit has been opened, letting loose the demonic locusts upon the earth.   The darkness is not the plague, in and of itself, the darkness is a result of the plague of demonic locusts. These locusts inflict damage both with their mouths and with their tails on human bodies already in agony from the oozing sores, and there is no escaping from them. This is also the time period in which no one on earth is able to die for five months, although many attempts are made to do so. This is truly the "night of the living dead."

This darkness was prophesied in Isaiah as happening right before the world acknowledges the Lordship and Kingdom of Jesus. The world will do exactly that when Jesus comes in battle to Armageddon and in triumph to the Mount of Olives. "Arise, shine, for thy light is come, and the glory of the Lord is risen upon thee.   For, behold, the darkness shall cover the earth, and gross darkness the people: but the Lord shall arise upon thee, and his glory shall be seen upon thee.   And the Gentiles shall come to thy light, and kings to the brightness of thy rising" (Isaiah 60:1-3).

"Who can stand before his indignation? And who can abide in the fierceness of his anger? His fury is poured out like fire, and the rocks are thrown down by him. The Lord is good, a strong hold in the day of trouble; and he knoweth them that trust in him.   But with an overrunning flood he will make an utter end of the place thereof, and darkness shall pursue his enemies" (Nahum 1:6-8).

We are told that the full force of this plague is aimed at Antichrist, although its effect is felt throughout earth. We also know that some of the people who were alive at the time of the First Vial are still alive at this point, because they are still blaspheming God on account of the gruesome sores caused by the First Vial.

SIXTH VIAL: DEMONIC SPIRITS UNLEASHED

Just as under the sixth trumpet, the malevolently powerful demonic spirits, which have been bound at the Euphrates River, are now unleashed and they will kill one-third of the people who somehow have managed to survive so far. As the four mighty angels are released, the Euphrates River dries up, allowing the kings of the east to strategically move against Israel as they prepare for the final war - Armageddon.

Independently of Antichrist they will move their forces into Palestine. Apparently, his reasons to conquer Israel are not their reasons to come against Israel, but yet the kings choose to do so. It may be that the plagues have so decimated the earth that Israel, The Beautiful Land, is the only place with enough food for the people left in the world.

The names of these nations symbolized by the three kings are not given because these nations did not exist in John's day. But we have some clues to their identity, which will soon be discussed, because this invasion is also foretold in Ezekiel 38 and 39 where Ezekiel mentions the same four groups that move against Israel. Both passages concern themselves with the same battle: Armageddon. The three nations that John calls the "Kings of the east", are called by Ezekiel, Sheba, Dedan, and the merchants of Tarshish. Besides this independent group of nations, there will be three other groups who will surround Palestine, but they will all be under the control of Antichrist.

THE INVADING ARMY: SATAN'S FORCES, NOT RUSSIA'S

Before looking at these four groups in more detail, it is necessary to set the stage of Ezekiel 38 and 39. Most eschatologists teach that this passage concerns itself with the invasion of Israel by Russia. This teaching seemed to become very prevalent after World War II when, coincidentally or not, Russia was seen by the United States as the primary threat to world peace. These eschatologists identify Russia as being Gog, the one identified by Ezekiel who comes against Israel. They buttress their argument with the fact that Russia is the only major world power located to the north of Israel, and so qualifies as coming out of the north parts, as Ezekiel 38:15 mentions. But God, Himself identifying Gog, asks the following in Ezekiel 38:17: "Art thou he of whom I have spoken in old time by my servants the prophet of Israel which prophesied in those days many years that I would bring thee against them?" Has God spoken of Russia in other places through His other prophets? No, absolutely not. But He has consistently spoken of two who would come against Israel, the apple of His eye, and those two are Satan and his man, Antichrist.

But what of the fact that the one to do so dwells to the north of Israel? Ignoring the fact that other nations lie to the north of Israel, Turkey and Syria being but two, notice what Isaiah 14:12-14 says about the dwelling place of Satan: "How art thou fallen from heaven, O Lucifer, son of the morning! How art thou cut down to the ground, which didst weaken the nations! For thou hast said in thine heart, I will ascend into heaven, I will exalt my throne above the stars of God: I will sit also upon the mount of the congregation, *in the sides of the north*: I will ascend above the heights of the clouds; I will be like the most High" (emphasis mine).

Satan, too, finds his dwelling in the very extreme (the sides) of the north. Furthermore, the Bible will name a king or a country "from the north," "from the south," etc. if the *attack* comes from that direction onto Israel, regardless of where the nation is located. The King of Babylon was called a king of kings from the North in Ezekiel 26:7 for this exact reason, even though Babylon is located to the east of Israel. Jeremiah 10:22 also prophesied that a great commotion would come *out of the north country* when speaking of the attack on Israel by Babylon. In other words, the country does not necessarily have to be located to the north of Israel in order to come out of the north, the warning and prophecy are simply to inform them that the attack is going to come from that direction. Ezekiel 39:2 gives that exact information when God, speaking to Gog says, "And I will turn thee back, and leave but the sixth part of thee, and will cause thee *to come up from the north parts*, and will bring thee upon the mountains of Israel" (emphasis mine). When Jeremiah talks about this time, he says the same thing, "Set up the standard toward Zion: retire, stay not: for I will bring evil *from the north* and a great destruction" (Jeremiah 4:6, emphasis mine).

WHO IS GOG?

Those that teach that Russia is Gog, point to the fact that Gog is called the prince of Rosh, Meshech and Tubal. Rosh, they say, is Russia, Meshech is Moscow, and Tubal is Tobolsk, a tiny town in Russia settled by gypsies under a royal land grant. Rosh is not Russia; *rosh* is the Hebrew word for "chief" or "first." One has only to consider the name of the Jewish New

Year, Rosh Hashanah (the first day of the year), or Rosh Hodesh (the first day of each month), to understand the meaning of *rosh*. So when Gog is called the prince of Rosh, he is literally being called the "chief prince." There is absolutely no etymological link between Rosh and Russia, between Meshech and Moscow, nor between Tubal and Tobolsk; there is only strained and wishful thinking on the part of those who would jam square pegs into round holes. One thing one does not do when interpreting prophecy in the Bible is to read it, pick out one Hebrew word and then find an English word that sounds a little bit like it. And unless the tiny, completely insignificant village of Tobolsk takes on giant importance at the end of time, importance not remarked upon by any of the prophets, it makes no sense at all for God to so emphatically declare Himself in opposition to it.

Furthermore, and most importantly, the Bible itself identifies both Meshech and Tubal, not as towns in Russia, but as being the grandson of Noah (Genesis 10 and 1 Chronicles 1:5). The Bible, along with historians, tells us where Meshech and Tubal settled. Meshech went north and settled between the Black and Caspian seas; an area which once was an independent country. History also tells us that Russia was settled from the *west* not from the south, as it would have had to have been had Meshech been the one to settle it. Tubal, along with another grandson of Noah, Gomer (also mentioned in Ezekiel 38), settled Turkey.

We only have to look at an atlas, then, to know the identities of the group of nations who are called Meshech and Tubal. They are Turkey and the nations around the Black and Caspian Seas below the Caucasus Mountains. Today, the nations of Georgia, Azerbaijan, and Armenia occupy that Territory. Those nations were indeed part of the USSR at one point, but the USSR is not synonymous with Russia. Furthermore, God, when addressing Gog in Ezekiel 38:17, says that many prophecies concerning Gog have been given, and been given by different prophets. Even those proponents of Russia as Gog, have no other prophecies that they can point to as referring to Russia. This fact in and of itself rules out the nation of Russia as being the meaning of Gog. Furthermore, Gog is not a nation, Gog is the leader of a nation and that nation is called Magog. Ezekiel 39:11 clearly states that Gog will be buried in Israel. A burial implies a death, and the Hebrew word here used for "buried" is a word that applies to a literal interment in the ground of a human being. It would be impossible to bury Russia or any other nation in that way.

Who, then, is Gog? Gog is the title of a human who will be completely led and possessed by Satan. In the last days, the only man spoken of in that way is Antichrist. And, whereas the prophets did not speak many times of Russia, they spoke over and over and over of a man who would rise up at the end of time who would wage war on both Israel and the saints; a man completely controlled and empowered by Satan; a man variously identified as the Antichrist, the Beast, the Chaldean, the Assyrian, the Raiser of Taxes, the Vile One, - Gog.

In fact, the man Gog is just the tool; the true enemy of Israel is the force behind the man. Amos 7:1, in the Septuagint Version of the Old Testament, says the following: "Thus has the Lord God shewed me; and, behold, a swarm of locust coming from the east; and, behold, one caterpillar, king Gog." We have seen in Revelation 9 how John has linked locusts with evil spirits. Here, Amos tells us the name of their king: Gog. It would be ridiculous to assert that Russia is the king over these evil spirits; it would not be ridiculous to assert that Satan is.

Another point to consider is that Gog is mentioned in Revelation 20, at least a thousand years after the Battle of Armageddon, when Gog again battles Jesus. Could this foe which dares come against Jesus Himself at the end of His thousand-year reign truly be Russia? I do not believe so. But we *are* told who shows up to battle Jesus at the end of the thousand years. And that one is Satan. Apparently, Satan will use another man to wage war on the people of God, just as he once used Antichrist, and that man, too, is identified as Gog. There has only been one constant enemy of both God and Israel, and that enemy is Satan. The human chosen by Satan to implement his plan is Gog, and the country of that man is Magog.

THE FOUR GROUPS OF NATIONS THAT COME UP AGAINST ISRAEL

Ezekiel 38 and Revelation 16 both name four groups of nations that come against Israel at the end. In Revelation, the kings of the east are one group. The three spirits out of the mouth of the dragon will be responsible for gathering together the remaining three groups. In Ezekiel, the prophet does not know what the names of some of the countries will be when Armageddon happens, but he recognizes the areas and so he identifies those countries by the names of their first settlers so that there could be no mistake as to which countries were involved. The first group of nations, already discussed, is comprised of the area settled by Meshech and Tubal; countries north of Palestine and most likely situated around the Black and Caspian Seas.

The second group mentioned consists of an alliance of Persia (Iran), Ethiopia, and Libya. Somehow, indeed, miraculously, Ezekiel knew that these particular nations would last for thousands of years and would still be in existence when the time of Armageddon came, and thus he could name them with impunity.

The third group of nations mentioned by Ezekiel is comprised of the lands settled by Gomer and Togarmah. We have already noted that Gomer settled Turkey along with Tubal. Gomer then moved across the Dardanelles into Northern Europe. Descendants of white Europeans are most probably descended from Gomer. His son was Togarmah who settled Southern Europe; the Latin countries in Europe. Thus, the third group of nations is comprised of European nations. All three of these groups are under the control of Antichrist and comprise the exact territory covered by the four visions of Daniel, symbolized by the lion, bear, leopard, and dreadful beast! Ezekiel adds that along with these three groups will be "many people with thee." Those people will be the scattered satellite nations of countries found in the three groups.

The fourth group mentioned by Ezekiel and referred to earlier, is an independent one. Ezekiel identifies those countries as Sheba, Dedan, and Tarshish and the "young lions thereof." Sheba and Dedan were grandsons of Abraham and his second wife, Keturah (Genesis 25:1 3). Sheba was a country of southwestern Arabia. Dedan's province is probably the Persian Gulf countries. Tarshish is Gibraltar. Gibraltar was the farthest known port in John's time, and it was the place to which Jonah fled to escape God. Here it represents a distant, unknown land; the far-flung corners of the world. Tarshish was used here in the same way we now use the phrase, "deepest, darkest Africa." It is possible that Ezekiel is referring to a merchant country in the Atlantic Ocean. The "young lions thereof" would be offshoot countries. Gibraltar is a British possession (although that has been a bone of contention with Spain) and so it is quite possible that England is the country in view here. The USA, Australia, and Canada could very well be the young lions. If so, this is the only reference to the USA in biblical prophecy.

Another amazing thing about Ezekiel's prophecy is that not only did he know what countries to name, he knew what countries to leave out. Two important end-time countries are omitted here: Babylon (in prophecy, the entire country of Iraq) and Egypt. Both will be destroyed by the time of the Battle of Armageddon

ARMAGEDDON: EZEKIEL AND REVELATION COMPARED

There are several other signposts that let us know that Ezekiel is talking about Armageddon in chapters 38 and 39. In Ezekiel 39:8 God says that "this is the day whereof I have spoken." The day whereof God has spoken, over and over, is the great and terrible Day of The Lord, not the hypothetical day wherein Russia invades Israel. Not only that, it is beyond argument that in that day, the Day of the Lord, Antichrist is in control of the world's political maneuvering, not Russia.

Second, Ezekiel 38:19-20 tells of an earthquake so intense that it affects the entire world to the point that all the mountains of the world will be thrown down: "Surely in that day there shall be a great shaking in the land of Israel; So that the fishes of the sea, and the fowls of the heaven, and the beasts of the field, and all creeping things that creep upon the earth, and all the men that are upon the face of the earth, shall shake at my presence, and the mountains shall be thrown down, and the steep places shall fall, and every wall shall fall to the ground."

Compare that passage to Revelation 16:18-20 which we will discuss shortly. The time is clearly Armageddon and John writes the following concerning what transpires: "And there were voices, and thunders, and lightnings; and there was a great earthquake, such as was not since men were upon the earth, so mighty an earthquake, and so great...And every island fled away, and the mountains were not found."

Can the mountains be thrown down twice? If so, when did God reform them so that they could be? That can only happen given major periods of geologic time. There is no such geologic age between what commentators say is the invasion of Russia into Israel and the Battle of Armageddon. No, the mountains are only thrown down once and both Ezekiel 38 and Revelation 16 record it, while Revelation 16 identifies it as being at the Battle of Armageddon.

Ezekiel and Revelation even give the same details concerning the cleanup from the great battle of Armageddon. Ezekiel 39 talks of the feast of the birds that God is preparing. Compare the following verses: "And, thou son of man, thus saith the Lord God; Speak unto every feathered fowl, and to every beast of the field, assemble yourselves, and come; gather yourselves on every side to my sacrifice that I do sacrifice for you, even a great sacrifice, upon the mountains of Israel, that ye may eat flesh, and drink blood. Ye shall eat the flesh of the mighty, and drink the blood of the princes of the earth, of rams, of lambs, and of goats, of bullocks, all of them fatlings of Bashan. And ye shall eat fat till ye be full, and drink blood till ye be drunken, of my sacrifice which I have sacrificed for you" (Ezekiel 39:17-19).

"And I saw an angel standing in the sun: and he cried with a loud voice, saying to all the fowls that fly in the midst of heaven, Come and gather yourselves together unto the supper of the great God; That ye may eat the flesh of kings, and the flesh of captains, and the flesh of mighty men, and the flesh of horses, and of them that sit on them, and the flesh of all men, both free and bond, both small and great. And I saw the beast, and the kings of the earth, and their armies, gathered together to make war against him that sat on the horse, and against his army" (Revelation 19:17-19).

It is clear that Revelation 19 is speaking of Armageddon as John retells the story a third time, and so it is only logical to assume that Ezekiel 39 is also speaking of Armageddon. Ezekiel 39:22 tells us that at this time God will punish Gog (Satan, or Satan's man) with pestilence, blood, and with an overflowing rain comprised of great hailstones, fire, and brimstone. These are the plagues that are under the trumpets and vials (bowls) in Revelation. Furthermore, the primitive weapons that are described in Ezekiel 39:9 are the only weapons that are left to man after God has finished with the plagues. If Ezekiel 38 and 39 were earlier in time, other weapons would have been available to Gog's forces.

Especially compelling is the fact that immediately after this war, God makes the following statement in Ezekiel 39:21-22, "And I will set my glory among the heathen, and all the heathen shall see my judgment that I have executed, and my hand that I have laid upon them. So the house of Israel shall know that I am the Lord their God from that day and forward." The glory that God sets among the heathen is Jesus Christ Himself and that happens right after Armageddon when Jesus sets His feet on the Mount of Olives, rending it in half, and then marches to the Temple in Jerusalem. This is never said to happen at a supposed Russian invasion of Israel. This is also the time that Israel accepts Jesus, turns again to God and never, ever departs again. This happens as a result of Armageddon, not as a result of a simple invasion. Hitler himself did not even make the Jews turn back to God. If an invasion was all that was needed to get Israel to accept Jesus, then why has it never happened before? The chronology is clear: The time of Ezekiel 38-39 is the time of Armageddon.

The very next chapters in Ezekiel, chapters 40 and on, concern themselves with the establishment of the new Temple wherein Jesus himself reigns. Zechariah 14 tells us that this happens right after the Battle of Armageddon: "Then shall the Lord go forth, and fight against those nations, as when he fought in the day of battle. And his feet shall stand in that day upon the mount of Olives, which is before Jerusalem on the east, and the mount of Olives shall cleave in the midst thereof toward the east and toward the west, and there shall be a very great valley: and half of the mountain shall remove toward the north and half of it toward the south...And the Lord shall be king over all the earth: in that day shall there be one Lord, and his name one...And it shall come to pass, that every one that is left of all the nations which came against Jerusalem shall even go up from year to year to worship the King, the Lord of hosts, and to keep the feast of tabernacles" (Zechariah 14, 3-4,9,16).

It is interesting to note that when Jesus touches earth again, the very ground cannot abide His glory nor His power, and the mountain splits in two!

SIXTH VIAL: THE EUPHRATES RIVED DRIED UP

The sixth trumpet concerned the river Euphrates; so, too, does the sixth bowl. This river has always been a formidable boundary, in part because it is 1800 miles long. It is also the northeastern-most limit to the lands promised to Israel by God. By drying up the Euphrates river, which allow the "kings of the East" to march upon Palestine, God is giving His permission for the time of Armageddon to begin.

Again we see that as much as Satan strives to control the times and seasons, they are ultimately up to God. But when God, under the sixth seal, lifts His restraint over Satan's forces, they immediately begin to mobilize. The three demonic spirits that come out of the mouths of the Dragon, the Antichrist, and the False Prophet summon the three groups under the control of Antichrist to march against Jerusalem. In addition to the groups under his control, Antichrist will work great miracles in order to convince the independent group of the kings of the east to send their forces into Palestine. As has been explained before, Satan will do great miracles at this time; it is part and parcel of the demonic deception that he must exert in order to convince the world to do his bidding. The miracles coupled with the drying up of the Euphrates River will convince the "kings of the east" of Antichrist's power and political acumen and they will join their forces with his to surround Jerusalem. Why the group of the kings of the east is independent of Antichrist's control at this point, and how that came about, is not addressed in Revelation. It will be very interesting to see, from the vantage point in heaven, how this situation works itself out on the earth when the time comes.

SATAN'S FORCES ASSEMBLE AGAINST ISRAEL

The terror that must fill Jewish hearts as the nations begin to assemble around them is almost unimaginable. Keep in mind that the Two Witnesses have been ministering to Israel before this time, although they have now been killed by Antichrist, and many Jews have turned back to God and many have accepted Jesus as Messiah. Interestingly, a prayer of Asaph is recorded in Psalms 83:1-5 that addresses itself exactly to this time: "Keep not thou silence, O God: hold not thy peace, and be not still, O God. For, lo, thine enemies make a tumult: and they that hate thee have lifted up the head. They have taken crafty counsel against thy people, and consulted against thy hidden ones. They have said, Come, and let us cut them off from being a nation; that the name of Israel may be no more in remembrance. For they have consulted together with one consent: they are confederate against thee:"

It is for this time that the warning in Revelation 16:15 is given, "Behold, I come as a thief. Blessed is he that watcheth, and keepeth his garments, lest he walk naked, and they see his shame." It is a reminder to hold fast, to watch expectantly for the return of Jesus and for their deliverance, and it is also an exhortation to be clothed in the Righteousness of Jesus (the alluded-to garments) instead of their own fleshly coverings of doubt and fear (their nakedness).

What we have not seen in this second rendition of the story from the vantage point of earth is something we were told in John's first telling from his vantage point in heaven. What he saw in heaven that, of course, he does not see from earth is that between the sixth and seventh trumpets/vials, Jesus takes formal possession of the earth and sea (recorded in Revelation 10). But although John does not see this now, Satan senses it, gathers his forces for battle, marches upon Palestine, and prepares to fight in the ultimate battle for total control over Planet Earth; for Jesus and His forces will meet Satan there at Armageddon. Truly, the unholy trinity of Satan has an appointment with a man called Faithful and True and this appointment between the two great forces will lead to the climax of the ages.

ARMAGEDDON

The following passages all prophesy the Day of Armageddon, and as the prophet Zephaniah proclaimed, it is truly "a day of wrath, a day of trouble and distress, a day of wasteness and desolation, a day of darkness and gloominess, a day of clouds and thick darkness." "Proclaim ye this among the Gentiles; Prepare war, wake up the mighty men, let all the men of war draw near; let them come up: Beat your plowshares into swords, and your pruning hooks into spears: let the weak say, I am strong, Assemble yourselves, and come, all ye heathen, and gather yourselves together round about: thither cause thy mighty ones to come down, O Lord. Let the heathen be wakened, and come up to the valley of Jehoshaphat [a king of Judah]: for there will I sit to judge all the heathen round about. Put ye in the sickle, for the harvest is ripe: come, get you down: for the press is full, the vats overflow; for their wickedness is great. Multitudes, multitudes in the valley of decision: for the day of the Lord is near in the valley of decision" (Joel 3:9-14).

"Now also many nations are gathered against thee, that say, Let her be defiled, and let our eye look upon Zion. But they know not the thoughts of the Lord, neither understand they his counsel: for he shall gather them as the sheaves into the floor" (Micah 4:11-12).

"Therefore wait ye upon me, saith the Lord, until the day that I rise up to the prey: for my determination is to gather the nations, that I may assemble the kingdoms, to pour upon them mine indignation, even all my fierce anger: for all the earth shall be devoured with the fire of my jealousy" (Zephaniah 3:8).

"Behold, he cometh with clouds; and every eye shall see him, and they also which pierced him: and all kindred of the earth shall wail because of him. Even so, Amen" (Revelation 1:7).

"And he gathered them together into a place called in the Hebrew tongue Armageddon" (Revelation 16:16).

THE LOCATION OF ARMAGEDDON

Armageddon means "the mountain of Megiddo" and is an ancient battleground situated by the town of Megiddo on the south side of the Plain of Esdraelon, ten miles southwest of

Nazareth, and about forty miles north of Jerusalem. It is at the entrance to a pass across the Carmel mountain range. Its location had immense strategic importance in ancient times because it was on the main highway between Asia and Africa, the Via Maris, which was a primary trading route for all traffic in the ancient world. A fortress was built at Armageddon that guarded the pass through the mountain range. Whoever controlled the pass, controlled the trade, so, because of its position at the entrance to the pass, the importance of Armageddon in the ancient world cannot be overstated.

Armageddon was also strategically located between the Euphrates and Nile rivers. Thotmes III, who made Egypt a world-empire, said, "Megiddo is worth a thousand cities." Because of its importance, it was the site of hundreds of battles between armies of the East and of the West even up to the time of World War I. It is said that more blood has been shed around this hill than at any other spot on earth. If that is not true now, it certainly will be true by the end of the Last Battle.

ARMAGEDDON/MEGIDDO'S HISTORY

There is no more appropriate place for this final battle than Armageddon. In ancient times, whoever controlled the Fortress of Megiddo controlled that part of the world. That is why 1 Kings 10:15 relates that Solomon wanted to control it. Furthermore, Armageddon has historically been a pivotal place between the forces of good and evil, having been the site of many battles between those forces. It was an ancient place of Baal (Satan) worship. Archaeologists have uncovered jars containing the remains of children sacrificed to Baal that they date to the time of King Ahab. Mount Carmel is the place where Elijah battled the prophets of Baal when he called fire down from heaven (1 Kings 18). Deborah, the Judge of Israel fought Barak at this spot (Judges 5:19), and good King Josiah was killed in battle here (2 Chronicles 35:22-25). But every battle ever fought here, every drop of blood spilled in order to determine whose sovereignty would prevail, pales in comparison to the battle which is now being prepared to be fought here. This final battle will determine which force, good or evil, is the stronger; which king, Jesus or Satan, will rule the world.

Satan is gathering his forces, not only in order to subjugate Israel, the apple of God's eye, but also to prevent the coming of Jesus and His saints, according to Revelation 19:19 which says, "And I saw the beast, and the kings of the earth, and their armies, gathered together to make war *against him that sat on the horse, and against his army*" (emphasis mine). Since the Great Rebellion in heaven, since the Garden of Eden when Satan got his toehold into the affairs of man, since Calvary when the Atonement was made, the universe has not seen a day, an event, so fraught with destiny for every creature in it. Whoever wins this battle will win the great cosmic war between Good and Evil.

THE CONFLICT BEGINS

When all the nations of the earth surround Jerusalem, Antichrist, at first, will prevail. The Two Witnesses will also be killed during this time, and because Antichrist has finally been able to kill them, it will seem to him and to his forces that his power is greater than that of God, and this will embolden Antichrist. As Zechariah and Luke tell us: "Behold, the day of the Lord cometh, and thy spoil shall be divided in the midst of thee. For I will gather all nations against Jerusalem to battle; and the city shall be taken, and the houses rifled, and the women ravished; and half of the city shall go forth into captivity, and the residue of the people shall not be cut off from the city. Then shall the Lord go forth, and fight against those nations, as when he fought in the day of battle" (Zechariah 14:2-3).

"And when ye shall see Jerusalem compassed with armies, then know that the desolation thereof is nigh. Then let them which are in Judaea flee to the mountains; and let them which are in the midst of it depart out; and let not them that are in the countries enter thereinto. For these be the days of vengeance, that all things which are written may be fulfilled. But woe unto them that are with child, and to them that give suck, in those days! For there shall be great distress in the land, and wrath upon this people. And they shall fall by the edge of the sword, and shall be led away captive into all nations: and Jerusalem shall be trodden down of the Gentiles, until the times of the Gentiles be fulfilled" (Luke 21:20-24).

(Note: the times of the Gentiles is not the same as the fullness of the Gentiles. The fullness of the Gentiles refers to the time in which the Gentiles can come to Jesus. That time historically began with the conversion of Cornelius and ends at the end of the Sixth Seal.)

This assault will take some time. Although we speak of the Day of the Battle of Armageddon, the time period will be much longer than just one day. The time of the demonic horsemen who ride at this time is given in Revelation 9 as being one hour, one day, one month and one year. Whether the time of the sixth seal is longer than that we do not know, but it is at least that long. We have just seen that half of the city will go into captivity. All this will take time and, as was said before, Satan, at first, will seem to prevail. But all that will change: "In that day shall the Lord defend the inhabitants of Jerusalem: and he that is feeble among them at that day shall be as David; and the house of David shall be as God, as the angel of the Lord before them. And it shall come to pass in that day, that I will seek to destroy all the nations that come against Jerusalem. And I will pour upon the house of David, and upon the inhabitants of Jerusalem, the spirit of grace and of supplications: and they shall look upon me whom they have pierced, and they shall mourn for him as one mourneth for his only son, and shall be in bitterness for him, as one that is in bitterness for his firstborn" (Zechariah 12:8-10).

Not only will Jesus and His saints defend Jerusalem and destroy her enemies, the Jews will accept that Jesus is, indeed, their Messiah; the self-same Jesus whom they had rejected thousands of years before. And when they do, curiously enough, Jesus will be coming to them as Conquering King, just as they always expected that He would.

SEVENTH VIAL: "IT IS FINISHED": JESUS IS SOVEREIGN OVER THE EARTH AND SEA

When the seventh angel pours out his vial onto the earth, the Voice from the Throne declares, "It is finished." This declaration is proof-positive that the angels under the trumpets and the angels under the vials are one and the same, for Revelation 10:7, speaking of the angels under the Trumpets, tells us, "But in the days of the voice of the seventh angel, when he shall begin to sound, the mystery of God should be finished, as he hath declared to his servants the prophets." And, indeed, when the seventh angel under the Trumpets sounds his trumpet, he says, "The kingdoms of this world *are become* the kingdoms of our Lord, and of his Christ; and he shall reign for ever and ever" (emphasis mine).

The declaration made here by God that "It is finished" was exactly what Jesus said on the cross right before He died. At Calvary, man's redemption was completed, the work was finished. Nothing more will ever have to be done again. Now, the redemption of everything else that was lost to sin, the earth and man's immortality, has been completed and the pronouncement is again heard from the throne where God dwells. Could this final pronouncement be said at two different times during the Tribulation? No. It is too profound and final a statement to be said at any other time than when Jesus has taken formal possession of the earth and sea, and that happens only once. "It is finished" has been uttered only once on the earth and "It is finished" will be uttered only once in heaven, but it is recorded twice by John in order to make clear that the time of the seventh angel under the Trumpets and the time of the seventh angel under the Vials is the same time. Jesus will declare from heaven that "it is finished" as He claims His sovereign right to the earth and seas. Every seal to the title deed to the earth has been broken and the deed lies open in the hand of the Lamb. Now He will descend from heaven with His saints to forcefully carry out what He has declared to be the case.

It is important to remember that in order to qualify to be a redeemer under Old Testament Law, one had to have the legal right, one had to be willing, and one had to be able. Jesus has the legal right to redeem us for He is our near kinsman, a "son of Adam." He proved His willingness at Calvary, but now what is so necessary here, is that He is able. Jesus, and only Jesus, is able to kick the Great Usurper, Satan, off of the disputed planet, earth. That is the purpose of the Great War of Armageddon. "It is finished" is stated in heaven, but it is heard from one end of the earth to the other, and its hearing will strike terrible fear into the hearts of all who have sided with Antichrist and rebelled against the King of the Universe.

THE ENTIRE EARTH IS SHAKEN

Immediately following that pronouncement, there will be other voices, thunders, and lightning in the sky, and then will occur the greatest earthquake that has ever happened upon the face of the earth. This earthquake topples the buildings in Dallas, Texas; this earthquake topples the buildings in Paris, France. This earthquake topples Algeria; this earthquake levels India; this earthquake destroys the cities of the world. The magnitude of this quake will change the topography of earth forever. It is possible that it will even bring forth a shift in the polar axis. Earth is now at a twenty-three-degree angle that many Bible scholars believe came about as a result of the Flood. They speculate that when the fountains of the deep broke up and bombarded the earth, they tilted it to a twenty-three-degree angle that caused the poles to freeze, trapping the water. The world's oceans and seas are probably also a result of the flood. If the earth were to be restored to a level degree, there would be a moderating of climates and winds.

Earth's mountain ranges now contribute to cold spots, storms, etc., but the Scriptures are clear on the fact that the mountains will some day be thrown down. When that happens, they will fill up the deep ocean basins while, at the same time, they will trap the displaced water into great subterranean reservoirs. The seas of the earth will once more resemble the pre-diluvian seas: smaller, both in depth and in breadth, and more or less uniformly distributed across the surface of the earth. This earthquake is what causes all of that to happen as the earth reels to and fro like a drunk. If the mountains were replaced by gentle hills, the climate would become far more temperate. Deserts, too, would disappear because rain would be equalized. The world would once again resemble the Eden that God initially created. That world had no uninhabitable places such as we now find on our earth. There were no vast, barren deserts, nor vast polar regions. And after the reshaping of the earth's topography that comes about under the seventh seal, neither will this world we now know.

The earthquake that changes all of this is prophesied about many times in the Bible. The following are some of those prophecies: "Therefore I will shake the heavens, and the earth shall remove out of her place, in the wrath of the Lord of hosts, and in the day of his fierce anger" (Isaiah 13:13).

"Fear, and the pit, and the snare, are upon thee, O inhabitant of the earth. And it shall come to pass, that he who fleeth from the noise of the fear shall fall into the pit; and he that cometh up out of the midst of the pit shall be taken in the snare: for the windows from on high are open, and the foundations of the earth do shake. The earth is utterly broken down, the earth is clean dissolved, the earth is moved exceedingly. The earth shall reel to and fro like a drunkard, and shall be removed like a cottage; and the transgression thereof shall be heavy upon it; and it shall fall, and not rise again. And it shall come to pass in that day, that the Lord shall punish the host of the high ones that are on high, and the kings of the earth upon the earth" (Isaiah 24:17-21).

"Every valley shall be exalted, and every mountain and hill shall be made low: and the crooked shall be made straight, and the rough places plain: And the glory of the Lord shall be revealed, and all flesh shall see it together: for the mouth of the Lord hath spoken it" (Isaiah 40:4-5).

"And it shall come to pass at the same time when Gog shall come against the land of Israel, saith the Lord God, that my fury shall come up in my face. For in my jealousy and in the fire of my wrath have I spoken, Surely in that day there shall be a great shaking in the land of Israel; So that the fishes of the sea, and the fowls of the heaven, and the beasts of the field, and all creeping things that creep upon the earth, and all the men that are upon the face of the earth, shall shake at my presence, and the mountains shall be thrown down, and the steep places shall fall, and every wall shall fall to the ground" (Ezekiel 38:18-20).

"For thus saith the Lord of hosts; Yet once, it is a little while, and I will shake the heavens, and the sea, and the dry land; And I will shake all nations, and the desire of all nations shall come: and I will fill this house with glory, saith the Lord of hosts" (Haggai 2:6-7).

THE QUAKE RESHAPES JERUSALEM, THE ISLANDS, AND THE MOUNTAINS

The result of this earthquake is that Jerusalem is split into three parts; the rest of the cities of the world are destroyed; and the islands and the mountains of earth are no longer to be found. Zechariah also prophesies that Jerusalem will be divided into three parts, and he gives us further details: "And it shall come to pass, that in all the land, saith the Lord, two parts therein shall be cut off and die; but the third shall be left therein. And I will bring the third part through the fire, and will refine them as silver is refined, and will try them as gold is tried: they shall call on my name, and I will hear them: I will say, It is my people: and they shall say, The Lord is my God" (Zechariah 13:8-9).

"And it shall be in that day, that living waters shall go out from Jerusalem; half of them toward the former sea, and half of them toward the hinder sea: in summer and in winter shall it be. And the Lord shall be king over all the earth: in that day shall there be one Lord, and his name one. All the land shall be turned as a plain from Geba to Rimmon south of Jerusalem: *and it shall be lifted up,* and inhabited in her place, from Benjamin's gate unto the place of the first gate, unto the corner gate, and from the tower of Hananeel unto the king's winepresses. And men shall dwell in it, and there shall be no more utter destruction; but Jerusalem shall be safely inhabited" (Zechariah 14:8-11, emphasis mine).

Springs of water will flow out of Jerusalem. One will flow north towards Galilee and one will flow south to the Dead Sea. Notice, too, that Zechariah prophesies that the city of Jerusalem will be elevated (lifted up). So, too, does Micah 4:1-2: "But in the last days it shall come to pass, that the mountain of the house of the Lord shall be established in the top of the mountains; and it shall be exalted above the hills; and people shall flow unto it. And many nations shall come, and say, Come, and let us go up to the mountain of the Lord, and to the house of the God of Jacob; and he will teach us of this ways, and we will walk in his paths: for the law shall go forth of Zion, and the word of the Lord from Jerusalem."

The book of Psalms tells us that Jerusalem will be the most beautifully situated place on earth. If we think that the natural beauty of a city like San Francisco is impressive, it will pale before the beauty of the natural setting of Jerusalem. "Beautiful for situation, the joy of the whole earth, is mount Zion [Jerusalem], on the sides of the north, the city of the great King," (Psalm 48:2).

BABYLON: SATAN'S RELIGIOUS, POLITICAL, AND ECONOMIC SYSTEM IS DESTROYED

It is at this point in time that God utterly destroys "great Babylon" with the cup of wine of His fierce wrath. This wrath that is visited upon Babylon encompasses more than simply the city of Babylon. In fact, the city of Babylon has already been destroyed by armies on earth. (This will be discussed in detail in the next chapters.) No, the "Great Babylon" referred to here is the entirety of Satan's system, religion, influence, and spirit of evil that have had play in the affairs of men since the time of the Garden of Eden. It is the source of all the evil and deceptions, of all the sin and depravity, of all the misery and torment that has oppressed the human race since the beginning of time. The wrath of God against this unspeakable horror and evil is unimaginable, and He now unleashes His long pent-up wrath against it and against all who have had a part in it. What a great and terrible day that will be!

"Howl ye; for the day of the Lord is at hand; it shall come as a destruction from the Almighty. Therefore shall all hands be faint, and every man's heart shall melt: And they shall be afraid: pangs and sorrows shall take hold of them; they shall be in pain as a woman that travaileth: they shall be amazed one at another; their faces shall be as flames. Behold, the day of the Lord cometh, cruel both with wrath and fierce anger, to lay the land desolate: and he shall destroy the sinners thereof out of it. For the stars of heaven and the constellations thereof shall not give their light: the sun shall be darkened in his going forth, and the moon shall not cause her light to shine. And I will punish the world for their evil, and the wicked for their iniquity; and I will cause the arrogancy of the proud to cease, and will lay low the haughtiness of the terrible" (Isaiah 13:6-11).

"And it shall come to pass in that day, that the Lord shall punish the host of the high ones that are on high, and the kings of the earth upon the earth. And they shall be gathered together, as prisoners are gathered in the pit, and shall be shut up in the prison, and after many days shall they be visited. Then the moon shall be confounded, and the sun ashamed, when the Lord of hosts shall reign in mount Zion, and in Jerusalem, and before his ancients gloriously" (Isaiah 24:21-23).

GREAT HAILSTONES FALL FROM HEAVEN: PEOPLE BLASPHEME GOD

As if the great earthquake is not enough, giant hailstones begin to fall upon the people. The Jewish talent, when weighing commodities, was equal to about 135 pounds. The Greek talent weighed about 86 pounds. Which weight John had in mind, one cannot say, however, either weight is prodigious. Factor in that it is a falling weight on a stationary object and one will soon understand that the destruction will be tremendous. This hail could very easily be a consequence of the shaking of heaven that God said He would do at the same time as He shook the earth. It could also be a consequence of the breaking up of polar ice caps during the great earthquake. Either way, none of this compels the people nor the armies to repent, nor even to ask for mercy from God. Their response is the same as it has been every time; they blaspheme His name.

Great hailstones fell on Egypt when God delivered Israel from the bondage of the Pharaohs and great hailstones fell on the kings of the Amorites when Israel was taking the Promised Land. The same thing happens now when God again delivers Israel from her enemies, it's just that, this time, her enemies are all the armies in the world, not just Egypt, not even just the Caananite nations. The scope and size of Israel's enemies do not matter to God, for, after all, He is God. And God knew that this day would come before He even created the world, and, further, He has made provision for this day millennia ago. Job, the most ancient book in the Bible, tells us this when God says to Job, "Hast thou entered into the treasures of the snow? Or hast thou seen the treasures of the hail, Which I have reserved against the time of trouble, against the day of battle and war?" (38:22-23). All things that have ever happened and will ever happen have been foreseen by God, and provision for each one of them has been made. How can one fear anything, when the

Lord of All Creation is in charge of the Universe? "Therefore my heart is glad, and my glory rejoiceth: my flesh also shall rest in hope" (Psalm 16:9).

PART FIVE: TRIBULATION AS SEEN FROM SATAN'S KINGDOM

Figure 5   Part 5: Revelation 17 - 22

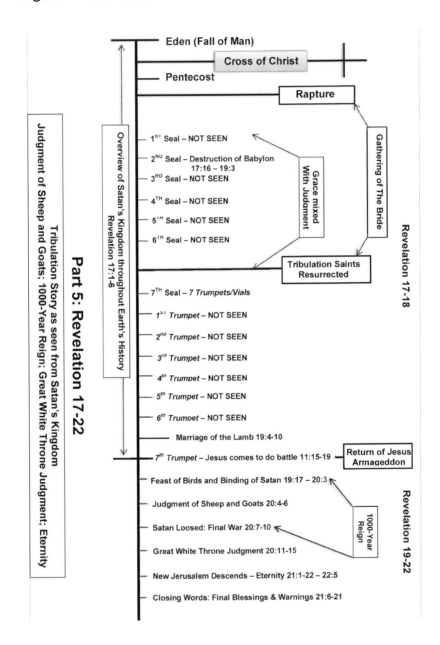

Eden (Fall of Man)

Cross of Christ

Pentecost

Rapture

Overview of Satan's Kingdom throughout Earth's History

Judgment of Sheep and Goats; 1000-Year Reign; Great White Throne Judgment; Eternity

Tribulation Story as seen from Satan's Kingdom

Part 5: Revelation 17-22

Overview of Satan's Kingdom throughout Earth's History
Revelation 17:1-6

1ST Seal – NOT SEEN

2ND Seal – Destruction of Babylon
17:16 – 19:3

3RD Seal – NOT SEEN

4TH Seal – NOT SEEN

5TH Seal – NOT SEEN

6TH Seal – NOT SEEN

Grace mixed With Judgment

Gathering of The Bride

Revelation 17-18

Tribulation Saints Resurrected

7TH Seal – 7 Trumpets/Vials

1ST Trumpet – NOT SEEN

2nd Trumpet – NOT SEEN

3rd Trumpet – NOT SEEN

4th Trumpet – NOT SEEN

5th Trumpet – NOT SEEN

6th Trumpet – NOT SEEN

Marriage of the Lamb 19:4-10

7th Trumpet – Jesus comes to do battle 11:15-19

Return of Jesus Armageddon

Feast of Birds and Binding of Satan 19:17 – 20:3

Judgment of Sheep and Goats 20:4-6

Satan Loosed: Final War 20:7-10

Great White Throne Judgment 20:11-15

New Jerusalem Descends – Eternity 21:1-22 – 22:5

Closing Words: Final Blessings & Warnings 21:6-21

1000-Year Reign

Revelation 19-22

CHAPTER 20
BABYLON
Revelation 17

EVENTS OF LAST DAYS AS SEEN FROM SATAN'S KINGDOM

The third telling of the story of the time between Rapture and Armageddon begins with Revelation 17. John has told the story once from the viewpoint of heaven, once from the viewpoint of earth, and now the third and final telling will be from the viewpoint of Satan's kingdom. Although it was the event of the Rapture that began both of the previous two accounts, Rapture will not be seen nor referred to this time. There is a simple reason for that; Rapture will not personally affect any person in Satan's kingdom. Furthermore, Satan has nothing to do with its execution, and although he will fight mightily against it after it does happen, it will catch him off guard at the beginning. Thus, the story of Rapture has no place in the story of the end as concerns Satan's kingdom.

"BABYLON" - WORLD SYSTEM, RELIGION, AND CITY

John devotes an impressive amount of space in the third and final telling of the story to one topic: Babylon. He devotes two and one half chapters to Babylon whereas he only gave two chapters to the story of the Church. Why? Because Babylon is far more than just a city that will assume great importance in the end of time: Babylon is a code term. Twice, John states that "Babylon" is a mystery. There is great symbolism and meaning attached to her. Throughout the history of man, there has been a "dark side" to the human existence; that fact is undeniable. But the form the darkness has taken has not always been the same. It had been up to the wise men and the people of God to try and figure out just exactly who was their enemy. It is soon clear to every person who lives that their staunchest enemies are sometimes shadow enemies; either not known or "friends" falsely trusted. Was there an overarching conspiracy of darkness or was there simply a random collection of evildoers? Philosophers and religious thinkers throughout time have been divided.

An analogy to this religious question could be found in medicine. Before the acceptance of the Germ Theory, which stated that infectious, contagious diseases, along with other medical conditions, were a result of microorganisms invisible to the naked eye, it was very easy to miss the fact that diseases had a common root cause. So, too, it was with the manifestations of evil. Were they linked or were they independent? After all what could the Pharaoh of Egypt really have in common with the evil emperor Nero? Were the "mystery religions" of Rome possibly linked to Baal worship? Revelation 17 answers this question with finality: all the evil governments and all the evil religions of all time have a common ancestry and root cause. "Babylon" is shorthand for the overarching system of Satan, and symbolizes *in toto* his complete opposition to God. God wanted John to have an overview of evil throughout history and John was astounded at the vision of evil that was given to him. God wanted John (and us) to understand that evil is systematic, not random nor haphazard.

But why the name "Babylon"? Because this system will culminate where it first began; in Babylon. Thus, "Babylon" comprises three different entities: A great city, a world system, and a world religion.

THE CITY OF BABYLON

The city of Babylon will be a great commercial center, a great political center, and a great religious center. In ancient times, the city of Babylon was one of the Seven Wonders of the World. The city will be even greater and more magnificent at the end of time. So much space is given to Babylon that it must be that she will assume more importance than any other city ever has. It was in this location that the powers of evil first made their assault against the human race in the Garden of Eden. It was here that the first murder was committed. In the time from Adam to Noah, wickedness increased to the extent that the entire race of man was imperiled. In a very short time, the onslaught of Satan against the human race had made such inroads that God decided that He needed to destroy the race of man. Genesis 6 records that fallen angels interbred with human women, the result being that the human race was now polluted. Many walking the face of the earth were not fully

Adamic (that is, of the race of Adam), many were a new race called by the Bible Nephilim. The Hebrew word *nephilim* literally means "fallen ones." When God chose to save one righteous man, Noah, and seven others of his family, the Bible makes certain to record his lineage, generation by generation, back to Adam; the point being made is that Noah was completely Adamic. The ensuing Flood destroyed the entire earth except for the eight souls who were safely aboard the ark. And when the ark landed on the mountains of Ararat, it could once again be said that every person on the earth knew and feared God. There was not an unbeliever alive, so Satan geared up for battle once more.

BABYLON FOUNDED BY NIMROD

Two hundred years later, Nimrod, the great challenger of God, established the kingdom of Babel (Babylon). He was the father of one-world government and despotic totalitarianism.

Initially, God had directed mankind to spread out over the earth and establish small settlements and communities. He knew that small groups would have more accountability from their citizens, they would have more flexibility, more humanness, and that there would be a greater overall sense of community in a small settlement. We still see that today in small towns. People are far less likely to commit crimes against people they know well, and if they do, the ostracism enforced by the community is both a powerful punishment and a powerful deterrent. Contrast that situation with that of very large cities or governments. It is there that one finds autocratic government, faceless bureaucracy, and inflexibility. Those are the places where crime and poverty thrive because the sense of overall connectedness has been destroyed and a state of anomie thrives for many.

BABEL - GOD IS DEFIED, LANGUAGE IS CONFUSED

In defiance of God, Nimrod convinced the population in all the surrounding areas to band together and use their combined strength to defy God. They decided on a place to make their stand: Shinar, known more familiarly as Babylon. And so, Nimrod's kingdom was established. Soon after, the building of the Tower of Babel was begun. The tower itself was never a threat to God. The very idea is ridiculous. What disturbed God was that He knew that Nimrod and his followers had their hands around some dangerous knowledge. God Himself said, "and now nothing will be restrained from them, which they have imagined to do," (Genesis 11: 6). In effect, God was saying: If they keep going, they will have every bit of knowledge including occult knowledge. Although that time of understanding will come for the human race, under Antichrist, God said, "The time of Nimrod is not the time." It was still early on in the history of the world and this compendium of knowledge was threatening the continuation of the earth. It was occurring too soon in God's timetable.

Given that, God intervened and confused their language. Up until now, all humans had spoken the same tongue, but God understood that the synergistic ability of their combined knowledge was too great. It was, as Sir David Lyndsay described it in Ane Dialog, "that Hyddeous Strength." Hideous Strength it was indeed, and so God put an impenetrable barrier, language, between the people, effectively retarding their compilation of knowledge. As an interesting footnote, we are fast moving toward a universal language once again and it is no coincidence that we are once again rushing towards Armageddon.

Another fact which reinforces the premise that Nimrod's rebellion was fueled by Satan is that the Assyrians cite Nimrod as the founder of their religion. As one recalls, the Assyrians were one of the earliest world empires; one of the seven world empires controlled by Satan. It is also interesting to note that one of the names given to antichrist is "the Assyrian."

BABEL - PEOPLE AND THEIR OCCULTIC PRACTICES SCATTERED

Now when God confused the common language, the Bible tells us that the people scattered into many different settlements, taking with them their bits of knowledge of the "dark sentences" of occultic religion. These remnants of the Babylonian culture soon showed up in different spots around the world. In the Middle East, they manifested themselves in the child sacrifices required by Baal and Moloch. The cruelty inherent in these sacrifices cannot be overstated. A metal image of the god would be heated white hot; the drums would pound; the chants would increase; and the people would be whipped into a frenzy until they danced up to the wide mouth of the white hot idol and placed their live children into it. The occultic practices of Babylon also showed up in far away South America. Consider the human sacrifices of the Incas as one example. Consider, too, the faces of demons that are displayed in African tribal worship, in the totems and kachinas of Native American worship, in the gods of the Hindu religion, and in the voodoo spirits of the Caribbean. The ziggurats found in Babylon are very similar to the Aztec temples unearthed by archaeologists in Latin America. The pagan expressions were all different but yet all the same. The seeds of the religion of Babylon were sown worldwide. The widespread corruption of the Babylonian system into the different societies and cultures is the main reason that God so sternly commanded the Israelites to stay away from the pagan societies around them.

BABYLON - SATAN'S INFILTRATION AND CORRUPTION WITHIN THE CHURCH

Many End-Times commentators have reduced Babylon to simply symbolizing the Roman Catholic Church. To say, as many Protestants do, that Babylon is the Catholic Church is a grievous error that completely ignores Satan's web of deception which he has been spinning since the Garden of Eden. The key to understanding of Revelation 17 is to grasp that Babylon is far more than any one person's pet loathing. It is not simply the Medieval Catholic Church, it is not simply the New Age Movement, it is certainly not simply one city such as New York or Rome, nor is it one country such as America. It is evil in its entirety; it is the genius of Satan in whatever form Satan wished it to take at any given moment in time.

The historical Church has not been exempt from Satan's lies and mutations. The attack on her from Satan did not even wait until the New Testament was fully written. Beginning with Gnosticism, the philosophy that taught that Jesus was not human, the seeds of apostasy continued through modern times as is evidenced in the heresy that is rampant in the "Jesus Seminar." Because of the tenet of Gnosticism that taught that

Jesus was not flesh and blood, two schools of early heretical thought arose. One was the school of the Ascetics which taught that the flesh was evil and thus it must be both denied and punished. The other was the school of the Libertines who taught that the flesh was unimportant, and thus, one could involve oneself in every conceivable gratification of the flesh with complete impunity. Both extremes were, of course, repugnant to God.

CORRUPTION - CATHARISM

Gnosticism soon took root in the early Middle Ages in a movement called Catharism, the most prominent medieval heresy. It also drew much from the religions of the East. Theosophy, Rosicrucianism, and Freemasonry owe at least part of their "secret doctrines" to Cathar influences. Cathars believed in an evil spirit and a good spirit that were supposedly equal in strength. In actuality, according to Cathar belief, the evil spirit had great advantage. For instance, Gnostic belief was incorporated in Catharism in the teaching that the good spirit could not inhabit a physical body, therefore Jesus of Nazareth could not have been the Son of God. The evil spirit, could, however, inhabit a physical body. In a further testament to the power of the evil spirit called by them Rex Mundi, it was the evil spirit who created the Universe. The good spirit was the god of love, but it was totally ineffective in the world other than exerting a good force through cosmic energy. Thus, the evil spirit was the primary force in the world; certainly, the force who needed to be appeased. How convenient for Satan!

Cathars venerated Mary Magdalene rather than Mary, the mother of Jesus, venerated by Catholics. Many of the Madonna and Child statues and paintings, the "Black Madonnas," and other relics, are actually Cathar tributes to Mary Magdalene whom, they taught, had a sexual relationship with Jesus. In the Cathar "Madonna and Child" relics, the child portrayed was not Jesus Himself, but rather the child of Jesus and Mary Magdalene. These Cathar beliefs warred against the established beliefs of the Church throughout the Middle Ages and, in some instances, resulted in two competing popes, one of which was usually a Cathar pope with a Cathar throne in a Cathar town. The Inquisition was initially undertaken trying to root out Catharism in the thirteenth century. As an interesting side note, Adolph Hitler was schooled under a Cathar Benedictine monk in Austria who shaped much of his thought. And Dan Brown, in his very popular Da Vinci novels, presents us with a new (but very ancient) Cathar gospel that has captivated thousands of modern readers.

CORRUPTION - ALCHEMY

The "science" of alchemy was another area of heresy during the Middle Ages. Although modern chemists and pharmacists sometimes trace their origin back to the Alchemists, the Alchemists were not simply proto-scientists of an ignorant age; they were occultists. Their symbol was the swastika, which, to them, represented transmutation. Many alchemists were wizards, sorcerers and magicians operating undercover in a hostile Christian culture. Victor Hugo well understood this, and incorporated it into his character of the evil priest who dabbles in the Black Arts in his book The Hunchback of Notre Dame.

CORRUPTION - THE KNIGHTS TEMPLAR

The Knights Templar was another example of heresy in the Medieval Age. It was a gnostic order of warrior monks in addition to being a secret religious society. According to many writings, they secretly repudiated Jesus Christ, blasphemed God, and worshipped a devil named Baphomet. Baphomet was pictured as a ram with curved horns and displaying the inverse pentagram - the symbol that, today, is most closely identified with Satanism. Templars practiced alchemy, astrology, sacred geometry, and magic. Pope Innocent III upbraided them for necromancy, and even as recently as the nineteenth century, historians routinely ascribed Satanism and devil worship to the order because of their black magic rituals that centered around Baphomet. Novices were initiated into the discipline of the order and were then raised by degrees into the secret doctrines of the group until they were fully illuminated. The concept of initiation by degrees would figure prominently in later occult-influenced movements also.

The Knights Templar were said to possess the Holy Grail. Adolph Hitler was fascinated by the legends of the Grail and, when the Nazis conquered France, sent Otto Rohn to the Pyrenees in order to look for it. Rohn, a professor, did not believe it to be a cup, but believed that it was a set of tablets on which a mystical secret doctrine was set down in ancient runic writing. Much grail information also came from the Arthurian legends. In them, the successful quester had to pass through a difficult series of steps that would make him pure enough to be counted worthy to view the Grail. Again, initiation into the mysteries of the Grail was necessary, and it was accomplished degree by Gnostic degree. Many times the minstrels who spread the legends of Arthur throughout Europe were, according to many medieval scholars, actually clandestine Gnostic missionaries, operating underground in a hostile Christian environment. Interestingly, Alastair Crowley, the infamous Satanist, was an avid scholar of the Arthurian tome, Percival, because he said there was so much information concerning the black arts contained within it.

The Templars amassed great wealth and gradually became the bankers to merchants, kings, and popes. As can readily be imagined, this greatly increased their power and influence. Their power became such a threat to the established system that King Phillip IV of France and Pope Clement V joined forces in order to attempt to eradicate them. Phillip and Clement failed, however, in their effort to completely wipe out the movement. Their extermination order was never carried out in Scotland, and many Templars escaped to there. Masonic tradition holds that Scottish Rite Freemasonry has its root in the Templars who escaped to Scotland. Certainly the Masonic order for young boys bears an interesting name, DeMolay, which is also the name of the last Grand Master of the Knights Templar, Jacques de Molay, who, in 1312, was slowly roasted to death over a low fire. Not only Scottish Rite Freemasonry, but York Rite Freemasonry seems to hold ties to the Knights Templar. The culminating degree in York Rite is the Knights Templar Degree, the equivalent of the 32nd degree in the Scottish Rite. To this day, many vestiges of Cathar Templar Ritual can be found in Masonic lodges throughout the world. The skulls seen in many lodges are extremely reminiscent of the devil Baphomet. One cannot underemphasize the intertwining of Freemasony, Rosicruicianism, and Theosophy with the current satanic underground. Nor should one dismiss those connections with the Illuminati plans for a one world government. Revelation 2:13 tells us that Satan's seat (his power, his authority) had shifted to Pergamum by the Fourth Century. The Pergamum Church time frame was exactly when this Gnostic/Templar/Cathar gospel was taking root. If you recall, Satan had just been defeated in his attempt to eradicate the Christian Church by means of government persecution and torture and it was necessary for him to launch a different kind of attack if he were to defeat God by defeating God's church. It seems clear to me that Satan began hatching that new plan to destroy the Church – a plan that has now taken almost two thousand years to come to fruition. It is a plan of world domination carefully tended and plotted and passed on from one satanic conspirator to the next and nurtured in the Cathar/Illuminati/Gnostic/Freemasonry groups that have been found in every generation since the Pergamum Age. They will come together to produce Babylon – the great one world system overseen by Satan's man, antichrist.

BABYLON - SATANIC CENTER OF WORSHIP FOR THE WORLD
Space does not permit the examination of other occultic heresies found within the Church such as Rosicrucianism, but it is interesting to note how little known today are the early heresies that ripped at the seams of the Church. Those heresies, along with the current systematic disbelief concerning the divine inspiration of the scriptures and even concerning the divinity of Jesus taught in many modern-day seminaries, the idolatry in Romanism, pagan belief, the Dark Arts, the false religions of Hinduism and Islam, and the current New Age mysticism will all combine at the end of time in the grand religion of Babylon. At that time the official religion of the world will be Satanism with only the Christians demurring. Paul taught in 1 Corinthians 8:5-6 that there are many gods in heaven and on earth but that there is but one God: "For though there be that are called gods, whether in heaven or in earth, (as there be gods many, and lords many,) But to us there is but one God, the Father, of whom are all things, and we in him; and one Lord Jesus Christ, by whom are all things, and we by him." Now, the many satanic gods will come together under

Antichrist in order to war against the One True God. Under Antichrist, Babylon will again become the satanic center of worship for the world.

The renowned historian, Arnold Toynbee, stressed in his writings that the site of Babylon would be the best place in the world to build a future world cultural metropolis. She is very near to the geographical center of the earth's land mass. She is within navigable distance of the Persian Gulf and she is also at the crossroads of Asia, Europe, and Africa. Right now, Babylon, located as she is in Iraq, is a miserably hot, dusty, poverty plagued, war-torn city. She will not remain as such; great changes are in store.

JOHN'S VISION OF THE GREAT HARLOT/WHORE

John's third vision begins when one of the seven angels with the seven trumpets/vials/bowls appears to him, carries him into the wilderness (Satan's realm), and shows him a great harlot sitting upon many waters. Symbolically, a woman always represents a religious system. This woman is called the "great whore," signaling to the reader that a very wide sphere of influence is presumed here. Indeed, the Whore represents both the religious and the political systems of Antichrist. The name given to this total system of influence and control of Antichrist's, and thus, by proxy, of Satan's, is Babylon. She is clothed in the colors of royalty and power that signal to the reader her political control. The colors are also indicative of her wealth as are the pearls and precious gems by which she is covered.

The meaning of the waters that she sits upon is consistent with the meaning of the sea which we have already posited in Revelation 4:6 when the Crystal Sea before the throne of God was in view. The sea was interpreted as being countless numbers of people. That interpretation is now corroborated, for in Revelation 17:15 we are told that the many waters upon which the Great Whore sits are symbolic of great numbers of people who are under the Whore's control and dominion. They have come out of every land and they speak every language. Thus we see that the woman is both extraordinarily evil and extraordinarily powerful, with her influence reaching into every culture and nation. Not only does she control and influence the people, she also controls and influences all of the rulers of the world and she does this through the power of her great riches. The kings of the world have made an unholy alliance with her in order to share in her wealth.

EVERY NATION IS SEDUCED BY THE WHORE

Keep in mind that this third vision of John's starts at the *beginning* of Tribulation, which commences immediately after the rapture of the saints. This system of Antichrist's already is in control *at* the Rapture; not immediately after, nor three-and-a-half years after the Rapture as many have taught. Antichrist has already appeared on the world scene at a time when it seemed that the earth would annihilate itself. Antichrist has successfully put an end to the wars, the internal strife, the *complete horror* that has defined existence for mankind in the years preceding. And with that pseudo-peace has come prosperity on a scale that mankind has never seen before. Great cities have been built, gold is used as pavement, wine and mirth are flowing freely, and every nation wants a piece of the action. And they can have it...for a price. The price comes in the form of their autonomy. And we see here in John's vision that they have all agreed to the price, for John is shown a vision of all of the kings of the earth and has been told that they have all committed fornication with the Great Whore. And because they have, their inhabitants are now drunk with the wine which comes from Satan, himself. They have surrendered their rationality, they have suspended disbelief, they are drunk on the system of Antichrist, symbolized here by the Great Whore.

HER GOLDEN CUP IS FILLED WITH ABOMINATIONS AND FILTHINESS

The Whore holds a golden cup in her hand. The contents of that cup are what have made the people so drunk. The cup is very costly and very beautiful and John must have been quite curious as to what it held. When he sees what is within, he is revolted because it is in such contrast with what the appearance of the cup promises. It is filled with "abominations and filthiness." As odd as this may seem at first, this is the exact nature of sin and depravity. It looks wonderful, exciting, and enticing on the outside, but that is its lure to trap mankind in its absolute filth and disease. It takes the mind and spirit of God to actually see sin as it really is, and few people ever do. Certainly, the world does not, and the people of this time have drunk so deeply from the Harlot's cup that they are drunk. They do not notice its filth nor its stench, they are aware only of its narcotic effect. Only John has eyes to see the contents as they really are.

This verse is interesting from another aspect. Remember when Jesus, in the Garden of Gethsemane the night of His betrayal, prayed that the cup would pass from Him? It was the horrible cup seen here. Jesus was forced to take and completely drink down the filthy, revolting contents found within. He took and consumed these very sins in order to free us from their bondage. We have known that intellectually, but here, John sees those sins and is overwhelmingly sickened by them. No wonder Jesus sweat blood at the thought of consuming this cup!

Jeremiah prophesied millennia ago that the world, in contrast to Jesus, would greedily seek after this cup when he wrote in 51:7, "Babylon hath been a golden cup in the Lord's hand, that made all the earth drunken: the nations have drunken of her wine; therefore the nations are mad." Understand that the nations are not mad as in "angry," the nations are mad as in "crazed." There is no sanity to be found anywhere in the earth!

SATAN - THE SCARLET BEAST
The Great Whore sits upon a red beast with seven heads and ten horns and which is covered in blasphemous names. The symbolism of the beast is clear: It is Satan in all his power throughout the history of earth. There have been six major world empires in the history of man: Egypt, Assyria, Babylon, Media-Persia, Greece, and Rome, and the coming world empire of Antichrist will constitute the seventh and final empire. All the empires throughout history have been in the power of Satan. John himself said, "And the whole world lieth in the evil one" in 1 John 5:19. As has already been noted, God wanted government systems to be simple and localized; in fact, He scattered mankind after Eden and again after the Flood. It is

Satan who has sought to create world empires because he knows that he will always be the control behind them.

The ten horns that arise out of the seventh head are synonymous with the ten toes of Daniel's vision. They are the nations of the Roman Empire which are brought together by Antichrist and which constitute the beginning of the final world empire. This is the last of Satan's empires, but it is but a continuation of the first six. The power, regardless of which nation has been featured, has always been Satan's.

THE WHORE'S NAME COMPRISES ALL FALSE RELIGIONS AND APOSTATE CHURCHES

The Great Whore has a name upon her forehead that identifies her. It was a Roman custom for harlots to wear a headband with the name of their owner upon it. This band reads: MYSTERY, BABYLON THE GREAT, THE MOTHER OF HARLOTS AND ABOMINATIONS OF THE EARTH. "Mystery" as used here in her name literally means "what is known only to the initiated." Only those who have the mind of God, or those who are initiated into the secrets of Satan, will understand that Satan is the power behind the empires of history and thus will understand the mystery of Babylon. The word "abominations" here literally means "idol worship." This is Satan's grand counterfeit of the Church. She is in every way the antithesis of the sun-clad woman in Revelation 12. Babylon takes to herself all the false religious and apostate churches that have ever existed. She is the system which Satan himself founded and spread throughout the world.

The message of Babylon is how he has ensnared man. Although there have been many diverse religions and governments, Satan has always been at the hub and the underlying system has always been the system of Babylon. Babylon is the culmination of Satan's lies throughout history; through the Garden of Eden, through the Tower of Babel, through the times of Baal worship, through the Mystery Religions of Greece and Rome, through the worship of Sun gods and other nature gods, through Hinduism and Buddhism, through the occultic thought behind Nazism, and through the New Age Movement of today. The very word "Babel" means "to confound," and that is exactly what Satan has done to the world ever since his appearance in the Garden of Eden.

SATANIC WORLD EMPIRE DRUNK ON THE BLOOD OF THE MARTYRED SAINTS

Besides providing the chalice that has made the nations of the world drunk, the harlot is drunk herself. And what has made her drunk is even viler than the abominations and filthiness which inebriated the nations, for she is drunk on the blood of the saints and the martyrs. When one gets past one's initial disgust, this makes perfect sense. What else could make Satan as euphoric as destroying the lives of the people who belong to his great enemy, Jehovah? As John looks upon this scene, it is unbelievably fascinating to him because he is able to see into the core of the complete hatred that Satan feels for God and His people. It is only the restraining hand of God that keeps His people from total destruction by Satan. This impresses itself so much on John, even though he, himself, had instructed the Church on the wiles and opposition of Satan, that he stands in amazement at the scene of the Great Whore. The angel then tells John that he will reveal to him the mystery of both the woman and the beast.

THE BEAST - HE WAS, IS NOT, AND WILL COME

The angel begins with the cryptic description that we have already looked at in connection with Antichrist and his fatal wound, "The beast that thou sawest was, and is not." He is not the same as before but yet he is the same. He will come forth in all of his power from the bottomless pit and yet he will ultimately be triumphed over and cast into hell, and the fact that he is vanquished will astound the entire world (all except for the Christian) because he is so exceedingly powerful that it seems that nothing should be able to prevail against him.

SEVEN EMPIRES, THEN A SEVENTH/EIGHTH EMPIRE

The seven heads of the beast are seven mountains; seven territories which have kings. Five heads have fallen, the angel says. That means that five of the kingdoms are now in the past: Egypt, Assyria, Ancient Babylon, Medea-Persia, and Greece. .

One head "is," the angel says. Keep in mind that the angel is speaking to John on the Island of Patmos in the first century. The head of the Beast which "is" is clearly the Roman Empire. She comprises the sixth head of the Beast. The seventh head has not yet appeared, says the angel, and when it does, it will be very short-lived. In its place will rise up an eighth, even though the vision of the beast does not show eight heads. That is because the eighth head is separate and yet of the seventh. It, too, will be cast into hell. This seventh/eighth head is Antichrist/Satan. Antichrist, the man, begins his reign, but within a very short space of time he is killed and a being identical to him, and yet different and even more vile, reigns in his stead. That is Satan.

Revelation 17:10 identifies the Beast as being the seventh head and yet Revelation 17:11 identifies the Beast as being the eighth head. He is both. This is the story of the fatal wound of Antichrist's told from the vantage point of Satan's kingdom! Daniel 11:20 prophesies the very same thing, "Then shall stand up in his estate a raiser of taxes in the glory of the kingdom: but within few days he shall be destroyed, neither in anger, nor in battle. And in his estate shall stand up a vile person, to whom they shall not give the honour of the kingdom [who will not be given the title of King]: but he shall come in peaceably, and obtain the kingdom by flatteries."

So of the seven heads, five are history, one exists in the time of John, and only one more will ever exist. That final kingdom will be the kingdom of Antichrist: Mystery Babylon. The final kingdom has ten horns, as John sees the vision. This is in complete accord with the ten toes and ten horns of Daniel's visions. The horns are the "ten" nation confederacy over which the Beast will rule. It is possible that the final number of nations will not be exactly ten. In prophecy, the number ten signifies a small, but indefinite number. Notice that verse 12 tells us that the confederacy of nations will have no power until the Beast comes to power. This is a complete contradiction of the commonly taught theory that the ten European nations will come together and produce the Antichrist. No, the Antichrist, according to both Daniel and Revelation, will come first and will pull together his confederacy of ten nations. He gives them power, not vice-versa. The angel says that they will have power for one hour, that is to say, for a brief time. They have only one common aim and that is to make war against the Lamb. This will happen at Armageddon when Jesus returns. Verse 14 bears out that Jesus will not return alone at Armageddon, rather, "They that are *with* him are called, and chosen, and faithful." In other words, when Jesus returns He will return with His Bride. There is no such thing as a post-trib Rapture.

ANTICHRIST'S KINGDOM DIVIDED - BABYLON DESTROYED

This vision of John concerning Satan's kingdom now gives us an amazing detail about the end of time. Verse 16 tells us that the ten horns and the Beast will end up hating the Whore and will destroy her with fire. Satan will himself destroy the city of Babylon! *Why* he will is not told to us, but *that* he will is certain. Although the *King James Version* reads that the ten horns are upon the beast, a literal translation of the passage makes a distinction between the beast and the horns. So apparently there is friction not only between Babylon and Antichrist, there is also friction between Babylon and the rest of Antichrist's empire. It will increase until Babylon is destroyed by her own allies. It may be that, as Babylon assumes more and more importance and power in the world, Satan becomes threatened by his own creation and so decides to destroy her. After all, Satan very well remembers his own rebellion towards his own creator, God, and so assumes that all powerful entities will react with the same treachery and violence. Whatever the reason, Jesus discussed this very thing - Satan warring against Satan - in Matthew 12:26, and He foretold what would happen as a consequence: "And if Satan cast out Satan, he is divided against himself; how shall then his kingdom stand?" The answer is simple: it won't. Satan and his kingdom are about to disappear off the face of the earth. Contrast Satan's treatment of his church with that of Jesus' treatment of His church! As incredible as that treatment may seem, the angel tells John the underlying reason for why it happens: "For God hath put in their hearts to fulfill his will." God uses even the wicked for His purposes.

BABYLON MEANS BABYLON

Lest there be any confusion about whom the Great Whore symbolizes, the angel repeats who she is in verse 18: She is the great city Babylon which reigns over the kings of the earth. It is interesting to me to listen to how this scripture is interpreted by many. Ignoring the fact that the Bible identifies her as Babylon many, many times, eschatologists insist that God did not really mean Babylon when he said Babylon. No, they argue, He meant Rome or He meant New York or He meant San Francisco. That argument sets dangerous precedent. There is no biblical basis for deciding that God really means other than what He says.

What if we take this approach of deciding that, although God says one thing He really means another as we study another passage such as Hebrews 11? Granted, the writer uses the phrase "by faith" numerous times, but so what? By the same method that dismisses the meaning of "Babylon," we could argue that what was really meant to be said here was "by works." The Scripture would then be preached as, "But without works it is impossible to please him [God]." It is immediately apparent that that would radically alter the point of the scripture. How, then, does one say that although God says Babylon - an actual, identifiable location - numerous, numerous times - He actually meant to say Rome? It is ridiculous. Rome was an actual, identifiable location at the time that Revelation was written; if God meant Rome He would have said Rome. So, when God names Babylon as being the name of that great and evil city we must assume that He means exactly that.

Granted, there have been spots upon the earth which have been Satanic strongholds, Pergamum being identified as one of those in Revelation 2. However, God Himself has identified for us the ultimate location of Satan's stronghold in the times of the end, and He has identified it as being in Babylon. Evil had its beginning on the earth in Babylon, and evil will have its culmination on the earth in Babylon. Perhaps people have had a difficult time with the idea that Babylon literally means Babylon because of the condition of modern-day Babylon. God, on the other hand, does not look at her condition in the early twenty-first century, He looks into the future and sees how she will appear at the time of Antichrist. Babylon will be rebuilt and will be exactly the city that we see portrayed in Revelation 17 and 18.

BABYLON REBUILT - BEFORE OR AFTER RAPTURE?

The obvious question is when is that great city built? Could it be after Rapture under the six seals when the world comes under complete war, extreme famine, when death and hell roam freely about the earth as the horsemen of the fourth apocalypse? Maybe it is during the time of the earthquake when men hide themselves in the dens and rocks of the mountains, or possibly in the time when the sun becomes black and the moon becomes blood. Absolutely not! It is ridiculous to postulate that the building of the greatest city that this world will ever see could be built in times like those.

Well, then, is it built under the seventh seal when, under the fourth trumpet, we see the earth hit with bloody hail that produces gruesome, pus-filled sores on people, turns water supplies bloody, and brings on extreme heat? Perhaps it is built when the world is overrun with the demonic creatures that torment night and day for five months, or maybe when the world is preparing to fight God and all of His forces at Armageddon. Ridiculous! To teach that Babylon is built at any time after the Rapture, during such a time of trouble as never was, is to ignore the entire book of Revelation. We are left with the only conclusion open to us after studying this book: If it can't happen after the Rapture then it must happen before the Rapture. If Babylon is not yet built, do not look for Rapture; it will not happen. But when it comes to pass that Babylon finally is restored as it must be, then, "look up, for your redemption draweth nigh"!

BABYLON DESTROYED - BEFORE OR AFTER RAPTURE?

When, then, will Babylon be destroyed? In the time after the Rapture and just before the Battle of Armageddon. Isaiah 13:1,9,10 tells us that it will take place in a time when the stars and sun are darkened. Isaiah 13:11-13 and Jeremiah 51:49 tells us that it will be in a time of judgment for all nations. Isaiah 14:4-23 tells us that her destruction is directly associated with the enslavement of Satan, which will happen when Jesus comes again at Armageddon. Isaiah 14:7-8 tells us that her destruction will be followed by a time of universal rest and peace.

Babylon's destruction will be complete. According to Isaiah 13:19 and Jeremiah 50:40 the city will become as desolate as Sodom and Gomorrah. It, too, will be burned completely with no remains whatsoever. Furthermore, the city will be forever desolate, with neither man nor beast entering it any more according to Isaiah 13:20 and Jeremiah 51:62. Although Babylon will be a city with both buildings and pavement covered in gold, no one will even scavenge through her remains for the treasures. Jeremiah 51:26 says that even the stones of Babylon will never be used in future construction elsewhere.

These are very important scriptures to consider when one is studying the prophecies concerning the destruction of Babylon because many will attest that all of the prophecies concerning her destruction have already been fulfilled. Really? When have both the sun and stars been darkened? How did the historians of the world miss the event of the judgment of all the nations? When was Satan enslaved? When has there ever been a time of universal rest and peace? Finally, is Babylon still intact in her former glory because no one has ever plundered the stones to use in later constructions? Of course not! We are left with the inescapable conclusion that the prophecies concerning Babylon have not yet been fulfilled! They await the rise of Antichrist.

CHAPTER 21
BABYLON IS FALLEN
Revelation 18

BABYLON - A GRAND CITY OF THE LAST DAYS

Much space in Revelation is given over to the discussion of Babylon. More space is given over to a discussion of her than is given to the entire seven letters to the Church! God is imploring us to believe Him and not dismiss the fact that this incredible city will actually exist at the times of the end. Yet and still, many eschatologists dismiss Babylon's actual existence. Just as Revelation 17 revealed Satan's church throughout history, so now does Revelation 18 reveal the form that she, Babylon, will take at the end of time. Revelation 17 deals with Babylon as a religion and as a system, Revelation 18 deals with Babylon as a city. Revelation 18 does not deal with a philosophy, it deals with the concrete form that the religion and system will assume.

The city of Babylon will be unlike any other city that has ever been seen on earth. The angel describes it as clothed in fine linens and decked with gold, precious stones, and pearls. Not a person alive has ever seen a city so grand. The gold and precious stones mentioned here are not found in the museums of Babylon; the gold and precious stones are the pavement and outdoor decorations of Babylon. The city must glitter as no other city ever has! The city is also draped in fine linen that the angel describes as being of purple and scarlet hue. In John's time, purple and scarlet fabric was enormously expensive and thus reserved only for royalty and the very wealthy. It is estimated that enough dye to color one pound of clothing would have cost $84,000 in today's dollars. The reason for this was that in order to extract an ounce of purple dye, about 12,000 murex snails had to be crushed by a very arduous method. Purple and red-purple (scarlet) fabric was considered to be treasure, much as was gold and silver.

When Alexander the Great conquered the Media-Persian Empire, he recovered 270,000 pounds of purple fabric that had been looted from Greece two hundred years before. The fabric color was still vivid. Now, imagine draping a city in such costly material. The elements, whether sunshine or rain, and the smog and pollution found in a city would make the care and cleaning of such decoration expensive and continual. Imagine the dry-cleaning bill! No matter, Babylon is rich. And the care and grooming given to the city must be in somewhat the same vein as the steam cleaning that Disneyland receives every night after the park closes. We who think we have seen beautiful cities have seen only hovels compared to the beauty that will be Babylon's.

BABYLON, THE EVIL CITY, IS FALLEN

While to the human eye, Babylon, exactly like the cup that the whore holds in her hand, will be enormously impressive and unbelievably rich, able to fulfill every human lust, to the eyes in heaven she is unbelievably filthy; the habitation of devils and the home of every foul spirit. While Babylon is still in the apex of its power, a mighty angel descends from heaven with a show of power and glory so amazing that it sets the entire earth aglow with its light. As that appearance amazes all of earth, an incredibly loud voice resounds throughout earth with an amazing pronouncement: Babylon is fallen; Babylon is history. This must seem completely ludicrous to the people living on earth because they can see with their own eyes that Babylon is still the magnificent city of the ages. But that does not negate the fact that God, who is not bound by time, has declared that it is destroyed. And once something is spoken out of the mouth of God, it is a sure thing.

JESUS VICTORIOUS OVER SYSTEM AND RELIGION OF BABYLON

Not only does God say that Babylon is now fallen, the very same thing was said by Jesus while He was on the earth. In Matthew 16: 13-20 we read the story of Peter's great confession of Jesus as the Son of God. Jesus had led His disciples to the coasts of Caesarea Philippi, a place notorious for its wickedness and idolatry. It had long been associated with Baal worship, and the ruins of steps to a "high place" or place of idol worship were still present there. Not only were the remnants of Baal worship still present, the worship of the Roman god of fertility, Pan, had long prevailed in Caesarea Philippi and many statues of Pan were set into the rock face which now looked down on Jesus and His disciples. When Jesus answered Peter that upon this rock He would build His Church, He was in the presence of the idolatrous rock face that assaulted His view.

Jesus was saying to the disciples that He would build a church that would take over that pagan rock and all the pagan religions, usurping them completely. And when He said that the gates of hell would not prevail against His Church, remember that the usage of the term "gates" calls to mind a defensive, not offensive image. Gates do not wage battle, they prevent entry and foreign domination. Jesus was emphatically stating that He would wage war into the very realm of evil itself and that the gates of evil would not be able to withstand Him and His church. His was a statement and a prophecy that His Church would triumph over the system and the religion of Babylon!

BABYLON'S FALL - THE THIRD TELLING

With the statement in Revelation 18 that "Babylon is fallen," the angel who proclaims it lets us know exactly where we are in this third time-line; the time line from Satan's perspective. That is because when the story was told from the viewpoint of the earth, the angel also proclaimed that Babylon is fallen (Revelation 14:8), and did so when the Second Seal was opened.

The question then arises as to why the third telling of the story begins with the Second Seal instead of the First Seal. What happened to the First Seal - the preaching of the gospel from heaven? Why is it not spoken of in this third telling? Because this third telling is the story from Satan's point of view and that point of view would not concern itself with the giving or hearing of the gospel. The preaching of the gospel will have no effect whatsoever on those who belong to Satan, and so, it is not included in the story. Therefore, the story line concerning Satan's kingdom commences with the Second Seal, the taking of peace from the earth and the announcement of Babylon's impending destruction.

BACKGROUND OF BABYLON'S RISE TO WORLD CONTROL

Some background to the rise of Babylon is given to us in Zechariah 5:5-11 which was a vision of the prophet, Zechariah. He recorded it as follows: "Then the angel that talked with me went forth, and said unto me, Lift up now thine eyes, and see what is this that goeth forth. And I said, What is it? And he said, This is an Ephah that goeth forth. He said moreover, This is their resemblance through all the earth. And, behold, there was lifted up a talent of lead: and this is a woman that sitteth in the midst of the ephah. And he said, This is wickedness. And he cast it into the midst of the ephah; and he cast the weight of lead upon the mouth thereof. Then lifted I up mine eyes, and looked, and, behold, there came out two women, and the wind was in their wings; for they had wings like the wings of a stork: and they lifted up the ephah between the earth and the heaven. Then said I to the angel that talked with me, Whither do these bear the ephah? And he said unto me, To build it an house in the land of Shinar [Babylon]: and it shall be established, and set there upon her own base."

Although this vision might be hard to understand at first, it is important to study it because much information is contained in it. To begin with, one must understand what is meant by an *ephah*. It was a common commercial measure in Hebrew times and was the largest unit of dry measure in use. Here in Zechariah's vision, the *ephah* is not filled with goods; it is empty and thus will be used as a large container for something. It is no accident that the *ephah* is a *commercial* measure, for that implies that the world of commerce and finance is involved in this prophecy as, indeed, it is.

In the middle of this symbol of commerce and finance is found an extremely wicked woman, the same woman we find in Revelation 17: The Great Whore. As Zechariah watches, two women come to move this woman from her current place of power and rule to her new place of power and rule. *From* where they move her is not revealed, but *to* where they move her is: it is Babylon. This signifies that although her influence is now centered somewhere else - New York? London? Rome? - it will end up being exactly where Revelation says it will be, in Babylon. This will be a spiritual move as well as a physical move. We know this because the two women who transport her are said to have wings like a stork, and the stork was listed in the Old Testament as being an unclean bird. Something deemed unclean by God very clearly has a negative spiritual connotation. Because the women have these wings, they are being identified as unclean women. In prophecy, women are always symbols of religions. Thus, two religions are going to come together at the end times and that marriage will precipitate the move to Babylon. The union of these two religions - whatever they are - will result in the persecution of the Christians and will be part of the machinery that is responsible for hunting down and killing the saints at this time. Which religions they are is not specified other than to note that they are ungodly (unclean) religions. When this prophecy begins to happen, know that great changes are in the offing. Satan is on the move!

One other thing to note about this vision in Zechariah is that, up until the move to Babylon, wickedness, although very much a reality in this world, has been controlled and contained to some degree. The woman is inside the *ephah* and the lid is on. When we see the vision of this woman in Revelation, things have changed. Not only is she set loose from the *ephah*, she is arrayed in royal garments and is in control of all of the kings of the earth. The horrible and inescapable conclusion to be drawn is that by the time of Antichrist, no longer is wickedness contained in any way. To the contrary, it is completely in charge.

GOD'S WARNING TO HIS PEOPLE - FLEE THE CITY
As noted in the previous chapter, Babylon, in every regard, will be the premier city of the world at this time. The East will meet West here in a city of unparalleled wealth, splendor, and sophistication. Verse 3 gives us more insight into the wealth of the city when it speaks of the delicacies that she provides for the other cities of the world. Babylon will be the place to see and be seen. But a voice is heard in the city warning the people of God, primarily the Jews, but also any Christian living in these Tribulation times, to flee the city. The reason given for fleeing is two-fold. One, Babylon's influence is so great and so intoxicating that it will prove overpowering even to the people of God. They must flee the overpowering temptation that Babylon

affords. The second reason given to flee is that Babylon will soon be destroyed and all who are found there will also be destroyed. Fair warning to leave before the destruction of the city is given to the Jews and Christians in Babylon, just as fair warning to leave was given to Lot and his family before Sodom was destroyed by God. It is up to the people of the city to either heed the voice of God or to disobey it. If disobedience is the response, no mercy will be forthcoming, just as it was not with Lot's wife who was turned into a pillar of salt when she disobeyed God as she was leaving Sodom.

This very warning to leave is also foreshadowed in Isaiah 52:11-12: "Depart ye, depart ye, go ye out from thence, touch no unclean thing; go ye out of the midst of her; be ye clean, that bear the vessels of the Lord. For ye shall not go out with haste, nor go by flight: for the Lord will go before you; and the God of Israel will be your reward." The promise of safety is given to all who will heed the warning of God.

For millennia, God has watched the corruption that the system of Babylon has foisted upon the world. He has witnessed the countless lives that have been destroyed by it, He has seen the pain and suffering that it has heaped upon the poor and the defenseless; he has seen the martyrdom of millions of His people by the henchmen of Babylon, and now He has had enough of it. The cup of Babylon's wickedness is now full, her sins have piled up all the way to heaven, and the time of judgment has now come upon her.

Jeremiah 51:6-9 echoes this warning to leave and prophesies the destruction to come when God Himself is quoted as saying, "Flee out of the midst of Babylon, and deliver every man his soul: be not cut off in her iniquity; for this is the time of the Lord's vengeance; he will render unto her a recompense. Babylon hath been a golden cup in the Lord's hand, that the nations have drunken of her wine; therefore the nations are mad. Babylon is suddenly fallen and destroyed: howl for her; take balm for her pain, if so be she may be healed. We would have healed Babylon, but she is not healed: forsake her, and let us go every one into his own country: for her judgment reacheth unto heaven, and is lifted up even to the skies."

GOD BRINGS JUDGMENT ON SATAN'S SEAT OF EVIL

At this time, God will remember every bit of pain that Babylon ever inflicted upon any helpless or innocent person and will return it to her in a double portion. The pain of that judgment will be unimaginable. But do not pity her; even she could have been healed by God, but she utterly rejected His grace and refused to repent of her cruelty and pride. She was the most sadistic of power-wielders; delighting in the sorrow and torment that was hers to inflict, priding herself in the fact that she was invincible to justice. She boasts that she has an all-powerful protector, a husband. She is speaking of Satan.

In past times, a woman without a husband was very vulnerable. The lot of the woman who had no husband to protect and provide for her put her at the mercy of circumstance. Unlike that fragile and defenseless woman, Babylon is protected. Not only is she protected, she boasts that she is invincible because her husband, Satan has the pre-eminent power on earth. But she is deceived on two counts. One, she is not a wife, she is a whore. The attention that she has received from Satan may have induced her to believe that she is loved by him, but she is not. She is used by him and she will ultimately be destroyed by him. Two, although Satan has held control over the world up until now, the situation is about to change as the seals on the title deed to the earth are broken one by one.

Babylon's insolence and arrogance have deceived her into believing that Satan's power will last forever; she has not reckoned with the fact of the second coming of the Redeemer. Although Jesus' first coming and the fact of the cross shook her confidence for a little while, nothing much that she could see really changed with the *systems* on earth. True, she lost some individual subjects in her kingdom, but worldly power stayed right where it always had: with her. And so, protected and provided for, by her husband, Satan, she has declared herself truly Queen of the World.

A HOUSE DIVIDED - SATAN TURNS ON BABYLON

It has never crossed Babylon's mind for an instant that Satan would ever turn on her. But turn on her he does, never seeing that in doing so he is fulfilling the plan of God for her judgment. And who better than Satan to destroy her?

God would most probably have a limit to His wrath and judgment; Satan will have none. No pain, no torment, no cruelty is beyond him - he is the origin of it all. And now, with his limitless resources of cruelty, he will destroy Babylon. She will suffer far more under Satan's hands than under the hand of God, and so God gives the destruction of Babylon over to Satan with these words: "Therefore hear now this, thou that art given to pleasures, that dwellest carelessly, that sayest in thine heart, I am, and none else beside me; I shall not sit as a widow, neither shall I know the loss of children: But these two things shall come to thee in a moment in one day, the loss of children, and widowhood: they shall come upon thee *in their perfection* for the multitude of thy sorceries, and for the great abundance of thine enchantments. For thou hast trusted in thy wickedness: thou hast said, None seeth me. Thy wisdom and thy knowledge, it hath perverted thee; and thou hast said in thine heart, I am, and none else beside me. Therefore shall evil come upon thee; thou shalt not know from whence it riseth: and mischief shall fall upon thee; thou shalt not be able to put it off: and desolation shall come upon thee suddenly, which thou shalt not know. Stand now with thine enchantments, and with the multitude of thy sorceries, wherein thou hast laboured from thy youth; if so be thou shalt be able to profit, if so be thou mayest prevail. Thou art wearied in the multitude of thy counsels. Let now the astrologers, the stargazers, the monthly prognosticators, stand up, and save thee from these things that shall come upon thee. Behold, they shall be as stubble; the fire shall burn them; they shall not deliver themselves from the power of the flame: there shall not be a coal to warm at, nor fire to sit before it. Thus shall they be unto thee with whom thou hast laboured, even thy merchants, from thy youth: they shall wander every one to his quarter; none shall save thee" (Isaiah 47:8-15, emphasis mine).

Besides reiterating the boasts of Babylon, Isaiah echoes the fact that the occult will be predominant in Babylon when he mentions the astrologers, the stargazers, and the prognosticators. Babylon is truly, as the angel in Revelation states, the habitation of devils, the hold of every foul spirit, and the cage of every unclean and hateful bird.

Isaiah and Revelation also both state that her destruction at the hands of Satan will come in an instant and with no warning. There will be no perceptible tension, no obvious buildup for her to heed. She will be astonished at the turn of events and enraged at the treachery of her husband. And then she will feel only pain as she is utterly consumed by fire. It will come at the hands of Satan, but it will come because of the judgment of God.

THE WORLD MOURNS AS BABYLON BURNS

The world, too, will be astonished. The kings of the earth will be overwhelmed with grief when they see the smoke rising from Babylon. Verse 10 gives us some very interesting information about the fire. It tells us that all who come to mourn are "standing afar off for the fear of her torment." It also tells again that the torment came in "one hour." One fate that would be almost instantaneous and would also demand distance even in mourning would be nuclear destruction, or possibly the next generation of warfare to come after nuclear warfare.

Note that John faithfully scribes what he sees even though he knows that in the first century, the century that will be the initial recipient of his vision, it is completely impossible to destroy a city in one hour. The early Church must also have looked askance at this pronouncement, but the faithful accepted it. In fact, only those who have been living in the last sixty years have had to do other than take it on faith. Only since the atomic bomb was successfully tested at Trinity Site, New Mexico, has this passage become empirically believable. One hour is now ample time to destroy most anything. We twenty-first century readers pride ourselves on our sophistication, but yet we, too, react in unbelief to other pronouncements of John's; pronouncements that Babylon will be rebuilt and will be the pre-eminent city of the world; to the fact that the gospel will be preached from heaven; to the fact that the Antichrist will come before the Rapture and will deceive the entire world including much of the Church. Refusal to accept the hard words of Scripture is not limited to any one generation of readers.

THE WORLD MOURNS OUT OF SELF-CENTERED GREED

The world does not weep for Babylon for any altruistic reasons such as the destruction of countless human lives. No it weeps for its own selfish reasons. First, and foremost, the primary market for their products is destroyed, and thus, their own income is seriously impacted if not completely destroyed. Second, the source of their own luxuries and lust is destroyed, for they have grown accustomed to the diversity of goods that could be found in Babylon. Third, much of the culture of the world is destroyed in one fell swoop when Babylon is destroyed. And fourth, Babylon as a vacation and honeymoon destination is not available to the world anymore; the preeminent playground of the world is gone. Thus, the mourning for the city is as shallow and vacant and full of indulgent self-pity as was the city itself.

Even a partial listing of the goods that were found for sale in Babylon is impressive. Every part of the world has come to Babylon for her gold, silver, precious gems and pearls, the most expensive clothing available, costly furnishings, ivory (which is now so scarce that its sale is outlawed in the United States), brass, iron, marble, spices, perfumes and lotions, wine and gourmet foods, the finest horseflesh and breeding animals, and all else that would entice mankind. Notice that no one is establishing orphanages or funding other charitable works with their money at this time. No, only the wicked and self-serving are prospering now.

The most macabre of the listings of the items for sale is the trading of "slaves and the souls of men." The human misery inherent in that phrase is bottomless. But the system of Babylon is corrupt to its core. It can be argued that merchandise listed in verses twelve and thirteen is listed in descending order of valuation by society at that time. We see gold and silver and precious stones mentioned first as the most valuable. We see the souls of men mentioned dead last. The well being of mankind has always been despised by Satan and now that he is in power, man will sink to his lowest level of worth since time began.

Even when there is scarcity in the rest of the world because of the judgments from God, somehow Babylon has continued to provide luxury to those who can meet her price. Now, that source will forever be gone and she will have disappeared off the face of the earth before the time of Armageddon arrives.

EARTHLY TREASURES DESTROYED

Verse 17 reiterates that her demise will come in "one hour" and that the world will be terrified to come too close to her location for fear of contracting her "torment." Even so, the despair which greets the world when they see their one source of goods and luxury destroyed, their one ray of hope in an otherwise decimated world completely gone, compels them to come as close to her as they dare. A perverse need to see for themselves brings people near to the scene of the tragedy. The ships hover in the seas as they watch her burning, their crews casting "dust" of some sort on their heads as obvious signs of lamenting as they wail over their loss. With Babylon gone, gone also is their own hope of prosperity. They have been like the war profiteers of earlier eras who have, although the rest of the world has been sunk in misery, been making a fortune off of that collective misery. Now, their own situation is the same as the wretched person on the street and they cannot contain their grief and horror.

During the buildup to this time, the gospel is being preached from heaven but it is completely ignored by these people. Instead of responding to that gospel, they trust in their wealth, ignoring God's warning to "love not the world, neither the things that are in the world". Their folly in so doing is now obvious. They have no eternal treasures and their temporal ones are now destroyed. If this reader has put his trust in the things of the world, he, too, shall end up desolate and destitute; if not before death, certainly afterward.

HEAVEN REJOICES AT GOD'S JUDGMENT ON BABYLON

Meanwhile, John has been a witness to all this; everywhere he has looked he has seen weeping, wailing, agony, distress, and mourning. But then, John happens to look *up* and he sees a completely different set of reactions. All of heaven is rejoicing because of Babylon's destruction, just as earth is wailing over it.   God has avenged His people exactly as He long ago promised.   Babylon has disappeared off the face of the earth in the very way that the prophets foretold thousands of years ago. So certain is this fact that the angel even acts out the destruction.   He drops a huge weight into the sea and says that in the same way something that destructive will fall out of the sky onto Babylon obliterating her forever.

ISAIAH'S AND JEREMIAH'S PROPHECY OF BABYLON'S DESTRUCTION FULFILLED

"And Babylon, the glory of kingdoms, the beauty of the Chaldees excellency, shall be as when God overthrew Sodom and Gomorrah.   It shall never be inhabited, neither shall it be dwelt in from generation to generation: neither shall the Arabian pitch tent there; neither shall the shepherds make their fold there.   But wild beasts of the desert shall lie there; and their houses shall be full of doleful creatures; and owls shall dwell there, and satyrs shall dance there.   And the wild beasts of the islands shall cry in their desolate houses, and dragons in their pleasant palaces: and her time is near to come, and her days shall not be prolonged" (Isaiah 13:19-22).

"For I will rise up against them, saith the Lord of hosts, and cut off from Babylon the name, and remnant, and son, and nephew, saith the Lord.   I will also make it a possession for the bittern, and pools of water: and I will sweep it with the besom of destruction, saith the Lord of hosts.   The Lord of hosts hath sworn, saying, Surely as I have thought, so shall it come to pass; and as I have purposed, so shall it stand" (Isaiah 14:22-24).

"So Jeremiah wrote in a book all the evil that should come upon Babylon, even all these words that are written against Babylon.   And Jeremiah said to Seraiah, When thou comest to Babylon, and shalt see, and shalt read all these words; Then shalt thou say, O Lord, thou hast spoken against this place, to cut it off, that none shall remain in it, neither man nor beast, but that it shall be desolate for ever.   And it shall be, when thou hast made an end of reading this book, that thou shalt bind a stone to it, and cast it into the midst of Euphrates: And thou shalt say, Thus shall Babylon sink, and shall not rise from the evil that I will bring upon her: and they shall be weary. Thus far are the words of Jeremiah" (Jeremiah 51:60-64).

AN ANGEL DECLARES THAT MYSTERY BABYLON IS "NO MORE"

As heaven rejoices, the mighty angel announces that Babylon and all that was found in her will be no more. The city will be no more, her music will be no more, her artisans will be no more, her culture will be no more, her crops will be no more, her light will be no more, her young people will be no more. Seven times the angel announces, "no more." As has already been noted before, seven is the number of completion. The judgment on Babylon is total and heaven's joy at this long-deserved and final judgment is overwhelming.

Again, the angel tells John that this overarching system of Babylon has been the primal source of worldwide deception, and also the seminal reason that every righteous person has been killed since time began. Beyond that, Satan and his world system have been the reason for every murder. The prophets are mentioned, denoting the righteous who were slain in Old Testament times; the saints are mentioned, denoting the righteous who were slain since the time of Jesus; and if that isn't egregious enough, the angel also states that Satan's system is the reason every person ever killed has been slain, righteous or not.

Satan's religion has been the one constant evil in the world since Satan first appeared to Eve in Eden, and will remain so until the time of his defeat. And although Satan himself and many of his forces are still living and powerful at the time of Babylon's destruction, Satan himself has destroyed one of his most potent weapons of deception, corruption, and cruelty: Babylon. How long it takes Satan to realize that is unclear to us, but we do know that he will have Eternity in which to rue his rashness. As Solomon observed long ago, "There is no wisdom nor understanding nor counsel against the Lord," (Proverbs 21:30). Satan has now found that out.

CHAPTER 22
THE MARRIAGE OF THE LAMB AND THE BATTLE OF ARMAGEDDON
Revelation 19

PRAISE FOR JEHOVAH

Three things of major importance happen in Revelation 19; two great suppers --- one involving the righteous and one involving the unrighteous; and the Battle of Armageddon.

After John witnesses the destruction of Babylon, he hears the voices of multitudes of people praising God saying *Alleluia* (Hallelujah). Hallelujah literally means "Praise the Lord" and is the only word of which I am aware that is exactly the same in every language found on the earth. It is the universal word of praise for God, and here it is sounded together by the multitudes from every tongue, tribe, and nation on earth. In Scripture, this word is used when God's enemies have been put down and defeated. Revelation 19 is the *only* place that *Alleluia* is used in the entire New Testament and here it is used four times in six verses. This is a powerful indication as to how heaven is responding to the destruction of Babylon and to the coming again of Jesus.

The first two times that the multitudes shout *Alleluia*, it is in praise of God's judgments upon Babylon, the Great Whore. They praise not only her judgment by God, but also the fact that the servants of God have finally been avenged. The third *Alleluia* is shouted by the multitude because of the fact that the smoke of her burning will forever rise from the site that Babylon once occupied. Why does this call forth such heartfelt praise? The place where man first settled after the Fall, Babylon, will be one of only three places where He will never again allow man to inhabit (the other two being Edom and Hazor, a town on the border of Edom and Judea), but the eternal smoke will serve as a constant reminder both to the fact of the evil that filled earth and to the fact that God has conquered it. When God performed some mighty feat in the Old Testament --- such as when He parted the Red Sea or the Jordan River, or when He delivered the people of Israel in a major battle, or when God came down from heaven and had an encounter with man, He would always command that a monument be built there to memorialize the event. If the people questioned why, God would, in essence, reply that it was "because it is in the heart of man and in the mind of man to forget my goodness and strength and power. And, yes, you will remember the great battle that was fought here and you might tell your sons and daughters, but somewhere down the line people are going to stop talking about it. So I want the child of age seven to come upon this monument and ask 'Daddy, what is this all about? What does this mean?' And then you will remind them of My greatness and My mercy and My power and the story of my beneficence will live on." Americans have done the exact same thing with the memorials in Washington D.C., with Independence Hall and the Liberty Bell, with the Alamo and Gettysburg. With the eternal smoke arising from Babylon, mankind will never, never forget that there once was a hideous strength called Babylon and that God utterly defeated it.

At the utterance of the fourth *Alleluia*, the multitude looks beyond the deliverance of their own planet and people, and they rejoice in the fact of God's glorious person and His rightful place on the thrones of both heaven and earth. This is a scene that mirrors the scene in Revelation 4; the very first throne-room scene awaiting John after his rapture where we see not only the countless multitudes praising God, but we see the four living creatures and the twenty-four elders falling on their faces and saying "Amen" and *Alleluia*. Each time that *Alleluia* is uttered even now, demons cringe and angels rejoice, because it foreshadows the time of God's victory.

A voice is heard from out of the Throne of God itself commanding every servant of God to praise Him, from the most humble to the most exalted, for God is over all who have ever lived and none can raise their eyes to His face unless He bids them to do so. But He does so bid them. Long ago, God commanded a blessing upon His people saying, "The Lord bless thee, and keep thee: The Lord make his face shine upon thee and be gracious unto thee: The Lord lift up his countenance upon thee, and give thee peace," (Numbers 6:24-26). Twice in this passage we are told that we are allowed to see His face because He has chosen to be gracious to us. The saints and creatures of heaven can lift their eyes to the face of God and praise His name because of the mercy given to every soul found there.

PRAISE THE LORD AT ALL TIMES

Even though we understand that to praise God is an honor, we seem only to praise Him in happy situations. Why? The Bible exhorts us to praise God in every situation and I think that there are several reasons for that. First of all, one must humble oneself in order to praise. Second, it demonstrates our reliance upon God, and third, it acknowledges that God can do something about the situation. Fourth, it recognizes that God is Good and God is Just and we bow before His sovereignty.

When we begin to understand the spiritual underpinnings of praise we begin to understand that in difficult situations it is even more crucial to praise Him than in victorious situations. We begin to see that when His name is invoked in times of stress and crisis, He enters and commands the situation. Now if I run into a car and begin to curse, scream, whine, growl, and gripe I am inviting Satan into the situation at a time when he least needs to be invited. I am empowering Satan to continue his destruction when I so react. On the other hand, if, when something ill happens to us, we fill our surroundings with praise, we immediately give control of the situation over to God to work it out however He wishes. Every situation that we find ourselves in needs and demands praise to God.

THE LORD ALMIGHTY REIGNS

Along with the multitudinous voices lifted in praise comes the very voice of Jesus - the voice of many waters and the voice of mighty "thunderings" --- announcing that The Lord God omnipotent (all powerful) reigns. The world has already seen the reign of mankind. The world has just finished experiencing the reign of Antichrist. No wonder heaven breaks out in glorious praise at the promise of the reign upon the earth of Jesus! The praise of David in Psalm 72:1-11 is about to be realized: "Give the king thy judgments, O God, and thy righteousness unto the king's son. He shall judge thy people with righteousness, and thy poor with judgment. The mountains shall bring peace to the people, and the little hills, by righteousness. He shall judge the poor of the people, he shall save the children of the needy, and shall break in pieces the oppressor. They shall fear thee as long as the sun and moon endure, throughout all generations. He shall come down like rain upon the mown grass: as showers that water the earth. In his days shall the righteous flourish; and abundance of peace so long as the moon endureth. He shall have dominion also from sea to sea, and from the river unto the ends of the earth. They that dwell in the wilderness shall bow before him; and his enemies shall lick the dust. The kings of Tarshish and of the isles shall bring presents: the kings of Sheba and Seba shall offer gifts. Yea, all kings shall fall down before him: all nations shall serve him."

Even the most righteous of human governments have had major flaws in them. Justice has not always prevailed, truth has not always dominated. For as long as man has been upon the face of the earth, mankind has had to put up with inferior government at best, and oppressive, corrupt, and evil government at worst. Never again will that be the case, for the Lord himself will now reign. Indeed, the reign of Jesus will stand in marked contrast to man's. Not a cry will go unheard nor unanswered. Not a need will remain unmet. Truly, the lamb will lie down with the lion and there will be complete peace and complete righteousness from the rivers in the heartlands to the ends of the earth.

THE SEVENTH ANGEL IDENTIFIES THE TIME OF JESUS' REIGN

By the recording of these praises in Revelation 19 we know exactly where we are in the time line of Revelation because Revelation 11:15-17 records the same scene that we have just read in chapter 19: "And the seventh angel sounded; and there were great voices in heaven, saying, The kingdoms of this world are become the kingdoms of our Lord, and of his Christ; and he shall reign for ever and ever. And the four and twenty elders, which sat before God on their seats, fell upon their faces, and worshipped God, Saying, We give thee thanks, O Lord God Almighty, which art, and wast, and art to come; because thou hast taken to thee thy great power, and hast reigned."

Revelation 11 puts this same scene under the seventh and final seal, so we know that this is also where we are in Revelation 19.

JESUS TAKES A BRIDE

"I will greatly rejoice in the Lord, my soul shall be joyful in my God; for he hath clothed me with the garments of salvation, he hath covered me with the robe of righteousness, as a bridegroom decketh himself with ornaments, and as a bride adorneth herself with her jewels" (Isaiah 61:10).

The time has finally come for the long-awaited marriage between the Son of Man, Jesus, and His Bride, the Church. This marriage feast happens under the seventh seal just before the Battle of Armageddon. It is at this point that the believers are henceforth referred to as the wife of Christ. In the first three chapters of Revelation, they were called the Church. When the Church was raptured and the institution, as such, no longer remained upon the earth, the believers were called saints. Now and forevermore, they will be known as the wife of Christ.

Here begins a new phase in their relationship with Jesus, "...for his wife hath made herself ready." She has chosen to accept the hand of the groom, Jesus. This has not been a forced or arranged marriage. Each saint who is part of the Bride is part of the Bride because of his or her own volition. Even though Jesus has known from the beginning of time who would say yes to Him and who would say no to Him, the choice has been left up to each human. "The Lord is not slack concerning his promise, as some men count slackness; but is longsuffering to us-ward, *not willing that any should perish, but that all should come to repentance*" (2 Peter 3:9, emphasis mine). "For God so loved *the world* that he gave his only begotten Son, that *whosoever* believeth in him should not perish, but have everlasting life" (John 3:16, emphasis mine).

The marriage of the Lamb will be the formal and solemn acknowledgment that those who belong to Jesus will join Him as co-rulers on His throne and sharers of His dominion and glory. This has to be done before He comes again to earth because we are coming with Him and His great love for His Bride does not allow Him to claim His glory, even though it is completely His, without her. Jesus could claim His victory over the forces of Satan and then come back for us but He does not. He loves us so much that He chooses to share all that He has with His Bride. To marry the King of the Universe would take an enormous dowry. Still, Jesus looked down on us and loved us with an indescribable love, knowing that we would never be able to come up with the required price. So Jesus chose to pay it Himself with His life on the cross, and now His father is throwing the celebration of the ages.

Supper will be catered by the One who thought up every delicacy found on the earth; the floral arrangements will be done by the One who created every flower in the first place. Just as Melchizedek, the King of Righteousness and Peace, brought food and drink to Abraham as he returned victorious from his battle with the five kings, so shall Jesus spread a banquet before His victorious Bride. Why is the Bride victorious? Because of the victory wrought for her by her Groom. And what has the Bride done that she is so blessed by Him? Nothing but say "yes" to His love for her.

THE BRIDE IS DRESSED IN THE RIGHTEOUSNESS OF CHRIST

The Bride is arrayed in fine linen, clean and white, which has been given to her. It had to have been given to her because it symbolizes her righteousness and that righteousness is not hers personally; it is the righteousness of Christ. That righteousness had to be given to her, it could never be earned. Her own righteousness would be as filthy rags and how terrible it would be to have to be married in the most regal ceremony ever performed while wearing filthy rags! Linen, in contrast to woolen garments, was also ordained to be priestly attire because one would not perspire in linen as one would in wool. Again, perspiration comes about as a result of effort, which speaks of works. The Bride is not here because of her own works. It was Jesus who paid a dear price, she has done nothing but accept His love.

Not a person present will feel that any of this is deserved, all will know otherwise. Each person will be humbled and awed and blessed to be there; never, never will one say "I got here on my own." This is in marked contrast to the response of the average person on the street calling himself a Christian, if asked why he is going to heaven. His answer would most likely be, "Because I am a good person." That is one of the most malicious lies that Satan has propagated, because when people are relying on their own righteousness to get them to heaven, they are going to be in for a terrible awakening just when it is too late to do anything about it, exactly as Satan has planned.

THE MYSTERY OF MARRIAGE

In Ephesians, Paul compares the marriage of a man and a woman with the relationship between Christ and the Church, and he calls marriage a great mystery. Now, many of us who are married, wonder at this statement. What is so mysterious about marriage? Paul is prodding us to realize that we don't begin to understand what is meant by true union, and further, that we will be astounded when we do realize what all is entailed in the marriage between Jesus and His Bride, the Church. Even though the Scriptures speak often of this marriage supper, we don't have much detail given about it. One fascinating detail that I cannot explain is that there will be other people in attendance at the feast besides the Father, the Groom and the Bride. There will be the friends of the Bridegroom and the companions of the Bride. Who are these people? I do not know. I only know enough not to argue with God's account of it. The angels, too, know something about the Marriage Supper, but what they reveal is also minimal. They hint at that knowledge in verse 9 when one of them says, in effect, "I'll tell you one thing, blessed are they that are invited."

Psalm 45 does give us a glimpse into this feast. Note especially the following description, "All thy garments smell of myrrh, and aloes, and cassia, out of the ivory palaces, whereby they have made thee glad. Kings' daughters were among thy honourable women: upon thy right hand did stand the queen in gold of Ophir. Hearken, O daughter, and consider, and incline thine ear; forget also thine own people, and thy father's house; So shall the king greatly desire thy beauty: for he is thy Lord; and worship thou him" (verses 8-11).

The honor of being the Bride of Christ is extremely difficult for human minds to grasp. An inexact but beginning basis for comparison of what it means to attend the Marriage Feast of the Lamb might be the following. Imagine that I received an invitation from Queen Elizabeth inviting me to the royal wedding of Kate and Andrew, and afterward, to the most exclusive of the royal receptions, all expenses paid. I am stunned because I didn't know that Queen Elizabeth knew I even existed. But I RSVP in the affirmative and put the date on my calendar. I spend months agonizing over what to wear, and finally break the bank choosing a gown that I really like.

When I get to Buckingham Palace, I walk in and sit down in the very back of the hall. I immediately notice that the gown that I have so carefully chosen is woefully inadequate for the reception and I stand out like a sore thumb. Queen Elizabeth notices me and, without a word, presents me with the most gorgeous gown I've ever seen. I put on her gown and am once again heading toward the back of the room when I am stopped and told that I belong up at the head table. I now realize that this entire banquet is in my honor. The whole banquet is being thrown for me! Queen Elizabeth herself comes and serves me my dinner, bringing me water refills, giving me a new salad fork when I drop mine, clearing my table and saying in every way, "This is for you." Now, it would be enough for me if she had just winked at me and said "I'm glad you could make it from Thousand Oaks," but this reception is beyond imagining.

As far-fetched as that scene might be as far as my life is concerned, it is still a most anemic parallel to the Marriage Supper of the Lamb. Instead of simply being the guest of the Queen of England, we will be the spouse and greatly honored guests of the King of the Universe, the Mighty Lamb of God, and Jesus will demonstrate to you and to everyone in attendance just how much He loves you. He will even wait on you in order to prove His great and complete love for you. It will only be at this point that we'll find out just how blessed we are to be invited to the Marriage Feast.

THE ANGEL PRONOUNCES BLESSINGS ON THE GUESTS AT THE MARRIAGE SUPPER

Possibly, John, too, is so overwhelmed by the magnificence of the ceremony and the promises given to the Bride that he needs reassurance that the whole thing is real. In any case, an angel now appears to John and instructs him to write the following, "Blessed are they which are called unto the marriage supper of the Lamb," reiterating that everything that John has seen and heard is the truth and will come to pass. At this, John is so overcome with the promise that is both his and every other believer's, that he falls at the feet of the angel in order to worship him. An amazing thing now happens. The angel tells John to get up and not to worship him because he, too, is a fellow believer. John is seeing another Christian in a glorified state!

Not only does this incident give us insight into the change that our own mortal bodies will experience (such change that John himself does not recognize the angel as being a fellow mortal!), it also is a stern admonition to the fact that no man nor angel is worthy of worship. God alone is worthy to be worshipped, and thus the practice of the adoration of saints or any other human is a forbidden practice in the eyes of God. This passage also gives credence to the fact that the angels who preach the gospel from heaven according to Revelation 14 are not necessarily heavenly angels. Nothing precludes them scripturally from being believers, and it is clear that the "angel" in chapter 19 is a believer, therefore we cannot rule out the possibility that this is the case also in chapter 14. Remember that the word "angel" simply means "messenger" and so sometimes they are heavenly angels and sometimes they are saints. Furthermore, the giving of the gospel is the work that God entrusted to the believers, and the angel in Revelation 14 is doing exactly that.

The glorified believer (the angel) now says something that succinctly and perfectly sums up the purpose of the Book of Revelation and every other book of prophecy and that is that the testimony of Jesus is the spirit of prophecy because the ultimate goal and purpose of prophecy is to testify and reveal to us more of the nature and person of Jesus. Its main purpose is *not* to foretell events that are to come, which explains why so many world events are left out of prophecy; the purpose of prophecy is not to tell us how the United States aligns itself in the end; the purpose of prophecy is not to foretell the rise of Napoleon, Hitler, or Stalin; the purpose of prophecy is to acquaint us with the spirit of our Lord. And when we know

Him intimately, we are ready for anything that will greet us on the world scene.

JESUS ABOUT TO RETURN TO EARTH TO MINISTER JUSTICE

John now sees heaven opened to reveal Jesus Himself, seated upon a white horse. The thrill that must have gone through John is unimaginable. Here was his best friend on earth, his dearest companion, now glorified and resplendent with all glory and majesty. What a sight it must have been! The name now ascribed to Jesus is that of Faithful and True. None other is so faithful, none other is so true; and in righteousness, He will now judge and make war. His coming is, in fact, the culmination of every promise and prophecy that has ever come out of the mouth of God. Jesus left heaven once before when He came to earth as the suffering savior. He has a different mission now; He is coming back to the earth as the minister of righteousness in order to fight a final and truly righteous war that will destroy all that is evil. He will now take back everything that has been lost to sin. This will be the Battle of Armageddon, where all the forces of darkness will oppose all the forces of light. It will be a physical and a supernatural battle all at the same time, for every magical and occultic device in Satan's arsenal of war will surely be used. It will be the Greatest War of all time.

Jesus is seated upon a white horse. We have seen a white horse coming out of heaven once before in Revelation 6 where it heralded the preaching of the gospel from heaven; now, it heralds the Lord of that gospel. When we see that Jesus Himself is seated on that horse, the common explanation that the previous rider, seen in Revelation 6 is the Antichrist becomes almost blasphemous. Then, as now, the white horse and his rider are reserved for righteousness.

The eyes of the rider are as flames of fire. Jesus will dispense perfect justice because He possesses perfect knowledge. Perfect knowledge is the symbolism of the eyes of fire. He also comes crowned with many crowns. The Dragon, Satan, had seven; the Beast, Antichrist, had ten. Then, and now, the accumulation of crowns signifies accumulated victories and dominion. Jesus comes as the one anointed by the King of the Universe, crowned with many crowns, and endowed with all the sovereignties of the earth as His rightful due and possession. It is gratifying to realize that at least some of these crowns are the crowns that the saints removed from their heads and placed at the feet of Jesus in Chapter Four. His victories and dominions include our very lives!

From this point on, Jesus will be known by a new name. It is not given here, in fact, at this point it is known only to Him. Names are very important to God and the name that Jesus will wear will encompass His entire character and nature. Remember that each overcomer has also been given a new name by God that is known only to that believer and it, too, will completely encompass his character and nature. Usually, when one marries, the bride takes on a new name. Jesus has already given His name to His beloved and therefore they are already called *Christ*ians. But each believer will receive a new first name also. It is my guess that at some point, in some glorious ceremony, all the names of the Bride and the name of the Groom will be revealed - maybe at the Wedding Feast itself - but for now, for reasons known only to God, the new names are undisclosed.

JESUS' BLOODSTAINED GARMENTS

Upon this white horse, crowned with many crowns, the rider is clothed with singularly arresting clothing. It is a vesture, a covering, which has been dipped in blood. If this is not unsettling enough, all of the armies that follow him out of heaven are clothed in fine linen, white and clean. The contrast could not be more amazing. What is the King of kings, the Word of God doing with the bloodstained garments while all those under His command have garments that are impeccably clean? It is only the visual expression of the eternal truth of salvation. His blood was the blood spilled; ours was not; He paid the price: we came in free. It is completely in the nature of Jesus that He would wear the soiled garments and save the clean for us. In like manner, all of the bodies in heaven will be glorified and perfect except for one. The one body in Heaven that is scarred is the body of the King - Jesus, while all of His saints will possess perfect, unmarred bodies. The scars of Jesus, which bear silent testimony to His sacrifice and suffering, are far too beautiful and precious to ever be erased.

John was not the first to see this vision of Christ. Isaiah saw it over seven hundred years earlier, and recorded it in Isaiah 63:1-4: "Who is this that cometh from Edom, with dyed garments from Bozrah this that is glorious in his apparel, travelling in the greatness of his strength? I that speak in righteousness, mighty to save. Wherefore art thou red in thine apparel, and thy garments like him that treadeth in the winefat? I have trodden the winepress alone; and of the people there was none with me: for I will tread them in mine anger, and trample them in my fury; and their blood shall be sprinkled upon my garments, and I will stain all my raiment. For the day of vengeance is in mine heart, and the year of my redeemed is come."

JESUS FOLLOWED BY ARMY OF SAINTS

The armies that follow Jesus were also foreseen. Consider Joel 2:11: "And the Lord shall utter his voice before his army: for his camp is very great: for he is strong that executeth his word: for the day of the Lord is great and very terrible; and who can abide it?" Who are the armies that follow Jesus out of heaven? The saints. We know that to be the case because the clothing is clearly the clothing of saints, but beyond that, the return of the saints with Jesus has been prophesied several times in the Bible. "For if we believe that Jesus died and rose again, even so them also which sleep in Jesus will God bring with him" (I Thessalonians 4:14).

"And Enoch also, the seventh from Adam, prophesied of these, saying, Behold, the Lord cometh with ten thousands of his saints. To execute judgment upon all, and to convince all that are ungodly among them of all their ungodly deeds which they have ungodly committed, and of all their hard speeches which ungodly sinners have spoken against him" (Jude 14-15).

"And ye shall flee to the valley of the mountains...and the Lord my God shall come and all the saints with thee" (Zechariah 14:5).

When Jesus comes back to earth, all who are still there will oppose Him, mourning and wailing at His coming (Revelation 1:7). It now becomes perfectly clear as to the reason that all of the earth will wail and mourn at the coming of Jesus. It is because all who love Him and belong to Him are with Him in the heavens, and are now coming back with Him to the earth. Clearly, the post-tribulation-rapture theory, the theory that says that the saints will not be raptured until after Armageddon, does not square with Scripture.

THE DESTROYING SWORD

The physical description of Jesus given as He rides out of heaven on the white horse is in perfect agreement with the description of Jesus that John gave in the first chapter of Revelation. The eyes of fire are the same and now we see the same sharp sword that comes out of the mouth of Jesus. That sword is the Word of God, and now that word will smite the nations of the earth that have aligned themselves with Antichrist and are gathering at Armageddon to oppose the forces of God.

When Jesus was in the Garden of Gethsemane with His disciples at the end of His life, an angry mob came to arrest Him. It was nighttime, and the crowd came with torches and swords to take Him by force. It must have been a scene somewhat like the scene in *Dracula* when the torch-bearing townspeople descended on the castle. The disciples must surely have panicked at the sight, watching their worst nightmare come true before their eyes as Jesus asks the mob, "Whom seek ye?" and they reply "Jesus of Nazareth." Then, in the midst of all this uproar and frenzy, Jesus simply answers, "I am he," and that terse utterance was so full of power that it caused Jesus' enemies to fall backward into a heap on the ground. If so mild an utterance prostrated His enemies then, what will happen this time?!

With a word from His mouth, God created the world; with a word from His mouth, He will now destroy every bit of evil found in the world. It won't take years, it will only take brandishing the sword of His word; the sword which proceeds out of His Mouth. He will utterly defeat the nations that have come to war against Him and His saints, and then He will rule them with a rod of iron. In other words, it will be a strict and unbending rule that will be necessary in order for the nations to learn His ways.

We are told in other books of prophecy and in the next chapter of Revelation that Jesus will rule over the nations from the holy city, Jerusalem. And we are also told that He will not rule over them alone; He has already given co-rulership over the nations to the overcoming saints who are now returning in power with Jesus. This is a fulfillment of Psalm 2:6-12, which prophesied: "Yet have I set my king upon my holy hill of Zion. I will declare the decree: the Lord hath said unto me, Thou art my Son; this day have I begotten thee, Ask of me, and I shall give thee the heathen for thine inheritance, and the uttermost parts of the earth for thy possession. Thou shalt break them with a rod of iron; thou shalt dash them in pieces like a potter's vessel. Be wise now therefore, O ye kings: be instructed, ye judges of the earth. Serve the Lord with fear, and rejoice with trembling. Kiss the Son, lest he be angry, and ye perish from the way, when his wrath is kindled but a little. Blessed are all they that put their trust in him."

There have been times and events in history that I would have given almost anything in order to have been present. I wish I could have heard Abraham Lincoln give the Gettysburg Address; I wish I could have witnessed the signing of the Magna Carta (especially because two of my direct ancestors were there!), or even the signing of the Declaration of Independence; I wish I could have heard Paul preach the sermon on Mars Hill or watched Moses part the waters of the Red Sea. But when Jesus rides out of heaven, I *will* be there to see it! I will be an eyewitness to the most glorious event ever to happen in the history of time.

THE NAME ABOVE ALL NAMES

Jesus displays a title as He rides out of heaven. He also displayed a title as He hung on the cross. That time, the title had been composed by Pilate and it read: JESUS OF NAZARETH THE KING OF THE JEWS. This time, it is composed by God and it reads: KING OF KINGS AND LORD OF LORDS. No greater title has ever been held and no one other than God Himself can claim it. It is found both on Jesus' clothing and on His very body at the site of His thigh. According to scripture, the thigh was the seat of authority. God commanded that each male Jew wear a prayer tassel, divided into four parts, which covered and rested upon the thigh. The purpose for the tassel was to remind each man of his standing before God and of the fact that he was accountable for everything that he did in his household. As he ruled over his household with authority, it was understood that his authority was; (1) derived from God and, (2) had to be held accountable to God. Thus, if he were to rule over his household in a cruel and despotic manner, he would ultimately be judged for that behavior. Jesus' name is on His thigh because His authority is found in His name. It is in Jesus' name that Christians find authority over Satan and the world when they pray.

The thigh was also indicative of power because a man's sword was worn upon his thigh. The power of Jesus is found also in His name. By that name the world was created, by that name heaven was established, by that name Satan will be put down. The name of Jesus is the most powerful force in the Universe. When one stops to consider that it is at the name of Jesus that every knee shall bow and every tongue confess that He indeed is King of kings and Lord of lords, and that the name of Jesus is above every other name which is found either in heaven or on earth, it is a staggering thought to realize that it is His name which He has given to each believer to wear.

The placement of Jesus' title upon His thigh is also significant because the thigh was the place where many times an oath was sworn. The person making the oath or promise would place his hand under the thigh of the person to whom the promise was being made, probably as an invocation of the posterity that proceeds from the loins. It thusly signified the intention to guard the oath and avenge its violation throughout succeeding generations. The promise made to Jesus by His Father is an eternal promise and one that is sure; so sure in fact that it is found upon Jesus' very person.

ARMAGEDDON AND THE GREAT SUPPER

John now sees an angel standing in the sun. Angels are commonly identified with stars. The sun is a star and it is possible that this angel's province is the sun. If so, this angel has been deeply involved with the history of Planet Earth. Regardless, it has been given to this angel to announce that the time for the great Feast of the Birds has now come. This is the feast in which the carrion fowl of the earth are called by God to feast upon the slain bodies which have fallen in the Battle of

Armageddon: The flesh of kings, captains, mighty men, horses, riders, and soldiers arrayed on the side of Antichrist. Such will be the horror of that battle, so great will be the carnage after that battle, that every carnivorous bird found in the earth will be called upon to help in the disposal of the bodies.

Because of the conditions that have been present on the earth for the last ten-and-one-half years --- famine, death, and destruction --- most of the species of the earth have been ravaged, including the human species. Only one species will have profited from all of the corpses and carcasses that have littered the landscape: The carrion birds. They, and only they, have had enough food, and their numbers must surely have exploded as the others dwindled.

Ezekiel also prophesied of the gathering of the birds at the time of the end at the same time that he prophesied that, in addition to the help from the birds, it would take seven months just to bury the dead slain in the battle. "And, thou son of man, thus saith the Lord God; Speak unto every feathered fowl, and to every beast of the field, Assemble yourselves, and come; gather yourselves on every side to my sacrifice that I do sacrifice for you, even a great sacrifice upon the mountains of Israel, that ye may eat flesh, and drink blood. Ye shall eat the flesh of the mighty, and drink the blood of the princes of the earth, of rams, of lambs, and of goats, of bullock, all of them fatlings of Bashan. And ye shall eat fat till ye be full, and drink blood till ye be drunken, of my sacrifice which I have sacrificed for you. *Thus ye shall be filled at my table with horses and chariots, with mighty men, and with all men of war, saith the Lord God.* And I will set my glory among the heathen, and all the heathen shall see my judgment that I have executed, and my hand that I have laid upon them. So the house of Israel shall know that I am the Lord their God from that day and forward" (Ezekiel 39:17-22, emphasis mine).

This Feast of the Birds is called by the angel in Revelation the "supper of the great God." It is, in fact, the second supper of the great God. The first took place a few verses back and it was the Marriage Supper of the Lamb. Everyone who will be feasted upon at the Feast of the Birds could have been an honored guest at the Marriage Supper of the Lamb, but they chose the wrath of God over the mercy of God. It is unimaginable that a person would do so, but yet we see people around us making the same decision every day!

CARRION BIRDS CALLED TO A GREAT FEAST

It will be an eerie sight indeed to watch the great ingathering of the carrion birds around Mount Megiddo as they respond to the call of the angel of the sun to assemble themselves. The armies of Antichrist have already sacked Jerusalem, completely overrunning the city, and now those "victorious" forces of evil are camped, awaiting the arrival of Jesus and His armies. Satan will be full of confidence at this point because he has just retaken Jerusalem, the holy city of God, and he has also finally been able to kill the Two Witnesses which he had striven to do but had not been able to do so for three years. It completely escapes the mind of Satan that the only reason that he was finally able to prevail against them was that God had finally allowed it. Instead, Satan figures that his power is waxing while God's power is waning, and he looks toward the sky in anticipation of that final battle at Armageddon. But first, instead of seeing the return of Jesus, Satan and his troops see large carrion birds beginning to assemble at the site. The birds come, roosting one by one until the limbs of the trees are groaning with them.

Usually, when these birds come, they smell blood, or something weak, or something dying, or something dead. This will not be the case here. Satan has assembled his forces with all of the power and all of the might that he can muster. There are no bleeding or weak people here. To the contrary, they are ready, rested, armed and geared for the fight of their lives. But the birds keep coming until the sky is black with them because the birds have heard the command to "assemble yourselves." Surely, some of the wicked will remember Alfred Hitchcock's movie, *The Birds*, at this point and it cannot help but strike terror in their hearts as they hear reports that every bird upon the face of the earth is now leaving its own habitation and is winging its way to the plains of Megiddo. They do not understand this yet, but this is the first sign of their imminent doom.

THE GREAT WAR AGAINST GOD IS CONCLUDED

John now looks toward the earth and also sees these forces that are called to make war against Jesus and His saints. He sees Antichrist and he sees the kings of the earth who are under the control of Antichrist along with all of the world's armies. What an ominous sight that must present to John! But the psalmist's words ring true: "Why do the heathen rage, and the people imagine a vain thing? The kings of the earth set themselves, and the rulers take counsel together, against the Lord, and against his anointed, saying, Let us break their bands asunder, and cast away their cords from us. He that sitteth in the heavens shall laugh: the Lord shall have them in derision" (Psalms 2:1-4).

John had seen the armies gather together at Armageddon in Revelation 16, but the story was interrupted in order to tell the story from the viewpoint of Satan's kingdom. Here, in Revelation 19, the stories finally unite because heaven has come down to earth, and Satan is about to meet God in a battle predestined from the ages. "Behold, the day of the Lord cometh, and thy spoil shall be divided in the midst of thee. For I will gather all nations against Jerusalem to battle; and the city shall be taken, and the houses rifled, and the women ravished; and half of the city shall go forth into captivity, and the residue of the people shall not be cut off from the city. Then shall the Lord go forth, and fight against those nations, as when he fought in the day of battle" (Zechariah 14:1-3).

As has been mentioned, this has already happened by the time of the gathering of the birds. The following is God's answer to it: "For, lo, I begin to bring evil on the city which is called by my name, and should ye be utterly unpunished? Ye shall not be unpunished: for I will call for a sword upon all the inhabitants of the earth, saith the Lord of hosts. Therefore prophesy thou against them all these words, and say unto them, The Lord shall roar from on high, and utter his voice from his holy habitation; he shall mightily roar upon his habitation; he shall give a shout, as they that tread the grapes, against all the inhabitants of the earth. A noise shall come even to the ends of the earth; for the Lord hath a controversy with the nations, he will plead with all flesh; he will give them that are wicked to the sword, saith the Lord. Thus saith the

Lord of hosts, Behold, evil shall go forth from nation to nation, and a great whirlwind shall be raised up from the coasts of the earth. And the slain of the Lord shall be at that day from one end of the earth even unto the other end of the earth: they shall not be lamented, neither gathered, nor buried; they shall be dung upon the ground" (Jeremiah 25: 29-33).

God utters a great shout and also a great and fearsome laugh (Psalm 37:13). To hear that laugh at such a time as this must be terrifying to His foes, and with good cause, for John records, "And the beast [Antichrist] was taken and with him the false prophet." Zechariah records, "And the Lord shall be king over all the earth: in that day shall there be one Lord, and his name one". Good will now conquer evil as this is the end result of the battle that has waged between God and Satan since the Great Rebellion took place in heaven eons ago.

THE LAKE OF FIRE - DESTINY OF ANTICHRIST AND THE FALSE PROPHET

When Jesus returns, the first thing He does is to come against Antichrist. It is clear, as we read the account of this battle, that Antichrist is a person, not a system. After all, a system cannot be thrown into the fire. A system exists, not in and of itself, but because people have chosen and empowered it. The only way to destroy a system is to conquer and destroy the followers. If the Beast were a system the followers would have been the first ones destroyed in order to defeat and dismantle the system. But the man is the first one destroyed, not some system, because the mark of the 666 is the mark of a man.

Both the Antichrist and the False Prophet are seized and thrown alive into the Lake of Fire. When this happens, it will comprise an inverse Rapture: punishment without first experiencing death. Just as the rapture will reunite our body soul and spirit, this time of inverse rapture could be when Antichrist's (the seventh beast) body and soul, unites with Satan's (the eighth beast) spirit. Isaiah prophesied this end for Antichrist in Isaiah 14:20: "Thou shalt not be joined with them in burial, because thou hast destroyed thy land, and slain thy people: the seed of evildoers shall never be renowned."

Daniel also foresaw the end of Antichrist. He wrote in Daniel 7:11, "I beheld then because of the voice of the great words which the horn [Antichrist] spake: I beheld even till the beast was slain, and his body destroyed, and given to the burning flame." There is a mystery involved with the destruction of Antichrist for it appeared to Daniel that Antichrist was as a dead man, whereas John makes it clear that he is very much alive when he is delivered to hell. The Apostle Paul weighs in about Antichrist's destruction in 2 Thessalonians 2:8-9 when he writes, "And then shall that Wicked be revealed, whom the Lord shall consume with the spirit of his mouth, and shall destroy with the brightness of his coming: Even him, whose coming is after the working of Satan with all power and signs and lying wonders." Here, Paul, along with John, includes both Antichrist and the False Prophet in this day of destruction, as it is the False Prophet who displays the signs and lying wonders. Apparently, Jesus speaks forth the word of their judgment and it consumes them without actually destroying them. Daniel saw them consumed, John saw them delivered alive to hell, and Paul describes what happens. These accounts are not contradictory, they simply add detail to the story. How it is that Jesus can consume the Antichrist and the False Prophet while not killing them, can begin to be contemplated when we remember that Jesus talked about the place where "the worm dieth not." In other words, punishment is all-consuming but also eternal. Full comprehension of how that is possible will have to wait until that day.

THE "WORD" DESTROYS ANTICHRIST'S ARMIES

The sword that proceeds out of the mouth of Jesus - the very word of God - will now commence to destroy the armies of Antichrist. This will not be hand-to-hand combat; no, with a word from the mouth of Jesus they will be destroyed. Isaiah reiterates this in Isaiah 11:4 when he writes, "But with righteousness shall he judge the poor, and reprove with equity for the meek of the earth: *and he shall smite the earth with the rod of his mouth*, and with the breath of his lips shall he slay the wicked" (emphasis mine).

The force of the word out of the mouth of Jesus will literally consume His enemies according to Zechariah 14:12-13, "And this shall be the plague wherewith the Lord will smite all the people that have fought against Jerusalem; Their flesh shall consume away while they stand upon their feet, and their eyes shall consume away in their holes, and their tongue shall consume away in their mouth. And it shall come to pass in that day, that a great tumult from the Lord shall be among them; and they shall lay hold every one on the hand of his neighbour, and his hand shall rise up against the hand of his neighbour."

After all, Hebrews 4:12 tells us that "the word of God is quick, and powerful, and sharper than any two-edged sword, piercing even to the dividing asunder of soul and spirit, and of the joints and marrow." Those in closest proximity to Jesus will be vaporized ("their flesh shall consume away while they stand upon their feet"), and this so horrifies the people who see this, that they panic and start slashing and killing those around them. This terror from God that will cause them to turn on one another is not a new tactic with God. He used the exact same tactic in Gideon's battle with the Midianites and it brought about a complete and total victory for Israel, even though she was vastly outnumbered by her foes.

The slaughter at Armageddon, however, will be unparalleled in human history. The blood is said to run as high as the necks of the horses, and, as has been stated, it will take seven months to bury the dead. As George Frederic Handel so aptly paraphrased the prophet Joel when he asked in his great work *The Messiah*, "For who may abide the day of His coming?" The answer is simple: Only those who belong to Him.

PART SIX: THE KINGDOM OF CHRIST

CHAPTER 23
THE THOUSAND-YEAR REIGN
Revelation 20

EVENTS OF REVELATION THAT PRECEDE CHAPTER 20

With chapter 20, John begins a new phase in Revelation. Remember that in Revelation 1 John recorded the circumstances of his being on the Isle of Patmos and his vision of the resurrected and transfigured Jesus Christ. Chapters 2-3 concerned the letters to the seven churches; letters which were also a prophetic account of the entire Church Age which will span the time from the first century until the coming of Jesus for His church at Rapture. Chapters 4-5 recorded the great throne-room-worship service as Jesus and His Father received the believers and prepared to take back Planet Earth from Satan. John saw a little book, sealed with seven seals, which was the title deed to the earth. The breaking of each of those seals comprised the period of time known as the Great Tribulation. The story of the Great Tribulation is then told three different times from three different viewpoints. Chapters 6-11 records the first telling of the story from the vantage point of heaven. Then chapters 12-16 told the story a second time, this time from the perspective of earth. The third and final telling of the story, this time from the viewpoint of Babylon, Satan's kingdom, was recorded in chapters 17-19.

Now, with chapter 20 John will tell the story of the thousand-year reign of Jesus and His Bride upon the earth. This time is commonly called the Millennial Reign of Jesus. It is not the beginning of a new age, it is the culmination of an old one. Just as the Sabbath comes at *the end* of the week, so the Millennium comes *at the end* of the age. It is not the end of human history, however. In fact, *most* of human history lies ahead.

SUMMARY OF THE THOUSAND-YEAR REIGN

Much of great importance will happen during the thousand-year reign of Jesus and His saints. Satan will be imprisoned and those who are still alive upon earth after the Battle of Armageddon will be judged. Jesus will establish His kingdom on earth; and for the first time since God first placed Adam in the Garden of Eden Right, not Might, will be the universal standard and rule for the human race. Finally, at the end of the thousand years, Satan will again be set loose upon the earth for a short time to try the souls of men. After he is consigned to the Lake of Fire, all who remain to be judged --- the dead who have not yet been raised --- will face their judgment at the Great White Throne of God.

CHAPTER 20 IS LITERAL NOT SYMBOLIC

This passage opens with the Greek word *kai*, translated into English as "and," but it indicates more than just a continuation of the story; it indicates that what is about to be read is a continuation of *literal* action. In other words, what Revelation 20 records is not symbolic, it is prophetic and will come to pass exactly as written. Chapter 20 is as literal as is chapter 19; the thousand-year reign is as certain as is the great war of Armageddon. Many people have argued against that, ignoring the implication of the word *kai*, and insisting that the thousand years spoken of here is purely symbolic. That is the viewpoint taken by the amillennialists who simply ignore the body of prophetic scripture that speaks of the Millennium. Why then, in the space of seven short verses, is the time of one thousand years reiterated SIX times?! Clearly, God is trying to get our attention by hammering the time of "one thousand years" over and over in our heads.

The Bible is never overstated nor is it hyperbolic. To the contrary, it is remarkably terse and understated. The mentioning of "one thousand years" six times breaks that pattern of terseness and it breaks that pattern for a decided reason: God wants us to take the time of one thousand years seriously. Even so, many do not. Some quote that Peter made the assertion that a day is as a thousand years to the Lord, and so possibly this whole time lasts only a day. When Peter made that statement, he was making the point that God does not live in time, and furthermore, He is not constrained by it. That does not mean that God did not create time and does not use it; He does. And here, He tells us what is in store for the earth in six different statements. Using the thousand years/one day argument here is as ludicrous as arguing that because the

Bible says that Jesus was in the grave three days, He was actually in the grave three thousand years! Note, also, how decimated the human population is at the beginning of the chapter in contrast to how vast are the numbers of people at the end of the chapter. That change will take time - the time that one thousand years gives.

A second group, the post-millennialists, teaches that man himself will get the world ready for Jesus before His return. In fact, they teach, Jesus cannot return until man has accomplished this task. Besides taking the return of Jesus out of the control of God that is completely refuted by Scripture, that position further errs by assuming that man will be able to effect the regeneration of the earth by his own abilities and effort. So far, all of human history, in addition to all of the Book of Revelation has debunked that theory in its entirety. As Revelation 5 asks and then answers, "Who is worthy to take the Book and open the seals?" Only the Lamb. Only the Lamb is worthy to lay claim to the title deed of the earth. Only the Lamb has paid the redemptive price; only the Lamb has the legal right. Mankind will never get the world ready for Jesus' return, in fact, the longer man remains in control of the earth, the worse and more degenerate it will become.

The third view of this time is the view supported by Revelation 20, and it is the view subscribed to by this author. It teaches that Jesus, and Jesus alone, will redeem and restore the world, coming in glory to rule and reign over earth for one thousand years, during which time Satan will be bound from any involvement in the affairs of man.

Although, the book in the Bible that was written last, Revelation, states this fact with certainty, so does the oldest book in the Bible, Job. "For I know that my redeemer liveth, and that he shall stand at the latter day upon the earth: And though after my skin worms destroy this body, yet in my flesh shall I see God," (Job 19:25-26). It is an incredible testament to the consistency of the Word of God that, long before Abraham, God revealed to a man the coming of a redeemer; the reign of that redeemer upon the earth; and the regeneration of his (Job's) own body that would allow him to witness it.

AFTERLIFE LOCATIONS: WHERE DO THE SPIRITS GO?

The armies of Antichrist have just been defeated on the Mountain of Megiddo, and the Antichrist and the False Prophet have been cast alive into the lake of fire. It is now time to deal with Satan himself. John sees an angel descend from heaven with a key to the Bottomless Pit which is the place spoken of in the Bible as being the hold for wicked spirits and demons. Remember that, according to the Greek, neither the angel nor the key is symbolic; what John is seeing is actually happening. This is given credence by other scriptures that speak of the Bottomless Pit, sometimes calling it "The Abyss," or "The Deep." Luke 8:31 records that the Legion of evil spirits which were cast out of the Gadarene demoniac begged not to be sent to the Abyss, and Matthew 8:29 adds that the demons were afraid of the torment awaiting them there. They reminded Jesus that the time had not yet come for their imprisonment in the place of the Deep.

Paul writes in Romans 10:7 that Jesus went to this place during the time that He was in the grave for three days and three nights in order to claim dominion and victory over the very place of the heart of evil.

There are several diverse places spoken of in the Scriptures as being habitations of the afterlife. The lower parts and the nether parts of the earth, the depths of the earth, Hades, and Abraham's bosom are all mentioned as being holding places for the human dead. Tataurus is the prison for the fallen angels, and the Abyss, as has been mentioned, is the place that is spoken of as holding the evil spirits in chains. We have already seen in Revelation 9 that the evil spirits can leave there for a time, with God's permission, but when they do, they always leave havoc and destruction upon the earth in their wake. Now, it is Satan's time to be delivered to the Abyss; to be held in chains for a thousand years in order that the world might have one thousand years wherein Satan's influence is not felt, but rather the righteous and peaceable reign of Jesus is the standard. We see at the latter end of this chapter that God is not entirely finished with Satan when He commits him to the Bottomless Pit. Because of that, he is not now destroyed by God, only imprisoned.

This great enemy of both man and God is identified by four different names in verse 2. There is no possibility of misidentifying him. Each of the names given here, dragon, old serpent, Devil, and Satan carry a unique connotation. The name of "dragon" makes reference to the powers and dominion that have been his on this earth since the time of Adam and Eve, and which have been seen most especially in the years since the rise of Antichrist to world prominence. Now, his earthly power is gone. The name "old serpent" refers to the fact that he has been in existence since human history began, when, of course, he took on the form of a serpent in the Garden of Eden. It refers also to his subtle poisonings and deceiving ways. Now, humanity is freed from his influence, at least for a thousand years. The name "Devil" literally means "liar and slanderer." Jesus called him the "father of lies," and we have already seen him slander the overcomers in Revelation 12 at the Bema Seat of Judgment. To be slandered is one of the most painful of human experiences. It means to be publicly verbally accused of something of which one is totally innocent. This slandering will never happen again. The name "Satan" means "accuser" and "adversary," and he is both the prototype and epitome of both of those characteristics. So with the naming of Satan, God completely identifies his nature and character and pronounces judgment against him by consigning him, in chains, to The Abyss - the Bottomless Pit - for a time of one thousand years. The chains used to confine Satan and the wicked spirits are not necessarily physical chains; indeed, I doubt that they are. But they are chains provided by God that are more than adequate to hold and confine the evil.

Isaiah 24:21-23 speaks of this humiliation of Satan: "And it shall come to pass in that day, that the Lord shall punish the host of the high ones that are on high, and the kings of the earth upon the earth. And they shall be gathered together, as prisoners are gathered in the pit, and shall be shut up in the prison, *and after many days shall they be visited*. Then the moon shall be confounded, and the sun ashamed, when the Lord of hosts shall reign in mount Zion, and in Jerusalem, and before his ancients gloriously" (emphasis mine).

This time of the capture and imprisonment of Satan is spoken of in other places in the Bible. God spoke to Ezekiel, in chapter 28, about Satan, calling him the King of Tyre (or Tyrus). It is a fascinating diatribe. I would like to especially note the following verses: "Moreover the word of the Lord came unto me, saying, Son of man, take up a lamentation upon the king of Tyrus, and say unto him, Thus saith the Lord God; Thou sealest up the sum, full of wisdom, and perfect in beauty. Thou hast been in Eden the garden of God; every precious stone was thy covering, the sardius, topaz, and the diamond, the beryl, the onyx, and the jasper, the sapphire, the emerald, and the carbuncle, and gold: the workmanship of thy tabrets [tambourines] and of thy piper [flute] was prepared in thee in the day that thou wast created. Thou art the anointed cherub that covereth; and I have set thee so: thou wast upon the holy mountain of God; thou hast walked up and down in the midst of the stones of fire. Thou wast perfect in thy ways from the day that thou wast created, till iniquity was found in thee. By the multitude of thy merchandise they have filled the midst of thee with violence, and thou has sinned: therefore [note *future tense here*] I will cast thee as profane out of the mountain of God: and I will destroy thee, O covering cherub, from the midst of the stones of fire. Thine heart was lifted up because of thy beauty, thou hast corrupted thy wisdom by reason of thy brightness: I *will* cast thee to the ground, I *will* lay thee before kings, that they may behold thee. Thou hast defiled thy sanctuaries by the multitude of thine iniquities, by the iniquity of thy traffick; therefore will I bring forth a fire from the midst of thee, it shall devour thee, and I will bring thee to ashes upon the earth in the sight of all them that behold thee. And they that know thee among the people shall be astonished at thee: thou shalt be a terror, and never shalt thou be any more" (Ezekiel 28:11-19, emphasis mine).

Isaiah prophesied that at this time the peoples of the world would take up a jeer and a taunt against Satan, whom he calls the King of Babylon now brought low: "Thou shalt take up this proverb against the king of Babylon, and say, How hath the oppressor ceased! The golden city ceased! The Lord hath broken the staff of the wicked, and the sceptre of the rulers. He who smote the people in wrath with a continual stroke, he that ruled the nations in anger, is persecuted, and none hindereth. The whole earth is at rest, and is quiet: they break forth into singing. Yea, the fir trees rejoice at thee, and the cedars of Lebanon, saying, Since thou art laid down, no feller is come up against us. Hell from beneath is moved for thee to meet thee at thy coming: it stirreth up the dead for thee, even all the chief ones of the earth; it hath raised up from their thrones all the kings of the nations. All they shall speak and say unto thee, Art thou also become weak as we? Art thou become like unto us? Thy pomp is brought down to the grave, and the noise of thy viols: the worm is spread under thee, and the worms cover thee. How art thou fallen from heaven, O Lucifer, son of the morning! How art thou cut down to the ground, which didst weaken the nations! For thou hast said in thine heart, I will ascend into heaven, I will exalt my throne above the stars of God: I will sit also upon the mount of the congregation, in the sides of the north: I will ascend above the heights of the clouds; I will be like the most High. Yet thou shalt be brought down to hell, to the sides of the pit. *They that see thee shall narrowly look upon thee, and consider thee, saying, Is this the man that made the earth to tremble, that did shake kingdoms; That made the world as a wilderness, and destroyed the cities thereof that opened not the house of his prisoners?* All the kings of the nations, even all of them, lie in glory, every one in his own house. But thou art cast out of thy grave like an abominable branch, and as the raiment of those that are slain, thrust through with a sword, that go down to the stones of the pit; as a carcase trodden under feet. Thou shalt not be joined with them in burial, because thou hast destroyed thy land, and slain thy people: the seed of evildoers shall never be renowned" (Isaiah 14:4-20, emphasis mine).

SATAN BOUND AND JUDGMENTS BEGIN

First, by John defining the breadth and depth of the power and hatred of our great enemy, Satan, which is done by naming all of his names in Revelation 20:2, and then by pronouncing Satan's judgment, there is thereby produced great joy for Creation now that this creature is in chains. It will now be a different world; at least until Satan is released at the end of the thousand years. Although at that time his deceptions and poisons will once again be given reign for a very short period of time once again, at *this* time, with Satan temporarily disposed of, Jesus sets about to put things aright as concerns the affairs of mankind. To that end, John sees thrones (note the plural) which have been set up upon the earth and he sees that those who sit upon those thrones are given the authority to judge the people who have lived through the coming of Jesus and the Battle of Armageddon. This is a fulfillment of the promise that was given to each overcomer by Jesus. But over whom will they sit in judgment? Not everyone on the face of the earth was killed at the great battle of Armageddon, and so the world is still populated with people other than the returning saints, including, possibly, children born to unbelievers in the last ten-and-one-half years. Those are the people who are about to be judged. Joel 3:12 prophesies the same judgment, "Let the heathen be wakened, and come up to the valley of Jehoshaphat [literally, "Jehovah hath judged"]: for there will I sit to judge all the heathen round about."

Apart from the multitudes who are about to be judged, but within the ranks of the returning righteous, John sees two groups of people; one group that now sits upon the thrones in judgment and another group whom he says will reign with Jesus during His thousand-year reign upon the earth. The first group is comprised of the raptured saints who both judge and reign; the second group is comprised of the tribulation saints who are said only to reign. However, both groups make up the Bride of Christ. Although many eschatologists have made a distinction between the two groups, saying that the tribulation saints are not a part of the Bride and are, indeed inferior to the raptured saints, here, Jesus allows both the raptured and the tribulation saints to sit with Him upon His throne, ruling and reigning over the earth. Earlier, in Revelation 6:11, John had also inferred that both groups were part of the Bride because both groups wore the clothing of the Bride, clothing given to them by the groom, Jesus.

JUDGMENTS NAMED: BEMA SEAT, NATIONS (SHEEP AND GOATS), GREAT WHITE THRONE

The saints of the Most High will now begin to judge, rule and reign with Jesus as was promised to them in Revelation 2:26, and prophesied by Daniel and by Paul. "And there was given him dominion, and glory, and a kingdom, that all people, nations, and languages, should serve him: his dominion is an everlasting dominion, which shall not pass away, and his kingdom that which shall not be destroyed...But the saints of the most High shall take the kingdom, and possess the kingdom for ever, even for ever and ever...and judgment was given to the saints of the most High; and the time came that the saints possess the kingdom...And the kingdom and dominion, and the greatness of the kingdom under the whole heaven, shall be given to the people of the saints of the most High, whose kingdom is an everlasting kingdom, and all dominions shall serve and obey him" (Daniel 7:14,18, 22,27).

"Do ye not know that the saints shall judge the world? And if the world shall be judged by you, are ye unworthy to judge the smallest matters? Know ye not that we shall judge angels? How much more things that pertain to this life?" (1 Corinthians 6:2-3).

THE JUDGMENT OF THE NATIONS (SHEEP AND GOATS)

This judgment is called the Judgment of the Nations, or, more commonly, as the Judgment of the Sheep and Goats and it was spoken of in great detail by Jesus Himself in Matthew 25:31-46. Most Christians have assumed that Jesus was speaking there of the judgment at the Great White Throne when all the non-Christians will be judged, but careful study of the two judgments show that this cannot be the case. Keep in mind that one of three judgments has already taken place: the Bema Seat Judgment of the Christians by Jesus. Two more judgments will occur; one at the beginning of the thousand years and one at the end but neither one of them will involve Christians in any way. They are entirely different judgments, based on different criteria and concerning different groups of people. How can God judge on the basis of different criteria and still be just? Consider that we accept that He does just that with the Christian and the non-Christian. The Christian is judged on his standing in Jesus, in the fact that the blood of Jesus covers him. The non-Christian is always said in the Bible to be judged on the basis of his works.

There is only one judgment spoken of concerning believers, and that is at the Judgment Seat of Christ. There are two judgments of unbelievers, one at the beginning of the thousand years, the Judgment of the Nations; and one at the end, the Great White Throne Judgment. Although both will be based on the works (the actions) of each person, there is a difference because the works that are judged at the Judgment of the Nations are far more specific in scope than those at the Great White Throne. At the Great White Throne, a person's entire life will be on trial and will be judged. This is not the case at the Judgment of the Nations. Jesus is very clear as to what will be the criterion at the Judgment of the Nations: it will be based on how each person who lived through the Tribulation and the Battle of Armageddon treated "these my [Jesus'] brethren." Those who are Jesus' brethren are both the Christian and the Jew at a time on earth when to be either of those classes of people meant certain death.

Judgment on those who mistreat the nation of Israel is a recurring theme throughout the Bible beginning in Genesis 12:3 when God said to Abraham, "And I will bless them that bless thee, and curse him that curseth thee." This promise will last right through to the end. Note carefully the following details that Jesus gives concerning this judgment: "When the Son of man shall come in his glory, and all the holy angels with him, then shall he sit upon the throne of his glory: And before him shall be gathered all nations: and he shall separate them one from another, as a shepherd divideth his sheep from the goats: And he shall set the sheep on his right hand, but the goats on the left. Then shall the King say unto them on his right hand, Come, ye blessed of my Father, inherit the kingdom prepared for you from the foundation of the world: For I was an hungred, and ye gave me meat: I was thirsty, and ye gave me drink: I was a stranger, and ye took me in: Naked, and ye clothed me: I was sick, and ye visited me: I was in prison, and ye came unto me. Then shall the righteous answer him, saying, Lord, when saw we thee an hungred, and fed thee? Or thirsty, and gave thee drink? When saw we thee a stranger, and took thee in? Or naked, and clothed thee? Or when saw we thee sick, or in prison, and came unto thee? And the King shall answer and say unto them, Verily I say unto you, Inasmuch as ye have done it unto one of the least of these my brethren, ye have done it unto me. Then shall he say also unto them on the left hand, Depart from me, ye cursed, into everlasting fire, prepared for the devil and his angels: For I was an hungred, and ye gave me no meat: I was thirsty, and ye gave me no drink: I was a stranger, and ye took me not in: naked, and ye clothed me not: sick, and in prison, and ye visited me not. Then shall they also answer him saying, Lord, when saw we thee an hungred, or athirst, or a stranger, or naked, or sick, or in prison, and did not minister unto thee? Then shall he answer them, saying, Verily I say unto you, Inasmuch as ye did it not to one of the least of these, ye did it not to me. And these shall go away into everlasting punishment: but the righteous into life eternal" (Matthew 25:31-46).

"For he that is not against us is on our part. For whosoever shall give you a cup of water to drink in my name, *because ye belong to Christ*, verily I say unto you, he shall not lose his reward" (Mark 9:40-41, emphasis mine).

"And whosoever shall give to drink unto one of these little ones a cup of cold water only in the name of a disciple, verily I say unto you, he shall in no wise lose his reward" (Matthew 10:42).

"For the Son of man shall come in the glory of his Father with his angels; and then he shall reward every man *according to his works*" (Matthew 16:27, emphasis mine).

Notice how carefully Jesus identifies the time of this judgment. It is not when the Christians are raptured, it is not at the end of the thousand-year reign which is where Revelation places the Great White Throne Judgment. No, it is right when Jesus returns to the earth *with his saints!* That is the time of Armageddon and this judgment immediately follows it. Notice, too, the criterion used to separate the sheep from the goats. It is not the criterion used to separate the saved from the unsaved; that criterion is the acceptance of Jesus as Lord and Savior. It is also not the criteria used at the Great White Throne Judgment. At that judgment, all of the works, both good and bad, are considered when meting out punishment. The criterion used here is far more narrow than that and it can be synopsized as consisting only of "how did you treat the people of God?" The word used here for "righteous" is used in conjunction with "the sheep" whose only works of righteousness seem to be kindness towards the brethren of Jesus. In the context of this passage, the word "righteous" literally means "just, without prejudice or partiality." In other words, they did not discriminate against the Christians and the Jews when the rule of the day was to do so or die.

It is necessary to stress once again that the Judgment of the Nations - the Judgment of the Sheep and the Goats - does not in any way concern Christians, even thought this judgment is usually explained as though it does. Remember that the Marriage Feast between the Bride, the Church, and the Groom, Jesus, has already taken place. There are no more Christians to be rounded up and included in the Bride; Jesus has not overlooked any who belong at His marriage feast.

The last ten-and-a-half years of the Tribulation have been worse than death camp experiences for the Jews and for the saints. They have been unable to buy food, they have been unable to buy drink, they have had absolutely no shelter available to them and their families, not even the meager shelter of new clothing upon their backs as the old wore out. No doctor's care was available to them as they died from disease and malnutrition; all that has awaited them was the prison cell and, finally, execution. Now, look at what Jesus says is the basis for being either a sheep or a goat. Did you feed my brethren? Did you ever even give them a cup of water? Did you clothe them, did you tend them in sickness, did you ever give them a moment of mercy as they waited for death in their prison hell holes? When my people were among you and destitute, did you show them the tiniest bit of mercy? If you did you may enter my millennium kingdom; not as rulers, not as Christians, but simply as subjects. Your drink of water to one of my suffering loved ones is enough to allow you that. Not because of who you are, but because of my great love for my Bride, and if you eased her suffering in any way, I, too, will have mercy on you.

Keep in mind that these people are not saved, they are not part of the Bride, they simply get to live, not die, and enter the kingdom of Jesus on earth. They will be subjects and servants, but they will live to enter the Millennium Kingdom; that is not at all the same as entering heaven. After all, Jesus and the saints will have to rule over someone; otherwise, what is the point of ruling and reigning?

The presence of Gentiles in the land of Israel in these days is also prophesied in Isaiah 14:1-2': "For the Lord will have mercy on Jacob, and will yet choose Israel, and set them in their own land: and the strangers shall be joined with them, and they shall cleave to the house of Jacob. And the people shall take them, and bring them to their place: and the house of Israel shall possess them in the land of the Lord for servants and handmaids; and they shall take them captives, whose captives they were; and they shall rule over their oppressors."

And what of those who had not the tiniest spark of mercy, what of those who inflicted or increased the suffering of the people of God? They go to hell, joining the Antichrist and the False Prophet who have already been thrown into the fire that will last forever.

The concept behind this judgment became very clear to me in the early 1980s as I watched a PBS documentary on the Holocaust entitled "Shoah." It consisted of interviews with people who were affected by the Final Solution, whether as victims, perpetrators, or witnesses. One interview with a very elderly person from the town of Sobibor, Poland, told of the death trains that would arrive in the little town awaiting clearance to deliver their human cargo to the ovens in the death camp. The Nazis could not kill the Jews as fast as they were being delivered, and the trains would back up into the main street of the little town. The witness told of the cattle cars full to bursting with the Jews who had been without food and water for days. It was bad enough in the winter, the man said, but it was worse in the summer because the trains, sometimes with metal roofs, would be stalled in the town square for hours and the combination of the mass of bodies (many only corpses by now), with the stifling heat made for hellish conditions. Adding to the mental torment was the fact that the town fountain was in clear view of the trains, sometimes, depending on where the train was stalled, just yards away. The Jewish prisoners, half-crazed with thirst, would call out, imploring a townsman to have mercy and bring them a sip of water. Most of the time, their cries went unheeded by the villagers because the Nazis had forbidden anyone, on penalty of death, to help the Jews in any way. But, continued the witness, every so often, someone would find the courage and have the mercy to risk his or her own life and would dip a cup into the fountain and sprint to the train, with the result that sometimes they were seen and were then shot on sight. I do not know if each of those people were Christians or not, but suddenly the scripture quoted above, that whosoever would give even a cup of water to these little ones would not lose their reward, sprang into my mind and I knew that the citizens of Sobibor who placed their own lives in jeopardy in order to show mercy would not be forgotten by Jesus. During the Tribulation, the hellish times will only increase, and Jesus' promise to reward even the slightest act of mercy will remain in force. Those people will live, not rewarded by any means in the same manner as are the overcomers, but still rewarded with the opportunity to live and to enter the Millennial Kingdom as subjects of Jesus and the overcomers.

JESUS WILL REIGN IN JERUSALEM

It is at this time, that the very name of Jerusalem shall be changed in order to indicate that Jesus is in residence there as King: "And the name of the city from that day shall be, The Lord is there" (Ezekiel 48:35b).

"Say among the heathen that the Lord reigneth: the world also shall be established that it shall not be moved: he shall judge the people righteously. Let the heavens rejoice, and let the earth be glad; let the sea roar, and the fulness thereof. Let the field be joyful, and all that is therein: then shall all the trees of the wood rejoice Before the Lord: for he cometh, for he cometh to judge the earth: he shall judge the world with righteousness, and the people with his truth" (Psalm 96:10-13).

"And many nations shall come, and say, Come, and let us go up to the mountain of the Lord, and to the house of the God of Jacob; and he will teach us of his ways, and we will walk in his paths: for the law shall go forth of Zion, and the word of the Lord from Jerusalem. And he shall judge among many people, and rebuke strong nations afar off; and they shall beat their sword into plowshares, and their spears into pruning hooks: nation shall not lift up a sword against nation, neither shall they learn war any more" (Micah 4:2-3). (See also Isaiah 2:3 which is almost an exact restatement of Micah 4:2-3.)

"And the Lord shall be king over all the earth: in that day shall there be one Lord, and his name one" (Zechariah 14:9).

"The king of Israel, even the Lord, is in the midst of thee: thou shalt not see evil any more" (Zephaniah 3:15b).

It has been said that the manifestation of a people's culture is seen in the details of that culture. That is certainly true of the Millennium Reign. Every detail described there speaks to the predominance of Jesus. According to Zechariah 14:20, even the bells that are worn around the necks of the horses will be inscribed, "HOLINESS UNTO THE LORD." Indeed, "The earth shall be filled with the knowledge of the glory of the Lord, as the waters cover the sea" (Habakkuk 2:14).

FULFILLMENT OF THE PROPHECY THAT THE MEEK SHALL INHERIT THE EARTH

Several millennia before, Jesus had made the statement in the Sermon on the Mount that "the meek shall inherit the earth." He did not say that the meek shall inherit heaven; no, the promise concerned Planet Earth and the time when earth itself will belong to the meek. The psalmist also prophesied the same saying, "But the meek shall inherit the earth; and shall delight themselves in the abundance of peace" (Psalm 37:11). He added in the same Psalm that "evildoers shall be cut off: but those that wait upon the Lord, they shall inherit the earth," and that "The righteous shall inherit the land, and dwell therein for ever."

The time has now come, with the coming of the thousand-year reign of Jesus from the City of Jerusalem, for the meek to inherit the earth. Until true justice is able to prevail in the government of the earth, the meek cannot possibly be safe and protected. But at this time the meek will finally inherit the earth because Jesus will have secured it for them.

Although it has commonly been taught that there will be a total of seven different dispensations of God's authority upon the earth, I have come to believe that there are only three. Rather than the dispensations of the Patriarchs, the Judges, the Kings, the Prophets, etc., I have found only three dispensations of authority addressed in the Bible. They are the dispensations of the Father, the Son, and the Holy Spirit. After all, logically, only God has legal authority concerning the affairs of man. The dispensation of God spanned the time from the creation of the world until the time of Pentecost that coincided with the coming of the Holy Spirit. During that time, all the nations of the world were forced to reckon with God himself. Egypt, Babylon, Assyria, and, of course, Israel, were judged by and were answerable to God.

The dispensation of the Holy Spirit spanned the time from Pentecost that was the beginning of the time when the Holy Spirit promised to indwell each believer, until the time of the Millennium Reign of Jesus. Jesus Himself declared that earth would be reproved and judged by the Holy Spirit, and also defined this time as the dispensation of the Holy Spirit in John 16:7-11 when He taught,

"Nevertheless I tell you the truth; It is expedient for you that I go away: for if I go not away, the Comforter will not come unto you; but if I depart, I will send him unto you. And when he is come, he will reprove the world of sin, and of righteousness, and of judgment: Of sin, because they believe not on me; Of righteousness, because I go to my Father, and ye see me no more; Of judgment, because the prince of this world is judged."

PERFECT GOVERNMENT: IMPERFECT PEOPLE

The dispensation of the Son will begin at the Thousand Year Reign at which time He will literally rule and reign in person, and earth and all the nations of the world will be accountable and answerable to Him alone.

The saints will also have a part in this dispensation. They are told that they will preside over other cities, some having one city, some having ten, but Israel will be judged by a special group of saints, for it is at this time that the Twelve Apostles will judge and rule over the Twelve Tribes of Israel. This was promised to them by Jesus while He was here among them. Matthew 19:28 records, "And Jesus said unto them, Verily I say unto you, That ye which have followed me, in the regeneration when the Son of man shall sit in the throne of his glory, ye also shall sit upon twelve thrones, judging the twelve tribes of Israel." Another biblical figure of renown will also rule over Israel: David will be Israel's king.

"And David my servant, shall be king over them; and they all shall have one shepherd: they shall also walk in my judgments, and observe my statutes, and do them. And they shall dwell in the land that I have given unto Jacob my servant, wherein your fathers have dwelt; and they shall dwell therein, even they, and their children, and their children's children for ever: and my servant David shall be their prince *for ever*" (Ezekiel 37:24-25, emphasis mine).

"And I will set up one shepherd over them, and he shall feed them, even my servant David; he shall feed them, and he shall be their shepherd. And I the Lord will be their God, and my servant David a prince among them; I the Lord have spoken it" (Ezekiel 34:23-24).

"And thine house and thy kingdom shall be established for ever before thee: thy throne shall be established for ever. According to all these words, and according to all this vision, so did Nathan speak unto David" (2 Samuel 7:16-17).

"For the children of Israel shall abide many days without a king, and without a prince, and without a sacrifice, and without an image, and without an ephod, and without teraphim: Afterward shall the children of Israel return, and seek the Lord their God, and David their king; and shall fear the Lord and his goodness in the latter days" (Hosea 3:4-5).

Although there will be perfect government, it will not result in a perfect world because people other than God-fearers will also populate the earth. Those who have been allowed to enter the Millennial Kingdom because they were merciful to the saints and the Jews during Tribulation are not holy people. They are in great need of reform in many areas of their lives. This becomes obvious to the reader because we are told that they will be ruled with a rod of iron, that is, sternly. If all in the Kingdom were righteous, this stern rule would not be needed.

There is a second group of people in the Millennial Kingdom who will need stern rule. Those are the ones who are born after Armageddon during the time that Jesus and the saints are ruling, but who, nonetheless, live unrighteous lives. This is so, because, even though Satan is bound and has his influence removed, some people will still choose to sin. How can this be? It is because Satan is not the only reason that people fall into sin; individuals' own desires, their own fallen nature also compel sin. The next thousand years will be the testing of people under ideal conditions, and yet some will still rebel against the will of God. Godly conditions and government have been forced on them, they have not chosen it; there has been no personal repentance, no heart-change with which to empower them to strive for holiness. And, as much as contemporary thought has advanced the notion that sin is simply a consequence of a bad environment, and thus society's fault and responsibility, the Bible makes clear that personal sin is always a result of personal choice.

At the start of the thousand years, the world will be in ruins both from the results of Satan's dominion and from the various plagues with which God has afflicted it in the last ten-and-one-half years. It will take seven months just to bury the dead! Especially because of the wars, males will be scarce, causing Isaiah 4:1 to prophesy, "And in that day seven women shall take hold of one man, saying, We will eat our own bread, and wear our own apparel: only let us be called by thy name, to take away our reproach." In other words, "We'll take care of ourselves and all our needs, just marry us so that we are not old maids!"

Death will still be functional; it is not abolished until the end of the thousand years, however; its power is greatly diminished. Consider the following verses: "Thus saith the Lord: I am returned unto Zion, and will dwell in the midst of Jerusalem: and Jerusalem shall be called a city of truth; and the mountain of the Lord of hosts the holy mountain. Thus saith the Lord of hosts; There shall yet old men and old women dwell in the streets of Jerusalem, and every man with his staff in his hand for very age" (Zechariah 8:3-4).

"For behold, I create new heavens and a new earth: and the former shall not be remembered, nor come into mind. But be ye glad and rejoice for ever in that which I create: for, behold, I create Jerusalem a rejoicing, and her people a joy. And I will rejoice in Jerusalem, and joy in my people: and the voice of weeping shall be no more heard in her, nor the voice of crying. *There shall be no more thence an infant of days, nor an old man that hath not filled his days: for the child shall die an hundred years old; but the sinner being an hundred years old shall be accursed.* And they shall build houses, and inhabit them; and they shall plant vineyards, and eat the fruit of them. *They shall not build, and another inhabit; they shall not plant, and another eat: for as the days of a tree are the days of my people, and mine elect shall long enjoy the work of their hands.* They shall not labour in vain, nor bring forth for trouble; for they are the seed of the blessed of the Lord, and their offspring with them" (Isaiah 65:17-24, emphasis mine).

The earth will soon see its decimated population resurge, in part because of the long lifespan which will be restored by God to the people. Isaiah 60:22 records, "A little one shall become a thousand, and a small one a strong nation: I the Lord will hasten it in his time." This will be a return to a pre-diluvian length of life. Given that Genesis 5 records names of those who lived 930 years, 912 years, 905 years, 910 years, 962 years, etc., up to the oldest, 969 years, and given the biblical assumption that one generation equaled approximately one hundred years and that the average family had between four and nine children, Harold H. Eyer in "A Topical Study of the Patriarchs, dated February 21, 1999, has projected that the world population at the time of the Flood stood at over nine billion people. Today's population stands at only around six billion people even though much more time has elapsed. It is easy to see that it will not take long to re-populate the earth.

THE THOUSAND YEARS BEGIN A WORK OF REDEEMING THE EARTH

The thousand years will begin the work of the reclamation of the earth. With Jesus and the saints ruling, justice and mercy will prevail over all the peoples of the earth and peace will be the norm. "And the streets of the city shall be full of boys and girls playing in the streets thereof. Thus saith the Lord of hosts; If it be marvellous in the eyes of the remnant of this people in these days, should it also be marvellous in mine eyes? Saith the Lord of hosts. Thus saith the Lord of hosts; Behold, I will save my people from the east country, and from the west country; And I will bring them, and they shall dwell in the midst of Jerusalem: and they shall be my people, and I will be their God, in truth and in righteousness. Thus saith the Lord of hosts; Let your hands be strong, ye that hear in these days these words by the mouth of the prophets, which were in the day that the foundation of the house of the Lord of hosts was laid, that the temple might be built. For before these days there was no hire for man, nor any hire for beast; neither was there any peace to him that went out or came in because of the affliction: for I set all men every one against his neighbour. But now I will not be unto the residue of this people as in the former days, saith the Lord of hosts. For the seed shall be prosperous; the vine shall give her fruit, and the ground shall give her increase, and the heavens shall give their dew; and I will cause the remnant of this people to possess all these things. And it shall come to pass, that as ye were a curse among the heathen, O house of Judah, and house of Israel; so will I save you, and ye shall be a blessing: fear not, but let your hands be strong" (Zechariah 8:5-13).

The promise of peace extends even to the animal kingdom and points to the fact that there will be no more carnivorous beasts of any type. This was certainly the case before the Flood, and it seems that it is the perfect will of God in the Millennium also. Therefore, the Great Feast of the Birds is also the Last Feast of the Carnivores.

"And it shall come to pass, that before they call, I will answer; and while they are yet speaking, I will hear. The wolf and the lamb shall feed together and the lion shall eat straw like the bullock: and dust shall be the serpent's meat. They shall not hurt nor destroy in all my holy mountain, saith the Lord" (Isaiah 65:25).

"And in that day will I make a covenant for them with the beasts of the field, and with the fowls of heaven, and with the creeping things of the ground: and I will break the bow and the sword and the battle out of the earth, and will make them to lie down safely" (Hosea 2:18).

It is possible to theorize, given the passage in Hosea, that mankind will no longer eat meat either. Certainly, the promise is given to the animal kingdom that they will be protected from the weapons of the hunt. A world free from hurt and pain and from suffering and want, is truly a regenerated world, harkening back to the first intent of God as was displayed in the Garden of Eden. Only the thousands of years of mankind's rule and Satan's influence will have interrupted God's eternal plan.

And eternal it is: "But Judah shall dwell for ever and Jerusalem from generation to generation" (Joel 3:20). "But

Israel shall be saved in the Lord with an everlasting salvation: ye shall not be ashamed nor confounded *world without end*" (Isaiah 45:17, emphasis mine). Not only will Judah dwell forever; the kingdom and territory of Jesus will never stop increasing, according to Isaiah 9:7: "Of the increase of his government and peace there shall be no end, upon the throne of David, and upon his kingdom, to order it, and to establish it with judgment and with justice from henceforth even for ever. The zeal of the Lord of hosts will perform this."

Although a carnivorous diet will probably be unknown in this new world, Ezekiel 42-46 seems to indicate that animal sacrifice will once again become part of the Temple worship. With the coming of Jesus to the world and with His ultimate sacrifice upon the cross, the need for the atoning sacrifice of animals was halted. However, they may again begin to serve a symbolic purpose at this time in human history. The reason for that is this: With Jesus ruling and reigning from Jerusalem over all of the earth, there will be no escaping His glory, power, and deity. What may fade from human remembrance is His humanity and humility as the Lamb slaughtered for the sins of humanity.

One summer, my teenage daughter went to Chile for a mission trip. In one of the very small towns in which they stayed, the townspeople had two barbeques for them. The first was a beef barbeque, but it was not an American style barbeque. When the teens arrived, they found that the cow that would provide the meat was still alive. It was roped and it sensed that it was about to be slaughtered. As it was led to the knife, it bellowed and mooed, it balked and resisted in every way that it could. Later on in the week, the teens were invited back to another barbeque. This time the live animal awaiting them was a lamb. It, too, was tethered and knew that it was about to be killed, but its demeanor was startlingly different. It did not make the smallest sound and, as it was led to the slaughter it went willingly; only in its eyes could you see a plea for mercy. This, of course, was exactly how Jesus died; so the animal sacrifice in that day, especially in an age with an enlightened sense of compassion toward all of God's creation, may be a very potent remembrance of the fact that all of the peace and prosperity of that day would not have been possible without the extreme suffering of the One who now rules over all the earth.

JERUSALEM, THE APPLE OF GOD'S EYE
Jerusalem will be the capital of the world. Not only will Jesus reign from there, the nations of the world will be commanded to make a yearly pilgrimage to her in order to worship Jesus in person and to keep the feast of tabernacles. Why keep this particular Jewish feast? In Greek, John 1:14 reads, "The word was made flesh and *tabernacled* among us" (emphasis mine). When Jesus returns to earth, He will tabernacle in Jerusalem, and thus, by keeping the Feast of Tabernacles, all nations will forever commemorate His coming again to dwell among men. If any nation neglects to do so, that nation, as punishment, will not receive any rain.

Mount Zion, the holy city, will be the most beautiful place in the entire world. "Beautiful for situation, the joy of the whole earth, is mount Zion, on the sides of the north, the city of the Great King" (Psalm 48:2). Furthermore, the glory of God will rest upon her in the same way that it went before the camp of the Israelites to supernaturally guide them as they wandered in the wilderness: "And the Lord will create upon every dwelling place of mount Zion, and upon her assemblies, a cloud and smoke by day, and the shining of a flaming fire by night: for upon all the glory shall be a defence" (Isaiah 4:5). Holy smoke will distinguish her during the day, and at night she will be visible for miles and miles, seemingly on fire with an otherworldly light.

RESURRECTIONS THAT OCCUR BEFORE AND AFTER THE THOUSAND YEARS
According to Revelation 20:5, all of the dead which now live and reign with Jesus during the Millennial Kingdom have been a part of the First Resurrection. There is one more final resurrection, but it does not occur until the end of the thousand years. The dead that were not raised at the time of the Rapture will continue to sleep on until the Second and Final Resurrection. As concerns the First Resurrection, however, there are two parts and two differently timed resurrections that comprise it. I say that because Revelation

20:4-5 make it clear that both the raptured saints and the tribulation saints are part of the First Resurrection, even though the two events are completely different and are also three-and-one-half years apart. The Rapture comprises the first prong of the First Resurrection, and the resurrection of all of the martyred tribulation saints at the end of the sixth seal comprises the second.

THE FIRST RESURRECTION: WHO IS INVOLVED AND WHAT IS THEIR FATE

The First Resurrection is the time when, according to Jesus in Luke 14:14, the just are resurrected. It is the time of the resurrection of the Bride of Christ and those who have a part in it are said to be both blessed and holy. The second death, hell, has no power over them and they are priests of God and of Christ. But Daniel 12:1-2, which concerns itself with the Rapture, indicates that another class of people may be involved also. Daniel writes: "And at that time shall Michael stand up, the great prince which standeth for the children of thy people: and there shall be a time of trouble, such as never was since there was a nation even to that same time: and at that time thy people shall be delivered, every one that shall be found written in the book. And many of them that sleep in the dust of the earth shall awake, some to everlasting life, and some to shame and everlasting contempt."

This passage divides the resurrection of the dead into at least two segments when Daniel says "and many shall awake". That implies that not all souls awake at that time. But we know that every soul will be resurrected to face judgment. This agrees with the passage in John 5 that also divides resurrection into two parts. The question, then, is this: if this passage concerns the Rapture, why are some raised to shame and everlasting contempt at this point?

At the very beginning of this book, I wrote: "There are two ways of approaching a passage of scripture. One way is to make it prove something which you have already decided, and if it doesn't quite fit, force it anyway, ignoring any inconsistencies. The other way is to find out exactly what the scripture says *regardless* of your current belief. The first way forces the scriptures to conform to your theology. The second method forces your theology to conform to the scriptures. God blesses only one of these ways with wisdom and insight from Him. The other method is the sure road of confusion. Sadly, the road of confusion has been the road most frequently taken. To paraphrase Robert Frost, our desire with this book is to take the road less traveled, the road whereon the scriptures are allowed to explain themselves. Then, the story, for the most part, will be clear." Daniel 12:1-2 truly puts the second way to the test, demanding that we honestly confront the Scriptures. The study of the Resurrection is an area wherein the Church has taken diverse and complicated scriptural information, and has reduced her understanding of it to the lowest common denominator. In reality, the study of the Resurrection is a very complex study.

Scripture very clearly teaches that with knowledge comes accountability: "And that servant, which knew his lord's will, and prepared not himself, neither did according to his will, shall be beaten with many stripes. But he that knew not, and did commit things worthy of stripes, shall be beaten with few stripes. For unto whomsoever much is given, of him shall be much required: and to whom men have committed much, of him they will ask the more" (Luke 12:47-48).

"Jesus said unto them, If ye were blind, ye should have no sin: but now ye say, We see; therefore your sin remaineth" (John 9:41).

"How then shall they call on him in whom they have not believed? And how shall they believe in him of whom they have not heard? And how shall they hear without a preacher?" (Romans 10:14).

As the parable of the Talents teaches in Matthew 25:14-30, if one has had the opportunity to hear the gospel, one is responsible for what has been received. If one takes and uses it, reward is the result. If one ignores it (here, burying the talent in the ground), one is not excused; to the contrary, one is held accountable and is punished. Indeed, Scripture teaches that those who have heard will be judged on their belief or on their unbelief: "Then began he to upbraid the cities wherein most of his mighty works were done, because they repented not: Woe unto thee, Chorazin! Woe unto thee, Bethsaida! For if the mighty works, which were done in you, had been done in

Tyre and Sidon, they would have repented long ago in sackcloth and ashes. But I say unto you, It shall be more tolerable for Tyre and Sidon at the day of judgment, than for you. And thou, Capernaum, which art exalted unto heaven, shalt be brought down to hell: for if the mighty works, which have been done in thee, had been done in Sodom, it would have remained until this day. But I say unto you, That it shall be more tolerable for the land of Sodom in the day of judgment, than for thee" (Matthew 11:20-24).

"For as Jonas was a sign unto the Ninevites, so shall also the Son of man be to this generation. The queen of the south shall rise up in the judgment with the men of this generation, and condemn them: for she came from the utmost parts of the earth to hear the wisdom of Solomon; and, behold, a greater than Solomon is here. The men of Nineveh shall rise up in the judgment with this generation, and shall condemn it: for they repented at the preaching of Jonas; and, behold, a greater than Jonas is here" (Luke 11:30-32).

"For if after they have escaped the pollutions of the world through the knowledge of the Lord and Saviour Jesus Christ, they are again entangled therein, and overcome, the latter end is worse with them than the beginning. For it had been better for them not to have known the way of righteousness, than, after they have known it, to turn from the holy commandment delivered unto them. But it is happened unto them according to the true proverb, The dog is turned to his own vomit again; and the sow that was washed to her wallowing in the mire" (2 Peter 2:20-22).

"I am the true vine, and my Father is the husbandman. Every branch in me that beareth not fruit he taketh away: and every branch that beareth fruit, he purgeth it, that it may bring forth more fruit...I am the vine, ye are the branches: He that abideth in me, and I in him, the same bringeth forth much fruit: for without me ye can do nothing. If a man abide not in me, he is cast forth as a branch, and is withered; and men gather them, and cast them into the fire, and they are burned" (John 15:1-2,5-6).

"Be not highminded, but fear: For if God spared not the natural branches, take heed lest he also spare not thee. Behold therefore the goodness and severity of God: on them which fell, severity; but toward thee, goodness, if thou continue in his goodness: otherwise thou also shalt be cut off" (Romans 11:20b-22).

"Now the Spirit speaketh expressly, that in the latter times some shall *depart* from the faith, giving heed to seducing spirits, and doctrines of devils" (1 Timothy 4:1, emphasis mine).

Scripture also teaches that some who assume that they are saved are not: "When once the master of the house is risen up, and hath shut the door, and ye begin to stand without, and to knock at the door, saying, Lord, Lord, open unto us; and he shall answer and say unto you, I know you not whence ye are: then shall ye begin to say, *We have eaten and drunk in thy presence, and thou hast taught in our streets.* But he shall say, I tell you, I know you not whence ye are; depart from me, all ye workers of iniquity. There shall be weeping and gnashing of teeth then ye shall see Abraham, and Isaac, and Jacob, and all the prophets, in the kingdom of God, and you yourselves thrust out" (Luke 13:25-28, emphasis mine).

Although many Old Testament prophets had been given insight into the Resurrection, not one of them understood it completely. But Jesus did; understanding both how the living would be affected and how the unseen world of the dead would be affected. With that in mind, consider the words of Jesus in which He told of a certain king who held a marriage feast for his son. Those who were initially invited refused the invitation, greatly enraging the king who had them destroyed. "Then saith he to his servants, The wedding is ready, but they which were bidden were not worthy. Go ye therefore into the highways, and as many as ye shall find, bid to the marriage. So those servants went out into the highways, and gathered together all as many as they found, both bad and good: and the wedding was furnished with guests. And when the king came in to see the guests, he saw there a man which had not on a wedding garment: And he saith unto him, Friend, how camest thou in hither not having a wedding garment? And he was speechless. Then said the king to the servants, Bind him hand and foot, and take him away, and cast him into outer darkness; there shall be weeping and gnashing of teeth. For many are called, but few are chosen" (Matthew 22:8-14).

The time that Jesus is speaking of is the time of the Great Marriage Feast, not the time of the Great White Throne Judgment, and yet even at the Marriage Feast there is a separation of those in attendance. Some are bidden to stay, some are cast into outer darkness. The implications of this parable strike deep at the over-simplification that the Church has made concerning the judgment of God of those raised in the First Resurrection. Remember Luke 13:25-28, quoted above. They *see* Abraham, Isaac, and Jacob along with all of the prophets *in the kingdom*; they remind Jesus that they have eaten and drunk in His presence, and have been present at His teaching; but yet and still, they are thrust out of the kingdom by the Lord. With that in mind, Daniel 12:2 becomes more understandable when we read: "And many of them that sleep in the dust of the earth shall awake, some to everlasting life, and some to shame and everlasting contempt."

RAPTURE, A PART OF THE FIRST RESURRECTION: WHO IS BEING JUDGED?

Jesus spoke often of those who had had opportunity to hear His words and yet dismissed them. They, He taught, would be judged, not on their works, but on their rejection of Him. It may be, then, that whereas as the Great White Throne Judgment, which will be discussed presently, is a judgment based on the works of those, both wicked and good, who never had an opportunity to hear the gospel; and whereas the Judgment of the Nations is a judgment based on the treatment of the world's people towards God's people; then the judgment that follows the Rapture is a judgment not only of those who have heard and accepted Jesus, but also those who have heard and rejected Jesus. This latter group would comprise those who heard the good news of salvation but never accepted it, those who were "fellow-travelers" (the almost-Christian and the pseudo-Christian), and also those who were apostates, people who accepted Jesus and then fell away, rejecting His grace, as Hebrews and 2 Peter describe; "For it is impossible for those who were once enlightened, and have tasted of the heavenly gift, and were made partakers of the Holy Ghost, And have tasted the good word of God, and the powers of the world to come, If they shall fall away, to renew them again unto repentance; seeing they crucify to themselves the Son of God afresh, and put him to an open shame" (Hebrews 6:4-6).

"For if after they have escaped the pollutions of the world through the knowledge of the Lord and Saviour Jesus Christ, they are again entangled therein, and overcome, the latter end is worse with them than the beginning" (2 Peter 2:20).

If that is the case, then all those who have had the opportunity to be saved would be raised at the First Resurrection, but only those who belonged to Jesus would be welcomed by Him; the others would be cast into outer darkness. I do not say categorically that this is the case, I only present it for consideration, however, I do say categorically that we have oversimplified the Judgments of God.

SATAN IS AGAIN ABLE TO DECEIVE MANY

Keep in mind that the thousand years is not the length of Christ's kingdom; the Thousand Years is the length of time that Satan is bound. This is made clear in Revelation 20:5-7 and, furthermore, we have not been told of any end to Christ's kingdom; indeed, that kingdom is eternal. The punishment of Satan is also eternal; the thousand years is simply the length of time that he is bound.

At the end of the thousand years, Satan will be released from his chains and will once again attempt to suborn the authority of Jesus upon the earth. He will immediately go out to deceive the human race (as always!), but the amazing thing is that, after a thousand years of perfect government and training, and with Jesus still on the throne, Satan will find that millions of people are more than willing to cross over to his, Satan's, side. The reason for this is that it is the nature of mankind to be deceived and to sin. Sin is not just a result of Satan's influence it is also a result of flesh. As James 1:14 so clearly states, "But every man is tempted, when he is drawn away *of his own lust*, and enticed" (emphasis mine). The viewpoint that man is perfectible by and of himself is completely refuted by the Bible. Man cannot be righteous on his own.

SATAN RELEASED, THE WICKED DESTROYED, AND SATAN CAST INTO GEHENNA

Gog and Magog are once again identified as the principles in this combat. The usage of the term "Gog" is a title, not a proper name, and Magog is his land. The title "Gog" indicates who it is that is being used as Satan's human puppet. The fight over Planet Earth has always been between God and Satan; this time is no different. To say that Russia (as most identify Gog) is the principle enemy of Jesus after all this time is a ridiculous statement. Russia is a minor player in the cosmic war between Good and Evil, not a principle one.

It appears that, once again, there will be a showdown at Jerusalem, the Beloved City, between the forces of God and of Satan, but in actuality, there is really no contest. Fire will be sent from heaven and it will destroy the forces of Gog and Magog. This is the prophetic fulfillment of the parable of Jesus, recorded in Matthew 13:24-30, 36-43: "Another parable put he forth unto them, saying, The kingdom of heaven is likened unto a man which sowed good seed in his field: But while men slept, his enemy came and sowed tares among the wheat, and went his way. But when the blade was sprung up, and brought forth fruit, then appeared the tares also. So the servants of the householder came and said unto him, Sir, didst not thou sow good seed in thy field? From whence then hath it tares? He said unto them, An enemy hath done this. The servants said unto him, Wilt thou then that we go and gather them up? But he said, Nay; lest while ye gather up the tares, ye root up also the wheat with them. Let both grow together until the harvest: and in the time of harvest I will say to the reapers, Gather ye together first the tares, and bind them in bundles to burn them: but gather the wheat into my barn...Then Jesus sent the multitude away, and went into the house: and his disciples came unto him, saying, Declare unto us the parable of the tares of the field. He answered and said unto them, He that soweth the good seed is the Son of man; The field is the world; the good seed are the children of the kingdom; but the tares are the children of the wicked one; The enemy that sowed them is the devil; the harvest is *the end of the world;* and the reapers are the angels. As therefore the tares are gathered and burned in the fire; so shall it be in the end of this world. The Son of man shall send forth his angels, and they shall gather out of his kingdom all things that offend, and them which do iniquity; And shall cast them into a furnace of fire: there shall be wailing and gnashing of teeth. Then shall the righteous shine forth as the sun in the kingdom of their Father. Who hath ears to hear, let him hear" (emphasis mine).

Many have taught that this parable applies to Rapture, but that cannot be. In this parable, the righteous stay and the wicked are gathered out of the world. The inverse is true at Rapture. Also, in this parable, the angels are the reapers, whereas at Rapture, Jesus Himself comes for His people. Finally, the timing of this parable is clearly given by Jesus: it is at the end of the world, not 1010½ years before the end of the world! Although the parable does not fit the time of Rapture, it fits perfectly the time of Revelation 20:8-9.

Even though all of the wicked perish by fire at this time, Satan is not destroyed. Instead, he will now be thrown into Gehenna, the lake of fire and brimstone that was expressly created with Satan in mind. As Jesus said in Matthew 25:41, "Depart from me, ye cursed, into everlasting fire, *prepared for the devil and his angels."* Hell is the place of Satan's punishment, not the site of Satan's kingdom. It has been there, waiting, since the first rebellion in heaven eons ago and now it will receive Satan in order to torment him throughout eternity. Some have tried to make the case that hell is not an eternal punishment; however, the verse just quoted above clearly says otherwise. Mark 9:43-48 reiterates six times that the fires of hell will never go out and also remarks three times that the prisoner of hell will never die either. Luke 16:9 tells us that the habitations waiting beyond the grave for evil men are everlasting habitations, and they surely must be so, because waiting for Satan in hell are the Antichrist and the False Prophet; still alive after one thousand years!

THE EARTH AND HEAVENS COMPLETELY CLEANSED

This is the last mention of Satan found in the Bible. Never again will sin, disease, pain, nor death plague any part of God's creation. The earth and, indeed, the universe, have been completely cleansed of the vile and evil effects of Satan and his angels, and as new civilizations throughout time and space are begun, the very memory of Satan will recede and dim. Out of all of God's creations, only the Bride will remember the savage and bloody battle that Satan waged against the human race.

THE GREAT WHITE THRONE JUDGMENT
The final verse of Revelation 20 tells of the Great White Throne Judgment. It is the story of the fulfillment of 1 Corinthians 15:24-28 which reads: "Then cometh the end, when he shall have delivered up the kingdom to God, even the Father; when he shall have put down all rule and all authority and power. For he must reign, till he hath put all enemies under his feet. The last enemy that shall be destroyed is death. For he hath put all things under his feet. But when he saith all things are put under him, it is manifest that he is excepted, which did put all things under him. And when all things shall be subdued unto him, then shall the Son also himself be subject unto him that put all things under him, that God may be all in all."

This is indeed the time that Jesus delivers up to God His kingdom on, cleansed of every evil man and of every sin. Hebrews 2:8 tells us that even though God has put all things in subjection to Jesus, all was not accomplished at the time of Jesus' resurrection. Some things remained to be done even then. But now, every enemy of God's has been defeated along with every enemy of man's, including death. God will now judge all that remains to be judged. It is such a solemn and grave time of judgment that even heaven and earth flee away. Note that they are never said to be destroyed, the original Greek says, literally, "a place was not found for them". This is because neither the earth nor the heavens are part of this judgment. This concerns only God and the unsaved dead.

Gone is any mention of the rainbow around the throne that was seen in Revelation 4. These people will not come under the grace of God; they will come under His judgment. As fear-inspiring as that thought is, one must remember that the judgment of God is completely fair and just. It is also interesting to note that Satan will not challenge this judgment, nor did he challenge the judgment of the sheep and the goats as he challenged the judgment of those who were raptured in Revelation 12. The reason for that is not that Satan has no interest in either of these judgments, instead, it is that Satan is not free to be present at either judgment. He has been bound for a thousand years which began at the judgment of the sheep and the goats, and he has been thrown into hell at the time of the Great White Judgment.

Who exactly are the people who now face God in His judgment? We know they are not the Christians because, one, the Christians were resurrected or raptured millennia ago, and, two, the Christians are already ruling and reigning with Christ. They are also not the wicked people and nations on earth who were alive at the Battle of Armageddon because they have already received their judgment at the Judgment of the Nations. These dead, then, are all of the rest of the people who have ever been born upon Planet Earth. They slept through the First Resurrection and they slept through the thousand-year Reign. Now they, too, will be raised and judged. The theology that every man and woman will be judged at the Great White Throne Judgment is not in accord with the scriptures. To begin with, no living people are found here at all. Furthermore, the dead in Christ have already been raised and judged and they will not be here either. Only the dead who have not already been raised will be present at this judgment. And now, the holding places of those dead - the ground, the sea, the crevices of the mountains, the quagmires in the swamplands; they all must surrender the dead which they have held for countless years.

Heaven keeps many books and now they are brought forth and opened. Only one of the books is named, although others are said to be opened at this time. The Book of Life is mentioned by name, however, do not confuse it with the Lamb's Book of Life. The Lamb's Book of Life is the book that records the names of all who belong to the Lamb. The Book of Life, on the other hand, records the names of every single human being who has ever lived. The names of the Christians are in both books; the name of every one else is found only in Book of Life. The Book of Life bears testimony to the existence of every person now found before the Great White Throne of God, but other books are also opened and the dead are judged on the basis of all of the records in all of the books that have now been brought forward. It is clear that the paths taken and the decisions made by each human being have been carefully noted by God, and it is the record kept of each life which will now determine the fate of each life. There can be no argument with that being the basis for this judgment. Rejection of Christ or the ignorance of Him is not the basis of the final judgment of these people, although it must be kept in mind that the rejection of, or ignorance concerning, Jesus has kept them from heaven and has already kept them from being part of the Bride. This judgment is a judgment of each person's works and life and that judgment will be handed down to each person present at the Great White Throne.

Revelation 20:12 very clearly states that, "the dead were judged out of those things which were written in the books, *according to their works*" (emphasis mine). But, because so many people have refused to accept this scripture and have argued that this judgment is based on a rejection of Jesus only, and further, that the uniform punishment of hell awaits every person here, we need to examine other corroborating scriptures: "For the Son of man shall come in the glory of his Father with his angels; and then he shall reward every man according to his works" (Matthew 16:27).

"Thy hardness and impenitent heart treasurest up unto thyself wrath against the day of wrath and revelation of the righteous judgment of God; who will render to every man *according to his deeds*" (Romans 2:5-6, emphasis mine).

"For when the Gentiles, which have not the law, do by nature the things contained in the law, these, having not the law, are a law unto themselves: Which shew the work of the law written in their hearts, their conscience also bearing witness, and their thoughts the means while accusing or else excusing one another; In the day when God shall judge the secrets of men by Jesus Christ according to my gospel" (Romans 2:14-16).

"Therefore if the uncircumcision [Gentiles] keep the righteousness of the law, shall not his uncircumcision be counted circumcision?" (Romans 2:26).

"How then shall [people] call on him in whom they have not believed? And how shall they believe in him of whom they have not heard? And how shall they hear without a preacher?" (Romans 10:14).

Paul recognizes the impossibility of accepting Jesus if one has never heard of him. It is true that Romans 1:20 tells us that no man has an excuse for claiming that they did not know that God existed because all of nature declares that there is a creator. But to infer that all of mankind is responsible for knowledge beyond that which God has revealed to them by His manifest presence in Creation is to stray from what this passage in Romans is saying. Again, this passage does not say that they understand God as *savior*, only that they understand God as *creator*.

Non-Christians, too, react negatively at the implausibility of the "Christian" concept that those in "deepest-darkest Africa" are going to hell simply because they have missed out on hearing the gospel. But Christians have held tenaciously to this doctrine. Keep in mind that God is completely fair and just in His judgment; humans beings are not. Humans can be petty, sadistic, vengeful and short-sighted. The Great White Throne Judgment is, thankfully, undertaken by God, not man. Even for the wicked, that is a very good thing. As Jeremiah 9:24 reads, "...I am the Lord which exercise lovingkindness, judgment, and righteousness in the earth: for in these things I delight, saith the Lord."

THE GREAT WHITE THRONE IS NOT A JUDGMENT OF SALVATION

To begin with, the Great White Throne Judgment is not a judgment of salvation. No one at this judgment will be part of the Bride of Christ. That point is self-evident because the marriage between the Bride and Jesus has already taken place. No one at this judgment will live in the holy city (heaven), no one at this judgment will rule and reign with Jesus. Having said that, not every one at the Great White Throne Judgment will receive the same punishment. The Bible clearly teaches that there are degrees of punishment. Consider the following verses: "Woe unto you, scribes and Pharisees, hypocrites! For ye devour widows' houses, and for a pretence make long prayer: *therefore ye shall receive the greater damnation*" (Matthew 23:14, emphasis mine).

"And that servant, which knew his lord's will, and prepared not himself, neither did according to his will, shall be beaten with *many* stripes. But he that knew not, and did commit things worthy of stripes, shall be beaten with *few* stripes. For unto whomsoever much is given, of him shall be much required: and to whom men have committed much, of him they will ask the more" (Luke 12:47-48, emphasis mine).

"Of how much *sorer punishment* suppose ye, shall he be thought worthy, who hath trodden under foot the Son of God, and hath counted the blood of the covenant, wherewith he was sanctified, an unholy thing, and hath done despite unto the Spirit of Grace?" (Hebrews 10:29, emphasis mine.)

"And the sea gave up the dead which were in it; and death and hell delivered up the dead which were in them: and they were judged every man *according to their works*" (Revelation 20:13, emphasis mine.)

"But I say unto you, That whosoever is angry with his brother without a cause *shall be in danger of the judgment*: and whosoever shall say to his brother, Raca, *shall be in danger of the council*; but whosoever shall say, Thou fool, *shall be in danger of hell fire*" (Matthew 5:22, emphasis mine).

This last passage clearly shows a delineation between the Judgment, the Council, and hell. In addition, the Bible speaks of a place of "outer darkness," of a place of "flaming fire," of a place where the sinner is punished by the absence of the presence of the Lord and His glory, of the place called the Abyss, and of Tartarus, the place reserved for the fallen angels. Furthermore, Acts 1:20, 25 tell us that there is at least one other place of punishment other than those already mentioned because Judas went to a place of judgment that was prepared expressly for him alone, in fact, it is called "his [Judas's] place." Judas' particular punishment is to be alone forever. His "place," therefore, could not be hell as we define it, for Judas would not be by himself in hell.

A careful study of John 5:24-29 tells us many things in connection with the different judgments as I indicate by my emphases: "Verily, verily, I say unto you, He that heareth my word, and believeth on him that sent me, hath everlasting life, and shall not come into condemnation; but is passed from death unto life. Verily, verily, I say unto you, The hour is coming, and now is when the dead shall hear the voice of the Son of God: and *they that hear* shall live. For as the Father hath life in himself; so hath he given to the Son to have life in himself; And hath given him authority to execute judgment also, because he is the Son of man. Marvel not at this; for the hour is coming, in the which *all* that are in the graves shall hear his voice, And shall come forth; they that have done good, unto the resurrection of life; and they that have done evil, unto the resurrection of damnation."

THIS THRONE JUDGMENT CONCERNS THOSE RAISED IN THE SECOND RESURRECTION

Jesus first tells His disciples that those who believe on Him will not come into condemnation, but have passed from death into life. Furthermore, He tells them that there is a time coming when He will call from heaven, and when He does, all who are able to hear His voice will come forth from their graves and will live again. Knowing that this is both new and amazing knowledge to His disciples, He goes on to tell them even more extraordinary things. He says to them to marvel not at the fact that those who belong to Him will rise to meet Him because there is a time coming when *every single person* who is in the grave will also here the voice of the Son of God and they, too, shall rise. And, concerning that second group, which contains no Christians (for they have been called forth from the grave at the first sounding of Jesus' voice), Jesus Himself says a most amazing thing: "And [they] shall come forth; they that have done good, unto the resurrection of life; and they that have done evil, unto the resurrection of damnation." It could not be more clear: the *second* resurrection, the resurrection of those who missed Jesus' call, will face a judgment based on whether they lived lives of good or lives of evil; and they will face different fates, depending on how they lived. That is *not* the basis on which Christians are saved and therefore we know that these people do not belong to Jesus; they are not His Bride. Nonetheless, some are spared and some are damned according to Jesus Himself.

Revelation 20:15 explicitly states that "whosoever was not found written it the book of life was cast into the lake of fire." That passage has most often been rewritten to state: "And absolutely no one was found written in the book of life and, furthermore, every single person there was cast into the lake of fire". But that is not what verse 15 states. If we are true to the intent of the passage we see that there is a delineation between those whose names were found in the book of life and those whose names were not found there, all the while keeping in mind that the Book of Life is not the same as the Lamb's Book of Life. The delineation, therefore, is between the spared (not the saved) and the damned. We can know with certainty that Jesus is not speaking of Christians here because, one, they make up the first resurrection, and, two, Christians are not judged on the basis of the works of their lives, they are judged on the basis of their faith.

No one present at the Great White Throne judgment is in the Lamb's Book of Life, however, verse 15 indicates that some of these people are found in the Book of Life while some have had their names blotted out. We must surmise that all at the judgment do not necessarily go to hell, although none are admitted into the holy city. Where they spend eternity is not indicated.

DEATH IS DEFEATED

"And death and hell were cast into the lake of fire. This is the second death." At long last that great enemy of man will be defeated as 1Corinthians 15:25-26 prophesied long ago, and all will be as God first intended it to be when He first placed man in the Garden. It will almost be as though those intervening millennia never happened except for two universe-shattering differences: that Jesus now has a Bride; that Satan has been utterly defeated. The promises of Genesis 3:15, Romans 16:20, and Acts 3:20-21 have come to pass: "And I will put enmity between thee and the woman, and between thy seed and her seed; it [the seed of woman] shall bruise thy head."

"And the God of peace shall bruise Satan under your feet shortly."

"And he shall send Jesus Christ, which before was preached unto you: Whom the heaven must receive until the times of restitution of all things, which God hath spoken by the mouth of all his holy prophets since the world began."

Jesus, the seed of woman and the God of peace, has prevailed and all things lost have now been restored. The great cosmic war between good and evil is forever over.

PART SEVEN: THE HOLY CITY AND ETERNITY

CHAPTER 24
A NEW HEAVEN AND EARTH AND THE NEW JERUSALEM
Revelation 21

THE EARTH REMAINS BUT IS RENEWED AND MADE FRESH

"And I saw a new heaven and a new earth," (verse1). The word here used for "new" is the Greek word *kainos*. It refers to freshness; it is never used with regard to chronological age. The word used for chronological age is *neos*, and *neos* is not the word John chooses to use because John knows what impression he is trying to get across: the heaven and earth are not newly made, they are refreshed. He does not see a brand new heaven and earth, he sees something entirely different. No unrecorded catastrophe has happened between chapters 20 and 21. John has not forgotten to record some cataclysmic event that has completely destroyed the earth; that earth which, by the way, Christ and the saints have spent one thousand years restoring and making perfect. John simply sees and records the result of that work of one thousand years.

The world is, once again, fresh, quite unlike the world that John knew, and we now know. This is corroborated in verse 5 when God explains to John what has happen. "Behold," He says, "I make all things new." Note that God did not say that He made all new things; He declares that He has made "all things new." There is a great difference between the statements. It is the difference inherent in the words "new" and "renewed." If I buy an old house and completely restore it and someone remarks that I have "made the house new," it is understood that it is the condition of the house that is being remarked upon, not the chronological age of the house. That is completely different from saying, "Oh, you have a new house!" Consider, also, that he does not make a new me when I go to heaven, he makes me new. I am the same person, only completely different. That seeming contradiction is the nature of the work of redemption and it applies both to people and to the earth.

Most eschatologists teach that something happens after the Great White Throne Judgment that annihilates heaven and earth. However, they are forced to admit that it seems that John did not feel that whatever happened was important enough to mention even in passing. After reading John's recorded details of every other action of God's upon the earth up until this time, one is forced to stop and consider how unlikely a scenario that is. One must come to the conclusion that the teaching of such a doctrine (the complete destruction of heaven and earth) is, indeed, adding to the Scripture. That is a terribly dangerous thing to do as the next chapter indicates, "For I testify unto every man that heareth the words of the prophecy of this book, If any man shall add unto these things, God shall add unto him the plagues that are written in this book" (Revelation 22:18). However, there is no need to explain the changed and renewed earth by adding an unknown catastrophe to history when the ones that John has already recorded will more than account for the changed topography and condition of earth. They were all found under the sixth seal in the trumpets/bowls of God's wrath that were poured out upon the world.

For instance, the most common teaching, which insists on an unwritten calamity between chapters 20 and 21 says that the unrecorded calamity is the fulfillment of 2 Peter 3:10 in which "the heavens shall pass away with a great noise, and the elements shall melt with fervent heat, the earth also and the works that are therein shall be burned up". They neglect to point out that Peter *specifically* states in the beginning of that verse that this will happen at the "day of the Lord." And it did. The earth was burned up with fervent heat during the time of the opening of several of the seals, but particularly upon opening the fourth one: "And the fourth angel poured out his vial upon the sun; and power was given unto him to scorch men with fire. And men were scorched with great heat, and blasphemed the name of God, which hath power over these plagues: and they repented not to give him glory" (Revelation 16:8-9).

2 Peter 3:10 must be taken greatly out of context in order to apply it to Revelation 21. Malachi also prophesies that it is at the day of the Lord that the world will burn as an oven. No prophet places the purging by fire at any other time.

Peter compares this purging by fire to the purging of the earth by water at the time of the Flood. But, after that purging by water, the world remained! That is emphatically stated in Isaiah 24:6 when he tells us that "therefore hath the curse devoured the earth, and they that dwell therein are desolate: therefore the inhabitants of the earth are burned, and few men left." *Few* men left; *not* no men left. No one argues that there was no world after the Flood; it was simply a world made new by the flood. The same is true of the world after it is destroyed by fire; it is a world made new.

In addition to the intense heat that has so changed the earth, the enormous earthquakes have done so also. Under the sixth seal, the earth has reeled to and fro as a drunken man; the sky has been rolled up as a scroll. Every mountain has been removed out of its place, as has every island. Now, here is a major topographical makeover of the earth! One need not look anywhere else for a cataclysm powerful enough to rework the planet. The time of the Great Tribulation is more than adequate!

Many times, in order to support the annihilation of the earth and heavens, Hebrews 11:10-11 is quoted; "And, Thou, Lord, in the beginning hast laid the foundation of the earth; and the heavens are the works of thine hands: They shall perish; but thou remainest: and they all shall wax old as doth a garment." According to Vine's Expository Dictionary of Biblical Words, "the idea is not extinction but ruin, loss, not of being, but of wellbeing."[29] This is in complete accord with the very next verse, 12, which is rarely quoted; "And as a vesture shalt thou fold them up, and they shall be *changed*: but thou art the same, and thy years shall not fall" (emphasis mine). The very clear meaning is that the earth is worn out (unlike God who never ages) and will need to be repaired and refreshed.

The day of the Lord has been over for one thousand years when John sees the new heaven and earth. During that time, Jesus and the saints have been in charge of the earth. It has been restored, replanted, and carefully tended. One final purging took place at the end of the Millennial Reign as the angels removed all the weeds and tares that were allowed to manifest themselves over time. Jesus has handed over to God a perfect, restored, renewed earth. God has made all things new, not all new things, and this time they will stay new. Sin and death have been done away with and nothing will corrupt the newness of the earth from now on.

THE EARTH, SUN, MOON AND STARS REMAIN FOREVER
It is important to understand that the earth was created to be eternal. God said to Abraham, "And I will give unto thee, and to thy seed after thee, the land wherein thou art a stranger, all the land of Canaan, for an *everlasting* possession; and I will be their God" (Genesis 17:8, emphasis mine). God said to Joel, "But Judah shall dwell [be inhabited] *forever*, and Jerusalem from generation to generation" (Joel 3:20, emphasis mine). Paul said to the Church, "Unto him be glory in the church by Christ Jesus throughout all ages, *world without end. Amen*" (Ephesians 3:21, emphasis mine). The psalmist tells us that the sun, moon, stars, heavens, and waters have been established forever with a decree that shall never end (Psalm 148:3-6). The psalmist also said, "The righteous shall inherit the land, and dwell therein for ever" (Psalm 37:29), and asked the question, "Who laid the foundations of the earth, that it should not be removed for ever?" (Psalm 104:5).

Isaiah declared the exact same thing when he prophesied, "Thy people also shall be all righteous: they shall inherit the land for ever, the branch of my planting, the work of my hands, that I may be glorified. A little one shall become a thousand, and a small one a strong nation: I the Lord will hasten it in his time" (Isaiah 60:21-22).

Consider Psalm 89:34-37: "My covenant will I not break, nor alter the thing that is gone out of my lips. Once have I sworn by my holiness that I will not lie unto David. His seed shall endure for ever, and his throne as the sun before me. It shall be established for ever as the moon, and as a faithful witness in heaven. Selah."

Jeremiah wrote: "Thus saith the Lord, which giveth the sun for a light by day, and the ordinances of the moon and of the stars for a light by night, which divideth the sea when the waves thereof roar; The Lord of hosts is his name: If those ordinances depart from before me, saith the Lord, then the seed of Israel also shall cease from being a nation before me for ever" (Jeremiah 31:35-36).

Solomon declared that "one generation passeth away, and another generation cometh: but *the earth abideth for ever*" (Ecclesiastes 1:4, emphasis mine). Now, Revelation 21:1 ends the story of redemption begun in the Garden of Eden. This is the "times of restitution of all things" Peter spoke of in Acts 3:21. So, the question becomes not if the earth remains, but rather, who is on the earth if the saints take up abode in the Heavenly City?

THE INHABITANTS OF EARTH

Isaiah 45:18 tells us that God Himself formed the earth and that He did so, not in vain, but in order for it to be inhabited. Now Satan intended to destroy the existence of man as a race and to take the mastery of the earth away from man. If, as is commonly taught by many Bible expositors, Satan fails to permanently take over the earth, but yet he does succeed in stopping the continued propagation of the race of man, then Satan has had some measure of victory over God! After all, it was the express purpose of God for man to "be fruitful, and multiply, and replenish the earth," and, further, this command was given before the issue of sin ever arose.

Consider what would have happened if man had not sinned. Adam and Eve would have lived forever, their sons and daughters would have lived forever, and their descendants would also have lived forever. Would there ever have been a cutoff of the race of man? No, the race of man would have continued throughout time. If Satan is able to alter that plan of God's in any way, something is lost by God and gained by Satan. Furthermore, Isaiah tells us that God intends that His government will continue to grow and expand forever, the earth abides forever and the race of man will continue forever. The confusion exists because commentators have mixed up the static and finite number of Christians (the saved who dwell in the holy city) and the finite number of those who will be damned, with the infinite and unfixed number of those who come after the thousand-year reign and who will continue to populate the earth, and probably the rest of the universe.

You see, sin and the Age of Sin are but a parenthetical paragraph in the history of God. The race of man will go on and will continue to increase. On the other hand, if, as is commonly taught, the whole solar system collapses and is destroyed, the earth ceases to be, and the race of man is stopped, who is ultimately the victor - the Creator or the Destroyer?

Mankind has an inherent desire for monuments, as witnessed by the Pyramids, Stonehenge, Gettysburg, the Statue of Liberty, the Alamo, Arlington Cemetery, even down to the graveyards that are in every community worldwide. God placed in man the desire to commemorate past events; not only that, He required and commanded the erection of monuments by His people. Now, earth itself will be a monument to God; it is the place where God's only Son was born and where He died. It is the birthplace of Jesus' bride. The footsteps of Jesus were on the earth. It is the territory where the costliest sacrifice *ever* was made; the soil of Planet Earth received the blood, sweat and tears of Jesus. It is the theater where the gravest war over the destiny of man was played out. Does it stand to reason that this place is of no significance to God? No! earth is a testament to God's greatness and victory; and the earth, as He promised, will abide forever.

OCEANS AND SEAS ON RENEWED EARTH REVERT TO PRE-FLOOD STATE

Verse 1 of Revelation 21 tells us that in this renewed earth there is no sea. Most of the time an erroneous extrapolation of that statement is made that includes all the bodies of water now found on earth: lakes, ponds, rivers, etc. John does not say that; he does not even imply that. He simply says that when he sees this new earth, he does not see enormous bodies of water, i.e. seas or oceans. This makes sense. As the earth exists today, approximately seventy percent of its surface is taken up by the oceans. That is a lot of wasted space that will be put to better use when the earth is put back aright. The Bible seems to suggest that the earth did not have these vast bodies of water at Creation; instead, they were a permanent result of the Flood. Genesis talks about separating the waters from the waters at the time of Creation, and placing the sky between them. That canopy of water over the earth would have produced enough water for the Flood and that is what Genesis 7:11-12 seems to indicate happened: "In the six hundredth year of Noah's life, in the second month, the seventeenth day of the month, the same day were all the fountains of the great deep broken up, and the windows of heaven were opened. And the rain was upon the earth forty days and forty nights."

Genesis 7:11 informs us that at the same time the "windows of heaven were opened," the "fountains of the great deep broke up." The vast oceans that we now see on earth may have been formed as a consequence of the deluge of water resulting from forty days and nights of hard and continuous rain resulting from the breaking up of the canopy of water over the earth, coupled with the great eruptions out of the bowels of the earth and the great tsunami waves which would have accompanied those eruptions.

If it took forty days and forty nights for it to empty, the canopy must have been enormous. Job describes the limits that God placed on that deluge when he records the following words of God: "Who shut up the sea with doors, when it brake forth, as if it had issued out of the womb? When I made the cloud the garment thereof, and thick darkness a swaddlingband for it, And brake up for it my decreed place, and set bars and doors, And said, Hitherto shalt thou come, but no further: and here shall thy proud waves be stayed?"(Job 38:8-11).

Psalm 104:5-9 describes the Flood and God's direction of it in much the same way: "Who laid the foundations of the earth, that it should not be removed for ever. Thou coveredst it with the deep as with a garment: the waters stood above the mountains. At thy rebuke they fled; at the voice of thy thunder they hasted away. They go up by the mountains; they go down by the valleys unto the place which thou hast founded for them. Thou hast set a bound that they may not pass over; that they turn not again to cover the earth."

Much geological evidence exists to support the fact that sea levels were once much lower. This, too, is in accord with the fact that the earth now holds much more water on its surface than it did originally.

Before that canopy was broken up, there had never been rain upon the earth, but everything flourished. That is certainly not the case now. Rain is a necessity. One other necessity to the continuation of life on earth is the existence of the ozone layer. The function of the ozone layer is to sift out certain lethal rays from the sun. Now imagine a pre-diluvian world in which the ozone layer, combined with the water canopy, would have shielded the earth. Combined, the protection would have been even more effective because water would sift out rays that pass through the ozone layer; possibly blocking those rays that allow or hasten decay. Food would not have spoiled as quickly and life spans would have been much longer (as, indeed, the Bible says that they were). Global temperatures would have been much more even and the light would have been softer. The water canopy might have produced the effect of air conditioning, making the earth a paradise.

The pre-diluvian world was different in other ways. Whereas before there had been gentle breezes, now the earth is subject to fierce winds. Extreme temperatures would have been unknown; now they are the norm. The vegetation of the earth would have been lush and ubiquitous, now there are vast deserts in the world. The new heaven and new earth seen by John now make it apparent that God has restored earth to its original state.

NEW JERUSALEM - CITY OF THE REDEEMED - COMES FROM HEAVEN

It is now that the holy city, the new Jerusalem, comes down out of heaven. It is a city filled top to bottom with sinners, but sinners who sing, "I once was lost but now am found," testifying to the amazing grace of the redemption. Indeed, the great glory of this city is found in the fact that it is the city of the redeemed and because of that, God will make His residence there. The promise of Jesus that has long been sought, the promise that "then shall the righteous shine forth as the sun in the kingdom of their Father," has now come to pass. The very city itself has also been promised to the overcomer: "But now they desire a better country, that is, an heavenly: wherefore

God is not ashamed to be called their God: for he hath prepared for them a city" (Hebrews 11:16).

"But ye are come unto mount Sion [Zion], and unto the city of the living God, the heavenly Jerusalem, and to an innumerable company of angels, to the general assembly and church of the firstborn, and to God the Judge of all, and to the spirits of just men made perfect, and to Jesus the mediator of the new covenant, and to the blood of sprinklings, that speaketh better things than that of Abel" (Hebrews 12:22-24).

"For here have we no continuing city, but we seek one to come" (Hebrews 13:14). (We are meant to be strangers in a strange land. If we are too comfortable here, something is wrong!)

John saw the Bride and the marriage ceremony take place one thousand years ago. The Bride ruled and reigned with her Bridegroom, Jesus, over the earth until He turned over His perfected work to His father. Now, with that task completed, Jesus is taking His Bride to her new home.

Millennia ago, God gave His promise that "I will walk among you, and will be your God, and ye shall be my people" (Leviticus 26:12). In all the ages of the human race since God walked with Adam, Eve, and a very few others such as Enoch, it is again possible for man and God to live together. To inhabit the same city as does God is an almost incomprehensible thought to the human mind. To have Him walk and live among us is even harder to comprehend, but such is the case. As a consequence of His presence, the experience of everyone in that city will be one of perfect joy. There will be no more tears, no more death, no more sorrow, no more pain. All of those experiences belonged to a fallen, imperfect, sin and disease-infected world. Every trace of that world is now gone. God has made all things new and this time they will stay that way.

REVELATION IS LITERAL

"And he said unto me, Write: for these words are true and faithful." This is a severe and solemn warning to all the readers and scholars of Revelation who have not taken its words literally. These words are not a coded message to a very few; these words are not a parable; these words are faithful and true, and the one who is Faithful and True will judge those who refuse to accept these words as such.

THE WORK IS DONE
"And he said unto me, It is done." This phrase is said by Jesus three times in the Scriptures, and each time a phase of redemption had been completed. It was first said by Jesus on the Cross (John 19:30). No other sacrifice would ever have to be made again. It was next said by Jesus at His second coming in Revelation 16:16 when Planet Earth was retaken. It will never have to be taken again. Finally, it is said here when Jesus delivers to God the perfected kingdom. It, too, will never have to be saved again, "For he hath put all things under his feet."

JESUS AND THE FATHER ARE ONE
In Revelation 1, Jesus appeared to John and told him that He, Jesus, was the Alpha and the Omega; the beginning of everything and the end of everything. In other words, Jesus is the sum total of everything. Now, in Revelation 21:6, God says the exact same thing of Himself. There is no escaping the significance of this: Jesus and the Father are one and the same. The sincere Jehovah's Witness who denies this, is at a loss to explain these two verses for there is no explanation other than the fact that Jesus is God and God is Jesus.

We are told here by God that He freely gives of eternal life to all who desire it. There is no cost borne by the supplicant; the cost is borne by God. There is also no turning away of any person who desires and thirsts after eternal life. God has not predetermined any to hell; anyone who is thirsty and so chooses may drink of the fountains of the water of life.

THE ONLY TRUE SON OF GOD IS AN OVERCOMER
Verse 7 tells us that anyone who has overcome, that is, who is saved, will inherit all things. There is no greater inheritance of one saint compared with another; there is no lesser inheritance of one saint compared with another. All present in heaven shall inherit all things. We are, as Paul told us, joint heirs. The term "joint heirs" is a legal term, meaning that the inheritance is not divided among the heirs; instead the heirs

hold all things in common. When Paul tells us that we are joint heirs, he is telling us that there are no classes of citizenship in heaven. There are no more desirable nor less desirable places in heaven. There is no varying level of communion with God found in the holy city. There are no lesser sons, there are no greater sons. Each one there is called a son of God. Remember, all the varying crowns of reward that we might have received have long since been reverently laid at the feet of Jesus.

It is sometimes easier for us to accept that Jesus loves us and is willing to rule and reign with us than it is for us to accept that the same is also true of His Father. But here, God extends to each believer the same status that is conferred upon Jesus: son-ship. God looks upon each one of us as another child of His, beloved by Him in the same way as is His first-born son, Jesus.

Verse 7 tells us who will be found in the City of God; verse 8 tells us who will not be. The fearful and unbelieving, the abominable and murderers, the whoremongers and sorcerers, the idolaters and all of the liars will have their part in the lake that burns with fire and brimstone. There has been a popular theology of late among Christians that teaches that God ranks all sin on the same level. He does not. True, any and all sin separates us from God, but the Bible is clear that God does not look upon all sin with the same gravity. Here is a prime example. Only eight sins are listed: one is forced to conclude that these are the most repugnant to the holy nature of God. The book of Proverbs tells us that there are six things that God hates and seven that are an abomination to him. They are a proud look, a lying tongue, hands that shed innocent blood, a heart that devises wicked imaginations, feet that swiftly run to mischief, liars, and one who sows discord among brothers. Adolph Hitler will receive a different punishment than will the basically decent man who never became a Christian. The Lake of Fire was created for Satan and his angels; only the human beings who align themselves with Satan by acting as Satan does will find themselves in the Lake of Fire. What are those actions? Revelation 21:8 enumerates them.

At first blush, it seemed rather severe to me to include the fearful among that damned group until God showed me that much of the evil that is done in the world is done either because people are afraid to stop the evil or they are afraid to do the godly thing. Many times injustice has prevailed because onlookers were afraid to confront it. Many times "good" people have done bad things because they were afraid to stand up for their own convictions. God despises this cowardice and will sternly judge those who fall prey to it.

Furthermore, it is sometimes only fear that keeps people away from Jesus; not a fear of Him, but a fear of the consequences of accepting Him. Being a Christian may mean the loss of one's life, one's marriage, money, status or reputation. Many times it only means that one is opened up to ridicule when others no longer see one as being sophisticated or educated. We have just witnessed the events that happened during the Great Tribulation and we have seen that many have rejected the gospel preached to them from heaven. Why did they reject that gospel? Did they believe it was false? No, they recognized its truth but something stronger held them in its grip: they were afraid. They were afraid of the Antichrist, of hunger, homelessness, pain, ridicule, loss of position, and ultimately of death. That fear will now earn them a berth in the lake that burns with fire and brimstone.

THE BRIDE AND THE HOLY CITY

John is now shown the Bride of Christ by one of the Seven Angels that was found under the seven seals. The last time John saw this angel, He was pouring out plagues upon the world. This time the angel shows John the reward of the saints. John, in the Spirit, is taken to a high mountain and is shown the Great City, the New Jerusalem, which is descending out of heaven. The Bride who was married in Revelation 19 is now going home. It is a home completely prepared for her by God; no human hand is on it. Even the inhabitants - the saints - are the workmanship of God. This is the heavenly Jerusalem spoken of in Hebrews, a city whose builder and maker is God. It is the Jerusalem that is above us; free, and the mother of all the saints, according to Galatians 4:26. She is bathed in a very soft and beautiful light because she is alight with the glory of God.

God does not judge a work by whether or not it is successful, but rather by whether or not it has His light. This should give us great comfort because there will be experiences into which God will lead us that will seem to go nowhere. And because of the results of those, we may begin to doubt whether or not we truly heard from God. But bear in mind that if God called you to teach a Sunday school class and only two people showed up, it does not matter. God does not judge whether there are two or two hundred people in attendance, humans do that, God judges whether or not we are listening to His call. Our results are not the point. Walking in His light is. Many Christians have given their lives in what seemed to be futile martyrdoms. Their deaths changed nothing politically, but did God discount their sacrifices because of their results? Absolutely not. Obeying His light is never futile; it is always glorious.

This work, the New Jerusalem, is both clear as crystal and like unto a jasper stone. Jasper is wavy with red and various other colors of the rainbow, and yet it is translucent. The light of a jasper stone is truly glorious and that is the description of the light that both fills and surrounds this city.

THE CITY IS DESCRIBED

There is a wall surrounding the city and, in that wall, twelve gates offer access to the city. There are three each on the north, south, east, and west. Each gate is named for one of the twelve tribes of Israel; stationed at each gate is an angel - truly a guardian angel. It is telling to note that the gates are named after the twelve tribes. This is a profound indication that Old Testament saints are part of the holy city; it is not limited to those who came after Jesus. This makes sense because we are told that Abraham looked for this very city. Abraham would not have looked for a city from which he was barred! Furthermore, Matthew 8:11 proclaims that Abraham, Isaac, and Jacob will be in the holy city for, "I say unto you, That many shall come from the east and west, and shall sit down with Abraham, and Isaac, and Jacob, in the kingdom of heaven."

The gates are named after the Twelve Tribes because it was to the nation of Israel that entry into the things of God was first given. The foundations of the city, however, are named after the twelve apostles of the Lamb, for it was upon the revelation of Jesus to them that the city rests. It is clear, then, that the holy city is made up of both Old and New Testament saints. Note that John mentions that the apostles named are the twelve apostles to the Lamb. There were more than twelve apostles in Church history; the New Testament, alone, names more than twelve. But the foundations are built upon the apostles to the Lamb. Those apostles are the original Twelve, without Judas and with the addition of Matthias. Paul is not one of those apostles, revered though he is by the modern church, for he was an apostle to the Gentiles, not to the Lamb. Neither is Barnabas one of those apostles; he was an apostle to the Church. Even the brother of Jesus, James, is not one of the twelve names on the gate. Although an apostle and the leader of the Church at Jerusalem, he became a believer after the resurrection of Jesus and so does not qualify as an apostle to the Lamb.

The holy city is a cube; a three dimensional city. It is fourteen hundred miles each way. As Henry Morris states in his book The Revelation Record, according to the measurements given, the city would reach from the top of Maine to the bottom of Florida. It would span from the Atlantic Ocean to Colorado. Figured another way, it would encompass all of Britain, Ireland, France, Spain, Italy, Germany, and Austria, plus parts of Turkey and Russia. And that takes into account but two of its three dimensions for it is as tall as it is large. Within this area, twenty-eight billion people could each have one-quarter mile completely to themselves. We now reckon that less that five people per square mile renders a place nearly uninhabited; the measurements of the holy city would allow for a sparser population even than that. In fact, Henry Morris, in his book, Creation and the Second Coming, calculates that if the city has twenty billion people, each person could have a personal space of a cube seventy-five *acres* in each direction. This puts to rest the uninformed notion that no one city could accommodate all of the saved throughout all of time. This one could do so easily.

The fact that the city is measured and that the measurements are given, indicates that the city has been both judged and evaluated according to God's standards. Each person there has been judged according to the righteousness of Christ, not according to his own righteousness, and so the city is perfect in its righteousness. It is truly the city of the redeemed.

Notice that the wall measures 144 cubits. Again the number 144 shows up as it did with the 144,000 Jews earlier in the book. The number 144 is the product of 12 times 12. The numbers are all significant. John further notes that human and angelic measurements are equivalent. Apparently, even though our concept of time is not in accord with heaven's concept of time, our concept of mathematics is in accord with heaven's. This idea has become more and more interesting to me as the culture in which I live has increasingly discounted the idea of absolute truth. Polls have shown that most Americans do not believe in an idea of absolute right and wrong anymore; truth is now judged to be relative. But mathematics is an obvious refutation to that belief system; after all, a positive one plus a positive one can never equal anything but a positive two. Humans grant the existence of absolute truth in mathematics, oh! If only we would grant its truth elsewhere, for it does exist and it is a reflection of the mind of God. What God considers right and holy is indeed right and holy, regardless of whether or not a society accepts it as a standard for right behavior. Conversely, what God considers to be profane and evil is indeed profane and evil whether or not it is judged that way by society. Mathematics is a God-given proof that truth is not relative and thus it is constant both in heaven and on earth.

THE WALL CONSTRUCTED OF PRECIOUS STONES

The wall surrounding the city is jasper, wavy and opalescent, but the city and her streets are built out of pure gold. This is not ordinary, earthly gold. This is gold the likes of which humans have never seen. It is gold of such purity that it, too, is transparent while retaining the characteristics of the gold that is more familiar to us. Keeping in mind that the city is a cube, the different colors of the foundations of each level are carefully described. The golden city rests first upon a layer of jasper, wavy translucent red; second, sapphire blue; third, chalcedony, a sky blue; fourth, emerald green; fifth, sardonyx, a deep red onyx; sixth, sardius which has a honey copper color; seventh, chrysolite, a pale green; eighth, beryl, a deep sea green; ninth, topaz, a yellow green; tenth, chrysoprasus, a gold-tinted green; eleventh, jacinth, a violet color; and twelfth, an amethyst purple. To have all of these hues and colors radiating through the city of gold as the light shines through will produce a breathtakingly beautiful sight. After all, this is the city brought to you by the maker of the rainbow! This light will replace the light of the sun and the moon even upon Planet Earth and the nations there will now walk in the light of the city. Such is the bounty of God that even the earthly nations will reap the benefit of the beauty of the holy city!

THE GATES OF PEARL

The twelve gates of the city, each emblazoned with the name of one of the Twelve Tribes, are each formed out of one pearl. When one considers that the width of the walls is two hundred feet (144 cubits), one realizes that the size of each of those pearls must be staggering. That the gates are made of pearl is very significant. When the contents of the treasury of Israel were listed in the Old Testament - the gold, silver, purple and blue fabrics, etc - pearls were never listed. That is because pearls were not valued by the Jews. When Jesus told them the parable of the man who sold everything he owned to buy the pearl of great price, the people probably wondered why on earth anyone would ever do that. It was as if they were told the man sold everything he had in order to buy some costume jewelry! Those listening must have wondered at the point of that parable. Now, in Revelation 21, we come to the heavenly city and we see that the gates are made of pearl. The significance is clear: pearls are the only jewels that are the direct result of an injury. An irritant invades an oyster and the oyster's response is to make a pearl out of the irritant. Now, when one enters this city, one must, of necessity, walk through God's answer to the injury to Jesus. One cannot walk through the gates of this city without realizing that the only reason anyone can enter is because God's answer to our sin was mercy in the form of the sacrifice of His Son. The pearl will become the most precious of the material treasures of heaven.

THE LORD GOD AND THE LAMB ARE THE TEMPLE AND THE LIGHT

There is also no Temple in the holy city, no church building, no central place of worship. There is no need for one because The Lord God Almighty and the Lamb are in residence there. A temple would be deserted, for who would have need of one when the One that the temple seeks to commemorate is present?! Likewise, there will be no special times of worship because worship will be continuous. One cannot help but worship in the presence of the Lord God Almighty and the Lamb.

There is also no sun nor any moon there, for the glory of God illumines it. This is the same glory that struck Paul down; the same glory that no man could look upon and live. Now we will live in it and breathe it in as it reflects off of the gold and foundation stones. Isaiah 60:19-20 prophesied this exact circumstance when he wrote: "The sun shall be no more thy light by day; neither for brightness shall the moon give light unto thee: but the Lord shall be unto thee an everlasting light, and thy God thy glory. Thy sun shall no more go down; neither shall thy moon withdraw itself: for the Lord shall be thine everlasting light, and the days of thy mourning shall be ended."

We in the holy city will be able to live in that light, but the nations will have it shining above them as we now have the sun. The nations will be utterly dependent upon the holy city. It is clear that the holy city is not a part of earth, it is above earth, but yet earth continues to be populated. We know that because a distinction is made between the saints who reside in the holy city and the people (nations) who reside on Planet Earth. One cannot escape the fact that the earth still exists.

There is no night in the city and the gates are always open. In ancient times, the gates surrounding the cities were always closed at nightfall as protection against enemies. The inherent promise in this verse, then, is that, *throughout the universe,* danger has ceased to be. And all the emotions that we have as a consequence of danger, imagined or real, will cease to have a purpose in the human experience, and thus will no longer exist or even be imagined.

Verse 26 seems to suggest that those who find glory and honor among the nations are allowed access to the City even though it is not their dwelling place, but it is undisputable that the gates are always open to the saints. The ramifications of this are profound. Gates function in two ways: they keep people in and they keep people out. As important as it is to understand that the gates allow entry to the saints, it is equally important to understand that they allow departure also. The saints are free to roam the ever-expanding Universe, coming and going from the city at will. Isaiah saw a vision of this in the passage of Isaiah 60 quoted above. He describes the earth in these days and says, "The Gentiles shall come to thy light, and kings to the brightness of thy rising." He continues to describe what he sees upon the earth, and then in verse 8, he apparently looks up into heaven and is amazed by what he sees. He does not know what to make of it and so records his question, "Who are these that fly as a cloud, and as doves to their windows?" He sees creatures that he describes as both cloudlike and dove-like who are leaving heaven. (We know that Isaiah is speaking of their leaving because in prophecy a door signifies entry and a window signifies departure.) He knows that they are not angels because he can recognize angels, so who are these creatures who fly out of the holy city? Isaiah is seeing the saints as they exit the open gates of the holy city.

The final verse of Revelation 21 leaves no doubt as to who it is who populates the city: only those whose names are written in the Lamb's Book of Life. Heaven is not the destination of all who have lived; the defiled, the abominable, the liars cannot enter in, for if they were to enter, they would bring with them their defilements and abominations and the perfect city would be no more. The inhabitants of the holy city will never again hear a cross word, will never again see an unkind act. While selfishness and evil acts were the standard experience on Planet Earth, the people of the holy city rose above that behavior and chose a higher standard for themselves; the standard of God. They have had more than enough of the experience of being strangers in a strange land while living on earth and now they have found their long sought after home, peopled only by others of like mind, the very mind of Jesus. This new home is now theirs for eternity.

CHAPTER 25
JESUS' FINAL MESSAGE
Revelation 22

THE CITY OF GOD - A BLESSED PLACE

John continues with his description of the holy city by noting the River of Life which finds its source in the very throne of God, and that wends its way through the middle of the city. One must keep in mind that this city is three dimensional - a cube - with twelve different levels differentiated by the twelve different stones described in Revelation 21. However, the different levels will create no barriers to the citizenry of the holy city, for they will move as effortlessly between them as Jesus did through walls. The River of Life most likely descends into each of the twelve levels much like a waterfall. The psalmist spoke of this river when he said, "There is a river, the streams whereof shall make glad the city of God, the holy place of the tabernacles of the most High" (Psalm 46:4). This river also takes us back to the initial dwelling place created for man, the Garden of Eden. It, too, had a river flowing out of it, forking into four separate rivers.

Also reminiscent of the Garden of Eden is the presence of the Tree of Life. It was initially found in Eden, but was removed after the Fall of man. It is now restored to the saints; indeed its restoration was the very first promise given to the Overcomers in Revelation 2:7. The tree is enormous. To begin with, the River of Life flows right through it, and the indication is given that the tree runs the length of the river. This strikes the human mind as impossible, but the workmanship of the entire city is "impossible," at least as concerns the human mind. The central part of the city, then, will be like one glorious park with the added glory of all of the aforementioned precious stones.

Note that the tree last seen in the Garden of Eden, the Tree of Knowledge, does not reappear along with the Tree of Life. The Tree of Knowledge will not be needed because we will no longer "see through a glass, darkly; but then face to face"; we will no longer "know in part; but then shall [we] know even as also [we] are known" (1 Corinthians 13:12). All knowledge will then be ours, but the sustaining of our very lives seems, even then, to be dependent on the mercies of God.

The Tree of Life, although a constant in the Eternal City, will also be cyclical. Eternity will still have, as part of its fabric, monthly and yearly cycles. The oft-taught "sameness" of eternity is completely refuted with this one verse. Change within constancy seems to delight God. We have witnessed it on earth, we will witness it in heaven. Each month for twelve months, the Tree of Life will produce a different fruit and then the cycle will begin again. That fruit is reserved only for the Overcomers, the citizens of the City. But the leaves from that tree will be given to the inhabitants of the other nations. Those leaves will have supernatural healing properties and will be used to heal and sustain the civilizations outside the holy city.

The information given us here by John has several implications. One, there will be people other than just the Christians who will continue to inhabit the universe. Two, those people, the various nations of the universe, will be dependent upon the holy city for their survival. They will walk in its light and they will be healed by its bounty. The word for "healing" used here is not indicative of sickness. It means "to give health to." Again, the city is the source of blessing for the universe, and the saints are the dispensers of its mercy. This is clear by the reference to the need by them for healing. Healing will be available but it will also be necessary even though death will no longer exist. And three, it will be the Christians who will dispense the benefits of the holy city to the rest of the Universe. We will bring the touch of God and His heaven to the worlds.

"And there shall be no more curse". Not only will the nations walk in the light of the city and be healed by its produce, they will also worship its King with no thought of rebellion. The curse of sin that presently rests on earth will be defeated at the end of the Age and Satan will be forever made impotent. Never again will sin be a part of, nor a threat to, any part of the Universe of God. There will never be another Fall. There will never be another curse.

WE SERVE FATHER AND SON BEFORE GOD'S THRONE

"The throne of God and of the Lamb shall be in it; and his servants shall serve him." We will now be given the ultimate pleasure of serving God. But our blessing does not end here. "Blessed are those servants, whom the lord when he cometh shall find watching: verily I say unto you, that he shall gird himself, and make them to sit down to meat, and will come forth and serve them" says Jesus in Luke 12:37. We will serve Jesus, but Jesus will serve us also. We will receive at His hand what we will finally be able to give to Him. This is the true nature of love; to give so freely and to receive so freely that the lines between giving and receiving are completely blurred. Both giving and receiving are delightful to those in love and we have never been in love the way we will be when we are in heaven.

How will we serve him? We do not really know. It stands to reason that our lives on earth have been lived and ordained with the thought of eternity clearly in mind, and that what we have spent a lifetime learning will not be wasted in heaven. But the scope of our service will extend farther than that. "Eye hath not seen nor ear heard, neither entered into the heart of man what God has prepared for those that love him" (1 Corinthians 2:9). That fact is what compelled Paul to write a most dramatic and extreme statement later in the same book. First Corinthians 15:19 says, "If in this life only we have hope in Christ, we are of all men most miserable." Most miserable! I, personally, would never have the courage to teach that if Paul had not written it. But Paul had been caught up to the Third Heaven and he knew what was awaiting the Christians, whereas, we do not. That is why he prayed so fervently "that the God of our Lord Jesus Christ, the Father of glory, may give to you a spirit of wisdom and revelation in the knowledge of him. I pray that the eyes of your heart may be enlightened, so that you may know what is the hope of his calling, and what are the riches of the glory of his inheritance in the saints, and what is the surpassing greatness of his power toward us who believe" (Ephesians 1:17-19a, NASB).

ETERNITY - WHAT IS IN STORE FOR THE OVERCOMER?

Although we cannot state with certainty what awaits the Christian in eternity, Paul goes on to tell us in 1 Corinthians

2:10 that "God hath revealed them [the things awaiting us in eternity] unto us by his Spirit: for the Spirit searcheth all things, yea the deep things of God." In other words, many clues abound in the Scriptures. One of those clues can be found in the very name of Jesus. When Isaiah prophesies the birth of God Himself on Planet Earth, he calls His name "Wonderful Counselor, the mighty God, the everlasting Father, the Prince of peace" [NASB]. Note that there are four nouns and four adjectives. We tend to think of this passage in terms of the phrasing of Handal's Messiah and create a pause between "wonderful" and "counselor". But Isaiah is saying that God is the wonderful counselor, not that God is wonderful and a counselor. All of the names are magnificent: mighty God, everlasting Father, Prince of Peace; however, Isaiah begins this awesome praise with the accolade of Wonderful Counselor. It is important to try to understand why.

The Hebrew word used for "counselor" is *yaats*, which, along with the meaning of "to advise," also means "to purpose, devise, or plan." Thus, to be a counselor in the Hebrew mind meant far more than just giving counsel or advise. It meant to purpose, (determine), devise (or think up), and plan. God is the supreme giver of advice, but He is far more, and this praise accords to Him His full breadth of acclaim and worship. Isaiah is declaring that God is the Wonderful Architect; the Planner of Great and Marvelous Things. And this is the *first* praise given to God, even before "everlasting father"!

Indeed, God is the Wonderful Architect, and just the example of our heavens and our earth bears that out. Paul says that God has made himself known to the inhabitants of earth simply by observing our world as it has the fingerprints of the nature of God all over it, showing Him to be unsurpassable in both design and whimsy. It also displays the extravagance of God in His love for us. Consider the multitude of different, odd, beautiful, and weird fish that God has formed. In reality, a few goldfish and maybe a Chinese fighter fish would have sufficed. But God wanted to delight us. And just in case we never got near the ocean, He did the same with thousands of different kinds of butterflies. And just in case we didn't notice them, He made thousands of different flowers with a thousand different smells. God has clothed the entire earth in unbounded creativity and beauty. God is the Wonderful Counselor. But what does this have to do with Christians and Eternity? It tells us that Eternity has a plan to it also; it is not just an unending stream of days. Furthermore, the plans for Eternity are a continuation of God's plans for the earth and thus to begin to understand Eternity, we must look once again at the history of the earth.

UNDERSTANDING GOD'S PLAN FOR ETERNITY

Genesis tells us that God's final work on earth during the Creation, was Man. Up until that time, His most glorious creation had been the angels, and within that creation there was one very special angel. Ezekiel says that God went to the outside limit when He created this angel, even saying that God could go no further than He had gone with this creation: "Thus saith the Lord God; *Thou sealest up the sum*, full of wisdom, and perfect in beauty" (Ezekiel 28:12, emphasis mine). This angel was the most beautiful, the wisest, most brilliant, and powerful creation that heaven had ever seen. To him was given the gift of music; to him was accorded the place closest to the Throne of God. His name reflected his position before God as he was called the Bearer of Light. He was so close to God that he caught and held the very light of God. In Hebrew the name given to him translates as "Lucifer," and after the Trinity, he held the most exalted position in heaven. But in the plan of God, Lucifer's position was not intended to transcend all other positions forever. That is because God, from the very beginning, had another position in mind, one not yet evidenced; and that position was one of a Bride for His Son. That Bride would eclipse Satan for she was destined to sit on the very throne of God.

Ephesians 1:4 and Revelation 13:8 both say that the names of God's chosen - the Bride - were known to Him as being His even before He created the earth. Matthew 25:25 says that the Kingdom was prepared from the foundation of the world. That is because, even though the saving grace of Jesus was given to all men, God knew who would respond to His call. Thus, there can be no denying that it was God's plan and intention, *before the world was created*, to have a Bride for His Son.

That fact becomes very interesting when coupled with the fact of Lucifer's rebellion. Were the two facts linked? I have come to believe so because the plan of a Bride would explain both Satan's rebellion against God even when he lived in the very glory of God, and why Lucifer in his fallen form, Satan, has been the arch-enemy of mankind ever since.

To begin with, all of creation knew that God would not choose an unworthy bride, one from an inferior order, for His only son. Just as I would not choose an ape, even the most handsome, intelligent, esteemed ape in all existence as a husband for any of my girls, neither would God choose a lesser being for His Son. She, too, must be a child of God; one of superior status, one who would have angels minister to her, one worthy to judge angels, one who would "shine as the brightness of the firmament" (Daniel 12:3). And, consequently, she would surpass Lucifer and displace him as the closest creation to the presence of God, and thus, be the new bearer of His light. (The commandment of Jesus to the Church to "let your light so shine" was no small commandment!) *But*, unlike Lucifer, she would become part of the very Family of God; *another* child of His - the only child other than Jesus that God had or would ever have!

Christians blithely sing about being a child of God, about being part of the family of God. Generally, they do not stop to reflect on what a miracle that is, and what that status implies. But Lucifer immediately understood, and I believe that that understanding is what led to his rebellion; to the first Great War in heaven.

We are told two things about Lucifer's fall and how he became Satan: one, that his pride came to the forefront, and two, that he became filled with violence. Satan must have decided that he had to prevent this idea of another child of God's at any and all costs. Satan decided that no one would be allowed to usurp his position, and by making that decision, he had to challenge God and His authority. This challenge resulted in rebellion at the highest levels of the universe, because one-third of heaven chose the side of Satan. Thus began the war over which one of only two possible outcomes would prevail: the "demotion" of Satan or the downfall of God. And so began the great cosmic war between good and evil.

When the Bible opens, the story of man begins in the Garden of Eden. God has created a paradise on Planet Earth and has given His new creature, Adam, dominion over it. Adam and Eve could not have possibly been misidentified as "god-like," but somehow Satan knew that God's future plans for a ride for His son centered on these puny humans and their offspring. This understanding of Satan's further points to the possibility that God made known His plans in heaven. Satan, who has lost in his attempt at a heavenly coup, now sees another opportunity. Knowing that, surely, God cannot possibly accept fallen, sin-filled creatures as a bride for His Son, Satan, sin-filled himself, knows he must see to the downfall of the human race. Twisting and misrepresenting God's plan to have these humans as His children, and thus as members of the family of God, Satan instead promises Eve that she will "be as God' if she will but disobey and sin against God by eating the forbidden fruit from the Tree of Knowledge of Good and Evil. She and Adam take the bait, reject God, and, by proxy, accept the dominion of Satan over them, and thus doom the race of mankind. It seems that Satan has succeeded completely. However, God replies, "You have indeed bruised Man's heel, but Man will bruise your head." Indeed, mankind is fallen, but a man from the very race of Adam is coming who will crush Satan's head.

What Satan did not understand was that God was not going to have a bride by direct creation; He couldn't. The Creator and the creation can never be equals. Nor can man, created a little lower that the angels, ever be capable of judging those angels. But we are told in 1 Corinthians 6:3 that we will judge the angels so something has to change in order for that to happen. What changes is man himself, but man changed by God. God is going to have this bride for His Son by redemption; by a group of created beings who would realize their own worthlessness and then, by their own decision, be changed into the image and very likeness of God through Christ His son.

You see, redeemed people are far more like God than created people. This is the promise of Ephesians 4:24: the new creature is in the **likeness** of God, created in holiness and righteousness. And although Satan hates these people and will war with them and tempt them for the entire length of time that they are alive, the redeemed will prevail and overcome on foreign soil, Satan's home ground, Planet Earth. God will use that very warfare, temptation, and opposition to mold them, ennoble them, change them, and purify them. And the end result of the persecution of these people will be a people who have overcome evil and who have been changed into the very likeness of God. Angels do not have to overcome temptation; angels live lives under perfect conditions. Only man chooses whether or not to succumb to temptation. When he chooses to resist, he becomes more Christ-like and less Adam-like each time. And now, each of those overcomers has found his place in the holy city.

UNDERSTANDING THE OVERCOMERS' ROLE IN ETERNITY

What will become of all these humans with their unique training forged upon a hostile planet? How will they be used? We are given another clue in Revelation 22:4-5, "And they shall see his face; and his name shall be in their foreheads. And there shall be no night there; and they need no candle, neither light of the sun; for the Lord God giveth them light: and they shall reign for ever and ever." Not only do the overcomers dwell with God, they are eternally marked as being His. Why, if they are the only people in existence, is that necessary? A conspicuous mark is meant to differentiate one group from another group; a mark is redundant when it is applied uniformly. The question is then, from whom are the Believers differentiated? In order to answer that, we must consider the Universe in the light of the fact that God is the Wonderful Counselor, the planner and creator of marvelous things...

Our earth revolves around our sun, taking one year to go around once. Our sun revolves around our galaxy - The Milky Way. Traveling at almost half a million miles an hour, it still takes two hundred million years for one revolution to take place because the Milky Way is immense! And there are millions of such galaxies. Our universe is already vast and it is continually expanding; it is not static. This makes sense because after all, God is "Creator," not "Creator, Retired." God never said, "I created once, but now I'm finished with all that." It is in God's very nature to create; He is never said to "out-grow" his creative nature as if it were but, simply, "a phase."

Harvard astronomer Harlo Shapely writes in his book <u>Climatic Change</u> that the necessary elements to support life on a planet like ours could be found in one in a trillion solar systems. Given those mathematical odds, there could be a hundred million earths like ours. There could be even more because God is not limited by mathematical odds. On December 5, 1022, the NPR program "All Things considered" reported that an earth-like planet has been found six hundred light-years away from earth. Even closer than that, at twenty light years away, an unconfirmed rocky planet three times more massive than Earth has been discovered by researchers at the University of California, Santa Cruz and the Carnegie Institution of Washington. Given the name Gilese 581g, the planet appears to have a heat source reaching its surface which is neither too strong nor too weak for liquid water to exist. As human knowledge increases, I am quite confident that more and more habitable spaces in the universe will be discovered. Says the Billion-channel Extra-Terrestrial Assay (BETA) director and Harvard physicist Paul Horowitz: "I have no doubts. Intelligent life in our galaxy? So overwhelmingly likely that I'd give you almost any odds."[30]

Sometimes we Christians remind me of the ants in the anthill in my backyard. To them, my backyard is their universe; there is nothing else out there. If I were to ask them about Paris, France, they would have no idea that Paris existed, they would probably deny the veracity inherent in my question. Humans are much the same way. When first born, the infant has no understanding that he is a separate entity from his mother. When that understanding first begins to dawn, the child faces anxiety. In fact we have a name for that anxiety; separation anxiety, and it will have to be resolved several times before the child is a toddler. After that understanding, the child continues to define his universe as consisting of his home and a very few other places. As he matures in understanding he acknowledges and accepts a broader "universe" of possibly his town only. We look with affection on the narrowness of that view but we, too, as adults, many times exhibit that same narrowness and childishness when we refuse to accept the concept of an existence outside our own planet. The idea that God would have bigger plans that involved more of the universe than just our little corner of it offends many. God, however, never changes His ways in order to appease our possible offense.

Not only do astronomers state with total certainty that the universe is expanding, this fact is in line with Scripture. Isaiah 9:7a says, "of the increase of his government and peace there shall be no end." Government and peace are not needed in uninhabited places. They are necessary only in communities and civilization. Thus, it is clear to see from this verse that God's plan is to expand His government throughout His universe. He is limited in scope only by the number of rulers that He has at His command, but who are His rulers? And from where do they come? After all, rulers have to be trained, tested, and, in order to represent God Almighty, they have to be changed into His very likeness. Only the saints qualify.

The saints have been trained on Planet Earth, sometimes in the most painful of situations, and they have triumphed because of the power of God Himself in their lives. They have learned to die to themselves and say, "for me to live is Christ." Now they will administer the government and peace of God throughout God's universe forever! Revelation 21:25 tells us that the gates of the holy city are always open. They are open because the saints will need to come and go throughout all God's universe, administering His rule. The Age of Fallen Man, spanning the time from the creation of Adam to the Second Coming of Jesus, is pivotal for Eternity. God has designed this age in order produce a bride for Jesus who will also rule and reign with Him as God's program for His ever expanding kingdom is carried out.

The reward and responsibility that is planned for the Overcomers is glorious beyond measure. Indeed, the human mind is unable to grasp what awaits the Christians as they walk into God's incredible plan for eternity. John has revealed to us the Throne of God. It is extraordinary, glorious, and holy. It is the focal point in the Capitol of the Universe, the source of the River of Living Water, and the origin of Light. Only two entities will share it with Him: His Son and His Son's Bride.

ETERNITY'S EVERLASTING STORY OF REDEMPTION

The earth and the universe will last forever. So, too, will the story of Jesus, the Redeemer. The new creations of God will undoubtedly have heard the phenomenal story of how Satan, the arch enemy of God, whose rebellion shook heaven to its absolute foundations, was defeated eons ago by the Son of God, and how then it was that that Son won His Bride. Ultimately, that is the story of the Bible from Genesis to Revelation, and that story will be better known and understood then than it is now.

Envision, if you will, the opening scene in the first Star Wars movie ever released. The movie screen is filled with thousands of stars and then words appear on the screen, unfolding like a scroll. "Long, long ago in a galaxy far, far away..." the words begin, and the story commences its telling. In Eternity, there, too, will be an everlasting story told from one end of God's universe to the other that *truly* begins "long, long ago in a galaxy far, far away..." And when the saints travel throughout the realm of their Father to administer His rule, they will be instantly recognizable as those very children of Everlasting God talked about in the Great Story because they will have a distinguishing mark upon them: the name of God upon their foreheads. That mark of distinction will belong only to those who have been redeemed by the blood of the Lamb; who lived victoriously in Satan's realm; who silenced the music of the angels with their songs of redemption; who are citizens of the glorious holy city, who rule and reign with Jesus; and who see God face to face. And, when they appear in the far-flung corners of God's universe, creation will cry, "Look! There is one of those people for whom Christ died. There is a child of the Living God, there is one of those who is a Bride of the Lamb and sits upon His throne!" Each of those saints will be the living embodiment of the fulfillment of the promise God made to His Son, eons and eons ago.

JESUS' REVELATION TO JOHN IS FAITHFUL AND TRUE

As God's revelation to John comes to a close, the angel solemnly declares to John that everything that he has seen and everything that he has heard is, indeed, faithful to God and true. John has not been deceived, this has not been a dream.

John must know that he has truly been present at The Day of the Lord and now he must bear witness of it to the Church. But John will not be alone in his witness; the Lord God and His angel (who, in verse 9 is identified as a fellow believer, now eternal) also bear witness to the truth of John's revelation. Not only do three persons bear witness to this, the fact that these words are faithful and true is stated three times. God Himself declares this in Revelation 21:5, and the angel/saint declares it here and in Revelation 19:9.

WILL WE BE FOUND FAITHFUL WHEN JESUS COMES?

"Behold, I come quickly: blessed is he that keepeth the sayings of the prophecy of this book" (verse 7). The Greek word translated here as "quickly" literally means "in haste." He is speaking of the manner of His coming, not the timing of His coming. He has not soon returned to earth, but when He does, it will be suddenly and in great haste. This has been greatly stressed in the Book of Revelation, it has been stated six times, twice as a warning and four times as a promise. Jesus is stressing that one must be ready at all times for His return. The question is, will He find us faithful when He returns? He is warning us that it is imperative that He does.

At the beginning of Revelation, a promise that those who heard the words of this prophecy would be blessed and, indeed, they were blessed with great insight into the very nature and character of God. They were also given much information as to what the future holds. Now, what they do with that insight and information is critical, for the blessing given in verse 7 applies to those who *keep* the Words of the prophecy. It is not enough to be hearers of the Word only, one must be a doer of the Word in order to inherit the promises given. And furthermore, it is specifically stated that the words in view here are the words in *this* book, not the Bible as a whole. These words are both a sacred trust and a powerful weapon. They equip the Church and also each believer in a critical way, and when the Church ignores this book she throws down one of her mightiest weapons.

GOD ALONE TO BE WORSHIPPED

Once before, John has unknowingly knelt in worship before an "angel" who turned out to be a fellow believer. It is difficult to imagine that, when he does so again at this point, he is making the same mistake. Perhaps he is again mistaking a mortal for an angel, but perhaps he is simply overcome by the message of what he has witnessed and heard and feels the need to acknowledge what he has been shown. John had known and loved Jesus more deeply than any other human ever had, except, perhaps, for Mary His mother. He knew this vision to be true, and it must have stirred in him a deep and profound reverence. Nonetheless, the angel once again admonishes him to stop. He further informs John that he, the angel, is both a fellow believer and a prophet. No other identification beyond this is given. (It is interesting, though, to ruminate on the saint whose reward involves being allowed to show heaven to the Apostle John!)

A more scathing indictment against the common practice of worshiping Mary and other saints cannot be found. It is repugnant in the eyes of heaven to worship a mere mortal, no matter how "sainted," he or she may be. Worship is reserved for God and God alone. And when we find ourselves in the presence of God Almighty we will completely understand this. Who else is Creator? Who else is Truth personified? Who else is Love, Beauty, and Justice in discernible form? No human would dare to allow worship for himself after glimpsing God.

THE PROPHECY OF THIS BOOK TO REMAIN UNSEALED

The human angel further states that he is a keeper of the sayings of Revelation, stressing again that God has a particular message for "this day." The man who is equipped with this knowledge is equipped for this day. Furthermore, this message is not to be "sealed" as was the book of the prophecies of Daniel. The Book of Revelation is a critical message for the Church and it has relevance throughout the entire Church Age. It is not to be hidden from the Church, it is not to be ignored. Its message is to be broadcast, and the organized churches who do not allow it, or do not encourage it to be taught and discussed, will answer for their actions on That Day. This is not a compendium of John's thoughts and interpretations, it is

521

a final message from God, given to, and concerning the Church. It is not a coded message; it is a vision of what will surely come to pass. The Bible is not complete without it and a study of the Bible is not complete without a study of Revelation. It is both a weapon that the Church has kept sheathed and a sacred trust that she has violated.

THE MESSAGE OF REVELATION IS TIMELESS
The time for its application and message is not solely future, as was Daniel's; Revelation's time "is at hand." The message is as timely now as it was then, perhaps more so. Without doubt, the prophesied events in Revelation will become clearer with time but, as was stated in the very first verse in the very first chapter, Revelation is a revelation of Jesus Christ Himself and who we are in Christ. When one confronts Jesus as God, not just Jesus as Man, but as Jesus the risen Christ, the Son who sits upon the throne of God, and the Lamb who was slain, one is able to understand, appreciate, trust, and therefore, love Him in a fuller, more complete way.

But what about all the possible misunderstandings which may ensue from its reading? What if Revelation seems to have no effect on various lives? Verse 11 addresses that when it says that he who is unjust will remain so, as will he who is filthy. But he who is holy and righteous will continue also. In other words, if one can hear both the hope of the gospel reward and the certainty of eternal punishment for the one who refuses the gospel, as unveiled in Revelation, and still choose to remain outside of the reach of Jesus' invitation, what more could possibly be said? Nevertheless, the message must be preached whether it heals or hardens. Many times I have heard people remark, "I would share the gospel but I just don't know how they would take it." It is not our responsibility to make the message enlighten the world; that is the job of the Holy Spirit. But it is our responsibility to proclaim the word, for "faith cometh by hearing."

Ezekiel 3:27 gives much the same message: "But when I speak with thee, I will open thy mouth, and thou shalt say unto them, Thus saith the Lord God; He that heareth, let him hear; and he that forbeareth, let him forbear: for they are a rebellious house." It is their responsibility for their rebelliousness only if they have heard, it is ours if they have not. Either way, Jesus is coming back and will bring with Him justice. Each person on the face of the earth will receive exactly what is due him and he will receive it at the hand of Jesus. There will be no denying the preeminence of Christ in that day. Buddha will not return, nor will Mohammed; no, they, too, will be judged. And in that Day they will receive justice from the hand of the Eternal Judge Jesus Christ. The claim of the pseudo-equality of all religious messengers, no matter what the religion, which is heard so ubiquitously today, will be seen to be a ridiculous claim on that Day. All will bow their knees, all will confess with their tongue that Jesus Christ is Lord.

JESUS DECLARES HIS DIVINITY

In verse 13 Jesus makes one of His strongest claims to divinity which can be found in the Bible when He says that He is Alpha and Omega, the beginning and the end, the first and the last. This can only be said of God, in fact, it is said of God in Revelation 1:8. Now Jesus is claiming that the same is true of Himself. To those who would acknowledge Jesus simply as a great man, one of many messengers from God, this verse offers no compromise.

C.S. Lewis addressed the fallacy of Jesus as "good man" with impeccable logic when he wrote the following: "I am trying here to prevent anyone saying the really foolish thing that people often say about Him: 'I'm ready to accept Jesus as a great moral teacher but I don't accept His claim to be God.' That is the one thing we must not say. A man who was merely a man and said the sort of things Jesus said would not be a great moral teacher. He would either be a lunatic - on a level with the man who says he is a poached egg - or else he would be the Devil of Hell. You must make your choice. Either this man was, and is, the Son of God: or else a madman or something worse. You can shut Him up for a fool, you can spit at Him and kill Him as a demon; or you can fall at His feet and call Him Lord and God. But let us not come with any patronising nonsense about His being a great human teacher. He has not left that open to us. He did not intend to."[31]

Revelation 22:14-15 again draw the line of dichotomy between those who find abode in the holy city and those against whom the city is barred; and once more God's view of what constitutes the vilest depravity is revealed. The unclean, those who practice witchcraft and seek after mind-altering states, adulterers and fornicators, murderers, idolaters, and liars are thus indicted as the basest of humans. In addition to being punished themselves, their offensive presence will never again have to be tolerated or suffered by the righteous.

"I Jesus have sent mine angel to testify unto you these things in the churches" (verse 16a). In light of this extremely solemn statement by Jesus, the fact that the Church, for the most part, has been silent on this book is a grave offense against God, indeed. Revelation is the one book specifically appointed to be read in the churches, it is the only Biblical book outside of Isaiah to record a physical description of Jesus. It is the only book in which the reading of it holds a specific promise of blessing, it is the only book which contains a direct word from Jesus after His ascension. Jesus, as He promised, has gone to prepare a place for His people, and after He had done so, He sent back word - via The Book of Revelation - as to its state of existence.

"I am the root and the offspring of David, and the bright and morning star." Jesus is testifying to, and affirming the fact that He is both human and divine. He does this by making a seemingly oxymoronic statement that he is both the father and child of David. As God the Son, He is the father of David; as a man, Jesus is the descendent of David. Jesus alone in all the Universe is both. God the Father is not both, nor, other than Jesus, is any human being who ever lived. This statement can apply to only one personage, and it is at His feet that every knee will bow.

The Morning Star that we are most familiar with, Venus, shines right before the dawn. In the same way, Jesus is saying that He is the Light that shines before the dawning of God's new day. Without Him, there is no light possible in this dark world. Lucifer, in Isaiah 14:12, was called the "son of the morning." It is Satan who, although seeming to be an angel of light, has plunged and kept this world in darkness. Those who follow Satan are blinded to the true light of God. Avowing that they are children of light, they are in complete darkness. Jesus is calling to just those people, emphatically stating that He, not

Satan, is the rising star whose coming heralds the dawn of the new day. And with that proclamation, the Spirit extends the greatest invitation to each human being that they will ever know. "Come," says the Bright and Morning Star, "I will accept you and I will love you, and I will even share My throne with you." The prophesied "Star out of Judah" that guided the wise men to Bethlehem will now guide all who will but let Him.

AN ETERNITY TO PARTAKE OF THE WATER OF LIFE

The Spirit says "come," but the Bride also says "come." This entreaty is both lateral and vertical on the part of the Bride. She beseeches Jesus to return, to come for her, and she also beseeches those who do not yet know Jesus as Lord and Savior to come to Him. The Spirit and the Bride work in tandem. The Bride, the Church, is to give the invitation of Jesus to the world, but it will only be authentic and efficacious if it is led and inspired by the Spirit. We can do no good work on our own; it must all be born of the Father.

"Come," which the Spirit and Bride say, is a present imperative. A better sense of the meaning would be to say, "Be coming." In other words, the prayer of the Church is not simply concerned with the final coming of Jesus, it also entails every event that must unfold itself before Jesus can come. It is a prayer that hands up to God the entire course of human events and trusts Him to work His work in it, knowing that human history's culmination will be His return.

Furthermore, the Church is not a closed society; all who are thirsty are invited to drink. And *"whosoever* will, let him take the water of life freely," says Jesus. His saving grace is not closed to anyone who will accept it. There are none who are predestined to rejection by God; how sad, if one were to hear this glorious story and then be told, "it is not for you". But Jesus here makes it plain that all are invited to drink of His water of life.

DIVINE WARNING: DO NOT ALTER ANY WORD OF THIS BOOK

Knowing that Revelation would be a book that would be a magnet for human tampering, Jesus sets an extremely stern injunction upon anyone who would attempt to alter it. Because it is "sensational" in the true meaning of the word, it would have been easy for the Early Church to tidy it up a bit before passing it on. I can just hear them saying, "Well, you know John *is* ninety now..." For that reason, verses 18 and 19 were written, and a more deadly warning can hardly be imagined:

"For I testify unto every man that heareth the words of the prophecy of this book, If any man shall add unto these things, God shall add unto him the plagues that are written in this book: and if any man shall take away from the words of the book of this prophecy, God shall take away his part out of the book of life, and out of the holy city, and from the things which are written in this book."

We saw in the very first chapter of Revelation that a blessing was given to anyone who would hear the words contained therein. That blessing is unique to Revelation and it tells us much about the value that God has placed upon the study of it. The injunction against tampering with the message found in this book has most often been broadened by Christians to apply to the entire Bible. This is incorrect. The warning found at the end of Revelation applies only to the vision that John received on Patmos. Out of the sixty-six books of the Bible this warning is given in regards to only one other section of Scripture: the Law. Deuteronomy 4:2 states: "Ye shall not add unto the word which I command you, neither shall ye diminish aught from it, that ye may keep the commandments of the Lord your God which I command you." The Law was critical and immutable and it had to remain through the ages just as it was given. Even so, the injunction concerning the Law was not nearly as dire and catastrophic as the one found in Revelation. Punishment for breaking this commandment from God could not be more severe.

WHY SUCH SEVERE CONSEQUENCES TO ALTERATION OF THIS BOOK?

One must ask oneself, "Why?" This book is crucial to the Church and it must accurately reflect the exact message of God to her. It is interesting to note that the Bible opens with God's word to Adam and Eve concerning the Tree of Knowledge of Good and Evil, and records that immediately after the giving of those words, Eve added to them as she related them to the Serpent. She was soon deceived and fell into sin. The words of

God must stand as they have been delivered to man. Consider that the message John was bringing back from Patmos would be perceived as being "fantastic." It would take all the credibility John had with the Church to allow her to accept from him this vision. In fact, of all men living at the time, John was probably the only one with the credibility to relate this message. Possibly, that was why he, alone, of all the Apostles was spared a martyr's death.

John would begin this book with the "impossible" declaration that he had actually been present on the Day of the Lord; he would speak of measuring the Temple, which no longer existed, and still does not to this day; he would talk of the whole world witnessing the ascension of the Two Witnesses millennia before there were television cameras; he would paint futuristic scenes of the most fantastic creatures and scenarios imaginable. And even if John were able to convince the First Century Church to accept this vision, there was the dire and ever-present fear that the next generation of "scholars" would edit it. And yet, according to the Lord God Almighty, the angel who was a glorified saint, and John, an earthly saint, this vision was accurate and true.

This was the exact word that Jesus wanted sent back to His church and it could not be altered in any way. Each detail was of critical importance. To tamper with this book is to tamper with the divine time-line of the most momentous things in the destiny of Christ and His people. And so a warning of death and plague was given to any who would add to these words, and a warning of the loss of salvation was given to any who deleted these words. And that, along with the providential care of God, has made it possible for twenty-first Christians to still have access to the words of Jesus, and thus have access to the blessings that are promised from Revelation.

That is not to say that these words have not suffered attack, they have. Christians have dismissed them, over-symbolized them, jumbled them, and refused to read them. But they are still there for the Believer if he will avail himself of them. The Spirit and the Bride still say "Come." And the last promise that Jesus made to the Church, "Surely I come quickly," continues to be met by faithful servants with the rejoinder "Amen. Even so, come, Lord Jesus."

"The grace of our Lord Jesus Christ be with you all, Amen" (Revelation 22:21).

Amen.

ACKNOWLEDGMENTS

Before writing this book, I never understood the need for acknowledgments. Now, I know that a book is never a solitary accomplishment. There are too many discouragements, too many dead-ends along the way. And then God sends special messengers and encouragers to the author at just the right juncture on the path. At least that is my story.

The first person that I must acknowledge is the late Arthur Bloomfield. Although our paths never crossed on earth, his scholarship, ideas, and books formed the structure for Wonderful Counselor. He opened Revelation for me and I cannot wait for the day that I meet him in heaven. Mr. Bloomfield, my book is because your books were.

Heartfelt thanks must also go to a handful of other people. Bill and Holland Hunter provided financial and emotional help at the very beginning of my writing, Sam Magno gave me a word from God that has sustained me to this day, John Helmuth spent hours on my graphics, TJ Kendall was my early proofreader and encourager, Linda McDill softened my sometimes direct approach to writing and also found my editor, Carol Lacey Pell, for me. Carol was extraordinary in that capacity and as a friend. Vince Raya designed my cover, Sandy Ange shot the photo for the book, Lily Woo, with her amazing eye for detail, both proofread my manuscript and is translating it into Chinese. My parents, Don and Lea Rost, both proofread and encouraged me every step of the way (and there were some steep steps), Finally, and most importantly, my husband, Pete, never ever let me stop before this book saw print. His vision for this book prevailed and I am eternally grateful to him and to the other angels that God sent to me. Each one of you freely contributed to this endeavor and that is amazing in and of itself. Thanks to you one and all, I have never for one moment forgotten your contributions. May God bless you all.

SELECTED BIBLIOGRAPY

Bloomfield, Arthur E., All Things New: The Prophecies of Revelation Explained, Minneapolis, Minnesota, Bethany House, 1959.

Bloomfield, Arthur E., Signs of His Coming, Minneapolis, Minnesota, Bethany House, 1962.

Bloomfield, Arthur E., The End of the Days: The Prophecies of Daniel Explained, Minneapolis, Minnesota, Bethany House, 1961.

Bloomfield, Arthur E., How to Recognize the Antichrist, Minneapolis, Minnesota, Bethany House, 1975.

Bloomfield, Arthur E., Before the Last Battle Armageddon, Minneapolis, Minnesota, Bethany Fellowship, 1971.

Cantrell, Ron, The Final Kingdom, Jerusalem, Israel, Bridges for Peace, 2000.

Carr, Joseph J., The Twisted Cross, Lafayette, Louisiana, Huntington House, 1985.

Christian History, Volume II, No. 1

Christian History, Volume II, No. 2, Issue 3

Christian History, Volume IV, No. 1

Christian History, Volume V, No.2

Christian History, Volume IX, No. 3

Christian History, Volume XI, No. 2

Christian History, Volume XII, No. 3

Christian History, Volume XIV, No. 4

Christian History, Volume XV, No. 1

Christian History, Volume XIX, No. 4

Christian History, Volume XX, No. 3

Christian History, Spring 2005

Christian History Institute's Glimpses, Number 1

Christian History Institute's Glimpses, Number 11

Christian History Institute's Glimpses, Number12

Christian History Institute's Glimpses, Number 14

Christian History Institute's Glimpses, Number 15

De Rosa, Peter, Vicars of Christ: The Dark Side of the Papacy, Crown Publishing, Inc., 1988.

Durant, Will, The Story of Civilization, International, Simon and Schuster, 1950.

Erickson, Carolly, Great Harry: The Extravagant Life of Henry VIII, New York, Summit Books, 1980.

Gibbon, Edward, The History of the Decline and Fall of the Roman Empire, Public Domain.

Harris, R. Laird, and Gleason L. Archer Jr., and Bruce K. Waltke, Chicago, Illinois, The Moody Bible Institute of Chicago, 1980.

Hendriksen, William, More than Conquerors, Grand Rapids, Michigan, Baker Book House, 1940

Hunt, Dave, A Woman Rides the Beast, Eugene, Oregon, Harvest House, 1994.

Hutchings, Dr. N.W., The New Creators: A Christian Analysis of Cloning and Genetic Engineering, Oklahoma City, Oklahoma, Hearthstone, 1997.

Jeffrey, Grant R., Armageddon: Appointment With Destiny, New York, Toronto, London, Sydney, Auckland, Bantam Books, 1990.

Jeffrey, Grant R., Apocalypse: The Coming Judgment of the Nations, Toronto, Ontario, Frontier Research Publications, 1992.

Lewis, C.S., Mere Christianity, New York, MacMillan, 1943.

Lewis, C.S., That Hideous Strength, New York, Scribner Paperback Fiction, 1996.

Lewis C.S., The Screwtape Letters, New York, Macmillan, 1961

Lotz, Anne Graham, The Vision of His Glory: Finding Hope Through the Revelation of Jesus Christ, Dallas, London, Vancouver, Melbourne, Word, 1996.

Marshall, Reverend Dr. Alfred, The Interlinear Greek-English New Testament, Grand Rapids, Michigan, Zondervan, 1958.

Morris, Henry M., The Revelation Record, Wheaton, Illinois, Tyndale House, 1983.

Morris, Henry M., Creation and the Second Coming, El Cajon, California, 1991.

Rutledge, Archibald, Life's Extras, Westwood, New Jersey, Fleming H. Revell Company, 1961.

Seiss, Joseph A., The Apocalypse: Exposition of the Book of Revelation, Grand Rapids, Michigan, Kregel Publications, 1900.

Smith, Chuck, <u>End Times,</u> Costa Mesa, California, The Word for Today, 1978.

Strong, James, <u>The Exhaustive Concordance of the Bible,</u> Madison, New Jersey, Abingdon, 1890.

Thompson, R. W., <u>The Papacy and the Civil Power</u>, New York, 1876.

Trench, Richard Chenevix, <u>Commentary on the Epistle to the Seven Churches of Asia,</u> Eugene, Oregon, Wipf and Stock Publishers, 1861.

Vine, W.E., <u>An Expository Dictionary of New Testament Words,</u> Old Tappan, New Jersey, Fleming H. Revell, 1940.

Walvoord, John F., <u>Armageddon, Oil and the Middle East Crisis</u>, Grand Rapids, Michigan, Zondervan, 1974.

Walvoord, John F., <u>The Prophecy Knowledge Handbook,</u> Wheaton, Illinois, Victor Books, 1990.

Wong, Daniel K.K., "The First Horseman of Revelation 6", Bibliotheca Sacra, April-June 1996: 212-226.

Young, Woody, and Chuck Missler, <u>Countdown to Eternity: Prologue to Destiny</u>, San Juan Capistrano, California, Joy Publishing, 1992.

DETAILED TABLE OF CONTENTS

TABLE OF CONTENTS   3

PART ONE: CHRIST   7

  CHAPTER 1   8

THE MESSAGE OF REDEMPTION OF EARTH AND MANKIND

AN INTRODUCTION TO THE BOOK OF REVELATION

    REVELATION - THE UNVEILING   9

    THE WRITER OF REVELATION   9

    REDEMPTION PROMISED TO MAN AND TO THE EARTH   10

    THE PURPOSE OF PROPHECY   11

    DANIEL - THE NATIONS   12

    EZEKIEL - THE JEWS   13

    REVELATION - THE CHURCH   13

    THE BLESSING OF REVELATION   15

    STRUCTURE OF THE BOOK   15

PART TWO: THE CHURCHES AND THE CHURCH AGE   17
    Figure 1 Part 2-3: Revelation 1 - 11   18

  CHAPTER 2   19

JOHN SEES THE DAY OF THE LORD

Revelation 1

    THE THEME   19

    THE REVELATION OF JESUS CHRIST GIVEN BY GOD   19

    THE BLESSING   20

    LETTERS TO THE SEVEN CHURCHES   21

    GOD EXISTS OUTSIDE OF TIME   22

THE SEVEN SPIRITS OF GOD	22
GOSPEL PROCLAIMED	23
CHRIST COMES AGAIN	23
JOHN'S VISION BEGINS	25
THE SEVEN CANDLESTICKS	26
DESCRIPTION OF JESUS	27
SEVEN STARS	29
THE COUNTENANCE OF CHRIST	30
THE KEYS TO DEATH AND HELL	31
JESUS HOLDS THE KEYS	32
THE BOOK'S MESSAGE OUTLINED BY JOHN	34

CHAPTER 3   **36**

THE CHURCHES OF EPHESUS AND SMYRNA
Revelation 2:1-11

THE CHURCH AGE	36
EPHESUS	38
HER CHARACTERISTICS, GOOD AND BAD	38
THE FOCUS OF LOVE - THE CHURCH OR JESUS?	39
THE NICOLAITANS - ECCLESIASTIC SEPARATION	41
SMYRNA	42
UNDERGOING PERSECUTION	43
POVERTY OR RICHES?	44
TARES IN THE CHURCH	45
FAITHFUL UNTIL DEATH	46
THE DAYS OF PERSECUTION	47
OVERCOMERS DELIVERED FROM SECOND DEATH	48
ROMAN PERSECUTIONS	48
POLYCARP	49
REIGN OF MARCUS AURELIUS	50
THE CHILDREN	51

REIGN OF SEPTIMIUS SEVERUS   52

REIGN OF DECIUS   53

THE REIGN OF DIOCLETIAN   54

CHAPTER 4   **55**

THE CHURCHES OF PERGAMOS AND THYATIRA

Revelation 2:12-29

CONSTANTINE   55

THE CITY OF PERGAMOS   56

THE MIXTURE OF CHURCH AND STATE   56

COMMENDATIONS BY JESUS   58

SATAN'S BASE OF EARTHLY POWER   58

THE MARTYR ANTIPAS   60

PERGAMOS'S FAULTS   60

BALAAM'S TEACHINGS   61

THE NICOLAITANS AGAIN   65

THE HIDDEN MANNA   66

THE WHITE STONE   67

THYATIRA   68

WORSHIP JESUS   68

JEZEBEL - CHURCH APOSTACY   69

THE CHURCH CORRUPTED BY POWER   70

CORRUPTION IN THE CHURCH   72

PURGATORY   73

FALSE DOCTRINES AND PERSECUTIONS   74

NICOLAITANS IN POWER   74

THE INQUISITION   75

INTERNAL REFORM   76

THE RESULTS OF PERSECUTION   78

THYATIRA REFUSES TO REPENT   78

THE BLACK PLAGUE   79

TRUE BELIEVERS HOLD FAST TO THE TRUTH   79

DOMINION OF EARTH RETURNED TO SAINTS
80

THE MORNING STAR 81

CHAPTER 5 **82**

THE CHURCHES OF SARDIS, PHILADELPHIA, AND
LAODICEA

Revelation 3

SARDIS 82

NO COMMENDATION FOR THIS CHURCH 82

THE CHURCH- ORTHODOX BUT DEAD 83

INFIGHTING 83

RESTORATION ONLY PARTIAL 84

A SELF-RIGHTEOUS CHURCH 85

PROMISES TO THE OVERCOMER 86

PHILADELPHIA 88

THE CHURCH UNITED 89

THE CHURCH WITH POWER 91

JESUS' NAME NOT DENIED 92

TARES IN THE CHURCH 93

THIS CHURCH ESCAPES THE TRIBULATION 94

THE OVERCOMERS' REWARD 95

THE CHURCH'S FINAL FORM 96

THE TRUE WITNESS 96

THE CHURCH DEPARTS FROM THE FAITH 97

THIS CHURCH NEITHER HOT NOR COLD 98

ALTHOUGH OUTWARDLY RICH, LAODICEA IS
WRETCHEDLY POOR 99

THIS CHURCH IS BLIND 100

THIS CHURCH IS NAKED 100

GOD'S DISCIPLINE LEADS TO REPENTANCE
101

JESUS CALLS US TO REPENTANCE 101

FROM TRIALS TO TRIUMPH TO HIS THRONE
102

PART THREE: TRIBULATION AS SEEN FROM HEAVEN'S VIEWPOINT   **103**
> **Figure 2**   Part 2-3: Revelation 1 - 11   104

CHAPTER 6   **105**

THE CHURCH AGE ENDS

Revelation 4

END OF THE CHURCH AGE - THE RAPTURE
105

THE FUTURE TOLD FROM THREE DIFFERENT VANTAGE POINTS   106

THE ORGANIZED CHURCH DEPARTS   107

JOHN SEES THE THRONE OF GOD   107

THE RADIANT GLORY OF THE LORD   108

THE RAINBOW   109

THE COVENANT OF GOD WITH THE EARTH 109

THE EARTH TO BE REDEEMED NOT DESTROYED   110

EARTH PURIFIED BY FIRE   112

THE EARTH NOT ANNIHILATED   112

THE EARTH WILL REMAIN FOREVER   114

THE TIME OF THE EARTH'S CLEANSING   115

THE TWENTY-FOUR THRONES AND THE TWENTY-FOUR ELDERS   116

LIGHTNINGS, THUNDERINGS, AND VOICES FROM THE THRONE   117

A SEA OF GLASS   117

THE CRYSTAL SEA REPRESENTED IN THE TEMPLE   118

THE FOUR LIVING CREATURES   119

WORSHIP BEFORE THE THRONE   121

CHAPTER 7   **124**

EARTH'S TITLE DEED REDEEMED

Revelation 5

EARTH IS YET TO BE REDEEMED 124

EARTH STILL IN THE HAND OF SATAN 124

GOD HAS OWNERSHIP OF EARTH 125

GOD'S LAW OF REDEMPTION OF THE LAND
126

THE TITLE DEED TO THE EARTH 127

THE TRICKERY OF SATAN 128

JESUS - OUR KINSMAN REDEEMER 129

THE LAMB 130

THE TITLE DEED TO EARTH IS RECLAIMED 131

THE CLEANSING OF CREATION 132

THE BEGINNING OF THE END 133

THE SONG OF REDEMPTION 134

CHAPTER 8   137

SIX SEALS – TRIBULATION MIXED WITH GRACE

Revelation 6

THE SEALED BOOK - AN OVERVIEW OF THE
TRIBULATION PERIOD 137

THE FIRST SEAL OPENED 138

THE WHITE HORSE AND RIDER - THE FIRST
HORSEMAN OF THE APOCALYPSE 139

THE FIRST HORSEMAN IS RIGHTEOUS, NOT
EVIL 140

THE PREACHING OF THE GOSPEL FROM
HEAVEN 142

THE ENTIRE WORLD HEARS THE GOSPEL 143

THE SECOND SEAL OPENED - THE SECOND
HORSEMAN OF THE APOCALYPSE 143

THIRD SEAL OPENED - THIRD RIDER OF THE
APOCALYPSE 145

FOURTH SEAL OPENED - THE FOURTH
HORSEMAN OF THE APOCALYPSE 147

DEATH AS A PERSONA 148

FIFTH SEAL OPENED 149

THE MARTYRS' BLOOD AVENGED 149

THE CHRISTIAN EXPERIENCE OF THE GRAVE
150

THE MARTYRS WEAR THE CLOTHING OF THE
BRIDE 150

RESURRECTION OF THE TRIBULATION SAINTS
151

THE SIXTH SEAL OPENED 151

THE AGE OF GRACE IS OVER 153

TOTAL REJECTION OF GOD BY THE WICKED
155

CHAPTER 9 **157**

144,000 JEWS SEALED AND THE TRIBULATION
SAINTS IN HEAVEN

Revelation 7

TWO GROUPS SAVED OUT OF THE
TRIBULATION 157

MAJOR CHANGES IN EARTH'S ENVIRONMENT
158

THE RIGHTEOUS PROTECTED FROM GOD'S
WRATH 158

GOD RENEWS HIS RELATIONSHIP WITH THE
JEWS 159

JEWS TO SUFFER TRIBULATIONS BUT FIND
JESUS 160

THE FIRST SAVED GROUP IN CHAPTER 7 -
JEWS FROM THE TWELVE TRIBES 162

THE SECOND SAVED GROUP IN CHAPTER 7 -
THE TRIBULATION SAINTS 164

THE SECOND PART OF THE FIRST
RESURRECTION 164

TRIBULATION SAINTS HERALD JESUS'
RETURN TO EARTH 165

THE TIME OF THE "GREAT TRIBULATION" 167

THE LAMB AND THE SHEPHERD 168

NO TEARS IN HEAVEN   170

CHAPTER 10   **172**

GOD'S WRATH ON EARTH: THE FOUR TRUMPETS
SOUND

Revelation 8

GOD'S WRATH IS USHERED IN BY THE
BREAKING OF THE SEVENTH SEAL   172

THE SEVEN TRUMPETS   172

PRAYERS GO UP TO GOD - JUDGMENT COMES
DOWN   174

THE FIRST TRUMPET - JUDGMENT OF FIRE,
HAIL AND BLOOD   175

THE SECOND TRUMPET – ONE-THIRD OF THE
SEA TURNS TO BLOOD   177

ONE-THIRD OF SEA CREATURES DIE, ONE
THIRD OF SHIPS DESTROYED   177

THE THIRD TRUMPET - FRESH WATERS
POISONED   178

THE FOURTH TRUMPET - CELESTIAL LIGHTS
DARKENED   178

JUDGMENT COMBINED WITH CLEANSING 179

AN EAGLE APPEARS IN HEAVEN WITH AN
OMINOUS WARNING   180

CHAPTER 11   **182**

THE LAST THREE TRUMPETS

Revelation 9

THE FIFTH TRUMPET -THE KEY TO THE
REALM OF DARKNESS   182

DEMONIC LOCUSTS   183

THE LOCUSTS HAVE BOUNDARIES   184

NO DEATH PERMITTED FOR FIVE MONTHS 185

KING OF THE LOCUSTS   186

SIXTH TRUMPET - FOUR SATANIC ANGELS
RELEASED   187

"GENERALS" OF AN EVIL FORCE   187

THE EVIL FORCE AND THEIR ACTIONS
DESCRIBED   189

JOEL'S VISION OF THIS SAME SATANIC ARMY
189

A SATANIC ARMY - NOT THE CHINESE ARMY
190

NO REPENTANCE - SIN FLOURISHES   191

CHAPTER 12   **192**

THE MYSTERY OF GOD IS FINISHED

Revelation 10

JESUS DISPLAYED IN HIS GLORY   192

THE MIGHTY ANGEL IS JESUS   192

JESUS TAKES FINAL AND LEGAL POSSESSION
OF EARTH   194

THUNDERS OF JUDGMENT   195

DELAY NO LONGER IN FINISHING THE
MYSTERY OF GOD   195

LENGTH OF TIME TO FINISH GOD'S WORK   196

UNDERSTANDING THE MYSTERY   196

DOMINION OF EARTH RETURNS TO MAN   197

OBTAINING THE PROMISED INHERITANCE IS
BOTH SWEET AND BITTER   198

WE WILL BE ETERNAL WITNESSES   199

CHAPTER 13   **201**

GOD'S TWO WITNESSES

Revelation 11

THE JEWS WILL COME TO JESUS   201

ISRAEL'S SPIRITUAL CONDITION ASSESSED
202

JUDGMENT UPON ISRAEL   203

THE TWO WITNESSES   204

WHO ARE THE TWO WITNESSES?   205

DOES THE RETURN OF ELIJAH AND MOSES
FIT JEWISH TRADITION?   209

IS ENOCH ONE OF THE TWO WITNESSES? 209

MOSES AND ELIJAH CONTRASTED 210

TWO WITNESSES KILLED ON GOD'S
TIMETABLE 211

WITNESSES' DEATH BRINGS SATANIC
CELEBRATION 213

TWO DEAD WITNESSES RESURRECTED 214

JEWS' RECOGNITION OF JESUS AS MESSIAH
IS PRECURSOR TO ARMAGEDDON 215

THE SEVENTH ANGEL BLOWS HIS TRUMPET/
THE KINGDOM OF DARKNESS BECOMES THE
KINGDOM OF LIGHT 216

WORSHIP IN HEAVEN 217

ARMAGEDDON ARRIVES 217

AWARENESS OF SIGNS THAT COME BEFORE
RAPTURE 218

THE HEAVENLY ARK IN HEAVEN 219

THE GREAT EARTHQUAKE 220

**PART FOUR: TRIBULATION AS SEEN FROM EARTH'S
VIEWPOINT** **221**
    Figure 3 Part 4: Revelation 12 - 16 222

CHAPTER 14 **223**

THE RAPTURE OF THE CHURCH AND WAR IN
HEAVEN

Revelation 12

JOHN'S VISION CONTINUES - THE FUTURE
DISCLOSED, NOT THE PAST 223

EVENTS OF REVELATION 4-11 NOW SEEN
FROM EARTH'S VIEW 224

A WOMAN - THE VISIBLE CHURCH 225

POWERFUL SATANIC CONFEDERATION
OPPOSES GOD'S PLAN 228

SEVEN HEADS - TEN HORNS - SATAN'S
HISTORIC POWER OVER KINGDOMS OF
WORLD 230

SATAN TAKES WORLD CONTROL 231

THE CHILD - WHO IS HE? 233

THE TRUE/VISIBLE CHURCH IS CAUGHT UP
BY THE RAPTURE 237

THE WOMAN IS NOT MARY - THE CHILD IS
NOT JESUS 238

THE WOMAN AND CHILD ARE FUTURE
EVENTS, NOT PAST 239

JOHN'S VISION IS A TRUE PICTURE OF THE
RAPTURE 240

SCRIPTURE CONSISTENT IN IDENTIFYING THE
TIME OF RAPTURE 241

TIMES SECRET BEFORE RAPTURE -
SPECIFIED AFTER RAPTURE 244

HOW THE RAPTURE WILL IMPACT THE WORLD
245

SATAN LOSES HIS PLACE IN THE HEAVENS 246

SATAN RULER OF THIS WORLD - NOT RULER
OF HELL 247

SATAN CAST TO EARTH - HIS DOOM IS
SEALED 247

SATAN IS STILL POWERFUL 248

ASCENT OF SAINTS - DESCENT OF SATAN 249

LEGALITY OF RAPTURE - SATAN ARGUES
BEFORE GOD 250

SAINTS' DEFENSE AGAINST SATAN'S
ACCUSATIONS 252

SAINTS ARE OVERCOMERS EVEN OF SATAN
253

SATAN'S RAGE DIRECTED AT THOSE LEFT
BEHIND AND THE TRIBULATION SAINTS 253

CHAPTER 15 **255**

THE RISE OF THE ANTICHRIST

Background to Revelation 13

DANIEL'S FIRST VISION 255

Figure 4 Antichrist's Empire 260

DANIEL'S SECOND VISION 260

DANIEL'S THIRD VISION 265

DANIEL'S FOURTH VISION 270

ANTICHRIST WILL APPEAR BEFORE THE
RAPTURE OCCURS 272

THREE PROPHETIC TIME ZONES BEFORE THE
RAPTURE 275

TIME ZONE ONE 276

TIME ZONE TWO 286

TIME ZONE THREE 304

THE RETURN OF JESUS FOR HIS PEOPLE 311

CHAPTER 16 **312**

THE BEASTS FROM THE SEA AND EARTH

Revelation 13

THE BEAST FROM THE SEA 312

SATAN'S FALSE SIGN OF "RESURRECTION" 320

ALL NATIONS WORSHIP THE POWERFUL
BEAST 321

SATAN RAGES AGAINST SAINTS BOTH IN
HEAVEN AND ON EARTH 322

NOT EVERYONE WORSHIPS ANTICHRIST 323

FOR THE TRIBULATION SAINTS JUSTICE WILL
SURELY PREVAIL 325

THE BEAST FROM THE EARTH: THE FALSE
PROPHET 326

SATANIC "PROOFS OF DIVINITY" 329

A SATANIC IDOL AND DEMONSTRATIONS OF
POWER 329

THE MARK OF THE BEAST AND ITS
CONSEQUENCES 330

THE BEAST: NOT A COMPUTER NOR A SYSTEM
BUT A MAN 332

CHAPTER 17 **334**

THE FIRST 3 ½ YEARS OF TRIBULATION REVISITED

Revelation 14

MOUNT ZION - SAFE REFUGE FOR THE
144,000 JEWS   334

144,000 SEALED WITH THE NAME OF GOD
AND JESUS   335

THE TASKS OF THE 144,000   335

HEAVENLY VOICE AND EARTHLY VOICES JOIN
IN A NEW SONG   336

144,000 VIRGINS   337

144,000 FIRSTFRUITS   338

JOHN AGAIN SEES THE SIX SEALS OPENED -
THIS TIME FROM THE EARTH   340

GOSPEL PREACHED FROM HEAVEN:
EXPECTED AND EXPERIENCED   343

GOD AS CREATOR IS FOUNDATIONAL TO
SALVATION   348

THE SECOND ANGEL FORETELLS THE FALL
OF BABYLON - ANTICHRIST'S CAPITAL   348

THIRD ANGEL GIVES WARNING CONCERNING
THE BEAST   350

TO LIVE IS HELL - TO DIE IS CHRIST   352

THE REAPING OF SOULS - SAVED AND
UNSAVED   353

CHAPTER 18   **355**

THE SAINTS VICTORIOUS OVER SATAN

Revelation 15

THE TRIBULATION SAINTS REAPPEAR - SAME
STORY, DIFFERENT VIEWPOINT   355

THE TRIBULATION SAINTS VICTORIOUS OVER
SATAN   355

GOD'S GRACE HAS TWO MANIFESTATIONS 357

THE SONG OF MOSES PROCLAIMS VICTORY
BOTH PAST AND FUTURE   360

GOD'S PERSPECTIVE   361

HOW DO WE RESPOND TO TRIALS?   361

JOHN'S VISION OF THE HEAVENLY TEMPLE

363

GOD DEALS WITH ISRAEL'S REBELLION WITH
JUDGMENT FROM HIS TEMPLE   363

SEVEN ANGELS WITH SEVEN VIALS
DISTRIBUTE GOD'S WRATH ON EARTH   364

GOD'S WRATH IS FOR CLEANSING THE EARTH
AND FOR JUDGMENT UPON THE BEAST   365

GOD'S WRATH IS HOLY, BLAMELESS AND
PURE   366

CHAPTER 19   **368**

SEVEN BOWLS OF WRATH

Revelation 16

FIRST VIAL: GOD'S WRATH BEGINS   368

SECOND VIAL: ADDITIONAL INFORMATION OF
THE SEA OF BLOOD   368

THIRD VIAL: FRESH WATER ALSO TURNED TO
BLOOD   369

HEAVEN'S HOSTS CONCUR WITH GOD'S
JUDGMENTS UPON THE EARTH   370

FOURTH VIAL: PURIFICATION OF THE EARTH
BY FIRE   371

REPROBATE HEARTS DO NOT REPENT EVEN
THOUGH IN FIERY TORMENT   372

FIFTH VIAL: DARKNESS, TERRIBLE PAIN, BUT
NO DEATH   373

SIXTH VIAL: DEMONIC SPIRITS UNLEASHED
374

THE INVADING ARMY: SATAN'S FORCES, NOT
RUSSIA'S   375

WHO IS GOG?   376

THE FOUR GROUPS OF NATIONS THAT COME
UP AGAINST ISRAEL   379

ARMAGEDDON: EZEKIEL AND REVELATION
COMPARED   380

SIXTH VIAL: THE EUPHRATES RIVED DRIED
UP   383

SATAN'S FORCES ASSEMBLE AGAINST ISRAEL
384

ARMAGEDDON 385

THE LOCATION OF ARMAGEDDON 385

ARMAGEDDON/MEGIDDO'S HISTORY 386

THE CONFLICT BEGINS 387

SEVENTH VIAL: "IT IS FINISHED": JESUS IS
SOVEREIGN OVER THE EARTH AND SEA 388

THE ENTIRE EARTH IS SHAKEN 390

THE QUAKE RESHAPES JERUSALEM, THE
ISLANDS, AND THE MOUNTAINS 392

BABYLON: SATAN'S RELIGIOUS, POLITICAL,
AND ECONOMIC SYSTEM IS DESTROYED 393

GREAT HAILSTONES FALL FROM HEAVEN:
PEOPLE BLASPHEME GOD 394

**PART FIVE: TRIBULATION AS SEEN FROM SATAN'S
KINGDOM** **397**

Figure 5 **Part 5:** Revelation 17 - 22 398

CHAPTER 20 **399**

BABYLON

Revelation 17

EVENTS OF LAST DAYS AS SEEN FROM
SATAN'S KINGDOM 399

"BABYLON" - WORLD SYSTEM, RELIGION, AND
CITY 399

THE CITY OF BABYLON 400

BABYLON FOUNDED BY NIMROD 401

BABEL - GOD IS DEFIED, LANGUAGE IS
CONFUSED 401

BABEL - PEOPLE AND THEIR OCCULTIC
PRACTICES SCATTERED 402

BABYLON - SATAN'S INFILTRATION AND
CORRUPTION WITHIN THE CHURCH 403

CORRUPTION - CATHARISM 404

CORRUPTION - ALCHEMY 405

CORRUPTION - THE KNIGHTS TEMPLAR 405

BABYLON - SATANIC CENTER OF WORSHIP
FOR THE WORLD   407

JOHN'S VISION OF THE GREAT
HARLOT/WHORE   408

EVERY NATION IS SEDUCED BY THE WHORE
                                             409

HER GOLDEN CUP IS FILLED WITH
ABOMINATIONS AND FILTHINESS   409

SATAN - THE SCARLET BEAST   410

THE WHORE'S NAME COMPRISES ALL FALSE
RELIGIONS AND APOSTATE CHURCHES   411

SATANIC WORLD EMPIRE DRUNK ON THE
BLOOD OF THE MARTYRED SAINTS   412

THE BEAST - HE WAS, IS NOT, AND WILL
COME   412

SEVEN EMPIRES, THEN A SEVENTH/EIGHTH
EMPIRE   412

ANTICHRIST'S KINGDOM DIVIDED - BABYLON
DESTROYED   414

BABYLON MEANS BABYLON   415

BABYLON REBUILT - BEFORE OR AFTER
RAPTURE?   416

BABYLON DESTROYED - BEFORE OR AFTER
RAPTURE?   416

CHAPTER 21   **418**

BABYLON IS FALLEN

Revelation 18

BABYLON - A GRAND CITY OF THE LAST DAYS
                                             418

BABYLON, THE EVIL CITY, IS FALLEN   419

JESUS VICTORIOUS OVER SYSTEM AND
RELIGION OF BABYLON   419

BABYLON'S FALL - THE THIRD TELLING   420

BACKGROUND OF BABYLON'S RISE TO
WORLD CONTROL   421

GOD'S WARNING TO HIS PEOPLE - FLEE THE
CITY   422

GOD BRINGS JUDGMENT ON SATAN'S SEAT
OF EVIL   424

A HOUSE DIVIDED - SATAN TURNS ON
BABYLON   424

THE WORLD MOURNS AS BABYLON BURNS426

THE WORLD MOURNS OUT OF SELF-
CENTERED GREED   427

EARTHLY TREASURES DESTROYED   428

HEAVEN REJOICES AT GOD'S JUDGMENT ON
BABYLON   428

ISAIAH'S AND JEREMIAH'S PROPHECY OF
BABYLON'S DESTRUCTION FULFILLED   429

AN ANGEL DECLARES THAT MYSTERY
BABYLON IS "NO MORE"   430

CHAPTER 22   **431**

THE MARRIAGE OF THE LAMB AND THE BATTLE OF
ARMAGEDDON

Revelation 19

PRAISE FOR JEHOVAH   431

PRAISE THE LORD AT ALL TIMES   433

THE LORD ALMIGHTY REIGNS   433

THE BRIDE IS DRESSED IN THE
RIGHTEOUSNESS OF CHRIST   436

THE MYSTERY OF MARRIAGE   437

THE ANGEL PRONOUNCES BLESSINGS ON
THE GUESTS AT THE MARRIAGE SUPPER   438

JESUS ABOUT TO RETURN TO EARTH TO
MINISTER JUSTICE   440

JESUS' BLOODSTAINED GARMENTS   441

JESUS FOLLOWED BY ARMY OF SAINTS   442

THE DESTROYING SWORD   443

THE NAME ABOVE ALL NAMES   444

ARMAGEDDON AND THE GREAT SUPPER   445

CARRION BIRDS CALLED TO A GREAT FEAST
447

THE GREAT WAR AGAINST GOD IS
CONCLUDED   448

THE LAKE OF FIRE - DESTINY OF ANTICHRIST
AND THE FALSE PROPHET   449

THE "WORD" DESTROYS ANTICHRIST'S
ARMIES   450

PART SIX: THE KINGDOM OF CHRIST   452

CHAPTER 23   453

THE THOUSAND-YEAR REIGN

Revelation 20

EVENTS OF REVELATION THAT PRECEDE
CHAPTER 20   453

SUMMARY OF THE THOUSAND-YEAR REIGN
453

CHAPTER 20 IS LITERAL NOT SYMBOLIC   454

AFTERLIFE LOCATIONS: WHERE DO THE
SPIRITS GO?   456

SATAN BOUND AND JUDGMENTS BEGIN   459

JUDGMENTS NAMED: BEMA SEAT, NATIONS
(SHEEP AND GOATS), GREAT WHITE THRONE
460

THE JUDGMENT OF THE NATIONS (SHEEP
AND GOATS)   461

JESUS WILL REIGN IN JERUSALEM   466

FULFILLMENT OF THE PROPHECY THAT THE
MEEK SHALL INHERIT THE EARTH   467

PERFECT GOVERNMENT: IMPERFECT PEOPLE
468

THE THOUSAND YEARS BEGIN A WORK OF
REDEEMING THE EARTH   471

JERUSALEM, THE APPLE OF GOD'S EYE   474

RESURRECTIONS THAT OCCUR BEFORE AND
AFTER THE THOUSAND YEARS   474

THE FIRST RESURRECTION: WHO IS
INVOLVED AND WHAT IS THEIR FATE   475

RAPTURE, A PART OF THE FIRST
RESURRECTION: WHO IS BEING JUDGED? 479

SATAN IS AGAIN ABLE TO DECEIVE MANY 480

SATAN RELEASED, THE WICKED DESTROYED,
AND SATAN CAST INTO GEHENNA   481

THE EARTH AND HEAVENS COMPLETELY
CLEANSED   482

THE GREAT WHITE THRONE JUDGMENT   483

THE GREAT WHITE THRONE IS NOT A
JUDGMENT OF SALVATION   486

THIS THRONE JUDGMENT CONCERNS THOSE
RAISED IN THE SECOND RESURRECTION 488

DEATH IS DEFEATED   489

PART SEVEN: THE HOLY CITY AND ETERNITY   490

CHAPTER 24   491

A NEW HEAVEN AND EARTH AND THE NEW
JERUSALEM

Revelation 21

THE EARTH REMAINS BUT IS RENEWED AND
MADE FRESH   491

THE EARTH, SUN, MOON AND STARS REMAIN
FOREVER   494

THE INHABITANTS OF EARTH   495

OCEANS AND SEAS ON RENEWED EARTH
REVERT TO PRE-FLOOD STATE   496

NEW JERUSALEM - CITY OF THE REDEEMED -
COMES FROM HEAVEN   498

REVELATION IS LITERAL   499

THE WORK IS DONE   500

JESUS AND THE FATHER ARE ONE   500

THE ONLY TRUE SON OF GOD IS AN
OVERCOMER   500

THE BRIDE AND THE HOLY CITY   502

THE CITY IS DESCRIBED   503

THE WALL CONSTRUCTED OF PRECIOUS STONES   505

THE GATES OF PEARL   506

THE LORD GOD AND THE LAMB ARE THE TEMPLE AND THE LIGHT   507

CHAPTER 25   **509**

JESUS' FINAL MESSAGE

Revelation 22

THE CITY OF GOD - A BLESSED PLACE   509

WE SERVE FATHER AND SON BEFORE GOD'S THRONE   511

ETERNITY - WHAT IS IN STORE FOR THE OVERCOMER?   511

UNDERSTANDING GOD'S PLAN FOR ETERNITY   513

UNDERSTANDING THE OVERCOMERS' ROLE IN ETERNITY   516

ETERNITY'S EVERLASTING STORY OF REDEMPTION   519

JESUS' REVELATION TO JOHN IS FAITHFUL AND TRUE   519

WILL WE BE FOUND FAITHFUL WHEN JESUS COMES?   520

GOD ALONE TO BE WORSHIPPED   521

THE PROPHECY OF THIS BOOK TO REMAIN UNSEALED   521

THE MESSAGE OF REVELATION IS TIMELESS   522

AN ETERNITY TO PARTAKE OF THE WATER OF LIFE   525

DIVINE WARNING: DO NOT ALTER ANY WORD OF THIS BOOK   525

WHY SUCH SEVERE CONSEQUENCES TO ALTERATION OF THIS BOOK?   526

ACKNOWLEDGMENTS   **529**

SELECTED BIBLIOGRAPY   **530**

DETAILED TABLE OF CONTENTS   **533**

ENDNOTES   **554**

ENDNOTES

Chapter 2

[1] Joseph Seiss, The Apocalypse: Exposition of the Book of Revelation, Grand Rapids, Michigan: Kregel Publications, 1987, pg. 18.

[2] Archibald Rutledge, Life's Extras, Toronto: Fleming H. Revell, 1961, pp. 53-54.

Chapter 3

[3] Richard Chenevix Trench, Commentary on the Epistles to the Seven Churches in Asia, Eugene, Oregon, Wipf and Stock, 1861, pg. 10.

[4] Frontline Faith, Vol 9, No. 5.

Chapter 4

[5] Will Durant, The Story of Civilization, International, Simon and Schuster, 1950, vol. VI, pg. 75.

[6] Cited in R.W. Thompson's, The Papacy and the Civil Power, New York, 1876, pp. 414-416.

[7] Carolly Erickson, Great Harry, New York, Summit Books, 1980, pp. 207-208.

[8] Louis Marie De Cormenin, History of the Popes of Rome, pg. 275.

[9] R.W. Thompson, The Papacy and the Civil Power, New York, 1876, pg. 466.

[10] Cited in Dave Hunt's, A Woman Rides The Beast, Eugene, Oregon, Harvest House, 1994, pg. 507.

[11] Peter de Rosa, Vicars of Christ: The Dark Side of the Papacy, Crown Publishers, 1988, pp. 99-100.

[12] Emelio Martinez, Recuerdos de Antano, pg. 390.

[13] Will Durant, The Story of Civilization, Simon and Schuster, 1950, vol. IV, pg. 784.

[14] R. Tudor Jones, The Great Reformation, InterVarsity Press, pg. 164.

[15] Dave Hunt, A Woman Rides The Beast, Eugene, Oregon, Harvest House, 1994, pg. 252.

[16] Will Durant, The Story of Civilization, Simon and Schuster, 1950, vol. VI, pp. 598-601.

Chapter 5

[17] Dr. Ernest Stoeffler, "Can These Bones Live?", Christian History vol. V, No. 2, pp. 9-10.

[18] ibid.

[19] Will Durant, The Story of Civilization, Simon and Schuster, 1950, vol. VI, pp. 453-457.

Chapter 9

[20] Dr. Joseph Seiss, The Apocalypse: Exposition of the Book of Revelation, Grand Rapids, Michigan, Kregel Publications, 1900, pp. 163.

Chapter 14

[21] Dr. Joseph Seiss, The Apocalypse: Exposition of the Book of Revelation, Grand Rapids, Michigan, Kregel Publications, 1900, pg. 298.

Chapter 15

[22] Gustl Kubizek, The Young Hitler I Knew, as cited by Joseph J. Carr, The Twisted Cross, Lafayette, Louisiana, Huntington House, 1985, pg. 24.

[23] Guido Knopp and Harold Shott, "Hitler the Commander", History Channel, 1995.

[24] Arthur Bloomfield, How To Recognize The Antichrist, Minneapolis, Minnesota, Bethany Fellowship, Inc., 1975, pp. 49-50.

[25] C.S. Lewis, The Screwtape Letters, New York, New York, The Macmillan Company, 1961, pp. 133-134.

Chapter 16

[26] Joseph A. Seiss, The Apocalypse: Exposition of the Book of Revelation, Kregel Publications, Grand Rapids, Michigan, 1987, pg. 336.

Chapter 18

[27] Cited in George Grant and Karen Grant's, Letters Home: Advice from the Wisest Men and Women of the Ages to Their Friends and Loved Ones, Nashville, Tennessee, Cumberland House Publishing, 1997, pg. 42.

[28] C.S. Lewis, God in the Dock, Grand Rapids, Michigan, Eerdmans, 1994, pg. 52.

[29] Vine, W.E., An Expository Dictionary of Biblical Words, Old Tappan, New Jersey, Fleming H. Revell, 1940.

Chapter 25

[30] Reader's Digest, "Are We Alone in the Universe?", May 1996, pg. 110.

[31] C.S. Lewis, Mere Christianity, New York, MacMillan Publishing Company, 1943, pp. 55-56.

Made in the USA
San Bernardino, CA
02 December 2013